T0386986

Sol

Volume I

Religions in the Graeco-Roman World

VOLUME 198/I

The titles published in this series are listed at *brill.com/rgrw*

Sol

*Image and Meaning of the Sun
in Roman Art and Religion*

VOLUME I

By

Steven E. Hijmans

BRILL

LEIDEN | BOSTON

Cover illustration: restored view of a third century vault-mosaic in mausoleum M of the Vatican necropolis. It depicts Sol as a male figure, standing in a chariot (indicated by a single wheel), drawn by four rearing, white horses. Sol is dressed in a *chlamys* and *chiton*, has raised his right hand and holds a globe in his left. Seven rays emanate from his head. Image by Anna Hijmans.

Library of Congress Cataloging-in-Publication Data

Names: Hijmans, S. E., author.
Title: Sol : image and meaning of the sun in Roman art and religion /
    Steven E. Hijmans.
Description: Leiden ; Boston : Brill, 2024 | Series: Religions in the Graeco-Roman world, 0927-7633 ;
    volume 198 | Extensive reworking of the author's thesis (doctoral)—University of Groningen, 2009,
    under the title: Sol : the sun in the art and religions of Rome. | Includes bibliographical references
    and index. | Contents: v. I. — v. II. |
Identifiers: LCCN 2022061079 (print) | LCCN 2022061080 (ebook) |
    ISBN 9789004406698 (v. I ; hardback) | ISBN 9789004514720 (v. II ; hardback) |
    ISBN 9789004516526 (hardback) | ISBN 9789004442405 (v. I ; ebook) |
    ISBN 9789004521582 (v. II ; ebook)
Subjects: LCSH: Sun—In art. | Sun—Religious aspects. | Rome—Religion.
Classification: LCC N8251.S6 H55 2024 (print) | LCC N8251.S6 (ebook) |
    DDC 704.9/49—dc23/eng/20230112
LC record available at https://lccn.loc.gov/2022061079
LC ebook record available at https://lccn.loc.gov/2022061080

Typeface for the Latin, Greek, and Cyrillic scripts: "Brill". See and download: brill.com/brill-typeface.

ISSN 0927-7633
ISBN 978-90-04-51652-6 (hardback, set)
ISBN 978-90-04-40669-8 (hardback, vol. I)
ISBN 978-90-04-51472-0 (hardback, vol. II)
ISBN 978-90-04-44240-5 (e-book, vol. I)
ISBN 978-90-04-52158-2 (e-book, vol. II)
DOI 10.1163/9789004442405 (vol. I)
DOI 10.1163/9789004521582 (vol. II)

Copyright 2024 by Koninklijke Brill NV, Leiden, The Netherlands.
Koninklijke Brill NV incorporates the imprints Brill, Brill Nijhoff, Brill Schöningh, Brill Fink,
Brill mentis, Brill Wageningen Academic, Vandenhoeck & Ruprecht, Böhlau and V&R unipress.
This book is printed on acid-free paper and produced in a sustainable manner.

For Margriet Haagsma

∵

Contents

Figures

Abbreviations

Abbreviations in this study follow:

1. The Lexicon Iconographicum Mythologiae Classicae (LIMC) vol. 1, XXXIV–LIV
2. Der Neue Pauly, Erweitertes Abkürzungsverzeichnis 3. Bibliographische Abkürzungen, and 4. Antike Autoren und Werktitel; https://referenceworks-brillonline-com.
3. Dyabola, Abk. Zeitschriften; www.db.dyabola.de
4. Additional abbreviations as listed below:

AGWien	Zwierlein-Diehl, E. 1973–1991. *Die antiken Gemmen des Kunsthistorischen Museums in Wien*, 3 volumes.
AR	*Archiv für Religionswissenschaft.*
Arachne	IDAI Objects Arachne. https://arachne.dainst.org/
BMCGrC	*Catalogue of the Greek Coins in the British Museum*, 29 vols. 1873–1965.
BMCR	*Bryn Mawr Classical Review*, https://bmcr.brynmawr.edu/
CBd	Nagy, A.M. 2010. The Campbell Bonner Magical Gems Database, http://cbd.mfab.hu/
CIMRM	Vermaseren, M.J. 1956–1960. *Corpus Inscriptionum et Monumentorum Religionis Mithriacae*, 2 volumes: Nijhoff.
EAH	Bagnall, R.S., Brodersen, K., Champion, C.B., Erskine, A., & Huebner, S.R. (eds.). 2013. *The Encyclopedia of Ancient History*. Wiley-Blackwell.
EEC	Ferguson, E. (ed.) 1990. *Encyclopaedia of Early Christianity*, New York & London.
EKM I.Beroia	Gounaropoulou, L. & Hatzopoulos, M.B. 1998. Επιγραφές Κάτω Μακεδονίας (μεταξύ του Βερμίου όρους και του Αξιού ποταμού). Τεύχος Α': Επιγραφές Βεροίας, Athens.
FS	Rüpke, J. 2005. *Fasti sacerdotum. Die Mitglieder der Priesterschaften und das sakrale Funktionspersonal römischer, griechischer, orientalischer und jüdisch-christlicher Kulte in der Stadt Rom von 300 v. Chr. bis 499 n. Chr.*, 3 vols., Stuttgart.
Gnecchi I–III	Gnecchi, F. 1912, *I medaglioni romani*, Milan.
ILB	Gerov, B. (ed.) 1989. *Inscriptiones latinae in Bulgaria repertae (Inscriptiones inter Oescum et Iatrum repertae)*, Sofia.
IRT	Reynolds, J. et al. 2009. *The Inscriptions of Roman Tripolitania*
JMP	Jaarboek voor Munt- en Penningkunde
LSA	*Last Statues of Antiquity Database*: https://www.ocla.ox.ac.uk/statues/

Lupa	F. Harl & O. Harl, *Ubi Erat Lupa*: http://lupa.at/
MER-RIC	Monnaies de l'Empire Romain/Roman Imperial Coinage AD 268–276: https://ric.mom.fr/en/info/present
NEsp	*Nouvel Espérandieu*: http://nesp.mmsh.univ-aix.fr/
PBASHum	Papers of the Bulgarian Academy of Sciences, Humanities and Social Sciences
RIB	*Roman Inscriptions of Britain*: https://romaninscriptionsofbritain.org/
Spätantike	D. Stutzinger & D. Becker (eds.) 1983. *Spätantike und frühes Christentum: Ausstellung im Liebieghaus, Museum Alter Plastik, Frankfurt am Main.*

Introduction

This study has been long in the making. I first became interested in Sol almost thirty years ago, when I set out to study the broader iconographic context of that famous image from mausoleum M in the Vatican necropolis that has been identified as Christ in the guise of Helios/Sol. I soon realized that there was no iconographic context to study as there are no other images in which Christ was actually depicted as the sun. This cast doubt on the identity of the so-called Christ-Helios, but in the process I also realized that we actually knew very little about the pagan Sol-imagery to which, iconographically, the Vatican image adhered. I decided to shift my focus from the non-existent Romano-Christian images of Sol-as-Christ to the Roman iconography of the sun. My new goal, somewhat naive, was to write a close analysis of the extant images of Sol, focusing on what those images could tell us about the chronology, origin, and nature of the cult of Sol in the Roman world.

Work progressed well and resulted in a number of articles (Hijmans 1994, 1995, 1996a and b, 1997), but it became increasingly clear to me that many of the images of Sol in my database did not depict *Sol*, if by Sol we mean the Roman Sun god. What they did depict was less clear to me, and more importantly, I was not entirely sure how to find out. At this point I found myself facing a choice between pragmatism and principle. With relatively little extra work I could have published an iconographic discussion of the kind that has a long tradition in our field. But its shortcomings, in this particular case, were simply too obvious, and in the final analysis I felt certain that I would come to regret that choice as a missed opportunity.

Once I had decided that there was no point in amassing a catalogue of images without knowing what intended meanings those images convey, I next spent a significant amount of time attempting to find a suitable body of visual or material culture theory to provide a framework for my planned analyses of the image groups in my database. I felt like an anthropologist attempting ethnographic fieldwork without really knowing prerequisite languages. To put it simply, I could not interpret the texts because I did not understand the words. The problem with Roman images is that they are not as straightforward as they often seem (or are deemed) to be. That social codes govern how images function is a given, of course, and that those codes are by definition neither universal nor transparent is also clear. What is often overlooked, however, is just how remarkably rigid and durable visual codes were in Rome. Consistently, for centuries, Romans depicted the sun as a youthful beardless male charioteer. This does not mean that Romans actually thought the sun was a youthful

© KONINKLIJKE BRILL NV, LEIDEN, 2024 | DOI:10.1163/9789004442405_002

beardless male charioteer, just as they did not think that Eternity, for example, was a woman bearing the severed heads of the sun and the moon on her out-stretched hands; it was simply the way they visualized the concept.

What concept? The obvious difference between image (beardless youth) and the depicted (ball of fire) underlines the importance of the social coding in Rome's visual system. To understand Roman art, one must be privy to those codes, which we often are not. But that is only part of the problem. Too many classicists still apparently assume that ancient images somehow speak for themselves, and hence "mean" whatever seems the most logical to the viewer. There is, for example, a tendency to ascribe "divine" or "solar" connotations rather indiscriminately to a wide range of Roman artistic conventions used to depict radiant light: emanating rays, radiate crowns of various types, nimbi, with and without rays, in various colours. These are routinely treated as roughly synonymous (and often explicitly solar) in meaning. But far from being solar, certain forms of symbolic light were actually *never* used in depictions of the sun. They did not convey "solar connotations" but quite the opposite, because the *fluent* Roman viewer knew unequivocally that a figure thus adorned could *not* be Sol. The fastidiousness with which such iconographic conventions and differentiations were observed by Roman artists is a testament to their impor-tance. Even seemingly minute details could change the meaning of an image through their presence or their absence.

While this system of conventions was by no means static, it was remarkably durable. Many of the rules governing how Sol was depicted remained stable for a millennium or more throughout the Greco-Roman world. We *must* pay those conventions the same painstaking respect that the Romans themselves did, for how can we hope to interpret images if we are ignorant of the rules governing their composition?

Yet even after we have learned the rules that allow us to establish securely that an image "is" Sol, we still hardly know what that means. One might think that we can side-step this problem by assuming that the Roman image meant the same as the most closely associated Latin word: the image of Sol is "*Sol*". But this would mean that an image of Sol and Luna would be *Sol Lunaque*, quod non; it has long been recognized that as a pair, Sol and Luna evoke, *inter alia*, the concept of *aeternitas*. It should in any case be obvious that verbal and visual modes of communication differ too profoundly to allow any such direct translation between the two. The primary dimension of verbal commu-nication is temporal, not spatial, whereas visual communication is primarily spatially organized, rather than temporally. An inscription is a poor alternative for a cult statue in visual terms, but to effectively make that argument you need words, not pictures.

To return to my search for a theoretical framework for my analyses: I soon found myself in the quandary so typical for our field, of knowing too little for a sophisticated art historical analysis and too much for the wide-ranging approaches of prehistorians. I realized that really I had no choice but to attempt to gain a more fluent understanding of the basic *potential* meanings of an image of Sol – the range of predefined possibilities a Roman would have in the back of her mind as she viewed a particular image – before trying anything more theoretically ambitious. This led me to loosely ground my study in a very basic semiotic framework, with as default position the assumption that meaning(s) associated with an image do not emerge naturally, but are socially constructed.

Equally important: images evoke meanings that cannot, or at least cannot easily, be expressed in words. How does one effectively recognize and define such meanings in our verbal academic discourse? How does one deal with all the other images that contribute to our understanding of the image of Sol? Do we know their meaning any better? What is the most effective methodology to decipher the social codes that govern the agreed upon meanings of a given type of image, and how does one deal with the inevitable gradual change of those meanings over time? These methodological and theoretical questions came to drive much of the research now presented here.

This study does not come close to answering these questions. Indeed in many respects it barely scratches the surface. But it does attempt to acknowledge their importance, and the impact that they have, or should have, on every step of the interpretative process. The common denominator in all these questions is that they force us to reflect on the complex factors at play in the interaction between viewers and the viewed. Tackling these questions challenged me to rethink some of our most basic ideas about the role and nature of the sun in Roman religion. They show that long-held notions concerning, for instance, the origins and chronology of solar cults in Rome, the nature and importance of those cults, the role of solar cult in the deification of emperors, and many other such occurrences must be reconsidered or even simply rejected. I believe this study demonstrates the potential of this type of visual analysis; the stark conclusions with which I open chapter one drive home its importance.

This study is a thorough, and quite extensive reworking of my PhD thesis. Previous versions of a number of chapters have also appeared as articles.[1] This book includes a very large number of images, for which I am deeply grateful to Brill. Images are at the core of this study and must be seen, not merely

---

1   Hijmans 2009 (thesis); Hijmans 1996 (chapter 11); Hijmans 2000 (chapter 9), Hijmans 2004 (chapter 8), Hijmans 2010 (chapter 5).

described (one anonymous reviewer even suggested that images of all entries in the catalogue be supplied). That said, neoliberal policies are making this type of visually grounded research exceedingly difficult, because of the often extraordinary fees one has to pay merely to obtain an image for research – not to mention what it costs to acquire the right to publish. Let me first stress that most museums provided digital images of objects in their collections free of charge or for a nominal cost. That said, a significant number of major museums demanded astronomical sums – up to \$200 – for a single image. Such prices are no doubt the result of political pressure on museums to generate revenue, but nonetheless remain completely unjustifiable. Every single illustration in this book is of a work in the public domain,[2] and museums have an obligation, both legal and ethical, to facilitate access to these objects, not restrict it.[3] By charging such high fees and by attempting to monopolize their right to provide images, these museums do the opposite. As stated, there are fortunately numerous museums that make high resolution digital images freely available on their websites, or provide them for a modest handling fee. It is in large part thanks to these museums that I was able to obtain a reasonable number of pictures illustrating objects in the catalogue.

I have deemed photographs and drawings made before 1920 to be in the public domain. Images produced after 1920 may also be, provided that have been released into the public domain by the rights holder. Such images are used in this publication in accordance with the license under which they have been released. The drawings made by my daughters Anna, Phoebe and Zoë are original works of art based on the objects they depict. These drawings may not be reproduced in any form without their prior written consent. Unless explicitly stated otherwise, the copyright of all other images remains with their respective copyright holders. I have gone to great lengths to ensure that I have all the permissions that can reasonably be required for each image in this publication and apologize for any inadvertent errors.

Numerous colleagues, friends, and family members have encouraged me to write this book, challenged my views, and provided assistance in various other ways. They include: Leonardo de Arrizabalaga y Prado, Peter Attema, Marion van Assendelft, Alessandro Barchiesi, Roger Beck, Natalie Boymel-Kampen,

---

2 All creative works enter the public domain no later than 100 years after the death of the author, artisan or artist who created the work has died. Anyone can use a public domain work, but no one can ever own it.

3 This is not the place to discuss the justifications museums give for monopolizing and profiting financially from their possession of objects in the public domain. See Petri 2014 http://doi.org/10.5334/jcms.1021217. I readily accept that in most cases it is not by choice but under neo-liberal political pressure that museums felt obligated to adopt such pricing policies.

Joe Bryant, Gino Canlas (index), Lucinda Dirven, Mariana Egri, Tristan Ellenberger, Sylviane Estiot, Kate Fenton, Arwen Fleming, Garth Fowden, Blair Fowlkes-Childs, Marjan Galestin, Richard Gordon, Andrew Gow, Philippe Gysen, Nathalie de Haan, Margriet Haagsma, John Harris, Tracene Harvey, Lion Hijmans, Adam Kemezis, Marianne Kleibrink, Hande Kökten, Amber Latimer, Chris Mackay, Katy Mackay, Matt McCarty, Shaun McKinnon, Hasan Malay, Carlos Márquez, Dragana Mladenovic, Eric Moormann, Frits Naerebout, Sarah Nash, Inge Nielsen, Andrew Palmer, Sanja Pilipović, Frances Pownall, Reinder Reinders, Jeremy Rossiter, Selina Stewart, Miguel John Versluys, Henk Versnel, the staff of the Netherlands Institute at Athens, the staff of the Netherlands Institute at Rome, untold numbers of critically inquisitive students, and many, many others.

I am humbled by all this support, and the more grateful for it because the publication of this book has a very personal extra dimension; it is my hardest fought victory in a long and losing war against Parkinson's, a disease I have been battling for two decades. This particular battle would have ended in defeat were it not for the tremendous effort put in by Frits Naerebout in particular, as well as Miguel John Versluys, Anna Beerens, and others. I also thank Gera van Bedaf, Tessa Schild and their colleagues at Brill for their help and patience. A very special word of thanks is due to my stepmother, Marianne Kleibrink, for her unflagging support and interest. Special thanks is also due to my parents, Ben Hijmans and Marion van Assendelft (a tireless editor), for instilling a love of Classics in me from an early age, and to my daughters Zoë, Anna, and Phoebe for keeping me sane, nonetheless. After so much help and advice, all remaining errors are, of course, my own.

This book is dedicated to my spouse, Dr. Margriet J. Haagsma, who, because of my illness, and despite her own academic obligations, prioritized the completion of the editing and indexing of this book. Throughout it all, she has proven to be the only truly *Invicta*.

Edmonton, December 17, 2023

CHAPTER 1

Art and Sol: Some Parameters for an Analysis of Images of the Roman Sun

Sol was a relatively minor, and primarily symbolic, cog in the Roman cosmic order, but he was by no means negligible. One need but explore the roles of Apollo and Sol in Augustan religion, the rise of Mithraism, the particular interest in Sol expressed by emperors such as Aurelian and Constantine, or the adoption by Christians of the winter solstice as birthday of Christ, to realize that the sun is a topic of considerable interest to the history of Roman religion and culture. Sol, then, is well worth studying. But anyone contemplating such a study faces a significant hurdle: there is a striking, indeed almost stunning disconnect between the traditional scholarly views on the solar cult in Rome and the actual evidence available.

The easiest way to demonstrate this is with a brief review of the most recent edition of the Oxford Classical Dictionary, which perfectly summarizes the traditional, established views.[1]

1 Two Sun Gods?

The OCD opens with the remarkable statement that Rome was home – at different times – to two "utterly different" solar deities: Sol *Indiges*, a Roman god, during the Republic, and Sol *Invictus*, a Syrian god, in late antiquity. That this has been the dominant view in classical scholarship for well over a century is mystifying, because there is quite simply no evidence to support the idea that there had been two distinct sun gods in Rome. On the contrary, all the evidence we do have actually shows, either implicitly or explicitly, that the Romans had venerated Sol as a god for as long as they could recall, and never ceased to do so until the demise of polytheism.[2] Literary sources place Sol (and Luna) among the gods introduced by Tatius, immediately after the founding of Rome;[3] Sol was

---

1 OCD, s.v. Sol, DOI: 10.1093/acrefore/9780199381135.013.5984. Retrieved August 5th, 2017. Cf., e.g., Preller & Jordan 1883: I 324–327 & II 408–16.
2 Hijmans 1996a; DNP s.v. Sol; Wallraff 2001; Matern 2002; Berrens 2004.
3 Varro *L* 5,74.

already portrayed on one of the earliest coins minted by Rome[4] and he continued to appear on Roman state coins for the next 500 years – sporadically until the end of the second century AD, and almost annually, often with multiple issues in one year, from the reign of Septimius Severus until the reign of Constantine.[5] This presence of Sol on Roman imperial coins is itself already conclusive evidence that the sun/Sun god was not deemed to be "foreign". Even the most popular non-Roman deities were only rarely (if ever) depicted on Roman imperial coins, in stark contrast to Sol.[6] Leaving that aside, there is the simple fact that in Roman art the iconography of Sol was firmly established well before the first century BC, and remained essentially unchanged in subsequent centuries. It is quite simply impossible, in the Roman world (and beyond), for two "utterly different" gods to be visually indistinguishable from each other. Likewise, in inscriptions we commonly find the sun referred to simply as Sol, without any epithet, from at least the first century BC to the end of antiquity. If, during this period, the Roman Sol was displaced by a much later and certainly foreign one, how are we to know which of the two was meant with "*sol*"?[7] There is also clear continuity in Sol's major "roles", which obviously cannot be if we are dealing with two different deities. For example: Sol was already well established as planetary day of the week in Pompeii (see catalogue E3.1–3), and retained that role throughout antiquity and beyond. The uninterrupted

---

4   An *uncia* minted between 217 and 215 BC (cat. L1.1). Various comparable coins were minted outside Rome in this period, and there is some discussion whether this coin was minted by Rome itself, or elsewhere under Roman jurisdiction. Cf. Thomsen 1961: II, 229–31; Crawford 1974: 150, 39/5.

5   On the iconography of Sol on Severan coins, see Williams 1999: 307–10.

6   While deities of non-Roman origin could be very popular in the Roman Empire – Isis, Sarapis, Jupiter Dolichenus, and Mithras are all ranked among the fourteen deities most mentioned in Latin inscriptions (MacMullen 1981: 5–7) – this popularity is not reflected in the official imperial Roman coinage. Of the 42.749 different coins catalogued on the Online Coins of the Roman Empire website (numismatics.org/ocre/ retrieved August 6th, 2017), only 141 (0.3%) depict foreign deities, namely Anubis (7), Diana Ephesia (11), Diana of Perge (6), Harpocrates (2, with Isis), Horus (9, with Isis), Isis (52, including coins with Anubis, Harpocrates, Horus, Nepthys, Sarapis, and Sothis), Isis Pharia (3), Jupiter Ammon (4), Lunus (1), Nepthys (2, with Isis), Sarapis (59, of which some with Isis), Sol Invictus Elagabalus (10), Sothis (2, with Isis), and Venus of Aphrodisias (1). For Sol, the same site lists 1410 different coins (3.3% of the total).

7   Cf., e.g. CIL VI 701–2 (23 BC), 3719 (AD 64–68), 52 (AD 102), Colini 1939: 122 (AD 150; Sol unnamed, only depicted), CIL V, 764 (AD 100–200), 1027 (AD 199), 2821 (AD 246), AE 1919: 52 (AD 286–293), etc. Iconographically, there is no essential difference between the depictions of Sol in the fourth century AD, (K6.2), in AD 246 (C2w.5), AD 150 (C2b.2), and the mid-first century in Pompeii (E1a.1–2).

presence of temples or shrines of Sol in Rome from the mid Republic or earlier[8] to the fourth century AD is also testament to this continuity.

A glance at the coins depicted in figure 1.1 perfectly illustrates this: if there were two entirely different sun gods in Rome, which of the coins depict the "early", Roman Sol, and which the "later", and "utterly different" Syrian one? Bear in mind that the oldest coin depicted is earlier than the establishment of *feriae* for Sol Indiges in honour of Caesar's victory at Pharsalus, and the youngest of this type dates to the reign of Constantine (L2.213, depicted in the catalogue, not here). The fact is that all evidence – be it archaeological, iconographic, epigraphic, or literary – is consistent in its lack of differentiation between a supposedly "early" and a "late" Sol. The obvious conclusion must be that there was one, continuous religious and cultural tradition in Rome concerning the sun as god.

That brings us to the epithets *indiges* and *invictus*, routinely used today to differentiate between the "early" Sol (*Indiges*) and the "oriental" Sol (*Invictus*). This convention is a modern invention, which does not have any basis in the actual use of those, and other, epithets for Sol in antiquity. We have already seen that it was common practice to simply use *sol*, without any epithet, throughout the Roman period. Almost all priests of the sun, for example, simply refer to themselves as *sacerdos Solis* or *pontifex Solis* without any qualifying epithet.[9] The primary sources for the Republican Sol, such as Varro, Tacitus, Quintilian, and Festus, likewise all simply speak of Sol when referring to his early cults and temples in Rome. In fact, *Indiges* is so rare an epithet for Sol that it occurs only in *Fasti* for August 9th and once in Pliny.[10]

The epithet *invictus* was much more commonly used for Sol. It made its first datable appearance with Sol in AD 158,[11] but the Sun god's association with victory precedes this. Sol is called *victor* around AD 100, and the connection is already tangible in the mid-first century BC, when *feriae* are instituted for Sol *Indiges* (!) on August 9th to commemorate Caesar's recent victory at Pharsalus.[12] More importantly, Berrens has shown conclusively that the epithet *invictus* was used entirely at random for Sol; it was an optional epithet that was not used to differentiate one Sun god from another in any meaningful

---

8   For a thorough discussion of the evidence for the pre-Republican phase of the cult of Sol in Rome, see Marcattili 2009: 37–50.

9   For a full list of *sacerdotes* and *pontifices Solis*, see Hijmans 2010: 408.

10   TLL VII.1, 1177 s.v. *indiges*, listing only the *Fasti*. For the *lucus Solis Indigetis* (Plin. *HN* 3.56) the TLL, without comment, still follows Barbarus' unnecessary emendation of *Iovis* for *Solis*, which goes against the unanimous mss. reading.

11   C2a.3.

12   See pp. 824–826.

FIGURE 1.1   Busts of Sol on coins. *Top row (from left to right)*: L1.5: 109/108 BC; L1.6: 76 BC;
L1.7: 51 BC; *second row*: L2.1: 19 BC; L2.11: AD 114–117; L2.12: 117–128; *third row*:
L2.23: 203–210; L2.75: 260–269; L2.76: 260–269; *fourth row*: L2.133: 276–282; L2.141:
282–283; L3.29: 305–311

way.[13] Furthermore, *invictus* was used for other deities (notably Hercules and Mars) and for the emperor as well, again without any suggestion that it altered their identities. In short, the modern practice to speak of Sol *Invictus* as a distinct, oriental sun god, is unfounded and must be abandoned.

The Oxford Classical Dictionary goes on to state that "Eastern sun-gods" had been making their way to the West for some time before emperor Heliogabalus first attempted to make the Syrian *Sol Invictus Elagabal* the chief deity of Rome. His attempt failed and the cult was checked, according to the OCD, until Aurelian "reintroduced" a similar cult, which was "also oriental." Once again Rose and Scheid, the entry's authors, perfectly summarize the longstanding consensus, and yet it too is untenable. To be sure, there can be little doubt that Heliogabalus attempted to impose his Ba'al of Emesa on the Roman pantheon during his brief reign (218–222). But the difference between Elagabal and the Roman Sol was carefully maintained. The Emesan god is consistently referred to as *Sol Elagabalus*, usually with the addition of *deus*, *invictus*, or both. Furthermore, the Roman Sol is depicted on coins before, during, and after the reign of Heliogabalus, retaining the same Roman iconography throughout (L2.19–41),[14] while Elagabal features on Heliogabalus' coinage only, always in his own standard iconography as a baetyl or conic rock on a cart, and identified as *Sanctus Deus Sol Elagabal* or designated as *Conservator Augusti*. After Heliogabalus' death, the baetyl disappears immediately from Roman coins, while the presence of the Roman Sol, on coins and in general, continues without a break.

Aside from this brief episode with Elagabal, oriental sun cults are actually extremely rare in Rome. The best (and almost only) example is the votive altar of Tiberius Claudius Felix, his wife Claudia Helpis, and their son Claudius Alypus (cat. C2r.1). In Latin it is dedicated to Sol Sanctissimus,[15] in Palmyrene to Malachbel. Iconographically, the image on side B (with the Palmyrene inscription) is distinctive because Sol is on a chariot drawn by two griffins. That is a clear digression from the Roman iconography of Sol, so that even without the Palmyrene inscription it would be clear that this altar was dedicated to a different sun god.[16] There is very little other evidence for oriental sun gods in

---

13   Berrens 2004: 194–8.

14   One coin minted under Heliogabalus may hint at an attempt to associate Sol with Elagabal (who was both solar and Jovian in nature), for it depicts Sol as a standing figure with a thunderbolt and carries the legend *Soli Propugnatori*. Both the thunderbolt (of Jupiter) and the epithet are used only this one time with Sol. See L2.29.

15   *Sanctissimus* as epithet for Sol is extremely rare; cf. CIL VI, 711. On the altar, cf. Fowlkes-Childs 2016: 203–12.

16   For the few other inscriptions mentioning Malachbel in Rome that I am aware of, cf. Hijmans 2010: 416–7. The nineteenth-century notion that the oriental Ba'alim were all

Rome.[17] This should not be surprising, for as Seyrig (1971 & 1973) has already shown, solar cults were not nearly as prevalent and important in the East as used to be thought.[18]

It is true that Sol Invictus Mithras was long held to be a clear example of an oriental sun god whose cult was gradually disseminated from the East to the West, but the chronology and geographic distribution of the cult cannot be reconciled with this diffusionist model. The oldest Roman Mithraic monuments are from the environs of Rome, followed by the Germanic provinces, and the vast majority of Mithraic sites are located in the Latin speaking West. Consequently, Mithraic scholars now reject the notion that this cult was gradually disseminated from the East, and while there is little consensus on how it did establish itself in Rome and her Empire, there is no evidence for Mithraism exercising "orientalizing" influences on traditionally Roman cults, including that of Sol.[19] On the contrary, as we will discuss in chapter four (pp. 153–174), Sol, in Mithraic art, has the effect of "occidentalizing" Mithras.

As for Aurelian, he certainly reformed the cult of Sol and boosted its prominence in Rome, but the sun god under Aurelian is iconographically indistinguishable from the long-established Roman Sol, amply and continuously present on imperial coins throughout the third century AD and in Roman art long before that. This continuity is also reflected in Aurelian's reforms. The introduction of a college of pontiffs for Sol, for example, which the OCD presents as "part of a policy of Romanizing the oriental god," does nothing of the sort because the new *pontifices Solis* simply replaced the *kalatores*, whose supervision of the cult can be documented for at least the first through third centuries AD, and probably went back much further.[20] The fact that *kalatores* are already mentioned in the oldest surviving Latin inscription, the *Lapis Niger* (mid to late sixth century BC), means that their religious status could not have been more quintessentially Roman. Hence replacing them with pontiffs cannot have made the cult of Sol more Roman than it already was. It did significantly raise the god's social status.

Aurelian's other "reforms" – building a new temple for Sol and instituting quadrennial games – are obviously also not grounds for assuming that Aurelian

---

       sun gods must, of course, be rejected; they are invariably identified with Zeus/Jupiter, with the partial exception of Elagabal.

17   On the Palmyrene temple in Rome cf. Fowlkes-Childs 2016; she also mentions one inscription from Rome dedicated to Sol Invictus Malachbel (CIL VI, 31036) and a third-century votive relief to Malachbel and Aglibol (Musei Capitolini 1206; IGUR 117).

18   Cf. also Noiville 1936.

19   Dirven & McCarty 2014: 130; Beck 1998; Clauss 1992. Seminal are Gordon 1975 and Merkelbach 1984.

20   Cf. pp. 845–7 for a full discussion of the role of the *kalatores* in the cult.

was introducing a new cult, let alone a Syrian one. If anything, Aurelian's games for Sol recall the Actian games for Apollo, founded by Augustus. As for the unique architecture of Aurelian's open-air temple for Sol, it finds its best parallel in a temple for Sol in Trastevere (hitherto overlooked or misidentified), which dated back to at least the mid first century AD.[21]

The general consensus, again admirably summarized by Rose and Scheid, has been that after Aurelian's reforms, the cult of Sol "remained the chief imperial and official worship till Christianity displaced it," and once again the evidence disputes this. Always overlooked, for example, is the fact that Aurelian's reforms established a clear hierarchy of pontiffs: members of the traditional college were henceforth referred to as *pontifices maiores* indicating that they took precedence over the *pontifices Solis*.[22] Likewise, while Aurelian's reforms resulted in Sol becoming one of the standard potential choices for patron deity of the emperor, there is no evidence to suggest that he was the most powerful or more popular choice. And while a small number of very rare and iconographically ambiguous coins minted in Serdica can be interpreted as a sign that Aurelian toyed with the idea of elevating Sol to the level of *dominus imperii Romani* ("lord of the Roman Empire"), what that means precisely is open to debate. We have no evidence that this idea was ever repeated, far less implemented.[23] There is, quite simply, no evidence that any emperor, including Aurelian, actually installed or attempted to install Sol to the level of supreme Roman deity.

This, then, is the stark conclusion with which we open this book, namely that generations of classicists have wrongly accepted the wholly unfounded notion that in late antiquity a Syrian Sun god, Sol Invictus, came to dominate the Roman pantheon. How classicists came to accept this oriental mirage is itself a fascinating piece of *Forschungsgeschichte*, which we will discuss in the final chapter of this book. How to replace this mirage with a more solid understanding of the roles of Sol in Roman religion (and beyond) is the topic of the rest of this chapter, which focuses on establishing a theoretical framework and methodology for studying the main body of evidence we have for Sol: the visual, material remains. For there lies the crux of the problem: the written sources on solar cult in Rome are so scant that they can be made to fit almost any overarching narrative. Far more abundant, but hardly studied, are the non-literary sources. What they can tell us about Sol is the topic of this book.

---

21   Infra, pp. 829–849. Cf. Hijmans 2010.

22   Infra, pp. 1012–1019.

23   Cf. pp. 1033–5.

In addition to the impact of its strange *Forschungsgeschichte*, two factors, then, make Sol difficult to study: the written evidence is sparse and the visual evidence, though quite extensive, is resolutely visual. Translating those visual expressions of the sun into a verbal understanding of his role(s) in the Roman world raises significant theoretical and methodological issues. We review the most important ones in this chapter. Some may feel that I am belabouring the obvious here, and I certainly do not claim to be saying anything revolutionary. My goal is simply to present my understanding of the principles of theory and practice in which this work is grounded.

2   Reading Roman Art – The Problem of the "Greek Norm"

Art, in the broadest possible sense of the word, was of major importance in the Roman world for the mediation and dissemination of social, political and religious dogmas, concepts, and concerns. As such, Roman art constitutes a rich trove of potentially informative "visual texts". The problem is that we lack convincing interpretative strategies to "read" Roman art in this manner. To understand why that is, we must first very briefly review the history of Roman art history.

Roman art has generally been treated as the heir to two important and conceptually very different artistic traditions. The closest tradition, geographically as well as artistically, was that of Etruscan and central Italian art. But it is the other influence, that of Greek art, that has most interested scholars. The reason for this is rooted in the views on classical art history that took shape in the latter part of the eighteenth and the earlier part of the nineteenth centuries and whose influence remains strong today. In these views, Rome was seen as unrivalled in its military and political ability to build Empire, but as culturally inferior to its illustrious predecessor, Greece.[24] The contention that Rome was capable only of absorbing and disseminating the superior culture of the

---

24   For a typical expression of this view, cf. Baumgarten et al. 1913: 219: "Wohl keinen größeren Gegensatz kann es zwischen zwei derselben großen europäischen Völkerfamilie angehörigen Völkern geben, als zwischen der griechischen und der römischen Nation. Ausgezeichnet durch größere körperliche Festigkeit, als der Hellene, hat der Römer vermocht, einen Menschheitstypus herber Männlichkeit zu entwickeln, wie er in gleich selbstbewußter Weise schwerlich unter den Kulturnationen der Welt wiederkehrt (...). Da sich nun die große Energie des nüchtern denkenden Volkes in überwiegendem Maße dem Staatsleben zuwandte, so ist es bis jetzt keinem Volke wieder vergönnt gewesen, eine Weltherrschaft über Kulturnationen aufzurichten wie es die römische war. (...) Die Menschheitskultur freilich konnte Rom nur verbreiten, weil dieses Volk mit seinem eminenten Staatsbewußtsein, seinem stolzen Selbstgefühl sich nicht im mindesten fremder

Greeks resonated widely. It resulted in a "de-Romanisation" of those areas of Roman – especially imperial – art and literature that were clearly inspired on Greece, and a denigration of those areas that were not. Discussions of Roman art and literature were framed in terms of imitation, stressing above all Rome's debt to Greece.[25] Of course, these unflattering views of Roman culture to some extent echo those of many Romans themselves, who saw the Orontes flowing in the Tiber, and complained that *Graecia capta Romam cepit*. Nonetheless, the modern view of Roman art as a (declining) continuation and (poor) imitation of the Greek was rooted more in the assessments of aesthetic quality championed by Winckelmann and his successors, than in an analysis and acceptance of ancient attitudes. Modern scholars have deemed Greek art to be the better not because that was what the Romans thought, but because they themselves idealized it as the more simple, unspoiled, and genuine, possessing (in Winckelmann's inimitable terms) that all-important *edle Einfalt und stille Grösse*.[26] Greek art, characterized by its ability to look beyond the mechanistic imitation of physical reality to explore ways to capture some divine, ineffable essence of beauty and truth, represented, in this view, all that one could desire from true art.[27] Roman art by comparison was inferior because it deviated from this path, even while it imitated Greek art. It often ignored such essentials as due proportions and natural relationships between bodies and space, and in its dryness distinctly lacked Greek art's focus on what art historians saw as true beauty. No matter that many surviving "Greek" works are in fact Roman; it is the Greek genius that makes noble simplicity and quiet grandeur shine through in even so tortured a figure as that of the Laocoon, just as it was Greek genius that allowed the divine spirit of beauty to be captured in and evoked by that greatest masterpiece of all: the Apollo Belvedere.[28]

Kultur verschloß. Das gilt vor allem dem Hellenismus gegenüber, aber auch die Kultur des Orients (...)."

25   Bolgar 1984: 431–2; Habinek 1992: 227–30, focusing in particular on Latin literature; cf. Boymel Kampen 2003: 375.

26   Cf. Morrison 1996: 64–7, for a clear description of Winckelmann's ideal of art. See also Scott 2006: 631–2.

27   Stocking 2014. Winckelmann felt that artistic development can be broadly understood within the framework of a "loss of" and "return to" nature (Käfer 1986: 99–100). Cf. Käfer's discussion (1986: 87–91) of Lessing's views on art, Homer, and nature. On the notion of nature as art's ultimate *exemplum* cf. Philostr. *Imag.* 294 K 8–10, praising the invention of μίμησις (*mimesis*) in painting as an εὕρημα πρεσβύτατον καὶ ξυγγενέστατον φύσει (a most ancient invention and most akin to nature).

28   Laocoon: Brilliant 2000: 50–62. On the traditional approach to Roman art: Ridgway 2005: 63 (cf. Ridgway 1994). On the practice of analyzing Roman statues as copies of Greek masterpieces and hence a source of insight in those masterpieces: Trimble & Elsner 2006: 202–4 (with useful references in notes 7 and 8), cf. Gazda: 2002.

To a degree, this is a perfectly valid approach to ancient art which is, after
all, as much our art today as it was their art then. But attributing universal
validity to those rules is a different matter. For anyone holding such normative views regarding the artistic and aesthetic superiority of Greek art, it follows that Romans would always have wanted to imitate and emulate the art of
the Greeks, which they knew intimately. The fact that they often did not do so
must then be taken as a sign that they could not, rather than that they would
not. In other words, it was the decline and fall of the Roman Empire that must
have caused art (understood to be Greek art) to degenerate.[29]

For a century and a half, the dogma of Greek genius reigned unchallenged. It
continues to inform our attitudes towards ancient art more than we realize.[30]
In the early twentieth century, however, two protagonists of the antinormative
Viennese school, Franz Wickhoff and Alois Riegl, rejected the aestheticizing
opinions about artistic quality that had dominated the debate until then.[31]
They argued that in particular the anticlassical art of the later Roman Empire
was not decadent but different, rooted in a shift in the *Kunstwollen* – to use

---

29   Cf. Riegl's 1927: 6–7 discussion of previous views on late Roman art: "Die bildende Kunst
     wäre von dem hohen Stande der Entwicklung, zu dem sie es bei den Mittelmeervölkern
     gebracht hatte, durch das zerstörende Eingreifen barbarischer Völkerschaften im Norden
     und Osten des römischen Weltreiches herabgeschleudert worden, so daß sie von Karls
     des Großen Zeit an eine aufsteigende Entwicklung vom neuen beginnen mußte." On the
     problem of quality as an intellectual category cf. Boymel Kampen 2003: 377 and n. 33.
30   Stocking 2014; P. Stewart 2004: 1–4. Cf. Ridgway 1986: 11 n. 28 and 2005, 63. On
     Winckelmann's view of his organic scheme of stylistic development as the inevitable out-
     come of a law of nature, and on the "logical acrobatics" he needed to make the ancient
     sculptural evidence fit the postulated universal scheme, cf. Fullerton 2003: 98–100.
31   Riegl 1927: 11 sets out the reasons why previous scholarship had misunderstood late
     Roman art in particularly clear and damning terms: "Was ist es nun, das (...) Forscher (...)
     verhindert hat, das Wesen der spätrömischen Kunstwerke mit unbefangenem Auge zu
     würdigen? Nichts als die subjektive Kritik, die unser moderner Geschmack an den uns vor-
     liegenden Denkmälern vornimmt. Dieser Geschmack verlangt vom Kunstwerk Schönheit
     und Lebendigkeit, wobei die Wage abwechselnd nach der ersteren oder der letzteren
     Seite neigt. Beides hat die vorantoninische Antike besessen (...), keines von beiden aber
     (...) die spätrömische Kunst. (...) Daß jemals auf Häßlichkeit und Leblosigkeit, wie wir
     ihnen in der spätrömischen Kunst zu begegnen glauben, ein positives Kunstwollen geri-
     chtet gewesen sein könnte, erscheint uns vom Standpunkte des modernen Geschmackes
     schlechthin unmöglich. Es kommt aber alles darauf an, zur Einsicht zu gelangen (...) daß
     das Kunstwollen noch auf die Wahrnehmung anderer (nach modernen Begriffe weder
     schöner noch lebendiger) Erscheinungsformen der Dinge gerichtet sein kann." Only a few
     decades earlier, Otto Seeck had still argued that in late antiquity, Roman society had been
     characterized by "eine entsetzliche Trägheit des Geistes. (...) Weder in der Landwirtschaft,
     noch in der Technik, noch in der Staatsverwaltung ist seit dem ersten Jahrhundert nach
     Christus eine neue Idee von irgendwelcher Bedeutung aufgetaucht. Auch Literatur und
     Kunst bewegen sich ausschliesslich in einer öden Nachahmung, die geistig immer dürft-
     iger, technisch immer schwächer wird." (Seeck 1910: 270–1).

Riegl's untranslatable term – of the age.[32] Wickhoff and Riegl thus became prime movers in a gradual rehabilitation of late Roman art – indeed of Roman art in general.

Riegl's notion of a shift in *Kunstwollen* injected an important new concept into the debate, but sustained the sense of a chronological evolution and differentiation of styles, and, by extension, of their exclusivity.[33] This monolithic view of style as an index of a specific region, group, and/or period continued to inform much subsequent study of Roman art history.[34] Some of the most important work focused on determining the unique qualities that made Roman art Roman. By the middle of the twentieth century, two major streams had emerged. The one continued to emphasize the debt to Greece of Roman art. A good example of this is Strong's insistence that "… at least until the late Empire, the Greek tradition is basically unchallenged, not simply because the artists were generally of Greek nationality but because classical Greek art was the acceptable standard of the Roman patron."[35] This school of thought continued to treat Roman art as essentially a continuation of the Greek in form, if not in achievement, and it downplayed the existence of any specifically Roman or Italian elements.[36] Hanfmann (1964, 19) goes so far as to deny the very existence of "Roman" art prior to Augustus, there having been only "art in Rome" that was, he feels, no more than "a marginal province of the frontiers of Greek art."[37] Not surprisingly, such scholars continued to discuss the art of late antiquity in terms of a decline from the Greek norm.[38]

---

32   For examples and discussion of attempted translations of *Kunstwollen*, cf. Elsner 2002b: 359–60.

33   Riegl 1927: 18 emphasizes the arbitrariness of giving specific dates defining specific periods, but in general supports the notion of an evolution of styles: "Es möge (…) sofort (…) bemerkt sein, daß manche charakteristische Züge der Kunst des vierten Jahrhunderts sich in stetig abnehmender Dichtigkeit bis in den vorchristlichen Hellenismus zurück verfolgen lassen." On Riegl cf. Elsner 2002b; Iversen 1993.

34   By far the best analysis of the history of Roman art history up to the 1950s and 60s is by Brendel 1979; cf. also Boymel Kampen 2003: 371–9.

35   Strong 1976: xix.

36   Strong 1976: xx–xxiv; cf. Hanfmann 1964: 15–18.

37   P. Stewart 2004: 1 quotes an unnamed "distinguished Oxford professor" who expressed an identical opinion to him. Cf. Scott 2006: 628–30 and Gazda 2002: 3 on the perpetuation of such concepts through museum displays.

38   Cf. Hanfmann 1964: 31: "'Folk art,' confined to carvers of shop signs and painters of wall posters under the early Empire, had subsequently played its part in the art of the lower status carried by the Roman legions to western Europe. Its 'anti-classical' expressionistic forms began to reach higher levels of art in the Antonine era, just as vulgarisms of common speech were becoming part of written literature in the *elocutio novella* of an Apuleius."

In continental Europe, German and Italian scholars in particular developed a slightly different approach, that stressed the dual nature of Roman art, its perceived tendency to eclecticism, and consequently its difference from Greek art.[39] Alongside the undeniably important influences of Greek artistic practice and traditions, these scholars pointed to what they saw as the continued vigour of an Italian tradition. Long associated with the lower strata of society as *Volkskunst* (Rodenwalt) or *arte plebea* (Bianchi Bandinelli), this Italian tradition was seen as having increasingly encroached on official or "high" art, so that by the third century it permeated all levels of artistic production in Rome. While much debate focused on determining what formal elements and spatial concepts characterized the Italian elements of Roman artistic traditions, and on establishing when and how they were adopted in "high" art, there appears to have been less interest in determining why the Italian and Greek artistic traditions were so different. For Bianchi Bandinelli (1976: 58), the class connections are paramount, and he argues that in the "plebeian" art of the first century AD we see

> ... il germe fondamentale di taluni aspetti artistici che preverranno quando l'apporto ellenistico si sarà esaurito e quando, respinta ai margini l'antica classe patrizia avversata dagli imperatori di quel tempo, le classi plebee formeranno la nuova ossatura dell'impero, nel III secolo.[40]

Others, like Felletti Maj (1977), stress ethnic connections.[41] In effect, therefore, there is, underlying these studies, still a concept of culture as something essentially immutable and intimately intertwined with specific ethnic or social groups.

---

39 Cf., e.g., von Heinze 1972: 5–13 whose emphatic pronouncement that Roman art "is anything but a continuation and culmination of Greek art" stands in marked contrast to the views expressed by Strong four years later. For a good overview of these schools, cf. Felleti Maj 1977: 19–39.

40 Cf. L'Orange 1965, who argues for a close link between the artistic changes and the sociopolitical transition from Principate to Dominate. Bianchi Bandinelli's emphasis on the marginalization of the ancient elite and the rise to prominence of the plebs is remarkably reminiscent of Seeck's discussion of the "Ausrottung der Besten", although their evaluations of the effects of this process differ fundamentally; Seeck 1910: 269–307.

41 Cf., e.g., Felletti Maj 1977: 37, who states that in the emergence of the anti-classical tradition in imperial art in the later second century it is obvious that "ideatori ed esecutori [sc. of the new style] non provengono direttamente dalle officine 'italiche', ma dalla schiera degli artisti più rappresentivi delle officine romane, nelle quali l'insegnamento classico era stato costantemente alimentato da artisti greci."

3   Greek Art and Etruscan Art

While such social or ethnic explanations for the coexistence of divergent styles
are not necessarily impossible, they fail to adequately explain one key characteristic of this phenomenon, namely that, in central Italy at least, the coexistence of different styles in the same context was already a characteristic of
archaic Etruscan art, and continued to be so throughout antiquity.[42] From the
outset, Etruscan art was clearly influenced by developments in Greece. The
similarities are often striking and consecutive stylistic developments in Greek
art quickly make their appearance in Etruscan art as well. Indeed, Etruscans
imported many of their prized possessions directly from Greece, and there
were also Greek artists at work in Etruscan centres. Of course, there were also
significant differences between Greek and Etruscan art – archaic Etruscan
males are clothed, not nude, for example – but such differences have generally
been understood as differences in cultural practice or as the result of regional
necessities (the lack of local marble leading Etruscans to rely heavily on terracotta, for instance). The important point is that the stylistic development of
Etruscan art is usually understood and discussed in the same terms as Greek
art. Indeed, it is often discussed as a poor and peripheral province of Greek art.
     And yet, throughout we see in Etruscan art a distinctly "ungreek" willing-
ness to forego mimesis. There is evident influence of archaic Greek art on the
heads and upper bodies of the couple reclining on the famous sarcophagus
from Cerveteri, now in the Villa Giulia museum, but in the transition to the
lower body and the articulation of the legs there is no attempt at natural proportions and positions whatsoever (fig. 1.2). This willingness to forego natural
proportions did not diminish in subsequent centuries. In fact, in the fourth
century and beyond the contrasts are even starker, with the easy naturalism of
locally produced sculpture[43] or the master draughtsmanship displayed on mirrors, for instance (figs. 1.3–1.5 and A1b.1), co-existing with elongated "ribbon"-
statuettes and the like (figs. 1.6–1.10). And we need but think of the strangely
proportioned and at times even grotesquely malformed figures atop many a
cinerary urn to see that this continues right into the first century BC (figs. 1.11,
1.12). No wonder then, that just as with Roman art, we see in discussions of
Etruscan art the problems caused by that normative paradigm that elevated
Greek art to the pinnacle of ancient artistic achievement. It is beyond dispute

---

42   As Boymel Kampen 2003: 371 puts it: "Sometimes every conceivable style short of Abstract
      Expressionism seemed to be happening all at once at some spot in the Empire." On the
      continued vigor of "classicizing" art throughout the fourth century AD, cf. Kiilerich 1993.
43   A famous example would be, e.g., the Capitoline Brutus, Cornell 1995: 392 fig. 31.

FIGURE 1.2   Terracotta sarcophagus, Rome, Villa Giulia Museum
PHOTOGRAPH COURTESY OF THE MUSEUM

FIGURE 1.3   Alabaster cinerarium, Princeton Art Museum 1986–68
PHOTOGRAPH COURTESY OF THE MUSEUM

FIGURE 1.4   Terracotta head of a Satyr, Princeton Art Museum 3369
PHOTOGRAPH COURTESY OF THE MUSEUM

FIGURE 1.5   Bronze mirror, New York, Metropolitan Museum 09.22116, Rogers Fund
PHOTOGRAPH COURTESY OF THE MUSEUM

that the Etruscans were acutely aware of Greek art and were inspired by it, and from the normative perspective one would expect no less. It is, however, equally undeniable that Etruscan art could digress radically from Greek practice. From the archaic canopic urns to the "ribbon"-statuettes of the third and second centuries BC, the Etruscans obstinately maintained the – to many scholars unsettling – habit of producing art forms that cannot by any stretch of the imagination be considered Greek, or even influenced by Greece.

It is interesting to observe how scholars attempted to explain this phenomenon without subverting the paradigm of Greek artistic superiority. Dealing with the earlier phases of Etruscan art, they resorted rather quickly to

FIGURE 1.6
Bronze statuette, Volterra, Museum
PHOTOGRAPH COURTESY OF THE
MUSEUM

FIGURE 1.7
Bronze statuette, Rome, Villa
Giulia Museum 236296
PHOTOGRAPH COURTESY
OF THE MUSEUM

FIGURE 1.8
Bronze statuette, Rome, Villa
Giulia Museum 244779
PHOTOGRAPH COURTESY OF
THE MUSEUM

FIGURE 1.9   Bronze statuette, New York Metropolitan Museum 96.9.418
PHOTOGRAPH COURTESY OF THE MUSEUM

FIGURE 1.10   Bronze statuette, New York Metropolitan Museum 1972.118.53
PHOTOGRAPH COURTESY OF THE MUSEUM

FIGURE 1.11   Cinerarium, Volterra, Museum
                PHOTOGRAPH COURTESY OF THE MUSEUM

describing un-Hellenized works as the products of primitive indigenous traditions of a not yet wholly Hellenized artistic community.[44] For later periods
(Classical, Hellenistic) proposals ranged from class arguments[45] to suggestions

---

44   Cf., e.g., Pallottino 1978: 166–71.
45   Bianchi Bandinelli 1973.

FIGURE 1.12   Cinerarium, New York, Metropolitan Museum 96.9.225a & b
PHOTOGRAPH COURTESY OF THE MUSEUM

that works produced in an un-Greek style were "ritually archaizing" or the product of "isolated backwaters".[46] In short, as with late imperial art, anything

---

46   On Etruscan art as "peripheral" to Greek art, cf. e.g., Hus 1980, who argues that in all ages there are "cultures directrices, créatrices des formes nouvelles et dispensatrices de progrès" and that in antiquity this was the role of Greek culture. Cultures that were "less advanced", such as Etruscan culture, "s'inspirent des modèles qui leur sont ainsi proposés

typically "Etruscan" in central Italian art of the Classical and Hellenistic periods was traditionally viewed as a problem – indeed, Pallottino (1978: 166) saw Etruscan art as a whole as a "problem" – with scholars attempting to explain in various ways how it could be that Etruscan art fell so far short of the aesthetic ideal embodied by the Greek art with which they were so well acquainted.

These attempts are fruitless. The reality is that in the six centuries of so-called Etruscan art (seventh-second century BC) the Etruscans consistently display perfect mastery at producing art à la grecque in one breath with art that clashes with the most basic principles (as we have understood them) of Greek aesthetics. There is no lack of genius here, but simply a difference of aims (or of tradition in achieving aims that were perhaps more similar than the differences in form imply). For it must surely be the case that any Etruscan of the third or second century BC who could afford an elaborately decorated alabaster cinerary urn could afford to have its lid carved in the Greek style, if they so desired. Hence the fact that so many of the urns produced in this period have lids that were, in fact, idiosyncratically non-Greek must mean that many Etruscans did not want one with Greek sculpting, not that they could not have one.

One could argue that style was not so much a matter of taste as a matter of topic, and that the main purpose of such urns was not to emote aesthetically but to express socially. The choice of style – "Etruscan" rather than "Greek" – could be determined by the intended communication.[47] Style itself becomes a medium for the message of the art-work, rather than an expression of some ineffable aesthetic desire of the artist or society. This could help explain why in the case of many cinerary urns, for example, the bodies of the deceased on the lid are strangely proportioned, but the figures in the scenes on the side are not (figs. 1.3, 1.11, 1.12). There is no sign here of lack of competence, no reason to speak of decline or dissolution. One glance at the reliefs is enough to show that clearly the Etruscan artisans who produced these works were perfectly capable of sculpting well-proportioned figures in a range of poses if they so desired.

---

et imitent, à la périphérie du foyer créateur, les techniques et les formes que celui-ci a élaborées." He proceeds to state that when, in the second half of the fifth century BC, political and economic decline had cut off Etruscan contacts with the Greeks, they missed the essential lessons of Classical Greek artistic development, reverting for that reason to their own more primitive, traditional forms. Brendel 1995: 36, 330 speaks of cultural backwaters, ritual archaizing, and "creative error" of Etruscan artists, who do not grasp the inner logic of Greek art, in order to explain the formal and stylistic "peculiarities". Others, like Torelli 1985 use a model of decline and decadence to explain the "dissolution" and "incoherence" of form that characterize disproportionate figures produced in Etruscan art of the Hellenistic era.

47   Fundamental for the notion of style as communicative tool in ancient art is Hölscher 1987.

Hence the fact that they often did not do so in the case of the figures on the lid was a matter of choice, and a common choice at that.[48]

Of course, this view of style as a tool requires that we abandon the monolithic and unwieldy connections between style and ethnicity, region, class or period, inherent to many older approaches (not to mention archaeological dating practices). If we wish to speak of Etruscan or Central Italian art we cannot focus on form, but must focus on expression. A third-century mirror from Praeneste, incised in a rich "Hellenistic" manner, is as integral to central Italian art as the contemporary abstract "ribbon"-statuettes, the terracotta Apollo-Helios from Civita Castellana (A1b.1), cinerary urns with their disproportioned figures reclining on the lids, the winged horses of Tarquinia, etc.[49] A major characteristic of art in this region happened to be that quite different styles of depiction could coexist not just contemporaneously, but actually within the same monument or composition.

This was the tradition that Rome was a part of and out of which Roman art evolved. Not an isolated or peripheral region that was incapable of doing more than garble the superior (Greek) art practices with which it came into contact, but a region with its own distinct artistic conceptions and, importantly, its own philosophy of art. Exploring that philosophy is well beyond the scope of this chapter, but one point should be made here: central to it, apparently, was the potentially *symbolic* rather than *mimetic* quality of the visual. For one consistent characteristic of Italian art is the ability to signify some concept or reality through art with little attempt to approximate that reality mimetically in the artwork. Art, in this tradition, is, or at least can be, autonomous in that the connection between representation and the represented can be to a significant degree arbitrary (i.e. based on social agreement) rather than iconic. At the same time, recognizability remains paramount. This is not abstract art, but visual communication bound by social conventions in which form is subordinate to meaning. It is effective, because its conventions are understood by society and individual artists are scrupulous in their adherence to established systems of depiction. Hence comprehension is always ensured, but the aesthetic qualities of Greek art are not necessarily desired. In short. the choice of style was dictated at least as much by the message and intended audience as by taste, which explains the characteristic coexistence of diverse, even conflicting styles throughout ancient Italian art.

---

48   On the specific role of Greek mythology and mythological imagery in Etruscan social discourse, cf. Massa-Pairault 1999. The use of "Greek" style for mythological scenes accentuates the specific nature of these scenes.

49   On the winged horses, cf. Bagnasco 2009.

4   **Greek Art and Good Taste**

But where does this emphasis on style as communicative tool leave Rome's documented admiration for Greek art? Surely it is clear from written sources that the Romans were not impervious to the aesthetic allure of Greek masterpieces. Caesar did not pay 80 talents for two paintings by Timomachus because of their clarity of message.[50] But while it is certainly true that Romans prized Greek art, Roman ambivalence towards the admirability of "great art" clearly shines through in their own assessment of the processes by which they discovered it. Pliny describes the earliest paintings in Rome as primarily informative victory tableaus and relates that Mummius was clueless when it came to appreciating the true value of the art he had plundered from Corinth (146 BC).[51] Others famously ascribe the beginning of Rome's admiration for Greek art to the sack of Syracuse in 212 BC and the art works sent back to Rome by Marcellus as booty.[52] What matters is not the accuracy of such assessments, but their symbolic function in Rome's understanding of its own past. For historians like Livy, ignorance of Greek artistic norms signalled the rustic simplicity prized in the Republican heroes, while the sophisticated tastes which admired Greek art heralded the abandonment of the *mores* that had made Rome great. Plutarch has the more dignified Romans complaining that Marcellus' booty was leading the Romans to idly converse about art and beauty, where formerly they had been rustic farmers who knew only how to till the land and defend it.[53]

By the first century BC, of course, Caesar was not the only Roman spending large sums of money to acquire Greek art.[54] In the spring of 67 BC, Cicero wrote to Atticus in Greece, asking him to acquire statues and herms suitable for his lecture hall ("quae γυμνασιώδη sunt") at his villa in Tusculum, and thanking him for the herms and Megarian statues he had already acquired on Cicero's behalf,

---

50   Plin. *NH* 7, 126; 35, 136.

51   Plin. *NH* 35, 22–4. When king Attalos paid Mummius 100 talents for one painting (of Dionysus) by Aristeides, Mummius assumed that there must be some quality to the painting of which he was unaware ("aliquid in ea virtutis, quod ipse nesciret"), and revoked the sale.

52   Liv. 25, 40. On the sentiments expressed by Livy, cf. Pol. 9, 10; Plut. *Marc.* 21. On Polybius' remarks, cf. Stewart 2003 :140–1. Cf. below. pp. 56–59.

53   Without, apparently, any irony intended, Plutarch (*Marc.* 21) quotes a line of the description of Hercules in the *Licymnius* of Euripides (Dramatic Fragments. 473, LCL 501, pp. 562–3), to describe the Romans as "plain and straightforward, and virtuous in the extreme," before Greek culture transformed them.

54   On art collecting in antiquity see Higbie 2017; cf. the papers in Fabbrini 2001 (focusing on the late Republic); Bounia 2004.

for the sum of 20 000 sestertii.[55] "Arcae nostrae confidito," he tells his friend. In this correspondence, Cicero is asking Attalus to spend substantial sums of money on his behalf to buy art which Cicero has never seen. Not surprisingly, therefore, the emphasis in Cicero's letters is on "suitable" or "correct"[56] rather than beautiful art. This does not mean that low quality or poor artistry will do. Cicero writes that he places his trust in the *elegantia* of Attalus, presumably referring not just the latter's good taste in matters of theme, but also in matters of artistic quality. But Cicero is already delighted with Atticus' purchases sight unseen,[57] stressing their aptness, and displaying no interest whatsoever in their style or artistry.[58] Indeed, when many years later Gallus managed to acquire some masterpieces for Cicero, the now retired statesman grumpily complained that they were far too expensive, and that he had no idea what to do with them.[59] Again Cicero displays no interest in the artistic quality, but

---

55 On Cicero's correspondence with Atticus concerning the acquisition of art for his villa, see Bounia 2004: chapter 9. Cf. Bravi 2014: 17–21; Marvin 1989 [1993]: 180–4. Assuming 6000 *denarii* to the talent, this is less than 1 talent (24 000 *sestertii*), a paltry sum compared to the prices Caesar was later to pay for his masterpieces. Cicero is delighted with Atticus for acquiring suitable sculpture for him at such a low price (*parvo*) (Marvin 1989 [1993]: letter 8).

56 "Dignum Academia tibi quod videbitur" ("what you think is worthy of the Academy") and "quae γυμνασιώδη maxime sunt" ("which are the most gymnasial"), Cic. *Att.* 1, 9 (5), 68 BC; "quae tu intelleges convenire nostro Tusculano" ("which you know will suit my Tusculan ⟨country home⟩"), Cic. *Att.* 1, 5 (1), early 67 BC; "velim (…) signa et cetera quae tibi eius loci et nostri studi et tuae elegantiae esse videbuntur" ("I would like statues etc. which you think suit that place, my interests, and your refined taste"), Cic. *Att.* 1, 8 (4), after Feb. 13th 67 BC; "οἰκεῖον eius loci" ("at home in that place"), Cic. *Att.* 1, 10 (6), middle of 67 BC; all translations by the author.

57 "Hermae tui Pentelici cum capitibus aëneis, de quibus ad me scripsisti, iam nunc me admodum delectant" ("the pantelic herms with their bronze heads, about which you wrote me, already quite delight me"), Cic. *Att.* 1, 8 (4), after Feb. 13th 67 BC; translation by the author.

58 This is clearest in his discussion of a Hermathena that Atticus had acquired for him, first expressing his delight before he had seen it: "Quod ad me de Hermathena scribis per mihi gratum est. est ornamentum Academiae proprium meae, quod et Hermes commune est omnium et Minerva singulare est insigne eius gymnasi." ("What you write me about the Hermathena is most welcome to me. It is an ornament proper to my Academy, both because Hermes is common to all and Minerva is especially significant to this gymnasium."), Cic. *Att.* 1, 4 (9), spring 66 BC; translation by the author. Location is again paramount once he has seen the statue. He says nothing about the statue itself, but writes to Atticus: "Hermathena tua valde me delectat et posita ita belle est ut totum gymnasium eius ἀνάθημα videatur." ("Your Hermathena pleases me greatly and it is so well placed that the whole gymnasium appears to be a dedication to it."), Cic. *Att.* 1, 1 (10), shortly before July 17th, 65 BC; translation by the author.

59 Cic. *Fam.* 7, 23.

stresses his desire to acquire ornaments suitable for the spaces they are to decorate and congruent with his personality; what is he, a man of peace, supposed
to do with a statue of Mars, he asks in exasperation.

Cicero is, of course, but one case and Gallus, one assumes, did not feel that
the statues he had acquired for Cicero were overpriced or unsuitable. Many
of the Roman elite were willing to spend large sums to acquire top pieces. But
as, among others, Bergmann (1995) has argued, we must not project our own
understanding of art even on these connoisseurs. Stewart points to the issues
of power (and its abuse) as among the many factors that were involved in the
appropriation, by whatever means, of public works of Greek art for the embel-
lishment of private Roman properties or public Roman spaces.[60] Other considerations played a role as well. Scholars are now largely in agreement that
the whole process of Roman appropriation of Greek "masterpieces" as well as
Roman "copying" of those masterpieces was a more complex and multifaceted
phenomenon than allowed for in the traditional approach which viewed it
simply in terms of Rome's admiration for Greek artistic genius and her more
or less faithful attempts to copy that. In particular the longstanding scholarly
practice of *Kopienkritik* has been the object of harsh criticism bordering on
ridicule.[61] The traditional interpretation of the handful of ancient sources that
discuss (Greek) art in Rome has also been criticized as too narrow and bent to
fit assumptions of Greek artistic superiority.[62]

This moving away from the notion of Roman copying of superior Greek
art is an aspect of the broader and rather substantial shift in attitude towards
Roman art that has been underway for some time and has gained momentum
in the past few decades. By moving it out of the shadow of Greek art, the way
has been opened to viewing Roman art on its own terms, which means that we
must view it with very different eyes. In fact, the whole notion of "Roman" art

---

60   Stewart 2003: 140–3. To further complicate matters, the difference between private and pub-
      lic is of course not a straightforward issue in the Roman sphere. Cf. Stewart 2003: 259–60.
61   For a concise and blistering critique, cf. Trimble & Elsner 2006: 202–4. Cf. Marvin 1989;
      Stewart 2003: 231–6 (with a good discussion of other critiques) and most recently
      Anguissola 2021. The practice of *Kopienkritik* is defended by others – particularly in
      Germany. While a degree of defensiveness is detectable, many of their arguments deserve
      to be taken seriously. The validity and usefulness of many aspects of *Kopienkritik* in the
      realm of ancient portraiture, for instance, is hard to deny, and there is no reason in principle
      why that cannot be extended to certain other works of art as well. Cf. Boschung 1993: 4–7
      or Bergmann 1978: 13–4 for the basic principles of *Kopienkritik*. Beard & Henderson 2001:
      221–4 discuss the locks of Augustus (the importance of counting locks (*Lockenzählen*) is
      defended by Boschung, *loc. cit.*). For potential and problems of *Kopienkritik* in the study
      of the portrait of Augustus: Smith 1996.
62   Stewart 2003: 225; Trimble & Elsner 2006: 208. On Pliny and art cf. Isager 1992.

as the unified or unifiable subject of a grand narrative has been largely abandoned. In its place a whole range of new approaches have emerged and continue to emerge focusing on gender, ethnicity, spectacle, power, emotion and the like, as mediated by different strands of art in the Roman world.[63]

5   The Iconographic Toolbox

A significant area of interest in this regard is the long-acknowledged, but insufficiently studied, communicative role of art in the Roman world which, mostly for the sake of convenience, I will continue to refer to as "Roman" art.[64] One can reasonably postulate that much of Roman art was primarily or even predominantly about communication, and hence concerned more with the visual meanings of the image than its aesthetic quality.[65] It is for this reason

---

63   For examples of newer approaches cf. Hölscher 1987; Elsner 1995, 2007; Stewart 2003, 2008; Marlowe 2013; Harris 2015; Anguissola 2021, and the wide range of examples discussed by Boymel Kampen 2003: 379–83.

64   Boymel Kampen 2003: 377 speaks of "Roman art as the arts of many social strata, ethnic groups, and power relations." This does not mean that there is no place for an element or notion of Romanness in the production of art in the Empire, just as there are clear Roman elements in other realms of imperial culture, such as law, government, religion, language, and the like. We must take care, however, with how we approach the "Roman" aspects of the arts of the Empire. The concept of romanization is undergoing a thorough reevaluation, much needed and focusing in particular on the Empire's multiculturality (Wells 1999; Webster 2001, 2003; Hingley 2005; Mattingly 2014; Alcock et al. 2016; Rowan 2022). The deconstruction of the binary opposition between Roman and provincial naturally has profound consequences for our understanding of "Roman" art. One problem that is often underestimated, however, is the extent to which art (in the broadest sense) was ephemeral. From body tattoos to tapestries and from wood carvings to precious metalwork, a very large proportion of, in particular, "provincial" art has left virtually no trace. What has survived the best is pottery and stone, two areas in which the arrival of Roman rule often revolutionized indigenous practices, especially in the western half of the Empire. This makes the evaluation of the "provincial" character of surviving regional art especially problematic. There can be no doubt about the hybrid nature of, for example, Nehalennia reliefs, Jupiter columns, or even the Adamclisi monument, from a Roman perspective. But locally all are exponents of profound, even revolutionary Roman innovations, ranging from the Latin of the inscriptions to the use of stone, the ornamental articulation (metopes, Corinthian capitals, *aediculae*), the figural conception, and the like. We simply do not know how this compared to pre-Roman and, perhaps, ongoing art production in less durable materials such as wood or cloth, making it very difficult to evaluate local attitudes towards such works in stone.

65   Hölscher 1987; Boymel Kampen 2003: 381; Tanner 2000, 2006: 235–300; Giuliani 1986. Tanner 2006: 233 describes art in the late Hellenistic and Roman periods as an "autonomous province of meaning."

that Roman art in particular was characterized by a strictly defined and highly durable iconographic toolbox, from which artists could, or indeed were obliged to draw to compose their images. The rigidity of this iconographic vocabulary was such that it was as impossible for a Roman artist to depict Sol with a beard as it was to depict Jupiter without one, or to place an owl (or any other bird) rather than a peacock next to Juno. It was this rich toolbox of standardized iconographic types that allowed Roman artists to produce the readily recognizable images that played a major role in the construction of the social ideologies of the communities in which they functioned. The main thrust of each image was readily apparent to a broad range of the viewing public, and each element of the composition contributed to making it specifically meaningful.[66]

---

66   On the recognizability of iconographical conventions, cf. Cic. *ND* 1, 81–3: "Nobis fortasse sic occurrit, ut dicis; a parvis enim Iovem, Iunonem, Minervam, Neptunum, Vulcanum, Apollinem, reliquos deos ea facie novimus, qua pictores fictoresque voluerunt, neque solum facie, sed etiam ornatu, aetate, vestitu. (…) Quid igitur censes Apim illum sanctum Aegyptiorum bovem nonne deum videri Aegyptiis? Tam, hercle, quam tibi illam vestram Sospitam. Quam tu numquam ne in somnis quidem vides nisi cum pelle caprina, cum hasta, cum scutulo, cum calceolis repandis. At non est talis Argia nec Romana Iuno. Ergo alia species Iunonis Argivis, alia Lanuinis. Et quidem alia nobis Capitolini, alia Afris Hammonis Iovis. Non pudet igitur physicum, id est speculatorem venatoremque naturae, ab animis consuetudine inbutis petere testimonium veritatis? Isto enim modo dicere licebit Iovem semper barbatum, Apollinem semper inberbem, caesios oculos Minervae, caeruleos esse Neptuni. Et quidem laudamus esse Athenis Volcanum eum, quem fecit Alcamenes, in quo stante atque vestito leviter apparet claudicatio non deformis: Claudum igitur habebimus deum, quoniam de Volcano sic accepimus." ("To us, perhaps, the suggestion is as you say, for from our childhood we have known Jupiter, Juno, Minerva, Neptune, Vulcan, Apollo, and the other gods, under the aspect which painters and sculptors have laid down for us, and so with regard to their insignia, and age, and attire. But the Egyptians, the Syrians, and almost the whole of the uncivilized world have not so known them. You would find amongst them a firmer belief in certain animals than amongst us in the holiest temples and images of the gods, for many a shrine has, as we see, been plundered by our countrymen, and the images of the gods taken away from the holiest places, but no one has even so much as heard tell of a crocodile, or ibis, or cat having been dishonoured by an Egyptian. What, then, is your opinion? Is it not that Apis, the sacred ox of the Egyptians, is regarded by them as divine? Of course he is, as much as your Juno Sospita is by you, that Juno whom you never see even in your dreams without a goat-skin, a spear, a small shield, and shoes turned up at the toe. As, however, neither the Argive Juno, nor the Roman, is of that description, it follows that the goddess is known under different forms by the Argives, the Lanuvinians, and ourselves. The form, moreover, of our Jupiter of the Capitol is different from that of the Jupiter Hammon of the Africans. Are you not ashamed, then, as a man of science, that is, an explorer and pursuer of nature, to seek a testimony to truth in minds imbued with habit? At that rate it will be open to us to say that Jupiter is always bearded, and Apollo beardless, that Minerva has grey eyes, and Neptune blue. There is, too, at Athens a much admired statue of Vulcan by Alcamenes, a draped, standing figure, in which a lameness which does not amount to

FIGURE 1.13
Ar. denarius, Rome
PHOTOGRAPH ANS 1944.100.1918

FIGURE 1.14
Ae. sestertius, Rome
PHOTOGRAPH IN THE PUBLIC DOMAIN

The strength and durability of this system were impressive. The description Cicero gives of the iconography of Juno Sospita (*supra*, n. 66) is not only borne out in every detail by Republican coin images, but remained as valid two centuries later under Commodus (figs. 1.13 and 1.14). In the case of Sol, the rules governing his depiction remained essentially unchanged for over half a millennium, from the first century BC (and in many respects earlier) to the fourth

deformity is slightly indicated. We shall, therefore, since we have received that account of Vulcan, think of the god as lame." (Translation by Francis Brooks 1896). Note how Cicero stresses the conventionality of these iconographic practices. How widespread and profound the knowledge of the actual conventions was, matters less than the acknowledgment and expectation of such conventions. Everyone knew that there was a right way to depict Juno Sospita, even if in most parts of the Empire they would probably not know what that right way was.

century AD and beyond.[67] From the sketchiest of productions to the most refined works, Sol was depicted with the same basic characteristics throughout this period and throughout the Roman Empire. In short, depictions of Sol were readily recognizable to the Roman viewer.

The mere fact that the Romans maintained the iconographic conventions for Sol over centuries is itself the clearest possible indication of the importance of that recognizability, and hence communication in Roman art. Roman artists worked within a framework of fixed conventions that spanned many generations over centuries, and Roman viewers viewed with the existence of those conventions in mind. These conventions extended well beyond the rules covering the iconography of individual figures. Complex compositions and image types with multiple figures were likewise firmly defined in ways that significantly limited artistic choice.

This can be illustrated with certain forms of ekphrastic literature, such as Philostratus' *Imagines*.[68] In it we see how the rhetor clearly expects his audience to grasp the manifold literary, philosophical, and visual allusions that permeate each of his "descriptions", challenging them to compose in their mind a "conventional" image that is wholly imaginary, yet brilliantly vivid.[69]

---

67   On the significance of the introduction of the raised right hand in the second century AD
      as iconographic characteristic of Sol, cf. ch. 2, pp. 64–66.

68   Squire 2013; Webb 2016, especially 187–90; Stewart 2003: 236–49. On *ekphrasis* in general
      see also Graf 1995; Elsner 2002; Trimble & Elsner 2006; Squire 2010.

69   The *Imagines* by Philostratus has only recently begun to receive the respect it deserves.
      For Squire 2013: 88, the book of descriptions "... amounts to one of antiquity's most
      sophisticated meditations on the phenomenology of seeing." Webb 2016: 188, too, stresses
      the profound sophistication of Philostratus' *ekphraseis*, pointing out that they are "... con-
      stantly dual. Within the fictional setting of the gallery they interpret a painting which is
      real and visible to the internal audience (...) But for the external audience of readers the
      words alone create the paintings, the speaker and his audience." Certainly we can aban-
      don the notion that Philostratus' rhetorical tour de force was, as Lehmann-Hartleben 1941
      and other past scholars would have it – and as Philostratus facetiously presents it – simply
      a series of straightforward descriptions of real paintings in a specific villa at Naples (cf.
      Kalinka & Schönberger 1968). Philostratus is purposefully vague about the actual location
      of the paintings he "describes", stating merely that he stayed in a villa facing the sea in
      an unnamed "suburb" outside the walls of the city (Philostr. *Imag.* 295K 22–23: ... ἔξω τοῦ
      τείχους ἐν προαστείῳ τετραμμένῳ ἐς θάλασσαν). This careful avoidance of specific informa-
      tion concerning the location and ownership of the villa would be most surprising if the
      paintings he is describing were real and could really be viewed. He sustains the vagueness
      in his subsequent description of the setting of the paintings, stating only that they were in
      the veranda-like *stoa* of "four, I think, or five levels" (ἐπὶ τεττάρων οἶμαι ἢ καὶ πέντε ὀροφῶν)
      and leaving both the host himself and the host's son (to whom the descriptions are nomi-
      nally addressed) unnamed (Philostr. *Imag.* 295K 20–23). Given Philostratus' Sophistic
      background as well as the numerous philosophical references in his frontal attack on

The extent to which he is playing his audience is particularly clear in the fifth description of book 1, concerning an image of the Nile in flood (Πήχεις).[70] First, Philostratus describes a reclining, bearded river deity of the standard three-dimensional type in Roman art, with little putti (the so-called πήχεις of the title) clambering over him and getting entangled in his beard. But in a pun on the multiple meanings of πῆχυς,[71] the putti gradually become little babbling streams and rivulets, and the Nile becomes the river in flood of the panoramic two-dimensional type well-known from the Palestrina Nile-mosaic. The description culminates with a god standing sky-high astride the river's source and unleashing the annual flood. As described, the picture is actually impossible, because it conflates two mutually exclusive, but equally common image types with which Roman art conventionally depicted the Nile: the three-dimensional reclining, bearded personification of the river with little babes clambering all over him, and the panoramic, two-dimensional bird's-eye views as in the mosaic of Palestrina. What his ancient audience admired was the skill with which Philostratus masked these impossibilities and tricked one into imagining these contradictory images.[72]

The suggestion that Philostratus' *ekphraseis* are meant to evoke virtual images in the mind's eye has clear implications for the nature of Roman viewing. It supports, and exploits, the contention – for which there is much

---

the Platonic view of art in this introduction, my colleague Selina Stewart suggests that it is tempting to view these four or five *stoai* as a reference to the four or five schools of philosophy. In the opening lines of his first description (Scamander), Philostratus states almost explicitly that the whole exercise is not about *real* paintings, to be viewed physically, but about the virtual images he hopes to evoke in the mind's eye. After stating that the painting of Scamander is "all Homer," his very first command to his fictitious 10-year-old (!) disciple is to *look away* (ἀπόβλεψον) from the picture in order to "see" all on which the image is based (ὅσον ἐκεῖνα ἰδεῖν, ἀφ᾽ ὧν ἡ γραφή. Philostr. *Imag.* 296K 6–10). This is an inversion of what his actual audience of readers must do, namely "see" the paintings through the texts he cites.

70   Philostr. *Imag.* 300K 23–301K 20.
71   πῆχυς = forearm, the length of the forearm, cubit, any small amount, and "cubit folk" metaphorically representing the rivulets of inundation of the Nile. Cf. Luc. *Rh.Pr.* 6.
72   Cf. Webb 2016: 187–90 for other excellent examples of Philostratus' play on representation and illusion. Concerning the Nile, it will be clear that I do not accept Moffitt's (1997) suggestion that Philostratus is not only describing a real painting, but actually one that was a copy of the Nile mosaic in Palestrina. To support this Moffitt alters the Nile-mosaic itself, postulating that there was once a depiction of a huge statue at the top of the mosaic representing the deity astride the source and unleashing the flood (it was no doubt lost, according to Moffitt, in one of the radical restorations of the mosaic), and he suggests that a reclining Nile statue of the Vatican type was set up in front of the mosaic. The painting described by Philostratus somehow copied this dual composition. On the Nile mosaic, cf. Versluys 2002: 52–5.

empirical evidence – that Roman art is composed to a significant degree of the kind of stock image-types that Philostratus can expect to evoke. One need but think of the rich mythological art, so well-known from Pompeii, for example. Many Roman depictions of a particular myth not only share the same iconographical conventions to identify the participants, but are also compositionally closely related. In terms of Roman viewing practices, the origin or the prototypes for these compositions were far less important than the recognizability of the basic typological schemes. To be sure, it is perfectly possible that an educated Roman viewer was aware that there was, for example, a famous painting of Medea in Rome by Timomachus of Byzantium. But even if we are correct in identifying two paintings from Herculaneum and Pompeii as copies or variants of that Timomachean masterpiece, this does not mean that the contemporary viewers viewed them as such. And for all we know Timomachus himself may have painted his Medea along the same lines, not as his invention but because they had already been established long before. That his painting's fame was due to his exceptional skill is clear, but that does not necessarily imply typological originality.

What was important to the Roman viewer of the Pompeian or Herculanean Medeas was the immediate recognizability of the type. Here is Medea in mental turmoil, in a deceptively calm scene immediately preceding her horrific murder of her two unsuspecting sons. Such images would evoke a range of associations in the educated viewer, but that does not mean that she would see these frescoes primarily as "copies" of some "masterpiece" any more than Galla Placidia would have considered the preening doves in her mausoleum to be a copy of Sosos' famous mosaic in Pergamum, produced some six centuries earlier. How such visual conventions came to be established, could vary. No doubt famous "originals", such as Sosos' preening doves, had a role in this process, but there is no reason to postulate an artistic masterpiece as source for each conventional treatment of a topic or theme. Once established, the conventions were just that: conventions that were sufficiently uniform for a Roman viewer to visualize their basic composition in his mind's eye simply at the mention of a theme or topos.[73]

But what do these images then mean, if anything, beyond "Medea about to kill her sons", or (to return to the topic of this study) "Sol"? Analysis of the meaning of such images has long been text-based. This is problematic, for the

---

73   Marvin 1989; cf. Beard & Henderson 2001: 26–31, 100–5. The two frescoes of Medea from
      Pompeii and Herculaneum are in the National Museum at Naples, Inv. 8976 and 8977; cf.
      Beard & Henderson 2001: figs. 21 & 22. On Timomachus' Medea, Gutzwiller 2004; on the
      preening doves of Sosos, cf. Plin. *NH* 36, 184; Westgate 2000: 266.

relationship between text and image is always a complex one, and this is pre-eminently the case in Roman art.[74] Not surprisingly, therefore, the Romans themselves show a clear interest in the different communicative potentials of word and image, as well as in the processes involved. Philostratus' *Imagines*, as we have seen, can be read as an exploration of verbal and visual modes of signi-fication. For not only does Philostratus use words to evoke images, but through-out his descriptions Philostratus has us "see" movement, "hear" sounds, "smell" scents, and "feel" textures supposedly transmitted by the images he evokes,[75] clearly exploring how, in the type of discourse between image and viewer that he postulates, metatexts can emerge that engage the viewer in both nonverbal and non-visual ways. In this way Philostratus challenges his audience to pon-der not only how we hear and allow words to construct virtual images in our minds, but also how we view and how meaning arises in these images that he/ we constructed in our mind's eye purely under the impetus of his rhetoric.

Philostratus does not provide answers, and the issues are no less debated today. But so much is clear: we cannot, in our analyses, assume that an image – of Sol, for instance – merely illustrates a word or verbal construct like *Sol* or *sun god*. There is now basic agreement that art, and indeed material culture in the broadest sense, cannot be thought of as simply reflecting externally defined concepts and meanings. On the contrary, material culture is actively involved in constructing them.[76] That this is so is quickly apparent if one imagines, for example, a statuette of Menelaos and Patroklos of the Pasquino type. It would be wrong to interpret this simply as a visual rendition of one of Homer's key passages (e.g., P 1ff or 717ff). The statuette is an object, not a text, visual rather than oral or aural, and as such it evokes and constructs its own traditions. It is an example of a statue type of which the potential "meanings" could vary greatly, depending on whether it was displayed in, say, a military barracks, a Greek library, among sculptural masterpieces in sumptuous imperial baths, or by a shrine to Antinous in one of Hadrian's private gardens. Likewise, its meanings change greatly over time. A modern viewer, for example, may well be reminded of Michelangelo's Pietà; other connotations today include free-dom of speech, from the practice, especially in times of censorship, of posting anonymous satirical poems on one particular and rather ruinous version of the statue type on a corner of the Via dell'Anima in Rome. The very term for such poems, pasquinade, is derived from the name of that particular statue,

---

74   Boymel Kampen 2003: 378–9; Squire 2009.

75   Movement: Philostr. *Imag.* 1, 2, 2 (297K, Komos); texture: 1, 2, 3 (297K, Komos), sound: 1, 5, 1 (300K Pêcheis); smell, taste: 1, 6, 1–2 (301–2K Erotes); etc. cf. Webb 2016: 189.

76   Knappert & Malafouris 2008; for art specifically, cf. Bredekamp 2010; Kautt 2019.

Il Pasquino. Obviously references to the *Iliad* would be of absolutely no use to anyone attempting to interpret, say, a cartoon of Silvio Berlusconi wishing to add *Il Pasquino* to his media empire.

6   The Semantics of Roman Art

This brings us back to the central issue of this chapter: the "meanings" of images in Roman art. Our field does not have a strong tradition of discussing ancient art from a semantic perspective, despite various concerted efforts.[77] Classicists have long had a tendency to tacitly imbue the ancient viewers with a method of viewing that upon reflection is quite remarkable and rather improbable, turning to texts in order to establish the meaning of a given image. At its best this approach can yield classic Panofskian iconographical analysis, for which Panofsky considered knowledge of the appropriate literary sources to be critical. On the other hand, at its worst this approach can be quite disconcerting. Most would agree, I think, that to rely solely or primarily on texts to interpret an image in isolation is problematic. Roman viewers did not consult texts the moment they saw an image. They relied on visual factors such as the visual vocabulary and tradition of the representation, the visual associations and connotations, the style and material, and the physical context of the object. These factors are not ignored in classical scholarship, but it is not exceptional to come across images interpreted primarily or even solely on the basis of textual parallels, especially in older classical studies, with results that are still widely accepted as correct today. A good example is the famous mosaic supposedly depicting Christ as Sol in mausoleum M in the Vatican Necropolis, which we discuss in chapter nine.

How Panofsky attempts to deal with this problem becomes clearer if we look briefly at his famous three steps of interpretation (pre-iconographical, iconographical, and iconological).[78] The first step is pure description of the image (Panofsky uses the example of a painting depicting thirteen men around a table). This is followed by the second stage in which the image is analysed in the narrower sense (the thirteen are Jesus and his twelve disciples). This is the stage that requires knowledge of the relevant literature such as the bible and Panofsky is careful to distinguish this iconographical analysis, which is still descriptive, from the analysis of the content or intrinsic meaning of the

---

77   Cf. most notably Hölscher 1987, 2012.
78   Panofsky 1962.

image which he terms the iconological analysis. This constitutes his third stage and deals with such matters as the patron's reasons for commissioning such an image and other aspects of its social and cultural meanings. It requires, in Panofsky's terms, synthetic intuition, based on a solid understanding of the "essential tendencies" of the mind. In other words, what the viewers themselves saw in the image and what the image meant to the viewer in sociohistorical terms is, Panofsky suggests, understood by the expert intuitively as a result of his expertise, experience and understanding of human nature.

This summary of Panofsky's approach is far too brief to do him justice, but is enough to illustrate the problem of what he terms the "intrinsic meanings" of images, that is, what (in our case) the Roman viewer actually saw in an image when she viewed it. Panofsky's suggestion that we rely on "synthetic intuition" and our knowledge of the essential tendencies of the human mind is unsatisfactory, because it provides no theoretical and methodological framework explaining how intrinsic meanings arose; they just did.[79] But it is precisely at that level of interpretation that we run into profound trouble in Roman art. We can describe an image of Sol, we can identify him in the "narrower" sense as Sol, but the intrinsic meaning of the image often remains unclear: sun or Sun god? Symbolic figure or deity? We certainly do not always "intuitively" know this, but we do know that it can be known.[80]

The theoretical foundations of art history have evolved immensely since Erwin Panofsky, but classical art history – long at the centre of any major debate on the philosophy of art – has been relegated to the sidelines.[81] Current debates in art theory are dominated by scholars of modern art, and theoretically sophisticated studies of ancient art have become few and far between. This lack of philosophical engagement, among classicists, with what it is that we study, and how we can most fruitfully do so, is a major concern for Boymel Kampen (2003) in her review of the state of Roman art history. She laments the dearth of meaningful discussions on the theoretical frameworks structuring our understanding of Roman art.

The problem is caused in no mean part by the fact that the Winckelmannian framework for classical art history has run its course, requiring a paradigmatic shift. Studying ancient art (and to a great degree, art in general) purely from the perspective of aesthetic achievement has become a thing of the past.[82] But

79   Pettersson 2001.
80   Jäger 2017: 670–1, citing Schade & Wenk 2011; Wohlfeil 1986: 92–3.
81   Lorenz 2016: 5.
82   Lorenz 2016: 170–1; Mitchell 1986, 1992.

what do we study, when we study Roman images?[83] The fact that we lack a clear answer is in part no doubt the result of what Lorenz sees as a lingering "investment in 'natural' meaning" reinforced by a reluctance to challenge the existing framework of interpretation.[84] Many scholars still approach ancient art as if it were not coded at all. They place themselves in the shoes of the ancient viewer and assume that she saw the same then as they do now.[85] At best the (often unarticulated) idea of a socially-based artistic *habitus* is invoked to explain stylistic and other idiosyncrasies of these otherwise "straightforward" images. In an excellent article in a *Festschrift* for Paul Zanker, Hölscher sketches the roots and limitations of such views, focusing in particular on the concept of "folk art/ *arte plebea/Volkskunst*". Hölscher rejects the notion of class- or culture-based artistic "habits" (*habitus*) in the Roman world, arguing instead for a Roman practice of deploying styles as communicative elements, supporting the overall meaning of the art work.[86]

Hölscher's longstanding emphasis on the communicative role of styles in Roman art marks an important break with tradition, and should stimulate a more comprehensive debate on the manner in which Roman images communicated with their viewers. Classicists have yet to fully engage with that debate, although there are certainly those who are taking important steps in that direction. A recent book by Lorenz (2016) is an example of this. She presents the whole study as an experiment, explicitly designed to foster debate on the best interpretative models for the study of ancient art. Lorenz subjects the mythological imagery on three ancient objects – a hydria of the late fifth century BC, a relief of the second century BC, and a sarcophagus of the second century AD – each to three established forms of analysis: iconological, semiotic, and what may be loosely termed post-processual (Lorenz prefers "image studies"). She opens each section with a concise but sophisticated introduction to the philosophies underpinning each approach, followed by the actual analyses. She closes each section with a discussion of the results, noting the relative strengths and weaknesses of the approach at hand.

Lorenz undertakes this experiment because, much like Boymel Kampen, she feels that classical art history is mired in a crisis of confidence, with many doing little more than amassing vast quantities of data without reflecting on

---

83   For a more extended analysis of what an "image" is, including reflections on the subtle differences in meaning between the German word *Bild* and the English word *image*, cf. Jäger 2017: 663–6; Lorenz 2016: 172–3.

84   Lorenz 2016: 166.

85   Zanker 1997: 179.

86   Hölscher 2012: 48–53.

the principles structuring their taxonomies.[87] Her iterative approach is well suited to stimulate comparative debate about the methodologies used and their theoretical underpinnings. It also refocuses the attention on the evidence, which she revisits with each of the different methodologies deployed. What Lorenz quite consciously does not do, is to explore the more fundamental, ontological questions these objects and images could raise.[88] She is not exploring "what" ancient art was, but rather what we can learn about ancient images, predefined (by us) as mythological and meaningful.

Bringing a sophisticated understanding of such interpretative approaches to bear on ancient art is very welcome, but within Classics, studies that do so are still too few and far between. This becomes apparent from the footnotes of some of the more theoretically informed studies. A recent article on provincial coins of the Roman Republic, for example, opens with a straightforward but refreshing emphasis on the role of ambiguity in the interactions with coins in this often liminal period.[89] This is not a difficult or abstract concept, but the author is forced to draw on literature dealing with other periods and materials to establish the parameters even for this part of her study. The closest she comes to the ancient world is nineteenth-century Britain and its appropriation of the Elgin marbles. Needless to say, she has to resort to similarly extradisciplinary literature for her other two sections, dealing with the social life of things and entanglement respectively (although for the latter there has been some interest from within Classics as well).[90]

Why is it that Classics seems incapable of fostering truly vigorous and informed philosophical debates on theory and methodologies best suited to the study of ancient art? Both Lorenz and Boymel Kampen observe that many

---

87   Lorenz 2016: 4.

88   Lorenz 2016: 237.

89   Rowan 2016: 25–34.

90   For the social life of things she draws on the work of W.J.T. Mitchell, and, through S. Mulhall, on Wittgenstein for the basic theory, and cites Kopytoff (an anthropologist) and Joy (a European prehistorian) for relevant discussions within the field of archaeology (Rowan 2016: 34). A bit further (p. 39) she also draws on M.J. Versluys' notion of "Objects in motion", one of the few truly Classical contributions to the debate. It is only when she comes to entanglement that Rowan has more Classical scholarship to draw on (Dietler and Whitley, as well as Versluys). The concept itself originated, of course, with the anthropologist and historian N. Thomas, and its important role in other areas of archaeology is well illustrated by the works of I. Hodder and P.W. Stockhammer, cited by Rowan (2016: 44). That there really is a dearth of theoretically informed research on ancient art can be well illustrated by the fact that of the 210 or so articles to appear in the long-running Theoretical Roman Archaeology Conference Proceedings between 2000 and 2016, barely five percent deal solely or predominantly with some aspect of Roman art.

have a "contemptuous distrust" of images as a source of meaning.[91] There is indeed a strong current in archaeology that denies the viability of analysing art and material cultural remains as sources for ancient concepts and ideas. This is not just the case in classical studies, where literary sources have long been privileged.[92] Kent Flannery and Joyce Marcus, both long active in Latin American archaeology, bluntly warn that iconographical interpretation can easily degenerate into "some of the worst archaeology on record." In fact, if pursued without the constraints of independent, documentary (i.e. verbal, literary) evidence, they feel that iconography is little more than a "bungee jump into the Land of Fantasy."[93] They argue that it can be "truly scientific" only when history or ethnohistory offer a solid foundation of knowledge, ensuring that we are well informed about the ideological and religious background that inspired the art under consideration. Where such external information is lacking, they feel that iconographical studies quickly become "science fiction."[94]

The notion that we can only know what something means if some source tells us, is problematic. Images never exist in isolation, but are inevitably produced within some sort of system, which structures the ways in which they signify and are perceived. The more elaborate and detailed the system, the greater the capacity of the artist to produce images intended to generate specific, circumscribed meanings. Of course, only people who are themselves cognizant of the system will be able to grasp the intended meanings easily, but deciphering a system is a very different proposition from deciphering a unique utterance. Roman art history as the study of the visual language(s) or system(s) of the Roman world, is not bungee jumping. It is a legitimate project to strive towards insight in the lexical meanings of the individual components of the Roman system(s) of visual communication, as well as the syntagmatic principles governing their composition into intelligible texts. It is also an essential project, for without such lexical and grammatical knowledge of the system, attempts to interpret individual works of art produced within it can indeed become the bungee jumps Flannery and Marcus warn against.

---

91   Lorenz 2016: 3; Rowan's article, being less programmatic, logically does not address the issue either.

92   Scott 2006.

93   Flannery & Marcus 1996: 351–2, 361–2.

94   Flannery & Marcus 1996: 358; they quote with approval a study by Olga Linares of Panamanian burial vessels from sites ranging from AD 500–1500, in which she makes use of eyewitness accounts of early Spanish conquistadores to support her interpretations (O. Linares, *Ecology and the Arts in Ancient Panama: On the Development of Social Rank and Symbolism in the Central Provinces*, Washington, 1977).

7   Matters of Methodology

An important *raison d'être* for this book is to contribute to the deciphering of
the Roman system(s) of visual communication, but simply saying so is not
enough. If Roman art history is to weather the withering criticism levelled at
it from within and without, its practitioners must engage in a robust debate
on the methodologies and philosophies that shape the field. Classical art history cannot do without theory. This does not mean that classicists need to
devise their own theories of art, of course. We can certainly follow Lorenz'
or Rowan's examples and situate our analyses within established theoretical
frameworks.[95] In terms of methodology, however, things are a bit more complicated. We cannot simply borrow established methodologies from adjacent
fields, because methodologies are devised to produce answers to the specific
questions asked of the specific material at hand. Methodologies common to
prehistoric archaeology generally transition poorly to classical archaeology,
because classicists are not engaged with the broad sweep of human evolution,
and deal with expanses of time that are far shorter, and with material cultures that are vastly more elaborate, than those studied by, say, scholars of the
Neolithic. Paradoxically it is the dearth of adequate sources, visual as well as
written, that often confounds us when we attempt to apply modern art historical methodologies to Roman or classical material. True, with carefully selected
objects such approaches can yield fascinating results, but even in Lorenz'
excellent study the inevitable blind spots and basic yet challengeable assumptions are manifold. Take the Louvre sarcophagus she discusses: we do not know
where it was found nor for whom it was made; she herself flags the grounds for
the date she gives a (potential) problem;[96] even the issue of the visibility of
the sarcophagus[97] – was it actually seen by many people – and, concomitantly,
the ontological status of the images in the consciousness of the Roman (non-?)
viewer, are open to debate. I must stress that this is not intended as criticism
of Lorenz' analyses of the sarcophagus imagery. She recognizes the limitations
of information fully. My point is that modern art historians would routinely
expect comparable information to be accurately available for the objects they
study, allowing them to perform much more detailed and intricate analyses
than classicists can normally aspire to.

95   Cf. Tanner 2000, who grounds his analysis in the action theory of Talcott Parsons and in
      Peircean pragmatism.
96   Lorenz 2016: 15 is careful to state that the date is based on stylistic grounds, an increas-
      ingly controversial system of dating, built at least in part on questionable assumptions
      and circular arguments, cf. Marlowe 2013.
97   Meinecke 2012.

Where does this leave us with regards to our basic question how to analyse images of Sol as sources of information about the Sun and his cult in the
Roman world? If the questions of modern art historical research are too intricate and those of prehistory too general for our data, then we must develop
our own questions that are adapted to our own field. Within established theoretical frameworks we must then develop methodologies aimed at answering
those questions and, through those answers, ultimately reflect back on the
theoretical frameworks that have informed our studies. That is the only way to
achieve both the overarching aim of this book – namely to contribute to our
understanding of the role of the sun in Roman religion and society, by adduc-
ing information that can be gleaned from the analysis of the visual evidence –
as well as its subsidiary aim, namely to do so without bungee jumping. Our first
task, then, is to choose a theoretical framework and methodology best suited
to helping us embark on this quest.

As we have noted, one of the most striking characteristics of Roman art was
its strictly defined and highly durable iconographic toolbox, which imposed
strict rules on how artists composed their images. The rigidity of this iconographic vocabulary was such that according to Cicero, even a child knew the
rules governing the iconographies of deities, for instance, down to the minor
details.[98] Cicero stresses the conventionality of these iconographic practices
throughout the Roman world, and although it is difficult to say how widespread
the knowledge of the actual conventions was, Cicero seems to take for granted
that his audience knew the difference between the iconographies of the Argive
and the Roman Juno, would recognize a North African Ba'al Hammon, and was
aware of such details as the correct colour of the eyes of Minerva or Neptune.
This means that he expects iconographic knowledge from individual Romans
that exceeds the combined knowledge of modern classical scholarship. I doubt
that we know enough of either the Argive or the Roman iconographies of
Hera/Juno to be confident that we could list the most important differences
as well as Cicero could have, not to mention such details as the correct colour
of a deity's eyes.[99]

---

98   Cf. *supra* footnote 66.

99   On the Argive Hera cf. Schoch 2009: 208–12. Beyond coin images and a rather brief
      description by Pausanias (2, 17, 4) we know nothing of her iconography. The "Roman" Juno
      is presumably Juno Regina, who was brought from Veii to Rome by M. Furius Camillus.
      She had a temple on the Aventine which housed the *xoanon* taken from Veii, and a temple
      in the porticus of Marcellus (which later became the porticus of Octavia) with a cult-
      statue by Polykles and Timarchides. No details of the iconography of either cult-statue
      are known with certainty (LIMC V, s.v. Iuno: 822–3). The original statue of Juno in the
      temple of Jupiter Capitolinus was destroyed in 87 BC, and both its iconography and the
      iconography of its replacement are also unknown (LIMC V s.v. Iuno: 823–4). On the other
      hand, as we have seen, when we do know more, as in the case of Sospita's iconography, for

It is no surprise, then, to find that the Roman iconographic conventions governing Sol's depiction were equally precise and strict, and remained essentially unchanged for over a millennium.[100] What is more, artists from all corners of the Empire adhered to those rules, irrespective of the style in which they worked or their religious background. From the sketchiest of productions to the most refined works, Sol was depicted with the same basic characteristics throughout this period and throughout the Roman Empire. As long as one knew the three basic image types used for Sol, recognizing images of Sol can almost never have been an issue in antiquity.

The fact that the Romans so carefully maintained the iconographic conventions for such image types as Sol over centuries, is itself the clearest possible indication of their importance. This emphasis on recognizability allows us to postulate that much of "Roman art" was primarily communicative, concerned more with the (visual) meanings, i.e. with the (semantic) function and agency of images, than anything else.[101] This is further borne out by the fact that such conventions extended well beyond the rules covering the iconography of individual figures. Complex compositions involving multiple figures and types were likewise covered by detailed rules. Roman artists were as restricted in how to depict a myth as they were in how to depict the individual participants.[102] As discussed above, the notion that many Roman works of art were "copies" of Greek masterpieces is a partial misunderstanding of this principle.[103]

Paradoxically, it was inevitable that the meanings associated with these rigidly defined images evolved in the course of the many centuries that they were in use. The Romans did not depict the sun as a charioteer because they thought the sun was one, but because that convention was so strong that in Roman art the sun could not take any other form. Even the straightforward depiction of the sun as a ball of fire – a classic component of children's drawings today – simply did not occur.[104] In fact, the convention was so strong that

---

example, the description Cicero gives is borne out in every detail. Whether Cicero is also correct that all Romans learned these iconographic details as children is immaterial. For a visual system like Rome's to function successfully, it was enough that people accepted that they could know, and that all artists should know such details.

100   All aspects of Sol's iconography are discussed at length in chapter 2.

101   Hölscher 1987; Boymel Kampen 2003: 381; Tanner 2000, 2006; Hijmans 2015. Tanner 2006: 233 describes art in the late Hellenistic and Roman periods as an "autonomous province of meaning."

102   Cf. Beard & Henderson 2001: 29–31 (on the iconography of Medea).

103   Marvin 1989; Gazda 2002; Perry 2005; Versluys 2015.

104   There are shorthand versions of the moon as a crescent, counterbalanced sometimes by an image type Sol, and sometimes by a star, which in that case presumably stands for the sun. The sun can also occur as a more-or-less round face with rays, usually to be interpreted as a bust of Sol, but sometimes it can be difficult to tell whether the sun or a

even in Roman-era synagogues, the sun was depicted in the guise of a divine charioteer.[105] That does not mean that Jews thought the sun was a god. It simply means that the anthropomorphic depiction of the sun was not iconic.

This brings us to the second point we need to make about Roman art, namely that, notwithstanding its adoption of many formalistic aspects of Greek mimetic traditions, it remained symbolic in nature, philosophically. This is a key element for the theoretical framework, research questions, and methodology of this study. The symbolic nature of Roman art allows us to approach Roman images as signs in a semiotic sense. Rather than assume that a Roman image somehow mimetically replicated the concepts that it conveyed, we should understand the relationship between the *signifier* (the physical form of the image) and its *signifieds* (the associated concepts) as potentially completely arbitrary. Such images made no attempt to embody mimetically the concepts they conveyed and one needed to be cognizant of the socially agreed upon signifiers in order to fully understand the associated meanings.[106] This should be uncontroversial. Nobody thinks that the image on Roman coins of a woman carrying the heads of Sol and Luna on her outstretched hands depicts some anthropomorphic goddess who has decapitated the sun and the moon; we know perfectly well that she actually visualizes the abstract concept of *aeternitas*. But we do not know that intuitively, and cannot just guess at it; we know because we have learned it.

There were countless such images in Roman art, and Romans understood them because they knew the conventional meanings associated with a given image, or, if they did not, knew that they needed to find out. Romans did not expect to understand their art without this knowledge any more than they expected to be able to read a poem without knowing the language in which it was written. Just as we need a Latin dictionary to look up the words we do not

---

gorgoneion (with rays rather than snakes?) is intended. Cf. e.g. CSIR Österreich 5 nrs. 401 and 411; a glance at the *stelai* nrs. 410–4 in that volume, shows that the various star-like discs vary too much in placement and number to warrant the conclusion that they symbolize Sol. Cf Schauenburg 1955. In the later fourth century AD, a small number of sarcophagi depict a crescent and a rayed disc as moon and sun (Rep. III, nrs. 63 and 282). Fındık 2021 argues that the rayed discs and other rosette-like decorative brickwork patterns commonly deployed in Byzantine architecture had solar roots, deriving ultimately from depictions of Sol.

105   See chapter 4, pp. 142–148.

106   Boschung 2014: 90–2 misses this point and argues that the lack of iconographical change reflected a remarkable stability (750 years) of traditional opinion. By this reasoning, that traditional opinion would have to be reflected even in fourth to sixth centuries synagogues (see previous footnote. Semiotic theory actually expects the relationship between signifier and signified to be dynamic, not passive.).

know, we need a lexicon of Roman art to look up unfamiliar image-types. It is to such a lexicon that this study aims to contribute an entry, discussing the three basic image types used in reference to Sol.

Treating these image types as signs in Rome's visual semiotic system has obvious implications for their potential meanings. In its simplest form, semiotics has three types of signs: iconic, indexical, and symbolic. *Iconic* signs are those in which the signifier closely resembles the signified. We recognize a pipe in a painting as a pipe because the painting closely resembles that which it represents, and by unspoken social convention we agree that it is possible to use paint, brush, and canvas to two-dimensionally depict something that is actually three-dimensional, made of wood or clay and has aromatic and tactile characteristics that – for a smoker – are the very essence of the object's *raison d'être*, but which the depiction lacks. That convention is so ingrained, that we are taken aback when Magritte states the obvious, namely that his painting *n'est pas une pipe*.

In the case of *Indexical* signs, the signifier points to the signified through an indirect, but distinct link, but does not directly resemble it. Tracks, for example, refer to the animal that made them; Trajan's column commemorates the wars depicted on it.

Symbolic signs are those in which the connection between signifier and signified is arbitrary, and known only to those who have learned it. In Roman art, the ubiquitous personifications, such as Concordia or Aeternitas, are typical examples of symbolic signs, as is the charioteer of a *quadriga* standing for the sun.[107]

This is very basic semiotics but it is enough to make quite clear why we should avoid calling the image types that this book proposes to study "images of Sol". The mere fact that the images all depict the sun in anthropomorph guise, strictly speaking makes them symbolic; the Romans knew as well as we do that the sun was actually an orb of fire. Hence, in the case of the sun in Roman art, the relationship between the form of the sign (the physical image) and its signified is established by social agreement. Obviously, in the case of symbolic signs in particular, we cannot simply assume we know the social agreements involved; we cannot assume to see what those in the know saw. To comprehend Roman visual signs such as the ones for sol, we need to (re)establish the relevant social conventions, and I do not think we always have; at least, not as well as we often imagine. The fact that we do not know the various

---

107   For a much more detailed discussion of semiotics and Roman art, cf. Lorenz 2016: 103–17, 154–66.

iconographies of Juno/Hera as well as Cicero expects us to (*supra* p. 46) is a case in point.

This brings us face-to-face with the major potential, but also a major problem of Roman art history. The care with which artists rendered their images *recognizable* by adhering to strict iconographic rules makes sense only if the alternative – misrecognition – were unacceptable. A correct reading of the image was clearly important, which means that the image conveyed specific meaning(s). Consequently, if we can gain the same fluency in reading Roman image-types that Roman viewers once had, then Roman art offers a wealth of visually informative imagery. But gaining that fluency will be quite a challenge. Not only are there many elements of the Roman visual semantic system that we do not (yet) understand, but classicists have also routinely presumed knowledge we do not actually have. Examples are legion of scholars assigning incorrect meaning to Roman images on groundless or spurious *a priori* assumptions.[108] Consequently, we not only have to learn a lot, but need to unlearn at least as much.

Some may feel that this is overly harsh, but this book amply illustrates the charge. To give one example: in his analysis of Roman coins depicting Sol, Berrens does not question what it was that a Roman actually saw when she recognized the image of Sol on a given coin. He assumes automatically that the image is the Roman Sun god. This is especially problematic because we are dealing not only with a highly conventionalized image, but also with coinage, arguably one of the most symbolic and conventionalized mediums for the dissemination of propaganda in the Roman Empire. As we shall see in this study, the type of Sol-images used on coins functioned primarily as symbols in Roman art, rather than as depictions of a fully-fledged deity. Various indexical or symbolic meanings have already been proposed in the past for such images, and Berrens actually rejects one, namely that on certain coins sol represents the East, and refers to Roman military campaigns in that region.[109] While Berrens is correct in this particular case, this does not *per se* diminish the likelihood that other indexical or symbolic *signifieds* were associated with the sol imagery on coins.

The matter is further complicated by the fact that the terms *Sonnenkult* and *Sonnengott*, which Berrens usually uses for the signified of the images he studies, are themselves problematic categories. The Roman concept of divinity does not coincide with the German one, and Romans almost certainly associated *deus Sol* with solar characteristics that we do not typically consider divine.

---

108   For an example concerning Sol, see the misidentification of Elijah as Sol, *infra* pp. 991–996.

109   Berrens 2004: 176–8.

One can think in particular of sol's perfect form (orb) and motion (circular). To the Romans these were quite literally quintessential aspects of the Sun as *deus*, but they are aspects which we would consider characteristic of the sun as "planet".[110] In other words, we cannot equate *D(d?)eus S(s?)ol* with *Sonnengott* because the Latin incorporates characteristics of the sun that the German certainly does not.[111] Add to this the fact that in written usage Latin authors often use sol in a manner that leads modern editors to write it with a lower case s rather than an upper case – i.e. *sun* rather than *Sun God* – and the problem of interpreting the image of Sol come into clear focus: does it depict Berrens' *Sonnengott*, the Roman *deus Sol*, simply *sol*, or some notion more or less arbitrarily associated with image types for sol?

The essential point here is that the image is visual and therefore by definition not synonymous with any given word. The concept(s) evoked by the signifier *S/sol* (the word, in its various orthographies) cannot be wholly identical to the concepts evoked by the signifier [sol] (the image type). For that reason, from here on, image type Sol will be the (unwieldy) term used whenever it is helpful to differentiate *S/sol* (image) from the *S/sol* (name/word). This may sound exaggerated; after all, the word *tree* may evoke the image of a tree and vice versa.[112] But we can never convey identical messages in systems based on formally different units or signs.[113] To see that this is so, imagine a

---

110   On the definition and divinity of the planets, deduced from their perfect shape and motion, cf. pp. 178–189.

111   Rothaus 2000: 1–7 opens his book with a warning against treating Roman cults as "christianities" with a different deity, pointing out that the differences were far more fundamental. Berrens' use and (implicit) concept of *Sonnenkult* and *-gott* is a good example of the problem to which Rothaus refers. On the problem of Christianizing assumptions in our approach to Roman religion, cf. Price 1984: 11–5 or Clauss 1999: 17–22.

112   This is why Saussurean semiotics, which prioritizes the verbal, is actually less suitable for discussion of the visual than Peircean semiotics. In Peirce's semiotic triangle the sign has three relations. In one corner is the signifier, which Peirce calls the *representamen*. In the other two corners are the *object* and the *interpretant*, which together fulfill the role of signified. The object is that to which the signifier/representamen refers, and the interpretant that which it evokes in the mind of the interpreter. Thus, the image type Sol can refer to an associated visual concept as object and yet evoke the word *sol* in the mind of the viewer as interpretant. That interpretant, whether a word or image, is itself a sign, though restricted by the associated representamen and object. This dialectic between object and interpretant allows for some of the issues that arise when we think about the object to which an image refers, because the object itself, as concept, is beyond the image or words the representamen evokes as interpretant. See Preucel 2010; Lorenz 2016: 103–17, 154–66; Lele 2006: 48–54 gives a good summary of Peirce's semiotic, followed by an analysis of its value for archaeological research; those daunted by semiotic theory in archaeology may find Harris & Cipolla 2017: 109–28 helpful.

113   Langner 2017.

richly decorated church and then try replacing every image or ornament with a word or text describing said image or ornament; the transformation is radical. Clearly, then, the answer to the question what the Roman viewer did see when she looked at Sol (image type) on a coin, or anywhere else for that matter, is not self-evident. It was also certainly not exactly the same as what words like *S/sol*, *deus S/sol*, *Sonne*, *Sonnengott*, etc. could and can evoke.

This brings us to a third important point about Roman art: we cannot routinely turn to language or literary texts to establish its visual meanings. We must concentrate on what Romans saw, and need to reflect more critically on the types of meanings that ancient art conveyed, how it conveyed those meanings, and what roles ancient viewers played in that process. By turning to texts, long common practice in our field, classicists tacitly imbue ancient viewers with a method of viewing that, upon reflection, would actually be quite remarkable. Roman viewers did not consult a library in order to understand what they were viewing. It was the visual language that engaged their attention and directly invoked the concepts depicted. Those concepts were no doubt also discussed in texts, but they are made present by images in manners that texts cannot duplicate. The inverse is also true. Images are incapable of duplicating literary language and meanings. The most important difference is that images are immediate, while words are deliberate. The essence of a verbal text is that it has chronological control. It determines the exact order in which it deploys each narrowly defined verbal sign, and that allows verbal texts to construct highly complex, precise, unambiguous statements. Conversely, visual signs and texts are spatial and immediate. Their task is not to produce a precise comprehension so much as an instantaneous sense. Hanging a crucifix on a wall has an immediate impact on the nature of a room, and in that sense the image is more immediately effective than any text could be. The same crucifix can also evoke a very direct sense of Christ's suffering in the viewer. The crucifix is useless, however, for the communication of theological reflections on that suffering; that requires verbal text. One might be tempted to say, in Cartesian terms, that the verbal system appeals to the mind, while the visual system is more of the body, but perhaps it is preferable, in the spirit of a post-Cartesian reuniting of mind and body, to associate the visual with what Kahneman (2011) identifies as "system one" or "fast" thinking (the immediate, visual, perception of the Christian nature of the room with a crucifix on the wall) and the verbal with "system two" or "slow" thinking (the sequential, verbal, explanation of what it is that renders the crucifix capable of affecting the room in that manner).[114]

---

114   I thank Lion Hijmans for bringing Kahneman's fascinating study to my attention.

Where does all this leave us? I have postulated that Roman art is a highly communicative system that we understand only imperfectly, and that we should study it independently from ancient literary sources. Against that background it will be clear why this study is not an attempt to collect, far less analyse, all iconographical and material sources relevant to the cult of the sun. That would require knowledge that I believe we do not yet have, namely the knowledge which images are, in fact, relevant to that cult. As I have argued in my critique of Berrens, above, we cannot equate the image type Sol with the word Sol. We also cannot assume that the image type Sol is the visual counterpart of the word Sol, if by that we mean sun / Sun / Sun god, because the image type Sol can function as a symbolic sign within its own, visual semantic system, i.e. be the depiction of some concept not directly related to sun god or solar cult.

The fact of the matter is that we do not know what concepts the basic image types Sol conveyed in Roman art. Therefore, this study is in the first place simply an analysis of the visual meanings associated with:

and/or

that is to say of the three specific image-types commonly found in Roman art and related to Sol.[115] The difference between this and a study of "imagery related to the Roman sun god", though subtle, is fundamental. Rather than study some group of images collected on the basis of non-visual criteria – all images deemed by us to pertain to a specific cult, or period, or region, or material object, or style for example – the analysis presented here deals with a distinct and visually clearly circumscribed group of three related iconographic signs. The material for this analysis has been collected purely on the basis of the formal criteria that define these signs, and the purpose of this analysis is to establish an initial sense of the range of visual meanings that these three image types had the potential to construct, with attention for the history, frequency, and contexts of their use.

Studying image types from Rome's visual semantic system is not the same as analysing an art work, of course. It is, however, an essential prerequisite for the analysis of any art work that is composed of some of those image types.

---

115   I would like to thank Zoë Hijmans for producing these drawings for me.

One needs to know the words before attempting to read a text. It is, in the first place, at this level of idiom that this study is most concerned with the image types Sol that it has collected. It takes that intermediate step of defining the basic potential meanings of the image types Sol, thus laying the groundwork for the analysis of specific images in which an image of Sol participates. That is why this is not an iconographical study of the Roman Sun god, but a semiotic study of three related image types that could be used to depict a range of concepts related, *inter alia*, to the Roman Sun god.[116]

8   The Interpretative Process – Understanding Manners of Meaning

The main goals of this study are now clear, as is its semiotic framework. Still to be discussed are the methodologies used to achieve these goals. The first question is how to define the social agreements that established the basic visual concepts and meanings associated with a given image type at a given time and place, bearing in mind that often knowledge of those agreements has been lost in part or in whole. This is where the largest issues arise in the classical tradition of studying imagery. The seemingly obvious step has always been to turn to the written sources in order to elucidate what the images depict. But as pointed out in the principles above, we cannot assume that the concepts associated with written signs are the same as those associated with comparable visual signs. For example, the bare feet of the Augustus of Prima Porta do not raise eyebrows; they characterize him as divine. Because we know that, we do not turn to texts discussing people walking *nudis pedibus* to deepen our understanding of what this status of divinity meant, but rather to texts discussing the phenomena of *divi*. The problem is that each component of an image, and each component image of a scene, can be similarly coded, quite possibly in ways that we are not aware of. Unless we have texts which explain that coding to us, we do not know which texts to turn to.[117] We cannot begin to analyse a particular Roman work of art or visual composition in communicative terms

---

116   Jäger 2017 argues cogently for the establishment of the "conventional meanings" of regularly recurring images or image types as the essential first step (*analytischer Einstieg*) in the historiographical study of images (*historische Bildkunde*). That is precisely what this study of the image types Sol intends to do.

117   A good example of a text that elucidates a visual code that would otherwise be hard to comprehend is Philostratus' fifth description in his *Imagines*. It shows that the dwarves that populate so many Nilotic scenes are in fact visualizations of a pun used to describe the rivulets that form the initial announcement of the coming flood of the Nile.

until we know what the component image types and visual conventions are contributing collectively to its meanings. It is at this level, as conventionally coded image types, that we will analyse the deployment of image types Sol.

All the various image types, selected by the artist for deployment in a given image, constitute the intermediaries between the visual semiotic system underlying Roman art and the actual images that constitute it. These image types are not actual symbolic expressions, but signs because, like signs, image types are virtual, having no author, no temporal existence, and no physical form. When an artist deploys an image type in a particular image that she is producing, the meaning of that particular image arises in the tension between the image type and the manner in which that type is instantiated in the actual image, as mediated by the viewer – and the artist – based on her/their knowledge of the conventional meanings associated with the image type. In this "tension" the image *type* forms the "constant", while the actual image is the variable. The closer the variable agrees with the constant, the less tension there is, and the more straightforward the actual meaning – intended and perceived – of the artist's image. It is important to remember, however, that the tension is not unidirectional, and that the "constant" therefore is not immutable. It, too, is affected by the tension, in the sense that lack of tension reinforces the constant's conventional meanings while increased tension provides impetus towards adjusting them. Both reinforcement and adjustment are dynamic processes which impact the image type, the former process making its meanings more entrenched, the latter making them more unstable. It is through these dynamic processes that image types also mediate the impact that actual images have on the visual semantic system through which artists generated them.

These "constants" are at the centre of the interpretative process where images are concerned, and that is why the image types Sol are the main focus of this study. One could consider the analysis carried out here to be a component of the hermeneutic contextual analysis, i.e., the placing of a specific image of Sol (actual symbolic expression) within its broader context of similar depictions which, taken together, provide the contours of an "image type" (or more). The pre-understanding with which I come to this contextual analysis is that the "context" – i.e. image type(s) – I wish to study is itself a component of an overarching visual semantic system with a specific, consciously maintained and imposed structure. I choose to understand that system in (loosely) semiotic terms as consisting of culturally agreed signs (which besides image types, can be styles, techniques, formats, material, positioning, size, and the like). By looking systematically at the actual deployment of the three basic image types Sol that are the object of this study, we can expect to discern patterns of occurrence which provide insight into the culturally agreed potential meanings of these image types within that system. We can also expect, through those patterns of occurrence, to gain further insight into the nature and functioning of the semantic system itself that this approach assumes Roman art to be.

The intended outcomes of this study, then, are new pre-understandings concerning the image types Sol and the visual system of signification to which they belonged, which can form the basis for new or further research in all three areas (images, signs, system). They are not conclusions, but beginnings of further study and hypotheses subject to confirmation, amendment, or rejection. One might be tempted to characterize this study in part as a "lemma" on image types Sol in a "lexicon" of Roman visual signs, but this can too easily be mistaken for a very static, systemic view of Roman art, with little acknowledgment of change over time and space, little attention for social strata and intercultural variation, and inadequate appreciation of the dynamism of the visual in Roman social discourse (and historical discourse, for that matter). Rather than a lemma, one should see this study as an attempt to re-establish an understanding of one of those two poles of tension, discussed above, namely the pole of the "constant". That there was such a "constant", a commonality of core meanings, is obviously a valid postulate, insofar as we can agree that an image of Sol can never be identified as Hades instead, or be mistaken for a goddess, or be taken for any of the countless things that an image of Sol is not. This core of meaning is the shared consensus that imbues the image type – in this case Sol – with its basic communicative ability. In many respects, pursuing those cores of meanings is the least exciting part of the study of image types – not much different from reading a dictionary.

It is in the deployment and manipulation of and by images that we find the real dynamism of the visual. This moves us beyond semiotics and puts us squarely in the field of what is now rather awkwardly called the entanglement of people and things.[118] But irrespective of what we call it,[119] we find ourselves dealing with what is to my mind one of the most exciting perspectives for the study of ancient art: its agency in creating *koine* (or its opposite) through transformation and manipulation. This is not a story of *Roman* art, empire building or acculturation; it is not the study of art as a tool in a process of "Romanisation". It is, if we limit ourselves to our field, the story of Mediterranean arts, of appropriation and rejection, of desire, of the psychology of possessing and being possessed. It concerns the agency of art in the transformation of identities, in

---

118   Hodder 2012.
119   Cf. Versluys 2015: 174 n. 72 on the fluidity of the various terms used for the processes under
       discussion here.

the keying of discourses – processes that can be slow and hidden or sudden and hotly debated.[120] An example is the famously controversial role of (Greek) art, mentioned above, in the aftermath of the conquest of Syracuse by Marcellus. The impact of his decision to strip Syracuse of much of its art and transfer it to Rome for display in his triumph and adornment of the city was something of a *topos* in Roman historiography.[121] Polybius (9, 10, 3–13) perhaps best captures the debate it aroused, arguing that the spoils of Syracuse transformed Rome from a peoples "leading the simplest of lives" to a peoples in danger of losing their victorious ways because it led them to "abandon the habits of the victors and to imitate those of the conquered."[122] This became the *communis opinio* of

---

120   One area where such dynamics play out is the issue of styles of art in the Roman world, and their connection with identities and/or meanings. Cf. Hölscher 1987, 2012; Webster 2003; Johns 2003; Hijmans 2016; Mladenovic 2016.

121   Polyb. 9, 10, 1–13; Liv. 25, 40, 1–3; Plut. *Marc.* 21. Cic. *Ver.* 2, 2, 4 seems to take a different view, but this is rhetorical rather than historical (cf. Cic. *Ver.* 2, 4, 115–6 and especially 120–1).

122   "As to whether in doing so [i.e. taking the art works of Syracuse to Rome] they [i.e. the Romans] acted rightly and in their own interest or the reverse, there is much to be said on both sides, but the more weighty arguments are in favor of their conduct having been wrong then and still being wrong. For if they had originally relied on such things for the advancement of their country, they would evidently have been right in bringing to their home the kind of things which had contributed to their aggrandizement. But if, on the contrary, while leading the simplest of lives, very far removed from all such superfluous magnificence, they were constantly victorious over those who possessed the greatest number and finest examples of such works, must we not consider that they committed a mistake? To abandon the habits of the victors and to imitate those of the conquered, not only appropriating the objects, but at the same time attracting that envy which is insepa- rable from their possession, which is the one thing most to be dreaded by superiors in power, is surely an incontestable error. For in no case is one who contemplates such works of art moved so much by admiration of the good fortune of those who have possessed themselves of the property of others, as by pity as well as envy for the original owners. And when opportunities become ever more frequent, and the victor collects around him all the treasures of other peoples, and these treasures may be almost said to invite those who were robbed of them to come and inspect them, things are twice as bad. For now, spectators no longer pity their neighbors, but themselves, as they recall to mind their own calamities. And hence not only envy, but a sort of passionate hatred for the favorites of fortune flares up, for the memories awakened of their own disaster move them to abhor the authors of it. There were indeed perhaps good reasons for appropriating all the gold and silver: for it was impossible for them to aim at a world empire without weakening the resources of other peoples and strengthening their own. But it was possible for them to leave everything which did not contribute to such strength, together with the envy attached to its possession, in its original place, and to add to the glory of their native city by adorning it not with paintings and reliefs but with dignity and magnanimity. At any rate these remarks will serve to teach all those who succeed to empire, that they should not strip cities under the idea that the misfortunes of others are an ornament to their own

the ancient historians who reflected on this series of events. Is it a matter of "Graecia capta Romam cepit"? It is not that simple of course, but it is no small thing when the introduction of works of art into a city is credited with (or held responsible for) so thoroughly transforming its inhabitants.

And yet this is only one incident of countless: whether it is the Hellenizing style of some Gandharan statues, the adoption of stone sculpture in parts of Rome's Empire where such had not existed before, the transport of obelisks from Egypt to Rome, or the depiction of image types Sol in mosaic floors of late Roman synagogues, all are examples of interactions with art in the Roman world that are far too complex, ambiguous, and, indeed, entangled to be swept under the mat of "acculturation" or "Romanisation". In fact, any concept that places the actual agency outside objects, reducing them to tools in a process rather than actors, falls short. This is also true of entanglement, at least as it is described by Rowan (2016: 48). She sees it as "an active process whereby 'foreign' goods are appropriated, transformed, and/or manipulated by individuals or social groups, resulting in new meanings and uses." That is fine as far as it goes, but what we need is a framework that also looks at art as *actor* in active processes whereby individuals or social groups are appropriated, transformed, and/or manipulated by "foreign" goods, resulting in new identities and discourses. Hodder (2012) stresses this aspect of things: "(...) In many ways things make us. There is an objectness, a stand-in-the-wayness of things that resists, that forms, that entraps and entangles."

The widespread, long-term, cross-cultural use of easily recognizable Roman image types suggests all manner of tantalizing entanglements. This is a direction of research that holds real promise for Roman art history, reinvigorating its role not just within classics, but within the broader discipline of art history as a whole. Nonetheless we are not pursuing it here, for reasons perhaps best explained with the help of Rowan's engagement ring. Such rings are the perfect example of entangled objects, she argues, because they undergo such transitions and take on such power through the manner in which they are used. Simply wearing one makes a strong statement; refusing or returning it can be devastating.[123] This is indeed an excellent example, but one which we can only explore fruitfully if we actually know that the object is an engagement ring. There is no point in trying to evaluate transformations without a strong sense of what is being transformed. Or, to return to image types Sol, we need to have a strong sense of their core meanings – the image type as

country. The Romans on the present occasion, after transferring all these objects to Rome, used such as came from private houses to embellish their own homes, and those that were state property for their public buildings." (Polyb. 9, 10, 3–13).

123   Rowan 2016: 44–5.

"constant" – before we can hope to study how that constant was expanded, manipulated, and transformed by its wide ranging contexts, and how it in turn expanded, manipulated, and transformed them.

Is our lack of knowledge in this regard really so dire? Do we know so little about Sol in Roman art that we still need to start, almost *tabula rasa*, with a basic, systematic analysis of its potential core meanings? This book will illustrate amply that this is indeed the case, not just because we know so much less about what image types Sol mean than we thought, but also because our field is still rife with studies that fundamentally misunderstand the manner of that meaning. As numerous examples will show, the ways in which ancient art engaged its audience and ambience are still far too often taken as self-evident. It was not. There is nothing self-evident about the step from image or object to meanings, and if there is one thing that this study illustrates clearly, it is that we must become far more disciplined in our viewing, and far more cautious in our interpretations of Roman art.

That note of caution notwithstanding, most of the actual analysis – the bulk of this study – is quite straightforward. We begin with chapter two, on the iconographic characteristics of the image types Sol. This is essentially an extensive affirmation of a major pre-understanding in the analysis, namely how to recognize the image types in the first place.

The next two chapters (three and four) provide a basic analysis of the images, in the form of a running commentary that focuses on identifying and interpreting meaningful patterns of usage as they emerge. The purpose is to identify potential meanings or connotations that could be associated with images of the Sol type, usually without going into specifics. A small number of minor "case studies" do offer further insights, but none of the discussions constitute an in depth analysis of specific images. The aim is to offer tentative proposals for potential meanings with which image types Sol may have imbued specific images. These chapters are followed by the core section of this study: the catalogue in which we present the visual evidence in the form of an extensive listing of images which consist of, or incorporate one (or more) of the basic image types Sol. This central place of the catalogue is intended to invite the reader to leaf through it, making it easier to visualize the number and variety of the images under discussion.

The remaining chapters present a number of case studies devoted to more detailed analyses of specific images or closely related topics. The aim of these case studies is to provide some initial tests of the hypotheses generated by the initial analyses, but here too the reader should not seek firm conclusions.[124] On

---

124 Chapter 5 establishes a continuous, uninterrupted presence of temples of Sol in Rome from an early date until the closure of all temples; chapters 6–9 deal with a variety of

the contrary, the case studies illustrate that we still have a long way to go before we can engage in more thorough analyses of the visual meanings involved.

One may wonder what the point is of this abstract chapter if the bulk of this study is so practical, preliminary, and down-to-earth. This chapter is necessary, however, not for the *what* of this book, but for the *why*. It is in many respects a quite personal attempt to put into words the broader perspectives to which this study hopes to contribute. Personal, because those well-versed in archaeological and visual theory will have recognized its deficiencies and have realized that I am by no means a theorist of material culture meanings. This chapter is not meant to be programmatic or an authoritative summary of relevant current theory, and those less conversant with the issues discussed should turn to the literature cited rather than to this chapter if they wish to gain an understanding of current trends and debates. This chapter should be read as a personal statement of my own understanding of the theoretical framework and horizon of this study. We all work within such a framework and with such a horizon, but we often fail to make them explicit, even to ourselves. I suppose that in a way this chapter is an attempt to pick up the gauntlet that Boymel Kampen threw down with her lament on the lack of theoretical and philosophical engagement among Roman art historians.[125] Certainly I agree with her that as scholars we need to engage with the basic theoretical and philosophical issues associated with our field and the knowledge we pursue. All too often we seem to take the what and why of our research for granted.

Because this is my personal understanding of the framework of my research, I have decided not to define certain key terms, such as "Roman", "art", "religion" and the like. The reason is simple: I am not very certain what I mean with those terms, particularly in the Roman (!) context. The hope is that further research building on this study will enhance and expand our understandings of what it means for something to be Roman or Roman art or Roman religious art, but in the meantime, I prefer to avoid even a working definition because it simply sets up arbitrary boundaries around concepts that I am not convinced are definable at all. Approaching such concepts with unarticulated and partially subconscious pre-understandings carries risks, but makes it easier for me to adapt my understandings in the course of this study (as I have certainly done

---

iconographical issues, such as the meaning of the radiate crown of emperors; chapter 10 discusses various aspects of the cult of Sol in the third and early fourth centuries, and chapter 11 returns to the previous research on Sol and attempts to understand how it managed to give rise to the wholly groundless notion that there was a Syrian god, Sol Invictus, in Rome in late antiquity, who was "utterly different" from the, by then supposedly defunct, Roman sun god Sol Indiges.

125   Boymel Kampen 2003.

and am still doing). For similar reasons I have not attempted to define "the Roman viewer". I am well aware that however we may seek, we will never find "the" Roman viewer because she does not exist and never has. There was no unified Roman view or gaze, but as many as there were Romans, and the individual experiences of past people are beyond the reach of the historian. The role of the Roman viewer in this study is to keep us firmly aware of the integral role of the viewer in the construction of emergent visual meanings through their art. We may not be able to relive the experience of individual Romans, but that does not mean that we need not incorporate it in our attempts at approximate understanding. Ultimately, what we seek is the otherness of collective experiences of (groups of) Romans and the light that otherness sheds on us. For the study of history is an essential component of the study of ourselves, or so we say.

Recognizing Sol: The Three Main Image Types

1 Introduction

The Romans had clear and easily recognizable iconographic conventions for what we have termed the three image types for Sol:[1] the youthful radiate bust, the standing figure with whip or globe, and the radiate charioteer of a *quadriga*. These are so clearly defined that there can rarely be any doubt whether a particular image is derived from one of these image types for Sol or not. They evolved out of classical Greek conventions for the depiction of Helios, and were largely in place by the fourth c. BC, replacing the Etruscan and Italic traditions which were somewhat different.[2] The last of the three image types to be established was that of Sol standing, perhaps under the influence of the Colossus of Rhodes in the early third century BC. The image types for Sol remained in use until well into the Middle Ages.[3]

With their consistency and durability, the image types for Sol meet the prime prerequisite of successful visual communication. This is in itself an important conclusion. It means that these image types were deployed to depict concepts that were common and important enough to make that degree of recognizability desirable. It does not mean that they conveyed a fixed meaning every time they were used. As we have seen, it is precisely the immutability of these image types, over such a long period of time, that allows them to take on more complex, conventionalized meanings.

Together, the three image types represent the prime forms by which *S/sol* was visualized by the Romans. Besides these three dominant types there were, of course, regional traditions with potentially very different iconographies for depicting the sun or solar deities, such as the wheel in Celtic regions, but we will not explore those here.[4] Another separate category is the depiction of myths in which Sol plays a role. Here Sol could be depicted more freely than

---

1 On the iconographic conventions, cf. LIMC IV, s.v. Helios/Sol; Roscher, ML, s.v. Sol; Bernhard 1933; Schauenburg 1955; Matern 2002: 47. No ancient discussions of the iconography survive, although some sources do provide pertinent information. Cf., e.g., Tert. *De Spect.* 9, 3. (*quadriga*), Verg. *Aen.* 12, 164 (radiate crown).

2 The Etruscan sun god could be depicted as charioteer of a *triga*, for example (section H5 of the catalogue).

3 Cf. the church of S. Maria en Quintanilla de las Viñas in Burgos (C4.28), the church of S. Mary at Beit She'an (D1b.2), the synagogue floor at Beth Alpha (D1a.6), etc.

4 Cf., e.g., C2i.1.

© KONINKLIJKE BRILL NV, LEIDEN, 2024 | DOI:10.1163/9789004442405_004

the strict rules of the basic three Roman image types normally allowed: seated on a throne receiving Phaethon, for example, or on horseback calming down the horses of the solar chariot after Phaethon had lost control.[5] Mythological images of Sol have been included in the catalogue.

A final category of "depictions" of Sol that we should not forget, is the sun's light itself. He could be integrated in the iconographic and architectural design of buildings through careful management of the admission of sunlight. A striking example of this could be found in the Serapeum in Alexandria, where a tiny hole in the wall, uncovered at the right moment, allowed rays of sunlight to fall precisely on the lips of the cult statue of Sarapis. This "kiss of Sol" is depicted on a fair number of lamps from Alexandria.[6] The oculus in the pantheon in Rome presumably also helped to integrate the light of the sun into its program of symbolic meanings, and in shrines of Mithras light effects were especially common. The use of light effects had a long tradition in the Mediterranean world.[7]

2   Criteria

The following are the main criteria by which to identify an image type of Sol.

2.1   *Youth*

Essential. Good examples: A3 (all images).

From Classical Greek art onwards, the sun is depicted without exception as a young and beardless male figure and this continues throughout the Roman period. A bearded figure cannot be Sol.[8] Neither can a mature or elderly figure. The youth of Sol is usually, but not always, further evoked by the abundant locks of thick loose hair framing the face, long but not quite the shoulder-length tresses of Apollo or Dionysus. These locks are generally not groomed, although sometimes there is a suggestion of a parting in the middle. At times the central locks above his forehead are brushed up and back in an *anastole*, and when this is combined with a slightly tilted head, strong brows, slightly opened mouth, and perhaps an upward gaze, the images are often taken to

---

5   Cf., *inter alia*, C3a1.1–13.

6   G1e and pp. 149–151.

7   Serapeum: Tran Tam Tinh 1984; Merkelbach 1995: 149–50; Sabottka 2008: 326; light effects at Hadrian's Villa in Tivoli: De Franceschini & Veneziano 2011 (with further imperial examples as well); Pantheon: Hannah & Magli 2011; Mithras cult: Clauss 2000: 120–30; Gordon 2017: 431–2; Hensen 2017: 393. On the use of light in Greek sacred architecture: Williamson 1993; Parisinou 2000; Patera 2010.

8   In archaic Greek art, Sol is sometimes bearded. Cf. Matern 2002: 47.

represent Alexander, or Alexander-Helios, rather than Sol. We have only a small number of coloured images of Sol, but from these it would appear that dark blond to deep (reddish) brown were the preferred colours for Sol's hair.

2.2 Rays

Very common, not essential. Good examples: B2.6; B2.26; E3.2, G1a (all images).

Rays or a radiate nimbus, symbolizing light, form the most recognizable element of the image types for Sol. Rays are the more common of the two, although the radiate nimbus was also quite popular. The rays are associated only with his head, and are generally depicted as emanating directly from it. In rare cases they may be depicted as if they were attached to a fillet of metal circling the head. The number of rays ranges from three to more than thirty, but arrangements of five, seven, or nine were the most common, as this allowed for a balanced, symmetrical depiction with one vertical ray emerging from the top of his head and an equal number of rays to either side.

Though important, the representation of emanating light is not an essential element of Sol's iconography, and in rare cases he can appear without any visualized radiance at all. How often this actually happened is now difficult to judge because in most cases when rays are lacking, one can assume that painted rays or metal rays, enhanced the image. We discuss divine radiance at greater length below, pp. 78–85.

2.3 Raised Right Hand

Very common, not essential. Good examples: A1a.8; B1.8, B1.9, B1.12; B1.13.

Particularly in the third and fourth centuries AD, one of the most striking elements of the image types Sol is his raised right hand. In that period, he was almost invariably represented with this gesture when depicted as a full-length figure, whether on or off a chariot.[9] The arm was usually outstretched, with the elbow lightly bent, and was raised only slightly above the shoulder so that the open hand was at about the same height as his head. The slightly bent elbow and loosely opened hand gave the pose a more relaxed appearance than the stiff stance of the fascist salute, nor was his posture threatening or apotropaic. It was most likened to the confident *adlocutio*-gesture of an orator commanding attention, or to an expansive gesture of power, blessing, or salutation, such as that of the emperor in many equestrian statues.[10] This aspect of Sol's iconography is relatively unremarkable, but requires some further comment

---

9   Matern 2002: 124–7 understates the number of depictions of Sol as charioteer with a raised right hand.

10   On the importance of hands and – by extension – hand gestures, see Corbeill 2004: 20–4; Cf. Aldrete 1999: *passim*; Brilliant 1963; Sittl 1890.

because Cumont, L'Orange, and others saw the raised right hand as a new iconographic element that heralded the introduction, in Rome, of a new, Syrian cult of the sun by the Severi. It was used, they believed, to differentiate this oriental Sol Invictus from the old Roman Sol Indiges.[11]

The raised right hand was certainly not a characteristic component of the image types Sol before the later imperial period, but its introduction was gradual, and began well before the Severans, starting with a coin minted on Crete under Vespasian.[12] A number of civic coins,[13] some reliefs, at least two bronze statuettes, and a fair number of intaglios[14] can also be dated to the Flavian and Antonine periods.[15] Thus when, in the fourth year of Septimius Severus's reign (AD 196) the first depictions of Sol as a full-length figure appear on Roman imperial coins, their iconography, which included the raised right hand, did

11 Cumont 1923: 69–72; L'Orange 1935: 93–4: "Da es nun gerade die Severer sind, die den orientalischen Sonnenkult in Rom einführten, da ferner der Gestus an sich dem orientalischen Ritual gehört, ergibt es sich ohne weiteres, daß das Motiv für den (…) Typ des neuen Sol, des Sol Invictus erst verwendet worden ist. Der Sol Invictus stammt demnach nicht nur seinem Begriff und Namen nach aus dem orientalischen Kultus, sondern es sind auch in der bildhaften Vorstellung des Gottes orientalische Elemente bestimmend geworden." Cf. the extensive discussion by Matern 2002: 129–47.

12 BMCGrC IX 3, 13. The figure cannot be securely identified as Sol and could be Augustus. Earlier, isolated examples include Helios with raised right hand on a chariot as early as the late fourth century BC in S. Italy; Naples Mus. Naz. 82244, from Canosa (Matern 2002: 210 Q21, fig. 4; LIMC IV, s.v. Helios 81) and Zurich, Roš Collection 66 (Matern 2002: 211 Q28, LIMC IV, Helios 78). Cf. some Bactrian coins of the second century BC, depicting Helios, standing, with a raised right hand (Matern 2002: 86, 298 M172–3). Also of interest are a pair of earrings from Bolsena, dated by some as early as the third century BC (J5.1).

13 Coins of the second century include: Aezani, Helios standing, with globe (BMCGrC XXV, 28 nos. 36–8; AD 180–192); Alexandria, Helios on *quadriga* left or right (RPC III, 4800.3, AD 114; Geissen 11974, AD 156/7, 2201, AD 178/9); Amasea (RPC IV, 5308, 5309, 10181, 10184, AD 180–192), Hierapolis Castabala (RPC IV, 4976, AD 161–180; cf. Matern 2002: 129–30); Bithynia-Pontus (RPC IV, 6139).

14 One of the statuettes has been dated to the first or second century AD by Kaufmann-Heinimann on stylistic and contextual grounds (B1.1); the other is dated to the Antonine period (B1.2); cf. also two statuettes of the second century AD in private collections (B1.3–4). The reliefs include a fragment of the Parthian relief in Ephesus (C1f.10, AD 166–169; hand and possible attribute lost); a marble relief in Naples, Museo Nazionale 6678 (C2a.5, probably M. Aurelius), possibly an altar in Newcastle-upon-Tyne, Black Gate Museum (C2j.1, after AD 150), a sarcophagus in Naples, S. Chiara (C3a8.1, AD 160–170), and a small bronze decorative element, now lost (K9.13, second century AD). Relevant intaglios dated to the first and second century include H1c.1–6, H1d.1–3, H2a,1, H3a,1, H3c.1, H3e.1–3, H4b.1, H4f.1, H6a.1–12, H6aa.1–5, H6ad.1, H6b.1, H6bd.1, H6be.1, H6i.1, H14.1, HA3A.1, HA6a,1–2, HA6aa.1, HA6b.1, HA6bb.1.

15 The actual number of surviving pre-Severan depictions is undoubtedly higher, for a large number of images of Sol with a raised right hand are dated rather loosely as "second–third century AD"; it is reasonable to assume that at least some of these date to the second, rather than the third.

not present a break with established practice.[16] It was simply one step in a process which saw the raised right hand increasingly become the norm, not only for the image type Sol as a standing figure, but also for representations of Sol on a *quadriga*.

This means that much of the debate about the significance of this gesture rests on two faulty premises: that the gesture appeared suddenly in Roman iconography, and that it was introduced from the East.[17] Neither is supported by the evidence. Hence, although it is still often claimed that the raised right hand differentiates one sun god ("Sol Invictus") from another ("Sol Indiges") this cannot stand.[18] There was in any case nothing to differentiate, for as the evidence amassed in the present study makes abundantly clear, there is no merit to the notion that there were two entirely different sun gods in ancient Rome. I will briefly return to L'Orange's arguments in the final chapter.[19]

2.4   *Chlamys*

Essential. Good examples: Figure 2.1; A1a.1; A1a.8; C2i.4. In Roman art Sol tended to be nude, but he was (almost) never depicted without a cloak. This cloak generally took the form of a *chlamys*, originally a military or hunting cloak of probably Macedonian origin.[20] A typical *chlamys* was fastened above the right shoulder with one fibula and would hang down behind Sol, covering his left shoulder and upper arm. But the cloak could also hang down from both shoulders or be depicted as billowing out behind him. The absence of a cloak was exceedingly rare. This means that all the other identifying factors must be quite unambiguous to warrant identification of a cloakless image as Sol. This is as true when he is otherwise nude as it is when he is clothed.

The *chlamys* was not a neutral article of clothing in the Roman world, but very much a symbol of power, with echoes of Alexander the Great. Baroin & Valette (2014) give some excellent examples of the associations evoked by the *chlamys* in Roman imperial circles when deployed in the elite's "*shows impériaux.*"[21] They remark *inter alia* on the impact the images of divine *chlamydati* had on these imperial discourses of power, singling out Hermes. One could readily add Sol to their examples, for it is fair to say that Sol's role was at least as important. This further strengthens their conclusion that the *chlamys* was

16   L2.19 (AD 196–198); cf. Williams 1999.
17   Matern 2002: 129–47 offers the most extensive discussion, with many references to earlier scholarship.
18   Cf., e.g., Gross 1985: 25–6.
19   Cf. also Hijmans 1996: 124–5.
20   Gerszke 2011: 104–9.
21   Baroit & Valette 2014: 58–64.

FIGURE 2.1   A model wearing a *chlamys*
DRAWING BY ANNA HIJMANS AFTER HEUZEY 1922, P. 125 FIG. 64

an article of clothing of great theatricality, both literally within the theatre, but especially beyond, in the pomp and portrayal of power.

2.5   *Chiton*
Optional. Good examples: C1e3.3; E1c.2. In Greek art, Helios was normally dressed in the long *chiton* of charioteers, generally with a high belt above the waist and sometimes with cross-belts over the shoulders. In Roman art, Sol was sometimes clothed, though usually not (see above). If clothed, he was invariably dressed in a *chiton*, usually of the long type common to Greek charioteers, but on rare occasions a shorter one.

2.6   *Quadriga*
The only type of chariot allowed for Sol. Good examples: H1–H4 (all images). One cannot identify a charioteer as Sol unless his chariot is drawn by four horses; Luna must have a *biga*, which may be drawn by bulls or horses.[22] On occasion, Sol as bust or standing figure may be accompanied by four horses, as a reference to his *quadriga*. In very rare cases a figure with only one horse has been identified as Sol, but these are all doubtful. Of course, this does not mean that every *quadrigatus* necessarily had solar connotations.[23]

In art as well as literature, Sol's horses are generally white. Hyginus names them as Eous, Aethiops, Bronte, and Sterope. In addition to these, he mentions Homeric names, but here the text is corrupt and only the name Abraxas can be salvaged with certainty, along with the probably mangled name Therbeeo. Finally, there are the four names given by Ovid: Pyrois, Eous, Aethon, and Phlegon.[24] The number of horses yoked to the *quadriga* invites numerical symbolism connected with the seasons. There was a significant amount of such symbolism connected with the *quadriga*, the circus, the circus factions, and Sol.[25]

2.7   *Whip*
Common, but not essential. Good examples: Fig. 2.2; A1a.1 (whip in right hand); C1c.2; C2b.2; E3.2. From the earliest representations in Roman art, a horse-whip (*scutica*) is a standard attribute of Sol. The *scutica* typically consists of an arm-length rod to which a single cord, or leather thong, is attached at one end. The

---

22   Tert. *De Spect.* 9, 3.
23   Dunbabin 1982.
24   Hyg. *Gen.* 183, Cf. Ovid *Met.* 2, 153.
25   The number of gates was twelve, equal to the number of months or signs of the zodiac. A race consisted of seven laps (planets, days of the week). There were four teams, with the whites representing winter, the reds summer, the greens spring, and the blues autumn (Tert. *Spect.* 9, 5). For a comprehensive discussion of such symbolism, cf. Lyle 1984.

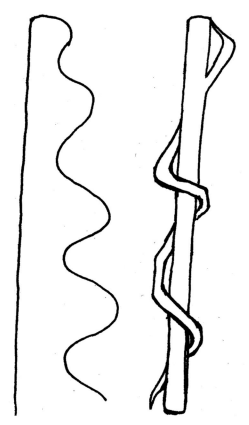

FIGURES 2.2A AND 2.2B
A Roman *scutica* (whip)
DRAWINGS BY PHOEBE HIJMANS

whip logically refers to Sol's role as charioteer of the solar chariot, and as such also occurs when Sol is represented as a standing figure or as a bust. The whip is not unique to Sol, as it is also is an attribute of Luna, but no other deities have a whip as a standard part of their iconography.[26] Thus, when any other male deity is depicted with a whip, this often can be taken as a reference to Sol.[27]

2.8   *Globe*

Common, but not essential. Good examples: E1a.1; L2.39. The globe (*globus*) was originally a teaching device for lessons in astronomy and astrology.[28]

---

26   Ginzrot 1817: 546. For human charioteers with whips of the same type, cf. e.g. Papini 2002: 95 and the references gathered there.

27   Cf., e.g., the iconography of Abraxas (LIMC I, s.v. Abraxas).

28   NP ant., s.v. Kartographie II. Globus; LCI II, s.v. Kugel; Schramm 1958: 1; Arnaud 1984: 60–3; cf. Laffitte 2012 for Greek and Near Eastern forerunners. For a surviving Roman celestial globe of the second century AD cf. Künzl 1996, Künzl et al. 2000.

Ancient cosmic globes should not be confused with modern, earthly globes. The former represented the cosmos, which was imagined to be round with earth at its centre, rather than simply the earth itself.[29] Often a diagonal band with or without figures of the zodiac crossed the globe and it may have been decorated with other astrological symbols and bands as well. Painted globes were usually coloured blue, with a red band for the zodiac.[30]

Both in form and function the globe was a useful iconographical symbol. It represented the cosmos, and thus any figure bearing the globe was represented as being a mover of (or in) the cosmos.[31] By the end of the Roman republic the globe had become an abstract symbol of (cosmic) power, with Jupiter, Dea Roma, and the Genius Populi Romani regularly represented bearing a globe, while Victory often stands on one. From Caesar onwards, all Roman rulers bear the *globus* as a sign of their power. Joint rule can be symbolized by the joint holding of a globe. Often the emperor was depicted as receiving a globe from a god, initially, usually Jupiter or Roma, but by the third century increasingly also Sol or Mars. By this time the globe had clearly become a conventional sign of supreme power, although that does not mean that its cosmic symbolism had been forgotten.

2.9   *Torch or Torches*

Rare. There is a small number of depictions of Sol with one or even two torches. These can sometimes be images that conflate Sol and Apollo, but that was usually not the case. Some have argued that torches are indicative of depictions of Sol from the East, but this is an argument based almost entirely on civic coinage which is itself overwhelmingly from the East.[32] The lack of compa-

---

29   In Antiquity, the notion that the earth was round was not unanimously accepted, but there is no consensus on how strong or widespread the opposition to it was. For contrasting views, cf. Arnaud 1984: 63–5 with Schramm 1958: 11. Sol holds a celestial globe, not a terrestrial one, and Arnaud 1984 gives compelling evidence that in Roman art all globes were, in fact, models of the cosmos, not earth.

30   For a fuller discussion of zodiac depictions, see Gundel 1992: 59–74 and *passim*.

31   Alföldi 1935: 77; Brilliant 1963: 75; Kantorowicz 1963; RAC 110, s.v. Herrschaftszeichen; Schneider 1997; Gordon 2013: 96–100.

32   E.g. Matern 2002: 95–8. For examples of Sol with a torch on civic coinage: BMCGrC XIII, 197 no. 20 (AD 193–211, Prusa ad Olympum); XX, 20 no. 13 (AD 161–180, Pessinus); XXI, 83 nos. 8–9 (AD 161–176, Hierapolis-Castabala, torch on ground next to Helios), 156 no. 66 (AD 245, Soli-Pompeiopolis); RPC IV, 1359, 1373, 1375 (AD 161–192, Philadelphia in Lydia); RPC IV, 1599, 1609, 1616, 3008, 3017 (AD 161–180, Tralles); RPC IV, 1896, 1897, 1899 (AD 180–192, Colossae, Phrygia); Matern 2002, 294 M121, fig. 110, (ca. AD 200); RPC IV, 7273 (AD 180–192, Germa = Matern 2002, 297 M167, fig. 115); RPC IV, 4861 (AD 161–169, Prusias

rable civic coinage from other parts of the Empire makes the argument difficult to evaluate. In media other than coins, representations of Sol with a torch
are very rare; it is worth noting, however, that the eight or so non-numismatic
images of Sol with a torch are about equally divided between East and West.

The majority of these representations date to the reign of Septimius Severus
or earlier.[33] In the case of the civic coins, the significance of this is difficult
to gage, given the general decline of civic coinage in the third century AD. It
is noteworthy, however, that the non-numismatic depictions also tend to be
earlier rather than later, as the majority date to the first or second century AD.

The torch is far more common as an attribute of Luna than of Sol, and when
the two are together, Luna is more likely to hold one. Likewise, Lucifer, preceding Sol, may be depicted with a torch. In general, the torch is associated
with night, rather than day – it is a standard attribute for Hecate, for instance –
which can explain its rarity as attribute of Sol.

2.10   *Staff*

Rare. In a small number of cases Sol is depicted holding a full-length staff.
Most are early in date, although on coins the staff can occur as late as the reign
of Severus Alexander.[34] Two early non-numismatic depictions are of known
provenance, namely Rome (E2.1, late first century BC or early first century AD)
and Germania (C2e.2, last quarter of the first century AD). There is also a later
example from Germania (C2e.29, ca. AD 200) Also of known provenance are
a number of civic coins from autonomous mints in the East listed by Matern,
although probably not all actually depict Sol with a staff.[35] The group is com-
pleted with a number of intaglios of unknown provenance.[36] This evidence
shows that the full-length staff was a rare attribute that occurred throughout

---

ad Hypium = Matern 2002, 289 M50); RPC VI, 6350 (AD 222–235, Selge = Matern 2002,
295 M139), Hypaepa (AD 193–217, Matern 2002, 291–2 M86–7), RPC IV, 5854, 6233, 11055
(AD 161–180, Ancyra, cf. Matern 2002, 297 M166); Matern 2002, 298 M169 (AD 193–217,
Tavium); Matern 2002, 286 M19 (AD 238–244, Hadrianopolis); Matern 2002, 295 M136a–b
(AD 244–249, Etenna).

33   Of the coins listed in the previous footnote, five date to the reign of Septimius Severus and
ten predate his reign, from a total of eleven cities. Five cities minted seven such coins after
Septimius Severus.

34   For Severan coins thought by some to depict Sol with a long staff or inverse spear, see
Berrens 2004: 43–4, and Matern 2002: 303 M243.

35   Matern 2002: 93–4, 288 M43 (Nikomedeia); 293 M107, M109 (Tralles); 294 M116 (Aizanoi).
On the coins from Tralles, Sol is holding a torch, rather than a staff according to the
RPC IV.2: 1599, 1616.

36   H6f, H6fa, H6g, H16 (all intaglios).

the imperial period, and that cannot be connected to a specific region of the Empire.[37]

2.11   *Sceptre*

Rare; suspect. Sol is sometimes described as holding a short sceptre (to be distinguished from the full-length staff discussed above). The identification of this attribute is problematic because of the close similarity with the short, solid staff of Sol's whip. Two examples can illustrate this. On an altar from the Aventine Dolichenum in Rome (C2b.2), Sol holds a short staff in the crook of his right arm with a slightly globular attachment at the top. The staff is very similar to the one held by Sol on another altar from Rome (C2w.5). On the latter, a thick rope is depicted curling downward over the staff, clearly indicating that it is a whip. On the former no such rope is immediately apparent, but on close inspection a thin ribbon-like string may be discernible just to the left of the top. This "string", if indeed it is that, is all but invisible on the photographs, but if we imagine the relief painted, and this cord in low relief picked out and continued in a sharply contrasting colour against the background, then the effect would be the same. In both cases the viewer would immediately recognize the "sceptre" as a whip, an expected attribute of Sol. On a relief in Naples (cat. C2a.5) the cord of the whip is equally invisible on most photographs, but clearly visible upon close inspection. A statuette of Sol in Leiden, from Laodicea (B1.21), holds a similar short staff in the crook of his left arm. There is no trace of a cord, but in view of the sketchy nature of the carving, which is very shallow and incised, a painted one cannot be excluded.

The number of depictions of Sol with a short staff without any extant trace of a cord is very low, and the potential for adding the cord in paint is significant. Therefore, in particular when Sol holds a short staff in the crook of his arm, this should be identified as probably a whip, even when no cord is visible.[38]

2.12   *Armour*

Not used for the image types Sol. There are a number of statuettes, reliefs, and the like that depict a youthful radiate figure in full Roman military attire, and with various attributes of Sol such as the raised right arm, a globe, and the like (figure 2.3).[39] These images adhere to one of the two basic full-length image-types inasmuch as they form a variant of the basic, nude Sol in a manner very similar to the figure of Sol dressed in a *chiton*. The difference is that the *chiton*

---

37   Matern 2002: 94 sees the staff as an oriental attribute on similar grounds as the torch.

38   Cf., e.g., an intaglio in Berlin, H6g.1.

39   For a discussion of such images, cf. Matern 2002: 120–2.

FIGURE 2.3
Statuette, Christie's sale 1466 lot 534,
June 8, 2004
IMAGE COURTESY CHRISTIE'S
NEW YORK

is an element with a strong Graeco-Roman tradition, and images of Sol dressed in a *chiton* can occur in all parts of the Empire. The figures in armour, on the other hand, apparently occur only in the Levant, and this suggests that the armour is a conscious, local digression from the Roman model (nude or *chiton*) to alert the viewer to the fact that this is not Sol, but a local or regional deity akin to him. The fact that Shamash and other local sun gods in the Levant tend to be depicted in armour supports this assumption. I have therefore excluded these images from discussion here.

2.13 Other Attributes

Rare. There are certain other attributes with which Sol could occasionally be depicted. Sometimes, these elements were used to modify the identity of Sol; examples include Syrian Solar deities in full armour or the Egyptian Souchos depicted with a crocodile.[40] In other cases, however, they appear to have left the identity of Sol unchanged. On a few coins in Asia Minor, Helios is depicted with a cornucopia;[41] Sol was occasionally depicted on horseback or riding a lion;[42] a coin in Rome minted under Heliogabalus[43] depicts Sol with a thunderbolt, and coins minted in AD 275 under Aurelian have him brandishing a bow and a branch.[44] There are other, comparable examples. As a general rule, it is safe to assume that ancient viewers would have noticed these variants as digressions from the norm, and – especially in the case of targeted audiences – would have understood the intended new references, which now may no longer be apparent or retrievable. For example, in the case of Heliogabalus's coin, the thunderbolt refers to his Emesan god Elagabal who, being a Ba'al, could be identified with Jupiter as well as Sol.[45] In the case of the bow and branch, the intent was clearly to emphasize Sol's connections with Apollo[46].

2.14   *Three Image Types*
More remarkable than the variants is the fact that there were so few. Throughout the Roman period the three image types for Sol adhered with striking consistency to the established iconographic norms. This leads to the following basic descriptions of each of the three image types:

2.14.1   The Standing Figure
The standing Sol is always youthful, beardless, with long hair, and almost always has divine radiance in the form of rays around his head, with or without a nimbus. He is usually nude with a *chlamys* or he is dressed in a *chiton*. His main attributes are a whip, a globe, or both. Any other attributes are rare. From the first century AD onwards, he can be depicted with a raised right hand, outstretched in a powerful gesture. This feature is initially rare, but becomes increasingly popular in the second century AD and by late antiquity it is one of his standard features. The standing Sol is usually depicted in contrapposto,

---

40   LIMC IV, s.v. Helios in peripheria orientali; LIMC VII, s.v. Souchos.
41   Cf. Matern 2002: 101.
42   HA12, H15ca–H15cd.
43   To avoid confusion between the emperor/priest and his homonymous god in this study, the former is called Heliogabalus and the latter Elagabal. On the history and meaning of the various forms of the name Elagabal, see Turcan 1985: 7–8.
44   L2.29 (thunderbolt) and L2.112 (bow and branch).
45   SHA *Elag.* 1, 5.
46   This had the effect of linking Aurelian to Augustus, as they both shared the "same" patron deity.

although on coins he is also often depicted walking or running, sometimes trampling one or more captives underfoot. Also on coins, the standing figure Sol can be depicted crowning emperors or bestowing a globe on them; it is rare to find Sol – standing or otherwise – engaged in a specific activity.

2.14.2 The Charioteer

Iconographically there are no distinguishing differences between Sol as a charioteer and Sol standing alone. The chariot itself is invariably a *quadriga*. In two dimensional depictions the *quadriga* is generally depicted in profile, but three-quarter representations and frontal *quadrigae* are not uncommon. In the case of frontal *quadrigae*, the horses are usually depicted jumping away in split pairs to either side, thus framing the central image of Sol. There are many charioteers depicted regularly in Roman art, and to identify a specific charioteer as Sol requires a number of his defining attributes, including rays, whip/globe, and/or raised right hand. In the case of small depictions, such as those on gems, attributes like the rays can often be difficult to see. Thus, access to very good photographs, impressions, or ideally the original object, are essential to confirm the identity of the charioteer.

2.14.3 The Bust or Head

Sol was very commonly depicted in bust or head alone, in which case the full range of defining attributes cannot be expected. Naturally the larger the bust, the more scope there is for additional attributes, such as a whip, globe, or raised right hand, and even a head alone can sometimes have a whip alongside it. In general, however, context takes the place of normal aggregation of attributes as deciding factor in the identification of a head or bust as Sol. For even with a head or bust, rays alone do not clinch the identity as Sol. This is not just the case when there are contraindications such as a beard, for example, or the wrong type of rays. There are examples of suitably radiate busts with portrait features dating to Hellenistic and Roman imperial date.[47] Furthermore, certain deities, such as Mên, recognizable by their own iconographic conventions, may also be depicted with rays.[48] Conversely, if the context is decisive enough even a non-radiate, youthful, beardless head or bust can be identified as Sol.

---

47   For a good example, cf. an intaglio portraying Trajan in Hannover, Kestner Museum, discussed by Bergmann 1998: 243 pl. 45.1.

48   Bergmann 1998: 70–2. The issue of divine radiance in Roman art is a complex one that is dealt with below (chapter 6).

Of the three basic image types for Sol in Roman art, Sol as charioteer has the longest tradition, closely followed by busts and heads of Sol. Both types have their origins in Greek art, and are common throughout the later Classical, Hellenistic, Republican, and Imperial periods. The first depiction of Sol on a Republican coin is of his head only. As Matern notes, the frequent occurrence of busts is noteworthy because in general deities tend not to be depicted in this manner. In part this may be the result of the importance of rays for Sol's iconography, making his reduction to bust easier to achieve without confusion about the identity than in many other cases. But Matern is no doubt right that this also reflects on the meaning of Sol in these images.[49]

There are virtually no surviving Greek or Hellenistic depictions of Sol as a standing figure. It seems likely, however, that the Colossus of Rhodes depicted Helios standing.[50] This is how he is portrayed on a Rhodian amphora stamp dating to about 100 BC (K9.6). In Roman art, standing figures of Sol occur from the first century BC, and soon become more common than Sol on a chariot.

Whether any of the Roman depictions are directly derived from lost Greek prototypes is difficult to say. Matern (2002) has dedicated a significant portion of her study to attempting to determine this, and has concluded that while in many cases no common prototype can be discerned, an exception must be made for Sol with the raised right hand, which she labels the "*invictus* type". She identifies a main type and two variant types of Sol with this gesture, the prototype of which she gives a *terminus post quem* on stylistic grounds of the latter part of the fourth century BC, tentatively suggesting that it may have been the Colossus of Rhodes itself.

In terms of Roman viewing many centuries later this issue is of secondary importance. Whether or not these specific subgroups were dependent upon a famous but long-lost original does not affect their recognizability, as they adhere to the standard iconography for this image type of Sol in every important respect. But although Matern's suggestion may not have significant consequences as far as the (Roman) viewing of these images is concerned, it is rooted in an understanding of their production which we must briefly discuss because it differs fundamentally from my own approach.

On stylistic grounds, Matern postulates that what she has termed the *invictus* type derives from older prototypes that are Greek rather than oriental.[51] She supports this with the following considerations:[52]

---

49   Matern 2002: 181–5.

50   Zusanek 1994; Hoepfner & Zimmer 2007; Vedder 2015.

51   Matern 2002: 147.

52   Matern 2002: 147–8.

1. The wide distribution of the "*invictus* type" throughout the Roman Empire;

2. What she considers a remarkable lack of variation ("erstaunlich wenige Abweichungen") in posture, arm position, and gaze ("Blickrichtung");

3. The observation that in certain cases the origins of images forming the context of a depiction of Sol can be traced back to Greek art, indicating a Greek prototype for the depiction of Sol himself as well.[53]

4. The general consideration that Roman cult statues were often copies of Greek originals.

Matern then proceeds with a lengthy analysis of the stylistic characteristics of, in particular, images of Sol with a raised right arm, identifying Polykleitan elements in their stance, a range of potential stylistic prototypes – including pre-Hellenistic ones – for the gesture with the right arm, and forerunners of the late fourth century BC for the hairstyle. She argues that a lack of torsion in the body suggests that the actual prototype cannot have been Hellenistic. This leads her to conclude that images of the "*invictus* type" themselves depended upon a full-scale Roman cult statue which, in turn, was inspired by a Greek statue which, on stylistic grounds, must be dated to the last third of the fourth century BC.[54] In her opinion, the best candidate for that statue is the Colossus of Rhodes, begun around 304 BC and erected 12 years later.[55] Although the Colossus itself collapsed in the 220s BC, Matern believes its iconography may have been preserved in various later cult statues, now lost, in places like Tralles, Philadelphia, and Rome itself.[56]

Matern herself identifies gaps in her evidence and acknowledges the speculative nature of her hypothesis: we do not really know at all what the Colossus looked like, and the chronological hiatus between the surviving statuettes and the postulated original is quite substantial (about 250 years). Nonetheless the obstacles to her hypothesis are even greater than she admits. To begin with, I simply do not see a sufficiently unified "*invictus* type" to postulate a single, physical "original". Matern speaks of a surprising lack of variation where I see quite a broad variety of postures, arm positions, and directions of gaze.[57] Many

---

53   Matern 2002: 147–8 gives two examples: the Sarcophagus in the Santa Chiara in Naples, where the depiction of the myth of Protesilaos is framed by Sol and Luna, both as full-length standing figures (C3a8.1), and the frieze-section from Ostia, now in Berlin, depicting various deities including Sol. Quoting Mattusch, she postulates late Classical prototypes for individual deities on the Ostian frieze, and a Hellenistic example for the frieze as a whole.

54   Matern 2002: 148–55.

55   Matern 2002: 155–62.

56   Matern 2002: 163–5.

57   Cf. B1.1, 2, 6, 7, 9, 10, 12, and 15, for example.

depictions of Sol without a raised right hand in other respects are as similar
to the examples Matern gives as these are to each other, not because they are
dependent upon the same original, but simply because Roman art takes a fairly
uniform approach to the depiction of nude, (semi-)divine youths.[58] The only
really definitive characteristic is the raised right hand, and this poses a real
problem for Matern's hypothesis. For from the outset the raised right hand is
not limited to standing figures of Sol, but also occurs with Sol as charioteer and,
albeit more rarely, even with busts of Sol.[59] This indicates that in the course
of the gradual introduction of the raised right hand as an iconographic characteristic of Sol there was no differentiation between the three basic image
types (bust, standing figure, *quadriga*). Thus the evidence does not support the
existence of an iconographically distinct group of the standing "*invictus* type"
postulated by Matern.[60]

In this context it is instructive to look at a number of medallions, a coin, a
fragment of a terracotta applique and a *phalera* all dating to the second half
of the second century AD and the first half of the third. All depict Sol rising
up in his *quadriga* over a series of clouds below which Tellus reclines; above
the clouds Lucifer precedes Sol.[61] On most, Sol does not raise his right hand,

---

58 Cf. the fresco of Sol in Naples (E1a.1, cf. E1a.2) which depicts the deity with the same gen-
    eral pose, gaze, and hairstyle as Matern's "*invictus* type", but lacks the raised right hand.

59 On provincial coins, Sol is depicted as *quadrigatus* with a raised right hand a number
    of times in the second century AD: cf. RPC IV 13883, 15089, 15122 (all from Alexandria,
    AD 156/7 and AD 178/9), and 5448 (Amaseia, AD 177–192). On Roman imperial coinage, cf.
    L2.20b. Cf. also various intaglios, such as a gem in Florence (H1c.1), four in Copenhagen
    (H1d.1–2, H3e.1 and H4f.1), an agate in Leiden (H2a.1), a carnelian in Paris (H3a.1), a helio-
    trope in a private collection (H4b.1), a heliotrope in Hamburg (HA3a.1), and possibly
    golden earrings in Paris (J5.1). For busts of Sol with his right hand raised, cf. a sarcopha-
    gus from Grave D at the Via Belluzzo in Rome (C3b3.4, mid-third century AD); a lamp
    in the Mus. Naz. in Rome (cat. G1a.64, second to third century AD); a relief in the Musei
    Capitolini in Rome (cat. C2c.84, fourth century AD), etc.

60 Matern 2002: 124–7 argues that the depictions of Sol as charioteer with a raised right
    hand are late and basically depict the statuary "*invictus* type" placed in a chariot: "Sie
    erweisen sich (...) als Umsetzung des Typus des stehenden Invictus (...) der in den
    Wagenkasten gestellt worden ist" (Matern 2002: 127). She downplays the number (and the
    relevance) of "early" depictions of Sol with a raised right hand on a chariot. She mentions
    no second century AD examples, only a few scattered cases in provincial coinage prior to
    Aurelian, and claims that on Roman imperial coinage Sol does not appear on a chariot
    with this gesture prior to Aurelian, which is incorrect (*supra* n. 50; 50). Without explana-
    tion she also changes the Severan date normally given to the relief in Baia (C1f.13) into
    "3. Jh. n. Chr.?" (Matern 2002: 222) and her dates for the intaglios she quotes also tend to
    be too late.

61 Phalera: K9.10; terracotta applique: F1b.11; bronze medallion of Antoninus Pius (ca. AD 154):
    L3.4; medallion of M. Aurelius minted in Nicaea: L3.3a; medallion of Commodus: L3.4;
    aureus of Septimius Severus (AD 197): L2.20a and b; medallion of Claudius Gothicus: L3.7.

but on the Severan aureus he does. The iconography of these medallions and the *phalera* is elaborate, and with the exception of the raised right arm on the Severan aureus, noteworthy for its consistency. Clearly, the Severan image is the same as the preceding ones, which means that the raised right arm is treated as no more than an optional iconographic characteristic of Sol which does not differentiate him or set him apart from the previous depictions without the gesture.[62]

Of course, the whole issue of "copies" and "originals" is fraught with difficulties. Too much has been made of Roman dependence on (superior) Greek masterpieces, more or less slavishly copied. The present study is premised on the understanding that as a communicative system, Roman art needed consistency in the depiction of key figures and concepts. The "remarkable lack of variation" and wide distribution of the "*invictus* types" are products of this necessary visual consistency and have nothing to do with long lost original masterpieces. Roman artists did not deviate significantly from the iconographic norm for the given image types because to do so would imply a change of meaning or intention.

3   Divine Radiance

No single aspect of Sol's iconography was essential, but clearly the most important, and also the most misunderstood aspect was his divine radiance. There are numerous examples in Greek, Hellenistic, and Roman art of both astral and non-astral deities represented as in some way radiant.[63] The depiction of their radiance was governed by precise iconographic conventions that differentiated between types of radiate light. These different types could not be used indiscriminately.[64] At what point this differentiation developed is difficult to say, but the following four categories of radiance can be discerned in Roman art by the first century AD; they were probably already in place much earlier.

---

62   Berrens 2004: 41; Bergmann 1998: 247–8 and Kantorowicz 1963: 128–9; cf. Kantorowicz 1961: 382–3, following Beaujeu and Alföldi, all believe that on the medallions of Commodus and Septimius Severus the charioteer is not Sol but the emperor in the guise of Sol, claiming that he is bearded. For a discussion and rejection of this view, cf. *infra*, pp. 937–940.

63   Cf. Bergmann 1998: 41–6. That symbolic radiance does not automatically imbue a figure with astral or solar characteristics is often forgotten, although Stephani 1859: 2 already scathingly dismissed scholars who believe that all forms of radiate light in Roman art are solar as "Gelehrte (...) denen Nichts unmöglich ist".

64   Cf. Bergmann 1998: 45–6; Matern 2002: 181–2.

3.1   *Nimbus Without Rays*

In Roman art, the nimbus is a circle or disc of symbolic light, generally blue or white, positioned behind the head.[65] Nimbi were used primarily in paintings and mosaics, rarely in bas-relief, and virtually never in three-dimensional art. Most gods and goddesses could be represented nimbate, and from Constantine onwards so could emperors,[66] but in Roman art the nimbus without rays is *never* an attribute of Sol.[67] Bergmann (2006: 159) notes that, although Roman artists adhered strictly to this rule, modern scholars are often unaware of it, leading many to make the incorrect claim that the nimbus was a primarily astral or even solar symbol.[68] In fact, the nimbus has the opposite effect, as it precludes a Sol-related identity.

3.2   *Rays and Radiate Nimbus*

Rays emerging from the head were commonly depicted in Roman art. They were often coloured yellow or golden, and usually took the form of lines or pointed spikes, but could also be more triangular in shape. With very rare exceptions rays are confined to male deities.[69] As we have seen above, they are important, but not essential components of the iconography of Sol.

In two-dimensional art (mosaics, paintings, low relief) the rays often occur in combination with a nimbus. In three-dimensional art this is understandably rare, and the few examples are rather awkward.[70] There appears to be no appreciable functional difference between the representation of rays alone and rays with a nimbus; Sol and astral deities are regularly depicted

---

65   Bergmann 1998: 45; Wallraff 2001: 145–51; Matern 2002: 181.

66   Wallraff 2001: 147. On Antoninus Pius depicted with the radiate nimbus of the Phoenix, cf. Bergmann 1998: 243–4 pl. 45.3.

67   In archaic and classical Greek art, Helios could be depicted with a nimbus only (Matern 2002: 181 n. 987), but Bergmann 1998: 45 notes that the differentiation between nimbus only and nimbus with rays had already begun in the Hellenistic era and was fully established in Roman art. I know of only four examples of Sol with a nimbus only (C2c.8, C2c.58, C2e.19 and E1c.1), and they either differ from the standard image type for Sol in so many ways that their identity is far from certain, or Sol's head is too poorly preserved to be certain that it was not radiate also.

68   Cf., e.g., Wallraff 2001: 129, 145. See also chapter 6.

69   Bergmann 1998: 70–2.

70   Matern 2002: 176–8, 181 distinguishes a separate category of rays, combined with what she describes as a *polos*-like object, and occurring predominantly in stone sculpture. I believe that Matern is right that this is not really a *polos*, but rather a three-dimensional "nimbus" with rays in relief on it. Cf. the statue of Sol in Copenhagen (A1a.5), and two busts from Egypt and Italy respectively (A3.2 and A3.11).

with either. But with non-astral deities combinations of these two forms of radiance are quite rare. In general, therefore, we can assume that rays and radiate nimbi were more specifically astral in character (though certainly not necessarily solar), and therefore not interchangeable with the less specific, non-radiate nimbi.[71]

3.3   *Radiate Crown*

Also known as a *Strahlenreif,* the radiate crown is depicted as if it were an object that actually existed. It has the appearance of a thin band of metal encircling the head just above the ears, to which vertical spikes have been attached as rays.[72] The suggested *reality* of this object is further accentuated in the manner in which the encircling band can disappear under the hair of the bearer.[73] Only Sol is depicted wearing a radiate crown of this type, and that only rarely.[74] Often, the rays disappear into a roll of hair and curls along the side of the head, implying (but not depicting) a hidden fillet under those curls to which the rays are attached.[75] The idea that Sol wore a removable crown of rays is voiced repeatedly in antiquity. As early as ca. 600 BC, Mimnermos speaks of the rays of Helios lying in his golden bedroom.[76] In the Aeneid (12, 164), Latinus wears a radiate crown *solis avi specimen*, i.e. of the same type as his forefather Sol.

3.4   *Radiate Crown or Wreath with Ribbons (Fig. 2.4)*

There is a minor but essential difference between the rare radiate crowns of Sol and the more common radiate crowns or wreaths worn primarily (but not exclusively!) by the emperors. The latter type invariably has ribbons or *lemnisci* at the back which hang down in the neck of the bearer.[77] Furthermore, the nature of the crown or wreath itself, to which the spikes or rays are attached,

---

71   Bergmann 1998: 72.

72   E.g. on certain late Republican denarii: Mn. Aquillius (109–108 BC), RRC 314 no. 303; C. Coelius Caldus (61 BC), RRC 457 no. 437. 1a. For an example in sculpture cf. A3.20.

73   E.g. certain dies of the obverse of a denarius struck by P. Clodius Turrinus in 42 BC (RRC 505 no. 494. 20a, pl. LIX. 494.20a).

74   The only exception to this rule that I know of is a rare coin of Geta with a radiate crown of this type, cf. Berrens 2004: 42.

75   E.g. on coins of Trajan of AD 116, RIC II 267 nos. 326–30, 341–2.

76   Mimn. fr. 10 G-P; cf. Ovid *Met.* 2, 40–1.

77   Bergmann 1998: 116–7. This is true for all two-dimensional depictions of the radiate wreath. We also have a small number of marble portrait busts with a radiate wreath of some kind, consisting of a rather thick band around the head just above the ears, into which holes were drilled to hold the rays. These appear not to have had *lemnisci*. For a further discussion of these busts see chapter 6.

FIGURE 2.4   Radiate crowns of Sol and radiate crowns of emperors compared. *Left column
(all Sol), from top to bottom, variants of*: L1.5 (109 BC), L1.7 (51 BC), L2.11 (AD 114),
L2.20 (AD 201), L2.74 (AD 260), L2.133 (AD 276), L2.213 (AD 310).
Right column (all emperors), from top to bottom: Augustus (after AD 14), Nero
(AD 65–68; RIC 197), Trajan (AD 98–117; RIC 385), Septimius Severus (AD 193–211;
RIC 680), Postumus (AD 160–169; RIC 68), Probus (AD 276–282; RIC 437), and
Constantine (AD 307–no later than AD 324; RIC 207). All images taken from coins
as indicated, except the portrait of Augustus, which is after a cameo in Cologne,
Romisch-Germanisches Museum 70,3
ALL DRAWINGS BY ANNA HIJMANS

shows greater variety. It can be depicted as a metal band, similar to that of the radiate crown of Sol discussed above, but it can also be broader and resemble a cloth diadem with rays. Other types include oak or laurel wreaths with rays.[78] The interpretation of these radiate crowns and wreaths with ribbons is a complex problem to which I return in chapter six. What is important to note at this point is that they are *never* an attribute of Sol or any other traditional deity. At a practical level the *lemnisci* thus immediately inform the viewer that the bearer of the wreath is *not* Sol or some other traditional deity. He is a person, usually an emperor, and usually alive.[79] Furthermore, whereas the nature of the radiance from Sol's head – a "real," removable crown, or simply rays of light – is often left unclear by the artist through his use of hair and curls to "hide" the fillet (if there "is" one), the same artists take great care to always clearly depict the reality of the radiate crown with ribbons, ensuring in particular that the ribbons themselves are always visible. Radiate crowns and wreaths of this type are worn by men only, not women.

Two basic forms of radiance can thus be discerned in Roman art. On the one hand, we have the clearly symbolic depiction of divine radiance in nimbi, radiate nimbi, and rays emanating from the head or the whole body. On the other hand, we have the rare radiate "crown" without ribbons of Sol and the radiate crown or wreath with ribbons of (mortal) men, which are both clearly *depicted* as if they were real objects rather than symbolic representations of light only.

The degree to which these forms of radiance have solar connotations varies. Nimbi without rays are suitable for most deities, but not for Sol. Rays and radiate nimbi have more specific astral connotations, but are not necessarily solar. The rare metal fillet with rays occurs with Sol only, and conversely the radiate crown or wreath with ribbons is never worn by Sol. Thus, despite an at first glance confusing range of types and contexts for the representation of symbolic radiance and the like, there were actually clear rules governing, and limiting, the acceptable usages of the different types of radiance. Given the longevity of these conventions and the consistency with which artists adhered to them, we cannot doubt that understanding these conventions was a part of normal visual literacy in the Roman Empire. This means that

---

78   For radiate laurel wreaths cf. Bastien 1992: 117–8. On radiate oak wreaths cf. chapter 6. Bardill's differentiation between radiate crowns with straight rays and with angled rays is not compelling, as the difference can invariably be explained as the result of purely artistic factors, Bardill 2012: 47–53. Cf. the position of the rays on the radiate oak wreath depicted on a soffit block in Nicopolis (fig. 6.21, p. 903.).

79   Cf. e.g. Bergmann 1998: 278 pl. 53.3 on a coin of Carus depicting the busts of Sol, radiate, and the emperor, radiate, facing each other.

the type of symbolic radiance becomes an important tool in identifying the figure – human or god, solar, astral, or divine. It also means that we must reject the still common tendency to assume automatically that the presence of symbolic light associates a figure with Sol. From the preceding it will be clear that certain forms of symbolic light actually have the opposite effect of precluding solar identification and hence, by extension, solar connotations.

This carefully differentiated series of conventions for the depiction of radiance in Roman art is an excellent example of the sophistication of Rome's visual semantics (table 2.1). It corroborates the evidence from ancient sources such as Cicero (quoted in chapter 1) that iconographic conventions even governed such details as the correct colour for a given deity's eyes. We cannot hope to understand the subtle differentiations between the different conventions unless we account for each consistently applied element – the presence or absence of the ribbons at the back of the radiate crown, for example (see chapter 6).[80]

TABLE 2.1   Overview of the usage of the Roman conventions for the depiction of radiance

	Sol	Male astral gods	Deities, post-Constantinian emperors	(Living) pre-Constantinian emperors and other humans
Nimbus without rays			x	(x)
Rays with or without nimbus	x	x		
(Metal) fillet with rays, *without* ribbon	x			
Fillet or wreath (oak or laurel) with rays, *with* ribbon (*lemnisci*)				x

80   On rare occasions, the emperor could be depicted as a full-length figure wearing a radiate wreath. On such coins, the scale of the image makes the *lemnisci* a truly minute detail that is nonetheless often still carefully executed. Cf. RPC 14510 (Alexandria, L. Verus), 14128, 16009 (Alexandria, M. Aurelius).

To summarize: the three image types for Sol that we will be studying here form a clearly defined and unambiguous group. In this group, he is depicted either on a *quadriga*, standing, or as a bust, young and beardless, radiate, holding a whip, a globe, or both, right hand often raised in a characteristic gesture, and nude except for a *chlamys* or alternatively dressed in *chiton* (generally long, rarely short) and *chlamys*. A combination of these basic characteristics is required to identify a figure as Sol, always bearing in mind that the omission of any one of these attributes is possible. Adding other attributes, however, or replacing one of these basic ones with something else, can cast doubt on the identity of the figure. Sol cannot normally be depicted with a sword, for instance, rather than a whip or globe. He cannot have a nimbus without rays, ride a *biga* rather than a *quadriga*, be dressed in a toga or cuirass, sit on a throne, or recline on a bed, or ride on horseback, and so forth. This does not mean that such depictions do not occur or are intrinsically impossible, but because they digress from the norm the viewer is alerted to the fact that the image is not a standard one of Sol. This book deals with the norms from which such images digress, not with digressions from those norms.

Understanding the Image Types for Sol: Main Definitions

1 Introduction

No more than a glance at the images catalogued here is enough to lead to some important conclusions concerning both the chronology and the cultural connotations of their use. **Chronologically**, the use of the three basic image types for Sol in Roman art is continuous and consistent. The images of Sol as *quadrigatus* and as bust are adopted from Greece into Roman art before the third century BC.[1] Sol as standing figure emerges a bit later and is initially rare, but well established before the middle of the first century AD.[2] These three basic image types remain in use, virtually unchanged, well into the Middle Ages, in regions as far apart as Spain and Palestine. **Culturally**, the iconography of Sol is wholly Graeco-Roman from the outset, and remains so throughout.[3] There are no subgroups which distinguish different types of Sol, aside from the rare depictions of Sol as an active protagonist in Greek myths. This means that the postulated differentiation between Sol Indiges and Sol Invictus[4] is not reflected in the visual evidence. The distinction between Sol and local solar deities, however, is always clear. Even though local sun gods do regularly adopt aspects of the image types Sol, they always maintain key traits that set them apart from the Roman Sol. Malachbel, for example, is always depicted in armour, Souchos always with a crocodile, Sol Invictus Elagabalus as an aniconic rock, etc. They cannot be confused with the Roman Sol, any more than one can mistake Jupiter Optimus Maximus Dolichenus for the Roman Jupiter Optimus Maximus.

Although we have already discussed this extensively in the first chapter, it is worth stressing again that these basic characteristics of our dataset fundamentally contradict the longstanding view that Rome had two entirely different sun gods, the former one Roman, the latter Syrian. How that tenet could arise, and how it remained largely unchallenged until the very end of the twentieth

---

1 Cf., e.g., F1a.1–17, L1. The Etruscan practice of depicting Usil in a *triga* is not continued in Roman art (cf. some examples listed under H5).

2 Cf. C2e.2, E1a.1–2, E7.2, H6a.2, H6aa.1, J5.1.

3 Stylistically, on the other hand, image types Sol were rendered in almost every style ever current in the Roman world, and geographically they occur anywhere Roman artistic conventions prevailed.

4 Supra pp. 8–9, 65–66.

century – indeed, it is still widely accepted today – is the topic of the final chapter of this book.[5] In all other chapters, including this one, we will largely ignore the old two-Sol paradigm. Our focus will be on what the images do convey, not on what they do not.

If the following discussion appears to ramble, it does so for a reason. One may think it preferable to provide crisp, concise definitions of the basic potential meanings of Sol images, with a few judiciously chosen examples from the catalogue to support them. But such definitions would actually obfuscate rather than illuminate the nature of Sol's potential visual meanings, because crisp, concise meanings are the antithesis of visual modes of signification. The aim in this chapter is not so much to explain what Sol images meant to the Romans, as it is to immerse the reader in the visual evidence, in the hope that he will gain a sense of how images of Sol functioned in the various contexts in which they occurred. This is the only way, I believe, to avoid an overly verbal "pinning down" of meanings which were, in fact, visual and hence to a significant degree ineffable. This chapter will focus on the broader picture, touching briefly on a wide range of images. The next chapter will present a series of more narrowly defined case studies. Before reading either chapter, it is strongly recommended that the reader simply leaf through the catalogue and, in particular, study the images that accompany it.

The catalogue of images of Sol illustrates the validity of treating the three image types Sol (standing figure, charioteer, and bust) as the basic visual signs which together communicated all visual meanings that came to be associated with images of Sol by Roman viewers. His iconography underwent only minor changes in the course of the almost 1000 years that it was in use: the early *Sonnengesichter*, frontal faces of Sol surrounded by rays, are very rare after the second century BC; in the course of the second century AD the raised right hand becomes increasingly common; from the latter part of the third century AD it also becomes slightly more common to depict Sol dressed in a long charioteer's *chiton*, rather than nude. But these are relatively minor and, more importantly, very gradual changes to an overall stable iconography. There are no patterns of usage which suggest any intent to systematically differentiate Sol clothed from Sol nude, for example, or Sol with raised arm from Sol without.

The anthropomorphic representation of Sol is clearly a matter of convention. This was the way one depicted the sun in Roman art, but it does not reflect the way Romans imagined the sun to be. Indeed, so fixed was this convention that Jews and Christians also availed themselves of the anthropomorphic image

---

5   See Hijmans 1996 for the first comprehensive refutation of the notion that a Syrian sun god played a dominant role in late Roman paganism. The final chapter of this book builds on that article.

types Sol in their art. Such usage constitutes unequivocal evidence that the three image types used for Sol cannot be equated with the Sun *god*, and this is confirmed by their general usage as illustrated and discussed in this catalogue. The Sun god as the object of religious cult is but one of a range of possible meanings for the image type, and not a very common one. In a large majority of cases the meanings of Sol images are more abstract. In semiotic terms the image types Sol are hence indexical or even symbolic signs, rather than iconic ones. They evoke concepts derived from Sol or even arbitrarily attached to the image types without any direct reference to the sun.

If images of Sol can evoke visual meanings that are only indirectly related to the Roman Sun god (if at all), this is even more the case when some non-solar image borrows from the iconography of Sol. Such borrowings attach elements of the visual meanings of the image type Sol to the borrowing image, but that does not necessarily assimilate the figure to the Sun god Sol. We have not explored hybrid images to any great degree in the catalogue, but I stress this point here as it follows logically from the preceding. If borrowing visual elements from the iconography of Sol – the image – were to automatically assimilate a figure to *Sol* – the Latin word – then the image Sol must equal the word Sol, which is not the case. Iconographic elements borrowed from image types Sol carry connotations associated with the visual meanings of that image type and/or the borrowed elements, not the verbal meanings of Sol, far less Sun god. They *may* associate the borrowing image with Rome's solar deity, but normally one should assume that the visual meanings of Sol-images in the cosmic-symbolic range and the like, are the ones being transferred. An example of this is the joint depiction of the emperor, radiate, and the empress with lunula. The reference here is not to *Sol* and *Luna* (the Latin words and their connotations), nor even to image types Sol and image types Luna independently, but rather to the composite image type Sol-and-Luna, that has its own specific meanings, which are at best only indexically related to the meanings of the independent images of Sol and Luna, and are yet further removed from the verbal meanings of the Latin words *Sol* and *Luna*. The image type Sol-and-Luna is discussed below (pp. 97–113).

This is an important point. We have, in the past, far too easily equated the image type Sol with the Latin word *Sol*, which we then casually translate as Sun god, *Sonnengott*, *dieu solaire*, and the like, helped no doubt by the anthropomorphic depiction of Sol in imagery. Of course, the Romans regularly spoke of *deus* Sol, but that does not mean that they conceptualized Sol as an anthropomorphic god on a chariot. This mythical image was part of their ancient heritage, but not of their contemporary understanding. What we see in the catalogue is that in the vast majority of cases the anthropomorphic image is deployed as (cosmic) symbol rather than deity. This emerges time and again as a key characteristic of Sol images.

As for the sun itself, the Romans thought of it as a cosmic body of a higher order and hence divine, with powerful symbolic potential, regularly exploited. Of course the sun had a long tradition of cult in Rome, which was scrupulously maintained, consonant with the Romans' powerful pride in their *religio*. But Roman cults did not define their deities. Knowledge of the divine was attained through philosophy. Cult was centred on ritual, not doctrine or dogma.[6] Ritual, hallowed by tradition, constructed identities and the associated social and religious order. It served as a conduit for experiencing the ineffable of those identities and orders. But ritual was not a matter of faith in or knowledge of the gods.

An anecdote may clarify this. At an ecumenical conference in Rome, around the time of the second Vatican Council, the participants representing different Christian denominations alternated their sessions with visits to early Christian sites in the city. One such site was the Mamertine prison, where a spring of fresh water is said to have appeared miraculously so that St. Peter could baptize his guards, having converted them during his imprisonment. A small pool still marks the spot of that miracle today and, nearby, a pillar is displayed to which, it is claimed, St. Peter had been chained (the chains themselves are preserved in the nearby church of S. Pietro in Vincoli). It so happened that on this visit a Russian Orthodox professor was the first to enter. He immediately dipped his hand in the pool, made a sign of the cross, and kissed the column. A Calvinist delegate, who happened to be next in line, somewhat hesitantly followed his example, after which the other scholars and delegates also, with varying degrees of self-consciousness, dipped their hands in the miraculous pool, made a sign of the cross, and kissed the sacred column.

Later, the professor who had led the way in this impromptu ritual, reflected on what they had done. Did they really believe a spring had appeared miraculously on this spot? Was there any evidence at all that St. Peter had been chained to that very column? Surely not! But, he argued, that was not the point. For over sixteen centuries, Christian pilgrims had dipped their hands in that pool and kissed that column, sharing this ritual with Christians from all over the world. That, he felt, was the only truth that mattered on this occasion. The little ritual at the Mamertine prison was not, then, an expression of belief in

---

6   The debate over the role and nature of ritual in Roman religion is complex and ongoing, and this is not the place to examine it in detail. Cf. Latham 2016; Martin 2013; van Nuffelen 2012; Várhelyi 2010 (especially chapter 5); Scheid 2005a (on which see Ando 2009); Price 1984 (still fundamental).

a rather unlikely story, but an avowal of kinship with all who over time had performed it.

The point of this anecdotal example is that rituals do not need to be an articulation of a deeply held credo, or article of faith – e.g. belief in the miraculous pool in the Mamertine prison – to be meaningful for those participating in it.[7] Historians of Roman religion, however, have long thought differently. There is a noticeable tendency to treat traditional paganism as ritualistic, almost obsessed with orthopraxy, and (hence) little involved with meaning and/or spirituality. Characteristic of traditional Roman polytheism was a "splitting-up of the divine powers," which "legitimized a precise, specific and finicky ritualism which avoided a frenzy for the supernatural but also correspondingly excluded any cosmic view, especially (...) when in the second century BC Greek philosophy arrived to shake up the calmly legal attitude of the Roman pontiffs."[8] As "a religion is successful only if it can monopolize the individual totally: body and soul, mind and senses," the "empty" rituals of Roman polytheism doomed it to failure, and ever since Cumont, many have argued that Rome's austere and formalized religion was supplanted by what are collectively termed "oriental cults" to fill the spiritual void it left.[9] More recently, notably under the impetus of John Scheid, there has been a marked change in attitude towards the orthopractic aspects of Roman polytheism, coupled with a re-evaluation of the "foreignness" of the "new" religions emerging in the Roman Empire.[10]

As far as Sol is concerned, this means that rituals in shrines of Sol with, presumably, a statue of Sol as focal point, need not be taken to be expressions of faith in an anthropomorph Sun god. We cannot infer directly from temples, priests, cult statues, and rituals for Sol how the Romans viewed the sun and its divinity. Certainly we cannot think of those participating in such rituals as forming a "congregation" of Sol-worshipers, with a shared Solar "theology".

---

7   I thank the late Ms Josepha Koet for sharing with me this anecdote. Cf. Sumi 2005: 8–12 on the difficulty differentiating ceremony and ritual in the Roman world. Van Nijf 2000 illustrates how the prime function of civic rituals was to provide a model both of and for society; religious sacrifices were a standard component of the many rituals he discusses, but in these contexts served primarily to co-define civic power-relations. Cf. Scheid 2013.

8   Turcan 2001: 22.

9   The literature is vast. Cf., to give one example, Turcan 2001, especially 1–27. Durand & Scheid 1994 sound a strong critical note; cf. Alföldy 1989; Stark 2001; Bonnet et al. 2006; Bonnet & Bricault 2013. The importance of rite in Roman religion is well articulated by King 2002: 299: "For the orthoprax Pagans, carefully performed rituals, not carefully purified sets of beliefs, were what the deities desired." See also: Gradel 2002; Rüpke 2007; Ando 2008; Pakkanen 2011.

10   Scheid 2005a & 2005b; Rothaus 2000.

This makes it easier to understand how Sol could evoke such a wide array of connotations, ranging from cosmic symbol to a divine power, and from metaphor to object of cult. Many of these connotations or meanings of the image types Sol are obscured if we use the term Sun god for Sol, because they fall outside the scope of what we consider to be divine. The same can be said of the Latin word *sol*. This does not mean that the Romans felt the same degree of contradiction. Indeed, one could equally well assume that the complex nature of Sol sheds an interesting light on Roman concepts of divinity.

2   Chronological Evolution and Meaningful Patterns

The chronology of the images presented in this catalogue has not played a major role in the discussions so far. This is because for many of the objects, simply establishing a reliable date is still a major problem, especially in view of a tendency to give later rather than earlier dates to depictions of Sol on the assumption that the sun god was a latecomer in Roman imperial religion. Accepting such dates uncritically obviously gives rise to circular arguments with regards to the chronology of usage of the image types Sol. Evaluating shifts in iconography, usage, and meanings of these image types thus depends in part upon improving the accuracy of the dating and requires a closer analysis than we can offer here.

In view of this unreliability of many of the dates given, we must limit ourselves to formulating certain general conclusions about the chronological evolution of the image types for Sol. It is clear that they were derived from Greek and, to a lesser degree, Etruscan predecessors and were routinely deployed in the Roman world from at least the mid Republican era (earliest Roman coinage, Calenian ware) until the early Middle Ages (late antique Greek lamps, Visigoth art in Spain, synagogue floors in Palestine, manuscript illuminations).[11] It is reasonable to assume that the visual meanings and connotations of these image types evolved over the course of those eight centuries and more, but our grasp of the chronology of the images is insufficiently precise to make close study feasible. To give one example: a terracotta roundel from Brindisi (C4.2) is variously dated as Hellenistic, first century BC, or third century AD. The earlier date is likely correct, which makes this an important early example in the Roman world of a full-fledged Sol-and-Luna image type (see below). But the dates given are too uncertain for the object to support any major chronological argument.

---

11   See catalogue sections L1, D, F, and G.

Certain categories of objects, such as lamps or, in particular, coins are more precisely datable, but we cannot extrapolate broad conclusions about the rise and decline of popularity of Sol in general on the chronology of Sol on coins or lamps only. This is particularly the case with Roman coins, as there is absolutely no correlation between the depiction of Sol on coins and the occurrence of Sol in general in Rome and the Empire. In the case of Roman coins we find that after a scattering of issues during the Republic, Sol becomes quite rare on state coins between the end of the first century BC and the end of the second century AD.[12] In marked contrast, significant numbers of accurately dated lamps of the first and second centuries AD depict Sol, as do many glass pastes and early imperial engraved gems, clearly showing that the relative absence of Sol from early imperial coins does not reflect an equal absence of Sol from Roman life in general. This is confirmed by the substantial numbers of reliefs and other images, as well as inscriptions, that can be dated to the first and second centuries AD. The virtual absence of Sol from imperial coinage in this period is hence simply the result of the manner in which coin-imagery was chosen, and ultimately all that we can conclude about the chronology of the image types Sol is that there is ample evidence to document their continued, uninterrupted use from at least the third century BC to the fifth century AD (and well beyond).

In general, the iconographic rules for the image types Sol were carefully adhered to in the depictions gathered in the catalogue. The main exception are the depictions of Sol in mythological scenes, where he is depicted much more loosely, as an active participant in the scene. As grieving father after the fall of Phaethon, for instance, Sol can be seated, nude, holding his head in his hand, and without even a single of the standard attributes of the image types Sol.[13]

There is some evidence that the image types were not entirely interchangeable. On intaglios, for example, the full-length figure of Sol with a raised right hand is far more likely to be depicted in mirror image (i.e. with the left hand raised so that the seal image would be correct) than Sol driving a chariot. There may be nothing more to this than the fact that the more crowded image of Sol as charioteer was less likely to yield a crisp, legible seal impression than Sol standing, but there are other examples as well. Both the image type Sol as bust and as charioteer can be found routinely as "framing" figure, but this is rarely the case with the full-length, standing Sol. This suggests that the three basic image types Sol were not wholly synonymous, but carried with them different connotations and shades of meaning. What those different flavours of

---

12   See catalogue section L2.
13   C3a1.6.

meaning were is at this point still hard to say. Perhaps the bust tended to be used more for symbolic imagery, the charioteer referred more to the cyclical and cosmic aspects of the sun (obviously closely related to the symbolic) while the standing figure presented the sun more as a divine power (statue type). This would allow for a significant degree of overlap between the use of the bust and the charioteer as images, while setting the standing figure more apart. But further research is needed to establish how strong and significant these differences were and how well they were maintained.

Key to the analysis of these images is the recognition of meaningful patterns, in the broadest sense. These can be chronological, geographical, iconographical, stylistic, contextual, or in some other manner conceptually significant. There is no finality to the number or types of patterns that we may discern, but there is a hierarchy, insofar as categorizations which affect all the images in the catalogue are more fundamental than those that do not. At this fundamental level we can see three main conceptual groups of images of Sol emerge from the catalogue:

1.   Sol as a deity and recipient of cult.
2.   Sol in mythological scenes.
3.   Sol as a minor figure: Sol, alone, with Luna, or with the planetary deities, as "symbol" (in the broadest sense).

3   Sol as a *Deity*

The four temples and numerous priests of Sol recorded in Rome (see chapter five) attest to a longstanding and continuous cult of Sol in the city. And yet, in the images collected here, Sol is rarely depicted as a full deity. One of the few examples is the votive relief from Naples, C2a.5, on which we see a sacrificial scene in front of a large statue of Sol. It is above all the context (altar, dedicants, high base) that establishes the nature of the image of Sol as cult statue, for there is no aspect of his iconography that sets him apart from any other image of Sol standing.

Unfortunately, the best candidates for actual cult statues of Sol all lack information about their original context.[14] It seems likely that at least some of the statues and statuettes were set up in (open air) temples or *lararia*, but we should not assume that this was the case for all of them, and cannot prove that it was the case with any of them. The statue from Cincari (A1a.3), for example, was probably one of the seven planetary gods in a monumental structure of

---

14   See catalogue A1.

some kind – possibly a nymphaeum. The recently discovered statue in Perge was also part of an impressive fountain complex of Severan date (A1a.8). As chance would have it, the only two objects in the catalogue that were found in *lararia* are both problematic. The statuette from Boscoreale does not conform to the criteria for an image of Sol (B4a.1), while the bust of Sol from Vaison-la-Romaine appears to be an appliqué (K1.3), i.e. a decorative element of some larger object. A few statuettes do have reported find contexts that could point to a *lararium*-group of which they were part.[15]

A number of full-size heads and busts, as well as a statuette of Sol as *quadrigatus*, come from Mithraic contexts, and are discussed more fully on pp. 153–174. We must keep in mind that in the rich and complex visual programmes of Mithraic shrines, it is by no means a given that an image of Sol stood alone, as full deity, rather than, for example, together with Luna as a Sol-and-Luna sign.[16]

Votive reliefs can usually be taken as a sign of cult, and the altar of Eumolpus and Pallas (C2b.1), which probably dates to AD 64–68, attests that Sol was the recipient of votives in Rome no later than the first century AD. Given the number of temples of Sol in Rome, it is actually a bit surprising that we have only few such votives dedicated specifically to Sol. The reason may simply be that the cult of Sol was not chic (until the reign of Aurelian). Neither the dedicants of the reliefs connected with Sol's shrine in Trastevere – the imperial slave Eumolpus (C2b.1), his son-in-law Anicetus (829–831) and the wine-merchant Daphnicus (C2a4) – nor the majority of the *sacerdotes Solis* belonged to the elite of the Empire.[17] Romans of less than top rank have left comparatively little trace in the epigraphic and archaeological record. Various factors, then, may be at play in restricting the amount of evidence we have for depictions of Sol as a god, which means that we must be especially wary of arguments from silence in this regard. The catalogue provides us with meagre, but unambiguous evidence for the cult of Sol in Rome. We will look at this more closely in chapter five.

4   Sol in Mythological Scenes

The rare depictions of the Sol of myth are interesting for the iconographic conventions used, or rather, ignored. In Phaethon scenes, Sol is clean-shaven, but

---

15   B1.1–2.

16   Cf. the pair of altars from the Aventine Dolichenum, C2b.2.

17   On the connection of Eumolpus and Anicetus with the shrine in Trastevere, and on the five *sacerdotes Solis* in Rome that we know by name, see chapter 5.

no attempt is made to incorporate any of the iconographic characteristics of the standard image types Sol. He can be recognized as the father of Phaethon through his position and role(s) in the scene, but viewed in isolation would not be identifiable as Sol. In fact, strictly speaking, most of the Phaethon sarcophagi do not belong in this catalogue because Sol is normally not depicted in these scenes in accordance with one of the three basic image types Sol that are the topic of this study. He is often without rays, whip or globe, and seated on a throne. In short, Sol as protagonist of a Greek myth is depicted in a very different manner from the standard Sol of the basic image types. This difference does not denote "different" suns – we find a depiction of the Phaethon myth even in a Mithraeum in Dieburg (Cat. C2c.8) – but does evoke a difference of substance. As the father of Phaethon in a mythical scene Sol is a matter of culture, not religion. He constructs meaning within the scene by invoking cultural knowledge – the *paideia* of the viewer – rather than through associations with cosmology, solar ritual, and cult. This does not mean that mythological sarcophagus reliefs cannot have a religious component or meaning. But the sarcophagi themselves do not present the Phaethon myth as religion any more than Ovid gives a religious dimension to myths in his *Metamorphoses*. The art of the sarcophagi follows established patterns for depicting the myth in contexts that are neither funerary nor religious and thus belongs to the same realm as the literature of Ovid, which is that of culture. In the case of sarcophagi it is the funerary context that gives these scenes added meaning, and this can also be expressed visually. On some Phaethon sarcophagi, for instance, we find the standard image type Sol-and-Luna on the short sides as cosmic "frame" for the main scene.[18]

On at least one sarcophagus this visual differentiation between what we could loosely term the "mythical" Sol and the "cosmic" one led to an interesting transferral of the standard image type from Sol to Phaethon. On the sarcophagus in Copenhagen (C3a1.6) Phaethon stands before Sol radiate, nude but for a *chlamys* and with a raised right arm. Though also radiate, Sol himself is seated and does not wear a *chlamys*, though he too raises his right hand in a responsive gesture. It is tempting to read these quotes of the standard image type of Sol's iconography as a reflection of the tension artists felt on the rare occasions that they depicted Sol in an iconography other than his standard one.

This iconographic differentiation between the Sol of myth and the standard image types Sol is further evidence of the extent to which the image types Sol had evolved to indexical signs by the second century AD at the latest (and probably much earlier). An image type Sol depicts a cosmic concept, but it was a soft-hearted divine father who succumbed to the pleas of his semi-divine son,

---

18   C3a1.3, 7, 12.

not a cosmic force, and hence he could, or even should be depicted differently. We find something of the same differentiation in the case of the three sarcophagi depicting the adultery of Mars and Venus, but here it is less marked.[19] Sol is depicted along with other gods next to Jupiter as one of the gathering of gods, integrated in the main scene rather than differentiated from it through size or position as is normally the case with the standard image types Sol.

The notion that there were separate iconographies or iconographic categories for "cultural" rather than "religious" or "cosmic" depictions of Sol is further supported by Mithraic imagery. Besides the bull-slaying scene, Mithraic art had a significant number of stock minor scenes in which Sol plays a role (see cat. C2c). As in the case of the mythological scenes just discussed, Sol can be depicted in positions or undertaking actions which are not part of the stock image type. As these images presumably narrate some aspect or event of the Mithras mythology, that is only to be expected. But the "myths" concerning Mithras were quite different from the Greek myths just discussed, both in terms of their presumed religious function (or at least context) and their culture. It is interesting, therefore, to note that in these Mithraic "myths" Sol does retain as much as possible of the standard iconographical conventions for the standard image type.

5   Sol as a Minor Figure

The great majority of depictions of Sol do not represent him as a "full" deity of either myth or cult. Sol may be placed in a marginal position, be depicted on a smaller scale, be uninvolved in the main scene, and – very often – may be paired with Luna, in which case the two jointly form a specific Sol-and-Luna sign. In all these cases he is depicted in a way that sets him apart from the main protagonist(s), supplementing the scene rather than participating in it. This establishes Sol as an emblem or symbol, rather than an actor in the image.

It is in this context that we find perhaps the most important role of Sol in Roman art, namely as one half of a derivative, composite image which consists of the depiction of Sol (usually either bust or charioteer, only rarely as standing figure) and Luna (likewise) as minor figures, often much reduced in size, framing the main scene or, more rarely, as attributes of the main figure. Used jointly in this manner they generate a range of meanings and connotations, explored below, that are not simply the sum of meanings that image types Sol and image types Luna can convey separately. The image type Sol-and-Luna is thus a semiotic sign in its own right.

---

19   C3a3.

Before we can embark on a closer discussion of this composite image type and its potential meanings, we need to reflect briefly on the implications of compound image types for verbal (academic) discourse. We have just posited that Sol-and-Luna as an image type means something thoroughly different from the compound meanings of separate images of Sol and Luna. A Roman viewer who saw a stele depicting a deity in a naiskos, with a small bust of Sol in the upper left corner and a small bust of Luna in the upper right, would not read the scene to herself as "deity, Sol, and Luna" but rather as "deity, sollunatized;" and she would do so without actually using words, because we rarely verbalize to ourselves what we see. To keep this in mind, I have opted, in this chapter at least, to consistently use "Sol-and-Luna" for the sign under discussion here, even when technically ungrammatical.

6 Sol-and-Luna 1 – Architecture and Liminality

We can trace the emergence of the classic Sol-and-Luna image type to the east pediment of the Parthenon, where Helios emerges in the left corner and Selene descends on the right.[20] The composite image type was present in Roman art no later than the third century BC.[21] At what point that included the incorporation of Sol-and-Luna on Roman temple pediments is hard to say. They were definitely part of the pediment of the temple of Jupiter Capitolinus after AD 82 (restoration of Domitian), and quite likely earlier. We find similar use of Sol-and-Luna on two small pediments, also from Rome.[22] In Syria, we find temples which deploy Sol-and-Luna in a rather different way, but probably with similar connotations. Rather than framing the main figures of the pediment, they frame the whole temple, with Sol taking up one pediment, and Luna the other.[23]

Although the number of pediment sculptures of Sol is low, it would be premature to conclude that Sol (with or without Luna) was not a common figure in temple pediments. The survival rate of pediments is not high, making it difficult to fully evaluate the evidence.[24] We should bear in mind that Sol occurs on the "pediments" of a substantial number of *naiskos*-shaped votive reliefs

---

20   Hurwit 2017.

21   Cf. L1.1, 4, 5.

22   C1a.2 and (probably) 6.

23   C1a.5 and potentially also C1a.1, 7 and 8.

24   One early example of, possibly, Sol from the roof of a temple is the terracotta statue from Falerii Veteres, (A1b.1), but both in date (fourth century BC) and type, this statue is too isolated to justify including it among the images discussed here.

and the like.[25] While these are not images of actual temples, they do actively invite the viewer to imagine a temple along the lines they portray – i.e. with an image of Sol, or Sol-and-Luna, on the roof or in the pediment. Many such reliefs occur in regions from which no actual pediment figures of Sol-and-Luna are known, such as North Africa or the Balkans. Whether the imaginary temples they evoke ever had real counterparts in local shrines or temples is hard to say, but they certainly show that such temple imagery was conceivable. The conclusion, then, must be that Sol, with or (more rarely) without Luna was a potential element of decorative schemata of pediments of sanctuaries – ranging from small shrines to major temples – in most if not all parts of the Roman Empire. A glance at the dates of the surviving examples as well as the *naiskos*-shaped reliefs suggests that this was the case throughout the (late) Republican and imperial periods.

Of interest, in this context, is the late-Antonine group of sarcophagus lids depicting the Capitoline triad flanked by Sol and Luna in their respective chariots. It is tempting to think that such an apparently large number of sarcophagi with the same basic scene, produced in such a short time-span (roughly AD 160–190), may indicate the commemoration of a specific event, presumably connected with the temple of Jupiter Capitolinus and involving weddings, as these lids cover sarcophagi with wedding scenes.[26] However, the variation in the composition of the main group of deities depicted on the front side of the lid suggests that it was at best intended to evoke the facade of the Capitoline temple, but not to copy it.[27]

The Sol-and-Luna pair is depicted in a more elaborate iconography on these sarcophagi than we will generally see. Both are preceded by flying personifications, usually male. Sol's companion is generally identified as Lucifer the light-bringer, while Luna is preceded by the personification of evening, Vesper/Hesperos. Below the horses of Sol's ascending chariot, the reclining bearded figure is Oceanus, the ocean. This enhancement of the image type

---

25   See, for example, sections C2d or C2f of the catalogue for numerous examples.

26   Wrede 2001: 28; Matern 2002: 74–5. Cf. Also the sarcophagus from Rome C3b3.2.

27   Sol and his chariot are preceded by a flying personification in five of the seven cases, but not always the same one, because on the sarcophagus in the S. Lorenzo in Rome (C3b1.4) the figure is female while in the other four cases it is male. This may not mean very much, given that the triad on the S. Lorenzo sarcophagus lid also differs from the norm – neither of the two goddesses is Minerva – so that the whole scene is anomalous, and may have been re-carved. But there are other variations as well. On five of the seven lids the Dioscuri also flank the central triad, but they are absent on the lids of St. Petersburg and Palermo (C3b1.3 & 7). Fortuna is sometimes included, but because some of the lids are significantly restored or fragmentary it is not possible to say with certainty how often she was omitted. The inclusion, in one case, of the three Parcae (C3b1.3) constitutes a further variant.

Sol, alone or more often with Luna, is fairly common, and stresses its cosmic symbolism. There is no corresponding figure below Luna's *biga* because it is descending, leaving no space, but on occasion she may be accompanied by Tellus.[28] Oceanus and Tellus (the latter by implication if not actual presence) symbolize the earth, Sol-and-Luna the heavens revolving around earth, and as a group they represent the cosmos as a whole. Depicted here together with the Dioscuri (representing the fixed stars, but also cyclical), Fortuna or the Parcae, and the Capitoline Triad they contribute to a group that articulates or evokes some of the fundamental aspects of the cosmos: supreme divinity at the centre, with whom fate or fortune are associated, flanked next by the fixed stars, the Dioscuri, who stand between the divine and the visible cosmos, represented by the liminal image type Sol-and-Luna who occupy the transitional space between the world (Oceanus, Tellus) and the divine (central triad). Together, the Dioscuri and Sol-and-Luna also represent the paradox of eternity: it is constituted of ceaseless change, perfectly captured by the never-ending cycle of life and death (explicit in the Dioscuri, implicit in the waxing and waning of the moon and the length of night and day). Yet underpinning this incessant change is the elegant and perfectly predictable motion of the (divine) heavenly bodies, guaranteeing a continuity that is eternal.

As usual we must stress that this is not "the" meaning of these scenes, but it is conceptually part of the range of associations such images could evoke. A lot of the components and connections that make up these concepts have old roots. It is worth noting, for example, that Sol and the Dioscuri were already emblematic on Calenian pottery in the early third century BC.[29] In fact, as Hurwit has recently argued very cogently, most of the cosmic symbolism is already deployed on the east pediment of the Parthenon, and may, in fact, have originated there.[30]

The pediment played an important role in the decorative scheme of the exterior of shrines and temples. It had a particularly defining, even narrative function, whenever it was decorated with sculptural figures, as was often the case.[31] The visual role of the pediment sculpture was sometimes supported by

---

28   C4.7.

29   F1a.6, 7, 9, 11.

30   Hurwit 2017: 529: "The gods are all at home on Mount Olympos, but the setting of the pediment is in fact broader and more complex than that: it includes the ocean stream that was thought to encircle the world, and it includes the heavenly sphere – sea and sky as well as earth, the cosmos entire." Cf. Ehrhardt 2004, who includes the occurrence of Helios and Selene on the bases of the Phidian statues of Athena in Athens and Zeus in Olympia in his analysis.

31   Temple doors could also be richly decorated, but were far less visible.

acroteria and other rooftop sculpture and narrative friezes and the like, but elsewhere on the temple exterior reliefs were primarily decorative. Geometric and vegetational designs predominate, ranging from the ubiquitous egg-and-dart and dental-frieze ornamentations and the like, to acanthus scrolls, rosettes, etc. Nonetheless, here figurative elements, though less common and more formalized in nature, also occur; one can think of the repetition of gorgoneia in the long row of antefixes along the side of the roof, but also of masks or heads in soffit blocks, bucrania, garlands, sacrificial implements, putti and other symbolic figures. A similar division in visual function and meaning of reliefs can be found in other public structures such as stoas and basilicas, theatres, and the like.

Though Sol is by no measure a common element of architectural reliefs, it is worth noting that he occurs both in more "narrative" contexts (such as pediments) and in more "decorative" ones (such as lintels, soffits, or antefixes).[32] If we leave aside the occasional mythical scene,[33] a closer look reveals that conceptually as well as physically Sol often actually occupies the middle ground between the decorative and the narrative in such buildings, especially when he is depicted together with Luna. This is almost literally the case with the pediments in which Sol-and-Luna occupy the corners. Sol emerges as it were from the "generic" part of the temple into the corner of the pediment which rapidly expands beyond Sol to its most narrative, central section and then recedes again to Luna who dives down from the other corner "into" the more generic part of the temple again. Together, Sol-and-Luna negotiate the transition from architecture to sculpture back to the building again.[34]

We see something similar in the architrave above the entrance of the *boukonisterion* of Oinoanda with its two soffit reliefs depicting Sol and Luna respectively (C1c.1). They do not define the entrance in the manner in which the central figure(s) of a pediment can define a temple – neither the entrance, nor the building to which it gives access, are "of Sol and Luna" – but they do enhance the entrance in a manner that goes well beyond what can be achieved with, say, a purely decorative set of geometrically patterned soffits. Similar "intermediate" functions between decorative and narrative can be assumed or conjectured with a number of other architectural reliefs of Sol.[35]

---

32   Lintels: C1f.21, 22, 29; antefixes: C1ca.1–4; soffits: C1c.1 and C1f.18; consoles: C1c.5–7; etc.

33   C1b.1, C1f.2, 16; in mythical scenes, Sol's role is conceptually different, and that difference is visually articulated by depicting Sol with a distinct iconography that differs substantially from the norm.

34   Besides all entries under C1a, cf. also C1f.17.

35   One can think of column capitals, for example (C1d.1–5), depending on the original location of the capitals and the context. Were all capitals decorated with busts, or only those flanking an entrance for instance?

This "mediation" is not limited to negotiating the transition from the narrative to the decorative (pediments) or between outside and inside (lintels, soffits, etc.). On the short sides of the arch in Orange (C1e.1) and again on the Arch
of Constantine in Rome (C1e.3) we find Sol and Luna in a comparable role, but
mediating as it were between the real and the surreal. Triumphal arches were
by nature highly artificial "gateways" which one transited without apparently
going from one space to another. This is not the place to explore the liminality –
virtual or real – of Roman freestanding arches in any detail, but we should note
that triumphal arches impose a line, a *limen* of some sort, across the road. That
line is possibly, but not necessarily, a "real" border, such as a border between
the profane and the sacred, or city and country, but almost never a physical
one, such as a wall. Along one axis of the Arch defined by the road which passes
through it, that symbolic "border" is spatially defined by the physical reality of
the Arch and the point of negotiation of whatever transition(s) that "border"
constructs is unmistakable. The decorative elements of the two long sides of
the Arch can be used to further articulate different sides of this notional border
or transition.[36] But while the continuity of the road renders the *limen* that the
Arch represents, perfectly intelligible along the road's axis, there is an inherent
tension between the physical reality of the Arch and the intangibility of the
transition it defines. That tension becomes quite clear when we view the Arch
along its other main axis, the one crossing the road from one short side of the
Arch to the other. The short sides clearly mark the physical ends of the Arch
but do not have any corresponding role for the notional "boundary" implied
by the Arch precisely because it is notional. In other words, the two main axes
defined by the Arch are fundamentally different in nature. One, the road, is
real and has an actual trajectory. The other axis is notional, except where it is
marked by the Arch and as such lacks a beginning and end. The two short *ends*
of the physical Arch thus stand in direct contradiction to the lack of such a
spatial dimension ("beginning", "end") of the *limen* the Arch implicitly defines.
One could say that the short sides are not *ends* at all, but are inconclusive. That
makes the short ends the parts of the Arch which most directly confront us
with the, almost by definition troubling, tension between the physicality of the
Arch and the purely conceptual nature of the transition it imposes on the road.
In a sense the short sides mark a transition of their own, a transition from the
physical Arch to the notional *limen*. It is on the indeterminate and transitional
short ends of these triumphal arches we sometimes find Sol-and-Luna.[37]

---

36   One of the examples is perhaps the Arch of Trajan at Benevento; cf. Gauer 1974.

37   The number of arches of which the short ends have survived intact is too low to allow
       any conclusion about the frequency with which the short ends were populated by Sol
       and Luna.

I must stress here that I am not trying to argue that Roman artists used Sol-and-Luna to *define* such spaces as transitional. Sol-and-Luna are too rare as architectural decorations for such a claim. My point is rather that Sol-and-Luna are *at home* in such transitional or liminal spaces, and that this potentially tells us something more about how Romans *read* their presence. Gutteridge (2010: 166) makes an interesting observation in this regard, noting that the Arch of Constantine, with its reworked and reused sculpture, elides the past and the present, a process strengthened by the "cosmic time" symbolized by Sol-and-Luna. That, too, is a form of mediation, between the real (present) and the aspired (an idealized past as the utopian future).

7   Sol-and-Luna 2 – Attributes of Aeternitas

Another way to look at Sol-and-Luna is suggested by a range of imperial coins that appeared in the Flavian and early Antonine period. On these coins, the personified Aeternitas is depicted bearing the heads of Sol and Luna on her outstretched hands.[38] Sometimes there is a small altar by her feet, and although there are no additional iconographic elements to identify the female figure, some coin legends give her name. Her identity is thus secure, and the heads of Sol and Luna are initially her principal attributes. In the middle of the second century AD, Aeternitas had adopted a new attribute, replacing Sol and Luna with the Phoenix. This may have occurred in response to a purported appearance of the Phoenix in Egypt in the mid-second century. The mythical bird was believed to come to Egypt on very rare occasions to replace the old and herald in the new.[39] But whatever the reason, the symbolism of both attributes suggests that they act as a sort of counterpoint to the figure of Aeternitas they accompany. They represent the cyclical nature, or the ebb and flow that characterize the ultimately stable cosmic permanence, through such references as the alternating light and darkness, birth and death, waxing and waning of the moon, lengthening and shortening of the days, and the like. They define the nature of the cosmic stability, which they symbolize, and in many respects Sol-and-Luna act to elevate an image that they frame to a level of cosmic timelessness.[40]

The emergence of Aeternitas as a personified theme on coins of the Flavians is chronologically interesting, as this is the formative period for many of the

---

38   L2.3, 6–7, 11 and 14–5, spanning the reigns of Vespasian, Titus, Domitian, Trajan, and Hadrian.

39   Van den Broek 1972: 113–32.

40   Cf., e.g., the *aurei* depicting Roma Aeterna holding the heads of Sol and Luna, L2.16.

religious iconographies in which Sol-and-Luna play a role. This appears to have been the time in which a range of local or regional cults were acquiring (or at least aspiring to acquire) a more supra-regional role in the Empire, and were developing appropriate "Romano-local" iconographies to express their place and status within it. Many "foreign" deities such as Mithras, Jupiter Dolichenus, Jupiter Heliopolitanus, Aphrodite of Aphrodisias, Saturn in North Africa, Jupiter in the Germanic provinces, the so-called Danube Rider cult, and others, incorporated Sol, usually with Luna, as either a potential or obligatory component of their new Roman guise.[41] Other, similarly "new" cults do not, so that Sol-and-Luna cannot be said to serve some function that was common to all new cults. But they do appear to be part of a series of symbolic figures, along with the Dioscuri, for example, that could be deployed for the Rome-oriented meanings they added to the image. This means that we need to study the presence of Sol-and-Luna in each context extensively to determine which of the potential meanings were deployed. To do so in detail is beyond the scope of this study, but a number of specific connotations of Sol-and-Luna will emerge with greater clarity as we briefly review more of the evidence.

8   Sol-and-Luna 3 – Cultic Reliefs

The images of Sol and Luna do not have to be physically connected (as parts of the same monument, for instance) to function jointly as Sol-and-Luna. A votive altar depicting Sol, discovered in the Aventine Dolichenum in the early 1930s, for example, was clearly twinned with a similar altar depicting Luna. Sol and Luna did not take centre-stage in that sanctuary, but stood out as "Roman" elements in a "foreign" context through their entirely Graeco-Roman iconography, presenting a marked contrast with the iconography of the deities of Doliche who are invariably depicted as "foreign". It must have been a conscious choice to depict Sol and Luna in their Roman guise, for there was no obvious reason not to depict them in a different iconographic tradition, more congruent with that of the Syrian deities of Doliche. The stark iconographic contrast does have the effect, of course, of binding Sol and Luna together. As Sol-and-Luna they could potentially have liminal associations, as we have seen, and those seem quite appropriate here, as they perhaps facilitate the transition between Rome and Doliche.[42]

---

41   In all these cases, the earliest *Roman* modes of depicting emerge in the first century AD.
42   C2b.2.

Sol-and-Luna are a fairly standard component of the bronze votive triangles
that are so distinctive of this cult. Only few such triangles have survived, but
most were no doubt melted down and reused in later times, so that it is reasonable to assume that they were a fixed element of Dolichenic shrines, which,
by extension, means that Sol-and-Luna were too. The sun and moon normally
appear as busts,[43] that is as less elaborate figures than others, like Jupiter, Juno,
and Victory. We see this particularly clearly on a triangle in Munich, on which
the busts of Sol and Luna are engraved, while all other figures are in relief
(C2d.13). Their function seems purely symbolic, contributing to the overall
symbolism of the triangles, but a close analysis of that symbolism is beyond
the scope of this study.

The Jupiter columns of the northeastern provinces bordering on the Rhine
offer another typical example of the combination of local and Roman-imperial
elements that one encounters in these "new" religions. Local elements include
the Sky god on horseback, the regular inclusion of local deities, the references to (holy?) oak trees, and the geographic limitation of the monument-
type. Roman-imperial are the identification of the sky god as Jupiter Optimus
Maximus, the use of the stone column-with-capital format, the iconography
of most deities and the Latin of the inscriptions. Sol, either alone, with Luna
or with the planetary deities, is depicted as a cosmic power in Roman guise.
As such, he constitutes a Roman-imperial and cosmic element in the overall
conception of the monument type.[44]

The stelae of Ba'al-Hammon or Saturnus in Numidia and Africa Proconsularis
are another example of a new cult limited to one part of the Empire with an
iconography rich in symbolic images, both neo-Punic and Graeco-Roman in
origin.[45] Punic, for example, are the Tanit figures that are depicted in particular on the stelae from the Kheneg, near Constantine.[46] Graeco-Roman is the
iconography of Saturnus, Sol and Luna, the Dioscuri, and often the dedicant
(wearing a toga), to give some examples. Stylistically the stelae range from
completely indigenous to substantially Graeco-Roman. The composition, iconography, and style naturally change in the course of the five centuries or so
that these stelae were produced, and can also vary from region to region.
Sol occurs on a substantial number of stelae, but still only a minority of the
total.[47] Generally Sol and Luna are depicted together characteristically as

---

43   On C2d.9 the two figures on the frontal split *quadriga* may be Sol and Luna.

44   C2e.

45   On Saturnus Africanus cf. McCarty 2015; Schörner 2009, 2013.

46   C2h.1, 4–6, 21–22, 24–25, 99 (from Sousse).

47   Ben Abid 2012.

small, peripheral or emblematic busts. On occasion, Sol is simply represented by a whip or perhaps some other symbol and somewhat more often Luna is depicted as a simple crescent. On rare occasions they are both depicted as full-length figures. There is no indication that the meanings associated with Sol-and-Luna sign varied according to the manner in which they were depicted. Quite striking, however, are two stelae on which the standing Sol and Luna are each accompanied by a single horse, suggesting that they doubled as the Dioscuri.[48] Whether this was to enhance the range of symbolic meanings conveyed in the limited space available or simply a stone carver's error is hard to say. The twins Castor and Pollux, much like Sol-and-Luna, appear often as "Roman" or cyclical figures in a non-Roman context.[49] Conflating their roles into one image is not completely without parallel. Certain sarcophagi dating to the late third or early fourth century AD have corner acroteria on the lids which conflate the images of Sol-and-Luna with theatre masks, thus expanding their respective symbolic meanings.

The combination of Sol-and-Luna with Saturn on these stelae brings together three adjacent deities of the week, but this is not emphasized. Preference is given to a central position for Saturn between Sol and Luna, which breaks the order of the days, but is logical given that Saturn is the recipient of the dedication. This does not mean that the planetary deities had no role to play. It is true that they are only rarely depicted in their anthropomorphic form,[50] but the seven-day planetary week could also be represented, directly or indirectly, through the inclusion of seven symbols on the stelae.[51] This suggests that there may have been a latent tension concerning the "incorrect" order of sun-saturn-moon which could explain why on a stele from the Philadelphia Baths in Timgad, Sol is in the middle, with Saturn to the left and Luna to the right, i.e. in their correct weekday order.[52] Generally, however, the peripheral and subordinate position of Sol and Luna as small busts sets them apart from the often more elaborate enthroned or reclining Saturnus and articulates them typically as the sign for cosmic *aeternitas*. This is reinforced by the presence of and in particular the conflation with the Dioscuri.

Sol-and-Luna also appear on the *ependytes* of Aphrodite of Aphrodisias, Jupiter Heliopolitanus, Artemis Eleuthera of Myra, Hecate, and an unidentified pair of gods, listed in the various sections of J2. The authenticity of the

---

48   C2h.65 and C2h.71.

49   Geppart 1996.

50   C2h.9 and C2ia.1.

51   One example of such symbols are the seven pine cones on reliefs from Tébessa: C2h.82–3, 84(?).

52   C2h.13.

pair of deities wearing a single *ependytes* (J2e.1) cannot be confirmed, and
the statue of the triple Hecate (J2d.1) is rather exceptional, but the statues of
the Aphrodisian Aphrodite and Jupiter of Heliopolis represent the standard
type for these deities as, apparently, does the statue of Artemis Eleuthera, even
though it is the sole surviving example. All are local deities and their iconography emphasizes their local roots. The sheath-like *ependytes* that encases and
effectively hides their bodies is one of the most important elements of this
local iconography. By Graeco-Roman standards it is distinctive in its foreignness. Nonetheless the iconography is Roman insofar as all surviving statues of
these particular versions of Aphrodite, Jupiter, and Artemis date to the Roman
imperial era. In the case of the Aphrodisian Aphrodite the provenance of most
statues is Italy, further emphasizing their Roman nature. The statues of Jupiter
Heliopolitanus are predominantly from the Levant, but could also travel, as at
least one made its way to Gaul (J2b.1). Artemis Eleuthera appears to have been
more strictly local.

This combination of Roman and local is reflected in the decoration of the
ependytes of these statues. The Aphrodisian Aphrodite has a range of distinctly
Graeco-Roman images adorning her dress: the three graces, Sol-and-Luna, a
nude, reclining Aphrodite seen from behind with a marine goat, and a number
of Erotes. All stand in marked contrast to the local guise of the statue in other
respects. The marine goat is particularly remarkable because the dominant
sign of the horoscope of Augustus was Capricorn. That Aphrodisias forged
close links with Augustus and his Julio-Claudian successors, is reflected, *inter
alia*, in the Sebasteion built between about AD 20 and 60. This monumental
arch and street leading to the temple of Aphrodite was replete with imagery
extolling Roman rule and the Julio-Claudian rulers.[53] The city's ancient and
venerable cult of Aphrodite naturally played a key role in this process, for it was
in Asia Minor that Aphrodite bore Aeneas, the Trojan ancestor of Augustus,
and in Asia Minor no cult centre dedicated to Aphrodite was more important
than that of Aphrodisias.[54]

It is tempting to include a redesigning of the cult statue among the
Aphrodisian projects undertaken to cement the bonds between their Aphrodite
and the Julio-Claudians.[55] This could quite literally have been a matter of new
clothes for the venerable cult image, particularly the richly decorated garment

---

53   Smith 1987, 1988b.

54   Aphrodisias was not the first city to forge links to Rome with a claim to shared mythical
      roots. In Pergamum in the early second century BC the emphasis on the role of Telephos,
      son of Hercules and father of Rhome/Roma had been deployed in like manner.

55   Reynolds 1996: 44 points out that under Tiberius, a reorganization of the cult led to
      Aphrodite of Aphrodisias being equated with Venus Genetrix and referred to as προμήτωρ

that is so characteristic of the statues and statuettes of the goddess dating to the Roman imperial era. That would give added relevance to the symbolic imagery in Graeco-Roman style with which the garment is adorned, the implication being that the imagery should help anchor the local goddess within the broader Roman Empire in general, and link it to its Julio-Claudian rulers in particular. The sea-goat/capricorn image can certainly be explained along these lines, and we have already postulated that the image type Sol-and-Luna could carry connotations of "Romanness". But this does not amount to proof that the design of the adornments was part of a conscious redefinition of the cult statue in the (early) Julio-Claudian era. Further research is needed both on the history of the cult image and the context of the transformations Aphrodisias underwent during the early imperial era. A similar line of reasoning could be valid for the Heliopolitan Jupiter and even Artemis Eleuthera, but again further research is necessary.

The enigmatic and misnamed[56] "Danube Rider" cult, known to us only through its small lead or marble votive plaques, makes ample use of Sol-symbolism, both alone and with Luna.[57] The plaques are richly decorated with a large number of images or symbols and show a significant degree of variation in content and organization, although there are a number of basic and fairly constant elements. Most plaques are divided into zones or registers, the most important of which are a celestial zone characterized by Sol alone in a frontal *quadriga* or Sol-and-Luna together as busts, and a terrestrial zone characterized by the goddess or priestess flanked by two approaching riders reminiscent of the Dioscuri. A third, symbolic, zone usually follows below, and incorporates numerous objects as well as the scene of a ram or ram's skin hanging from a tree to which various other figures may be linked. On the lead plaques we often find a fourth zone as well, above the symbolic one, but below the riders, depicting diners on a couch by a table.

Sol is invariably depicted in his standard iconography. As charioteer he often has his right hand raised, and holds a globe and/or whip in his left hand. As bust he is always clean-shaven and usually radiate. Together with Luna, he is the only figure whom we can identify with certainty. For all other figures, various possibilities have been put forward, but none are conclusive.[58] This

---

τὴν Σεβαστήν. Brody 2007, however, sees no connection between the iconography of Aphrodite and the Julio-Claudians.

56   The main figure, in the centre of the cult plaques, is a woman; whether she is a priestess or goddess is unclear.

57   C2f.

58   For a good summary of earlier opinions: Mackintosh 1997: 368–73. A recent, concerted attempt to identify the protagonists based on new finds, is presented by Szabó 2017.

obviously makes it difficult to further analyse the role of Sol on these plaques. It is generally assumed that the cult involved was a mystery cult that required initiation.[59] The comparison with Mithraism presents itself, and some have interpreted the cult as an actual lunar counterpart to that solar cult. In this interpretation the woman flanked by the twin riders is identified as Luna.[60] Mackintosh (1997, 372–3) argues that, as in Mithraism (for which she cites various studies by Beck), most of the main components of these plaques can be related to constellations or planets: the twin riders to Gemini, the ram to Aries, the fish (on the table before the priestess/goddess and/or below one of the riders) to Pisces, the lion to Leo, the snake to Hydra, and the vase to Crater. At the same time the various scenes (banquet, skinning of the ram) would refer to elements of the cult myth or initiation. This is a promising approach which requires further analysis, for instance to establish the type of coherence that Beck can demonstrate for the Mithraic star chart of the tauroctony. Szabó's suggestion that we can now identify the main figures as Dom(i)na and Dom(i)nus does not materially affect the necessity of this project of careful, contextual analysis of the visual evidence, which remains critical for further progress in the study of this cult. His suggestion that Sol, on the plaques, represents Dominus is not in keeping with the visual meanings the Sol imagery on the plaques generally evokes. Here too, the comparison with Mithraism and its enigmatic solar deity may prove fruitful. As further evidence of a possible connection between these two cults, one can point to the fact that both avail themselves of small marble votive reliefs sculpted in a very indistinct and idiosyncratic style. These are quite similar to each other in form, though not of course in content.[61]

But all of this remains open to further study. The identification of the central woman/goddess as Dom(i)na, and Sol as Dom(i)nus, for example, is by no means conclusive, for example, because iconographically there is nothing to connect her to Sol in one of the various ways that Sol and Luna can be visually paired. She may be Domna, but there is nothing very lunar about her (*pace* MacKintosh 1997). Conversely, Sol's identity as Sol is beyond question, but there is nothing to suggest that he is Domnus.[62] The problems are compounded by the fact that no Danube rider temples or shrines have been

---

59   Mackintosh 1997.

60   Mackintosh 1997: 370–3; Popovic 1991 appears less committed to this view than Mackintosh suggests.

61   Hijmans 2015.

62   The suggestion that she is Luna is based on two Danube rider reliefs. On one there are two crescents next to her head, on the other a painted crescent is visible above her head. Mackintosh 1997: 371. For other suggestions cf. Zotović 1998; Plemić 2013.

identified and we have no large-scale Danube rider art. Whether in lead or marble, the Danube rider reliefs are always small enough to be carried with ease by one person. As indicated above, this suggests a much more person-bound rather than place-bound function for the plaques.

The fact that Sol occurs without Luna with some frequency is worth noting,[63] but the Sol-and-Luna pattern is the more common on these plaques. Interestingly, the Sol-and-Luna sign is fairly often inverted, with Luna in the upper left, and Sol in the upper right corner.[64] On these plaques, day is making way for night, suggesting that the main scene is set at night. The depictions of Sol only, without Luna, strengthen this notion. Sol is not a participant in any specific action, so that it would appear we must read him as a symbol again, and the fact that he can be replaced by Sol-and-Luna or Luna-and-Sol corroborates that. Given that Sol as symbol is normally part of a larger, cyclical image, notably Sol-and-Luna, there must be a latent expectation of some counterpart to Sol alone on these plaques. Luna is the most obvious possibility, which could support those who see Luna in the central figure. But Sol alone can also be found representing eternal sky and light to counterbalance decay, earth, and underworld, as is the case in Mausoleum M in the Vatican necropolis, for example (see chapter nine). It is impossible to be more precise about the range of meanings of Sol on these plaques, until we have a better understanding of their complex iconography overall.

There are at least fifteen other deities with whom Sol appears on occasion, but is not normally associated. In addition, there are images in which Sol forms part of a group of deities that are not commonly depicted together in this manner or are altogether rare in art. Being the anomaly, Sol is not part of a pattern of meaning in these cases, but forms a foreign element in any pattern that may normally be present. In most cases the first step should therefore be to establish whether there is a common pattern without Sol, which is varied or changed by the presence of Sol. This requires thorough analysis and discussion of the iconographies of the fifteen or so deities involved, which is beyond the scope of this study. In the majority of cases, Sol-and-Luna are depicted in conjunction as cosmic framing pair,[65] but the two are also fairly regularly depicted on par with the other deities present.[66] Sol alone is also sometimes depicted as a smaller, more symbolic figure,[67] but more often as a figure on par with the

---

63   C2f.1–35, 51–54.

64   C2f.55–57, 60–62, 65–66, 73–74, 87, 92, 104.

65   C2k.1, C2l.1–2, C2p.2, C2s.1, C2t.1–2, C2v.1, C2w.2(?), 4–5, 10, 17–18.

66   C2o.1, C2u.1, C2w.11–16.

67   C2k.1, C2n.1, C2p.1, C2w.1, C2x.1(?).

others.[68] With rare exceptions, such as the Ara Casali (C2w.3), Sol is not performing any particular action. On the Ara Casali his role in the discovery of the adultery of Mars and Venus is depicted.

It is interesting that the conventionalized use of Sol, with or without Luna, as "cosmic symbol" extends to these exceptional cases, which come from almost every part of the Empire. The fact that the deployment of Sol as smaller additional figure is possible in these instances shows that the combined Sol-and-Luna image type has the capacity to convey meanings outside of its normal contexts. In other words, it confirms that such components could be and were read as independent signs contributing meaning to the visual context in which they were deployed, irrespective of what that context was.

9   Sol-and-Luna 4 – Sarcophagi

On sarcophagi, mythological as well as non-mythological, we mainly find Sol-and-Luna as framing figures along the lines of their basic image type. Exceptions are the quite unconventional Endymion sarcophagus in the S. Paolo at Rome (C3a2.3), the Meleager sarcophagus (Cat. C3a6.1) with a shield decorated with a head of Sol, the sarcophagus of La Gayolle in the museum of Brignoles (C3b4.1), and an early Christian sarcophagus in the Vatican (C3b4.2). Where Sol-and-Luna are depicted as framing deities, their symbolic function is, as usual, indicated by their marginal position and, often, size. In a few cases the images are full-sized, but on the short sides of the sarcophagus, with Sol in a *quadriga* on the left side and Luna in her *biga* on the right.[69] Their marginality is indicated by their placement as well as in the execution of these figures, which is more shallow than that of the figures on the main relief. Normally, however, Sol-and-Luna are depicted in the main relief, but as small and minor figures driving their *quadriga* and *biga* respectively. Sol usually occupies the upper left hand corner, Luna the upper right hand one.

On the Endymion sarcophagi, this means that Luna can be depicted in two ways: as the protagonist of the myth, and as framing figure with Sol.[70] This is further evidence of the substantial difference between the mythical and the symbolic, iconographically conveyed by these sarcophagi. The framing Sol-and-Luna pair has an indexical, conventionalized meaning that differs fundamentally from the type of meaning conveyed by Luna stepping off her *biga* to

---

68   C2j.1–2, C2m.1, C2q.1, C2r.1, C2w.5–9, C2x.2.
69   C3a1.7, 12, C3a2.1, C3b3.2.
70   On Endymion sarcophagi in general, cf. Koortbojian 1995; Borg 2014; Elsner 2014.

view Endymion. This is not a double depiction of the mythical Luna, for when such double images do occur, to depict Luna's departure as well as her arrival, the scale of both images of Luna is the same.[71] Instead, we have Sol-and-Luna as symbolic pair contributing specific meaning to the image that does not conflict with the presence of Luna as protagonist of the main scene.[72]

While Sol-and-Luna are generally depicted in the standard way that we have come to expect, there are a few noteworthy exceptions. On a Prometheus sarcophagus in Naples (C3a4.3) Sol is in the right hand corner, but heading left into the scene while Luna, in the left-hand corner, is heading to the right. Not only are Sol and Luna inverted, but they are also headed towards each other, a clear allusion to the chaos that preceded the creation, which is the theme of the main scene. On an Endymion sarcophagus in the catacombs of Domitilla (C3a2.6), Sol is also in the upper right hand corner and Luna is on the left. Here Sol is leaving the scene rather than entering it from the left as is normally the case, and the rise of Luna heralds the arrival of night – appropriate for what Luna has in mind. Luna is omitted as Sol's counterpart on the Endymion sarcophagus from the S. Paolo in Rome (C3a2.3), perhaps indicating that there was a lingering sense that in the image type Sol-and-Luna the gods Sol and Luna were depicted, while Luna, of course, already takes centre stage in the main scene.

Closer analysis of Endymion sarcophagi is needed than I can offer here, in particular because the image type Sol-and-Luna is not a standard component of the iconography. However, of the connotations of Sol-and-Luna that we have previously discussed – cosmic/eternity, Romanness, and liminality – the liminal aspect and eternity seem the most appropriate here. Endymion, asleep, is in the liminal state between life and death. Luna's love for Endymion crosses the border between human and divine, and more generally there are the issues of love and loss, arrival and departure, and the like. There is a great deal of information packed into these sarcophagus reliefs, and they deserve close attention.

10   Sol-and-Luna 5 – Alone, without Context

Sol and Luna are fairly commonly depicted together without being part of a larger setting: on lamps (G1c) or intaglios (H7d, H7e), for example, or some of the reliefs listed under C2b. Here, their meaning – if any specific meaning

---

71   Koortbojian 1995: chapter 4 n. 35.
72   The depiction of Sol and Luna on the short sides of some Phaethon sarcophagi is comparable; cf. C3a1.3, 7, 12.

was intended – is still symbolic for the simple reason that their default meaning when depicted together is Sol-and-Luna, not Sol and Luna, unless otherwise indicated. I don't know of any example where that is the case.[73] On the other hand, there are numerous examples of busts of Sol above a crescent, or in some other way associated with a crescent.[74] Many describe such busts as Luna rather than Sol, taking the crescent as part of the iconography of the bust and ignoring the fact that Luna is never radiate. I take the crescent to be part of the image as a whole rather than an attribute of the bust, which makes these a type of Sol-and-Luna image which reduces the moon to crescent in order to underline (almost literally) the symbolic nature of Sol.

One particular context deserves some extra attention here, namely that of the exceptionally abstract god or gods Hosios and Dikaios. It is interesting that on votive reliefs dedicated to the Holy and Just god(s), Sol should appear in a less formulaic and abstract form than is usually the case. Here Sol is on par with Hercules (C2g.1, 3), Cybele (C2g.5), Zeus, Mên and Dionysus (C2g.7), Apollo Lykaios (C2g.10), and other deities (C2g.6), not to mention Hosios and/or Dikaios (C2g.8–10). This is a marked difference from the small-scale, framing figures of Sol and Luna common on for instance tauroctonies, or the planetary deities as on the Jupiter columns, or the cosmic sky of the Danube rider plaques. We should be careful not to read too much into this, however, as Sol is not a very common figure on Hosios and Dikaios reliefs.

Arnold (2005, 441–2) stresses the moral role of Hosios and Dikaios, as well as other Anatolian deities, as overseers of correct conduct and punishers of transgressors. In that role, according to Arnold, these deities are mediators or emissaries of the divine. Perhaps we should see all deities depicted on these monuments as guarantors of all that is sacred and just – as elements, that is, of the divine forces that comprise Hosios and Dikaios. But this is speculation and further pursuit of the meanings of Hosios and Dikaios reliefs is beyond the scope of this study. As far as the images of Sol are concerned, there is no clear pattern of context or manner of depiction suggestive of a specific symbolic meaning. Clarification of his role here requires further research.[75]

---

73   We know nothing of the temple of Sol and Luna on the Aventine, and therefore cannot exclude the – in my opinion likely – possibility that it, too, celebrated the two as cosmic pair. Cosmic symbolism played a major role in the circus and, presumably, Sol's temple there, and it appears that at some point that temple took over the functions of the Aventine Sol and Luna temple (if, indeed, the two were ever separate at all).

74   There are far too many to list. Cf. G2a.1–3, 6, 8, 10–14, 16, 18; H7b, H7h, etc. Other examples can be found in any catalogue section listing busts of Sol.

75   The iconography of Helios/Sol is also not consistent. On a recently discovered stele from a small village near Eskişehir, dedicated to Helios, Hosios, Dikaios, and Apollo, the left-hand

11 Sol-and-Luna 6 – Early Middle Ages

We should also briefly mention the post-Roman examples listed under C4.29, as well as K9.29 and K9.30. Strictly speaking, they do not belong in the catalogue, but I have included them as good examples of the post-Roman survival of the image type. Probably the most striking is the placement of the two architraves depicting Sol and Luna in the Visigothic church of S. Maria de Quintanilla. The iconography of the two reliefs betrays a good knowledge of Roman art, which clearly inspired the *imago clipeata* type, here with supporting angels rather than Roman Erotes, Victories, or the like. In addition, the reliefs are placed quite appropriately as support for the arch separating the chancel area from the transept, a quintessentially transitional space in a church. Taken together, this suggests a more than superficial understanding of and admiration for Roman visual practices on the part of the Visigothic builders.

This continued use of the Sol-and-Luna sign in a Christian setting is not an isolated anomaly. We see the same in the via Latina catacombs (E6.1), on bronze fittings of *pyxides* (K6.2), early Byzantine censers (F3.3 & 5), etc.[76] This is comparable to the depiction of Sol on the floors of late antique synagogues and churches (D1a.2–7). Déonna (1948) gives a lengthy discussion of the medieval history of the Sol-and-Luna pair, and into a long continuity in the Middle Ages.[77]

12 Sol Alone, as Minor Figure or in Complex Scenes

Analysis of Sol's potential meanings becomes more difficult when he is depicted alone, without context, on private and personal objects such as pottery, lamps, engraved gems, and the like. Nonetheless, these objects do provide important added information about the chronology, the geographical range, and the iconographic consistency of depictions of Sol. Calenian ware, for example, provides us with secure, early dates for canonical images of Sol, including one of Sol within a zodiac circle.[78] Lamps provide important evidence for the occurrence

---

figure is undoubtedly Helios but he is dressed in a long garment (not a *chiton*), and has none of the image type's attributes except the radiate nimbus. Cf. Erten & Sivas 2011.

76   The catalogue lists only a very few, random examples of Sol-and-Luna in Christian scenes such as the crucifixion, included only to illustrate, not for research. See E6.1 (Joseph's dream); K6.2; K6.9; F3.3 and F3.5 (crucifixions).

77   Deonna 1948. Felicity Harley at Yale University is currently preparing a new study of the Sol-and-Luna image in medieval art.

78   F1a, and in particular F1a.13 (zodiac), all third century BC.

of Sol in the first century AD,[79] and equally noteworthy are the very late lamps depicting Sol well into the sixth century AD.[80] What these lamps and plates also show is the broad social and geographic distribution of Sol in his standard Roman iconography, as production and provenances span the whole Empire.

In mosaics, Sol is also normally depicted as a symbol or sign of some sort.[81] Exceptions are the two mosaics depicting the Phaethon myth, and a mosaic depicting Sol and an unidentified woman as one of a series of divine couples.[82] The remarkable mosaic floors of certain late antique synagogues prominently depicting Sol within a zodiac circle are discussed in chapter four (pp. 142–149), and the so-called depiction of Christ in the guise of Sol is discussed in chapter nine.

Noteworthy, again from a chronological perspective, is the relative frequency with which Sol is depicted in frescoes from Pompeii, either as symbol,[83] as mythical figure,[84] or, in one case, in an unknown role.[85] These obviously pre-date AD 79, and include one clear example of the Sol-and-Luna imagery, as well as a number which depict Sol as one of the planetary deities.[86]

Before we turn to our largest group of images – the intaglios – we can summarize some of the main points which emerged so far concerning the meanings that images of Sol could bring to the table. Rarely is he depicted as a fully fledged god in his own right, but there is unambiguous evidence that he could be. In myth, likewise, the sun had a role to play as a main actor, albeit only on rare occasions. The vast majority of the images depict Sol in a much more symbolic mode, mainly as part of a composite symbol or sign Sol-and-Luna. Together, they are the attributes of Aeternitas, reconciling the seemingly irreconcilable opposites of change and permanence. Through their reference to light and darkness, waxing and waning, rising and setting, lengthening and shortening, etc., Sol-and-Luna make constant, cyclical change an essential characteristic of Eternity.

A connection between eternity and liminality may not be immediately apparent, but we did see clear cases of Sol-and-Luna enhancing and defining liminal spaces – both on the pediments and on the sides of triumphal arches,

---

79   G1a.1–39, G1b.1, G1g.1, G2a.1–12.

80   G1a.71–110.

81   D1 (Sol with zodiac), D2 (Sol as planetary deity), and D3 (Sol and the seasons); cf. also D5.1, 6 and 8.

82   D4.

83   E1a.1–2, E1b.2, E2.2, and E3.1–3.

84   E4.1–4.

85   E7.2. On frescoes of the *Sternenstreit* in which Hesperus is often misidentified as Sol, cf. Hijmans 1994.

86   E2.2 and E3.1–3.

for example. As transition points between one state and another, *limina* are the fulcrum of change and the antithesis of permanence. As we remarked above, Sol-and-Luna are by no means standard images at every liminal place, but one can well see how they would be considered appropriate images in such contexts.

Finally, we noted that Sol-and-Luna as well as Sol alone, are important symbols in the iconographies of a notable number of non-Roman cults. These cults have little in common as a group, and come from almost all corners of the Empire: Germany (Jupiter columns), N. Africa (Saturnus), Lebanon (Jupiter Heliopolitanus), Syria (Jupiter Dolichenus), "Persia" (Mithras), Asia Minor (Aphrodite of Aphrodisias), and the lower Danube regions (Danube rider cult). It is too early to say too much about this, but the notion that they introduce a Roman element into these cults, is enticing. Sol-and-Luna quite literally frame or encapsulate the images to which they are attached, and they are invariably depicted in a purely Roman iconography, an aspect that defines them and makes them stand out. In Mithraic art, which we have yet to discuss, the contrast between the explicitly non-Roman garb of Mithras, Cautes, and Cautopates, and the wholly Roman iconography of Sol-and-Luna is particularly striking. On the *ependytes* of Aphrodite of Aphrodisias, Sol-and-Luna are Roman, not just through iconography this time, but also through the context of other images, such as the three Graces, who are equally Graeco-Roman in their manner of depiction, contributing to the tension between the Romanness of Sol-and-Luna and the explicit non-Romanness of the cult involved. That iconographic tension, which all these cults share, must have been intentional, because in most or even all cases it could have been avoided by simply adopting a regional sun and moon deity, and depicting them in their own traditional iconography.

13   Intaglios

We close this first round of discussion with a slightly more detailed look at one specific class of artefacts, the engraved gems or intaglios. These form the largest material group of representations of Sol, barring coins, and for this reason alone the group deserves special attention. Furthermore, intaglios provide important information concerning both the chronology and the diversity of iconographic themes related to the image type Sol, and as such they were often intensely personal objects with significant symbolic values and functions.[87] A close look at them will give us some insight into how Romans interacted with

---

87   Platt 2006.

images of Sol. These engraved gems are so small, however, that it is difficult to use them as primary sources for iconographic practices, which is why we have not discussed them earlier in this chapter. We will first briefly discuss the production and ownership of intaglios, and then review the occurrence of the image types Sol.[88]

Intaglios were produced by engraving the desired design into a semi-precious stone (*intagliare*) which could then be used for a variety of purposes, ranging from seal stamp to amulet. A by-product of intaglios were glass pastes. An impression, usually in clay, was made of an intaglio, which served as a mould into which heated glass paste was pressed. Thus, whereas each intaglio is unique, there are potentially countless glass pastes with identical designs. In some cases more than one glass paste still survives from the same mould.[89]

With very few exceptions all stones used for intaglios in antiquity were semi-precious. Confusion still reigns when it comes to describing the types of stone used, for there are many discrepancies between modern mineralogical terminology and the names traditionally given to gems by scholars.[90] This has resulted in a somewhat mixed use of terms over the years, with different scholars using different names to denote the same stone. I have, where possible, standardized the terms used in this catalogue, opting for the "classicist" terminology. Chalcedony is thus used only for more or less translucent, white stones of that family. For other chalcedonies the terms carnelian (red, translucent), sard (brown, translucent), plasma (dark green, opaque), prase (green, translucent), jasper (opaque, various colours), agate (banded chalcedonies in a variety of colours), sardonyx (stratified chalcedony in which white layers alternate with layers of sard), and nicolo (stratified chalcedony of two layers, a dark one underneath and a bluish one above) are used. In addition to the monochrome varieties of jasper, I use the term heliotrope to denote green jaspers mottled red. In the case of Sol, stone types not of the chalcedony family include garnet, lapis lazuli (almost invariably modern intaglios), onyx, haematite, serpentine, magnetite, silex, citrine, quartz, opal, amethyst, aquamarine, and pyrites.[91] All

---

88   On intaglios and their meanings in general see most recently: Lang 2018; Scott et al. 2018; Thoresen 2017. There are also numerous important contributions in: Entwistle, & Adams 2011.

89   Cf. H7.62, 64 and 66 (glass pastes in Berlin, London, and Geneva).

90   To further complicate matters, terms used in antiquity to denote one type of stone may now be used for a different type: in Plin. *NH* 37, 60 the term *sappir* is used for *lapis lazuli*, to give but one example (Maaskant-Kleibrink, pers. comm.). Cf. Thoreson 2017.

91   On stones used in antiquity cf. Guiraud 1996: 28–36.

are rare, and together they account for less than 7% of the intaglios. It should be noted that over a quarter of intaglios produced in antiquity were glass pastes.[92]

Intaglios and the moulds for glass pastes were produced by *gemmarii* active in various parts of the Empire. According to some scholars, the vast majority of Roman intaglios were produced in a very limited number of production centres, from where they were shipped to all corners of the Empire.[93] Others believe that there were countless *gemmarii* all over the Empire in every major economic centre.[94] We have very little firm information, but evidence from Pompeii suggests that at least two *gemmarii* were active in one district of that city alone. The house of one of these, Pinarius Cerialis, revealed *inter alia* 114 uncut gems and finished intaglios in a box, as well as gem-cutting instruments. This evidence from Pompeii is potentially valuable in helping to determine the social status and affluence of *gemmarii*. However, the problem with Pinarius Cerialis is that we cannot be certain that he actually was a *gemmarius*. On the one hand, Pannuti (1975, 187–188) remarks on the widely differing style and quality of the 30 engraved gems in Pinarius's box, which suggest that they may not all have been made by the same person. On the other hand, he points out that as they were found together with 83 (sic) uncut stones, one can hardly speak of Pinarius as a collector of intaglios either. This leaves open the possibility that Pinarius was a jeweller who used both the intaglios and the uncut gems in the jewellery he produced. The presence of three different glass pastes in the box supports this view. It seems unlikely that these were produced by Pinarius, as glass paste intaglios were mass-produced and one would then expect a larger number of identical glass pastes to have been found in his house. If the glass pastes were produced elsewhere, the same may hold true for some or all of the other intaglios, but this would leave unexplained the evidence of gem-cutting instruments found there. The most probable conclusion thus remains that Pinarius did actually produce at least some of the intaglios himself. Perhaps he worked with assistants or apprentices, as this could explain the wide range of quality of the intaglios found in his house.[95]

---

92 Guiraud 1996: 36 bases this high percentage on data from excavations, pointing out that glass pastes, being artistically less accomplished, are underrepresented in major gem collections.

93 AGWien 3, 15–6.

94 Henig 1978: 27–30; Guiraud 1996: 76–8.

95 Cf. Sena Chiesa 1985: 11. On the location of gem production centres she takes an intermediate position and suggests that there was a limited but nonetheless significant number such centres, including Pompeii. Funerary inscriptions for *gemmarii* have been found in Rome (CIL VI, 245, 9433–9436), Pompeii (CIL IV, 8505), and Forum Novum (Vescovio) (CIL IX, 4795).

The house of Pinarius Cerialis is quite modest, showing little sign of wealth.[96] Yet of the 30[97] cut stones, some were of exceptionally good quality. Clearly, therefore, even a *gemmarius* capable of above average work (or a jeweller utilizing such work) could be a normal member of the artisan class, living comfortably enough, perhaps, but hardly well-to-do.[98] Two inscriptions found in Rome mention *gemmarii* who were freedmen, a third a *gemmarius* who had dependent freedmen.[99] All these *gemmarii* in Rome conducted their business along the Via Sacra, including the well-to-do *gemmarius* M. Lollius Alexander, who may have been the personal *gemmarius* of the wealthy Lollii family, notorious for commissioning jewellery worth 40 million *sestertii*.[100]

Even if Pinarius himself was not a *gemmarius* but a jeweller handling gems engraved by others, there must have been countless like him in the Roman Empire – we have already mentioned at least one other in the same district in Pompeii (Henig 1978, 29) – implying that the average intaglio was well within financial reach of Romans with even only a modest income. This is particularly the case if one includes the inexpensive, mass-produced glass pastes, although these had almost ceased to be used by the latter part of the first century AD. Other evidence for the ownership of intaglios also suggests they reached broad segments of Roman society. They are not limited to rich graves, and are not set in precious metals only, but also in bronze and iron rings. Finds from legionary camps suggests that many soldiers had rings with engraved gems,[101] and the

---

96   Pinarius has been described as relatively affluent in view of the quality of the frescoes in the house. Actually, only two small rooms (a & b) were decorated with high-quality frescoes, the frescoes of the Peristile and the *triclinium* being of very modest quality. De Vos (PPM III, 436) suggests that the *gemmarius* had ordered the fine paintings first, but finding that these were beyond his means, was forced to let a lesser *bottega* complete the decoration of his house. It is more likely, however, that the fine paintings were meant to impress visitors and customers. The two finely decorated rooms belong to the most public part of the house, and it was no doubt here that Pinarius transacted his business. Thus, the decoration of these rooms enhanced and underlined the status of his own artistic work (which was considerable; cf. Henig 1978: 29). On the differentiation between public and private in Roman houses cf. Wallace-Hadrill 1988: 77–96 (on business in the house esp. 84–6), and Wallace-Hadrill 1994: 17–61. The box containing the gems, cameos, and glass pastes was found in the southeastern corner of the Oecus.

97   Pannuti 1975 catalogues 24 intaglios (three glass pastes, the rest gems) and six cameos. De Vos speaks of 28 engraved stones (PPM III, 436).

98   As Cerialis was apparently also active in politics, his social position was certainly not negligible (NotScav 1927: 101).

99   CIL VI, 9434–5 (freedmen), 9433 (patron of freedmen).

100   Plin. *NH* 9, 117; Mratschek-Halfmann 1993: 92–3, 113. Augustus also had his personal *gemmarius*, Dioskourides (Plin. *NH* 37, 8).

101   Kaić 2016; Greene 2014.

number of gems that were lost accidentally in bathhouses and ended up in the drains also implies that many visitors to the baths wore rings with intaglios.[102] Consequently, when dealing with the iconography of intaglios and glass pastes, we are dealing with subjects and themes which, potentially at least, were common currency within broad strata of Roman society.

Traditionally, gems were used to make impressions (Henig 1978, 24) in soft material (clay or wax, e.g.), which would serve as signature or guarantee of the owner or as seal to close and safeguard a document. They were thus the personal possession of one owner or institution, and the choice of theme was hers or his. In private as well as public archives, sealed documents could be stored, sometimes for generations. If an archive was destroyed by fire, baking the clay seals, these seals (known as *cretule*) are preserved, sometimes in large numbers. The Maison des Sceaux on Delos yielded a large number of such *cretule*.[103] Seals could be used in a similar manner to secure property, sealing doors or securing the lids of containers. Clement of Alexandria stresses that for Christians these are the only reasons to own an intaglio. They are permitted one golden ring, not as ornament, but

> for sealing things which are worth keeping safe in the house in the exercise of their charge of housekeeping. For if all were well trained, there would be no need of seals, if servants and masters were equally honest. But since want of training produces an inclination to dishonesty, we require seals.[104]

By Clement's time, however, intaglios had long since acquired a broader range of functions. For the early imperial period, Zazoff (1983: 329) identifies three types of production: aristocratic glyptic art, popular glyptic art, and imperial glyptic art. The first represents the traditional intaglios, of high to superb artistic quality, reflecting the taste and culture of the owner and serving as his personal seal. The second group represents far more hastily executed, simple intaglios, and include magical gems and amulets, thus betraying a broader range of functions than simply that of a personal seal. Finally, imperial glyptic art includes what Zazoff describes as a flood of propagandistic gems, to which

---

102   Zienkiewicz 1986.

103   Boussac 1992. A well-preserved archive at Elephantine in Egypt yielded documents of the Hellenistic period with seals still attached; Rubensohn 1972 [1907]. There have been numerous other significant finds of *cretule*, but I have largely limited myself to Delos in the catalogue.

104   Clement *Paedagogus* 3, 1.

he adds collections of gems deposited in temples, where they had both a propagandistic and a popularizing effect.[105]

This division recognizes the broader range of uses made of intaglios, but
is still too simple. The vast majority of intaglios, and certainly most of those
in our catalogue, belong to Zazoff's category of "popular" glyptic art, and this
category in particular is rather under-defined, betraying the strong art historical emphasis in much of glyptic research until recently. From an aesthetic
and artistic perspective most "popular" intaglios, of mediocre quality at best,
truly have little to offer and aside from brief entries in museum catalogues and
corpora such as the LIMC they receive scant attention. From a social perspective, however, such intaglios are as significant as the "aristocratic" or "imperial"
ones. They rank among the most personal and personally important possessions a Roman had.[106] As personal seal they stand for the person whose seal
they are, functioning as their guarantee and word of honour. That alone gives
the engraved gem a protective function, securing and safeguarding the integ-
rity of a document, the contents of a vessel, or the like by sealing it shut, or a
powerful promise or bond through exchange or gifting of the intaglio itself.
This protective function could be enhanced to the point where the intaglio
became an amulet with magical properties through the nature of the image,
often divine or magical and sometimes including incantations and the like, as
well as through the properties of the gemstone itself.[107] While it is common
practice to treat amulets as a separate group of "magical" gems, this distinction
is thus misleading. A wide range of engraved gems had at least a certain degree
of amuletic qualities through their stone type, as well as their role as seal, safeguard, and guarantee.

In other respects as well, intaglios and the rings in which they were set
were socially significant. In Roman society clothes most definitely defined the

---

105   The term propaganda is perhaps not the best choice for what Zazoff has in mind. Unlike
        coins, gems themselves did not circulate, i.e. they did not carry a message from one (the
        minting authority, i.e. the emperor) to many. Intaglio's and perhaps even glass pastes
        could be distributed as gifts, and as such convey specific messages from a patron to a
        client. Thus, gems could enhance the status of patrons or, more importantly, serve as a
        tangible token of his patronage and appreciation, enhancing the status of the client.
106   Platt 2006: 234–7.
107   On magical gems: Bonner 1950; Delatte & Derchain 1964; Philipp 1986; Mastrocinque &
        Duyrat 2014, and the online Campbell Bonner Magical Gem Databse at http://classics
        .mfab.hu/talismans/visitatori_salutem (February 1, 2019) with an excellent bibliography.
        A gem did not have to bear a "magical" image and/or words to have amuletic qualities.
        The most important ancient source on the properties of gemstones is Thphr. *Lap*. A typi-
        cal example of a protective amulet is one against drunkenness – a certain type of gem
        inscribed with the words *Sol* and *Luna* – described by Plin. *NH* 37, 124.

person and at all times there were clear – if shifting – codes establishing what dress and jewellery it was appropriate to wear. Often attempts were made to enshrine these codes in law. Traditionally, for example, only Roman ambassadors and, later, Roman senators had the right to wear a gold ring, and in the first century BC one still had to be at least a knight to wear one, although sometimes patrons could bestow this distinction (and the honours which went with it) on lesser men.[108] Others wore iron rings, which were very common in the Republic, generally with glass pastes or intaglios.[109] During the Empire, rings continued to carry a message of social rank, albeit a watered-down one.[110]

We can identify five major, and sometimes partially overlapping functions of rings in the Roman Empire: jewellery, signet rings, status/class-denoting rings, award rings, and pledge rings. Rings can have judicial, religious, magical, or symbolic meaning. There were official rings, bestowed by the state, an official, a *corpus* and the like, and private rings, often given as gifts to a friend or loved one. To this we can add military rings, wedding rings, magical rings, and the like.[111] Naturally, not all engraved gems came from rings, although it is reasonable to suppose that the majority did. Even so, without further information (context) it is difficult if not impossible to establish the function of the ring (and thus the gem).[112] This does not diminish the semiotic power of intaglios, but merely makes it more difficult for us to grasp.[113]

The significance of intaglios and the rings in which they are set does not automatically translate into a particular significance of the images on intaglios. Clearly, the image can have great relevance for the significance of the intaglio as a whole; one thinks in particular of the images of magical gems. But besides image and stone type, much of the meaning of intaglios is derived from *whom* it represents, as that person's seal, rather than what it depicts. The significance of Pliny's seal stone, which depicted a *quadriga*, lies primarily in the fact that it represents Pliny. The fact that the engraving in the stone depicted a *quadriga* does not automatically mean that *quadrigae* (or their *aurigae*) had special significance for Pliny. The engraved gem is but part of the ring as a whole, and that ring may have come into his possession as a gift, through inheritance, through membership of a particular association of some sort, or through purchase.[114] Of course, Pliny's *quadriga* is not meaningless either. There must have been a

---

108   Marshall 1908: xviii–xix; Henkel 1913: xxiv–xxvi; cf. Cic. *Fam.* x, 32, 2.
109   According to Henkel 1913: xxvi iron rings without intaglios did not exist.
110   Marshall 1908: xx–xxi. For the broader context, cf. Schenke 2003.
111   Henkel 1913: 330–40.
112   Henkel 1913: 350–1.
113   Platt 2006: 237–8.
114   Plin. *Epist.* x, 74, 3. Cf. Platt 2006: 241.

reason why it was engraved into the stone in the first place. But the connection between ring, image, and owner is not straightforward and the complexity of an intaglio's semiotic potential is clear.

The issues at play in the choice of images are further complicated by the fact that certain medium-related factors will also have influenced their choice or perceived suitability. In Gaul, for instance, popular local deities such as the Matres, Epona, and others, well represented in sculpture and relief, are completely absent from intaglios.[115] This may be an indication that Gaul lacked important centres of intaglio production. The tradition of producing intaglios was Graeco-Roman and Oriental, and this may be why typically Egyptian or Near Eastern deities do show up on Roman intaglios. But at least one major production centre, Aquileia, was so close to regions where Epona and the Matres, for instance, were popular that unfamiliarity with these deities cannot have been the reason why they were not depicted.

It follows that we should not seek to pin down what the image type Sol meant on specific gems for specific owners. There are simply too many options: Sol would be appropriate for an amulet of a chariot racer, a suitable image for a ring sealing an oath, a logical choice for the signet ring of, say, Iulius Anicetus,[116] an obvious adornment for a ring given to someone upon attaining the rank of Sun-runner in the Mithraic mysteries, in astrological terms the preferred choice of someone born on a Sunday, etcetera. Various emperors could well have chosen to distribute rings with intaglios engraved with Sol as gifts to soldiers or other dependents; Aurelian and Constantine in particular come to mind, but one can also think of Gallienus or Heliogabalus. Chance may also have played a role; the ring may simply have caught the buyer's fancy because of the colour of the stone or the shape of the ring itself. It is true that Clement of Alexandria urged his Christian followers to take care to choose appropriate designs for their rings:

> And may our seals be either a dove, or a fish, or a ship sailing before the wind, or a lyre, as Polycrates had, or an anchor, which Seleucus had engraved as his seal; and if it is an angler, he will recall the apostle and the children drawn out of the water. For we are not to engrave the images of idols, as we are prohibited to adhere to them. Neither should we depict a sword, nor a bow, being followers of peace, nor drinking-cups, being temperate.[117]

---

115   Guiraud 1988: 62–7.
116   See chapter 5.
117   Clement *Paedagogus* 3,12.

But there is no suggestion here that the image should hold particular meaning for the owner, and the implication is that owners did not give the images on their rings much thought. That, at least, appears to be Clement's concern. Why else would he need to warn Christians against choosing images of pagan gods?

It will be clear that the importance of intaglios for the present study does not, therefore, lie in the meanings the image types Sol conveyed and constructed through these intaglios. Too many factors contributing to those specific meanings are personal and beyond recovery. But the mere fact of the substantial number of rings on which image types Sol occur in one form or another is significant. They further enhance our understanding of the social, geographic, and chronological distribution of the overall image type in its basic forms. They also contribute further examples of the image type Sol "in action" as a contributing element to complex images. In short, intaglios further enhance our insights into the social roles of the image type Sol.

Virtually all intaglios bearing Sol can be dated to the later Hellenistic, late Republican, and Roman imperial periods. Greek, Etruscan, and earlier Hellenistic or Republican intaglios with Helios, Sol, or Usil are quite rare. That said, it should be noted that the dating of intaglios is notoriously difficult. It should also be noted that intaglios in general became vastly more popular in the first century BC.[118] For the dating of intaglios I have opted for an approach that favours external criteria over internal ones. This means that where possible factors such as find-context or ring type are taken into account to establish a *terminus ante quem*. Material can also be of help: glass paste intaglios, with the exception of imitation nicolos, can rarely be dated before the first century BC or beyond the first century AD.[119] Imitation nicolos, by contrast, were introduced in the first century AD, only to disappear and then reappear in the course of the second century AD, remaining in use in the third century. Comparable are garnets (rare), which were used in the late Republic and early Empire only.[120] Unfortunately, only a small percentage of intaglios have a stratified find-context or are set in a typologically datable ancient ring, so that we are left with style and engraving technique as the main dating criteria. It must also be kept in mind that external *termini ante quem* have only limited value, as intaglios could remain in use for long periods; an intaglio buried in the third century may well have been produced in the first.[121]

---

118   Raselli-Nydegger 2005: 64–5.
119   Guiraud 1996: 36–7.
120   Zwierlein-Diehl 1991: 14, however, points out that material should never be the primary criterium as exceptions can occur.
121   Zwierlein-Diehl 1991: 13 and n. 24.

Fortunately, important advances have been made in the past 30 years in establishing the chronology of Roman gems along stylistic and technical lines, taking intaglios with clearly established *termini ante quem* as point of departure. Consensus is building on these dates, although it has not yet been achieved as far as the terminology for the various styles and techniques is concerned.[122] The most notable result has been that the previous tendency to date good workmanship earlier and mediocre workmanship later has proven to be unsustainable.[123] Many gems in stiff, hasty styles such as the imperial small grooves style or imperial plain grooves style can be dated to the first century AD, as is shown by their presence in Velsen I or Pompeii. Even such very crude styles as the imperial rigid chin-mouth-nose style or the imperial incoherent grooves style can be shown to have been in existence as early as the late first century AD.[124]

Although the evidence for these early dates is incontrovertible, and broad consensus on them has been reached among specialists, the traditional tendency to date mediocre workmanship to the later second and third centuries AD is still found in many fairly recent corpora (such as some volumes of the AGD, the LIMC, etc.). This means that published dates can be unreliable. Where possible, I have either studied gem impressions or clear photographs together with Prof. Marianne Maaskant-Kleibrink (MK) to establish the date of the intaglio. Unfortunately, these were not always available, and often the published photographs are inadequate, leaving me no choice but to accept the given date (if any). In establishing and dating the forms of rings, I have followed the typologies of Guiraud (1988) and Zwierlein Diehl (1991).

The catalogue lists 593 intaglios with Sol.[125] No stone type predominates, but carnelian (24%) and heliotrope (19%) together account for over two-fifths of all intaglios. The percentage of glass pastes (13%) is quite low, especially in view of Guiraud's (1996: 36) estimate that in fact glass pastes constitute over 25% of all intaglios produced in antiquity. The low percentage of glass pastes with Sol may simply be the result, however, of the fact that glass pastes are under-represented in the major published museum collections.

122　Zwierlein-Diehl 1991: 11–2 gives an overview of the different terms currently being used.

123　This tendency is clearly recognizable, e.g., in the dates suggested by Walters 1926.

124　Cf. Zwierlein-Diehl 1991: 13, for a survey and examples. On the problem of style and dating, cf. Fullerton 2015.

125　This includes some gems which have been published elsewhere as authentic, but which I believe to be modern. Not included in this total are the 39 gems listed under H1f representing *quadrigae* (r.) with a driver who cannot be securely identified for lack of clear attributes as well as all gems in sections H17 and H18. The *cretule* have also been excluded.

The intaglios date from the third century BC to the fifth century AD. The second and third centuries AD account for about 50%, the first century BC and the first century AD for about 28%. Around 19% of the intaglios remain undated due to the unavailability of good impressions or photographs.

Few intaglios have known provenances, but those that do, come from all parts of the Roman Empire. I have not attempted to map provenances, however, because the statistics are overly skewed by the rather haphazard publications of corpora of *Fundgemmen* (Aquileia, Gadara, Caesarea Maritima, Britain, France, etc.). This, together with the fact that the provenance of the vast majority of intaglios is unknown, makes any statistics concerning provenance misleading rather than illuminating.

The range of representations of Sol on intaglios is large and includes variants or themes not preserved in other media. The following discussion begins with the three main image types Sol, followed by remarks about some of the rarer images on intaglios. The discussion is meant to give an impression of the range of images but is neither comprehensive nor exhaustive.

Sol is represented on a *quadriga* on about 24% of the intaglios.[126] This group is dominated by Sol on a *quadriga* to the left (H1, over 52 %), followed by Sol in a frontal *quadriga* (H3 & H4, over 41%). Only eleven gems depict Sol on a *quadriga* to the right (H2). The earliest gems in this group depict Sol on a frontal or three-quarter *quadriga*, and date to the latter part of the first century BC. This includes the superb carnelian from Naples, which both technically and iconographically is in a league of its own (H4h.1). Sol on a *quadriga* in profile appears about a century later. In general, Sol as *quadrigatus* is most popular in the second and third centuries AD.

Sol was obviously not the only charioteer of *quadrigae*. When the charioteer is radiate, and/or has a raised right hand or is holding a globe, it is usually safe to assume that he is Sol (barring the presence of other attributes, not connected with Sol). However, *quadrigati* with no distinguishing attributes can be anyone.[127] As long as the intaglio is clear and well preserved, there need be no doubt whether Sol is meant or simply some anonymous charioteer.[128] Problems arise, however, when the intaglio is damaged, worn, or vague due to poor workmanship (as is the case with many glass pastes, *cretule*, and some

---

126   This does not include the inconclusive gems of H1f.

127   Pliny, as we have seen, describes the design of his ring as a *quadriga*, and it would be fair to assume that if Sol was the *quadrigatus*, Pliny would have said so. He does not: *"signata est anulo meo, cuius est aposphragisma quadriga"* (Plin. *Epist.* x, 74, 3).

128   For *quadrigati* who are *not* Sol, alone or in circus scenes, cf. Maaskant-Kleibrink 1978: nos. 187, 258, 268, 636, 637, 716, 792, 892, to give some random examples.

gems in styles such as the imperial incoherent grooves style).[129] Especially in older corpora, illustrations are too poor to make it possible to determine which charioteers may be Sol. Under H1f I have included a quite random selection of such intaglios, mainly from two large collections, simply to give an impression of the numbers and the material involved. They range from stones which almost certainly depict Sol (H1f.8) to ones which almost certainly do not (H1f.27–38). I have not included the intaglios of H1f in my computations in this section.

In general, the representations of Sol as charioteer are straightforward, without iconographic surprises: Sol is usually nude but for his *chlamys*, or is sometimes represented clothed in *chiton* and *chlamys*. His main attribute – logically – is a whip, but he sometimes has a globe or a torch. He is also often shown with his right hand raised, on which more below. There are a few intaglios with more complex representations, such as H1da, with a bust of Luna above the horses and a snake in front of them, or H1f.1, H1fa, H4da where Sol(?) is surrounded by a zodiac circle; and H1i, where he is preceded by Phosphorus. In each of these cases, the intaglio's authenticity cannot be verified. This leaves only three intaglios in this group with more complex scenes which are undoubtedly authentic: the famous Naples carnelian of the first century BC (H4h.1, Oceanus and a Nymph below Apollo-Helios on a *quadriga* to the left); H2ca, Sol crowned by a Victory, and H4f, a glass paste of Sol (probably, but not completely certain) on a frontal *quadriga* between the two Dioscuri.

Two additional groups of intaglios show Sol as a charioteer. The first consists of *a globolo* scarabs of the third century BC on which he is depicted on a frontal *triga* (H5). I have listed only the four from Paris.[130] The identity of the charioteer as Sol is based on two of the four (H5a.1–2), on which the charioteer is clearly radiate. Both iconographically and chronologically these intaglios form a distinct group, however, which is unrelated to the other intaglios presented here, and which has no direct relevance for this study. They have been included in the catalogue only as an indication of their existence.

The two intaglios of Sol as the charioteer of a *biga* present a more difficult case (H14.1–2). There can be little doubt that both are authentic, and no doubt whatsoever that Sol is meant (radiate, right hand raised). There are no parallels

---

129   Sometimes the gesture, traces of an attribute, or general iconography provides sufficient evidence to merit their identification as Sol, despite the fact that in the corpus they are merely described as a charioteer. Cf. Maaskant-Kleibrink 1978: no. 1116, where the charioteer is clearly Sol (raised right hand), although he is not radiate, and is therefore not identified as Sol by Maaskant.

130   I would like to thank Mme. M. Aviseau-Broustet for calling my attention to these scarabs and sending me excellent impressions of them.

for Sol on a *biga* (normally reserved for Luna), and I can offer no explanation for this deviation from the norm that Sol's chariot is drawn by four horses.

Intaglios depicting Sol standing comprise about 28% of the total, and can be divided into two main groups, namely Sol standing alone (79%) and Sol standing with other figures. Standing alone, Sol is depicted with his normal attributes (including whip, globe, staff or sceptre, torch). The globe, however, is relatively rare, while the staff or sceptre is relatively common, in comparison to depictions of Sol in other (larger) media. Sol is usually nude, but sometimes wears a *chiton*. The *chiton* is not restricted to specific types of scenes or iconographies. On a number of intaglios he stands next to a burning altar, and on one he is faced by a small orant.[131] The dates of these intaglios reach back to the first century AD, and the group includes one intaglio in a second-century ring (HA6aa.1) and one excavated in a later second-century context (H6aa.3). Known findspots are in Italy, Gaul, Britain, Pannonia, and Syria.[132] This group of gems further supports our conclusion that Sol had a role as a Roman god, with cult and sacrifice, continuously throughout Roman imperial times, in most if not all parts of the Empire. On four intaglios he faces Jupiter (alone on three, accompanied by Hera and Mercury on one);[133] once he faces Nemesis and Minerva,[134] once Saturn,[135] and once an unidentified bearded male;[136] on one intaglio he is crowned by Victory.[137] Intriguing is an intaglio depicting Sol standing next to a very large altar, together with an unidentified male figure of equal size, who is pouring a libation on the other side.[138] The fact that the libant is as large as Sol is puzzling. More magical than religious is the scene on an intaglio in Paris with Sol as one of seven figures on a Nile boat, surrounded by an Ouroboros.[139] The fact that two, or possibly three of the other six are animal-headed confirm the Egyptian milieu of this scene, in which Sol participates in his traditional, Graeco-Roman iconography. Finally, there is one intaglio depicting Sol embracing Luna.[140]

Of the intaglios and *cretule* depicting the bust of Sol, about 75% depict Sol facing left, only 3% show Sol facing right, and the rest depict a frontal head or

---

131   H6aa, HA6aa, H6ad, H6ba, H6ca, H6fa, H6n.
132   H6aa.6, 8, H6ca.1.
133   H6bc, H6bd, H6be, H6k.
134   H6ac.
135   H6bf.
136   HA6bb.
137   H6bg.
138   H6bh.
139   H6bi.
140   H6l.

bust of Sol. On the majority of intaglios in this group, Sol is depicted alone;[141] on almost all the rest he is portrayed with Luna, depicted as a bust or, more often, as a crescent.[142] In most cases the crescent is below the bust of Sol, but in one case it is next to his head,[143] and in Delos it was often above him.[144] Sometimes, there is a star on each point of the crescent. On one intaglio, Sol and Luna are joined by Saturn.[145] Three early frontal busts of Sol are surrounded by a zodiac circle.[146] One frontal bust is being crowned by two Victories.[147] In a few cases Sol is accompanied by animals or star signs.[148]

Sol is not always easily recognizable, especially on the earlier intaglios, for lack of attributes. As we have seen, the radiate crown alone is not enough to identify Sol securely. On Roman coins and later intaglios this problem was solved by clearly depicting the radiate crown of humans as an actual object, fastened at the back by carefully depicted ribbons. On late Hellenistic intaglios, this differentiation was apparently not made, and a fair number of Hellenistic radiate busts have been published as portraits of often unidentified rulers.[149] Most such portraits have not been included in the catalogue, but I am not convinced of the validity of the assumption a high-quality late Hellenistic male bust – radiate or not – was always a portrait. An unpublished carnelian from Paris dating to the first century BC could readily be taken for a portrait, were it not that there is a whip, barely visible, behind the bust's left shoulder. The conclusion that in this case Sol is meant is thus almost inescapable.[150] In fact, bearing in mind how rare radiate portrait busts of rulers were on Hellenistic coins, I would prefer to take the perspective that our default position should be that such busts are *not* portraits unless they can be unambiguously identified as such.[151] This problem is not, of course, confined to intaglios depicting Sol. One need but think of the sculptural busts of Sol that have been confused with Alexander the Great.

Early dates predominate in this group. A significant number of the intaglios predate the imperial period and relatively few postdate the second century AD. The early dates are supported by four intaglios in rings of the first century AD,

---

141 H7, H7a, H7bc, H7g, H8, H9, H9a (modern), H9b.
142 H7b, H7ba, H7bb, H7c–e, H7h, H8b, H9c, H9f.
143 H7c.
144 H7h, H9f.
145 H9e.
146 H9b.
147 H9d.
148 H7bb, H7f, H8a, H8c.
149 Cf. H7d.1.
150 H7a.1.
151 Bergmann 1998: 5, 58–67.

one of which was found in Pompeii.[152] These early dates also include gems with Sol and Luna.

Finally, it should be noted that this group includes a few of the earliest intaglios depicting Helios/Sol. One *cretula* (from an excavated, dated context) dates to the fourth or third century BC. It shows a frontal radiate bust, and I have no reason to identify it otherwise than as Helios/Sol.[153]

Sol as a minor figure, with or without Luna, also occurs on intaglios with some frequency, but is proportionally less common than in most other media, except coins.[154] This is quite simply because engraved gems and coins provide such a small surface area for the image that incorporating Sol as a minute minor figure requires significant additional effort and skill. The dates for Sol in this type of iconography tend to be early, though rarely pre-imperial: almost two-thirds of the intaglios are dated to the first or second century AD. Of the remainder about half are undated. This group provides further evidence that the iconographical convention of representing Sol, alone or with Luna, as a minor, symbolical figure, was well established by the late Republican period.

There are numerous subgroups, of which a few deserve specific mention. Interesting are the groups with two Fortunae or with Fortuna and Victory facing each other.[155] These ring stones, sometimes with the inscription χαρά (joy), clasped hands, and other additional images, are excellent examples of how the Romans constructed fairly detailed messages through visual means. The combined images of Fortune, Power, Concord, and Joy, all eternal and stable (Sol/ Luna) compose an evocative message when – as seems likely – such a ring was given as a (wedding?) gift.

Other intaglios which deserve mention are those with Mithraic representations and those showing the Danube riders.[156] The dates of the Mithraic gems are noteworthy as they, too, are quite early: two are dated to the first century AD and one to the first or second century AD. Unfortunately, the early dates cannot be confirmed by independent means (ring or find-context). There is, however, sufficient other evidence for Mithraic monuments in the first century AD to support the possibility of these dates.[157] The three dated intaglios with Danube rider depictions (all third century AD) conform to what is known about the late emergence of this cult.

---

152   HA7.1–3, HA9b.
153   H9.1.
154   H10 and H11.
155   H10i, H10ia, H10ib, H10l, H11c, H11ca–d, H11da–c; 14 intaglio's in all, of which six with inscription χαρά.
156   H11a and H11b.
157   Beck 1998, Clauss 2000: 21–3.

The intaglios depicting Diana of Ephesus or Venus enthroned flanked by tiny busts of Sol and Luna represent compositions that, as far as I am aware, have not survived in other media. Besides these examples on which the image type Sol is fully depicted, there is a reasonable number of similar gems that simply depict a star and a crescent in the place of the busts of Sol and Luna. Such representations have not been included in the catalogue, but do have a place in discussions of the significance and occurrence of Sol and Luna as a symbolic pair.[158]

Remarkable are ten intaglios, all fairly late (insofar as can be determined) that depict Sol riding on horseback.[159] Strictly speaking they do not belong in this study as they do not adhere to one of the three basic image types Sol, but I have included them as a reminder that Sol or sol-like figures were not wholly restricted to those three image types. Unfortunately, our knowledge of this group is limited. Iconographically, the rider, radiate, right hand raised, holding a whip in his left hand, strongly echoes Sol, and one wonders whether we are dealing with a regional assimilation or some other variant of the standard Roman Sol.[160] This is further suggested by a relief from Corbridge (C2d.7) on which Sol is also depicted on horseback. In this case the horse is winged, but in other respects the iconography is closely reminiscent of Sol on these intaglios. The relief, originally part of the Dolichenum of Corbridge, also includes a Dioscure and Apollo. Irby-Massie (1999, 68–9) remarks on the extended nature of the pantheon represented at this Dolichenum, which also included Brigantia, a Celtic goddess here closely identified with Dea Caelestis and Juno Dolichena. Her name implies local roots, but whether we can extend that to include Sol in his exceptional iconography is difficult to say.

The remaining intaglios in the catalogue either depict complex scenes in which Sol has a minor role, or serve as examples of hybrid iconographies incorporating aspects of the standard iconography of the image types Sol.

The iconography of Sol includes an element – the raised right hand – that confronts the engraver of gems with an interesting dilemma: which image is the more important one, that of the gem, or its mirror image produced with each seal or impression made with the gem? In Roman art, Sol was *never* depicted with his left arm and hand raised, rather than his right, a rule that included all the (numerous) coin issues on which Sol is depicted with a raised

---

158   H11e and H11f. Cf. e.g. Maaskant-Kleibrink 1978: 672, 674.

159   H12.

160   For an intaglio depicting Sol riding a dromedary, cf. Raspe & Tassie 1791: 217 no. 3102 (images are hard to find, but some can be found online at www.beazley.ox.ac.uk.). Cf. Also the equestrian statue of Helios in Termessus (A2f.2).

right hand. In the case of coins the die engraver faced a similar situation as the gem engraver as he had to deal with two images, that of the die and its mirror image, the coin. But the dominant image was obviously the coin, so that dies were invariably carved in the mirror image of the intended coin design. Gems, however, did not have an obvious dominant image. As amulet or jewellery the stone itself and its engraving were the important image, but for signet rings the gem, like the coin die, is the conduit for the actual image which is the impression or seal. Signet rings were also jewellery of course, and there was no reason why an amulet could not double as a seal. As we have seen, a strict division between the two was not possible. *De facto*, then, intaglios had two images, the one engraved into the stone and the other its mirror image, the intaglio's impression. To what extent these images were interchangeable depended on the iconographic conventions governing the image, but in the case of Sol with his raised right hand, only one of the two images can be correct while the other clearly is not. The engraver had to choose which that would be: the intaglio itself or its impression.

Overall, Sol is almost as likely to be depicted with his right hand raised on gems (intaglio itself the preferred image) as with his left hand raised (intaglio the mirror image of the preferred one). In many cases, therefore, it was the impression that presented the correct image rather than the intaglio itself. That in itself is interesting, but does not tell us whether this was a matter of choice or of chance. In the case of profile images of Sol, however, it is not just the arm, but also the direction of the profile that changes from gem to impression. Here we find clear evidence that gem engravers took into account which image – intaglio or impression – was to be the more important. On the vast majority of intaglios depicting Sol in a profile *quadriga*, he is riding to the left (H1), while only a small number depict the *quadriga* in the opposite direction (H2). Of the intaglios with the *quadriga* riding to the left, 27 depict Sol with a raised right hand and only one or perhaps two with a raised left hand,[161] while of the twelve gems depicting Sol's *quadriga* to the right, six depict him with a raised hand, and in all six cases it is his left hand. This shows that the latter were clearly meant to produce a seal as dominant image, on which Sol would be depicted riding left with his right hand raised. It also shows that in the case of intaglio images the correct direction for Sol to face is left. This is in marked contrast to other depictions of Sol in a chariot, which almost always face right in all media except coinage. I have no explanation for this, but it is in itself noteworthy that even a seemingly insignificant iconographic detail such as the direction of Sol's chariot was fixed by convention in Roman glyptic art.

---

161   The exceptions are H1g.1 and H19a.1.

In the case of frontal images (Sol standing, Sol on a frontal chariot) the impression does not differ essentially from the intaglio except in which hand is raised. It would appear that intaglios depicting Sol in a frontal chariot were also generally not meant primarily for sealing. Sol's right hand is raised on 26 intaglios of H3 while the left hand is raised on six. Of the intaglios of H4, only four depict Sol with a raised hand at all, once his right hand, the other three his left. Interestingly, matters are different with Sol as standing figure. A large majority of these gems depict Sol with a raised hand, in most cases his left (about 80%). Of those in which he raises his right, almost half are multiple-figure scenes). In the case of the frontal chariots as well as the standing figure of Sol it is impossible to establish whether it is chance or purpose which determined with which arm Sol was depicted making his striking gesture. Just as for the profile *quadrigae*, however, there can be no doubt that the dominant direction of Sol as standing figure also was left and that each intaglio was designed in such a manner to ensure that in the dominant image Sol faced left and had his right hand raised. The left-facing preference extends to busts of Sol, the vast majority of which also face left (H7). By analogy with the profile chariots, one could argue that the intaglios with busts of Sol facing right were therefore also designed to produce the dominant image in the seal.

The care with which the left-facing direction of Sol is maintained on intaglios is further evidence of how strictly defined such iconographical conventions were in the Roman world. This was maintained over a considerable period of time, for the intaglios on which Sol has raised his right arm include gems dated to the first and early second century AD, with the early dates backed up by the evidence of fairly early (first–second century) ring types.[162]

Perhaps the most interesting result, however, is the fact that a far larger percentage of intaglios depicting Sol standing are engraved in mirror image, i.e., with the left hand raised so that the impression is the correct image, than the percentage of intaglios depicting Sol as charioteer. Does this mean anything? Quite possibly it simply shows that gems that for sake of the mirror image had to be "wrong" on *two* counts – wrong hand raised and wrong direction – were too jarring and hence avoided. The result would then be, of course, that these gems could not easily be used as seals, which in turn would mean that when it came to Sol as seal-image the standing figure or bust was the preferred choice, rather than Sol as charioteer. Consequently, a ring with an intaglio depicting Sol as a standing figure would have a slightly different set of associated meanings than one depicting Sol as charioteer.

---

162   Cf. H1c.1, H1d.1–2, H2a.1, H3a.1, H3c.1, H3e.1–2, H4b.1, H4f.1, H6a.1–3, H6aa.1–2, H6ad.1, H6be.1, HA6a.1–2, HA6aa.1, HA6bb.1.

This again suggests that different shades of meaning, however slight, existed between the three basic image types Sol, which should not surprise us, although we have not, so far, pursued that possibility. It corroborates the other evidence for such shades of meaning, mentioned above, namely that as minor, framing figure with Luna, Sol can be depicted as bust or charioteer, but rarely as standing figure. Separated from his chariot, yet depicted full-length rather than as a bust, Sol was at his most independent. He is not engaged in the eternal cosmic cyclical motion implied by the chariot, nor has he been abbreviated to a bust, but he is autonomous and ready for, if not actually engaged in, self-directed action.

To what extent these shades of meaning mattered and how strongly they were felt, is difficult to say and requires further research. One area to look at is obviously that of coins, that are as it were the "seals" of the intaglio-like coin dies. The standing figure is by far the most popular on coins. He is normally depicted with a raised hand, and invariably it is his right. Sol is occasionally depicted in a profile *quadriga* on Roman imperial coins, and the dominant direction is to the left as it is on intaglios. Often, Sol has raised one arm, and again it is invariably the right.[163] Busts or heads of Sol are also not terribly common on Roman coins, and surprisingly here the direction is the opposite: contrary to the left-facing busts of most intaglios, busts of Sol on coins face right almost exclusively.[164] Thus, coins and intaglios do not fully complement each other, unless we take the numismatic evidence to indicate that all left-facing busts and heads of Sol on intaglios were meant to produce right-facing seals in concord with the coins.

The direction profile busts or *quadrigae* take on intaglios or coins is clearly not random, but the direction varied between image types and genres. It would appear that while consistency mattered, the actual direction was a relatively meaningless convention. The alternative is to postulate that right-facing busts have a different connotation from left-facing *quadrigae* by virtue of the

---

163 Sol in a *quadriga* riding to the left: RIC IV.1, 250–251 nos. 265a–h, 254 nos. 282a–f, 256 nos. 294a–c, 302 nos. 543a–b, 304–7 nos. 551, 556, 562, 566, 570, RIC V.1, 63 nos. 421–2, 174 nos. 497–8, 351 nos. 17–8, 360 nos. 114–115, RIC V.2, 45 no. 267, 100–1 nos. 767–74, 113 nos. 871–4, 250 no. 152, 478 no. 170, 498 nos. 408–9. Sol in a *quadriga* riding to the right: RIC II, 360 nos. 167–8, RIC V.1, 274 no. 77, RIC VI, 638 no. 143.

164 Busts of Sol facing right: RIC I, 63 nos. 303–4, RIC II, 267 nos. 326–30 and 341–2, 309 no. 803, 340–1 nos. 16 and 20, 345 nos. 43a–b, 357 no. 145, 426 no. 661, RIC III, 379 no. 119, RIC IV.1, 126 no. 282, 320 no. 50, RIC V.1, 301 no. 319–20, RIC V.2, 32 no. 138, 40 no. 209, 187 no. 355, 362 no. 317, 390 no. 33, 395 no. 96, 509 no. 542, RIC VI, 173 no. 83. 227 nos. 886–95. Bust of Sol facing left: RIC V.2, 535 nos. 872–4.

direction they face. That is not impossible, but would require more evidence than we have at present.

Our review of the image types Sol on intaglios has raised a number of interesting points. Iconographically, the range of images is rich, but contains few real surprises. Most noteworthy are the gems depicting Sol on horseback, but their number is too small to warrant the conclusion that they represent a separate image type Sol, the more so because there are virtually no parallels outside glyptic art. We know from the relief in Corbridge (C2d.7), the epigraphic evidence from Asia Minor and Termessus that solar statues on horseback were possible, but cannot say how they were perceived to relate to the standard image types Sol.

Because of their restricted size and specific use, we did not find much in this section to enhance our understanding of what Sol could mean. We can note, however, that the intaglios adhere to the iconographic rules for the basic image types, which means that those rules must have been known to wide swathes of Roman society. The gems also provide striking evidence of the rigidity of those rules, which, as we have seen, even governed such aspects as the correct direction for a chariot of Sol (left, not right).

Understanding the Image Types for Sol: Specific Cases

The following "case studies" of Sol in Roman art are discussed separately here for a variety of reasons. They may concern images, image groups or religious contexts that have drawn more than average scholarly attention; or they may be in some other way exceptional and thus deserve to be discussed at greater length and with more specificity than would have been possible in the previous chapter.

1   Sol and Alexander

It is not uncommon for depictions of Sol to take on elements that are also considered typical of portraits of Alexander, such as the *anastole*, the tilt of the head, the slightly parted lips, etc. This can happen to such a degree that scholars disagree on who is portrayed, which leaves us with a fair number of images that have been interpreted as representations of Sol by some, but as Alexander or Alexander-Helios by others.[1] The problem is particularly acute in the case of sculptural busts or heads of Sol (cat. A3.1–22).

This is true even if we restrict ourselves to the six busts which can be identified as Sol with the greatest degree of certainty on the basis of their iconography and/or context (cat. A3.2, 7, 8, 11, 14 & 16).[2] Common elements of all six busts are their hellenistically inspired, baroque style, their youthful features, and their long, unruly hair, usually springing out wreath-like over the forehead and ears from under a fillet. To a greater or lesser extent, they share Alexander-like traits such as the *anastole* and sometimes the upward tilting of the head and gaze. All but one of these six busts are radiate.

---

1 Approaches range from Bieber 1964, who ignores the whole concept of Alexander-Helios (barring one short remark on p. 71) to Vermeule 1985, who treats virtually all Roman representations of Sol as manifestations of Alexander-Helios (*passim*, cf., e.g. p. 29). The problem of identification is not, of course, limited to Alexander-Helios, but is a general one where Alexander is concerned. As Nielsen 1993: 140 puts it, one gets "the unpleasant feeling that the criteria for identification (sc. of Alexander) vary according to individual taste." Cf. Blum 1914 (on cat. A3.9); L'Orange 1947: 34; Kleiner 1957: 101; Hölscher 1971: 43–5; Stewart 1993; Schörner 2001; A. Stewart 2004; Miller 2012, and Hijmans 2022.

2 Of the three main image types of Sol, busts have the fewest defining characteristics; if one of these is lost, this can leave the identity ambiguous.

As we have seen in chapter two, none of these iconographic elements themselves offer conclusive grounds to identify these as sculptural busts of Sol.
The matter is clinched in three cases by the context, as the busts were found
in Mithraic shrines.[3] The presence of Sol is mandatory in Mithraic temples,
whereas the presence of Alexander would be unexpected, making it a fore-
gone conclusion that these three busts represented Sol and were viewed as
such. In the other three cases it is the iconography itself which is decisive. The
radiate bust from Schloss Fasanerie near Fulda (A3.16) rests on four very small
horses drawing a chariot of which only the pole is visible. As the *quadriga* is a
standard part of the iconography of Sol this additional iconographic element
establishes beyond reasonable doubt that this bust too represents Sol. The two
busts in Venice and Madrid respectively (A3.2 & 11) have such an elaborate
radiate nimbus that their identification as Sol also seems beyond dispute.

Yet none of this has restrained scholars from recognizing Alexander and
others in these busts. Krug (1969) identifies the Venetian Sol as Mithridates VI
assimilated to Alexander-Helios.[4] She cites the Lazzeroni-Sol (!) in Schloss
Fasanerie as a prime example of the latter. Hannestad (1993: 66–8) discusses
the three busts from Mithraic temples, offering a different identification for
each. Only the radiate one from the Mitreo degli animali in Ostia (A3.7) is actually a Sol, according to him. He believes that the S. Clemente bust (A3.14) is a
portrait of Alexander, later reworked to transform it into a bust of Sol, while
he interprets the non-radiate bust from the Mitreo del palazzo imperiale in
Ostia (A3.8) as a mask of Alexander. Hannestad virtually ignores the context
of these three busts – Mithraea – and hence does not explain how a Mithraic
adept would identify the bust in the Mitreo degli animali as Sol, yet recognize
Alexander in the one in the Mitreo del palazzo imperiale, and Alexander-Sol in
the S. Clemente Mithraeum. Surely, he would see Sol in all three, even though
the bust from the Mitreo del palazzo imperiale was not radiate.[5]

This may simply mean that the Mithraic context diluted the impact of
the Alexander elements in the iconography of these individual busts to the
extent that they could be ignored. But from the point of view of Roman visual
semantics, that is unsatisfactory, as it makes context, rather than iconography, the deciding factor in determining the meaning of the image. That would
appear to fly in the face of the precision and attention to detail that we have

---

3   A3.7 (Ostia, Mitreo degli animali), A3.8 (Ostia, Mitreo del palazzo imperiale), and A3.14
     (Rome, Mithraeum of S. Clemente).
4   Smith 1988a: 182 C8 rejects Krug's suggestion.
5   One must remember that the bust need not have had metal rays of some sort to "shine"; it
     could have been placed in front of some hidden source of light coming from behind or above,
     for instance. On the extensive use of special light-effects in Mithraic shrines, see Clauss 2000:
     127–30. Cf. C2c.62.

emphasized in Roman iconographical practice. And yet, that is precisely the conundrum Alexander portraits appear to set us, for if there is one thing scholars agree on, as far as Roman-era portraits of Alexander are concerned, it is that recognizing them is not straightforward. Smith (1988: 59) is quite clear about this lack of clarity:

> The Alexander-like appearance of a head, especially one of evident Roman date, is not a sufficient criterion for detecting an Alexander – not even a Roman Alexander, still less a copy of a fourth-century or Hellenistic Alexander. More of its context and function must be known, but they rarely are. In other words, unless a head has unmistakable portrait features, one can never be sure whether a given Alexander-like head is actually an Alexander or merely a mythological or ideal figure borrowing from the Alexander iconography.

Though useful as a *caveat*, this offers little practical help, for how is one to determine "unmistakable portrait features"? Krug (1969) finds the features of Mithridates VI in the Venice-Sol to be very clear; Smith (1988: 58) does not.

So how does one go about identifying an Alexander-portrait? Stewart (1993: 44) suggests that "one must take each case on its merits and attempt to plot a given piece's position within widening circles of probability: the probable, the possible, the unlikely, and so on." In other words, there are no clear criteria and it all depends on the individual scholar's taste and intuition.[6] Lauter (1988) argues that we have at best only a handful of real portraits of Alexander, and Nielsen (1993: 137) goes even further, claiming that we have none and stating that we would not recognize Alexander if we came face to face with him.

Clearly there is no consensus on how to recognize a portrait of Alexander, caused by the fact that there are no clear iconographic elements by which to identify him. This ambiguity is at odds with the care Roman artists take to avoid just that, which suggests that we can agree with Nielsen that for the Roman era in particular we simply have no portraits of Alexander. The generic features that, according to others, formed the main elements of his so-called portraits are simply used too widely to have had that function. The upward gaze, the tilt of the head, the powerful brow, the rich locks of hair, the *anastole*, the parted lips were all not deployed as identifying features of the historical individual. They were simply generic elements in the artist's toolbox with which he could imbue an image with the qualities of youthful power and passion. As such,

---

6   Cf. Nielsen 1993: 140. In general, on approaches to Alexander-portraits, cf. the excellent summary given by Stewart 1993: 56–70; Ridgway 1990: 108–36 (especially 134–6).

they were appropriate for a whole range of figures.[7] A Roman viewer did not read them as elements derived from the portrait of Alexander, but rather as features appropriate to it. They were not deployed to supply an image with an identity, but to imbue it with certain qualities.

This goes to the core of the question how Romans viewed. If we accept that the supposedly Alexander-like traits were in fact conventional artistic tools that did not refer to an individual – Alexander – but to an heroic concept, then we must not only reject Hannestad's (1993: 62) view that we are dealing with the "likeness of Alexander", chosen as the "model" for the specific figure depicted, but even Nielsen (1993: 141), who suggests that in such cases "contemporary viewers were possibly meant to waver among Alexander, Achilles, Perseus, Apollo, Argus etc."[8] Instead, we should read these traits as simply examples of Roman artists deploying elements of Rome's rich visual vocabulary. In the case of Sol, they serve to define him as the Roman pantheon's quintessential deity of fiery youth and invincibility.

This means that images of Sol with such features do not represent "Alexander-Helios".[9] Bergmann (1998: 73–9) has already shown that it is impos-

---

7   Cf. Spencer 2002, with the *caveat* that her fascinating study focuses on the reception and interpretation of the historical Alexander by the Roman elite of the later Republic and early Principate, as evidenced by their writings. See also A. Stewart 2004.

8   As Smith 1988: 59 puts it, "… the strongly idealized image of Alexander (especially in the posthumous portraits) became so well known that it entered the common stock of Greek iconography in the Hellenistic and Roman periods and was absorbed into a whole range of other images, divine and mythological." Cf. Smith 1991: 22; Vasilieva 2004.

9   The external evidence for Alexander-Helios, adduced by A. Stewart 1993: 334 is not convincing. Although Diodorus 17, 89, 3 and Curtius 9, 1, 1 state that Alexander offered sacrifice to Helios in thanks for being allowed to conquer the East, this hardly constitutes evidence that Alexander claimed any special bond with Helios (cf. Arrian, V.10, who states simply that Alexander offered to the Gods, without special mention of Helios). The radiate coins of Ptolemy III Euergetes (246–222) and his successors, as well as those of Antiochus IV Epiphanes (215–163) and his successors, are not examples of "fully fledged solar imagery," as A. Stewart would have it (cf. Grimm 1978). Smith 1988: 42, 44 rightly rejects the notion that rays on Hellenistic royal portraits referred specifically to Helios, stating rather that they represent "the radiance of royal-divine epiphany." Therefore, even if we leave aside the gap of over 80 years between Alexander's death and the first radiate Hellenistic coin-portraits, there is nothing here to suggest an Alexander-Helios prototype for this imagery. *Anth. Gr.* 16, 121 (A. Stewart 1993: 117) mentions αὐγαί, but they represent the bright light of Zeus (Διός); Helios is not mentioned, nor is any specific link suggested in the text between Zeus (let alone Helios) and Alexander. The "sunless" lands referred to in Plut. *Mor.* 330D remain so, because they cannot "look towards one rule of justice as though toward a common source of light." The point Plutarch makes is that, *if* Alexander had not died so young, these lands *would* have been united under one rule of justice, which would have enlightened them. No suggestion here that Alexander was like or akin to the sun. The relevance of Plut. *Alex.* 22, 9 and 63, 4–5, to which A. Stewart refers in support of the concept of "blazing" Alexander, is not clear to me.

sible to find any definitive criteria by which any radiate image can be securely identified as Alexander or Alexander-Helios rather than Sol or some other radiate deity.[10] We can actually extend that to almost all supposed portraits of Alexander in the Roman era, because we lack definitive criteria by which they can be securely identified. It is this lack of workable criteria which shows that what I have referred to as "generic" traits of youthful power were not, in fact, all characteristics derived from the portrait of Alexander. The notion that they represent an *imitatio Alexandri* when they are deployed in Roman art over-emphasizes Alexander and semantically is too restrictive a reading of these elements.[11] In those rare cases where we may, in fact, be dealing with an actual Roman-era portrait of Alexander, they were deployed to render his portrait meaningful (as opposed to being rendered meaningful by his portrait).[12]

The widespread use of these elements is not in imitation of Alexander, but does, of course, bring with it connotations and meanings that are also evoked by portraits of Alexander. And really, here we should remind ourselves that we are dealing with visual signification. Besides power, youth, and passion, these generic iconographic elements evoke associations with, or connotations of powerful, passionate youths, such as Sol, Alexander, Achilles, Apollo, the Dioscures, and others who could be depicted with such traits. As part of the viewer's fast thinking, these associations remain liminal, undifferentiated, but nonetheless seminal for the understandings the image evokes. Especially in the case of Alexander, whose portrait, we have seen, is so hard to pin down, those understandings would be fuzzy, diffuse, and wide-ranging. But above all, the associations are not merely verbal or nominal, but far more encompassing.

This can be well illustrated with one of the examples of a supposed *imitatio Alexandri* proffered by Trofimova (2012: 220 no. 118), a tauroctony relief now in St Petersburg (C2c.108). Iconographically, there is nothing remarkable about this relief beyond the fact that it is incomplete. The scene is the standard one of Mithras killing a bull, repeated countless times on similar reliefs across the Empire. Stylistically, however, it belongs to a relatively small group

---

10   Even when there are specific iconographical elements pointing away from Sol, this does not automatically lead to Alexander. A bronze statuette in Paris (Louvre Br 344), for example, that depicts a radiate figure with a raised right hand, full body armour, and "Alexander-like" features, is not Sol because of the cuirass, but probably also not Alexander, given that – as Seyrig has already noted – the iconography is that of a Syrian solar deity influenced by that of Sol. I thus disagree with Bergmann 1998: 76–7 pl. 14.1–3, who believes that the possibility that this statuette is Alexander is "fairly strong," as well as with Matern 2002: 120–2, who argues that it is Helios. Cf. Seyrig 1970: 110. Cf. also a statuette in Ankara (arch. mus. 19332), likewise in the guise of a warrior, and hence likewise not Sol (Bergmann 1998: 79 pl. 14.4).

11   On the supposed *imitatio Alexandri* in Roman portraits, see Kovács 2015; cf. Spencer 2002.

12   For the opposite view, cf., in particular, Trofimova 2012. See also: A. Stewart 1993, 2004; Vasilieva 2004.

of tauroctony reliefs that are sculpted in a highly Hellenizing style. This is in significant contrast to the majority of tauroctony reliefs, which are products of what Bianchi Bandinelli would have termed *arte plebea*. The *imitatio Alexandri* which Trofimova discerns in the features of Mithras, is a by-product of the use of the Hellenistic baroque style (loosely defined) for this relief. In iconographical terms, the difference in style has no impact, for there is nothing to indicate that the identity of Mithras here is in any way different from Mithras on "plebeian" reliefs. Stylistically, the difference did affect the tauroctony's meaning, insofar as it made clear at a glance (fast thinking) that this tauroctony belonged in a Mithraeum that catered to the upper class or had been donated to its Mithraeum by a member of the elite. Alexander has no role to play in the "Alexander-like" traits, because they do not change the identity of Mithras. They do colour the identity of the Mithraeum, in a manner that is totally devoid of Alexander-related associations.

The potential connotations and associations of all the various components of the St Petersburg tauroctony do not end there, of course, but for the viewer in fast thinking mode their presence is primarily intuited as a potentiality. Only if he shifts to slow thinking does he begin to actively parse them. That is characteristic of all visual signs in Roman art. They carry with them wide arrays of potential meanings, including the potential to construct complex meanings in association with other signs, but they generally are viewed in the fast-thinking mode only, and rarely invite or undergo a thorough exegesis of those potentialities. That is why the image is almost the opposite of a word, for the image conveys an immediate sense at first glance, and gradually expands in meaning if it is subjected to further consideration, whereas a word's meaning is progressively made more precise and restricted by the text in which it is deployed. This speaks again to the reasons behind the distinction between sol (image), *sol*, and Sol.

Where does this leave us in practical terms, as far as the issue of Alexander and Alexander-Helios is concerned? On the present evidence, it seems safe to assume that, if an image adheres to the basic iconographic conventions of Sol, then it *is* Sol. So-called Alexander-like features, no matter how strong, are no more than visual conventions portraying Sol's youth, ardour, and invincibility. Only strong contextual evidence could mandate the identification as Alexander in such cases, but to date there is no conclusive evidence that any of the extant radiate "Alexanders" must be Alexander and cannot be Sol.[13] If

---

13   It is unfortunate that so often we do not know the intended context. A radiate "Alexander" set up in a villa among the portraits of other rulers may well have been a possibility in antiquity.

an image does *not* adhere to Sol's iconographic conventions, as in the case of the cuirassed statuettes in Paris and Ankara, for instance, then he is not Sol, but neither is he then necessarily Alexander. Only closer examination of such radiate, non-solar depictions with Alexander-like features may yet reveal a particular type of radiate or radiant Alexander portrait (perhaps with a star over his head?), but that takes us outside the scope of the present study.

It should be noted that the basic principles I have outlined do not provide a clear answer in every instance. I have not taken possible regional variations into account, for instance, and at least one problematic case remains: a late Hellenistic or Roman imperial bust of a statuette in Brooklyn (B4b.3). A short discussion of this piece can well illustrate the intractability of the problems.[14] The alabaster bust, from Egypt, is presumably an acrolith, in which case it is reasonable to assume that where the extant bust ends the clothing of the statuette, in a different material, began. This would mean that the statuette was not clothed in a *chiton* or *chlamys* as Sol should be, although an unfastened *chlamys* hanging over the left shoulder cannot be wholly excluded if the acrolith was part of a bust rather than a full statuette, or a component of some larger, elaborate composition. The head is slightly tilted and the gaze, beneath pronounced brows, is upwards, while the lips are slightly parted. The hair is arranged in rich, deeply carved and drilled curly locks around the face with an *anastole* above the forehead. Set in the hair are seven deep holes, presumably for metal rays. No diadem is visible in the hair, but on the back a ribbon in low relief appears to emerge from below the hair, where there may be a reworked knot, onto the left shoulder.

Is this Sol or Alexander-Helios? The apparently non-solar clothing and the *lemnisci* in the nape of the neck suggest the latter. Bergmann also points to the similarities with busts in Paris (from Egypt) and Berlin (from Priene), both with diadem but without rays, and both identified as Alexander.[15] I do not know of any depiction of Sol in the type of dress implied here, although Helios can sometimes be dressed in a *himation* in the Greek world.[16]

As problematic as the lost context, is the fact that the two closest parallels adduced by Bergmann are not radiate, an important consideration with regard to the seven holes. We cannot be certain that they held rays, although that seems likely. More importantly, we have no way of knowing when they were drilled. Too little is known about the find-circumstances of this bust to determine when it was deposited, but it is perfectly reasonable to assume that it had

---

14   Bergmann 1998: 74–5.
15   Paris, Louvre N7807; Raeder 1984: 33 no. 1.
16   Bergmann 1988: 74 n. 445 cites a small number of Rhodian coins.

been around, for some time, as an alabaster head of this quality would surely not have been blithely discarded after the metal had been sold. With reuse a possibility, why not go one step further and entertain the possibility that the holes were drilled at a time of reuse, transforming a bust of Alexander into one of a new statuette of Sol?

This is rampant speculation, of course, and my point is not to postulate that this is what actually happened. I simply want to stress that we cannot take for granted that the seven holes were part of the bust from the outset, especially because the closest parallels have no such holes. The original non-solar elements of the iconography (*lemnisci*, type of clothing) could have been neutralized by new solar attributes (rays, aspects of the lost parts of the statuette) as well as by a new, explicitly solar context. We have absolutely no way of knowing this, and are hence left with an insoluble problem.[17]

Aside from the alabaster bust in Brooklyn, I do not know of any representations which combine Alexander-like features with a conflation of solar and non-solar attributes with equal clarity. The other images adduced by Bergmann are either clearly not Sol, or Sol without any defining characteristic of Alexander (defining characteristics taken to be those that would be acceptable with Alexander, but not with Sol).[18]

2   Sol in the Synagogue

An issue that has raised equally debated problems of identification, though for entirely different reasons, takes us to a number of late antique synagogues in Palestine. These were decorated with iconographically similar, but stylistically very disparate mosaic floors. In the main naves of these synagogues, the floors are divided into a few large panels of which the most prominent one contains a depiction of Sol in his frontal chariot within a zodiac circle, with the

---

17   Bergmann 1998: 67 explores the possibility that Egyptian portraits of Alexander dating to the Roman imperial era may have depicted him radiate or with a star above his head.

18   Cf. Bergmann 1998: 73–9. Not Sol: Cameo, formerly in the treasury of the Cathedral at Cammin; two bronze busts, one in Boston (B4b.2) and one now lost (formerly Fouquet collection), both depicting a youth with an *uraeus* and a quasi-radiate crown of a type that is rare and certainly never sported by Sol; the aforementioned bronze statuette in the Louvre and marble statuette in Ankara, both in Roman armour, and a bronze equestrian statuette sold in Zurich in 1979. Sol, but not Alexander: a bronze statuette from the Forman collection (B1.17), sold at auction in 1899, which certainly cannot have carried a sword and have held a lance, as Bergmann 1998: 75–6 tentatively suggests (rejected by Matern 2002: 104–5). Whether this bronze, which I know only from an 1899 auction catalogue photograph, is authentic is open to question; cf Hijmans 2021.

seasons in the four corners. Iconographically almost identical, these central panels range stylistically from the classicizing mosaic of Hammath Tiberias (D1a.2) to the almost exaggeratedly naive style of the mosaics of Beth Alpha (D1a.6). In all cases there can be no doubt that these mosaics served as the floor of a synagogue; the contexts are unambiguous and the mosaics themselves have Hebrew inscriptions and panels above and below the central one in which old testament scenes or Jewish religious objects such as the menorah and ark are depicted.

The following synagogues have mosaics of this type:[19]

1. **Hammath Tiberias (D1a.2).**[20] The synagogue at the ancient site near this thermal spa was discovered accidentally in 1947 and fully excavated in 1961–1963. The excavator, M. Dothan, recognized four main levels of occupation (with level I the most recent and level IV the oldest). The synagogue floor with Sol and the zodiac belongs to level IIA. This level represents the refurbishment of the synagogue of level IIB, which according to Dothan took place in the first quarter of the fourth century AD. He believes that the synagogue was destroyed about a century later by an earthquake in AD 419. Dothan's chronology of the site has recently been challenged by Magness. She argues for a later date and proposes that the synagogue floor of stratum IIA with its mosaic of Sol and the zodiac was laid down just before AD 400 and remained in use until at least the third quarter of the fifth century AD.[21] While this re-dating is certainly possible, it pushes the synagogue to the latest possible date. In two dedicatory inscriptions incorporated in the mosaic, the dedicant Severus describes himself as the pupil (*threptos*) of the "most illustrious" Patriarchs.[22] The Greek *lamprotatos* corresponds to the Latin *clarissimus* and is an adjective that indicates that the Patriarchs were of senatorial rank. Patriarchs were still *viri clarissimi* in AD 392, but had been downgraded to *viri illustres* by AD 397, with further downgrades following rapidly until the last Patriarch, Gamaliel VI, was executed in AD 425. As the title *lamprotatos* was imperial, not Jewish, to continue using it for the Patriarch after he had been officially downgraded would in effect be a dangerous rejection of imperial authority. Given that all the archaeological evidence is

---

19 The literature is extensive: cf. Fine 2014; Hachlili 2009: 35–56; Wadeson 2008; Magness 2005; England 2003; Levine 2003; various contributions in Levine & Weiss 2000. Fine 2005: 199–200 gives a very brief summary of previous views. A map with the locations of these synagogues can be found in Magness 2005: 3 fig. 1.

20 Dothan 1983.

21 Magness 2005: 8–13.

22 Dothan 1983: 55, 60.

compatible with a date even many decades before the 390s, the *terminus ante quem* provided by the inscriptions is reasonable.

The image of Sol at Hammath Tiberias, though damaged by a wall that was later built over it, is easily recognizable and adheres in every respect to the long-established standard image type. Sol has a radiate nimbus (seven rays), is dressed in a blue sleeved *chiton* and red *chlamys*, has raised his right hand in his characteristic gesture, and holds a blue globe in his left hand. He is driving his *quadriga*, but the horses have been destroyed by that later wall.

2. **Huseifa (D1a.4).** The synagogue lies below modern buildings and could only be partially excavated in 1930 by Avi-Yonah. Extensive mosaics covered the floor of the complex, but all were heavily damaged by the later building activities. The eastern panel of the central nave of the synagogue consisted of a zodiac circle, only part of which survives, around a central figure who is lost, but widely accepted to have been Sol. There is no direct evidence for the date of the synagogue, but it appears to be later than the one at Hammath Tiberias, giving it a late fifth century date.[23] It appears to have been destroyed around the middle of the sixth century AD.[24]

3. **Sepphoris (D1a.5).**[25] This is one of the most recently excavated and, from the perspective of this study, the most interesting synagogue in this group. The synagogue lies in the northern part of Sepphoris and was excavated in the early 1990s. It was built in the first half of the fifth century AD and destroyed in the early seventh century AD. The synagogue is 20.70 m long and 8 m wide and consists of a nave with only a single aisle along the north side. The entire synagogue is adorned with an elaborate mosaic floor with biblical scenes, Jewish symbols, and in a prominent, central position a panel with the circle of the zodiac, the four seasons in the corners, and within the zodiac the sun in a *quadriga*. In this case the sun is not depicted in the standard image type Sol, as in Hammath Tiberias, but as a long pole surmounted by a disc with eight broad rays. Next to the disc are a star and the lunar crescent.[26]

4. **Beth Alpha (D1a.6).**[27] The synagogue at Beth Alpha was excavated in 1929 by E. Sukenik. The complex as a whole is 20 m × 14 m, and the prayer hall 10 m × 8 m. The mosaic floor of the synagogue has an inscription that

23   Hachlili 2009: 35.
24   Avi Yonah & Makhouly 1933.
25   Weiss 2005, 2011; Kühnel 2000; Weiss & Netzer 1996.
26   The only parallel I know for this manner of depicting Sol is an undated round altar from Pergamon, now in the Antikensammlung in Berlin, inv. AvP VII 420, Arachne 175333.
27   Stewart 2016; Sukenik 1932.

dates it to the reign of a Justin, generally assumed to be Justin I (518–527) but possibly Justin II (565–578).[28] It consists of two smaller panels with a biblical scene (the Sacrifice of Isaac) and Jewish symbols respectively, and a larger one in the centre with a zodiac, the four seasons, and Sol on a frontal *quadriga*.

5. **Na'aran (D1a.7)**. The synagogue at Na'aran was discovered towards the end of the first World War, and excavated in the early 1920s. Its prayer hall was almost 15 m wide and well over 20 m long (the exact length could not be established). The mosaic floor of the prayer hall, deliberately vandalized by iconoclasts, consisted of four panels.[29] Upon entering, one first came across a panel decorated with a geometric pattern of polygons and circles once containing depictions of animals, later destroyed. The next panel is slightly smaller, and depicts the zodiac ring, the four seasons, and Sol in his chariot, radiate and wearing a star-studded *chlamys*; and again, all figurative images have been destroyed. The other two panels contain a biblical scene (Daniel in the lions' den) and Jewish symbols respectively. The floor cannot be dated with precision, but belongs to the sixth century.[30]

6. **Susiya.**[31] The prayer hall of this synagogue measured 15 m × 9 m. It was built in the fifth century and survived until the eighth or even ninth century, during which time it was repeatedly refurbished. In its present state, the floor belongs to a late stage of the monument and only slight traces remain of what may have been a zodiac circle in an earlier phase of the floor.

7. **Yaphia.** This synagogue, like the one in Huseifa, is beneath a modern building and only a small part could be excavated when it was explored in 1951. The prayer hall was about 15 m wide and almost 20 m long. Its mosaic floor was heavily damaged but traces of twelve circles around a large central circle suggest we may be dealing with a variant of the zodiac circle here. Only one recognizable figure in one of the smaller circles survives and may be the sign of Taurus. The fragment of an inscription next

---

28   Justin II seems an unlikely candidate, because Jews and other non-Christians were under considerable pressure during his reign. Also, there may already have been a rise in Jewish iconoclasm as early as the second half of the sixth century AD.

29   Prigent 1990: 32–5 dates Jewish iconoclasm as early as the latter part of the sixth century AD. Fine 2005: 84–5 places it significantly later, in the eighth or ninth century AD, linking it to the influence of Islam.

30   Late sixth century, according to Hachlili 2009: 35.

31   Gutmann 1981.

to an adjacent circle cannot be reconciled with this interpretation, as it suggests the twelve Tribes of Israel may have been depicted.[32]

8. **Huqoq** (D1a.8). The excavations at Huqoq (near Capernaum) began in 2011, and the mosaics in the main nave of the synagogue floor were discovered in 2014 and 2015. The mosaic floor is divided into five panels, with Sol and the zodiac taking up the central panel. the two panels north of it depict Noah's ark (with animal pairs) and the Egyptian soldiers drowning in the Red Sea respectively. The two panels to the south depict Jonah being swallowed by three fish and the Tower of Babel respectively. The mosaics are dated to the early fifth century AD.[33]

Not surprisingly, these synagogue mosaics have given rise to considerable discussion and controversy. The presence of figural art in late antique synagogues was itself unexpected, and largely unknown until the discovery of Na'aran, because it was deemed contrary to Rabbinic law. The presence of an apparently pagan image of the sun god within a zodiac circle was even more problematic. It is not my aim to review the various explanations proposed for the iconography of these floors. These mosaics are somewhat beyond our chronological limits, and the Jewish context also introduces a wholly different set of iconographic, religious, and cultural elements. I do not, therefore, intend to reflect on the meaning of Sol in this particular context, but propose to focus instead on what his occurrence in this context tells us about Roman art.

Sol in a frontal chariot within a zodiac circle has at least one mosaic parallel outside the region and religious context of these floor mosaics. In 1895, a mosaic was discovered in the reception hall of a Roman villa in Münster-Sarmsheim dating to the third century AD (D1a.1). One large panel of this mosaic depicted Sol in a frontal *quadriga* within a zodiac circle. The only substantial difference between this mosaic and the ones in the synagogues listed above is that it does not have seasons in the four corners, but vases flanked by fish. Other mosaics show the bust of Sol alone or Sol and Luna together within a zodiac circle (D1a.3, D1b.1–2). Sol and the zodiac form a logical combination, and occur together in the Roman world as early as the second quarter of the third century BC (F1a.13; also early are H9b.1–2). Though not especially common, the image of Sol within a zodiac circle remained in use throughout the late Republic and imperial period.[34]

---

32   Magness 2005: n. 12. In En Gedi, a mosaic inscription lists the twelve tribes and then the twelve signs of the zodiac. Cf. Magness 2005: 7.

33   Scant traces of possibly a zodiac circle discovered at Wadi Hamam may indicate that there was a similar depiction of Sol in the central panel of the main nave floor-mosaic of that synagogue as well; cf. Miller & Leibner 2018: 172–3.

34   C1f.7, C4.11, E3.4, G1c.3, H1fa.1, H1ha.1, H3aa.1, H4da.1, H6cc.1, H6h.1 (doubtful), H9b.1–2, HA9b.1, K1.14, K9.10, 12, 15, 24. Sol and the zodiac could also appear on coins, particularly

When the first synagogue floor with zodiac circle, image type Sol, and the four seasons was designed, presumably sometime in the fourth century,[35] there was nothing to differentiate that particular section or panel of the mosaic from mainstream Roman imperial art. What was adopted into the floor design was an astrological composition composed of a series of standard and widespread Roman image types. That the designers were aware of this cannot be doubted. Severus, who donated the oldest surviving mosaic floor of this type, in the Hammath Tiberias synagogue, was closely associated with the Patriarchs, which puts him in touch with the imperial elite, for the Patriarch was of senatorial rank and very close to the top of the imperial hierarchy in the region. To function successfully at this level, a thorough education in Graeco-Roman culture was a *conditio sine qua non*. To be senatorial, one had to be well versed in senatorial culture.

The zodiac design of these floors, then, was not a Jewish invention, nor was it introduced into the synagogue by people who were not fully aware of its range of meanings within Roman imperial art. For most scholars the main question that this raises is simple: "Why did certain Jewish congregations place the figure of the Graeco-Roman Sun god in a central position in their synagogues?"[36] Thus formulated, the question itself is in large part the source of the "problem". The image of Sol is assumed to mean the Sun *god*, which is a misreading of the image. It is true that the genesis of the anthropomorphic depiction of the sun was related to the ancient Greek concept of anthropomorphic gods, but that takes us back more than a millennium.[37] In Roman art, as we have seen, Sol, though still anthropomorphic, had long since evolved into a visual sign, not just for the sun in all its aspects, but for concepts at best indexically related to the sun. As such, this image type was the prime way to depict the sun irrespective of whether he was to be viewed as divine, cosmic, symbolic, or metaphorical. In fact, the anthropomorphic image was the *only* image type for the sun available to Roman art.

---

of local civic mints (the following represent an incomplete selection). In the zodiac series issued in AD 145 in Alexandria, we find a zodiac circle around the jugate busts of Sol and Luna: RPC IV.4, 15280, 15281, 15476, 16967, and 16976; we also find an outer circle of the zodiac and an inner circle of planetary deities (heads) around the bust of Sarapis: RPC IV.4 14869 and 15284 (note the order of the planetary deities!). Cf. RPC VI, 3570 (Tium, AD 218–222); 3772 (Cyzicus, AD 222–235); BMC Thrace 157 no. 58 (Perinthus AD 222–235); SNG Levante Suppl. 390, (Eirenopolis AD 243).

35 The date is based on the assumption that the Hammath Tiberias mosaic has a *terminus ante quem* of circa AD 395.

36 Magness 2005: 7.

37 The earliest surviving anthropomorphic image of the Greek god Helios is possibly on an amphora from Thera dating to 670/60 BC (LIMC V, s.v. Helios 1), but it does not become common until the late archaic period.

In other words, from the perspective of Roman visual practice there is nothing inherently surprising about finding Sol in a synagogue. The sun was not a matter of (pagan) belief – nobody denied his existence – and if, for whatever reason, one wanted to depict the sun, this was the way to do it. This does not mean that the roots of the image types Sol in pagan religious anthropomorphism had been forgotten, but they had become (almost) irrelevant. The clearest evidence for this comes, paradoxically, from the mosaic in Sepphoris. That the figure of Sol was here replaced by a rayed disc on a pole is a unique and unprecedented change in iconography that indicates that the Jewish designers of such floors were not completely unconcerned by the pagan religious connotations of the anthropomorphism of the image type. But the disc and pole are still depicted as "charioteer" of a *quadriga* of horses. This shows two things: that the charioteer on the synagogue mosaics definitely was not intended to depict the Graeco-Roman Sun *god*, for in that case the Sepphoris innovation would be inexplicable, and, secondly, that the iconographic prescripts which governed art in the Roman world were so widely known, so deeply rooted, and so immutable, that even the late antique and early Byzantine Jewish mosaicists in these synagogues felt bound by them, to the point that the mosaicists in Sepphoris retained the chariot and thus the link to the Graeco-Roman iconography of the image type Sol. There is no "logical" link between the radiant orb of the sun in their mosaic and a chariot with horses, so that one had to be awkwardly created by placing the disc on a pole, and the pole in the chariot. This awkwardness may explain why this particular attempt at Sepphoris to divest the image of its lingering pagan religious roots was apparently not copied elsewhere, but it does not explain why it was not attempted along different lines elsewhere. We can only conclude that the issue was not urgent.[38]

The presence of Sol in these synagogues thus provides strong support for our contention that in Roman art such image types were indexical or even arbitrary signs in the semiotic sense. In the case of the synagogue mosaics, the zodiac circle and the busts of the seasons leave the viewer in no doubt as to the cosmic context of these particular Sol images. The synagogue itself reinforces this religiously neutral understanding of Sol, as does the fact that these are floor mosaics. Floors are not a location one associates with divine or sacred images. Placing a statue or relief of Sol on the wall or ceiling of a synagogue would have been quite a different matter.

That Jewish mosaicists in late antiquity introduced the Graeco-Roman image type Sol into their synagogues in Palestine is a remarkable testimony to

---

38   The two surviving rays of Sol in the mosaic of Huqoq (D1a.8) are compatible with an image of the sun similar to Sepphoris, but there can be no certainty that this was the case.

the pervasive influence of Roman iconographic conventions and principles. Just as the words *S/sol* and *H/helios* were used as a matter of course by pagans, Jews, and Christians alike, so too the image types Sol could be used by all three groups.

3 A Divine Kiss on the Lips

On a group of nearly identical lamps from Egypt, dating to the third century AD, the frontal bust of Sarapis is depicted next to a profile bust of Sol, who is kissing him (G1e). These lamps are of particular interest because they can be securely linked to a specific ritual, and thus may shed light on more cultic aspects of Sol.

The lamps depict an event that regularly took place at the Serapeum at Alexandria, about which Rufinus and Quodvultdeus inform us in some detail.[39] A small, hidden "window" was situated in such a way that when it was opened at a precisely calculated moment it admitted a beam of sunlight that struck the statue of Sarapis on the lips. In addition, there was an image of Sol and his *quadriga* made of "very pure" iron that could be set in motion with the aid of hidden magnetic rocks in the ceiling so that the statue appeared to the viewers to rise into the air of its own accord. This "kiss of Sol" was a renowned event, and it would appear that these lamps were sold as souvenirs at or near the temple. That in itself places us squarely in the religious sphere, at one of the most spectacular temples of the Roman world. At first glance, therefore, one would conclude that here, surely, we are dealing with images of Sol depicting the traditional Sun god. But if we look more closely at the evidence it becomes clear that matters are not so straightforward.

Neither the lamps nor the passages in Rufinus and Quodvultdeus indicate to what extent Sol was presented as, or perceived to be an independent actor in this kiss. According to Rufinus, an attendant proclaimed: "surrexit Sol, ut valedicens Serapi discedat ad propria" ("the Sun has risen to return to his own, saying farewell to Sarapis") as the iron statuette began to move, but that still does not tell us very much. Was Sol considered to be a god in the same league as Sarapis, or was his (uncontested) divinity of a different type? Perhaps the question should not be framed in these terms. Instead we should note that there was, apparently, no reason to differentiate, iconographically, between Sol kissing Sarapis and the standard image types Sol, except that his arm may be depicted embracing Sarapis; he is clearly depicted performing an action,

---

39 Rufinus *HE* 11, 23; Quodvultdeus *Liber promissionum et praedictorum Dei* 3, 42. Cf. Tran Tam Tinh 1984. On Quodvultdeus cf. Nazzaro 2001.

namely kissing his counterpart. Iconographically, then, there is a clear difference with the mythological scenes in which Sol's iconography was much
freer and noticeably more independent of the standard image types Sol. What
we have here is the standard image type uncharacteristically performing an
action. The closest parallels for this are the Mithraic panel scenes in which
Sol and Mithras are depicted in various actions. The Mithraic scenes are much
more elaborate, however, than the small images on the circular discs on oil
lamps under discussion here.

As with coins we should bear in mind that these lamp-disc images could
evoke a famous monument or, in this case, event without incorporating in
detail the more subtle iconographic (and ritual) pointers that may contain
information essential to that main monument or ritual. In fact, it is safe to
assume that the lamps transmit in visual shorthand an aspect of the ritual
that, if it had been photographed, would actually have appeared quite different. They illustrate the actual ritual moment when the rays of sunlight briefly
fell upon the lips of the statue of Sarapis after the hidden window was opened.
We should bear in mind that these rays of light admitted into the cella of the
temple did not symbolize the sun just as the statue did not symbolize Sarapis.
The ritual was not a re-enactment of some far-off meeting of the two. Rather,
the rays *were* the kiss of the sun falling on the lips of the cultic embodiment
of Sarapis. The ritual was not symbolic, but the real thing. The lamps translate that actual, witnessed kiss of Sol into Roman visual language, in which
Sol stands for those rays of light and, by extension, their source, the sun. What
the image evoked, in the mind's eye of the intended viewer, then, was not Sol
striding across some heavenly floor to kiss his counterpart Sarapis, but rather
the rays of light that struck the lips of Sarapis' statue at the *moment suprême* of
a major (and no doubt impressive) ritual.[40]

A Roman artist wishing to depict the rays of sun touching the lips of
Sarapis, poetically described as a kiss of Sol and ritually enacted because of
its significance, was bound by the strict visual conventions of Roman art and
did not have much choice in how to do so. To depict the bust of Sol embracing and kissing the bust of Sarapis is, therefore, a logical way to visualize the
rays of sunlight on the lips of the statue according to the norms of Roman
visual communication, irrespective of whether the attendant, announcing the
departure of the sun *ad propria sua* thought of the sun as *sol* or *Sol*. In fact, the
image is incapable of depicting such a contrast, which means that when we,
in our publications of that quote, decide whether to capitalize Sol or not, we

---

40   I see no indication that the image on the lamp refers to the iron statuette. It rose into the
        air, but did not kiss Sarapis, and it symbolized Sol's departure, not his embrace.

are imposing a differentiation between the meanings of Sol and *sol* that was absent in antiquity.

Thus, we have here an excellent example of the problems that arise in translating ancient ritual into ancient art, and ancient art into modern academic text. In particular, it illustrates how careful we must be not to imagine an anthropomorphic sun *god* as the signified of the anthropomorphic signifier Sol (or sol).[41]

4   Funerary Altar of Julia Victorina

This funerary altar (C3f.1), discovered near the Lateran in Rome, is virtually unique and its meanings are not clear.[42] It is decorated with two female busts, one on the front and one on the back. Both busts are presumably portraits of Julia Victorina, the deceased. The bust on the front has short hair in loosely falling locks framing the face. Her forehead below the fringe of hair is smooth, the eyebrows thin but pronounced, her gaze direct. Her nose was (probably) straight but is damaged. She has a small, straight mouth with fairly thin lips and a pronounced chin. Full cheeks give her face the roundish contours of a child. Her ears are shapely and fairly large, and she is wearing small round earrings. An upturned crescent rests on the top of her head.

The radiate bust on the back has a different hairstyle, consisting of nine carefully arranged round curls framing the face from ear to ear. The short curls leave free a high, straight forehead. Below the thin eyebrows fairly deep-set eyes gaze straight ahead. The nose is straight and quite narrow, the mouth small with thin straight lips, the chin strong. The jawline is fairly straight and the cheeks flatter, giving the face a slightly more triangular shape than the counterpart on the front. The shapely ears are proportionately smaller and she is wearing the same earrings. Seven straight rays emerge from a fillet running over the top of the head from ear to ear. Set side by side, the differing hairstyles, the different shapes of the face, and the proportionate difference in the size of the ears make the radiate portrait on the back of the altar that of an adult woman who has lost the more child-like features of the portrait on the front.[43]

---

41   As for the ritual itself, here too we must be careful not to take its meaning as obvious too easily. The kiss has important religious connotations in a variety of religious traditions. Cf., e.g. Bähring 2018.

42   Comparable is the compital altar found in Trastevere and now in the Museo Nazionale inv. 58640, Berti 1989, n. 60; CIL VI, 36851.

43   It should be noted, however, that the loss of the nose enhances the childish features of the latter; a straight, adult nose would have diminished the contrast with the portrait on the back.

The fact that they are both wearing the same earrings confirms that the same person is meant, and that she is Julia Victorina. It is widely accepted that she is depicted on the front as the ten-year-old girl she was at the time of her death, and on the back as the adult she never was.[44]

The problem is that this leaves the *lunula* and rays of the respective portraits unexplained. The first question to ask, therefore, is whether this altar in any way echoes the image type Sol-and-Luna. Basically, it does, of course, but only to a certain degree. The crescent on the one portrait and the rays on the other inevitably evoke Luna and Sol, or, more likely, the Sol-and-Luna type, but only in a limited way. The lunula and the radiate crown do not make the identity of the busts ambiguous. Their identity is reinforced by their placement. The two portrait busts are not placed in a flanking or subordinate position, which would have made them more Sol-and-Lunalike; they are not on the sides of the altar for instance, but on the front and the back, and they are clearly the main images. The two sides are each decorated with a laurel tree with birds. In short, the two busts borrow from the Sol-Luna imagery, but do not copy it. This is not Julia Victorina assimilated with Luna and Sol respectively, but two busts that at best stand to each other as Luna stands to Sol.

In normal social hierarchy the adult portrait on the back would be more important than the child on the front. This is reinforced by the attributes of Sol and Luna, for the light of Sol is more powerful, and in art he is generally granted the dominant role, rising in his four-horse chariot from the left into the scene while Luna descends out of the image in her *biga* of oxen or horses. In terms of Roman gender inequality as well, Sol, being male, has the dominant role in the image type Sol-Luna. And yet if we return to the portraits, the one on the front, despite its youth and association with Luna, is by virtue of its position the preeminent one, for it is surely safe to assume that the inscription was on the side one approached first. How visible was the back at all? Is the deeper relief of this side of the altar meant to counteract reduced visibility because of placement or lack of light? Could one walk around the altar? One assumes that this was the case, and that the viewer thus went from the child who had died to the adult who never lived, back again to the child who had died.[45] Circling around the altar thus involves the viewer in two major transitions, from childhood to adulthood and from life to death. The interwoven

---

44   Cumont 1942: 243–4 argued that the portrait on the back represents the maturity and
      immortality that she will attain during the sojourn of her soul in the sphere of the moon
      as it begins its ascent through the spheres. Nock and Beazley 1946: 143 have their doubts
      about his rather precise and detailed interpretation, but admit to having no alternative
      explanation for the unique imagery of this remarkable piece. Cf. D'Ambra 2006: 66–7;
      Kleiner 1987: 119–21 n. 15; Wrede 1981b: 264–5 n. 183.

45   On circumambulation in Roman funerary rites, cf. Davies 1997: 56–7.

quote of the Sol-Luna iconography with its liminal connotations subtly reinforces this element of transition; the *aeternitas* reference which is also part
of the general meaning evoked by the image type Sol-Luna is likewise appropriate. But that does not yet explain why Julia Victorina is "Luna and Sol", for
the same effect could be achieved with a small depiction of Sol and Luna on,
say, the sides. There must be a reason why the Sol-Luna imagery is integrated
into the two portraits, depicting the ten-year-old as the moon in relation to
her adult, solar self that was never attained. But any attempt to find such a
reason must take into account the laurels (of Apollo as Helios?) on the sides,
the ornamentation, comparable funerary altars, and other such elements, all
essential components of any comprehensive study. That is clearly beyond the
scope of the present discussion. What I do hope to have shown is that the basic
connotations of the Sol-Luna imagery offer a good point of departure for the
analysis of this funerary altar.

From our perspective, however, more interesting than what the altar says
is the manner in which it says it. The imagery constructs a significant part
of its meaning by adopting elements of an image type, Sol-and-Luna, which
itself borrows two images (Sol and Luna) to construct meanings that, in semiotic terms, are only indexically related to the actual signifiers. The image type
Sol-and-Luna itself does not denote a meeting of Sol and Luna; in the case of
the portraits of Julia Victorina the references to moon goddess and sun god
are even further removed. The crescent and the radiate crown enable an elegant and at first glance straightforward funerary altar to construct, in typically
Roman visual fashion, a complex of meaningful associations that enhance the
impact of that altar. At no point, however, can there be even a suggestion that
Julia Victorina is somehow being *identified* with Luna and Sol.

What we see here is one of the clearest examples yet in this study of symbolic signs in Roman art in the form of the upturned crescent and the crown of
rays deployed on this altar in a manner that has nothing to do with Luna and
Sol anymore. The capacity of Roman art to deploy these two symbols in this
manner will prove to be an important key to the understanding of the imperial
radiate crown (see chapter six).

5 Mithras

Sol Invictus Mithras, protagonist of the mysteries of Mithras, has loomed large,
perhaps overly so, in studies of Roman imperial religion.[46] The relevance of

---

46   The literature on Roman Mithraism is vast. Beck 1984 gives an excellent overview, which
      is supplemented (up to 2001) by Martens & de Boe 2004; cf. since then Beck 2006; Gordon

this cult for the study of the Roman image types Sol is not easy to establish because the evidence is complex, even somewhat contradictory. On the one hand we have, in Mithraic art, a standard use of the image type Sol-Luna in the upper corners of all tauroctony reliefs: Sol, as bust or charioteer, is (almost) always in the upper left hand corner, Luna in the upper right hand one.[47] In addition to these, we have a fair number of reliefs on which Sol reclines next to Mithras at a banquet, as well as various minor scenes in which Sol plays a subordinate role to Mithras. Sol follows the same iconography of the standard image types in these cases, but his pose is adapted to the scene.

It is noteworthy that Mithras and Sol are always depicted separately, because in his name, Sol Invictus Mithras, the protagonist of the cult is normally presented or addressed as a single deity. What is even more remarkable, while Mithras is invariably depicted in Persian rather than Roman garb, Sol is always portrayed in his normal Roman guise. The cult of Mithras thus raises two fundamental questions for our study: what is the relationship between Sol and Mithras, and what is the relationship between the Sol within Mithraism and Sol outside it? In this section, we will explore these two questions to some degree, but will make no attempt to answer them comprehensively. That is not only beyond the scope of this study but probably beyond the scope of surviving evidence altogether. In fact, one may wonder whether Mithraists themselves felt it necessary or even possible to articulate a definitive "answer" to either question.[48] The main purpose of this section on Mithraism is to pursue and explore strategies for the effective study of the image types Sol, where the cult of Mithras forms a concrete setting, with relevant material and important issues. This section is therefore primarily intended to tease out ways in which we can conceptualize and analyse the meanings of the image types Sol, and should be read with that in mind. I make no attempt to provide a coherent interpretation of Sol within Mithraism (far less of Mithraism as a whole).

Throughout this section, I rely heavily on Beck, not so much because I share his conclusions (which I do find quite persuasive), but because in terms of the interpretation of visual evidence I find his approach the most methodologically rigorous and theoretically informed.[49] Beck's actual interpretation of the

---

2009; Martens 2009; Witschel 2013; Dirven 2015; Turcan 2016; Gordon 2017: 93–9; Hensen 2017; Mastrocinque 2017; Panagiotidou & Beck 2017.

47   For exceptions cf. C2c.40, C2c.75, C2c.86.

48   Beck 2006: 64: "No blood was spilled, as far as we know, in reconciling the singularity of the sun with the distinct personae of Sol and Mithras."

49   Adrych et al. 2017 take a very interesting approach to Mithraism overall, discussing the occurrence of Mithras in a range of cultures and periods, with attention for noteworthy continuities (such as the consistently important role of the sun). Their chapter on the

evidence is of less importance to this section, as I do not intend to go far down that route.

5.1 The Mithraic Cult

Of all the cults with a major profile in the Roman world, Mithraism was the one most closely associated with Sol. It flourished in the Roman Empire from before AD 100 to the end of paganism. Its shrines are small, closed structures, often underground, with a simple plan. A "typical" Mithraeum is a fairly narrow rectangular room with an entrance on one short side opening on to an aisle that leads directly to the altar at the other end. Along the length of the walls to either side of the aisle are two low platforms on which initiates attending a ceremony could recline. The shrines rarely offer space for more than thirty initiates and often far fewer.[50] The floor and sides of the aisle as well as the wall behind the raised platforms could be decorated with a variety of frescos, mosaics, and sculpture, but the most prominent decorative element of the Mithraeum was without a doubt the depiction of Mithras slaying a bull – the tauroctony – which dominated the short side opposite the entrance. Depictions of the tauroctony were usually reliefs but were sometimes painted. Three-dimensional sculptural tauroctonies were also not uncommon.

There is no consensus among scholars about how the association between Mithras and Sol is to be interpreted, as this obviously depends on how the cult of Mithras itself is understood; and on that, opinions vary widely. The traditional view, developed primarily by Franz Cumont and, in his wake, Maarten Vermaseren, seeks the roots of the cult in Persia and further east and understands the dissemination of the cult in terms of a continuous historical process that was already two millennia old by the time Mithraism reached Rome. Proselytizing adherents of the cult were credited for its rapid expansion in the Roman Empire, the first Roman Mithraists being thought to have been soldiers posted on the Empire's eastern border, where they came into contact with the cult and its Persian adherents.

This understanding of the origins of Roman Mithraism has come under sustained attack since the 1970s. An alternative school of thought, represented notably by German scholars such as Reinhold Merckelbach and Manfred

---

Roman tauroctony scene (pp. 15–38) is excellent for its discussion and critique of past approaches to the analysis of this scene, but has little to offer that is truly new in terms of methodology or interpretation. Their discussion of Sol and Luna (pp. 23–4) falls short, if only because their focus on free-standing tauroctonies has masked the fact that Sol and Luna were not "frequently" present, but were in fact essential components of the tauroctony.

50 On Mithraic shrines, see the important contribution of Hensen 2017.

Clauss, argues that there were no direct links between the Roman cult of Mithras and the Persian Mitra either in terms of continuity of cult or the nature of their respective ideas. In this view, the cult of Mithras in its Roman form was a Roman invention and was founded in either Rome or Ostia in the first century AD and spread from there to other parts of the Empire.[51] Gordon (2017) takes a comparable position, arguing that the arrival of Mithras in Rome was more a matter of appropriation than of reception of the Persian cult.

A third view, proposed by Roger Beck, sees the kingdom of Commagene as the missing link between Persia and Rome, and proposes that Mithraism entered Rome when the Commagenian royal family – to which the renowned astronomer Ti. Claudius Balbillus was closely connected[52] – was exiled to Rome in AD 72.

Views on the nature or content of the cult vary as widely as views on its origin and cannot all be reviewed here. Most scholars have assumed the existence of a distinct Mithraic doctrine, the text of which has not survived. Some see that doctrine as rather simplistic, others as quite sophisticated, with suggested influences ranging from Platonism to Zoroastrian dualism. There has been general agreement, however, that whatever the doctrine was, key concepts of it were expressed in Mithraic art through the representation of significant events in a postulated Mithraic mythology.[53] More recently, however, the very existence of a (more or less detailed) Mithraic doctrine has been called into doubt.[54] In this view the cult of Mithras was focussed on ritual experience rather than theological doctrine, with no more than a loose cluster of general ideas underpinning the rituals.[55]

That opinions about ancient Mithraism can differ so widely is the direct result, of course, of our lack of sources. It has an obvious impact on our goal to explore the deployment of the image types Sol in Mithraic art. This is particularly the case because the different schools of thought about the nature of Mithraism deploy, or at least assume, very different modes of reading Mithraic art. Those who see the cult of Mithras as firmly rooted in a carefully defined and detailed Mithraic doctrine tend to study the art of Mithraea primarily as

---

51   For a concise statement of this position, see Clauss 2000: 7. Merkelbach sees the founder of Roman Mithraism as someone with extensive knowledge of Persian religions; cf. Beck 2006: 50–3.

52   Balbillus' daughter was the wife of Epiphanes, the son of Commagene's last king Antiochus IV.

53   Clauss 2000: 16–7 (role of art); Boyce & Grenet 1991 (Zoroastrianism); Turcan 1982 (Neoplatonism); Swerdlow 1991 (unsophisticated cult).

54   Discussed by Beck 2006: 51–2; cf. also Alvar 2008: 74–6.

55   Beck 2006: 52 and n. 30.

a source for key concepts of that doctrine. The primary function of Mithraic images, they feel, was to illustrate Mithraic beliefs, and therein lies their value for the modern scholar.[56] The problem with this approach is that it is particularistic and potentially circular. It relegates to images the role of reflecting meanings constructed verbally, in a written and/or oral doctrine. As we have seen in chapter one, this is not the best approach. Narrating verbal constructs as complex as religious doctrine is neither the task nor the strength of visual communication.

Those who downplay the importance of Mithraic doctrine take a different perspective. In their opinion Mithraic art's main task was to create a (ritual) environment. This is not a trite dismissal of the art as wallpaper or window dressing but quite the opposite. It is a key notion which Beck in particular explores in detail.[57] In his view the Mithraeum in all its material and visual facets was the "material representation of the initiate's cognized environment."[58]

In practice, this means that we currently are dealing not only with competing hypotheses concerning the cult of Mithras, but also with two very different approaches to reading Mithraic art: the one sees Mithraism as a cult with a specific, elaborate doctrine that was *taught* to the initiates and illustrated by the art; the other sees it as a cult centred on meaningful rituals that were *experienced* by the initiates in an environment constructed by Mithraic material culture. For our purposes, the second hypothesis provides the more fruitful and dynamic context for our analysis of the image types Sol, because it approaches the art and material culture of Mithraism in a more sophisticated and theoretically informed manner.

5.2 *The Mithraeum according to Beck*

Notably Beck (2006) has devoted much attention to analysing the visual and experiential meanings of Mithraic material culture as a whole, focusing strongly on the question in what manner initiates apprehended the Mithraeum (as opposed to "Mithraism"). He approaches this from various perspectives, some quite controversial,[59] but from a theoretical standpoint Beck's approach to the material culture is without a doubt the most stimulating, which is why I have chosen his study to form the backdrop for our discussion.[60] As I stated

---

56   Martin 2014: 21; Alvar 2008: 74–105; Beck 2006: 17–9; Clauss 2000: 62 describes this
       approach as "thumbing through a picture book."

57   Beck 2006: *passim* but see in particular chapter 7.

58   Beck 2006: 141.

59   His reliance on cognitivist approaches to locate religion physically and neurologically in
       the brain, for example, is bound to raise questions.

60   Cf. Martin 2014.

above, this does not mean I necessarily agree with Beck, or that I am suggesting that his interpretations are the most convincing. Once again it is not my aim to solve the issues involved – in this case the place of the Roman Sol in the cult of Mithras – for that is beyond the scope of this study. My aim is simply to explore the issue(s) and avenues of approach towards a greater understanding of the concepts and images involved.

Basic Roman cosmology (see below, pp. 178–189) provides the backbone for Beck's analysis of Mithraic space, in particular the Mithraeum.[61] In his view this "cave" was a model of the cosmos,[62] instantiating the northern hemisphere of the celestial sphere. "North" is defined by the axis around which the sphere rotates, the upper point of the axis being the northern pole of the celestial sphere, and the lower point the southern pole. The southern hemisphere is not incorporated in the Mithraeum but notionally extends below the floor of the shrine. The north-south axis is a line running straight down from the midpoint of the ceiling to the midpoint of the floor of the Mithraeum. The entrance into the Mithraeum thus marks the transition from "outside" the cosmic sphere to inside it, with the entrant walking, so to say, at the level of the celestial equator. The further details of this model – the benches along the side as the celestial equator *and* ecliptic, the position of the equinoxes and solstices, the seasons and the planets, the signs of the zodiac, etc., as defined in Beck's "blueprint" of an ideal Mithraeum – need not concern us here.

Important from our perspective is a more general point Beck stresses when he explores the manner in which initiates perceived or apprehended the Mithraeum. He contends that in their experience the Mithraeum was not a model or representation of the cosmos, but a real universe which the initiate apprehended as such, just as he experienced the rituals there not as enactments but as "already so", i.e. as "actual". Beck's arguments in support of this are too complex and multifaceted to be presented here, and are drawn from a wide variety of sources and disciplines, ranging from work done on other ancient mystery cults to modern neurology and even avian biology.[63] In the conclusion of his "blueprint" of the Mithraeum, however, he stresses an aspect of the Mithraic "experience" that is worth quoting in full:

---

61   Beck 2006: 61.

62   Beck 2006: 102–18.

63   Beck 2006: 119–52. Avian biology enters the discussion on pp. 149–50, where Beck analyses the cognitive implications of the Indigo Bunting's demonstrated ability to navigate by the stars.

> The problem is not so much the inability to enter other minds as the 'ineffability' of the experience. It is literally indescribable. This is not because it is or pretends to be something particularly grand or 'sacred'. It is simply that language cannot do the job. (...) Language is linear, sequential, left-brain, and so cannot narrate a quintessentially right-brain experience (viseo-spatial, simultaneous or non-temporal, holistic). (...) The experience simply cannot be captured in normal descriptive narrative. Metaphor is the best that normal language can do.[64]

By focussing on space and ritual in this manner, Beck's approach represents a major advance in that he, most importantly, allows the visual, material evidence to "speak" with its own voice. It is important to realize that this does not merely *allow* him to redefine Mithraic doctrine but *obliges* him to do so.[65] The evidence we have points to great care and much attention devoted to the physical and visual articulation of the Mithraeum. This is valuable information for the experiential, ineffable aspects of Mithraism but offers little information on possible narratives and doctrines. In fact, we have no hard evidence for the existence of extensive doctrines in Mithraism, which, as we have seen, leads some, including Beck, to argue that Mithraism was held together by a fairly loose set of general principles drawn from standard Roman cosmology.[66]

Beck defines some of these main principles early in his study and returns to them in his conclusion.[67] He begins with two fundamental sacred postulates or "axioms", namely (1.) that Deus Sol Invictus Mithras is the god of the cult and (2.) that there is "harmony of tension in opposition," a notion which Beck derives from Porphyry, *De antro* 29, and traces back ultimately to Heraclitus. These axioms are expressed in a wide range of motifs, such as ascent and descent or light and darkness, and operate in various domains, four of which Beck identifies specifically: 1. the myth or story of Mithras' deeds; 2. the cosmos; 3. earth; 4. the destiny of human souls. "Domains" can thus be spatial (2, 3), but need not be (1, 4). The axioms and motifs were conveyed by a symbol system that had two forms, one physical and one organisational. The physical symbol system is that of the Mithraeum and its art, with a particularly important role for the tauroctony, the definitive icon of the cult of Mithras.[68] The

---

64   Beck 2006: 150.
65   Beck 2006: chapter 4.
66   Beck 2006: 57–8.
67   Beck 2006: 5–8, 257–60.
68   Beck 2006: 7 presents the Mithraeum and the tauroctony as two separate and distinctive structures of the physical symbol system. I believe that this assumes too great a dichotomy between architecture and art. In my opinion neither is complete without the

seven grades of initiation constitute the organisational symbol system. In addition to this symbol system Beck argues that Mithraism communicated with the idiom of what he terms star talk, the "language" of the stars and planets that is "spoken" through their meaningful movements. In Beck's view, initiates apprehended all this in four modes: 1. through ritual; 2. through meaningful iconography; 3. verbally; 4. by leading their life in accordance with the ethical principles of Mithraism.

This is the framework of Mithraism as Beck perceives it, and which his book explores and tests. We do not have space here to elaborate on Beck's understanding of the cult of Mithras in greater detail, nor do we need to, given the very preliminary nature of our own analyses. Let me emphasize again that the value of Beck's work for our purposes does not reside in his conclusions, but in its theoretical and methodological basis. Notably his attention to semiotics, and his concern to establish *how* Mithraic cult means rather than focussing on *what* it means, resonate with some of the major theoretical concerns of this study and are much needed steps forward in Mithraic research.[69] In this context we should note again Beck's emphasis on the importance of ritual, visual, material, and in general experiential meanings in Mithraism that cannot be adequately conveyed with words.

5.3 *The Tauroctony*

Sol plays a role in a range of stock themes in Mithraism's rich iconography, including the most common and, presumably, most important "icon" of the cult, the tauroctony. In this scene, which depicts Mithras in the act of stabbing a bull, Sol and Luna are two of the indispensable figures. They occur on every tauroctony without exception.[70] Their role is minor, however, and their position, as we have seen, marginal. They are depicted on a much smaller scale than the main figures – Mithras, the bull, a snake, a dog, a scorpion, a raven,

---

other and in particular with three-dimensional tauroctony-statue groups it is impossible to establish clearly where the tauroctony ends and the Mithraeum begins. In fact, if – as seems likely – actual rays of light admitted under carefully controlled circumstances served to link Sol with Mithras in the manner of the extended ray on tauroctony reliefs, then the Mithraeum is integral to the tauroctony.

69   E.g., Beck 2006: 8.

70   This holds true for all two-dimensional tauroctonies (reliefs, frescos). Sculptural groups of Mithras slaying the bull were also popular, but in such cases adjacent figures such as Cautes and Cautopates, Luna, Sol, and the raven, either had to be dispensed with or were produced and placed separately. There is evidence that with sculptural groups of the tauroctony the actual depiction of Sol could be replaced by lighting effects which allowed beams of light to illuminate Mithras in appropriate fashion. Cf., e.g., the Mithraeum of the Baths of Mithras in Ostia (Pavolini 2006: 126–7).

and two torchbearers known as Cautes and Cautopates – either as small busts or driving their respective chariots (a *quadriga* of horses for Sol, and a *biga* of horses or oxen for Luna).[71] Sol is generally, but not always, radiate,[72] and nude but for a *chlamys*. His attribute is usually a whip, sometimes a globe, often nothing. In short, iconographically there is nothing that sets this Sol apart from the standard Sol-types of the Roman Empire.

The tauroctony depicts Mithras in the act of killing a bull with his dagger. A dog and a snake catch the blood from the wound while a scorpion grabs the testicles of the bull. It is normally understood to be a depiction of a major event in Mithraic mythology, but as we have no Mithraic texts, we do not know the narrative of the myth nor can we hope to grasp the precise doctrinal significance Mithraists may have attached to the tauroctony, types of information that the image itself cannot communicate in any detail. This may seem obvious, but it actually has significant implications. For it raises the question whether the tauroctony was meant to communicate Mithraic myth and/or doctrine at all and, if not, to what degree knowledge of that myth or doctrine was necessary for the Mithraic viewer to understand the image. I do not doubt that there was a Mithraic narrative of some sort in verbal form – Beck's domain 1 – but there is no hard evidence that the cult revolved around that myth or doctrine. On the contrary, in the context of Roman religion in general one would expect the ritual and experiential aspects of the cult to have been central.[73] The function of ritual is neither to teach nor to elucidate doctrine. Ritual is not about understanding but about mediation between the participants and the divine. In the cult of Mithras, according to Beck, that mediation took a specific form typical of initiation cults. Mithraic ritual allowed its initiates to experience that which it is impossible to describe. In Mithraism's case, so Beck believes, this is the descent and ascent of the soul through the seven spheres of heaven.[74]

Whether or not Beck is correct in the details does not really matter for the more general point, namely that ritual in cults such as Mithraism allows the initiates to *experience* the teachings of the cult in a manner that is ineffable, beyond words. The site of the ritual – in this case the Mithraeum – and its trappings play an integral role in the ritual, and that must particularly have been

---

71   *Quadriga* and *biga*: C2c.1 (Mithras behind Sol!), 4, 30, 37 (Sol on a *biga* of horses, Luna oxen), 48, 53 (only Sol in his chariot, Luna not in hers), 58, 99; busts: C2c.2–3, 5–7, 10–14, 16–22, 24–25, 27, 29, 33–34, 36, 38–41, 43–44, 46–47, 50, 52, 57, 59, 61, 63, 67, 69, 72, 757–6, 79–83, 87–94, 96–98, 100–101. Sometimes four horses or protomes of horses accompany the bust of Sol: C2c.15, 31, 68, 78.

72   For busts of Sol without rays cf., e.g., C2c.50, 53, 78.

73   Beard, North & Price 1998: 47–9; Beck 2006: 128–34.

74   Beck 2006: 41–4, 284 (index) under "soul, descent and ascent of".

the case with the tauroctony, prominent as it is in every Mithraeum. In line with the nature of the cult we must consider the tauroctony in the first place to be a ritual object contributing to the experience the initiate underwent. Under such circumstances any narrative content recedes to the background. Interpretation of the primary meanings of the tauroctony should then focus on its ritual roles rather than on the story behind the picture.

We can return, for a moment, to the crucifix of chapter 1 to illustrate my meaning more clearly.[75] Classrooms in Catholic schools normally have a crucifix on the wall, which plays an important role in establishing an identity for the classroom and the school as a whole. But both the event the crucifix depicts and all related doctrine are irrelevant as far as understanding its function and meaning in that classroom is concerned. Such crucifixes are not tools to disseminate Catholic doctrine, but identity markers used to create an atmosphere that in many respects cannot be clearly communicated with words. This does not mean that there is no doctrine behind the crucifix. Invariably, for example, the wound in Christ's side is depicted, from which both blood and water had gushed forth,[76] and this wound and the water that came out of it have been the subject of intense theological debates. But no one would turn to such debates to help explain the role of our classroom crucifixes, any more than they would consider the crucifix a useful source for understanding the wound and its theological meanings.

I am not suggesting that the tauroctony played the same role in the Mithraeum as the crucifix of our example in a classroom. Neither am I suggesting that there is an equally elaborate Mithraic doctrine behind the tauroctony frieze as there is a Christian one behind the crucifix. My point is simply that irrespective of the nature of Mithraic doctrine (elaborate and detailed or loosely grouped and general) it is important to realize that the primary function of the tauroctony was not didactic or doctrinal. Any lost Mithraic text(s) reflected in such images as the tauroctony provided non-essential narrative detail, that is, narrative that is integral to the image, but that does not need to be fully apprehended in order for one to understand the visual meanings of that image or to experience its full impact.

This lack of narrative purpose in the ostensibly narrative tauroctony is not exceptional in Roman art. There are numerous cases in the Roman world where we find an inscribed narrative that does not establish the visual meaning. In an ontological sense, the narrative is apparently an essential component of the

---

75   P. 52.
76   John 19, 34.

monument in these cases, but in semantic terms that monument is not, or not primarily, intended to convey the narrative.

5.4   *"Illegible" Narrative Imagery*

The column of Trajan is a prime example of an ostensibly narrative monument whose primary visual meanings are non-discursive. The column consists of an exceptionally long and minutely detailed sequential narrative in visual form which was and is, in any practical sense, illegible. The higher portions of the column cannot have been visible at all to the unaided eye of a Roman, and even if they were, the sheer exertion required to crane one's neck and walk around the column of Trajan 23 times to peruse the 190 m long frieze of increasingly minute figures is such that no artist in his right mind would have even considered communicating a narrative in this fashion – if that were the main message, or if apprehending that narrative in any detail were a prerequisite for understanding the monument.[77] Consequently we cannot maintain that the purpose of the column was to communicate the events depicted on its frieze.[78]

Paul Veyne sees no reason to be troubled by this indifference to the viewer and visibility. "Cette indifférence s'explique bien simplement: le décor de la colonne est une expression d'apparat impérial et non une information de propagande communiquée au spectateur."[79] To the extent that Veyne means that the column constructs an aura of Trajanic imperial power – further on Veyne

---

77   On this difficulty of "reading" the frieze of the column of Trajan, cf. Settis 1998: 202–5; Coulston 1990: 298; Huet 1996; Davies 1997: 44–5 (quoting a range of earlier studies) and 58–60; Veyne 2002; Hijmans 2015. It has been suggested that the higher scenes were still legible because the use of paint enhanced the visibility of the images. Others have said that the two libraries flanking the column of Trajan may have had balconies from which one had a good view of the upper scenes. In almost all cases, it has been taken for granted that the inscribed scenes were *meant* to be viewed and an answer is sought to the question *how* that was achieved (Veyne 2002: 5–6 n. 10 & 11, gives examples ranging from 1916 to 1996). But there is no satisfactory answer to that question. The proposed balconies, for example, would require the viewer either to constantly run up and down the stairs from one balcony to the other, or to give up on following the sequence of the narrative as it winds its way around the column. The only alternative is to postulate connected balconies on all four sides of the column area, which is highly unlikely. Rather than bend over backwards to come up with some way in which Romans could "read" the whole column, we should simply accept that this was, in any meaningful way, impossible, which means that it was unimportant (unless the artist was an idiot, which does not seem likely). If that conflicts with our notions of how to view (and produce) such a monument, then the Romans apparently did not share those notions – which makes it all the more interesting to answer the question why so much effort was expended on producing such a carefully detailed, unviewable visual narrative. On the column in general, see Settis 1988.

78   Davies 1997: 58–60 cogently rejects suggestions that the column's design was flawed.

79   Veyne 2002: 9.

uses the term *charisme* for the power of Augustan imagery[80] – this is perhaps an example of what we have termed "visual meanings". Veyne resolutely rejects the term "propaganda" for such art-works as Trajan's column, because it imbues images with meanings that are too precise and specific and misreads the nature of that which the imagery expressed. But Veyne underestimates the semantic power of Roman images in a Roman context. Like so many scholars, he treats coins, for instance, as self-contained vehicles of imagery, rather than as part of a more concerted program of events, ceremonies, and other ephemeral images; this leads him to downplay their semantic potential and impact too strongly.[81] As for images in general, Veyne assumes (without clear evidence) that most were only comprehensible to a privileged few.[82] This does not take into account the preponderance of image *types* for complex scenes which rendered individual depictions far more readily recognizable. Veyne is no doubt correct that few professors in the Sorbonne could say what sculpture adorns their university's main entrance, but his referent is irrelevant because underlying that sculpture is a different type of *force pragmatique*. A closer parallel to Roman visual literacy is perhaps the museum guard in Athens who, upon learning my three daughters' names, could describe with significant accuracy the iconography and attributes of each of their patron saints. The difference is not in the degree of knowledge, but in the awareness that in Greek Orthodox visual culture the correct and appropriate image for a given situation or context is quite narrowly defined.

As a consequence of this, Veyne exaggerates the difference between *expression* and *information* in the case of the column of Trajan. It, too, did not stand in isolation, but was part of a much broader range of initiatives, expressing its visual meanings in consort with them. That the sculptural detail is not central but supportive of those meanings certainly makes them more visually expressive rather than verbally informative, but that affects the manner, not the degree, in which they communicate with the viewer.

A completely different approach to the problem is that of Davies (1997). She proposes that the column of Trajan, being a funerary monument, was decorated with its spiral frieze to impose upon the viewer the necessity to walk around the monument in a manner reminiscent of the ritual circumambulation associated with tombs. Thus, in her reading the ritual experience of the monument subordinates the narrative, and the impossibility of reading the

---

80   Veyne 2002: 25.

81   Veyne 2002: 16–9. On this topic cf., e.g., Howgego 1995, 2005; Manders 2012, and for various case-studies, the contributions in Elkins & Krmnic 2014.

82   Veyne 2002: 14–6.

entire frieze is inconsequential; reading only a small part is enough to achieve the desired effect: the ritual of walking around the tomb a few times. At the same time, the presence of the frieze imbues the column with a narrative of which the broad outlines (war, victory) can be sensed, without being actually read, by anyone viewing the column. To those for whom it was important, the details of the narrative were available nearby, but in a different format; for it is safe to assume that a copy of Trajan's *Dacica*, the written account of his Dacian campaigns, was deposited in the adjacent Latin library.

Whether we agree with Veyne, Davies, or neither in their understanding of Trajan's column, need not concern us here. Our main point is clear. The column of Trajan is one of the clearest examples of "illegible" narrative imagery in the ancient world. It is not the only one,[83] nor were "illegible" narratives restricted to visual imagery. The content of many inscriptions was also essentially inaccessible because of the inscription's length, placement and/or letter size, and, of course, widespread illiteracy. One example, quite closely related to Trajan's column, is the *Res Gestae* of Augustus, inscribed on two bronze stelae at the entrance of his mausoleum. We do not know the size of these plaques, but the lettering must have been quite small, significantly reducing the inscriptions' legibility in practical terms.[84] The point is not that long inscriptions with tiny

---

83   Perhaps the most famous example is the Parthenon frieze (Boardman 1999: 306–7); cf. Veyne 2002: 10.

84   According to the inscription in Ankara (CIL III, p. 772), line 3, the *Res Gestae* were incised "in duabus pilis aheneis quae su[n]t Romae positae," i.e., on two pilasters (*stelai* in the Greek version of the inscription) of bronze set up in Rome. Suet. *Aug.* 101, 4 speaks of bronze *tabulae* (plaques) which were to be placed *ante mausoleum*. Buchner 1996: 167–8 has identified two rectangular foundations to either side of the entrance as the base for the bronze-plated pilasters, which he reconstructs as stelae that were 5 Roman feet (almost 1.50 m) wide. The *Res Gestae* has roughly 2600 words totaling over 15600 letters. To calculate how much space that would occupy on the two bronze stelae we can take the inscription on the base of the column of Trajan as an easily legible benchmark and starting point. Its letters are about 11.5 cm high and on average it has about 10 letters per metre horizontally, and 6 lines per metre vertically, i.e. 60 letters per square metre. Let us assume that the letters covered the stele over almost the full width (1.40 m) and that both sides of each stele were used for a total of four sides. We can then make the following calculation: 15600 ÷ 4 = 3900 letters per side; 14 letters per line × 6 lines per vertical metre = 84 letters per vertical metre. 3900 ÷ 84 = 46.4. This means that if each line was 1.40 m long, and the same letter size and proportion was used as on the later Trajanic inscription, the inscribed portion of each stele would have to be 46.4 metres high – an obvious impossibility. If we reduce the letters of the *Res Gestae* to one-fifth that height (i.e., to 2.3 cm) and maintain the same proportions, we arrive at 70 letters per line and 30 lines vertically, i.e., 2100 letters per vertical metre. Each inscription would then still be almost 2 m high on each stele, which means that, if one includes a base of about 0.7–1.0 m., the top lines would be a metre or more above the top of an adult viewer's head. Of course, we can

letters could not be read at all, but that they are not practical if reading them was the main purpose. These, too, are visual monuments of which the text is an integral part, but whose main message requires only that the viewer apprehend the *presence* of the text and its general nature, not its precise contents.[85]

5.5   *Sol and the Rhetoric of the Tauroctony*

Roman visual culture was accustomed, then, to monuments that could theoretically be read as a detailed text, but for which the presence of the text was more important than its precise content. Returning to the tauroctony, this means that there was no automatic assumption that the tauroctony reliefs were about the tauroctony. Indeed, as the primary function of the tauroctony cannot have been to narrate Mithraic myth, it is possible, even likely, then, that much of the *visual* meaning(s) of the tauroctony was instantiated independently of the (verbal) myth and doctrine associated with Mithras killing a bull. This means that it is to be expected that the meanings that Sol brings to the tauroctony are not, or at least not wholly, defined by the role of Sol – whatever it may have been – in the mythology and/or doctrine of the cult of Mithras.

As we have seen, the image type Sol-and-Luna used to "frame" the main image of the tauroctony was widely used in Roman art, and was established well before the first Roman Mithraic art emerged at the end of the first century AD. There can be no doubt that any visually literate person in the Empire would immediately recognize it as a common visual motif bringing its own specific meanings to the scene. In one significant respect, however, the Sol of the tauroctonies does differ from the normal Sol-and-Luna sign. Mithras is invariably depicted looking back over his shoulder at Sol, and often one of Sol's rays is extended all the way to Mithras. A raven is also depicted flying from Sol to Mithras. This link between Sol and Mithras is remarkable, because it

---

fiddle more with the parameters. Buchner proposes letters of 1.5 cm high for an inscribed surface, on each of the four sides, of 1.40 m high, but however one reconstructs it, restricting the inscription to two stelae flanking the entrance was a decision that significantly limited its legibility. On the mausoleum of Augustus, cf. LTUR s.v. Mausoleum Augusti; on the *Res Gestae*, cf. Güven 1998; on inscriptions as "monumental writing", cf. Woolf 1996.

85   Other good examples of inscriptions whose primary purpose cannot have been that they were read, include the *tabulae Iliacae* and the like with their minute lettering; cf. Habinek 2009: 124–36; on the *tabulae Iliacae* in general, cf. Squire 2011. Cf. also the inscriptions on the backs of the statues at Nemrud Dağ (CIMRM 32), the famous Epicurean inscription at Oinoanda (Chaniotis et al. 2009), the imperial decrees and letters inscribed on the "archive wall" of the northern *parodos* of the theatre at Aphrodisias (Kokkinia 2016), etc. A modern parallel of sorts could be the Vietnam Veterans Memorial in Washington. The 58,256 inscribed names are absolutely integral to the monument but one does not need to read them all to experience the monument's devastating impact. Cf. Graham 2013.

emphasizes the connection between the two, and brings out Sol's participation in the event depicted. In other words, Sol is depicted as part of the standard visual image type Sol-and-Luna, which almost by definition had a conventionalized, non-narrative role, and at the same time Sol is depicted connected to Mithras in a manner which no doubt referenced specific Mithraic concepts.

Sol, then, is one pole in two dualistic units. The one is the image-type Sol-and-Luna which evokes essential, timeless dualities of light and darkness, heat and cold, ascending and descending, male and female, and the like, all related to the cyclical or dualistic essence of eternity or totality. The other is defined by his connection with Mithras. In a shrine dedicated to the cult of Sol Invictus Mithras it is through this connection that the tauroctony as main image brings into focus the complexity as well as the contradictory nature of the identity of the cult's protagonist. Not only is Sol Invictus Mithras depicted as two separate figures, respectively Sol and Mithras, but the two are also portrayed as profoundly different in identity and nature from each other. Sol is essentially static, either fixed and immobile as bust, or engaged in his eternal, predictable cyclical motion as solar charioteer partnered with Luna. Mithras is the very opposite of this cyclical yet immutable, timeless image. He is in the act of killing the bull, the single culminating moment of a fierce struggle and in Mithraic mythology presumably a *moment suprême*. Thus, in connecting the eternal Sol with Mithras in his moment of victory, the extended ray, the raven, and the gaze of Mithras are in effect uniting two opposites, each in his/its own way *invictus*. This tension of connected opposites was clearly an element of its visual rhetoric, which one can extend to include the peripheral (Sol) and central (Mithras), Roman (Sol) and Persian (Mithras; note the chiastic contrast with the previous), small and large, sky and earth, light and the darkness of the Mithraic grotto, etc.

One essential characteristic of the tauroctony, then, is its rhetoric of tension/connection between opposites, not just in Sol and Mithras, but also in others, such as Cautes and Cautopates.[86] Being visual communication, the tauroctony naturally does not define or prescribe precisely which opposites one should think of, nor does it limit its communication to such juxtapositions. At the narrative level, the tauroctony depicts a significant event in Mithraic mythology, at which Mithras, in consort with the sun, kills a bull. It has also been argued that the tauroctony is a star chart and contributes to the definition of the Mithraeum as a whole as a model of the cosmos, thus representing

---

86   On Cautes and Cautopates as the "principal expression" of this theme or axiom, cf. Beck 2006: 6.

the theological foundation of the cult of Mithras.[87] In short, the tauroctony is a complex, polysemous image that narrates an event of central importance to Mithraism with a rhetoric of tension/connection between opposites in a form that explicitly symbolizes the cosmological foundations of the cult.

5.6   *Sol in Other Mithraic Scenes*

Sol also occurs in other roles in the rich Mithraic iconography. On elaborate tauroctony reliefs, he may appear as one of the seven planetary deities, either as bust or as full-length figure.[88] Often the seven planets are evoked simply by seven stars, sometimes seven altars.[89] He also appears in a number of other scenes of Mithraic myth. The most important of these is a banquet of Sol and Mithras together. Usually, this is depicted as a minor scene below a tauroctony, but it is sometimes depicted on the reverse of revolving tauroctony reliefs or independently on a relief on its own.[90] A number of other Mithraic scenes involving Sol occur with some frequency, usually on small panels to either side of a tauroctony. We find him as charioteer for Mithras who steps into the chariot behind him; or kneeling before Mithras, radiate crown removed, while Mithras holds an unidentified object over his head; or shaking hands with Mithras; or roasting meat over a burning altar together with Mithras.[91] In addition we have a few examples of other, less common scenes in which Sol was depicted,[92] and numerous depictions of Sol alone, found in Mithraea but not directly "mythological" or connected with a tauroctony.[93] Some of these may have been accompanied by images of Luna.

Leaving aside (to some degree) the images depicting Sol alone, most of these images are unique to the cult of Mithras, and strictly speaking they do not

---

87   For a concise summary of the tauroctony as star chart, see Beck 2006: 194–7, with numerous references to more detailed discussions on p. 194.

88   Sol, standing, with other planetary deities: C2c.29; bust: C2c.54, 67.

89   E.g., CIMRM 1818, fig. 471.

90   Small panels with dining scene: C2c.8, 10, 23, 29 (!), 34, 36, 38–39, 58, 63–65, 77, 82, 89; two-sided reliefs: C2c.1, 5, 29 (!); separate relief: C2c.28, 42. Note that on C2c.29 the dining scene is depicted twice.

91   Mithras stepping onto Sol's chariot: C2c.2, 8, 27, 29, 34, 39, 58, 63–66, 73, 77, 80, 82, 89; Sol kneeling before Mithras: C2c.29, 34, 39, 58, 63–64, 66, 77, 80, 89; Sol and Mithras shaking hands over an altar (or roasting meat): C2c.29, 58, 66, 73, 82.

92   Examples include Sol carrying a disc of some sort (C2c.58), Sol and bearded figure, *capite velato* (Saturn? C2c.88), and Sol and Phaethon (C2c.8).

93   Examples include C2c.9 (statue base), 26 (altar), 32, 45 (lead plaque, rays cut out), 49 (marble plaque, rays cut out), 51, 55 (altar with Cautopates; busts of Sol and Luna), 56 (votive altar, bust of Sol, rays cut out), 60 (votive altar, bust Sol), 62 (altar, Sol, rays cut out), 70 (altar; Mithras and Sol holding meat above burning altar), 71 (altar, full-length figure of Sol with whip and globe), 74 (Sol, raised right hand, billowing cloak), 84, 102.

adhere to the norms of the standard image type Sol, as he is depicted engaging in a range of activities. Nonetheless, in most respects Sol in these scenes is governed by the same conventions and practices as those of Sol outside the cult. In the first place, it is noteworthy that while Mithras is depicted in Persian attire, the depictions of Sol in all scenes of Mithraic myth always adhere to the established Graeco-Roman iconography.[94] This Roman attire of Sol is striking and, in my opinion, forms a major element of the rhetoric of tension of opposites in the tauroctony: the Roman Sol versus the Persian Mithras.

5.7 The "Romanness" of the Sol-Image in Mithraic Art

Irrespective of whether we follow Beck (2006: 5–6) or not in seeing this contrast between Mithras and Sol as a deliberate visualisation of one of his two main axioms of the cult of Mithras, "harmony of tension in opposition", we cannot escape the visual contrast that is consistently maintained in Mithraic art between Sol and Mithras. Just as the word Sol would introduce a Latin element if it were used in an otherwise Persian text – indeed it does so in the name Sol Invictus Mithras – so the images of Sol (and Luna) inject a Roman iconographic element into a self-styled "Persian" representation: the tauroctony. What meaning(s) this duality conveyed to Mithraists we do not know, but for our purposes the mere presence of the contrast reinforces the "Romanness" of the Sol-image itself and thereby its connotations of Rome, i.e. empire.[95]

Connoting Rome and the associations of empire and order that Rome evoked is not, of course, *the* meaning (or function) of Sol-and-Luna, either in the tauroctony or outside the Mithraic sphere. But it has emerged as one of the numerous elements that Sol (with or without Luna) can inject into the palette of meanings of an image or context in which he figures. And while the notion of "Romanness" is vague, it is still too denotative to capture the fluidity and potential breadth of that aspect of the Sol-image. Inherent in visual communication is that much of the "message" is achieved through the evoking of associations, and I use "Romanness" as an imperfect catchall for one specific group of associations Sol appears to have evoked in Mithraic art. In a verbally oriented culture such as our academic one, the fluidity of these evoked associations grates, and we are tempted to try and pin down the meaning(s) of

---

94 In some cases, Sol has removed his radiate crown and it is hanging on the wall behind him or lying on the ground next to him. Note that on these reliefs Luna is likewise depicted in her Graeco-Roman iconography, while Cautes and Cautopates on the contrary wear a Persian cap and clothes similar to Mithras's.

95 Given the name of the cult's protagonist – Sol Invictus Mithras – it is striking to see how little attention is paid to the roles and meanings of Sol or Sol-and-Luna in tauroctony scenes. Martin 2014: 44 mentions them only once in all his collected essays.

the image and its associated concepts more precisely. But in Roman society (and other societies) the visual played (and plays) a far more central role in the communication and construction of concepts. It did not supplement the verbal definition of these concepts, or evoke the words, or stand *in loco verborum* (see chapter one); the images themselves and the experiences associated with them instantiated the concepts. The "message" was itself visual and experiential and recipients of such messages visualized and experienced rather than verbalized them.

Beck (2006) emphasizes this within a broader framework in his analysis of the Mithraic experience, quoting among others Jonathan Z. Smith on the nascence of the "western world view" under the impetus of the Reformation, in which ritual is no longer "real", but has become a symbol, and not necessarily a symbol of reality.[96] In the world of Mithraism, according to Beck, there was no conception of such a gap between ritual and reality. "If we are to understand the Mithraeum or, more to the point, to understand the initiate's apprehension of his Mithraeum, we have to ... reseal the gap" that *we* think exists, because the Mithraists did not perceive it. Hence, for the Mithraic initiate in imperial Rome there was no symbolic relation between the Mithraeum and the universe it represented: "the Mithraeum *is* the universe; the authorized microcosm *is* the macrocosm" (Beck's emphasis).[97] This brings us back to that fundamental issue which I raised in chapter one: the Roman mode of viewing and the nature of visual meanings in the Roman world. Beck's exploration of a Mithraist's experience of Mithraism further illustrates how necessary it is not to take Roman viewing and visual experience for granted, as it was probably very different from ours. Indeed, the richness of the visual experience in Mithraea is further indication of the importance of that experiential aspect of the visual.[98]

If we project that importance of the experiential onto the figures of Sol and Luna in Mithraic art again, we must first of all take to heart the problem of symbolic meanings. To paraphrase Beck, Sol and Luna do not symbolize, they *are* Sol and Luna – not the Sol and Luna of "raw" reality, which we cannot apprehend, but in this case the Mithraic Sol and Luna apprehended through the Mithraic mental template internalized by the initiate.[99] It is not that they do not mean, nor that they do not mean symbolically, but that they do not symbolize verbal concepts. The visual meaning of Sol and Luna was by its very

---

96   Beck 2006: 112–3; cf. Martin 2014: 23–5.

97   Beck 2006: 113.

98   One can think in particular of the obvious importance of light effects, evident, for instance, in the practice to cut out Sol's rays so that they would literally shine if a lamp or torch were placed behind. See C2c.45, 49, 56, 62.

99   Beck 2006: chapter 7.

nature – that is by virtue of being visual – to a significant degree ineffable. To what degree depends on our interpretation of the specific image or image category, but for the purpose of this study it is enough to establish the importance of that ineffability.[100]

In the "Romanness" of Sol and Luna we find a possible example of this that is relatively straightforward. One could argue that the "harmony of tension in opposition" of Sol and Mithras in their unified duality of "Roman" (Sol) and "foreign" (Mithras) embodied a fundamental feature of the "Roman experience", of what it "meant" to be an inhabitant of the Roman Empire. Sol and Luna represent the "Roman" or "imperial" in each inhabitant, Mithras the "other" or "regional" which was also part of almost every inhabitant's identity, and Sol Mithras the successfully achieved harmony of these aspects seemingly at odds with each other. This is certainly not what the tauroctony or Mithraism as a whole is *meant* to symbolize in any discursive sense. But it is precisely such non-discursive meanings – or should we speak of effects? – of art that we are seeking to stress. To quote Tanner (2001: 260): "'Expressive symbolism', objectified as 'art'..., is the primary medium through which *affect* or *feeling* is culturally shaped and socially controlled ... thereby motivating commitment to certain social rules or systems of cultural representation" (my emphasis). Without expressly verbalizing it, the Mithraist may have intuitively felt recognition and acknowledgement of his own "duality" in the duality of Mithras and Sol. If that was the case, there can be little doubt that the cult of Mithras helped shape his attitudes towards that duality as well. For while Mithraic art acknowledges and indeed stresses the cultural differences between the Roman Sol and Persian Mithras, the resulting tension is resolved and, ultimately, harmonious unity is stressed.

One may counter that on certain side scenes Sol appears to pay homage or submit himself to Mithras, hardly the way Rome could or would have been depicted vis-à-vis non-Romans. I believe that this submission too could have been read at different levels, but that is not my point. I am not trying to establish what the tauroctony "meant", but am trying to circumscribe just one of the numerous ways in which it may have been felt or experienced by some Mithraists. As such, it is but one example of the many types of non-discursive meaning an image like the tauroctony could have embodied. For the present study, it suffices to stress the potential of an image such as the tauroctony to reflect and shape unarticulated feelings in the viewer – feelings of identity in our example, but by no means restricted to that.

---

100   Beck 2006: 150–2.

This is important, because just as with ritual we cannot assume that Roman Mithraists placed as little worth on the experiential aspects of Mithraic art as we have. To grasp the essence of the visual meanings of Mithraic art we must realize that if, as seems likely, Mithraists experienced ritual as "real" rather than "symbolic," it follows that the visual and architectural elements incorporated in the ritual – the Mithraeum and its art – partook of that unsymbolized "reality", which has implications well beyond the cult of Mithras for Roman art (and architecture) in general. The manner in which carefully orchestrated effects of light and darkness were apparently deployed in Mithraea illustrates the importance attached to enhancing the experience and effect of the rituals involved.[101] Comparable is the "miraculous" statue of Sol moving to kiss Sarapis in the Serapeum at Alexandria, discussed above. This is not the place to explore this experiential dimension of viewing further, but more research into Roman interaction with the visual is badly needed. Such research may be well served by recent work on embodiment, which is much more focussed on the non-discursiveness of meanings than, for instance, the semiotic approach taken in this study can be.[102]

5.8   Sol and "Star Talk"

As stated above, we did not discuss the possible connotations of "Romanness" of Sol and Luna in Mithraic art to argue that this was an important element of their meanings or even to establish that it was part of their meanings at all. The possibility that Sol and Luna carried connotations of Rome and Empire is still a hypothesis requiring further research. Far less hypothetical is a more obvious area of meaning that cannot be ignored here: the cosmological dimension of Sol (and Luna). Long an advocate for the importance of ancient astronomy as key to understanding the main concepts of Mithraism, Beck is well known for his interpretation of the tauroctony as a rendering of the main constellations from Taurus to Scorpio. This reading, and the astral nature of Mithraism in general, appears to me to be quite compelling,[103] although it is still often rejected.[104] Indeed, Beck (2006) interprets the Mithraeum as a whole as a model of the cosmos and the tauroctony, one of the focal points in the Mithraeum and, presumably, its rituals a very significant "statement" of the stars. This is where the notion of "star talk" becomes important, a concept that

---

101   E.g., C2c.24, 62; cf. C2a.12.
102   Joyce 2005. For examples of archaeological studies employing embodiment theory, cf. Hamilakis et al. 2001b; Bachand et al. 2003; Lesure 2005; Knapp & van Dommelen 2008; and contributions by Bohak, Gawlinski, Naerebout, and Várhelyi in Raja & Rüpke 2015.
103   Beck 2006: 31 argues this on statistical grounds.
104   Cf. Gordon 2007: 394–5; Prescendi 2006; Beck 2006: 30–9; Clauss 2000; Swerdlow 1991.

Beck has coined for the "language of the heavens",[105] that is the figurative language stars utter through their movements, either as speakers themselves or as tools of some higher power.

The stars "talk" through their actual motion, but in order to speak there must be a language, and where there is a language, it can be used by those who know it to speak. Beck argues that the tauroctony as a whole is an example of the Mithraists doing just that, namely using the idiom of star talk to convey the message of the triumph of Sol over Luna in an "ideal" month.[106] This "ideal" month is one in which the sun is in its most important house, Leo, while the other heavenly bodies – most notably the moon – are in an "ideal" or idealized position which in reality could never occur. The details of this notion as developed by Beck involve rather complex astronomical explanations with which we will not concern ourselves here, but in general terms, the sun's victory in the "ideal" month counterbalances the solar eclipses that actually could occur in a given "real" month. These "victories" of the moon over the sun, Beck postulates, were a cause for concern despite their predictability and transience. With the tauroctony the Mithraists use star talk to express an ideal response.

For our purposes the precise details of Beck's exegesis of the tauroctony as a text in star talk do not matter. What is important are the broader principles. Rather than as a straightforward illustration depicting the main event of Mithraic myth, now lost to us, Beck reads the tauroctony as a polysemous image with multiple levels and types of meaning, rooted in a non-verbal language. The small, marginal figures of Sol and Luna play a minor role in Beck's analysis.[107] They in effect duplicate Mithras (sun) and the bull (moon), but Beck stresses that this is not a problem, as it is typical of the way various strands of meaning are constructed, indeed must be constructed simultaneously in a visual "text".[108]

Within the star talk text the strand of meaning constructed by Sol and Luna in the upper corners is connected with Cautes and Cautopates in particular, according to Beck, in a sometimes supporting, more often chiastic juxtaposition.[109] The sun and Cautes refer to ascent (and all its connotations), the moon and Cautopates to descent. But their meanings extend well beyond this specific Mithraic one. In the language of Roman art Sol and Luna are also cosmic, as we have seen, signifying eternity and related concepts. In that sense,

---

105   On the concept of star talk and the notion of star talk as a language, see Beck 2006: 153–89. For examples of the application of "star talk" see Beck 2006: 190–239.

106   Beck 2006: 190–239, in particular 236.

107   Beck 2006: 197–8, 206–8, 214.

108   Cf. Beck 2006: 198.

109   Beck 2006: 206–8.

they serve in the tauroctony as markers of its cosmological dimension or meaning in general. Again, this is not their "primary" meaning, nor is it something
that can be conveyed through the Sol-Luna pair only. The Seasons, the four
Winds, the Dioscuri, and the Planetary deities can all contribute to or elaborate on aspects of this.

5.9   *Image, Narrative, and Meaning*

Beyond serving as a marker of cyclical cosmic eternity, we also find Sol and
Luna mediating a transition of sorts, in this case between two types of reading of the tauroctony, the "narrative" and the "cosmological". At the narrative
level, the tauroctony presents itself as a myth, a story with a sequence of events
of which Mithras killing a bull was apparently the climax, with other events
including Mithras carrying the dead bull to a cave, a festive dinner of Mithras
and Sol, etc. Sol, we have seen, plays an active role in a number of scenes in this
story, including the tauroctony itself, in which he sends forth a raven and a ray
of his light to Mithras. But the static, symbolic nature of the Sol-Luna pair on
the tauroctony is at the same time also a marked contrast to the dynamic event
being depicted and signifies another dimension of the depiction, cosmological
rather than narrative. In it, the role of Sol and Luna as counterparts to Cautes
and Cautopates was again modest, but not negligible, and just as the importance of the climactic narrative "event" of the tauroctony is clear, so too the
theological importance of the ideal cosmic event depicted is evident.

This, then, raises the question what role the Mithraic images, such as the
tauroctonies, played in Mithraism. Our usually unspoken assumption has
been that their purpose is to evoke or trigger the (verbal) narrative of Mithraic
myth and/or doctrine. While this is certainly possible, I have argued that in
the Roman world it was not uncommon to find visual monuments such as the
column of Trajan that were not meant to communicate a narrative despite the
fact that a significant portion of the monument was dedicated to the detailed
visualisation of that narrative. The story, in such cases, is apparently integral to
the message, but the message does not consist of the narration of the story. The
viewer does not have to read the story to understand the monument.

If we transpose this to Mithraic images such as the tauroctony, it means
that the presence of Mithraic myth/doctrine may be integral to the tauroctony without implying that communication of that myth/doctrine is the
tauroctony's purpose. The tauroctony may depict Mithras killing a bull without meaning to tell the story of Mithras killing the bull. This opens the way to
a whole range of different understandings of the tauroctony in which only the
essence, not the narrative of Mithraic myth/doctrine plays a role. I have toyed
with one such understanding, suggesting that the tauroctony may embody

the duality of identity – Roman and local – that was characteristic of so many inhabitants of the Roman world. While this may serve as an example of the (many) *types* of understandings the tauroctony could evoke in Mithraic viewers, I am certainly not suggesting that it was one of the main "meanings" of the tauroctony, or indeed that it was one of the intended meanings at all. I do think that this hypothesis, and others like it, offer promising approaches for further research of Mithraic art.

6   Preliminary Results

This brief examination of Mithraic art in this chapter has yielded a number of useful results. At the fundamental level of Roman viewing and visual practice, we have explored the seeming contradiction between content and medium in Mithraic art, suggesting that we can "read" Mithraic art in numerous different, more direct fashions where visual communication is at its strongest (and far more effective than the verbal) and have argued that the mere fact that a complex, seemingly extended narrative is inscribed upon a visual monument does not mean that the monument is necessarily meant to portray or disseminate that narrative. The crucifix uses what it depicts – the crucifixion of Christ – to engage in its own discourse, which is not, or at least not necessarily, about what it depicts This understanding of Roman visual signification reinforces the importance of differentiating between verbal meaning(s) of *Sol* and visual meanings of the image types Sol, or if one prefers, between modes of communication geared to system two (slow) thinking and those geared to system one (see p. 52 above).

But many of the issues we have tentatively broached here are far more complex and go to the heart of the problems of visual communication. The very notion of discursive images is controversial, with many theorists positing that images are essentially presentational and therefore completely non-discursive.[110] This is predicated in part on the notion that there is no visual syntax which allows for the coherent organization of images into a visual narrative in a predictable and widely understood fashion. Others see this differently, and the semantics and rhetoric of art have received much attention in recent decades.[111] There are two trends contributing to the greater respect

---

110   See Langer 1953 for the classic division between verbal discursive meanings and visual non discursive meanings. Cf. Mitchell 1992.

111   Barthes 1977; Bal & Bryson 1991; Kress & van Leeuwen 1996: 18; Rose 2001; Verstegen 2014; Groarke et al. 2017.

accorded to the communicative power of the visual. There is the increased recognition of the agency of verbal communication, i.e. the structuring role of language.[112] Concomitant with this is the increased attention for what can be loosely termed non-discursive signification. But, although a strict division between art as non-discursive and language as discursive is now widely debated, I do not think art historians have sufficiently recognized the degree to which Roman visual practice would appear to challenge that division. I say "would appear", because we still have so much to learn about Roman modes of visual signification, but as we have seen, Roman art was to an important degree a sophisticated and remarkably durable semantic system which deployed not only iconographies, but also style, material, location, and context to construct often complex meanings. The polysemous tauroctony is a case in point, but more in general we can state that Roman images did not signify in isolation and were not intended to have one precise meaning. That is why understanding that an expression of an image type Sol does not mean the same as the utterance of the Latin word *Sol* (which in turn is not synonymous with "Sun god"), is so important. It explains how the trajectories of evolving meanings of image types Sol can differ from those of *Sol* (the Latin word), allowing for situations to arise in which new or evolving visual meanings have an impact on their verbal counterparts. We will see an example of this when we discuss the *Carmen Saeculare* of Horace (chapter eight).

In this sense, Roman art was very much a language, with a vocabulary and syntax, capable of producing a wide array of readily comprehensible messages.[113] Both the syntactic dimension and the "vocabulary" require further research, however, far beyond what is offered here, and I do not raise these issues with the aim to further explore them. That would require a more thorough analysis of the fundamentals of Roman visual communication than I think is currently feasible, set against a stronger understanding of current visual theory than I can offer. What I do hope to achieve is an awareness of how important it is for us to examine our pre-understandings concerning the process(es) of viewing (Roman) art. I believe that this will not only enhance our understanding of Roman visual practice. The remarkably "linguistic" nature of that practice may also contribute to the further development of visual theory, given that in

---

112   This is a main concern of various schools of twentieth century philosophy. Besides the "linguistic turn" (Rorty 1967; White 1973; cf. Spiegel 2005, in particular the chapters by Eley and Stedman Jones), one can think of Gadamer's philosophical hermeneutics, of Foucault, Derrida, etc.

113   Cf. Liverani 2007; Beck 2006: 157–64; Hölscher 1987.

its structure Roman art differs so strongly from the modern and postmodern artistic practices which constitute some of the dominant referents today.

Despite these considerations and caveats, I feel that the preceding analyses and discussions nonetheless allow us to formulate a number of preliminary conclusions about the potential meanings of image types Sol.

1. **Sol**

    The Roman Sol has a continuous, uninterrupted presence among the gods of Rome from as early as we can trace Roman religion until the demise of paganism. He stands to regional sun gods as every Roman deity stands to regional counterparts, e.g., as Jupiter to Dolichenus.

    1.a **Sol Invictus Mithras**

    Sol outside Mithraism cannot be iconographically differentiated from Sol within Mithraism. This would not be remarkable – Sol has a place in the iconographies of numerous cults – were it not that Mithras elides a visually conspicuous differentiation from Sol under the verbally unified name Sol Invictus Mithras. This is an example of Mithraic harmony of tension in opposition, in which Mithras (foreign, deadly, in the moment, cave dweller), is united with the Roman, life-giving, eternal, sky-commanding Sol. That unity cannot be extended to Sol in other, non-Mithraic contexts. Hence, while Sol is of central importance to Mithras' identity, Mithras is not an essential part of Sol's identity in the Roman world.

2. **Aeternitas**

    Sol-and-Luna as pair can be interpreted as representation of (cosmic) eternity, in line with the meaning scholarship has long associated with them.[114]

3. **Liminality**

    The *aeternitas*-role of Sol-and-Luna is enhanced, both by their placement relative to other figures and by additional iconographic features, so that they also occupy an intermediate position between the two major potential readings or states of existence.

4. **Romanness**

    In name and iconography Sol (and Luna) are manifestly Roman elements that stand in clear contrast to the non-Roman. Consequently, they inject a fairly strong element of "Romanness" when they are associated with self-styled local cults.

---

114   Déonna 1948.

These are simply working hypotheses with various degrees of strength. The first two are not new and appear to be increasingly secure. The other two have yet to stand the test of repeated evaluation that all such working hypotheses must constantly undergo. New insights in the potential meanings of the image Sol can add to our understanding of his role and meanings in Mithraic art; further study of Mithraism promises also to shed further light on the potential meanings of the Sol-image in general.

This ends our general discussion of the many depictions of Sol, begun in the previous chapter. It has revealed how widespread and common the symbolic use of Sol was as an easily recognizable cosmic image of some sort. This is not to downplay his role as a deity or as mythological figure, but purely in experiential terms, a Roman was far more likely to see Sol depicted as a day of the week, or – together with Luna – as a symbol of "cosmic eternity", than as a figure of myth, let alone as an object of cult. This dominant cosmological context must have played an important role in the overall understanding Romans had of both Sol-the-image and Sol/sol-the-word. Therefore, we end this chapter with a closer look at a few of the basic principles of Roman cosmology in order to better understand this context and its implications.

7   Sol: The Planet

By the (late) Classical era, Greek astronomers and philosophers generally understood the cosmos in terms of the perfect shape (sphere) and movement (circular).[115] The basic form of their model for the universe had the earth at the centre, surrounded by eight spheres. The outer sphere was that of the fixed stars. The seven other spheres were for the planets. All spheres were thought to rotate around the earth from East to West every 24 hours, but in addition to this universal motion the seven planetary spheres were deemed also to rotate in the opposite direction, each at its own speed. In this way, Greek astronomers attempted to explain why the planets do not have a fixed spot in relation to the stars, but instead gradually travel through the constellations, from West to East. It takes the moon a month, the Sun a year, and Saturn 30 years to complete their courses through the constellations. The band of constellations through which the planets travel is the zodiac.[116]

Spherical forms and circular motions were the foundation for the explanation of stellar and planetary movements because circle and sphere were

---

115   Laffitte 2012: 195–6.
116   For a fuller but still concise description, cf. Beck 2006: 77–9.

deemed to be the perfect shapes of movement and form, and hence emblematic of the perfection of the cosmos. This cosmic perfection formed the basis for the tenet that the heavenly bodies were of a higher, i.e. divine, order. As the motion of the planets became more clearly documented, however, they began to form a serious problem for this notion of cosmic perfection and divinity, for the planets did not appear to adhere to the basic principle of circular motion They vary in brightness (correctly surmised to mean that they are not always equidistant to earth) and their eastward motion (through the constellations) is not uniform in speed, but varies and can even be retrograde. This erratic movement of the planets appeared to seriously undermine the fundamental assumption that heavenly motions were simple, circular, uniform, and regular.

It is not clear when this was first recognized as an important issue. If we follow Simplicius (as most scholars do), then it was none other than Plato himself who challenged his students to find a solution that explained planetary wanderings in terms of the postulated principles of heavenly motion, i.e. in terms of circular movements only. There is, however, no firm evidence for careful planetary observations in Greek astronomy prior to the second century BC and it has recently been argued that the whole issue did not arise until that time.[117] But irrespective of when the Greeks began to explore this issue in full detail, there were, by the Roman era, complex models that explained all those seemingly erratic planetary movements in terms of combined motions

---

117   The view that this goes back to Plato is based on Simp. *in Cael.* 488.3–24 (Eudem. fr. 148). Accepting this as an accurate reference by Simplicius to Eudemus is problematic. Baynes (2002) points out that this does not meet the bar set by his very sensible "Rule of Ancient Citations". He argues that there is no evidence Greek astronomers became aware of the stations and retrogradations of the planets until the second century BC and that the project of "saving the phenomena" (explaining the anomalous movements in terms of simple, universal principles), in his opinion, thus cannot be attributed with confidence to Plato's legacy (Baynes 2002: 165–6). His basic point is that Simplicius is writing with an agenda, and, because we cannot corroborate the accuracy with which he cites earlier sources, we need to find other evidence that Plato's successors (notably Aristotle and his circle) had the knowledge and concerns with regards to planetary motions that Simplicius ascribes to them. Baynes argues that there is no such evidence, and that what evidence we have actually implies the opposite, namely that Aristotle was not aware of planetary stations and retrogradations. A significant weakness in Baynes' argument is that Babylonian astronomers were already aware of the intricacies of planetary motions by the seventh century BC (Baynes 2002: 165), but that does not prove that the Greek philosophers of the fourth century BC shared the same knowledge, or, if they did, that they found it troubling. Thus, Baynes' basic point remains valid: we do not *know* that the issue of saving the phenomena arose in the latter part of the fourth century simply because Simplicius states this to be so over 800 years later. For the traditional position on "saving the Phenomena": Duhem 1982 [1908]; cf. McMullin 2013.

of circles within circles, supported with impressive calculations.[118] This culminated in the model proposed by Ptolemy in the second century AD that remained unchallenged until long after the Roman era.[119]

7.1 *The Religious Aspect*

The religious impact of these models has, I think, been underestimated.[120] In part at least, this is because few historians of ancient religion are well-versed in ancient astronomy – Roger Beck is a notable exception – and few historians of ancient astronomy are interested in the religious side of their field. We know a fair bit about Greek (and Roman) astronomy, but it is mostly studied (and admired) by historians of science, in particular because of the mathematical advances achieved in this period. As a result, the ancient astronomy of many modern studies is divested of its astrological and theological components.[121] Ancient astronomers would have found that division puzzling. For them, studying what the movement of the stars *meant* was the ultimate goal of astronomy.[122] This is clearly expressed by Ptolemy in his introduction to the *Almagest*. He considers astronomy to be a form of theoretical philosophy which he divides into three main branches:
- theology, being the philosophy that deals with the immutable that is beyond perception;
- mathematics, being the philosophy that deals with the immutable that is perceptible;
- physics, being the philosophy that deals with the changeable and perceptible.[123]

Stars and planets are perceptible, and wholly predictable in their movements and seeming changes (such as the waxing and waning of the moon), and in

---

118 Evans 1998: 297.
119 For a detailed explanation of the evolving models of planetary motion, see Evans 1998: 289–391.
120 This underestimation is probably in part caused by the wild claims made in "some of the wackier corners of cyberspace" (Gordon 2007: 334), and the vehemence with which some of the protagonists, such as David Ulansey, have defended their claims.
121 This is at the root of the line of reasoning followed by Cumont 1935, probably with an agenda (cf. Beck 2006: 34). A good, recent example is Evans 1998. Lehoux 2007: 35–9 neatly summarizes certain issues that make "some of the distinctions we might like to draw between astronomy and astrology, physics and superstition, or more generally between science and pseudo-science, anachronistic" (Lehoux 2007: 37). Cf. similar comments by Beck 2006: 33, who graphically describes historians of ancient astronomy as panning "for astronomical gold in a stream of astrological grit and gravel."
122 McMullin 2013.
123 Ptol. *Synt. Math.* 1, 4–5.

that sense immutable quantities. They differ materially from earthly matter, because on earth things change in an unpredictable manner. This material difference between earth on the one hand, and the planets and stars on the other, is fundamental. It was thought to manifest itself not only in the immutability of the cosmos, but also in its patterns of motion. On earth natural motion is linear and downwards as all matter is pulled towards earth. The natural motion of the stars and planets, however, was, as we have seen, deemed to be circular and consonant with the spherical shape of the cosmos; heavenly motions were also regular rather than unpredictable, uniform rather than varied, and simple rather than erratic. This qualitative difference in motion was associated with the notion that the heavenly bodies were of a different matter than the four earthly elements of water, earth, fire, and air. This fifth essence (from which our word quintessence) was variously interpreted by different schools of thought, but, however it was viewed, it was invariably understood to be of a higher order than matter on earth. It is in this sense of a "higher order" that the divinity of the cosmic bodies was generally understood.[124]

The urgency with which astronomers attempted to explain the planetary movements is thus clear. If the planetary movements were not perfect, the whole framework on which the understanding of the cosmos was built would be fatally undermined.[125] That framework was quite elegant, and went well beyond the limits of astronomy as we understand it. One need but think of the harmony of the spheres, which linked the discovery of the exact proportions governing music to the notion that the celestial spheres were similarly proportioned.[126] Broadly speaking, this notion of cosmic interconnectedness or *sympathia*, to give it its Stoic name, was in one form or another widely shared. No wonder, then, that astronomy was a wide-ranging branch of philosophy that was of major importance. For astronomy was concerned with that which is perceptible but also perfect in its immutability, and about which fixed knowledge was hence possible. That attainability of fixed knowledge made astronomy a member of the mathematical branch of theoretical philosophy, but because the objects of astronomical research – stars and planets, their

---

124　Wright 1995: 109–25. Cf., for example, Plut. *De Fac.* 922B. The stoics deemed the matter of heavenly bodies to be fire, rather than a fifth element, but divine nonetheless. Highly influential, in antiquity, was the notion that the human soul was of this divine substance, descending down from the stars to enter the (earthly) body at the beginning of its life, and ascending back to the stars upon the body's death. Beck 2006 sees this idea as one of the cornerstones of Mithraism. The most accessible ancient account is Cicero's *Somnium Scipionis*.

125　Wright 1995: 49; McMullin 2013.

126　Wright 1995: 45–7, 135–8; cf. Pl. *Rep.* 617b–c; Cic. *Somn.* 6, 18–9.

movements and other astronomical phenomena – were divine or divinely inspired, astronomical research logically extended into the realm of theology. Because heavenly bodies have an unmistakable influence on earth (one need but think of sunburn or *luna*cy, but also of more theoretical issues such as harmony), astronomy also logically extended to the realm of physics, the field of philosophy which dealt with earthly matters.

7.2   *A Divine Cosmos*

Of course, this is not to suggest that there was only one school of astronomy in antiquity, but we are not concerned with the philosophical debates and the details of their differences of opinion. What we find is that from Plato to Ptolemy and beyond the basic principle of a divine cosmos was mainstream science and understanding that cosmos was a matter of philosophy. Mathematics and physics had a role to play, but primarily a supporting one (except in materialist philosophies). Thus, Aristarchus of Samos (ca. 310–230 BC) probably did not arrive at his heliocentric hypothesis as a result of superior scholarship and mathematics but, as far as we can tell, by a much simpler logic. Having measured the sizes of the sun, earth, and the moon, he concluded that the sun's diameter was seven times greater than earth's diameter. This conclusion may have led him to hypothesize that the sun, rather than the smaller earth, should by rights be at the centre of the universe. While his hypothesis happened to be correct and was later mathematically corroborated by Seleucus of Seleucia (ca. 150 BC),[127] it did not gain many followers, because it was deemed to cause greater problems than it solved. For having the divine fire of the sun in the centre disturbed the logic of the order of the spheres, which was deemed to be from divine perfection (outer sphere) down sphere by sphere to the most mundane (earth, with its lesser elements). It is telling that Cleanthes, the successor of Zeno in the Stoa, wrote a treatise against Aristarchus in which one of his charges was impiety.[128]

The divinity of the planets was thus not a trifling matter. On the contrary, the whole idea of "saving the phenomena", whether Platonic or late Hellenistic

---

127   According to van der Waerden 1987: 527–9 this is how we should understand Plut. *Quaest. Plat.* 8 (see his translation on p. 528). Besides lacking sufficient accurate observations, van der Waerden argues that the trigonometrical methods required to prove Aristarchus' hypothesis were not developed until after Aristarchus' death, but would have been available to Seleucus.

128   Plut. *De Fac.* 923a; cf. Diog. *Laert.* 7, 174. There were other objections besides the religious ones, notably that the stars had to be unimaginably far away for the stellar parallax, caused by the earth revolving around the sun (and thus sometimes being closer, sometimes further from certain stars), to be immeasurable.

(*supra* n. 117), was driven in part by the desire to preserve the postulated "divinity" of the heavenly bodies. If the stars and planets were not of a higher order, then the apparently erratic movements of the planets would not have been an issue. But planetary motion did matter, and explaining their movements within the postulated framework of simple, uniform circular motion afforded the ancient astronomers deep satisfaction. It confirmed, so they felt, that divine order and stability that lay at the root of even seeming cosmic anomalies.

Modern historians of science have deplored the detrimental effect of this philosophical framework on the advances in Greek science, but that does not diminish its importance (although it has diminished the willingness to acknowledge its importance and explore its influence).[129] Indeed, from our perspective, that philosophical framework is the issue, not the mathematical and observational advances of Hellenistic scholars. Nor do we need to immerse ourselves in the debates about that framework among the intellectual elite. We should bear in mind that preserved treatises by ancient scholars at the cutting edge of ancient science are not representative of the broader social impact of the advances in astronomy of the late Hellenistic and early imperial era. It is that impact that is of interest to us, and that impact was very real. The significant advances in ancient astronomy in the Hellenistic era profoundly affected almost all levels of society.

No doubt the most obvious impact was the Julian calendar reform, which thoroughly redefined the Roman year and its months. The introduction of a stable system of time reckoning which would never again need periodic realignments, must have made a deep impression on the man in the street.[130] It transformed the abstract philosophical notion of cosmic stability and perfection into a fact of life experienced by all at the level of one of the most fundamental organizing principles of human existence: time. It is hard for us to imagine just how profound the impact must have been, but we get a taste of the enthusiasm spawned by the Hellenistic advances in astronomy from the public projects they engendered. The (predictive) achievements of astronomy were monumentalized and thus literally (and impressively) put on display in such *tours de force* of calculation and design as the Horologium of Andronicus in Athens or Augustus' immense sundial in the Campus Martius in Rome, to

---

129   One of the most influential twentieth-century historians of Greek astronomy, O. Neugebauer, was quite emphatic about the detrimental influence of philosophy; cf. e.g. Neugebauer 1975: 572. See also McMullin 2013. Gordon 2013 points out that this emphasis hinders our understanding of the role of cosmology in ancient religion.

130   Cf. Gee 2001: 520; Wolkenhauer 2011: 237–70.

name but two examples.[131] Small portable devices such as the Antikythera Mechanism attest to the wide diffusion of the practical effects of new astronomical discoveries.[132] What that meant in religious terms is hard to say, but it seems likely that the visible, and now apparently demonstrated harmony of perfect motion of *all* heavenly bodies will have enhanced the sense of the divine associated with the cosmos. True, McMullin is no doubt right that scholars like Ptolemy remained aware of the tension between the methodologies and results of mathematical and philosophical cosmology respectively, but that does not mean the average Roman necessarily had doubts. Beck points out that even early Christian authors did not easily abandon the notion of divine stars and planets.[133]

7.3   *The Julian Calendar Reforms and the Planetary Deities*

In a sense, then, I agree with Wallraff that there was an upswing in cosmological religion in the early Empire. This was not, however, a re- or digression from Hellenistic science, but rather the outcome of it. The Romans did not revert back to revering the planets as gods, for they (and the Greeks with them) had always accepted the fact that the stars and planets were of a higher order. Hellenistic astronomy and philosophy reinforced this understanding, and while the astronomers among them will have known that not all astronomical problems had been solved completely, and those schooled in philosophy were aware of the strong differences of opinion between the various major schools, these were at best concerns of a small elite.[134] Most Romans (including most scholars) must have felt confident that there was some form of divine inspiration behind the harmony of perfect shapes and motions that characterized the cosmos as they understood it.[135] That still left ample room for discussion and disagreement, about the nature of the divine for instance, not to mention the nature of the traditional gods and their cults. But those discussions need not concern us here. How the seven planetary deities were conceptualized did

---

131   On the *horologium* of Andronicus, better known as the Tower of the Winds in Athens, cf. Kienast 1993, 1997a, 1997b. On the sundial in the Campus Martius, see Rehak 2006. Displays of astronomical knowledge were widespread and took on many forms. Varro *Rust.* 3, 5, 9–17, for example, describes an aviary on the grounds of a villa which included revolving morning and evening stars and the like, and which some interpret as replete with cosmological symbolism; cf. Green 1997: 440–3; Sauron 1994.

132   Beck 2006: 124–5; Evans 2020.

133   Beck 2006: 164–70.

134   The stark differences between philosophical schools as understood by one member of the late Republican elite are clearly presented by Cicero in his *De Natura Deorum*.

135   Cf. The Stoic view as expressed by Cic. *ND* 2, 33–44. Cicero himself expresses a preference for the Stoic view in the final sentence of book 3 (*ND* 3, 95).

depend, of course, on where one stood in those discussions. But irrespective of where one stood, the planet Venus was not the ravishing goddess born from the foaming mix of sea and the semen of Kronos, wife of the lame Hephaestus, and lover of Ares. If the shift in the nomenclature of the planets discussed by Cumont (1935) and cited by Wallraff (pp. 186–7) reflects a shift in conceptualization, it is not that the planets came to be viewed more as gods, but rather that the gods came to be viewed more as cosmic powers, such as planets. The planetary deities represented cosmic, not mythical concepts of divinity.

The seven planets were the most anomalous heavenly bodies in terms of movement and – in the case of the sun and the moon – visibility and they had posed the greatest challenge to Hellenistic astronomers. It is thus fitting that they became in a sense emblematic of the perceived scholarly success in solving the riddles of their movement and proving cosmic perfection. Though hard to prove, it seems to me more than likely that this sense of achievement was one of the connotations the depiction of the seven planets evoked, certainly initially.

As we have seen, the planets were thought to be related to seven concentric spheres revolving around the earth.[136] This meant that the planets were not all the same distance from the earth. To determine their relative position, Hellenistic scholars referred to the rate with which each planet travelled through the zodiac, assuming that the faster the planet travelled, the closer it was to earth. On this basis, Saturn, with its 30-year trip through the zodiac, was identified as the planet farthest away, while the moon, which needs a mere month, was deemed to be closest. Next to Saturn was Jupiter (12 years) and then Mars (2 years), but the relative positions of Mercury, Venus, and the sun were less obvious as all three need about the same length of time – one year – to complete their circuit of the zodiac. Various options were proposed, but by the first century BC the one that prevailed placed the sun in fourth position, i.e. in the middle with three planets to either side, as befit what was obviously the brightest wandering star. In third position came Venus, followed by Mercury next to the moon.[137] The basic order was thus: Moon, Mercury, Venus, Sun, Mars, Jupiter, and Saturn.

A glance at the catalogue shows that this is not the order we find in Roman depictions of the planetary deities. Normally, they are depicted (from left to

---

136 On the complex revolutions each planet was thought to perform within its particular sphere, which served to explain the seemingly erratic movements of the planets, see Evans 1998: 289–443.

137 Beck 2006: 77–9; 1988: 4–7; Rüpke 1995: 456–60.

right) as Saturn, Sun, Moon, Mars, Mercury, Jupiter, and Venus.[138] This is an astrological order and a fundamental division of time into seven-day cycles (out of which our week emerged) running from Saturn for the first day to Venus for the last day of the cycle.[139] This order has its roots in Hellenistic astrological practice of assigning a planet to each of the 24 hours of a day, beginning with Saturn for the first hour of the first day and proceeding inwards with Jupiter for the second hour, Mars for the third, the Sun for the fourth, Venus for the fifth, Mercury for the sixth, the Moon for the seventh, and then Saturn for the eighth again. The 24th hour of the first day is thus governed by Mars, and the first hour of the second day by the Sun, which consequently also governs the eighth, fifteenth, and twenty-second hour of the second day, so that Mercury governs the 24th hour of the second day and the Moon the first hour of the third day, and so on. There being only seven planets, the week started anew on the eighth day.[140]

One of the earliest testimonies for the seven-day week in Rome is its inclusion on the *Fasti Sabini* of Augustan date, and it is well attested in Pompeii (cf. Cat.E3.1), making it safe to say that the seven-day week was well known in the Roman world no later than the beginning of the first century A D.[141] It thus seems safe to see the arrival of the seven-day week as a corollary of the Julian calendar reforms (though not as an official part of it). There is no proof for this, however, and considerable debate about the source of the Roman practice. Some stress Jewish influence and argue that the seven-day week arrived in the wake of the practice, purportedly adopted by Augustus and others of the Roman elite, to observe a day of rest every seventh day (on Saturn's day) in imitation of the Jews.[142] The extent to which this Jewish practice was adopted by non-Jews is difficult to establish. Certainly not as widely as Flavius Josephus would have us believe, with his sweeping claims.[143] Most of our sources simply document an awareness, not an adoption of the practice,[144] and Rüpke concludes that there

---

138   The only example of the astronomical order in the catalogue in K9.37, a copper amulet of unknown provenance, Roman imperial in date.

139   On the order of the days on Roman monuments, cf. Duval 1953.

140   Dio 37, 18, 1–2. On the seven-day week: Girardet 2006: 280–2; Rüpke 1995: 456–61, 587–92; Beck 1988: 8–9; Colson 1926.

141   Cf. Cat. H1oka.1; K5c.1. Also, from Pompeii are two inscriptions: CIL IV, 6779, 8863; cf. Petron. *Cen.* 30, 4. Some further examples in Schürer 1905: 25–9.

142   Wallraff 2001: 92–3; for the opposite view, cf. e.g., Gandz 1949: 216–7.

143   J. *Ap.* 2, 282. Wallraff 2001: 88, 90–1 also quotes Justin and Tertullian.

144   Wallraff 2001: 92 n. 11 refers to Suet. *Aug.* 76, 2; Ovid *Rem.* 219–220; Hor. *S.* 1, 9, 69–70; Aug. *Civ.* 6, 11 (quoting Seneca); Philo *V. Mos.* 2, 20–21. In n. 14 he also refers to Tac. *Hist.* 5, 4, 3 and Tib. 1, 3, 17–18. The latter does not refer to Saturn's day necessarily as a Sabbath, but more likely simply as a day to be careful; it is basic astrology – quite literally, cf. Valens

is no evidence that the Jewish example was widely followed.[145] Wallraff on the contrary argues forcefully for a two-stage introduction of the seven-day week, centred initially on the adoption of a Jewish-style rest day on Saturn's day in the latter part of the first century BC, followed a century or so later by the fully fledged planetary week.[146] The evidence does not support this notion of two stages. To be sure, Roman awareness of the Jewish Sabbath on Saturn's day can be dated to Augustus and presumably goes back earlier. But the evidence for a seven-day week goes back as far and from the outset is plausibly connected with planets and astrology, rather than Jewish-style Sabbath practices.[147] More importantly, in the Roman week Saturn is invariably the first day, not the seventh, as was the case for the Jews, nor the sixth, as it became for the Christians. As we have seen, there was a good astronomical reason for this, namely that Saturn was the furthest star and hence a "logical" point to begin counting (see above, on the astrological practice of assigning a planet to each hour). But it means that if the Romans first adopted the Jewish system of a Sabbath on the seventh day and then grafted onto that the planetary week, they either 1. did not choose Saturn for the Sabbath, or 2. changed the Sabbath from Saturday to Friday when they adopted the planetary week, or 3. celebrated their "Sabbath" as the *first* day of the week. There is no evidence for any of this, and none of these possibilities is at all likely.

The best interpretation of the evidence, then, is that the seven-day week had entered Rome by the late first century BC and should be understood initially as a concept connected with the astrological scholarship of the Hellenistic Greek world. There is nothing inherently religious about the seven-day week, nor was any day particularly sacred, as with the Jewish Sabbath or the Lord's day of the Christians.[148] It was, however, an exponent of the stable continuity represented

---

Anth. I,1 – that certain planets were beneficial, others not, and Saturn was generally not; cf. Beck 2007: 73–5; Girardet 2007: 280–1; Riley 1995: 27.

145   Rüpke 1995: 458.

146   Wallraff 2001: 90–3.

147   The evidence from Pompeii clearly indicates that the full sequence of deities was so firmly established by the mid first century AD that Wallraff's chronology is untenable. Frescoes from Pompeii (e.g. E3.1) in particular indicate this. They date to the mid first century AD (Long 1992: 498) and their context (similar medallions with the four seasons and the twelve months) is unambiguous. We should bear in mind that there is no reason to think that these oldest surviving examples happen to be also the very first instances in the Roman world.

148   Tertullian (*nat.* 1,13) suggests that in his day it was common for pagans to reserve one day a week to rest ("ex diebus ipsorum [sc. deorum planetarum] praelegistis, quo die lavacrum subtrahatis aut in vesperam differatis, aut otium et prandium curetis"), and links it to the Sabbath and Saturn's day ("non longe a Saturno et sabbatis vestris sumus"). Given the importance of Saturn in North Africa – there was an important shrine of Saturn

by the divine cosmos. In that sense it is very telling that our Roman depictions of the planets normally show them in the order of the week, rather than in astronomical order. The representation is not of the planets as they are, but of the planets as they act. By setting the seven planets in this order, they articulate the role of the heavenly bodies in the organization and measurement of basic rhythms of time on earth. Set the planets in a different order, and the message changes, and this was in fact the case on occasion within Mithraism.[149] Representing this specific role of the planets in this way asserts their fundamental relevance for earthly matters. That relevance is very real, of course. Nobody can deny the influence of the annual cosmic cycle, which manifests itself in such fundamental things as weather patterns and the regularly recurring seasons. It was an empirical reality that the planets affect earth, but earth does not affect the planets. This not only reasserts cosmic divinity but also articulates the mediating role of the heavenly bodies between earth and the unknowable and immutable divine beyond the spheres.

Depicting the planets in this manner evokes a specific aspect of the cosmos, namely its construction of time, and offers an accessible way to apprehend the passage of time with precision. In doing so, it also brings to the fore the structuring role of the cosmos. How much of our daily life the heavenly bodies structured was open to debate, and still is, as is quickly apparent if one forays into the literature on the topic today.[150] But the contrast between the never ending and never changing dance of the stars and the harsh clash of unstructured and unpredictable movement on earth was very real.

Between them, the two major cosmic symbolic "signs" in Roman art in which Sol partakes – that of Sol-and-Luna and that of the planetary gods – capture two of the major features (from an earthly perspective) of the heavens: divine stability of the stars (Sol-and-Luna) and their structuring prowess on earth (seven-day week). From the concept of Roma Aeterna, to the cosmic symbolism attached to the circus, we know how widely cosmic symbolism was deployed in the Roman Empire.[151] It may seem obvious, therefore, that this

---

overlooking Tertullian's Carthage at Djebel Bou Kournein – this reference to Saturn may not be as straightforward as it seems. In any case, Tertullian seems to be pushing his case a bit too hard, trying to pin the label 'Sabbath' on a series of practices that were much more informal. Though no day was specifically sacred, the days certainly differed in character. If we follow Valens *Anth.* 1, 1, Saturn and Mars were not beneficial planets, Jupiter, Venus, and Luna are beneficial planets, and Mercury and Sol are ambivalent, although Valens discusses them in predominantly positive terms. Cf. Beck 2007: 73–9.

149   For example, the order of the planets associated with the seven stages of initiation into the cult of Mithras; Beck 1988.

150   For contrasting views: Lilienfeld 2010; Foster & Roennenberg 2008.

151   Paschoud 1967; Lyle 1984; Feldherr 1995; Rehak 2007.

is the topic *par excellence* for us to pursue in this study. It is not. A glance at previous literature on this broad topic will show that it is dominated by literary sources. There is nothing wrong with that, but as I have argued in chapter one, visual signification differs fundamentally from the verbal. To understand how Romans structured their cosmos-inspired ideologies visually and spatially, we need to have just as sophisticated an understanding of the elements contributing to and participating in those visual discourses, as we do of the Latin and Greek used to construct the verbal ones. As this study shows, we have not yet come close to being as fluent visually as we are verbally, and the one thing we do not need, at this time, is a hubristic foray into the intricate visual discourses on cosmic imperium in the Roman Empire, in which we derive or intuit the meanings of every poorly understood visual component from verbal texts. This book will continue to focus on strengthening our understanding of image types Sol in Roman culture, and in that way contribute to making such forays more feasible in the future.

The Images: Catalogue and Discussion

1   Table of Contents

© KONINKLIJKE BRILL NV, LEIDEN, 2024 | DOI:10.1163/9789004442405_007

2   **Introduction**

This catalogue constitutes the core of this study. Its main purpose is to present the visual evidence pertaining to the basic image types for *S/sol*. It consists of a catalogue of images and a discussion of those images, either individually or as a group. Given the importance of the visual element of the evidence for this study, an attempt has been made to illustrate as many of the listed objects as possible.

The catalogue is fairly straightforward. The objects are organized according to type (statue, statuette, relief, lamp, engraved gemstone, etc.), and each group is subdivided according the iconographic themes or motifs (but with no attention to style or execution). The objects were initially listed per sub-group in chronological order per century, but this could not be sustained, and after ca. 2007, new entries were simply added at the end of the relevant category. Each entry begins with the current location of the object, followed by the provenance, material, date, a very brief description, and a restricted bibliography. On occasion, some brief comments follow.[1] Information about the date, provenance, material, and other specifics is usually based on what is reported in the most accessible secondary literature. If the relevant information is not immediately available I have listed it as "unknown", although no doubt in many cases a more extensive search of secondary literature, or consultation of museum archives and the like can reveal more accurate information. The dating of the objects in particular should be treated with caution, because especially in older literature there was a tendency to give a late date to depictions of Sol on the assumption that his cult belonged to the late imperial period. In the case of intaglios I have often provided my own dates after consultation with Marianne Maaskant-Kleibrink on the basis of seal impressions, photographs, or, in the case of intaglios in Athens and Berlin, direct inspection. Whenever scholars differ on the date of an object, I tend to view the earlier date as the *lectio difficilior* in a scholarly environment that has long persisted in treating Sol as a late Roman phenomenon, and hence as the date more likely to be correct.

Descriptions and references are generally limited and intended only to offer a starting point for scholars seeking further information about the object in question. I have not attempted to give measurements. These are often not readily available, and when they are, they naturally pertain to the object as a whole rather than to the depiction of Sol in particular. If the object is listed

---

1   To avoid confusion, the catalogue numbers are the same as the ones in my unpublished (but accessible) PhD thesis. This means that later additions to the catalogue were placed at the end of the relevant section, rather than in their correct chronological place.

in the LIMC s.v. Helios or Helios/Sol and/or in Matern's 2002 catalogue, this is invariably indicated in the references provided.

The catalogue's subdivisions are a little idiosyncratic, at times overly detailed (especially section H), and in format not entirely consistent. One can easily see that the catalogue is the oldest part of this book in that its format has remained unchanged the longest. I have considered completely reorganizing it and renumbering all entries, but decided against this. It would be a lot of work with the risk of many errors because it would not only entail the catalogue itself, but it would also oblige me to change all the references to the catalogue in my texts and notes. Thus while I agree that such catalogue numbers as H7bc.2 (a nice bust of Sol above a crescent) really are a bit over the top, I do not think that the benefit of a more streamlined catalogue outweighs the risks of such an overhaul, nor does it merit the amount of labour involved.

The catalogue is limited to depictions of Sol according to one of the three basic iconographic types, as well as Sol in mythological scenes. Depictions of Apollo as the sun, of regional solar deities, and other sun-related images are not included, except occasionally as *comparanda*. Only "Roman" images are included, being defined as images produced in a region under Roman rule at the time of production. In the case of unknown provenance, the Late Hellenistic period is generally taken as a *terminus post quem* for inclusion. The fifth century AD is the lower chronological limit, although a few early-medieval images of the sixth and seventh centuries AD have been included to illustrate the continued use of the image types sol.

The vast majority of the objects listed are in museums, others in private collections. A limited number of objects are known to us only through sale catalogues of auction houses or antiquities dealers. Including objects on the art market in a catalogue such as this can raise serious ethical problems. The iconographical information embodied by these objects is of valid academic interest, but their incorporation into a bona fide academic publication can give them unwarranted legitimacy and increase their monetary value. According to the AIA code of ethics, any archaeological object that cannot be documented in a public or private collection prior to December 31, 1970, should be considered an undocumented artifact which cannot be ethically sold or possessed. In accordance with this, I have deemed it ethically acceptable to include any objects on the art market which can be documented prior to that date. Furthermore, I have also considered it acceptable to list objects in my catalogue that have already been listed in the LIMC or in Matern (2002). That leaves a very small number of objects whose mention may raise ethical issues because they cannot be documented before 1971, but whose inclusion I felt was nevertheless important. In these cases, to counteract any benefit that may accrue from their inclusion in the catalogue, I have added an explicit note stating that under the AIA code of ethics it is unethical to own or sell these objects.

Following the catalogue proper, there are brief discussions which review any problems of date or identity of specific images in the main sections, and provides a summary of the types of images present, their date range and their geographical distribution. No analysis of images should be expected in these discussions. Chapter three contains the basic analysis of the range of potential meanings that can be associated with the various image groups identified here. The primary purpose of this study, it should be remembered, is to present and analyze the visual evidence for the Roman sun (god) at an overarching, lexical level, so that scholars of Roman religion can access and further analyze the information encoded and encapsulated in these images at the level of image groups. A small number of case studies in subsequent chapters offer a more in-depth analysis of specific images or image groups. There is no attempt to treat all aspects of the material in equal detail. The role of Sol in ancient magic, for example, is not discussed in this study.[2]

The level of analysis achieved here may therefore appear very modest, but that is unavoidable. Consider the challenges we face if we aspire to analyze, in depth, a group of synagogue floor mosaics of the fourth to sixth centuries AD which prominently depict a large image of Sol within a zodiac (D1a.2, 4–8). Other components of these floors include Old Testament scenes, Jewish religious objects, and the like. To establish what the role of Sol and the zodiac is in those synagogues is a major research topic, and inevitably well beyond the scope of this book and its author; I am not a specialist in late Roman synagogues. This book does give other, more qualified researchers useful information when they tackle that issue, in the form of a better understanding of the way the image types for Sol "worked". In the case of these floor mosaics, for example, the research and results presented here show it to be unlikely that any reference to a sun *god* is intended. The vast majority of the sol-images are not cultic, and refer to the sun without any implied reference to Sol as a god with temple and cult, anthropomorphism notwithstanding. The sun was and is not a matter of faith, but a matter of fact. What modern scholars often forget is that the Romans depicted that factual sun in the same anthropomorphic guise as the sun god. That does not explain why the sun was depicted in these floor mosaics, but it does show that the premise of, e.g., Emmanuel Friedheim (2009), that the images should be directly linked to the cult of Helios/Sol Invictus, is actually the least likely way to interpret Sol here. Image type, medium, context, location and placement all make it exceedingly unlikely that

---

2 On Sol in magic, cf. Fauth 1995.

we have here "an *interpretatio Iudaica* of Helios/Sol Invictus and his rite".[3] If we were really dealing with a shrine in which the believers had "syncretistically merged the supremacy of the Creator with that of Sol Invictus,"[4] it would be unprecedented to place the image of that syncretized Creator on the floor to be trampled underfoot. I do not know of any shrine or temple in antiquity (or any other period) in which the deity revered was depicted on the floor. Of course, Friedheim may disagree with me, but he will then have to explain why the image type sol in these mosaics must be numbered among the rather rare depictions of Sol (the god) rather than the far more common depictions of sol (the sun) with its various symbolic and cosmological meanings.

This example well illustrates the necessity for the approach taken here. It is based on the premise that understanding images such as the ones on these mosaic floors is not a straightforward process, and that Roman modes of viewing and apprehending them are still poorly understood. A significant part of the issue is the fact that every type of narrative around material culture entails its "translation" to verbal culture. This was as true in antiquity as it is today, which means that when we set out to interpret the image types for Sol in the Roman world, we first need to get a sense of what a Roman *saw*. We can gain that only by immersing ourselves in the images at a visual level. As we engage in this visual dialectic with images of Sol, patterns of usage emerge experientially, which structure and circumscribe the basic meanings of the visual "texts" in which we have immersed ourselves. Our next step is then to try to reconstruct how a Roman would verbalize those visual structures of meaning, before turning to the question how we would translate their verbalisations into our modern academic discourse. In other words, *pace* Friedheim, an image of Sol ≠ *sol* (the Latin word) ≠ sun (the English word), far less Sun god (as English speakers perceive a god to be).

Coming to grips with the various and diverse strands of the visual construction of meanings through the image types for Sol is thus a complex dialectical process in which patterns can emerge at various levels: meaningful variations and innovations in the manner of composing the image type (raised right hand of Sol for instance); impact of (and on) context (Sol with Luna, as attributes of Aeternitas for instance); repetition and variation of visual patterns (Sol and Luna riding in opposing directions on the Prometheus sarcophagus in Naples (C3a4.3), for instance), etc. Each recognized pattern generates its own research trajectory to be pursued, and its own feedback to the broader topic of the role of images of Sol in Roman visual communication. In terms of our understandings of the meanings encoded in images of Sol and their roles in Rome's visual

---

3   Friedheim 2009: 126.
4   Friedheim 2009: 125.

system of communication there is a great deal more that we can learn. This study is only a first step.

As far as the Roman practice of viewing and engaging with its visual culture is concerned, each exploration of an hypothesized "strand of meaning" can also be deemed a preliminary test of an hypothesized mode of viewing. That does not make this a theoretical study – I have no intention of dealing comprehensively with the thorny issue of Roman viewing – but it does mean that it approaches the analyses of these images with certain pre-understandings, some of which concern the Roman modes of viewing. In that sense the issue of Roman viewing is very much "at play". It is hence important to make these pre-understandings as visible as possible, and this has been a consideration in determining the organization of the catalogue and this chapter.

The decision to organize the catalogue by object rather than by image or theme makes it possible to subdivide the material into relatively objective, relevant categories. The type of object one is dealing with has bearing on the meaning of the image, but can be determined without taking account of the image. One cannot assign the same meaning to an image on a lamp as one does to a cult statue, even if the two are iconographically identical; the type of object is an important factor in defining the image. But one doesn't need to define the image in order to determine which object is a lamp and which a statue. In the subdivision of the main categories, definition of images was sometimes unavoidable, but here too I have attempted to keep the sub-categories as free of interpretation as possible.

Once the images were organized, the logical next step was (and is) to look at them more closely in the order in which they appear in the catalogue, and attempt to identify meaningful patterns. That is done in chapters three and four, but with no claim to comprehensiveness. Countless factors can contribute to the definition of more or less coherent image groups, and most of those groups will not be centred on Sol; magical imagery is a good example. Needless to say, there can be no point to an attempt to interpret sol's role in ancient magic without taking the full range of magical imagery into consideration. That is a major research project in itself, and far beyond the scope of this study. The in-depth study of any of the patterned image groups in which Sol participates invariably requires that the material be explored within a broader framework of Roman visual culture. As a consequence of all this, the discussions in chapter three and four, though wide-ranging, are by no means comprehensive. Subsequent chapters illustrate that by building on some of the understandings we arrive at in chapters three and four.

I have made every attempt to obtain the necessary permissions for publishing the photographs that illustrate this catalogue. Images are at the core of this study, and my ability to pursue my research and disseminate its results is wholly dependent upon my ability to access and disseminate the images I study. This should not be difficult. The images/objects themselves are inevitably in the public domain by virtue of their age, and in most cases museums hold these objects in trust for the public good. Many museums have indeed been very helpful, but some major museums have such prohibitive pricing policies for images that they impede rather than facilitate research such as mine to the point that it has become almost impossible to carry out, let alone to disseminate it in an academically justifiable manner. Fortunately, in cases where an image was essential, but unobtainable, I have been able to rely on my three daughters, Anna, Phoebe and Zoë Hijmans, to make accurate drawings based on images available in older publications or in the public domain. Given the above it will be clear that no image in this catalogue may be published, reused, or copied in any way without prior written consent of the copyright owner, unless the image is explicitly identified as being in the public domain.

3   Catalogue

   A. Free-Standing Sculpture, Life Size or Larger[5]
      A1. Full Statues
      A1a. Identification as Sol Certain or Probable
1.   Plate 11.2
      Rome, Palazzo Barberini.
      Rome?
      Marble.
      Mid 2nd c. AD (Antonine).
      Statue of Sol, standing, nude but for a *chlamys* covering his left shoulder, fastened with a fibula over the right shoulder. With his restored left hand, extended forward from the waste, he grasps a fold of his cloak, but it may be that he held a globe in this hand originally. In his lowered right hand he holds the upright staff of his whip up to his shoulder, letting it lean back lightly in the crook of his arm. The cord of the whip, fastened at the

---

5   This section lists life-size and colossal sculpture – statues as well as busts. Besides certain or near certain representations of Sol it includes a selection of sculptural works that do not adhere to the defined image types for Sol but are often identified (incorrectly) as Sol or as assimilations with Sol. Certain famous and less famous statues of Sol known only from written accounts have also been included.

top, hangs down, circling the staff twice. The head does not belong to the statue. It is a portrait of an unknown man, bearded, and dates to the reign of Hadrian.

Papini 2002.

Although the head is lost, the identity of the statue as Sol appears to me to be certain.

Image: drawing ©A. Hijmans.

2.   Plates 11.3, 23.1
      Château de la Mauvoisinière, Bouzillé, France, private collection (formerly Richelieu collection).
      Rome?
      Marble.
      Mid 2nd c. AD (Antonine).
      Statue of Sol, standing, nude but for a *chlamys* covering his left shoulder, fastened with a fibula over the right shoulder. He stretches his restored (?) left hand forward from the waste, but it may be that he held a globe in this hand originally. In his lowered right hand he holds the upright staff of his whip up to his shoulder, letting it lean back lightly in the crook of his arm. The cord of the whip, fastened at the top, hangs down, circling the staff twice. The head of a youth does not belong to this statue.
      Papini 2002: 85, fig. 3.
      Image: drawing by A. Hijmans; photograph after Papini loc. cit.

3.   Plate 23.2
      Utica, Museum?
      Henchir Tounga (Cincari).
      Marble.
      2nd c. AD.
      Sol standing, nude but for a *chlamys*, long wavy hair, right arm and right leg missing, left arm missing below elbow and left leg missing below the knee. The statue was found at the Septizodium of Cincari (Henchir Tounga). For another Septizodium that may have contained statues of planetary deities, cf: Janon 1973: 229–37 (Lambaesis). Lusnia (2004: 526, 533) assumes that the Severan Septizodium in Rome was also adorned, inter alia, with statues of the planetary deities.
      Picard 1961: 85–6, fig. 4; Longfellow 2011: 176–8; Duval & Lamare 2012: fig. 23.
      Image: photograph after Picard loc. cit., with permission.

4. Plate 23.3
    Stuttgart, Landesmuseum Württemberg RL 295.
    Ofterdingen, near Rottenburg.
    Sandstone.
    2nd–3rd c. AD.
    Male figure, nude but for a *chlamys*, right arm missing, whip in left hand;
    front part of head, and legs below the knees missing. Probably part of a
    relief rather than a freestanding statue with unfinished rear. Insufficient
    attributes for the identification as Sol to be certain.
    LIMC Helios/Sol 113; Espérandieu, Germanie, 624; Ubi Erat Lupa 7678.
    Image: Landesmuseum Württemberg, Ortlof Harl.

5. Plate 23.4
    Copenhagen, Ny Carlsberg Glyptotek 623.
    Rome, Esquiline, near Sette Sale.
    Aphrodisian (not Carrara) marble.
    Contested: third or fourth quarter 4th c. AD (Kiilerich & Torp 1994: 312
    n. 30); early 4th c. (Stirling 2005: 123–4); 2nd c. AD possible (Moltesen
    2000; Attanasio 2015).
    Sol standing, nude but for a *chlamys*, long curly hair, radiate nimbus
    with triangular rays sculpted in relief, right arm raised (broken above the
    elbow), left arm held an attribute but is broken below the elbow; one
    horse as a support. The reconstruction of this statue is dubious.
    LIMC Helios/Sol 460–1 (the head listed as a separate monument in the
    LIMC under 461 is in fact the head of this statue); Matern 2002: 114, 177,
    238 I42 (with incorrect inv. number); Castillo Ramirez 2014: 69; Attanasio
    2015.
    Image: Ny Carlsberg Glyptotek, Copenhagen; Ole Haupt.

6. Plate 24.1
    Istanbul, Archaeology Museum 5059.
    Silahtarağa.
    Marble.
    Late 4th c. AD (Kiilerich & Torp 1994: 314–6; Stirling 2005: 214, with good
    arguments for rejecting the date of AD 150–190 given by Chaisemartin &
    Örgen 1984).
    Sol standing, nude but for a *chlamys* over his shoulder, long, curly hair,
    both arms missing from the shoulder, legs missing below the knees.
    Behind the forehead, the cranium has been cut away horizontally, with

a hole in the center to fasten in place whatever addition was made separately for this part of the head. Not Apollo, as Chaisemartin & Örgen propose, but probably Helios/Sol (Kiilerich & Torp 1994: 314–6).
Chaisemartin & Örgen 1984: 13–5 pl. 4–6; Matern 2002: 115, 238 I41, fig. 53; Longfellow 2016.
Image: Arachne D-DAI-IST-78/112, W. Schiele; https://arachne.dainst.org/entity/2038846.

7.   Plate 24.2
Berlin, Staatliche Museen, Antikensammlung SK 177.
Probably Lyconopolis (Assiut), not Alexandria (Fendt 2009: 51).
Thasian marble.
Early Antonine (130–150).
Sol standing, nude but for a *chlamys*, outer fringe of long wavy hair provided support for a wreath or radiate crown, right arm lowered, broken below the elbow, *chlamys* draped over lower left arm (outstretched, but lower arm broken off); hand and patera are modern restorations. Fragmentary inscription on plinth: διὶ ἡλί[ῳ] / τουμα[... / αντι[... Found together with a female statue, also now in Berlin (SK159). The inscription on the base of the female statue (Arachne 204473) implies a connection with Sarapis (Fendt 2009: 51); perhaps we can identify them as Sol and Luna in a Sarapis temple.
Matern 2002: 15 n. 109, 98, 173, 229 G31; Papini 2002: 108; Fendt 2009.
Image: Arachne: photo Johannes Laurentius; arachne.dainst.org/entity/3413269.

8.   Plate 13.1
Alanya, Museum Prg.2014/199.
Perge, Nymphaeum F5.
Marble.
Late 2nd–early 3rd c. AD.
Statue of Sol, standing, radiate nimbus (edges broken), nude but for a *chlamys*, right hand raised, left hand and lower arm broken, but could have held a globe. Excavated in 2014.
Kara 2015: 17–9, fig. 15.
Image: drawing © Anna Hijmans.

A1b. Identification as Sol possible, but uncertain

1.   Plate 24.3
Rome, Museo Nazionale Etrusco di Villa Giulia 2670.

Città Castellana (Falerii Veteres).

Terracotta.

Late 4th–early 3rd c. BC.

Torso, nude, of a young, male figure with long wavy hair; right arm missing completely, left arm missing from the elbow. A groove in the head implies the statue once had a (metal?) crown of some sort, quite possibly radiate. The statue, which is part of a group of statues which adorned the roof of a temple, ends at the waist (finished, not broken) and presumably stood in a chariot.

Ensoli 1995: 400 (with references); Comella 1993.

Image: CMiBACT, Museo Nazionale Etrusco di Villa Giulia; Mauro Benedetti.

2. Plate 24.4

Raleigh, North Carolina Museum of Art 84.1.

Unknown.

Marble.

Late 2nd–early 3rd c. AD.

Statue of a youth, nude but for a *chlamys*, right arm stretched forward (lower arm broken off), left arm partially broken off, but traces remain of some object held in the hand and leant against the shoulder. On his head the youth wears/bears a strange, polos-like gear, the top of which is rough and unfinished. Along the edge of this gear are 12 holes. By his left leg is the protome of one horse as support. Lack of attributes make secure identification impossible; equally possible that this is one of the Dioscuri, cf. chapter 6.

Vermeule 1990; Hijmans 1994; Matern 2002: 112–3, 181, 238–9 I43; Papini 2002: 108.

Image: courtesy North Carolina Museum of Art.

A2. Full Statues, Lost (Selection)

A2a. Sol Alone, in Chariot

1. Rome, Palatine, Temple of Apollo.

No indication.

Augustan.

Propertius describes the temple, and states that there was a chariot with Sol on the roof: "In quo Solis erat supra fastigia currus;" (Prop. II,31,11; 2). Cf. the Carmen Saeculare of Horace (see chapter 8). On the temple of Apollo in general, see Zink 2008.

2. Rome, Circus Maximus, Temple of Sol.
   Unknown.
   Terminus ante quem: Tacitus refers to the temple as a *vetus aedes*, making a Republican date for the statue a reasonable possibility.
   The presence of a statue on the roof seems certain, but whether it was Sol in a *quadriga*, as Guarducci believes, is less clear. Cf. Tert Spect. 8,1. On the temple cf. Humphrey 1986: 62–3, 91–5; Marcattili 2009: 37–59. It is depicted on various coins. One of the clearest is a sestertius of Trajan, illustrating the Circus Maximus, with the temple of Sol and a minute radiate head on the roof (Guarducci 1983 (1959): 144 fig. 5; cf. BMCRE III: 180 nos. 853–5, pl. 32, 2–4), and coins of Caracalla (BMCRE V: 477–8 nos. 251–2, 259†; Gnecchi II: pl. 109,5).
   Guarducci (1983 (1959): 145–6) suggests that the phalera K9.10 was dedicated in this temple and copies a famous representation of Sol connected with it. The evidence for this is circumstantial and inconclusive.

3. Greece, Corinth, Lechaion-Gate.
   Gilded bronze.
   Terminus ante quem: ca. AD 150.
   ἐκ δὲ τῆς ἀγορᾶς ἐξιόντων τὴν ἐπὶ Λεχαίου προπύλαιά ἐστι καὶ ἐπ᾽ αὐτῶν ἅρματα ἐπίχρυσα, τὸ μὲν Φαέθοντα Ἡλίου παῖδα, τὸ δὲ Ἥλιον αὐτὸν φέρον.[6]
   Paus. II.3,2; LIMC Helios 123;
   Edwards 1994.
   For coins showing the Lechaion gate and (possibly) its *quadriga* of Sol cf. Papachatzis 1980: fig. 72 nos. 12.

   A2b. Sol Alone, Standing

1. Rome, Golden House, then near the Colosseum.
   Bronze.
   AD 64–68 or 69–79.
   Colossal bronze statue, originally of Nero, but transformed into Sol by Vespasian.
   LIMC Helios/Sol 446; Bergmann 1994; 1998: 190; Albertson 2001; Marlowe 2006.

---

6 As you leave the market-place along the Lechaion road, you come to an arch on which are two gilded chariots, one carrying Phaethon the son of Helios, the other Helios himself. (Translation: author).

2. Greece, Isthmia, Temple of Helios.
    Unknown.
    Late 1st to early 2nd c. AD (before Hadrian).
    Cult statue of Helios in the temple of Helios at Isthmia, restored or
    replaced by P. Licinius Priscus Iuventianus when he also restored the
    temple.
    LIMC Helios 338; Ritti 1981: no. 6; IG IV, 203. For the dating of Iuventianus'
    activities, cf. Camia 2002.

3. Syria, Emesa, Temple of Elagabal.
    Unknown.
    Before AD 274.
    Statue, presumably of Sol, found in the temple of Elagabal in Emesa.
    Verum illic [sc. in templo Heliogabali] eam formam numinis repperit,
    quam in bello sibi faventem vidit. Quare et illic templa fundavit donariis
    ingentibus positis et Romae Soli templum posuit maiore honorificentia
    consecratum (...).[7]
    HA Aurel. 25, 46. On the temple of Elagabal in Emesa: Young 2003; Lipinski
    2011.

4. Rome, Temple of Sol.
    Palmyra.
    Ca. AD 274/5.
    Cult statue of Sol, standing (?) in the temple of Sol built by Aurelian in
    Rome.
    ἐν τούτῳ καὶ τὸ τοῦ Ἡλίου δειμάμενος ἱερὸν μεγαλοπρεπῶς τοῖς ἀπὸ Παλμύρας
    ἐκόσμησεν ἀναθήμασιν, Ἡλίου τε καὶ Βήλου καθιδρύσας ἀγάλματα.[8]
    Zos. 1,61,2.

5. Romania, Mahmudia.
    No indication.
    317–324.
    Dei sancti solis / simulacrum consecr(atum) / die XIV kal(endas)
    decemb(res) / debet singulis annis / iusso sacro d[d(ominorum)]
    n[n(ostrorum)] / licini aug(usti) et licini caes(aris) / ture cereis et

---

7 And in fact there he found that form of divinity, as he had seen supporting him in battle. And
   therefore he built temples there [sc. Emesa], depositing great gifts, and in Rome for Sol he
   built a temple consecrated with even greater honorifics.

8 At this time he also built that magnificent temple of the sun, which he ornamented with all
   the sacred spoils that he brought from Palmyra; placing in it the statues of the sun and Belus.
   (Translation: author).

profu/sionibus eodem die / a praep(ositis) et vexillat(ionibus) / in cast(ris) salsoviensib(us) / agentib(us) exorari / val(erius) romulus v(ir) p(erfectissimus) dux / secutus iussionem / descri⟨p=b⟩sit.[9] Liebeschuetz 1979: 281 n. 4; ILS III: 8940.

6.   Romania, Corabia, Museum 300/2355.
       Sucidava.
       Marble.
       No indication.
       Left foot and base of a support of a statue on a base, inscribed ...]li inv(icto) pro s(alute)/...]rinus et iuli(anus) p(osuerunt); Berciu and Petrolescu restore the inscription as Deo Soli Invicto pro salute / eorum Marinus et Iulianus posuerunt.[10]
       Berciu & Petolescu 1976: 43–4 no. 33, pl. XXII.

       A2c. Sol and Luna
1.   Greece, Elis, Agora.
       Stone.
       Terminus ante quem: ca. AD 150.
       Sol radiate, Luna with crescent moon.
       ἑτέρωθι δὲ Ἡλίῳ πεποίηται καὶ Σελήνη λίθου τὰ ἀγάλματα, καὶ τῆς μὲν κέρατα ἐκ τῆς κεφαλῆς, τοῦ δὲ αἱ ἀκτῖνες ἀνέχουσιν.[11]
       Paus. 6.24,6; LIMC Helios 375.

2.   Greece, Thalamai (Laconia), Sanctuary of Ino-Pasiphae.
       Bronze.
       Terminus ante quem: ca. AD 150.
       χαλκᾶ δὲ ἕστηκεν ἀγάλματα ἐν ὑπαίθρῳ τοῦ ἱεροῦ, τῆς τε Πασιφάης καὶ Ἡλίου τὸ ἕτερον: αὐτὸ δὲ τὸ ἐν τῷ ναῷ σαφῶς μὲν οὐκ ἦν ἰδεῖν ὑπὸ στεφανωμάτων, χαλκοῦν δὲ καὶ τοῦτο εἶναι λέγουσι.[12]
       Paus. 3.26,1; LIMC Helios 376; cf. RE XVIII 4, 2070–1 s.v. Pasiphae.

---

9   The statue of the holy god Sol (which was) consecrated on the 18th November, by order of our lords Licinius Augustus and Licinius Caesar, must be decorated with incense, candles and libations, every year on the same day, by the commanders and military units garrisoned in the barracks of Salsova. Valerius Romulus, of perfectissimus rank, commander (dux), wrote this down, obeying order. (Translation: LSA 2604, U. Gehn).

10   Marinus and Iulianus erected this for the god Sol Invictus for their salvation. (Translation: author).

11   Elsewhere there are the statues of the sun and of the moon made of stone; horns project from the head of the one, rays surround the other's [head]. (Translation: author).

12   Bronze statues stand in the open-air part of the sanctuary, of Pasiphae and the other of Helios. But the one in the temple it was not possible to see very well, because of the

3. Baalbek/Heliopolis.
   Baalbek.
   Limestone.
   Undated.
   Latin inscription recording the erection of a gilded statue of Victory between two previously erected statues of Sol and Luna, in honour of the emperor: I(ovi) O(ptimo) M(aximo) H(eliopolitano) C(aius) Tittius / [ca]rmacus plumbarius qui sta/tuas solis et lunae consacravit locum / inter eas medium ad statuam victori/[ae] auro inluminatam pro sal(ute) imper(atoris) / [con]locandam consacrandam oc/[cupa]vit.[13]
   CIL III: 14386d; Hajjar 1977: 42–5 no. 24.

A2d. Sol and Planetary Deities

1. Lost.
   Italy, Vervò.
   No indication, but bases said to be satis magna.
   No indication.
   Six inscribed bases for statues of the planetary deities; base of Sol missing.
   Ianovitz 1972: 92–3; CIL V: 5051–6.

A2e. Sol and Other Gods

1. Greece, Acrocorinth, Temple of Aphrodite.
   No indication.
   Terminus ante quem: ca. AD 150.
   ἀνελθοῦσι δὲ ἐς τὸν Ἀκροκόρινθον ναός ἐστιν Ἀφροδίτης· ἀγάλματα δὲ αὐτή τε ὡπλισμένη καὶ Ἥλιος καὶ Ἔρως ἔχων τόξον.[14]
   Paus. 2.5.1; LIMC Helios 377.

A2f. Constantine Possibly in the Guise of Sol

1. Figures 7.1 and 7.4.
   Constantinople (lost).
   From Ilium.
   Bronze.

---

garlands, but they say it too is of bronze. (...) Pasiphae is another name for Selene, not that of a goddess native to Thalamai. (Translation author).

13 Gaius Tittius Carmacus [or Arraeus], a leadworker, who consecrated the statues of Sol and Luna, reserved the place between them for the placement and consecration of a gold-decorated statue of Victory in honour of Jupiter Optimus Maximus Heliopolitanus for the well-being of the emperor. (Translation: author).

14 Going up to the Acrocorinth there is a temple of Aphrodite; the statues are of her, armed, of Helios, and of Eros with bow.

AD 325–330.

Constantine, radiate, globe in left hand, spear in right, probably clothed, not nude.

Not Constantine/Sol but merely Constantine with imperial radiate crown.

LIMC Helios/Sol 448 (with references); Fowden 1991: 125–31; Tantillo 2003b.

2. Termessus (Pamphylia).

Bronze?

Ca. AD 324.

Equestrian statue of Constantine/Sol? Only the dedicatory inscription survives: Κωνσταντείνω Σεβ(αστῶ),/ Ἡλίω / Παντεπόπτη, / ὁ δῆμος.[15]

TAM 3(1): 45; Fowden 1991: 129 n. 95; Tantillo 2003a; LSA 615.

A3 Heads/Busts of Sol

1. Plate 25.1

Boston Museum of Fine Arts 95.68.

Egypt, Ptolemais Hermiou.

Carrara (!) marble.

150–100 BC (Stewart); 2nd c. AD; 19th c. AD.

Long wavy hair, hair band, no holes for rays. Same type as A3.6 below, but without the holes for rays. Identification as Sol not certain.

LIMC Helios 170; Bieber 1945; Hoffmann 1963: pl. 25; Comstock & Vermeule 1976: 81–2 no. 127; Stewart 1993: 333–4 (Alexander, not Sol).

Image: Photograph © 2019, Museum of Fine Arts, Boston.

2. Venice, Museo Archeologico Nazionale 245.

Egypt.

White Thasian marble.

1st c. BC–1st c. AD.

Long, wavy hair blown back against a nimbus with holes along its edge for metal rays. I concur with Smith (1988, 182 C8) that this is simply Sol, not Mithridates VI assimilated to Alexander-Sol (pace Krug 1969).

Krug 1969 with lit.; EA 2444/5; Beschi 1983; cf. Smith 1988: 182 C8; Bergmann 1998: 68; Matern 2002: 116, 172–3, 247 B18, fig. 69.

---

15   To Constantine Augustus, to the all-seeing Sun; the people (demos) [set this up]. (Translation: LSA 615, U. Dehmig).

3. Plate 5.3, 5.4
   Formerly Jena, Schott collection; current location unknown.
   Unknown.
   White marble.
   Late Hellenistic?
   Fairly short, wavy hair; seven holes for rays.
   EA 1465/6; Matern 2002: 171, 245 B9 fig. 66.
   Images: 3a after EA 1465 and 3b after EA 1466; in the public domain.

4. Plate 25.2
   Arles, Musée Départemental Arles Antique FAN.1992.140.
   Arles.
   Limestone.
   1st c. AD (Espérandieu).
   Head of Sol with wavy curls and seven holes for rays.
   Espérandieu III: 370 no. 2532; Rothé & Heijmans 2008: 764–5.
   Image: photograph courtesy Musée Départemental Arles Antique

5. Rome, Musei Capitolini 15725.
   Rome, Circus of Maxentius.
   Marble.
   Late 1st or early 2nd c. AD.
   Badly weathered male bust with short hair, unspecified number of holes
   for rays.
   Identification as Sol doubtful.
   Pisano Sartorio & Calza 1976: 194 pl. 22.12.

6. Plate 25.4, 25.5
   Rome, Musei Capitolini 732.
   From the Vatican, probably entering the Capitoline collection as a gift of
   Pius V in 1566.
   Greek marble.
   1st or 2nd c. AD.
   Head turned, long wavy hair, 7 holes for rays.
   LIMC Helios 169; Ensoli 1995: 401; Kiilerich 1993: 88–9; Stewart 1993: 333–
   4; Matern 2002: 178, 180, 246 B12.
   Image: photograph courtesy Arachne Mal80-11_15994; arachne.dainst
   .org/entity/1075824.

7.   Plate 25.3
     Vatican, Museo Gregoriano Profano 10747.
     Ostia, Mitreo degli Animali.
     Marble.
     Around AD 160.
     Long, wavy hair; seven holes for rays.
     LIMC Helios/Sol 12; EA 2257; Ostia II: 91 pl. 32,4; Vorster 2004: 113–4, 61
     Pl. 79.14. 80.4.
     Image: courtesy Vatican Museums.

8.   Plate 8.3
     Vatican, Museo Gregoriano Profano 10758.
     Ostia, Mitreo del Palazzo Imperiale.
     Italian marble.
     Second half 2nd c. AD.
     Long wavy hair; back of head damaged. According to Becatti (Ostia II),
     this head originally wore a Phrygian cap, in which case it is Mithras, not
     Sol (pace Letta in LIMC).
     LIMC Helios/Sol 13; Ostia II: 56, 92 pl. 32,1.2.
     Image: courtesy Vatican Museums.

9.   Plate 5.5, 5.6
     Bologna, Museo Civico Archeologico Inv. Rom. 1929.
     Anzio.
     Yellowish white, fine-grained marble.
     2nd c. AD.
     Bust of Sol with long wavy hair and five holes for metal rays.
     LIMC Helios 176; Brizzolara 1986: 56–7, fig. 17, pls. 37–8; Matern 2002: 171,
     245 B7.
     Images: 9 and 9a Courtesy of the Photo Archive, Bologna, Museo Civico
     Archeologico.

10. Plate 25.6
     Rome, Art Market.
     Unknown.
     White marble.
     2nd c. AD.
     Long wavy hair, 7 holes for rays, *chlamys*; 3 corn ears on *chlamys*.
     EA 811 (cf. remark concerning this bust at EA 1172); Matern 2002: 170, 180,
     246 B13; Christie's antiquities sale 5488, London October 7, 2010, lot 151.
     Image: EA 811 (photograph in the public domain).

11. Madrid, Prado 367.
     Unknown, probably Italy.
     White marble.
     2nd c. AD.
     Long wavy hair, roughly rendered; nimbus with holes along the edge for
     metal rays.
     EA 1614/15; Blanco 1957: 122–3 no. 367-E, pl. LXXXII; Matern 2002: 116, 173,
     246 B10; Schröder 2004: 149.

12. Plate 25.7, 25.8
     Athens, Agora Museum S 2355.
     Athens, Agora House C, room 7, well P.
     Marble.
     Mid 2nd c. AD, buried deliberately ca. AD 530 together with a bust of Nike
     and a portrait of a bearded man.
     Long wavy hair, 15 holes for metal rays.
     LIMC Helios 175; Shear 1971: 273–4; Frantz 1988: 37, 41, pl. 40b; Matern
     2002: 13 n. 96, 179, 245 B6.
     Images: 12 and 12a courtesy of the American School of Classical Studies
     at Athens.

13. Plate 25.9
     Private Collection.
     "Eastern Mediterranean".
     Marble.
     Second half 2nd c. AD.
     Bust of Sol, wavy hair, holes for rays (modern rays of wood), *chlamys*, on
     globe (bust and globe carved from one piece of marble).
     Matern 2002: 245 B5 fig. 64.
     Photograph courtesy Kallos Gallery, London.

14. Rome, formerly S. Clemente Mithraeum, now lost (stolen in 1991).
     Rome.
     Marble.
     2nd–3rd c. AD.
     Long wavy hair, five holes for rays.
     LIMC Helios/Sol 64; CIMRM 343; Matern 2002: 179, 246 B14.

15. Toulouse, Musée Saint Raymond.
     Unknown.
     Red marble.

Late 2nd–early 3rd c. AD.
Long wavy hair, six holes for metal rays.
Espérandieu, Recueil II: 1028; Matern 2002: 171, 247 B17.

16.   Plate 5.1, 5.2
        Fulda, Schloss Fasanerie (Adolphseck), formerly Rome, Pal. Lazzaroni.
        Unknown.
        Yellowish marble.
        2nd c. AD.
        "Wreath-coiffure", seven holes for metal rays, *chlamys*. The bust rests on
        four small horses pulling a chariot.
        LIMC Helios/Sol 141; EA 1172; Krug 1969: 192 no. 10; L'Orange 1947: 34 &
        fig. 15; Matern 2002: 58, 170, 245 B8 fig. 65; von den Hoff & Dobler 2005:
        48–9 no. 16.
        Images: 3.16 and 3.16a Arachne FA5257-08_131198; arachne.dainst.org/
        entity/60065.

17.   Plate 26.1, 26.2
        Sevilla, Casa de Pilatos, main patio.
        Rome?
        Marble.
        AD 140–170.
        Long wavy hair, upward turning head, heavenly gaze, triangular stone
        rays (restored, but remnants of the original rays still present).
        Gomez-Moreno & Pijoán 1912: 67–8 Fig. 29; Matern 2002: 171, 246–7 B15;
        Trunk & Witte 2002: 230–2 no. 47.
        Images: 17 and 17a courtesy of the Fundación Casa Ducal de Medinaceli.

18.   Vatican, Gardens.
        Unknown.
        White marble.
        Undated.
        Long wavy hair; holes for rays. The head does not belong to the torso in
        the photograph of EA.
        EA 776.

19.   Plate 27.1
        Private collection.
        Unknown.
        Marble.

Undated.
Long wavy hair, hanging down to the shoulders, *anastole*, marble trian-
gular rays. Significantly smaller than most of the busts gathered in this
section (17 cm); perhaps originally part of a (sarcophagus-)relief?
Matern 2002: 245 B4.
Image: photograph courtesy Christie's London.

20. Plate 26.5
Istanbul, Archaeology Museum 388.
Kyme.
Marble.
Undated.
Head of Sol, relatively short hair emerging from under a fillet in a fringe
of curls. Holes in the fillet for rays.
Stewart 1993: 426–7 fig. 137.
Images: 20 and 20a respectively Arachne D-DAI-IST-77-91_146357,04 and
D-DAI-IST-77-90_146357,06; arachne.dainst.org/entity/124354.

21. Plate 26.3
Malibu, Getty Museum 77.AA.3.
Unknown.
Marble.
1st–2nd c. AD.
Badly battered head of Sol, radiate (eleven holes for rays), long wavy hair,
anastole.
Grossman 2001: 57 no. 4.
Image: Digital image courtesy of the Getty Museum's Open Content
Program.

22. Plate 26.6
Grosseto, Museo Archeologico e d'Arte della Maremma
Roselle, Augusteum
Marble
1st–2nd c. AD
Bust of Sol, radiate (holes for rays), long wavy hair, *anastole*.
Romanò 2013: 174, 197.
Image: Wikimedia Commons, photo by Sailko, CC BY 3.0 https://com
mons.wikimedia.org/wiki/File:Helios,_50-150_dc_ca,_da_augusteo_di
_roselle.JPG.

23.   Sparta, Museum?
       Gytheum, Roman Theatre.
       Marble.
       AD 325–375.
       Badly damaged head of Sol with seven holes for rays immediately behind
       the curls of a wreath coiffure. The bust appears to portray an older per-
       son, and the curls of the wreath coiffure may in fact be a very worn and
       damaged wreath. I agree with Deligiannakis, however, that on balance
       and as preserved an identification of the bust as Helios/Sol is the most
       likely.
       Deligiannakis 2017.

24.   Coligny, Bodmer Foundation.
       Egypt.
       Marble.
       Head of Sol, long wavy hair and *anastole*; thirteen holes for rays.
       Kleiner 1957; LIMC Helios 174; Matern 2002: 244, B1.

25.   Varna, Museum.
       Histria.
       Marble.
       Probably Roman Imperial.
       Colossal head of Sol, damaged, with long wavy hair, *anastole*, and around
       fifteen holes for rays.
       Bordenache 1961: 194–196, fig. 9. Matern 2002: 244, B3.

       A3a. Sol and Luna
       Vacat (see B2a)

       A3b. Lost Busts
1.   Megalopolis, Agora, Enclosure of the Great Gods.
       Unknown.
       Terminus ante quem: ca. AD 150.
       Herm (?) of Sol Soter: κεῖται δὲ ἐντὸς τοῦ περιβόλου θεῶν τοσάδε ἄλλων
       ἀγάλματα τὸ τετράγωνον παρεχόμενα σχῆμα, Ἑρμῆς τε ἐπίκλησιν Ἀγήτωρ
       καὶ Ἀπόλλων καὶ Ἀθηνᾶ τε καὶ Ποσειδῶν, ἔτι δὲ Ἥλιος ἐπωνυμίαν ἔχων Σωτὴρ
       εἶναι …[16]

---

16   "Within the enclosure of the goddesses are the following images, which are all square in
     shape: Hermes with the added name Agetor, and Apollo and Athena and Helios also, with
     the eponym saviour (…)." (translation author).

Paus. VIII.31,7.

Papachatzis (1980: 315) suggests that Pausanias is describing herms.

B. Small Free-Standing Sculpture[17]

B1. Statuettes, Sol Standing Full-Figure

1. Plate 27.2

Paris, Bibliothèque Nationale de France, Cabinet des Médailles, 114.

Chalon-sur-Saône.

Bronze.

1st–2nd c. AD (Kaufmann-Heinimann).

Sol standing, nude but for a *chlamys*, radiate (seven rays), right hand raised, whip in left hand.

LIMC Helios/Sol 115; Reinach RépStat I 238,6; Babelon-Blanchet 1895: 114; Aghion 1993; Kaufmann-Heinimann 1998: 250; Matern 2002: 102–3, 161 n. 901, 162, 172, 236–7 I8, fig. 38.

The statuette was found 1763 together with a number of others, all dated to the 1st or 2nd c. AD.

Image: Sketch by Anna Hijmans, after Reinach.

2. Plate 9.1

Boston Museum of Fine Arts 1996.3.

Asia Minor (formerly in the collection of a Greek refugee family from Smyrna, living in England).

Bronze.

Antonine.

Sol, nude but for a *chlamys*, radiate (only one ray survives), right hand raised, his left hand held an object, lost, possibly a whip.

Unpublished, but see Matern 2002: 102, 107, 148, 231 I7, fig. 37 (= this statuette).

Reportedly found together with statuettes of Hygieia, Aesculapius, and Isis.

---

17 This section lists free-standing statuettes of Sol that must have stood on a fairly high support such as a shelf, a ledge or low wall, a table, a niche, or the like to engage the viewer. Most statuettes are quite small (ca. 0.10–0.20 m high), but a few are larger (ca. 0.40–0.60 m). The category is rather imprecise, because often the original function or usage of a "statuette" can no longer be determined. A number of objects gathered here may actually have been appliques, i.e. decorative elements of some larger object such as a vessel or container, a piece of furniture, a cart or chariot, and the like (cf. e.g. B1.5). This is particularly the case with heads or busts, although these can also have belonged to statuettes. Most statuettes of Sol are made of bronze, but the list also includes statuettes of gilded silver: B1.6; bronze and silver: B2.12, B2.13 marble: B1.21, B4b.1; steatite: B2.1; ter-racotta: B2.8; and red sandstone: B3.1.

Image: photograph © 2019, Boston Museum of Fine Arts; Frank B. Bemis Fund, William E. Nickerson Fund, Otis Norcross Fund and Helen B. Sweeny Fund.

3. Art Market.
Unknown.
Bronze.
2nd c. AD.
Upper part of a statuette (?) of Sol, wearing a short *chiton* and *chlamys*, right hand raised, globe in left hand, seven rays.
Matern 2002: 239 I48, fig 55. Sotheby's London auction July 13–14 1987, lot 443.

4. Art Market.
Unknown.
Bronze.
2nd c. AD.
Upper part of a statuette (?) of Sol, wearing a *chiton* and *chlamys*, right hand lost, globe in left hand, seven rays.
Matern 2002: 239 I49, fig. 58. Sotheby's London auction July 9–10, 1992, lot 482.

5. Foggia, Museum, Inv. 72 OR 50.
Ordona, Villa "Posta Crusta".
Bronze.
2nd–3rd c. AD.
Sol standing, nude but for a *chlamys*, radiate (seven rays), right hand raised, globe in left hand. The statuette ends just above the knees, from where there is a pin with which it was fastened onto some other object.
Ordona V: 31 no. 3; NotSc XXIX (1975): 528 fig. 36; Matern 2002: 109, 161 n. 899, 172, 236–7 I32.

6. Plate 28.1
Lyon, Musée et Théâtres romains inv. 93.1 104 20.
Lyon-Vaise.
Silver, gilded.
2nd–early 3rd c. AD. Found in depot 1 in section B below a house of the 3rd c. AD, used as a potter's workshop in the 4th c. AD. The relationship of deposits 1 and 2 (close together, but distinct) to these buildings is not clear, making it difficult to give a firm date of deposit (depot 2 contained

coins, giving a terminus post quem in the latter part of the 3rd c. AD; depot 1 contained no coins).

Statuette of Sol, radiate (five holes survive, rays lost), nude but for a *chlamys*, right arm raised, globe in left. Inscription: Num(ini) Aug(usti) rat(iarii) / Eburod(unenses) frat(res?).

Frei-Stobla & Luginbühl 2011: 204; AE 2003: 1176; Baratte 2003; Matern 2002: 103, 107, 148, 231 I5; Aubin 1999.

Image: photograph by Ursus, in the public domain under CC BY-SA 3.0 license.

7. Plate 9.2
   Paris, Louvre BR 1059.
   Montdidier.
   Bronze.
   2nd–3rd c. AD.
   Sol standing, nude but for a *chlamys*, radiate (seven rays of which one lost), right hand raised, left hand with attribute lost.
   LIMC Helios/Sol 115; F. Braemer, in: Altherr-Charon et al. 1979: 37 n. 64 pl. 13,15 (with references, date); Matern 2002: 103, 131 n. 702, 161, 232 I9, fig. 39; Vedder 2015: 37 n. 89.
   Image: © RMN-Grand Palais / Art Resource, NY; photo Hervé Lewandowski.

8. Plate 27.3
   Unknown.
   Acre (Israel).
   Bronze.
   2nd–3rd c. AD.
   Sol standing, nude, radiate (twelve rays), right hand raised, globe in left hand.
   LIMC Helios/Sol 117; Reinach RepStat III 30.7; Matern 2002: 110, 173 n. 953, 237 I35, fig. 51.
   Image: after Reinach, loc. cit.

9. Plate 28.2
   Geneva, Musées d'art et d'histoire Inv. 012482.
   Sainte-Colombe-les-Vienne (Rhône).
   Bronze.
   2nd–3rd c. AD.

Sol standing, nude but for a *chlamys*, radiate (seven rays), right hand raised, left hand holding a whip of which the rope hangs down by his hip.
LIMC Helios/Sol 116; Braemer 1963: 57 no. 224 pl. 20; Matern 2002: 109, 172, 236 I31, fig. 48.
Image: photograph © Musées d'art et d'histoire, Ville de Genève / Bettina Jacot-Descombes.

10.   Plate 28.3
London, British Museum 1865.0712.17.
Rhodes.
Bronze.
2nd–3rd c. AD.
Sol standing, nude but for a *chlamys*, radiate (5 rays of which one lost), right hand raised (? broken just above the elbow), attribute in left hand lost.
LIMC Helios/Sol 117; Walters 1899: 1015, pl. 28; Matern 2002: 102, 131 n. 702, 160, 173 n. 953, 231 I4, fig. 35.
Image: © Trustees of the British Museum.

11.   Plate 28.4
Sofia, Museum (could not be located in 2018).
Bulgaria.
Bronze.
2nd–3rd c. AD.
Sol standing, nude but for a *chlamys*, radiate (seven rays), globe in right hand, whip in left hand.
LIMC Helios/Sol 117; RA 1923: 26; Matern 2002: 90, 227 G14, fig. 25.
Found together with a statuette of Luna.
Image: after RA 1923, 26.

12.   Plate 29.1
Antakya, Hatay Museum 15346.
Antakya.
Bronze.
2nd–3rd c. AD.
Sol, radiate (5 rays), nude but for a *chlamys* (unfastened, hanging over left shoulder), right hand raised, remnants of a whip in his left hand.
Matern 2002: 103, 230 I1, fig. 31.
Image: courtesy Hatay museum.

13. Plate 27.4
   Rome, Museo Nazionale Romano.
   Unknown.
   Bronze.
   2nd–3rd c. AD.
   Sol standing, nude but for a *chlamys*, radiate (seven rays), right hand raised, object in his left hand is probably a whip.
   LIMC Helios/Sol 116; Reinach RépStat II, 110,4; Matern 2002: 109, 237 I34 fig. 50.
   Image: after Reinach.

14. Plate 12.3
   Munich, Antikensammlung AS 3146.
   Unknown.
   Bronze.
   2nd–3rd c. AD.
   Statuette of Sol, radiate (seven rays), nude but for a *chlamys*, right arm raised, globe in left hand.
   Matern 2002: 103, 231 I6, fig. 36.
   Image: © Staatliche Antikensammlungen und Glyptothek, Munich; photograph Renate Kühling.

15. Plate 9.3
   Paris, Bibliothèque Nationale de France, Cabinet des Médailles 113.
   Unknown.
   Bronze.
   2nd–3rd c. AD.
   Sol standing, nude but for a *chlamys*, radiate (seven rays), right hand raised, attribute in left hand (whip?) lost.
   LIMC Helios/Sol 115; Reinach RépStat I, 238,8; Babelon-Blanchet 1895: 113; Matern 2002: 109, 161 n. 899, 172, 237 I33.
   Image: photograph © Bibliothèque National de France, Cabinet des Médailles et Antiques; 15a drawing by A. Hijmans.

16. Plate 29.2
   Paris, Bibliothèque Nationale de France, Cabinet des Médailles 115.
   Unknown.
   Bronze.
   2nd–3rd c. AD.

Sol standing, nude but for a long *chlamys*, radiate (six? rays), right hand raised, holding whip, left hand missing.
Babelon-Blanchet 1895: 53, no. 115; Matern 2002: 90–1, 226 G11.
Image: sketch after Babelon-Blanchet loc. cit.

17.   Unknown, formerly Forman collection.
       Unknown.
       Bronze.
       2nd–3rd c. AD.
       Sol standing, nude but for a *chlamys*, radiate (five rays), right hand raised, left hand outstretched, palm upwards, attribute lost. The right hand may have held some iron or metal object, the remains of which are oxidized against the palm.
       LIMC Helios/Sol 115; Smith 1899: 17 no. 104; Reinach, RépStat III 30,1; Bergmann 1998: 75–6 pl. 13.3; Matern 2002: 104–5, 232 I10, fig. 41; Vasilieva 2004: 152.

18.   London, Art Market.
       Unknown.
       Bronze.
       2nd–3rd c. AD.
       Statuette of Sol, radiate (seven rays), nude but for a *chlamys*, right arm raised.
       Matern 2002: 104, 172, 230–1 I3, fig. 32.

19.   Milan, Museo Civico Archeologico A 994.05.01.
       Switzerland, art market.
       Bronze.
       Undated.
       Statuette of Sol, radiate (five rays), nude, right arm raised, whip in left hand leaning back against his shoulder. The fact that the statue depicts Sol completely nude is problematic.
       Marensi 2004.

20.   Trier, Rheinisches Landesmuseum 91, 74.
       Trier.
       Bronze.
       Undated.
       Sol stands, radiate, globe in lowered right hand, dressed in a long *chiton*.
       Matern 2002: 91, 227 G15.

21. Plate 29.3
    Leiden, National Museum of Antiquities 1884.
    Laodicea.
    Marble.
    Undated.
    Statuette of Sol, radiate nimbus, dressed in *chiton* and *chlamys*, sceptre or whip in left hand, right arm largely missing.
    Matern 2002: 87 n. 519, 98, 177 n. 772, 229 G28, fig. 27.
    Image: © National Museum of Antiquities, Leiden; photograph R.J. Looman.

22. Marseille, Musée d'Archéologie Méditerranéenne 2249.
    Egypt.
    Bronze.
    Undated.
    Statuette of Sol, nimbate (? Froehner speaks of a "disque solaire"), nude but for a *chlamys*, right (? Froehner says left) hand raised. Prof. G. Tallet (personal communication) informs me that the statuette is not radiate. Probably a Dioscure rather than Sol.
    Froehner 1897: 151–2 no. 749.

23. Deva, Museum.
    Sarmizegetusa, Mithraeum.
    Marble.
    Late 2nd c. AD.
    Upper part of a statuette of Sol, radiate (six rays); the ends of the rays are connected with a "nimbus".
    LIMC Helios/Sol 30; CIMRM II, 2035, fig. 544.

24. Plate 29.4
    Hannover, Kestner Museum 1995.1.
    Lyon?
    Bronze.
    Antonine.
    (Formerly B4.2) Sol, nude (no *chlamys*), right hand raised, left hand outstretched, palm upward to support an object (globe?) now lost, no rays nor trace of rays. Inscription: M(arcus) Aurel(ius) Sila actar(ius) ped(itum) / sing(ularium) pro se et suos (sic) v(otum) l(ibens) s(olvit).
    Wiegels 2013; Matern 2002: 230 I2 (confuses this statue with the next); cf. B1.25, and the comments there.
    Image: photograph N. Bettermann, in the public domain under CC BY-SA 4/0 license.

25. Lost.
    Apulum.
    Bronze.
    Antonine.
    Statuette of Sol with a separate radiate crown with five rays; initially com-
    plete, then broken off its base at the ankles, arms also broken off, then
    lost completely (according to Wiegels 2013: 3–4). Inscription: M(arcus)
    Aurel(ius) Sila a/ctar(ius) eq(uitum) / sing(ularium) pro se et suos (sic)
    v(otum) l(ibens) s(olvit).
    This statuette cannot be the same as B1.24 for a number of reasons: 1. The
    inscriptions, though similar, differ in lettertype (Hannover: incised,
    Apulum: dotted), number of lines (Hannover: two, Apulum: three), and
    content (Hannover: actarius peditum. Apulum: Actarius equitum). 2. Size
    of the statuette (Hannover: 0.50m., Apulum: 0.30m.); 3. Reported damage
    to the statuette from Apulum, not visible in the statuette in Hannover.
    Furthermore, the statuette in Hannover, acquired at auction from a pri-
    vate collection, was reportedly found near Lyon. Taken together, this indi-
    cates that two separate dedications by Aurelius Sila have been found, one
    when he was an actarius peditum in Lyon, and one (now lost) when he
    was actarius equitum in Apulum. It seems reasonable to think he made
    both dedications to the same deity, and in view of the (separate) radi-
    ate crown associated with the lost statuette from Apulum, the identity of
    the statuette from Hannover as Sol seems assured, even though, strictly
    speaking, not enough attributes survive to conclude this beyond doubt,
    in particular given the unusual absence of a *chlamys*.
    Wiegels 2013: 3–4; Stauner 2004: 383 no. 330; AE 1962, 208.

26. Archaeological museum of San Pedro in Saldaña (Palencia, Castile and
    León).
    Roman villa La Olmeda.
    Bronze.
    2nd–3rd c. AD.
    Statuette of Sol, radiate (seven rays), nude but for a *chlamys*, right hand
    raised, whip in left hand leaning back against his shoulder. Feet missing
    Abásolo 2013.

        B2. Busts, with or without *Chlamys*

1. Plate 30.1
    Boston, Museum of Fine Arts 2004.2233.
    Possibly from Egypt.

Steatite.
1st c. BC–2nd c. AD.
Bust of Sol, radiate, *chlamys*.
Unpublished.
Image: photo © 2019 Museum of Fine Arts, Boston.

2. Plate 1.1
Paris, Louvre AO 7530.
Lebanon (Tripoli).
Bronze.
1st c. AD.
Bust of Sol, *chlamys*, long wavy hair, radiate (seven rays).
Jucker 1961: 184 fig. 83; Dussaud 1903: 379 fig. 18; Matern 2002: 249 B37;
Fani 2016: 213 no. 2.
Image: © Musée du Louvre, Dist. RMN-Grand Palais / Thierry Ollivier /
Art Resource, NY.

3. Lost.
Tripoli (Lebanon).
Bronze.
1st c. AD.
Bust of Sol, radiate, (seven rays).
Matern 2002: 250 B40; Jidejian 1980: fig. 38.

4. Private Collection.
Unknown.
Bronze.
1st–2nd c. AD.
Bust of Sol, radiate (nine rays), *chlamys*.
Vasilieva 2004: 135–138 (with fig.).

5. Plate 30.2
Paris, Louvre, ex Collection de Clercq.
Tortosa.
Bronze.
2nd–3rd c. AD.
Bust of Sol, *chlamys*, radiate (seven rays), on an octagonal base.
De Ridder 1905: 151 no. 224 pl. XXXVII.2; Matern 2002: 182, 248 B29.
Image: photograph after de Ridder loc.cit., in the public domain.

6. Plate 31.5
    Chalon sur Saône, Musée Denon 81-723.
    Valence.
    Bronze.
    2nd–3rd c. AD (Matern); 1st–2nd c. (Kaufmann-Heinimann).
    Bust of Sol, radiate (seven rays), *chlamys*.
    Matern 2002: 248 B25; Kaufmann-Heinimann 1998: 250–252, fig. 202.
    Image: courtesy Musée Denon.

7. Plate 30.3
    Bad Deutsch-Altenburg, Museum Carnuntinum 11971.
    Carnuntum (illegal find).
    Bronze.
    2nd–3rd c. AD.
    Bust of Sol, *chlamys*, radiate (five rays), "wreath coiffure".
    Fleischer 1967: 106 no. 134; Schön 1988: 105 no. 125; Matern 2002: 182,
    247–8 B22.
    Image: Landessammlungen Niederösterreich, Archäologischer Park Car-
    nuntum (photograph: Nicolas Gail).

8. Vienna, formerly with the Limeskommission.
    Carnuntum.
    Terracotta.
    2nd–3rd c. AD.
    Bust of Sol, radiate.
    Schön 1988; 105 no. 126; Fundberichte aus Österreich 21 (1982): 281
    fig. 748.

9. Lost.
    Lauriacum (Lorch).
    Bronze.
    2nd–3rd c. AD.
    Bust of Sol, radiate.
    Schön 1988: 201 no. 231.

10. Plate 30.4
    Paris, Bibliothèque Nationale de France, Cabinet des Médailles 117.
    Rimat, near Saïda, Syria.
    Bronze.
    2nd–3rd c. AD.

Bust of Sol, head slightly turned to the left, radiate (twelve rays), "wreath-coiffure" of carefully arranged locks and curls, upward gaze, *chlamys*. Found in 1849 together with a Kriophoros (Cab. Med. 450) and an applique (K1.6) in a small, vaulted room of about 1 m × 1.5 m.

F. Lajard, ArchAnz 1851: 50–51; Babelon-Blanchet 1895: 54 no. 117; Matern 2002: 182, 249 B 33; Fani 2016.

Image: sketch after Babelon-Blanchet.

11. Barcelona, Museo d'Arqueologia de Catalunya M5610.
Unknown.
Bronze.
2nd–3rd c. AD.
Bust of Sol.
Jucker 1961: 185 n. 1; LIMC Helios/Sol 66.

12. Paris, Louvre, ex Collection de Clercq.
Unknown.
Bronze, silver plated.
2nd–3rd c. AD.
Bust of Sol, radiate (seven rays).
De Ridder 1905: 151–2 no. 225.

13. Art Market.
Unknown.
Bronze with silver inlay.
2nd–3rd c. AD.
Small bust of Sol, eyes of inlaid silver.
Matern 2002: 248 B26.

14. Székesfehérvár, Szent István Király Múzeum 69.350.
Gorsium (Tac).
Bronze.
3rd c. AD.
Small bust of Sol, radiate (seven rays), *chlamys*.
Fitz 1998: 108 no. 209.

15. Plate 30.5
St. Germain-en-Laye, Musée d'Archéologie Nationale 26054.
Unknown.
Bronze.

3rd c. AD.

Highly corroded head of Sol, wreath coiffure, radiate (nine? rays, of which one missing and most damaged). Either a bust or a fragment of a statuette.

LIMC Helios/Sol 16.

Image: © Musée d'Archéologie nationale.

16. Lost. Cast of the original in the Museum in Strasbourg.
     Strasbourg.
     Bronze?
     3rd c. AD.
     Bust of Sol, radiate, five rays.
     Matern 2002: 250 B39.

17. Mulhouse, Musée Historique 1016.
     Ehl?
     Bronze.
     Undated.
     Head of Sol, radiate (five rays).
     Matern 2002: 248 B30.

18. Naples, Museo Nazionale 5110.
     Unknown.
     Bronze.
     Undated.
     Bust of Sol, radiate, seven rays.
     Matern 2002: 172, 182, 248–9 B31 fig. 70.

19. Plate 30.6
     Karlsruhe, Badisches Landesmuseum F870.
     Unknown (formerly in Thiersch collection, acquired by the museum in 1860).
     Bronze.
     Undated.
     Bust of Sol, radiate, emerging from leaves.
     LIMC Helios/Sol 66; Schumacher 1890: no. 280.
     Image: courtesy Badisches Landesmuseum, Schloss Karlsruhe.

20. Plate 30.7
     Munich, Antikensammlung 3113.
     Unknown.

Bronze.
Undated.
Bust of Sol, wreath coiffure, five rays.
LIMC Helios/Sol 66 (without ref.).
Image: Staatliche Antikensammlungen und Glyptothek München; photo by Renate Kühling.

21. Plate 30.8
Munich, Antikensammlung 3114.
Unknown.
Bronze.
Undated.
Bust of Sol, wreath coiffure, five rays.
LIMC Helios/Sol 66.
Image: Staatliche Antikensammlungen und Glyptothek München; photo by Renate Kühling.

22. Vienna, Kunsthistorisches Museum VI 374.
Unknown.
Bronze.
Undated.
Bust of Sol (applique), radiate (nine rays), long wavy hair, *chlamys*.
Sacken 1871, 77 pl. 36,6.

23. Art Market.
Unknown.
Bronze.
Modern?
Head of Sol, long wavy hair, five or seven rays.
Froehner 1885: 196–7 no. 946.

24. Plate 31.1–3
Munich, Archäologische Staatssammlung 1993.3509.
Pförring, Eichstatt.
Bronze.
2nd–3rd c. AD.
Bust of Sol, radiate, twelve rays. Probably an applique, possibly from a Dolichenic triangle.
Wamser et al. 2000: 404 no. 177c.
Image: 24, 24a & 24b Archäologische Staatssammlung Munich, photographs Manfred Eberlein.

25. Plate 31.4
    Paris, Louvre MA 2608.
    Samsun.
    Marble.
    Undated.
    Head of Sol, radiate nimbus.
    https://www.photo.rmn.fr/archive/12-536779-2C6NU08T5A9V.html
    (1 August 2017).
    Image: © Musée du Louvre, Dist. RMN-Grand Palais / Stéphane
    Maréchalle / Art Resource, NYImage.

26. Plate 31.6
    Paris, Louvre AO 1226.
    Tripoli (Lebanon).
    Bronze.
    Undated
    Head of Sol, radiate, seven rays.
    Fani 2016: 213 no. 1.
    Image: © Musée du Louvre, Dist. RMN-Grand Palais / Thierry Ollivier /
    Art Resource, NYImage.

27. Beirut, National Museum.
    Rimat, As-Suwayda.
    Bronze.
    Undated.
    Bust of Sol, radiate, twelve rays, *chlamys*.
    Fani 2016: 213–4 no. 3.

        B2a. Busts of Sol and Luna
1. Plate 31.7
    Sofia, National Archaeological Museum 4076.
    Nicopolis ad Istrum.
    Marble.
    Late 2nd–early 3rd c. AD.
    Busts of Sol and Luna above a plaque bearing the inscription: Aemilia
    Bettia pr[o] / nepotes svos pos(uit). Sol is radiate (seven holes for rays),
    has long wavy hair and an *anastole*, and wears a *chlamys*. His bust rests on
    a globe.
    Matern 2002: 247 B16; Gerov 1989: 196 no. 426.
    Image: courtesy National Archaeological Museum, Sofia.

B3. Sol with *Quadriga*

1. Plate 32.1
Bad Homburg, Saalburg Museum inv. St. 143.
Stockstadt, Mithraeum I.
Red sandstone.
Last quarter of the 2nd c. AD.
Sol, nude but for a *chlamys*, in a *quadriga*. Head and arms of Sol lost.
Identification as Sol likely, given the Mithraic context.
LIMC Helios/Sol 123; CIMRM II, 1174; Matern 2002: 214 Q39. CSIR
Deutschland II, 13, p. 79 no. 83, pl. 27.
Image: Römerkastell Saalburg, Ernst Künzl.

B4. Identification Uncertain
B4a. Standing, Full-Figure

1. Plate 33.1
Baltimore, Walters Art Gallery 54.
Boscoreale.
Bronze.
Early 1st c. AD.
Standing male figure, nude but for a *chlamys* draped loosely over the
shoulders and the left arm, right hand lowered and holding an unclear
object, and likewise some object (sword?), now lost, in lowered left hand;
wreath coiffure, radiate (?), and a smooth, peaked cap on the back of the
head behind the "rays".
LIMC Helios/Sol 114 (placing the statuette mistakenly in New York MMA);
Hill 1949: 29 no. 51, pl. 5.
Found in a lararium together with two statuettes of Jupiter, one of
Mercury, and one of Isis-Fortuna.
The "rays" of the "radiate crown" are exceptionally thick. Notably the central "ray" must be interpreted as a support of something-a star perhaps,
above the head-for it cannot be a ray. This suggests that the other, broad
"rays" may be the leaves of a wreath. Combined with the peaked cap, the
unfastened *chlamys*, the unidentified object in the left hand, and the general posture of this figure these elements all suggest that this is not Sol.
Too many attributes are broken off to allow a secure alternative identification, but possibly he is one of the Dioscuri.
Image: photograph courtesy the Walters Art Gallery, Baltimore, under
creative commons zero: no rights reserved-license.

2. vacat (cf. B1.24)

3.   Sion (Switzerland), Musées Cantonaux du Valais 653.
Muraz/Anchettes.
Bronze.
2nd–3rd c. AD.
Two appliques, found together, of Venus and Sol (?) being all that remain of the seven gods of the week? Sol nude but for a *chlamys*, standing on a globe, right hand raised to his head, whip (reported, but not visible to me on the photographs at my disposal) in his left hand; curly hair surmounted by a radiate nimbus (?). Although the context may suggest that this figure is Sol, the strange headdress has no direct parallels.
LIMC Helios/Sol 290 (ref.).

4.   Art Market.
Unknown.
Bronze.
2nd–3rd c. AD.
Sol (?), nude but for a bit of cloth hanging over his left shoulder, right hand raised with elbow at right angle, left arm lost, 5 holes (for rays?) in his head.
Matern 2002: 232 I11, fig. 42.

5.   Plate 33.2
Copenhagen, National Museum 10151.
Tommerby, Jutland.
Bronze.
Ca. AD 500 (Poulsen 1993); late 4th c. (Bergmann); early 4th c. (Calza).
Large statuette of a beardless man, dressed in high-girt *chiton* and *chlamys*, radiate (twelve rays) with a central jewel above the forehead, right hand raised (hand missing), left hand outstretched (missing). The statue presumably stood in a chariot. Identification as Constantine in the guise of Sol (LIMC) rejected by Bergmann; Poulsen (1993) suggests Theoderic.
LIMC Helios/Sol 449; Poulsen 1993; Spätantike 507–8 no. 114; Bergmann 1998: 2878.
Image: photograph © National Museum Copenhagen, with permission.

B4b. Busts

1.   Caracal, coll. Ilie Constantinescu.
Romula.
White marble.
2nd–3rd c. AD.

Head of Sol (?), long wavy hair, 5 holes for rays (?). The back of the head, spherical, unworked, was presumably covered by some (metal?) object. Identification as Sol not certain, as this hinges on the missing headgear: radiate nimbus (= Sol), conical cap (= Dioscuri), Persian cap (= Mithras)? Berciu & Petolescu 1976: 43 no. 31, pl. xix–xx.

2.   Plate 33.6
Boston, Museum of Fine Arts 1964.316.
Bought in Jerusalem.
Bronze.
2nd–3rd c. AD.
Head of a statuette; long curly hair, radiate crown, uraeus.
LIMC Helios/Sol 15; LIMC Helios 337; Comstock & Vermeule 1971: 99 no. 105; Matern 2002: 182, 248 B24.
Image: photograph copyright 2019 Museum of Fine Arts, Boston.

3.   Plate 33.4, 33.5
Brooklyn, Museum 54.162.
Egypt.
Alabaster.
1st c. BC–1st c. AD.
Bust of an acrolithic statuette of a young man, with upturned head, deep-set eyes, slightly parted lips, long locks of hair, brushed back in an *anastole* above his forehead, and seven holes for rays. A broad ribbon (?) is visible on his right shoulder, and (reworked?) traces of a knot at the base of the neck.
Image: Brooklyn Museum, Charles Edwin Wilbour Fund, Creative Commons-BY, photograph: Brooklyn Museum / Gavin Ashworth.

B4c. Sol on Horseback
1.   Plate 33.3
Antakya, Arkeoloji müzesi.
Unknown.
Terracotta.
Undated.
Sol, radiate nimbus (six or seven rays), nude but for a *chlamys*, on horseback, holding reins in both hands.
Artefacts.mom.fr STE 4081.
Image: photograph M. Feugère, courtesy Artefacts.mom.fr.

B5. Lost, Iconography Unknown

1.   Plates 200.8

Zurich, Schweizerisches Landesmuseum.

Augst.

Brass.

Undated.

Small plaque for the base of a statuette, with inscription: Deo Invicto / typum aurochalcinum / solis.

Furger & Riederer 1995: 174. CIL XIII, 5261.

Image: photograph courtesy M. Clauss.

C. Reliefs[18]

C1. Architectural Reliefs[19]

C1a. Pediments

1.   Delos, Iseum (Temple I of the Serapeum).

In situ.

Marble.

130 BC.

In the centre of the tympanum: frontal bust of Sol, heavily damaged, identification uncertain.

LIMC Helios 297.

2.   Plate 34.1

Rome, Musei Capitolini 2977.

Rome; acquired in the 18th c. from a marble-dealer near the Capitoline.

---

18   Section C is devoted to a wide range of objects that are solely or predominantly decorated in relief. This extensive section is divided into five main parts: architectural reliefs (C1), votive reliefs and other religious reliefs (C2), funerary reliefs (C3), reliefs with another or an unknown function (C4) and reliefs on which the identity of Sol is doubtful (C5). "Reliefs" do not form a strictly defined or definable category. Statues, such as the Augustus of Primaporta, can be decorated with scenes in relief on their breastplate for instance, and there are numerous small objects with relief decoration. These are not discussed here, but separately. The distinctions between the types of reliefs gathered here and those grouped in other sections are primarily pragmatic. In some cases a different aspect of the object formed the basis for the category. Lamps, for example, are collected under the rubric "lamps" rather than here under reliefs, notwithstanding their relief decorations. In other cases the reliefs decorate an element or aspect of an object that would normally not be considered a "relief". The Augustus of Primaporta is a statue, but the image that interests us is a decorative element of his breastplate. Hence the object is catalogued as decorated breastplate in section K2a.

19   Architectural reliefs are reliefs that formed decorative architectural elements of buildings or arches. The section is subdivided into: Pediments (C1a), Metopes (C1b), Architraves (C1c), Antefixes (C1ca), Capitals (C1d), Triumphal Arches (C1e), and Other/unknown (C1f).

Marble.

Mid 1st c. AD (Hommel); late 2nd–early 3rd c. (Lancellotti).

Tympanum of a small shrine (original width slightly more than one m.). In the centre Dea Caelestis riding side-saddle on the back of a lion; she is flanked in the corners by Luna (right, lost) and Sol (left), emerging, waste upwards, with his *quadriga*, radiate, nude but for a *chlamys*, possibly a whip in his right hand.

LIMC Helios/Sol 353; Hommel 1954: 50–1; Cordischi 1989; Matern 2002: 71, 221 Q95, fig. 14; Lancellotti 2010: 77.

Image: photograph © Capitoline museums.

3. Rome, temple of the Capitoline Jupiter.

Lost.

Various.

AD 86.

Two reliefs preserve somewhat vague indications of the sculptural decoration of the pediment of the temple after its restoration under Domitian:

3a. Plates 34.2 & 35.1

Paris, Louvre 978 and 1079.

Rome, Trajan's Forum.

Marble.

Early 2nd c. AD.

Two drawings of a relief depicting a gathering of Roman priests and other dignitaries attending an extispicy in front of the Capitolium. When it was discovered in the 1540s in the Forum of Trajan, most of the depiction of the temple facade still survived. At some point after the late 16th century, that part of the relief was destroyed. What survived was transported in 1808 from the Villa Borghese (where it had been housed since 1650) to Paris. Drawings by Pierre Jacques (1576) and an anonymous sixteenth century artist preserve the lost portion of the relief. In the temple front (now lost, but preserved in the drawings), Sol (left) and Luna (right) in a *quadriga* and *biga* respectively (but both drawn as *bigae*) flank the Capitoline triad, each riding towards them. Along the raking sima atop the roof, the planetary deities were depicted, apparently as full length statues. From right to left they were: Luna, heading up the roof to her left in her *biga*; Mars, nude, helmeted, holding an upright spear; Mercurius, though he was already too much damaged to be recognizable when the drawings were made; and at the apex, Jupiter, also in a chariot (only faint traces of the chariot survived at the time of drawing). Continuing from right to left the next figures would have been Venus, Saturn and Sol, but no trace of them survived.

LIMC Helios/Sol 354; LIMC Ares/Mars 280 (with bibl.); Tortorella 1988; Matern 2002: 69, 221 Q93.

Images: C1a.3a1: drawing by Pierre Jacques, 1576, published in Jacques 1603: 48; photograph in the public domain. C1a.3a2: anonymous drawing preserved in the Codex Vaticanus Latinus 3439, fol. 83; photograph in the public domain.

3b.   Plate 36.1
       Rome, Musei Capitolini 807.
       Rome, Forum, Arch of M. Aurelius, later used as decoration in the church of S. Martina, and moved to the Palazzo dei Conservatori in 1515.
       Marble.
       AD 176.
       M. Aurelius brings sacrifice in front of the temple of Capitoline Jupiter, depicted tetrastyle though it was in fact hexastyle. On the gable, a frontal four-horse chariot, flanked to each side on the lower end of the roof by two poorly preserved acroteria. The detailed relief in the pediment depicts Jupiter in the centre above an eagle with outstretched wings. To the left of Jupiter (i.e. by his right side) Juno, to the right Minerva (helmet). To the right of Minerva are seven figures, of whom the central and most prominent one is Sol in his chariot (only one horse depicted) ascending to the left towards the centre. Between Sol and Minerva are Mercurius (above) and below him Asclepius. To the left of Asclepius, next to the eagle, a woman, possibly Salus (Cafiero), but also identified as Iuventas, the wife of Hercules (Simon). The three figures in the far right corner are probably Cyclopes forging thunderbolts for Jupiter (Cafiero), as are the three corresponding figures in the far left corner, towards whom Luna, left of Juno, is driving her chariot (only one horse depicted). The small nude male figure behind her chariot is usually identified as Hercules.
       Matern 2002: 221 Q94 (with refs.); Cafiero 1986; Simon 1990: 114–8; Sobocinski 2014.
       Image: Arachne photograph G. Fittschen-Badura, FittCap71-75-02_26248, 08.jpg; arachne.dainst.org/entity/1085698.

4.   Varna, Museum?
       Dionysopolis (Balchik).
       Marble.

3rd c. AD.

Pediment of an aedicula inside the naos of the temple of Magna Mater. Depicted is the bust of Sol, radiate (eleven rays), *chlamys*, between the protomes of four horses, two to either side of him.

Lazarenko et al. 2010: 26; fig. 13.

5. Plates 37.1, 37.2

Aïn Hersha (Hermon, Syria), temple.

In situ.

Limestone.

Early 2nd c. AD.

Busts of Sol and Luna on the Eastern and Western tympanum respectively. Sol has long, wavy hair, a radiate nimbus (nine rays), and is wearing a *chlamys*.

LIMC Helios in per. or. 25; Freyberger 2006: 231, 242–9, pl. 28b.

Image: photographs 5 and 5a Arachne D-DAI-DAM-StF-d-D17-048_SYRHER and D-DAI-DAM-StF-d-D17-045_SYRHER; https://arachne.dainst .org/entity/5967887 and arachne.dainst.org/entity/5967884.

6. Plate 36.2

Berkeley, Phoebe Hearst Museum of Anthropology 8-4282.

Environs of Rome.

Marble.

Ca. AD 225 (LIMC); 150–200.

Small pediment, only left-hand corner preserved, depicting Sol emerging upwards in the corner in his *quadriga* towards a reclining Oceanus with rudder; Sol (no rays) is dressed in *chlamys* and *chiton*; his right hand, now lost, was raised.

LIMC Helios/Sol 355; Matern 2002: 71, 221 Q92, fig. 13 (with refs.); Lattimore 1975.

Image: © Phoebe Hearst Museum of Anthropology, University of California at Berkeley.

7. Plate 38.1

Milete, Serapeum, West-facade.

In situ.

Marble.

Second half 3rd c. AD.

In the centre of the tympanum: bust of Sol, radiate (11? rays), *chlamys*.

LIMC Helios 136; Matern 2002: 177 n. 972, 182 n. 991, 261 B117; Milet VII.1, pl. 125.
Image: Photograph author.

8.   Plate 38.2
Qasr Naus (Ain Akrine), Lebanon, Eastern Tympanum.
In situ.
Limestone.
Undated.
Fragment of the eastern tympanum, with badly damaged bust of Sol, radiate nimbus (nine rays), *chlamys*.
LIMC Helios in per. or. 26; Jucker 1961: 147 sketch 12; Freyberger 2006: 243, pl. 28d.
Image: photograph courtesy J. Lendering.

9.   Dmeir (42 km East of Damascus), "temple".
In situ.
Limestone.
Mid 3rd c. AD.
In the tympanum of the eastern facade, busts of Sol and Luna to either side of a window. Quite worn, but still recognizable.
LIMC in per. or. 28; Klinkott 1989: 121.
The nature of this building is uncertain; cf. Klinkott 1989: 109–10; Lenoir 1999.

C1b. Metopes

1.   Corinth, Museum 572.
Corinth, Theatre.
Marble.
1st quarter 2nd c. AD.
Eighteen fragmentary panels with reliefs depicting the battle of Gods and Giants; on one: Helios and Giant. Identification uncertain.
Sturgeon 1977: 40, slab 18, G35, pl. 29; LIMC Helios 379; LIMC Gigantes 481 panel XVIII; Matern 2002: 189, 284 K44.

C1c. Architraves

1.   Plate 38.3
Oinoanda.
Oinoanda, agora.
Marble.

193–211 (dedicatory inscription to Septimius Severus).
Partially preserved soffit relief of the architrave of the boukonisterion at
Oinoanda. Bust of Sol, radiate (nine rays), *chlamys*. In the space below Sol
a whip and below the whip a bird (eagle?). The companion relief depicts
Luna with 8 stars. The boukonisterion is interpreted as a building con-
nected with athletics; cf. Milner 2015.
Matern 2002: 262 B119; Coulton 1986: 76–7 & pl. VIII b; Milner 2015: 1945.
Image: drawing © by Anna Hijmans.

2.   Plate 39.1
      Sens, Musée Municipale.
      Sens, City Wall (spolium).
      Limestone.
      Early 2nd c. AD.
      Fragment of an architrave with bust of Sol, radiate nimbus, whip over left
      shoulder.
      LIMC Helios/Sol 29; Espérandieu IV, 67–8 no. 2858; Matern 2002: 262
      B125.
      Image: photograph Musées de Sens-J.P. Elie.

3.   Plate 38.4
      Cincinnati Art Museum 225.
      Khirbet et-Tannur, inner temenos enclosure frieze.
      Limestone.
      First half 2nd c. AD.
      The seven planetary deities form part of the decoration of the tetrastyle
      facade (engaged columns) of the inner temenos enclosure; a doorway
      between the two central columns opens to the altar platform beyond.
      Busts of four framed deities are depicted above the engaged columns.
      Poorly preserved, they are identified tentatively as a storm god, Apollo,
      a moon god, and Tyche (McKenzie et al. 2014: 219; cf. Fig. 331). The seven
      planetary deities (busts of Helios, Saturn, Jupiter and Mercury survive in
      identifiable state) are grouped on the architrave between the columns.
      Alternating with the planetary busts were Nikes. The bust of Sol, dam-
      aged, has long, curly hair, a radiate nimbus (6 of probably twelve rays pre-
      served), a *chlamys* fastened above his right shoulder, and a torch behind
      each shoulder.
      LIMC Helios in per. or. 18; McKenzie et al. 2014: 219; 95 fig. 129; 216 fig. 374.
      Image: Arachne D-DAI-DAM-02.391-Khirbet-At-Tannur-Heiligtum
      _SYRHER; arachne.dainst.org/entity/5908579.

4.   Plate 39.6
      Petra, Museum.
      Qasr el-Bint (temple of Dushares).
      Limestone.
      Late 1st c. BC.
      Medallion of a doric frieze depicting the bust of Helios, long wavy hair,
      radiate, *chlamys*.
      Matern 2002: 250, B44; Zayadine et al. 2003: 18, 222 pl. 100; McKenzie et al.
      2014: 275, 278 fig. 432.
      Image: Lupa.at/24040 photograph Andreas Schmidt-Colinet.

5.   Plate 39.2
      Split, Museum AMS 73525.
      Split, Diocletian's Palace, console of the architrave of the temple.
      Stone.
      Late 3rd–early 4th c. AD.
      Bust of Sol, facing, radiate (six rays survive), long hair in neatly arranged,
      deeply drilled curls.
      Cambi 2017: 30, fig. 8.
      Image: courtesy museum Split / Zrinca Buljevic.

6.   Split, Diocletian's Palace, console of the architrave of the temple.
      In situ?
      Stone.
      Late 3rd–early 4th c. AD.
      Bust of Sol, facing, radiate (six rays survive), long hair in neatly arranged,
      deeply drilled curls along the top of the head and hanging down in thick
      bangs to the shoulder; Cambi sees traces of a quiver, but I believe this
      may be a whip.
      Cambi 2017: 32, fig. 11.

7.   Plate 39.4
      Split, Diocletian's Palace, console of the architrave of the temple.
      In situ
      Stone.
      Late 3rd–early 4th c. AD.
      Bust of Sol, facing, radiate (nine? triangular rays survive), long hair,
      chlamys.
      Cambi 2017, 31: figs. 910.
      Image: photograph author.

C1ca. Antefixes

1. Plate 99.5
   Speyer, Historisches Museum der Pfalz.
   Rheinzabern.
   Terracotta.
   1st c. AD.
   Antefix: frontal head of Sol, twelve rays. Below, two horses facing each other.
   Arachne 616550. For the type see: Leogrande 2022.
   Image: Arachne ILEO-131_616550.jpg; arachne.dainst.org/entity/5334242.

2. Plate 99.6
   Rheinzabern, Terra Sigillata Museum.
   Rheinzabern.
   Terracotta.
   1st c. AD.
   Antefix: frontal head of Sol, 12 (?) rays. Below, two horses facing each other.
   Arachne 616539. For the type see: Wesch-Klein 1988: 223.
   Image: Arachne ILEO-120_616539.jpg; arachne.dainst.org/entity/5334232.

3. Plate 99.7
   Speyer, Historisches Museum der Pfalz.
   Rheinzabern.
   Terracotta.
   1st c. AD.
   Antefix: frontal head of Sol, 12 (?) rays. Below, two horses facing each other.
   Arachne 616544.
   Image: courtesy of the Historisches Museum der Pfalz

4. Speyer, Historisches Museum der Pfalz 58/143.
   Rheinzabern.
   Terracotta.
   1st c. AD.
   Antefix: frontal head of Sol, 12 (?) rays. Below, two horses facing each other.
   Arachne ILEO-861_617280.jpg; Arachne.dainst.org/entity/5334397.

C1d. Capitals

1. Qasr Rabbah, Jordan; reused in a house.
   Qasr Rabbah, temple.
   Limestone.

Early 2nd c. AD.

Capital of a pillar: bust of Sol, radiate nimbus, *chlamys*.

LIMC Helios in per. or. 21; Glueck 1966: 58, 303 fig. 137a, 454–5.

2.   Plate 39.3

Cussy-la-Colonne.

Removed from the column of Cussy and long used as well-head, until it was returned to the column in the 19th century.

Limestone.

Late 2nd–early 3rd c. AD.

Partially preserved capital of the "Column of Cussy", with busts of deities on each side: Sol, radiate nimbus; bearded god; Luna (only crescent remains); fourth deity completely destroyed.

LIMC Helios/Sol 264; von Mercklin 1962: 106–7 no. 288, figs. 522–4 (Sol fig. 524); Matern 2002: 261 B113.

Image: photograph author.

3.   Plate 39.5

Reims, Musée Lapidaire.

Durocortorum (Reims).

Sandstone.

Early 3rd c. AD.

Capital (fragment), with head of Sol, radiate, head of Luna (crescent uncertain) and two heads of bearded gods without defining attributes.

LIMC Helios/Sol 264; von Mercklin 1962: 110 no. 301, figs. 541–3, 546 (Sol: fig. 541).

Image: Arachne photograph Mercklin_91374; arachne.dainst.org/entity/ 1116653.

4.   Plate 39.7

Rome, Museo Palatino.

Rome, Palatine, Domus Severiana.

Marble.

First half 3rd c. AD.

Capital of a pilaster (fragment): frontal bust of Sol, long wavy hair, radiate (nine rays, some missing), *chlamys*, in a tondo above a garland carried by two amorini.

LIMC Helios/Sol 200; von Mercklin 1962: 128–9 no. 342, fig. 649; Matern 2002: 262 B124.

Image: arachne.dainst.org/entity/1116743

5. Formerly Rome, Albergo Costanzi.
Rome.
Unknown.
Roman Imperial.
Capital of a pilaster with busts of Dionysus, Attis, and Sol (*chlamys*, right hand raised).
Von Mercklin 1962: 167–8 no. 403 (not illustrated).

C1e. Triumphal Arches

1. Orange, Arch.
In situ.
Limestone.
AD 26–27.
Under an arch in the tympanum of the lateral sides, between cornucopiae, Sol (East), radiate (ten rays) and Luna (west). The face of Sol is much damaged.
LIMC Helios/Sol 361; Amy e.a. 1962: 140, pls. 21, 70; Paar 1979: 233–4; Matern 2002: 262 B121; Stilp 2017; Fellague 2017.

2. Tripoli, Archaeological Museum Y7655.
Leptis Magna.
Marble.
Early 3rd c. AD.
Relief-fragment from the Arch of Septimius Severus: head of Sol, radiate nimbus (7? rays).
LIMC Helios/Sol 2; Bartoccini 1931: 92, 97 fig. 65; Bacchielli 1992;

3. Plate 40.1–40.5
Rome, Arch of Constantine.
In situ.
Marble.
AD 312–315.
Sol is represented five times on the Arch of Constantine.
1. (40.1, 40.2) Eastern arch, West side, bust of Sol, radiate, nude but for a *chlamys*, right hand raised, left hand (now lost) holding globe. Across from Sol bust of Constantine with *chlamys* and cuirass, right hand (now lost) raised, left hand (now lost) holding globe. The other two busts presumably depicted Licinius and Jupiter.
2. West side, frieze, profectio, two soldiers carrying statues of the dii militares Victoria and Sol, standing, radiate, *chlamys*, right hand raised (lost).

3. (40.3, 40.4) East and West side, tondi with Luna in *biga* (West) and Sol in *quadriga* (East), radiate, dressed in *chiton* and *chlamys*, right hand raised (hand lost), globe in left hand, preceded by Lucifer with torch, Oceanus lying below the horses.

4. Postament-relief. Soldier carrying a standard surmounted by statuette of Sol (much damaged).

5. (40.5) postament-relief 19. Soldiers carrying standards surmounted by Victoria and Sol (damaged) respectively.

LIMC Helios/Sol 201, 362, 408; L'Orange & v. Gerkan 1939: 55, fig. 10, pl. 7b; 57–8, 126 – pls. 32 c–d; 138–9, pl. 33 c,d; 162–3, fig. 1, pl. 38a; Matern 2002: 106, 110, 126–7, 224 Q106, 233 I118–9, 237 I37a–b; Gutteridge 2010: 166; Pensabene & Panella 1999; Pensabene 2016.

Images:

1. Arachne, D-DAI-ROM-35.605_29237; arachne.dainst.org/entity/1088583.

2. Arachne, D-DAI-ROM-35.612_29235; arachne.dainst.org/entity/1088581.

3. Arachne, D-DAI-ROM-32.70_29232,02; arachne.dainst.org/entity/1088578.

4. Arachne, D-DAI-ROM-32.69_29233; arachne.dainst.org/entity/1088579

5. Arachne, D-DAI-ROM-35.622_29251,01; arachne.dainst.org/entity/1088597.

Cif. Other/Unknown

1. Plate 41.1

Corinth, Museum S195.

Corinth, Agora.

Marble.

Late 1st c. BC–early 1st c. AD or 2nd–3rd c. AD (v. Hesberg).

Three panels of a coffered ceiling; from left to right: bust of Luna, with a crescent behind her shoulders; bust of Sol, radiate (seven rays), *chlamys*; and a partially preserved coffer with a rosette.

LIMC Helios 296; v. Hesberg 1983: 228 pl. 46,1; Corinth I.2, 83 fig. 57; Matern 2002: 12 n. 81, 115 n. 264, 261 B116.

Image: photograph courtesy American School of Classical Studies at Athens, Corinth Excavations.

2. Bolsena, Duomo.

Unknown.

Terracotta.

Late 1st c. BC–early 1st c. AD.

Fragment of a frieze. At the left: Sol, only partially preserved, nimbate (no rays?), possibly seated, presumably towards Phaethon (lost). To the right, two women (Horae) preparing the chariot of Sol.

LIMC Helios/Sol 180; LIMC Phaethon I, 4; Gabrici 1911; Matern 2002: 186, 278 K2.

3. Plate 42.1
    Vienne, Musée Lapidaire.
    Vienne.
    Marble.
    1st c. AD, or Renaissance.
    Corner fragment of a large relief showing Sol emerging from waves, radiate nimbus (originally nine rays), *chlamys*, torch in raised right hand.
    LIMC Helios/Sol 27; Matern 2002: 97, 229 G30.
    Image: Centre Camille Jullian photograph number 131534.

4. Plate 41.2
    Aphrodisias, Museum.
    Aphrodisias, stoa of the agora.
    Marble.
    AD 14–29.
    Frontal bust of Sol between garlands, radiate nimbus (twelve rays).
    LIMC Helios/Sol 304; LIMC Helios 137; Matern 2002: 19, 177 n. 972, 182 n. 991, 260 B 110.
    Image: photograph author.

5. Aphrodisias, Museum.
    Aphrodisias, Sebasteion, South Building.
    Marble.
    Early 1st c. AD.
    Base relief on the D-level of the facade of the s. building, with bust of Sol, radiate, (sixteen rays) *chlamys*.
    Matern 2002: 19, 182 n. 991, 260 B109; Smith 2013: 282–3 D-base 15, fig. 230, Pl 168.
    Based on the findspot, this relief was paired with a relief depicting Luna at the centre of the facade, each equidistant from the end, separated from each other by two other D-bases (only the fragment of one appears to have survived). The other D-bases are decorated with rosettes, primarily, as well as Medusa and Satyr-heads, and one with two cornucopiae.

6.   Plate 42.2
      Florence, Uffizi 72/sculture.
      Rome, Aventine.
      Italian marble.
      Late 1st–early 2nd c. AD.
      Front of a pilaster decorated in relief with a depiction of many hundreds
      of weapons. On a shield: frontal bust of Sol, radiate nimbus (nine rays).
      Next to it a shield with crescent. A bit higher, bust of Luna with crescent
      on an Amazon shield. On the left side of the pilaster a second shield with
      bust of Sol.
      LIMC Helios/Sol 1; Matern 2002: 261 B114 (both mention only representa-
      tion on the front); Crous 1933: 101, xx, pl. 1, top, pl. 8.
      Image: photograph author, reproduced with permission.

7.   Paris, Louvre N4570.
      Rome?
      Terracotta.
      Ca. AD 114–117 (LIMC), ca. AD 120 (Gundel).
      Fragment of a terracotta plaque, which formed a complete scene with
      five others, now lost. On the preserved fragment: three signs of the zodiac,
      part of the radiate head of Sol and his right hand holding a torch, part of
      a radiate circle and part of an inscription: ...] q r f f optimo pr[incipi....
      For a reconstruction of the whole scene cf. Cumont 1940. The meaning of
      q r f f is not known.
      LIMC Helios/Sol 424; Gundel 1992, 238 no. 98; Cumont 1940.

8.   Plate 93.5
      Berlin, Staatliche Museen, Antikensammlung SK 913.
      Ostia.
      Marble.
      Mid 2nd c. AD.
      Restored relief depicting deities, of whom the second from the right
      (head and right arm restored), dressed in *chiton* and *chlamys*, is almost
      certainly Sol because he is holding a whip in his left arm. The frieze in
      Berlin is part of a longer frieze, portions of which were found (reused in
      later buildings) in Ostia in 1938 and 1970 respectively (Museum inv. 148
      and 18853). They depict the birth of Minerva, the birth of Vulcan, Vulcan
      thrown off the Olympus, and (from r. to left) Mercurius, Sol, Minerva,
      Jupiter, Juno, Apollo, Venus, Mars, and Neptune.
      Matern 2002: 118, 147–8, 239–40 I50, fig. 57.
      Image: courtesy of the Staatliche Museen, Berlin.

9. Corinth, Museum.
   Corinth, Odeum.
   Marble.
   Ca. AD 175; Late 1st c. AD (LIMC). I base the date of AD 175 on the remarks
   of Broneer, Corinth X, 114, who compares these fragments stylistically to
   pilaster capitals belonging to the second phase of the odeum which is
   dated to around AD 175.
   Numerous fragments of marble slabs, which presumably decorated some
   part of the scaenae frons of the odeum. Each square slab appears to have
   consisted of a square border connecting the ends of a superimposed +
   and x which fill the square, and a mask in the centre. The bars of the +
   and x have been interpreted as rays, implying that the masks represent
   Helios. The masks differ greatly, however, and some, at least, appear to
   have been theatre masks (e.g. Corinth X, fig. 109 no. 101).
   LIMC Helios 300.

10. Plate 10.1
    Ephesus, Museum.
    Ephesus.
    Marble.
    Ca. AD 170.
    Fragment of a relief of the Parthian monument. Sol ascends a chariot
    to the left (only one wheel remains, horses lost), preceded by a youthful
    figure dressed in *chiton* with sleeves and a cloak. Sol is nimbate and radi-
    ate (7 metal rays, fixed in holes, lost), has a raised right arm (upper part
    lost) and held some object in his lowered left arm, possibly a torch or a
    cithara (rejected by Matern). The chariot was drawn by griffins, rather
    than horses, which suggests that this was perhaps Apollo-Helios, rather
    than simply Sol.
    Matern 2002: 70 n. 444, 79–8, 224 Q110. Oberleitner & Landskron 2009,
    116–8, 254–7, figs. 204–211.
    Image: drawing © Anna Hijmans.

11. Plate 42.3
    Vienna, Kunsthistorisches Museum I 867.
    Ephesus.
    Marble.
    Ca. AD 170.
    Apotheosis of L. Verus. Sol (?), radiate nimbus, *chlamys* and *chiton*, torch
    in his left hand, precedes the *quadriga* together with Virtus.

LIMC Helios/Sol 423; LIMC Artemis/Diana 280. Oberleitner & Landskron (2009: 255) argue that this figure cannot be Sol because he is now known to be present on an adjacent plaque (10), that was discovered in 1990. Image: courtesy KHM-Museumsverband.

12.   Rome, Villa Medici.
      Unknown.
      Marble.
      2nd c. AD.
      Two tondi with the busts of Luna (crescent moon behind her shoulders) and Sol (?) respectively; the head and face of Sol are largely modern, leaving only the association with Luna to suggest that this is, indeed, Sol.
      Cagiano de Azevedo 1951: 55 pl. XI.

13.   Baia, Museum 9.
      Misenum, shrine of the imperial cult.
      Marble.
      Severan.
      Sol rides a *quadriga* to the left. He has a radiate nimbus (6? rays), is dressed in a *chiton* and *chlamys*, has raised his right arm, and holds a whip in his left. Below him, Oceanus.
      Matern 2002: 127, 222 Q98; Adamo Muscettola 2000: 43–5 fig. 6; Laird 2015: 210–11 fig. 82.

14.   Plate 42.4
      Myra, Theatre.
      In situ.
      Marble.
      Mid 2nd c. AD (terminus post quem of AD 141, when the theatre was destroyed by an earthquake and rebuilt).
      Frontal bust of Sol, radiate (probably nine rays, of which 7 survive at least in part), long, wavy hair, and *chlamys*.
      Knoblauch & Özbek 1996.
      Image: photograph courtesy J. Lendering.

15.   Plate 42.5
      Perge.
      Perge, Nymphaeum F3.
      Stone.
      c. AD. 120–140.

Fragment of a frieze, depicting the bust of Sol, radiate nimbus (twelve? rays), *chlamys*.

Mansel 1975a: 83–92 fig. 51 (cf. Mansel 1975b); Matern 2002: 172, 177 n. 972, 182 n. 991, 262 B122 fig. 85. On the nymphaeum in general see Özdizbay 2012: 62–6, 2479.

Image: Arachne D-DAI-IST-R4387_156317; arachne.dainst.org/entity/1149160.

16.   Antalya, Museum 18.23.93.
      Perge, Theatre.
      Proconessian marble.
      Third quarter 3rd c. AD.
      On slab G4 of the gigantomachy frieze of the theatre, Sol, radiate (holes), dressed in a belted and sleeved *chiton* and *chlamys*, moves right on a *quadriga*. His left arm points forward (hand broken off), and with his bent right arm he raises a now lost object behind his head, possibly a whip. A small nude figure stands before Sol on the chariot. Below and behind Sol is the upper body of a reclining woman, possibly Tellus, and to the right of her, below and ahead of Sol, Oceanus or a river deity with a jar from which water flows directly into the mouth of a defeated giant. The four horses, led by a female figure, trample on two giants.
      Matern 2002: 12 n. 81, 81, 222 Q97; Alanyalı 2013: 127–128 figs. 142–149.
      Luna, moving left on a *biga* of bulls, is depicted on G10.

17.   Antalya, Museum.
      Perge, Nymphaeum F2.
      Marble.
      Ca. AD 200 (Severan).
      To either side of the tympanum, reliefs depicting the busts of Sol and Luna.
      Mansel 1975a: 65–71; Matern 2002: 172 n. 946, 182 n. 991, 260 B108, fig. 84.

18.   Perge.
      Perge, Propylon H.
      Marble.
      Ca. AD 200 (Severan).
      Two soffits, iconographically identical but stylistically very different, depicting the rape of Ganymede in a central lozenge-shaped panel, between two tondo's depicting the busts of Luna (right) and Sol (left), radiate, one with twelve rays, the other with 13. The latter bust has a

garland around the neck and a *chlamys*; the former bust is unfinished below the face.

Mansel 1975a, 71–75, fig. 32a–b; Matern 2002: 180 n. 985, 182 n. 991 and n. 998, 262 B123a and b, figs. 878.

19.   Newcastle, Great North Museum NEWMA 1960.21,A.
Vindolanda (Chesterholm).
Sandstone.
Early 3rd c. AD.
Fragment of a relief; preserved are the upper part of the face of Sol with a radiate nimbus (six rays, representing about half the total) and next to the head the top of Sol's whip.
CSIR Britain I, 6, p. 52 no. 131, pl. 35.

20.   Balat, Miletus Museum 2121.
Didyma.
Marble.
3rd c. AD.
Coffer of a ceiling with bust of Sol (damaged), radiate.
Matern 2002: 177 n. 972, 182 n. 991, 260–1 B111.

21.   Hatra, Palace.
In situ.
Stone.
Undated.
Lintel, relief, decorated with a frontal bust of Sol, radiate nimbus (8? rays).
Jucker 1961, 178, fig. 68.

22.   Plate 42.6
Ira (As-Suwayda district, Syria), reused locally in the walls of a house.
Said to be from Si'.
Stone.
Undated.
Fragments of a lintel. Busts of Sol and Luna.
LIMC Helios in per. or. 20; Glueck 1966, 304 pl. 138, 472; Dentzer-Feydy 1992, 81–2 fig. 24; Freyberger 2006, 235–6 pl. 31b–d.
Image: Arachne D-DAI-DAM-StF-n-O6-209-34_SYRHER / Stefan Freyberger; arachne.dainst.org/entity/5977335.

23. Damascus, National Museum 8.652.
    Khirbet et-Tine (near Homs).
    Basalt.
    Undated.
    Fragment of an architectural frieze decorated with busts; only the bust of
    Sol and traces of the arm of an adjacent bust remain. Sol is radiate and
    wears a *chlamys*.
    Image: https://arachne.dainst.org/entity/5947061/image/5947061.

24. Lost; cast in Carlisle City Museum Inv. 39–1894.2.
    Carlisle, Annetwell str.
    Stone.
    2nd–3rd c. AD.
    Medallion in the form of a laurel wreath enclosing a frontal bust of Sol,
    curls, radiate (eleven rays), *chlamys*, whip above his right shoulder.
    CSIR Britain I, 6, 161 no. 484, pl. 109.

25. Niha Temple A
    In situ.
    Stone.
    Early 3rd c. AD.
    On the North (right hand) ante of the temple an unfinished bust of Sol,
    not (yet) radiate, long hair, *chlamys*, above an unfinished wreath. On the
    South ante, Luna (?).
    Freyberger 1999; Freyberger 2006: 242, pl. 30a.

26. Plate 4.4
    Ma'bad Helios, As-Suwayda district (Syria). In situ.
    Stone.
    Undated.
    Large relief-bust of Sol, radiate (three rays survive), possibly a nimbus,
    long wavy hair, from the peripteral temple. Heavily damaged.
    Arachne 5970612. On the temple (dedicated to Rabbos rather than Helios)
    cf. Segal 2013: 197–199.
    Image: Arachne D-DAI-DAM-StF-d-D27-406_SYRHER; arachne.dainst
    .org/entity/5970612.

27. Plate 37.3
    Slim, As-Suwayda district (Syria) in a garden.
    Found locally.

Stone.

Undated.

Relief bust of Sol, radiate, long wavy hair.

Arachne 5973128.

Image: photograph courtesy J. Lendering.

28.   Plate 39.8

Slim, As-Suwayda district (Syria) in the wall of a house.

Stone.

Relief bust of Sol, radiate (eleven rays), long wavy hair, in a tondo, between torches; the edge of an adjacent tondo to the left is also preserved.

Arachne 5990121.

Image: Arachne D-DAI-DAM-DA-d-S146-034_SYRHER; arachne.dainst .org/entity/5990121.

C2. Religious and Votive Reliefs[20]

C2a. Sol Alone

1.   Pula, Museum 251.

Pula. Said to come from the temple of Roma and Augustus.

Limestone.

1st c. AD. The first c. AD date for the altar is given in Inscriptiones Italiae x, 10, no. 22 "ex forma monumenti". Ianovitz (1972: 16 n. 38) feels that this makes the date "difficilmente valutabile, affidato com'è (...) a considera-zioni personali", but Degrassi (1970: 629) does accept it and I see no rea-son to reject it. Ianovitz was probably uncomfortable with this early date because of his tendency to link all references to Sol with Mithraism.

Votive altar; in the centre, bust of a deity, probably Sol (heavily damaged); inscription: soli // n(umerius) placen[tius] / atticus. Whether the altar was actually associated with the temple of Roma and Augustus cannot be certain. In 1860, the temple became a depot for antiquities, and it was subsequently no longer clear which objects were found in context with the temple and which were removed to it in the years after 1860; cf. Reichel 1893, 6–7 no. 89.

---

20   This section is comprised of reliefs with a religious or votive function, broadly defined, that were erected as more or less self-contained objects. The most frequent are votive altars and votive reliefs of all sizes. The section has been subdivided into groups according to the principal deity or deities to whom the relief was dedicated or in whose context Sol is depicted.

Ianovitz 1972: 15–16 (with refs.); CIMRM I, 757 (incorrect transcription of the inscription); Degrassi 1970: 629.
Image: http://db.edcs.eu/epigr/bilder.php?bild=$InscrIt-10-01_00022 .jpg;pp (February 1, 2019).

2. Benghazi, Museum.
Berenice.
Limestone.
Mid 1st c. AD. Date based on stratigraphy and find context.
Votive (?) stele. Sol on frontal *quadriga*, radiate nimbus (face and most rays destroyed), dressed in *chiton* (?) and *chlamys*.
Bonanno 1978: 63, G38, pl. 4,38; Matern 2002: 53, 213 Q38.

3. Plate 43.1
Rome, Musei Capitolini NCE 1866.
Rome, via Patrizi.
Marble.
AD 158.
Votive altar. At the top, a small bust of Sol, radiate (seven rays), *chlamys*, with whip (right hand) and globe (left hand). Below: inscription: soli invicto deo / ex voto suscepto / accepta missione / honesta ex nume / ro eq(uitum) sing(ularium) aug(usti) p(ublius) / aelius amandus / d(onum) d(edit) tertullo et / sacerdoti co(n)s(ulibus). This is the oldest accurately dated use of invictus as epithet for Sol.
Schraudolph 1993: 236 L144, pl 40 (with refs.); Matern 2002: 39 n. 305, 172, 256 B79, fig. 81 (with refs.).
Image: Arachne Mal162-06_16366; arachne.dainst.org/entity/1076181.

4. Plate 44.1
Vatican, Galleria delle Statue 550.
Rome, near the Porta Portese, at or near the shrine of the Syrian gods (according to Palmer).
Marble.
2nd c. AD.
Altar; above inscription in tondo, frontal bust of Sol (face restored), radiate (seven rays, restored), *chlamys*. The tondo flattens and widens towards the bottom, so that it resembles a crescent. In front of the lowest Part of the tondo is a small eagle with outspead wings. Inscription: d[eo] / soli vi[ctori] / q(uintus) octavius daphnicu[s] / negotia(n)s vinarius a se[p/r?.. / tricliam fec(it) a solo inpe[nsa] / sua permissu

kalator(um) pon[tif](icum) / et flaminum cui immunitas / data est ab
eis sacrum faciend[i]. There is no room for lost letters prior to VI of vic-
tori, and therefore no grounds for the reading invicto. The end of line 4
has been variously restored as A SEP[tem Caes(aribus) (Marini) or A
SER[api (Mommsen); cf. Palmer 1981: 368 n. 3). Palmer accepts Marini's
restoration, but it is almost certainly too long, although it has the advantage of a parallel in CIL IX, 4680 which records another vinarius a septem
Caesaribus. Perhaps Daphnicus used the abbreviation Sept(em), which
occurs in some inscriptions (e.g. AE 1982, 928b, a much later inscription;
CIL III, 10577; 14141; CIL IV, 10580; CIL V, 6176; CIL VIII, 1040). There may
conceivably be room for A SEP[T(em) Caes(aribus), in particular if one
looks at the apparent length of line 6 and accepts a slight variation in the
length of the lines.

LIMC Helios/Sol 37; Amelung 1908: 416b pl. 61; CIL VI 712; Palmer 1981:
372–381; Chausson 1995: 666–7; Matern 2002: 42 n. 328, 170, 184, 257 B83,
fig. 80 (B107 in her catalogue is the same altar); Fowlkes-Childs 2016: 206–
7, fig. 10.5.

Image: courtesy of the Vatican Museums.

5.   Plate 16.3
      Naples, Museo Nazionale 6678.
      Rome.
      Marble.
      Ca. AD 175 or ca. AD 215.
      Votive relief; in the centre a statue of Sol on a base; Sol's head is missing,
      but above his right shoulder traces are visible of his long hair and a nim-
      bus. He is nude but for a *chlamys*, his right hand is raised, and he holds a
      whip in his left hand. In front of the statue-base stands a small, portable,
      tripod altar, burning. Between the altar and the base a dead bull lies on
      the ground; to either side of the altar two men in toga, bare-headed, of
      whom the right-hand one is in the act of placing something on the altar.
      Behind him a boy is holding a pyxis. The inscription, in the field, identi-
      fies the dedicants as L. Arruntius Philippus, Quintus Codius Iason and
      the latter's son Mercurius. The emperor in whose honour the dedica-
      tion is made can be either Marcus Aurelius or Caracalla. Inscription: pro
      sal[u]te et m[em]oria / imp(eratoris) caes(aris) m(arci) aureli(i) antonini
      aug(usti) / l(ucius) arruntius / philippus / q(uintus) codius / iason / et /
      mercu/rius / filius / huius / d(onum) d(ederunt).

LIMC Helios/Sol 189; von Hesberg 1981, 1054–5 no. 5b; CIL VI 1018; various drawings were made of the relief, with restored head: Vermeule 1960: 21 no. 182; Vermeule 1966a: 16 no. 8282; Matern 2002: 110, 164, 237 I36; Huet 2017: 15–17, fig. 2.4.
Image: drawing © Anna Hijmans.

6. Side, Museum 1957.
Side.
Limestone.
2nd c. AD.
Altar with bust of Sol, face hacked away, radiate (nine rays), draped. Below, inscription: Ερμες ηλιω ευχην
Matern 2002: 101 n. 578, 182 n. 991, 196, 257 B86.

7. Plate 43.3
Vatican, Museo Gregoriano Profano 9906.
Rome, Via del Mare (near theatre of Marcellus).
Marble.
2nd–3rd c.; Antonine (Liverani).
Votive altar, on the front bust of Sol, radiate (five rays), whip; on the back crescent and star; on either side, sacrificial bowl and jug respectively. Inscription invicto / soli / felicissimus et philocurius aed(em) / d(onum) d(ederunt).
Schraudolph 1993: 237 L152 pl. 41; Matern 2002: 237 B84; Campbell 2017: 92.
Image: Arachne FA2174-05_21537.jpg; arachne.dainst.org/entity/257627.

8. Ancona, Soprintendenza delle Marche 173.
Fano.
Marble.
Second half 2nd c.–early 3rd c. AD.
Altar bearing an inscription: soli / invicto / q(uintus) valerius / eutyches / d(ono) d(edit).
Altar found in conjunction with a headless statue of Abundantia, the torso of a seated man, fragment of a relief depicting a winged man standing next to an altar around which a snake is curled, small base on which three statuettes (two, headless, preserved) of women in long *chiton*, and a head of Hercules with a lion's skin over his head.
Bernardelli Calavalle 1986; Battistelli & Deli 1983: 77, 81, 91; AE 1990, 331.

9.   Plate 43.4
      Carnuntum, Museum Carnuntinum Car-S-109 (22600).
      Carnuntum, Petronell (Traun collection).
      Stone.
      2nd–3rd c. AD.
      Sol, bare-headed, nude but for a *chlamys*, whip (?) in raised right hand, in a *quadriga* to the right.
      LIMC Helios/Sol 143. CSIR Österreich Carnuntum Suppl. 115 nr 210, pl. 60.
      Image: Landessammlungen Niederösterreich, Archäologischer Park Carnuntum (Photograph: Nicolas Gail).

10.   Burdur, Museum R 2 6 91.
      Unknown.
      Marble.
      2nd–3rd c. AD.
      On the front, bust of Sol, radiate (eight rays); on the sides: grapes (left) and wreath (right).
      Matern 2002: 171 n. 945, 177 n. 972, 182 n. 991, 253 B61, fig. 77.

11.   Formerly Beirut, private collection; current whereabouts unknown.
      Unknown.
      Stone.
      2nd–3rd c. AD.
      Baetyl, decorated with a standing, half-nude Helios, radiate, right hand raised, within an oval zodiac circle.
      Gundel 1992, 229 no. 74; Matern 2002: 123, 136, 178, 241 I60.

12.   Plate 43.2
      Aix-en-Provence, Musée Granet 839.8.1.
      La Torse, Aix-en-Provence.
      Sandstone.
      2nd–3rd c. AD.
      Altar. In a niche, framed by two columns, Sol in a frontal *quadriga*, radiate (7 holes for rays), nude but for a *chlamys* billowing out behind him and filling the apse of the niche, right hand raised, left hand broken off. The heads and forelegs of four small horses rising up above waves are all that is visible of the *quadriga*. Inscription above and below the niche: p(ublius) tallius one/simus/v(otum) s(olvit) l(ibens) m(erito).
      LIMC Helios/Sol 122; Matern 2002: 214–5 Q46; Espérandieu I, 77 no. 94.
      Image: photograph © Musée Granet / Bernard Terlay.

13. Plate 43.5
Newcastle-upon-Tyne, Great North Museum, NEWMA 1822.42a.
Vercovicium (Housesteads), Mithraeum.
Sandstone.
3rd c. AD (?)
Altar with inscription; on the border above the inscription bust of Sol, radiate (seven rays), *chlamys*, whip over right shoulder. Inscription.: d(eo) soli / herion / v(otum) l(ibens) m(erito).
RIB 1601; Harris & Harris 1965: 35, pl. 5.2; CIMRM I 858/9 (inscription incorrect); CSIR I, 6, p. 52 no. 130, pl. 35; Matern 2002: 255, B75 (inscription incorrect).
Image: https://romaninscriptionsofbritain.org/inscriptions/1601 (February 1, 2019).

14. Plate 10.2
Rome, Musei Capitolini 2969.
Rome, Forum of Nerva.
Marble.
4th c. AD.
Triangular votive relief, lower right corner missing. Sol standing, radiate (seven rays), dressed in *chiton* and *chlamys*, right hand raised, globe in left hand. Below his feet a face. On the three borders, inscription: [si] mulacrum restitu / tum deo soli invicto / [s]acratis speleus pat(er) et ap[...
Schraudolph 1993: 236 L146, pl. 40; Matern 2002: 118–9, 240 I52.
Image: Arachne D-DAI-IST-R 11.1177; arachne.dainst.org/entity/1096474.

15. Plate 43.6
Aquileia, formerly Chiesa di S. Felice, then in the house of Geronimo Susanna (early 16th c.), lost when the house was torn down in the later 17th c.
Aquileia?
Stone.
Undated.
Votive altar. A head, probably of Sol, radiate (? only a rough sketch survives). Inscription: soli / deo / invicto / sacrum / feronius censor / signi(fer?) / v(otum) s(olvit) l(ibens) m(erito).
Calderini 1930: 131 no. 9; Ianovitz 1972: 51–2; CIL V, 807; CIMRM I, 752; Buonopane 2009: 409–416 (with 16th c. sketch and complete bibliography).
Image: after Buonopane loc.cit.

16.   Plate 6.4
       Yalvaç, Museum E 1481 (350).
       Antiocheia in Pisidia.
       Limestone.
       Undated.
       Altar with on one side a bust of Sol, radiate nimbus (eleven rays), draped.
       On the next side to the right: Cybele.
       Matern 2002: 177 n. 972, 182 n. 991, 258 B88.
       Image: Arachne D-DAI-IST-R 11.177; arachne.dainst.org/entity/2007251.

17.   Unknown.
       Gelendos.
       Limestone (?)
       Undated.
       Small altar with a worn bust of Sol, radiate nimbus, *chlamys*.
       Matern 2002: 258 B91.

18.   Plate 44.3
       Original lost; drawing preserved in the Royal Library, Windsor Castle: Dal
       Pozzo-Albani Drawings II, Fol. 52 no. 8380.
       Unknown.
       Marble?
       Undated.
       A variety of pantheistic symbols crowned by a bust of Apollo-Helios,
       radiate (nine rays), *chlamys*, quiver behind right shoulder.
       Vermeule 1966b: 24 no. 8380.
       Image: Royal Collection Trust / © Her Majesty Queen Elizabeth II 2018.

19.   Budapest, National Museum 97.1909.2.
       Dunaúváros/Intercisa.
       Limestone.
       Undated.
       Votive altar, no inscription, on the two sides small bust of Sol, radiate
       (eight and ten rays respectively).
       Barkóczi e.a. 1954: 366; Ubi Erat Lupa 8060 (with image).

20.   Budapest, National Museum, North depot cellar.
       Unknown.
       Limestone.
       Undated.

Votive altar (?), no inscription; small bust of Sol, radiate nimbus (12? Rays), between two horses to either side.
Ubi Erat Lupa 9893 (otherwise unpublished).

21. Plate 44.2
Carnuntum, Museum Carnuntinum Car-S-429.
Carnuntum?
Limestone.
Undated.
Smallish head of Sol, broken at the back, with longish hair and a nimbus with holes for 9(?) rays.
CSIR Österreich Carnuntum Suppl. 115 no. 211, pl.60. Ubi Erat Lupa 23441 (no image).
Image: Landessammlungen Niederösterreich, Archäologischer Park Carnuntum (Photograph: Nicolas Gail).

22. Plate 44.4
Cluj-Napoca, National History Museum of Transylvania v. 51139.
Apulum.
Limestone.
Undated.
In the tympanum above the inscription a small facing head of Sol, radiate nimbus (twelve rays). Inscription: invicto / myth{i}r/ae chr/estion / v(otum) s(olvit)
CIMRM II, 1945; CIL 3, 1112.
Image: photograph courtesy National History Museum of Transylvania, Cluj-Napoca.

23. Lyon, Lugdunum Musée Gallo-Romain inv. 2001.0.326.
Lyon, montée de Choulans.
Limestone.
2nd–3rd c. AD.
Shallow niche with a radiate bust of sol (seven rays) with long, wavy hair. The rays extend onto the unadorned aedicula-shaped frame of the niche. On the frame, to the right of Sol, the thong of a whip is indicated in shallow carving, lighly curled around the (lost) painted rod of the whip.
NEsp LYO 044; Savay-Guerraz 2013: 106.

24. Plate 45.1
Antalya, Museum.

Arykanda, Helios-temple.
Stone.
Undated.
Votive altar with image of Sol, radiate (five rays), *chlamys*.
Bayburtluoglu 2005.
Image: photograph courtesy J. Lendering.

25. Çorum, Archaeological Museum 2883.
Sungurlu area.
Limestone or marble.
Undated.
Frontal head of Sol, radiate (twelve rays), longish, wavy hair, worn and lower part too damaged to make out anything below the neck.
İbiş 2022: 95–6, fig. 47.
İbiş identifies the material as marble (mermer) in the caption with the image, and as limestone (kireçtaşı) in the text.

C2b. Sol and Luna

1. Plate 45.2
Florence, Museo Archeologico 86025 (formerly Villa Casamorata).
Rome, Trastevere.
Marble.
Neronian (?), possibly Flavian (cf. Bergmann 1998: 194–5).
Bust of Sol, radiate (ten rays), *chlamys* (?); inscription: eumolpus caesaris / a supellectile domus / auriae (sic) et claudia pallas f(ilia) / soli et lunae donum posuerunt. Bergmann sees conscious echoes of Nero's features in the bust of Sol.
CIL VI, 3719 = 310331; Matern 2002: 254 B65; Bergmann 1998: 194–201.
Image: courtesy of the Ministero per i beni e le attività culturali-polo museale della Toscana-Florence.

2. Plates 18.2, 18.3
Rome, Musei Capitolini 9775.
Rome, Aventine, Dolichenum.
Marble.
Ca. AD 150.
Votive altar dedicated to Sol, and set up together with a twin altar dedicated to Luna. Sol is standing, not radiate, nude but for a *chlamys*, whip in right hand, globe in left.

Speidel 1978: 26; Colini 1936:, 151–2 fig. 8.; Hörig & Schwertheim 1987: 223–4 no. 356 pl. lxx; Matern 2002: 94, 229 G29; Corradini 2015.
Image: 2 and 2a Arachne Malı701-03_39447.jpg; arachne.dainst.org/ entity/6473547, and Malı701-04_39446.jpg; arachne.dainst.org/entity/ 6473548.

3. Plate 45.3
   Paris, Louvre MA 2754.
   Janiculum, Syrian Sanctuary; entered the Louvre in 1816.
   Marble.
   Ca. AD 100–135.
   Candelabrum resting on a triangular block with on each side respectively a relief of Sol (radiate bust, seven rays), Luna (bust) and a bull (walking to the right). Below Sol an inscription: doryphorus pater, added in the 3rd c.
   Bouillon 1821, III, Candelabres p. 3, pl. 3.1; Froehner 1874: 387–8 no. 424; Gauckler 1912: 160; LIMC Helios in per. or. 10; Matern 2002: 171–2, 182 n. 998, 256 B77, fig. 79.
   Image: © Musée du Louvre, Dist. RMN-Grand Palais / Art Resource, NY.

4. Damascus, National Museum.
   Duweir (near Sidon).
   Stone.
   AD 295.
   Busts of Sol (radiate, whip) and Luna to either side of a date palm. Below them two staggered bulls on each side of the palm.
   LIMC Helios in per. or. 4; Bossert 1951: no. 533.

5. Székesfehérvár, Szent István Király Múzeum 496.
   Zámoly, from a tomb of the 4th c. AD.
   Wood, originally plated with metal.
   4th c. AD.
   Side A: bust of Sol, radiate (twelve rays), *chlamys*, whip; inscription so[l].
   Side B: Bust of Luna, inscription [lu]n[a].
   LIMC Helios/Sol 303; Kádár 1962: 39–40 pl. 3,5; Fitz 1998: 107 no. 208.

6. Destroyed in 1870.
   Nehwiller-pres-Woerth.
   Sandstone.
   Undated.

Remnants of a depiction of Sol and Luna below an inscription: soli et
lun(a)e sac(rum) / edullius visurionis / [ex] iu[s]su so[l(vit) l(ibens)]
m(erito).
Espérandieu VII, 211 no. 5622; CIL 13, 6058.

7.   Beirut, National Museum.
       Tyre.
       Stone.
       Undated.
       Altar. On the front an eagle above a thunderbolt, and two bulls; on the
       two sides busts of Luna and Sol, radiate nimbus (eleven rays), *chlamys*.
       LIMC Helios in per. or. 6; Cumont 1927.

8.   Beirut, National Museum.
       Aaqoura.
       Stone.
       Undated.
       Altar decorated on four sides, with a thunderbolt, a bull, and busts of
       Luna and Sol, radiate nimbus (eleven rays), *chlamys*.
       LIMC Helios in per. or. 7; Cumont 1927.

9.   As-Suwayda, Museum.
       Si'
       Basalt.
       Undated.
       Naiskos with an eagle in the tympanum between the busts of Luna (left)
       and Sol (right), the latter rendered as a Sonnengesicht on a radiate disc.
       LIMC Helios in per. or. 29.

10.   Cremona, Museo Archeologico MC 250.
       Calvatone.
       Botticino marble.
       1st–2nd c. AD.
       Altar with frontal heads of Sol (left) and Luna (right). Sol is radiate (twelve
       rays), and Luna has a large crescent behind her head.
       CSIR Italia Regio X Cremona, pp. 123–5 (image p. 124).

11.   Lost?
       The island Ayas across from the harbour of Aigeai, Cilicia
       Limestone
       Undated.

Altar dedicated to Eternal Zeus (ἀφθίτῳ Διί). On the sides, Sol and Luna. Freyberger 2006: 242; Hajjar 1977: 315–6 no. 266.

C2c. Mithraic (Selection)

1. Plate 46.1
   Wiesbaden, Stadtmuseum am Markt SNA 239.
   Nida (Heddernheim).
   Sandstone.
   late 1st–early 2nd century AD.
   Two-sided Mithraic relief, one side depicting a tauroctony, the other Mithras and Sol at a banquet. Sol is dressed in a long *chiton* and a *chlamys*, holds a whip in his left hand and is receiving food (?) on his outstretched right hand. He is bare-headed, having removed his radiate crown and placed it over a Persian cap on a post between Mithras and himself. The main relief revolves within a frame decorated with minor scenes. On the slab above the main scene, between two tondi depicting wind gods, Sol with *quadriga* and Luna on a *biga*. Mithras is depicted ascending the *quadriga* behind Sol.
   LIMC Helios/Sol 245; 252; Merkelbach 1984, 342–4 figs. 101, 103; CIMRM II 1083; Lupa 7109.
   Image: modern copy (detail), Archaeological Museum Frankfurt.

2. Wiesbaden, Stadtmuseum am Markt.
   Nida (Heddernheim).
   White marble.
   AD 85–200. This relief comes from the oldest Mithraeum at Nida, Mithraeum 1, that was built in about AD 85, and abandoned in AD 210. Small Danubian-style marble relief, round top, depicting a tauroctony. In the upper left corner, above the cape of Mithras, a sketchy bust of Sol. Below and separated from the main scene, three minor scenes. From left to right: man laying hand on kneeling man; Sol and Mithras at banquet; Mithras ascending chariot behind Sol.
   LIMC Helios/Sol 252; 254; CIMRM II 1084 fig. 276.

3. Rome, Museo Nazionale Romano.
   Nesce, Mithraeum.
   Marble.
   AD 172 (Clauss 1992, 49).
   Tauroctony. In the upper left-hand corner bust of Sol, *chlamys*, whip, no rays; in the right-hand corner, Luna.

LIMC Helios/Sol 373; Merkelbach 1984: 322–3, fig. 73; von Hesberg 1981: 1086–7 no. 10; CIMRM I, 6501.

4.   Plate 46.2
     Paris, Louvre MA 1023.
     Rome, possibly from a Mithraeum on the Capitoline Hill.
     Marble.
     2nd c. AD.
     Tauroctony in grotto; above in the left-hand corner: Sol, bare-headed (not radiate) nude but for a *chlamys*, whip in right hand, in an ascending *quadriga*, preceded by Phosphorus; in the right hand corner, Luna in descending *biga*, preceded by Hesperus.
     LIMC Helios/Sol 377; CIMRM I, 415.
     Image: © Musée du Louvre, Dist. RMN-Grand Palais / Philippe Fuzeau / Art Resource, NY ART482220

5.   Plates 46.3, 46.4
     Paris, Louvre MA 3441.
     Fiano Romano.
     Marble.
     Second half 2nd c. AD.
     Two-sided relief. Side A: Tauroctony, upper left-hand corner, frontal bust of Sol, radiate nimbus (eleven? rays), upper right hand corner frontal bust of Luna. Side B: Sol, nude but for a *chlamys*, radiate nimbus (eleven? rays), whip, dining with Mithras; in upper left-hand corner Luna.
     LIMC Helios/Sol 252; 370 (inaccurate description); CIMRM I, 641.
     Image: © Louvre, (Museum), Paris, FrancePhoto: Erich Lessing / Art Resource, NY: ART200834.

6.   Cincinnati, Art Museum 1968.112.
     Rome.
     Marble.
     Second half 2nd c. AD.
     Tauroctony. In the upper left-hand corner a frontal bust of Sol, radiate (eleven rays), *chlamys*; right-hand corner lost.
     LIMC Helios/Sol 369; Vermeule 1981, 237 no. 198.
     Image: Sailko, CC BY 3.0, via Wikimedia Common.

7.   Copenhagen, National Museum 2229.
     Acquired in Rome.
     Greyish marble.

2nd c. AD.

Fragment of a Tauroctony-relief. Preserved are Cautes and above him bust of Sol with radiate nimbus.

LIMC Helios/Sol 373; CIMRM I, 597 fig. 169 (not fig. 171).

8. Plates 15.1, 47.1, 48.1
Dieburg, Museum Schloss Fechenbach 22052.
Dieburg, Mithraeum.
Red sandstone.
Late 2nd c. AD.

Two-sided relief, revolving on a pivot. Side A: a total of 11 panels. There is a central panel (Mithras on horseback, hunting), with one large panel above (3 scenes) and one below. The central scene of the upper panel depicts a temple-like building (dystyle in antis) in which a bull is lying. In the tympanum are two busts, possibly Sol and Luna, to either side of a goose (Vermaseren) or eagle (Spätantike) on a globe. On the large panel below (divided into two by an inscription), the right-hand scene depicts Sol, nude but for a *chlamys*, radiate (? not visible on the images available to me), whip, on *quadriga*, with Mithras stepping up from behind. The inscription in and around this panel (upper border, central baulk, lower border) reads: d(eo) i(nvicto) m(ithrae) / silves/trius / silvi/nus / et silvestrius pe[rpetuus et a]urelius nepos v(otum) s(olverunt) l(ibentes) l(aeti) me(rito). Four small panels are arranged vertically along each side (lower right hand corner: Mithras and Sol, with nimbus, no rays, dining). An additional inscription on the borders of the lower left scene reads: Perpetu(u)s frater / artis sutor(iae); on the borders of the lower right scene: Silvinus ar/tis quadratari/ae aureli[us] d(ono) d(ederunt). Side B: the scene is enclosed by a circular border. In the four corners outside the border: the four winds (busts). In the centre of the main scene, Sol, nude but for a *chlamys*, head lost, whip (?) in his left hand, is seated on a throne on a two-stepped dais in front of a tetrastyle temple with an imago clipeata in the centre of the tympanum. Below him the bust (three-quarter en face) of Caelus, with velum above and behind him, between the reclining Tellus (right), with cornucopia, and Oceanus (left), holding a jar on its side. On the lower left step of the dais, Phaethon, nude but for a *chlamys*, beardless, short hair, bare-headed, stands with his right hand raised towards Sol's right hand (lost). On the lower right hand step of the dais, an almost nude woman (Summer); above her, behind Sol's left shoulder, a woman, dressed and capite velato (Winter); behind Sol's right shoulder a half nude woman with her hand above Sol's head (Spring) and next to her a fourth woman, behind Phaethon, also half nude and bearing a tray of fruit (Autumn). Four youths, two to either side, are arranged around the scene; they are nude, but for a *chlamys*, clean-shaven, bare-headed, and each holds a horse by his bridle. They each hold a conch-shell in their left hand, identifying them as the four winds. Inscription: silvestrius silvinus et silvestrius perpetu(u)s et silvestrius aurelius d(eo) s(oli) i(nvicto) m(ithrae).

This scene directly reflects the Phaethon-iconography of contemporary sarcophagi, and barring the inscription on the encircling band contains no direct reference to Mithras.

LIMC Helios/Sol 173, 218a; Spätantike 537–540 no. 144; Merkelbach 1984: 358, 261 fig. 123; Matern 2002: 186, 278 K4; CSIR Deutschland II, 13, pp. 154–6 no. 272, pls. 100–101; CIMRM 1247; Matijević & Wiegels 2004: 222–227.

Image: 8 and 8a © Museum Schloss Fechenbach Dieburg, photograph: Gelfort.

9. Plate 49.1
    Poetovio (Ptuj), Pokrajinski Museum RL 144.
    Poetovio (Ptuj), Mithraeum I.
    Marble.
    Mid 2nd c. AD.
    Statue-base. On the left side, frontal bust of Sol, radiate (nine rays), *chlamys*, whip above his right shoulder; on the right side bust of Luna. On the front: inscription. petrae / genetrici / felix / prudentis antoni / rufi p(ublici) p(ortorii) vil(ici) vic(arius) / ex viso.
    LIMC Helios/Sol 308; CIMRM II, 1489–90; Selem 1980: 101 no. 34.
    Image: photograph courtesy photo dokumentation Regional Museum Ptuj-Ormož.

10. Jerusalem, Israel Museum 97.095.0019.
    Syria.
    Limestone.
    2nd–3rd c. AD.
    Tauroctony. Frontal bust of Sol, radiate, left, and Luna right. Lower right: Sol (radiate) and Mithras at the banquet. The relief includes a number of other scenes, some unique.
    De Jong 1997.

11. Rome, S. Clemente, Mithraeum.
    In situ.

Marble.

Ca. AD 200.

Altar with relief of the tauroctony; upper corner left, frontal bust of Sol; upper corner right, frontal bust of Luna.

LIMC Helios/Sol 368; Merkelbach 1984: 299, fig. 43; CIMRM I, 3389.

12. Rome, Musei Capitolini 1203.

Rome, Salita delle Tre Pile.

Marble.

2nd–3rd c. AD.

Tauroctony. In the upper left-hand corner, frontal bust of Sol, radiate nimbus, *chlamys*; upper right-hand corner frontal bust of Luna.

LIMC Helios/Sol 368; CIMRM I, 417.

13. Rome, Musei Capitolini 1204.

Rome, Via di Borgo S. Agata.

Travertine.

2nd–3rd c AD.

Tauroctony; in the upper left-hand corner, bust of Sol, radiate (with one long ray extending to Mithras); upper right, bust of Luna.

CIMRM I, 366.

14. Vatican, Museo Chiaramonti 1379.

Rome, near the church of S. Lucia in Selci.

Marble.

2nd–3rd c. AD.

Tauroctony; upper left-hand corner bust of Sol, radiate nimbus (eleven rays), *chlamys*; right-hand corner bust of Luna.

Merkelbach 1984: 304 fig. 50; CIMRM I, 368; Amelung 1903: 692–3 no. 568, pl. 74.

15. Rome, Museo Nazionale Romano 164688.

Tor Cervara.

Marble.

2nd–3rd c. AD.

Tauroctony; in the upper left-hand corner, bust of Sol, radiate (seven rays), *chlamys* and *chiton*, globe in left hand and right hand raised, above the protomes of four horses; in the upper right-hand corner bust of Luna. After it was discovered in 1964, some parts of the relief ended up in Karlsruhe (acquired through a Swiss dealer) while most others were

entered in the Museo Nazionale in Rome. In 2013 all parts were reunited and the restored relief is now permanently on display in Rome.
LIMC Helios/Sol 381.

16.   Rome, private collection.
       Uncertain, presumably Rome.
       Marble.
       2nd–3rd c. AD.
       Mithras standing on the back of the slaughtered bull; upper left-hand corner bust of Sol, radiate nimbus (seven rays), *chlamys*; upper right-hand corner bust of Luna.
       LIMC Helios/Sol 372; Merkelbach 1984: 298–9 fig. 42; CIMRM I 334.

17.   Brussels, Art and History Museum A 9096.
       Rome, reportedly found between the Porta Portese and S. Pancrazio.
       Marble.
       2nd–3rd c. AD.
       Upper part of a tauroctony; in upper left corner bust of Sol, radiate, *chlamys*, damaged above Cautopates, in upper right corner bust of Luna (damaged) above Cautes.
       LIMC Helios/Sol 368; CIMRM I, 585 fig. 162.

18.   Plate 49.3
       Berlin, Staatliche Museen, Antikensammlung SK 707.
       Rome.
       Marble.
       2nd–3rd c. AD.
       Tauroctony; in the upper corners busts of Sol (left), *chlamys*, radiate, and Luna (right).
       LIMC Helios/Sol 374; Merkelbach 1984: fig. 69; CIMRM I, 598.
       Image: © Staatliche Museen zu Berlin.

19.   Plate 46.5
       Paris, Louvre MA 1025.
       Rome?
       Marble.
       2nd–3rd c. AD.
       Tauroctony, in the upper left-hand corner, bust of Sol, seven rays.
       LIMC Helios/Sol 373; CIMRM I, 588 fig. 164.
       Image: Musée du Louvre, Paris, FrancePhoto: © RMN-Grand Palais / Stephane Marechalle / Art Resource, NY: ART522067

20. Palermo, Museo archeologico regionale "Antonino Salinas" 751.
Local origin (Panormus) doubtful; possibly from Rome.
Marble.
2nd–3rd c. AD.
Tauroctony; in the upper left-hand corner bust of Sol, nimbus (?), no rays;
in the right-hand corner bust of Luna.
CIMRM I, 164; Merkelbach 1984: 282 fig. 23; cf. Clauss 1992: 54 n. 59.

21. Vatican, Cortile del Belvedere.
Ostia.
Marble.
2nd–3rd c. AD.
Tauroctony. Upper left-hand corner: bust of Sol, radiate (four or five rays),
upper right-hand corner bust of Luna. Other Mithraic scenes along the
border, including: Mithras crowning Sol.
LIMC Helios/Sol 244; 284 (incorrect description); Merkelbach 1984: 297
fig. 41; CIMRM I, 321.

22. Plate 49.2
Clamecy.
Intaranum (Entrains).
Sandstone.
2nd–3rd c. AD.
Upper left hand corner of a tauroctony; with the head of Sol, radiate
(eight rays) and the raven. The surviving part of the relief is in two pieces
which fit together; see photograph in Espérandieu. One (or more?) of the
youthful, upturned heads with long wavy hair found at Entrains may be
Sol rather than Bacchus (as Espérandieu identifies them), but this would
depend on the context (e.g. within the Mithraeum); cf. Espérandieu III
2286 (quite likely), 2288 (possible), 2291 (possible).
LIMC Helios/Sol 368; Espérandieu III, 260 no. 2275; CIMRM I, 945.
Image: Lupa.at/25879 photograph Ortolf Harl.

23. Lisbon, Archaeological Museum.
Caetobriga (Troía).
Marble.
2nd–3rd c. AD.
Part of a large Mithraic relief. Of the main scene, only a small section at
the right, with the frontal bust of Luna above Cautopates with lowered
torch, are preserved. To the right, in a separate panel, Sol, *chlamys* and *chiton*, radiate nimbus (eleven rays), right hand lowered and outstretched,

palm outwards, drinking horn in left hand, lies together with Mithras on a couch; two servants.

LIMC Helios/Sol 250; Bendala Galán 1986: 398 β1, pl. XI; CIMRM I, 798.

Image: mithraeum.eu/monument/245

24. Bonn, Rheinisches Landesmuseum.
     Dormagen.
     Limestone.
     2nd–3rd c. AD.
     Fragment of a Tauroctony relief. In upper left hand corner, above Cautopates, bust of Sol in high relief, *chlamys*, long wavy hair, holes for rays. Inscription: deo soli i(nvicto) m(ithrae) p(ro) s(alute) th(?)urat(?) r(?)[al]is didil[ae f(ilius)] / dup[l(arius)] al(a)e noricorum ci[vis t(h)rax v(otum) s(olvit) l(ibens) m(erito)]

     LIMC Helios/Sol 373; CIMRM II, 1014; Schwertheim 1974: 13 no. 8b.

     Image: https://edh-www.adw.uni-heidelberg.de/edh/inschrift/HD063838.

25. Stuttgart, Landesmuseum Württemberg.
     Fellbach.
     Sandstone.
     2nd–3rd c. AD.
     Tauroctony; in upper left-hand corner, frontal bust of Sol, and in right-hand corner Luna.

     CIMRM II, 1306; Merkelbach 1984: 348 fig. 109.

     Image: http://lupa.at/7358 (February 1, 2019).

26. Formerly Hanau, Schloss Philipsruh (destroyed in WWII).
     Gross Krotzenburg.
     Red sandstone.
     Late 2nd–first half 3rd c. AD.
     Altar; head of Sol, radiate, between two bulls' heads. Dedicatory inscription: deo soli / invict(o) mytrae / iul(ius) macrinus / immun(is) leg(ionis) / viii aug(ustae) ex voto / suscept(o) solvit / l(ibens) l(aetus) m(erito). Found together with a Tauroctony relief (upper left part), and another altar, similar but slightly smaller, dedicated to Luna by Lucius Fabius Anthimus, who was a member of the Cohors IIII Vindelicorum (if the much damaged text of the lower part of the altar was correctly read and reconstructed).

LIMC Helios/Sol 187; Merkelbach 1984: 363 fig 127; CIMRM II, 1150–1; CSIR Deutschland II, 12, p. 129 no. 283, pl. 104.
Image of a cast: http://lupa.at/6993.

27.   Plate 52.1
      Karlsruhe, Badisches Landesmuseum. C16.
      Heidelberg-Neuenheim.
      Red sandstone.
      2nd–3rd c. AD.
      In the main field, Tauroctony, with busts of Sol (left), radiate, and Luna (right). The main panel is framed above and to the left and right by a series of smaller panels with various Mithraic scenes. These include: (above, third and fourth scenes from left) Sol in *quadriga*, jumping upwards (right), with Mithras behind him, and Luna, in *biga*, going downwards. Remains of a Jupiter-Giant pillar were found in close vicinity to this Mithraeum (CIMRM II, 1282, 1284, 1286), but according to Clauss (1992, 111 n. 68) were not in any way connected with it.
      LIMC Helios/Sol 255 (ref. to Spätantike incorrect); Merkelbach 1984: 354–5, fig. 116; CIMRM II, 114–5, 1283.
      Image: © Badisches Landesmuseum Karlsruhe, photograph: Thomas Goldschmidt.

28.   Plates 49.5, 49.6
      Ladenburg, Lobdengau-museum.
      Lopodunum (Ladenburg).
      Sandstone.
      2nd–3rd c. AD.
      Sol, nude, and Mithras, nude but for a *chlamys*, reclining behind a three-legged table.
      LIMC Helios/Sol 249; Schwertheim 1974, 144 pl. 42; Beck 1984: pl. 3.
      Image: 28 and 28a Lupa.at/25600 Photographs Ortolf Harl.

29.   Hanau, Schloss Philippsruhe inv. A 2878.
      Rückingen.
      Sandstone.
      First quarter 3rd c. AD.
      Two-sided Mithraic relief. Side A. Lower part: tauroctony under an arch decorated with the signs of the zodiac; in the two corners busts of Sol (left) and Luna (right). Upper part divided into four horizontal registers,

of which the top one is almost completely destroyed. The registers depict various scenes; Sol is included in the following: Top register, right hand corner: 1. Sol kneeling, being crowned by Mithras; third register, centre: 6. Sol in *quadriga*; fourth register: Sol, standing, globe, among the planetary deities (? – if so, they are in arbitrary order over two registers); 4. Sol and Mithras shaking hands; 5. Sol and Mithras dining. Side B depicts two scenes: the upper half shows Mithras on horseback; the lower half: 5. Mithras and Sol dining.

LIMC Helios/Sol 244; 247; 252; Merkelbach 1984: 364–5 figs. 128–9; CIMRM II, 1137; Beck 1988: 15–6 n. 35; CSIR Deutschland II, 12, pp. 112–3 no. 228, pls. 90–91.

30.   London, Museum of London (City Hall Museum) A16933.
       London.
       Marble.
       2nd–3rd c. AD.
       Tauroctony within a zodiac circle. In the upper left-hand corner, Sol (head missing) in *quadriga* rising upwards; in upper right-hand corner Luna in *biga* descending.
       LIMC Helios/Sol 382; Merkelbach 1984: 329 fig. 81; CIMRM I 810–1; Gundel 1992, 222 no. 53.

31.   Graz, Joanneum 266.
       Pohanica (Zgornje Pohanca).
       Marble.
       2nd–3rd c. AD.
       Tauroctony. In the upper left-hand corner bust of Sol, whip, behind the heads of four horses; in upper right-hand corner: Luna in *biga* of oxen (only the hindquarters of one of the oxen survive).
       LIMC Helios/Sol 380; CIMRM II, 1458 fig. 372; Lovenjak 1998, No. 55.
       Image: http://lupa.at/6136 (February 1, 2019).

32.   Deva, Museum.
       Sarmizegetusa, Mithraeum.
       Marble.
       2nd–3rd c. AD.
       Bust of Sol, *chlamys*, radiate nimbus (seven rays), *chlamys*.
       LIMC Helios/Sol 31; CIMRM II, 2132 fig. 578.

33. Plate 49.4
    Deva, Museum.
    Sarmizegetusa.
    Marble.
    2nd–3rd c. AD.
    Tauroctony, fragment. In the upper left-hand corner frontal bust of Sol, radiate (six rays, seventh ray hidden behind the raven), *chlamys*.
    LIMC Helios/Sol 368; CIMRM II, 2062 fig. 549.
    Image: © Deva Museum, Cristina Mitar.

34. Timişoara, Museum.
    Varhély-Sarmizegetusa.
    Marble.
    2nd–3rd c. AD.
    Two fragments of a tauroctony-relief. Above, left, bust of Sol, right, bust of Luna. Some of the surrounding Mithraic scenes also survive, including (all below the main scene): Sol crowned by Mithras, Sol and Mithras dining, and Mithras ascending a *biga* behind Sol.
    LIMC Helios/Sol 368; CIMRM II, 2052 fig. 543.

35. Plate 50.1
    Bucharest, National Museum.
    Acbunar (Mircea Voda).
    Marble.
    2nd c. AD.
    Tauroctony-relief, Sol and Luna in the upper left and upper right corners respectively.
    Römer in Rumänien, Ausstellungskatalog Köln, Cologne 1969: 209, F 77.
    Image: Arachne FA-612-09_3312.jpg; arachne.dainst.org/entity/3462085.

36. Plates 51.1–51.4
    Alba Julia, Muzeul Unirii 455.
    Apulum.
    Marble.
    2nd c. AD.
    In the centre: tauroctony, with busts of Sol (left), radiate, and Luna (right). Above and below, Mithraic scenes, including (both below): Sol and Mithras dining; Mithras ascending the *quadriga* behind Sol. Inscription:

d(eo) i(nvicto) m(ithrae) t(itus) aur(elius) f(abia) marcus vet(eranus) leg(ionis) XIII G(eminae).

LIMC Helios/Sol 252; Merkelbach 1984: 384 fig. 152; CIMRM II, 1958 (omits description of two Mithraic scenes below).

Image: 36, 36a, 36b, and 36c courtesy Muzeul Unirii; photographs author.

37. Plates 52.2–52.5
      Alba Julia, Muzeul Unirii 8 (204/II).
      Apulum.
      Sandstone.
      2nd–3rd c. AD
      Relief in three registers. In the upper register, at the left, Sol, nude, head lost, in *quadriga* (not a *biga*, as Vermaseren says) heading right, and in the right-hand corner Luna in *biga* (oxen) heading left (!). The upper and lower register (left part lost) also contain Mithraic scenes, including Mithras ascending the *quadriga* behind Sol.
      LIMC Helios/Sol 257; Merkelbach 1984: 385 fig. 153; CIMRM II, 1972.
      Images: 37, 37a, 37b, and 37c courtesy Muzeul Unirii; photographs author.

38. Sibiu, Bruckenthal Regional Museum 7161.
      Apulum.
      Marble.
      2nd–3rd c. AD.
      Tauroctony. In the upper left-hand corner bust of Sol; in the upper right-hand corner bust of Luna. A series of Mithraic scenes surround the main scene (some lost); these include (below the tauroctony): Sol kneeling before Mthras; Sol and Mithras dining; Mithras ascending the *quadriga* behind Sol.
      LIMC Helios/Sol 244; 252; 368; Merkelbach 1984: 383 fig. 150; CIMRM II, 1935/6.
      Image: http://lupa.at/17299.

39. Sibiu, Bruckenthal Regional Museum 1826.
      Apulum.
      Marble.
      2nd–3rd c. AD.
      Tauroctony. In upper left-hand corner bust of Sol, in upper right-hand corner bust of Luna. A series of Mithraic scenes surround the main scene; these include (below the tauroctony): Mithras crowning Sol; Sol and Mithras dining; Mithras ascending the *quadriga* behind Sol.
      LIMC Helios/Sol 252; 368; Merkelbach 1984: 386 fig. 154; CIMRM II, 2000.

40. Plate 50.2
    Constanţa (Rumania), National Museum of History and Archaeology 40 (33118a).
    Tirguşor.
    Sandstone.
    2nd–3rd c. AD.
    Tauroctony. In the upper corners the busts of Luna (left) and Sol (right), radiate nimbus (seven rays). Note the inverted positions of Sol and Luna.
    LIMC Helios/Sol 368; CIMRM II 2306, fig. 639.
    Image: Lupa.at/21199 photograph Ortolf Harl.

41. Ptuj, Pokrajinski Muzej Ptuj Ormož inv. 52.
    Poetovio (Ptuj), Mithraeum II.
    Marble.
    Last quarter of the 2nd c.–3rd c. AD.
    Fragment of a tauroctony relief. In the upper left-hand corner bust of Sol, radiate, *chlamys*.
    LIMC Helios/Sol 368; CIMRM II, 1576 fig. 398.

42. Sarajevo, Museum.
    Konjic.
    Limestone.
    2nd–3rd c. AD.
    Two-sided relief. On one side the tauroctony (damaged, Sol missing). On the other side the banquet of Sol and Mithras (damaged). Sol is most likely the right-hand figure on the couch, bare-headed, wearing a *chiton* and *chlamys*.
    LIMC Helios/Sol 251; Merkelbach 1984: 381 fig 148. CIL III 14617. CIMRM 1896, figs. 4901.
    Image: http://lupa.at/22318 (February 1, 2019)

43. Split, Museum (lost in WWII).
    Pritok-Jezerine (near Bihać).
    Sandstone.
    2nd–3rd c. AD.
    Tauroctony; in upper left-hand corner bust of Sol, radiate (seven rays); in upper right-hand corner Luna.
    LIMC Helios/Sol 373; CIMRM II 1907 fig. 496.

44. Zagreb, Museum Arch. 123.
    Raetinium (Golubić, near Bihać, Bosnia).

Yellow limestone.

2nd–3rd c. AD.

Tauroctony. In the upper left-hand corner bust of Sol, radiate nimbus, *chlamys*, whip (?) in raised right hand; in the upper right-hand corner bust of Luna.

LIMC Helios/Sol 368; CIMRM II, 1910 fig. 498.

Image: http://lupa.at/8830 (February 1, 2019).

45.   Rome, Mithraeum of S. Prisca.

In situ.

Lead.

Ca. AD 225.

Lead plaque with 3/4 head of Sol, radiate (seven rays); the rays were cut out to allow light to shine from behind.

CIMRM I, 494; Vermaseren & van Essen 1965, 346 no. 46, pl. 80; Merkelbach 1984: 313 fig. 62; Matern 2002: 264 B139.

46.   Rome, Mithraeum near the Circus Maximus.

In situ.

Marble.

Second half 3rd c. AD (Clauss 1992, 28).

Tauroctony. In the upper left-hand corner bust of Sol, radiate; in the upper right-hand corner, Luna.

LIMC Helios/Sol 368; Merkelbach 1984: 308 fig. 54; CIMRM I, 435/6.

47.   Rome, Mithraeum near the Circus Maximus.

In situ.

Marble.

Second half 3rd c. AD (Clauss 1992, 28).

Tauroctony. In the upper left-hand corner, bust of Sol, radiate; in the upper right hand corner, bust of Luna.

LIMC Helios/Sol 373; CIMRM I, 437, figure 123.

48.   Rome, Museo Nazionale Romano 205837.

Rome, Mithraeum of the Castra Peregrinorum (S. Stefano Rotondo).

Marble.

Late 3rd c. AD.

Tauroctony. In the upper left-hand corner, Sol in *quadriga*, radiate (four or five rays), nude but for a *chlamys*, globe in left hand, reins in right; in the upper right-hand corner, Luna in *biga* preceded by Hesperus.

LIMC Helios/Sol 379.

48a.   Rome, Museo Nazionale Romano 205838.
       Rome, Mithraeum of the Castra Peregrinorum (S. Stefano Rotondo).
       Marble.
       Late 3rd c. AD.
       Small tauroctony. In the upper left-hand corner, bust of Sol, radiate (five
       rays), *chlamys*, and in the upper right-hand corner, bust of Luna.
       Lissi-Caronna 1986.

48b.   Rome, Museo Nazionale Romano 205839.
       Rome, Mithraeum of the Castra Peregrinorum (S. Stefano Rotondo).
       Marble.
       3rd c. AD.
       Five fragments of a small tauroctony in the Danubian style, with well-
       preserved polychrome painted details. In the upper left-hand corner, bust
       of Sol, radiate.
       Lissi-Caronna 1986.

49.   Lost.
       Rome, Baths of Caracalla, Mithraeum.
       Marble.
       3rd c. AD.
       Originally head of sol, radiate (seven rays, cut-out and meant to be illumi-
       nated from behind), raised right hand; small bust of Luna above his left
       shoulder. The actual head of Sol is completely lost.
       LIMC Helios/Sol 307; Merkelbach 1984: 309 fig. 55; CIMRM I, 458.

50.   Richmond, Va., The Virginia Museum of Fine Arts, Glasgow Fund 67–58.
       Unknown, possibly Rome.
       Marble.
       Late 3rd c. AD (Vermeule).
       Tauroctony. Busts of Sol and Luna in the upper corners. Sol's bust (left) is
       in profile facing right. He has long, wavy hair, but no rays.
       LIMC Helios/Sol 376; Vermeule 1981: 236 no. 197.
       Image: https://www.vmfa.museum/collections/search-collections/?key
       word=Mithras (February 1, 2019).

51.   Plate 53.1
       London, British Museum 1873,0820.260.
       Ostia, possibly from the Aldobrandini Mithraeum.
       Bronze.
       3rd c. AD.

Plaque with dedicatory inscription; at the top, in relief, in the centre, bust of Sol, radiate (seven rays), between a sacrificial knife (left), and patera (right). Inscription: sex(to) pompeio sex(ti) fil(io) maximo sacerdoti soli invicti m(i)t(hrae) patri patrum q(uin)q(uennali) corp(oris) treiect(is) togatensium sacerdotes solis invicti m(i)t(hrae) ob amorem et merita eius semper habet

LIMC Helios/Sol 458; Walters 1899: 169 no. 904; Merkelbach 1984: 291 fig. 33; CIMRM I, 234/5; Becatti, Ostia II, 42 pl. 5.1.

Image: photograph © Trustees of the British Museum.

52. Naples, National Archaeological Museum.
      Puteoli (Puozzoli).
      Marble.
      3rd c. AD.
      Tauroctony-relief; upper left-hand corner bust of Sol, *chlamys*, radiate (six rays, of which one extended to the mantle of Mithras).
      LIMC Helios/Sol 373.

53. Plate 53.3
      Vienna, Kunsthist. Museum I 624.
      Aquileia, Monastero.
      Marble.
      Mid 3rd c. AD (or 2nd c. AD according to Vermaseren), but cf. the dates of inscriptions from the same group in the 240s; (Clauss 1992: 63–4).
      Tauroctony. To the left, Sol (no rays) in *quadriga*, to the right, bust of Luna (no *biga*).
      CIMRM I 736 FIG. 203.
      Image: courtesy KHM-Museumsverband.

54. Bologna, Museo Civico Archeologico, stolen.
      Bologna? Danube region?
      Marble.
      3rd c. AD.
      Tauroctony. Above the main scene, busts of the planetary deities, running from Sol (left) to Luna (right) with Sarapis rather than Jupiter in the centre. Sarapis is facing, the others are in profile or three-quarter view, looking towards Sarapis. Below the main scene, variations on Mithraic scenes including: Mithras dining with Cautes and Cautopates; winged putto ascending *quadriga*. There is some discussion as to whether the

four central planetary deities are original, or 19th century restorations; cf. Beck 1988, 101–106.

LIMC Helios/Sol 283; Merkelbach 1984 320–1, fig. 71; CIMRM I, 693; Beck 1988: passim, especially 101–6.

55. Plate 53.2
Trier, Rheinisches Landesmuseum.
Augusta Treverorum (Trier).
Sandstone.
3rd c. AD.
Altar. In the main scene, Cautes within a zodiac circle. In the upper left-hand corner, above the tympanum, bust of Sol, radiate (seven rays), and in upper right-hand corner, largely destroyed, bust of Luna.
LIMC Helios/Sol 328; Merkelbach 1984: 336 fig. 90; CIMRM I, 985.
Image: © GDKE/Rheinisches Landesmuseum Trier, Foto: Th. Zühmer.

56. Bingen, Museum am Strom, inv. 2464.
Bingen.
Limestone.
Ca. AD 235.
Votive altar to Mithras, adorned with a frontal bust of Sol (largely destroyed), radiate (seven rays), *chlamys*. The rays pierce the altar to allow illumination from behind. Inscription: in h(onorem) d(omus) d(ivinae) soli / invicto mitrae / aram privati se / cundinus et ter / tinus et confinis / ex voto privati / tertini v(otum) s(olverunt) l(ibentes) l(aeti) m(erito).
CIMRM II, 1241–2; Merkelbach 1984: 361 fig. 124; CSIR Deutschland II, 14, 57–9 no. 15, pl. 8.
Image: http://lupa.at/27231 (February 1, 2019)

57. Plates 6.5, 55.1
Speyer, Historisches Museum der Pfalz.
Gimmeldingen.
Sandstone.
AD 235.
Tauroctony. In the upper left-hand corner bust of Sol, radiate nimbus (thirteen rays); in the upper right-hand corner bust of Luna.
LIMC Helios/Sol 368; CIMRM II, 1314 fig. 348; Clauss 1992: 110.
Image: Lupa.at/25549 Photograph Ortolf Harl.

58.   Plates 55.2, 55.3
      Karlsruhe, Badisches Ladesmuseum C 118.
      Osterburken.
      Yellowish sandstone.
      Ca. AD 225 (Clauss 1992, 118, with ref.).
      In the main field the tauroctony below an arch with the signs of the
      zodiac. Above the arch in the left hand corner Sol standing in a *quadriga*,
      preceded by Lucifer; Sol is nude but for a *chlamys*, has a nimbus, and
      holds a whip in his raised right hand. Behind Sol the head of a Wind-god;
      various Mithraic scenes are also depicted in his corner. In the upper right
      corner Luna in *biga*, Hesperus, a Wind-god, and various Mithraic scenes.
      The central panel above the zodiac between these scenes contains the
      twelve gods. To the left and the right, the Tauroctony is framed by small
      panels with Mithraic scenes; these include: (left side, second panel from
      below) Sol (?) carrying disc; (right side, third panel from the top) Mithras
      ascending a *quadriga* behind Sol; (fourth panel from the top) Mithras
      holding an object (piece of meat?) over Sol's head; (fifth panel) 4. Mithras
      and Sol shake hands above a burning altar; (seventh panel) Mithras and
      Sol (nimbus) dining.
      LIMC Helios/Sol 247; 252; 378; Merkelbach 1984: 350–3, figs. 112–5;
      CIMRM II, 1292.
      Images: 58 and 58a Lupa.at/13799 Photographs Ortolf Harl, courtesy
      Badisches Landesmuseum, Karlsruhe.

59.   Plate 54.2
      Bad Homburg, Saalburg, Museum.
      Stockstadt, Mithraeum I.
      Silver.
      3rd c. AD.
      Fragmentary aedicula-shaped silver-foil relief of the tauroctony. In the
      upper left-hand corner, bust of Sol, radiate (bust of Luna in right-hand
      corner lost).
      Espérandieu, Germanie 281; CIMRM II, 1206.
      Image: © Römerkastell Saalburg, Claudia Rothenberger.

60.   Plate 54.3
      Bad Homburg, Saalburg Museum inv. St. 78.
      Stockstadt, Mithraeum I.
      Yellow sandstone.
      3rd c. AD.

Altar. On the front, bust of Sol, radiate (eleven rays), whip emerging from behind his right shoulder. Face completely hacked away.
LIMC Helios/Sol 35; CIMRM II, 1201 fig. 315; CSIR Deutschland II, 13, 72 no. 67, pl. 20.
Image: © Römerkastell Saalburg, Gerhard Kunze/Sebastian Röhl.

61. Aschaffenburg, Stiftsmuseum 373.
Stockstadt, Mithraeum II.
Bronze, silver-plated, traces of gilding.
3rd c. AD.
Relief plaque, fragment. Tauroctony (most of the scene missing); above: heads of Sol, radiate (left) and Luna (right), each accompanied by a second youth (Lucifer and Hesperus or two of the Wind-gods).
LIMC Helios/Sol 393; CIMRM II, 1216 fig. 319.

62. Newcastle-Upon-Tyne, Great North Museum NEWMA 1956.10.30.
Brocolitia (Carrawburgh), Mithraeum.
Stone.
Later 3rd c. AD.
Altar with half-length representation of Sol, nude but for a *chlamys*, radiate, whip in right hand. The rays of Sol are triangular holes cut through the altar to a recess at the back of the altar which held a lamp. Inscription: deo invicto / mitrae m(arcus) sim / plicius simplex / pr(a)ef(ectus) v(otum) s(olvit) l(ibens) m(erito).
LIMC Helios/Sol 456; Smith 1974, no. 9; CIMRM I, 847; Matern 2002: 255 B76; RIB 1546 (with image online).

63. Plate 54.4
York, Yorkshire Museum.
Eboracum (York).
Limestone.
3rd c. AD?
Tauroctony. In the upper left-hand corner, bust of Sol, very worn; in the upper right-hand corner Luna. Below: Mithras crowning Sol, Mithras and Sol dining, Mithras ascending the *quadriga* behind Sol.
LIMC Helios/Sol 244; 252; 254; LIMC Mithras 137; CIMRM I, 835.
Image: CC BY-SA 4.0.

64. Enns, Museum Lauriacum R X 131
Lauriacum (Lorch).

Limestone.

3rd c. AD.

Tauroctony. Left and right angle of the arched border above lost (presumably Sol and Luna were depicted there); the rest of the upper border depicts Mithraic scenes, as does the lower border. Among the latter: Mithras crowning Sol; Sol and Mithras dining; Mithras ascending the *quadriga* behind Sol.

LIMC Helios/Sol 252; 254; CIMRM II, 1422 fig. 364.

65.   Linz, Schlossmuseum.

Lentia (Linz), Tummelplatz.

Marble.

Last quarter of the 3rd c. AD.

Small roundel depicting the tauroctony. The upper part (with busts of Sol and Luna) lost; in exergue, Mithraic scenes, including: Mithras and Sol dining, Mithras ascending the chariot behind Sol.

LIMC Helios/Sol 252; 254; CIMRM II, 1415 fig. 362.

66.   Plate 56.1–56.4

Klagenfurt, Landesmuseum Kärnten Lapidarium 19b.

Virunum (Zollfeld).

Marble.

3rd c. AD.

Pilaster, fragment, with various Mithraic scenes including: 1. Mithras preparing to crown (or hit?) kneeling Sol, radiate, nude but for a *chlamys*; 4. Sol, radiate (ten rays), nude but for a *chlamys* and Mithras shaking hands; 6. Mithras ascending the *quadriga* behind Sol, radiate.

LIMC Helios/Sol 244; 247; CSIR öst. II.4 (1984), 300b pl. 6; Merkelbach 1984: 367 fig. 131; CIMRM II, 1430.

Images: 66, 66a, 66b, and 66c photographs Lupa.at/5860 Ortolf Harl.

67.   Budapest, National Museum 6.1943.1.

Brigetio (Komárom).

Bronze.

3rd c. AD.

Tauroctony. In the four corners tondi with busts of the four seasons; next to the two upper ones, busts of Sol, radiate, whip, and Luna. In a frieze below the main scene the busts of the seven planetary deities; Sol, radiate, whip, second from the left.

LIMC Helios/Sol 288, 393a; CIMRMM II, 1727; Merkelbach 1984: 378, fig. 143.

68. Székesfehérvár, Szent István Király Múzeum 8641.
    Sárkeszi, Mithraeum.
    Limestone.
    Around the beginning of the 3rd c. AD.
    Tauroctony. In the upper left-hand corner, bust of Sol, radiate, and the
    protomes of two horses; upper right-hand corner, Luna.
    LIMC Helios/Sol 380; CIMRM II, 1816 fig. 470; Fitz 1998: 102 no. 186.

69. Plate 52.7
    Poetovio (Ptuj), Mithraeum III.
    In situ.
    Marble.
    3rd c. AD.
    Six fragments of a tauroctony-relief. In the upper left-hand corner bust of
    Sol, radiate, *chlamys*.
    LIMC Helios/Sol 376; CIMRM II, 1600 fig. 410.
    Image: © Photo documentation Regional Museum Ptuj-Ormož.

70. Plate 15.3
    Poetovio (Ptuj), Mithraeum III, RL 293.
    In situ.
    Marble.
    AD 262–268.
    Altar decorated on three sides. Front: Mithras and Sol, radiate (five rays),
    nude but for a *chlamys* hold a dagger (?) with meat (?) upright above a
    burning altar while a raven pecks at it from above. Sol holds an unclear
    object in his left hand, possibly a small globe, definitely not a dagger
    (pace Merkelbach). Left side: dagger, bow, and quiver. Right side: Mithras
    shooting rain from a rock.
    LIMC Helios/Sol 246; Merkelbach 1984: 374 fig. 138; CIMRM II, 1584,
    fig. 403.
    Image: © Photo documentation Regional Museum Ptuj-Ormož.

71. Poetovio (Ptuj), Mithraeum III, RL 295.
    In situ.
    Marble.
    AD 253–268.
    Altar. Inscription on the front; on the right-hand side Sol, radiate (twelve
    rays), nude but for a *chlamys*, whip in his raised right hand and globe in
    his left hand, standing on a small pedestal, the heads of four horses in
    low relief by his right leg; on the left-hand side a man with mural crown,

cornucopia, and patera by an altar. Above the moulding on either side a reclining lion.

LIMC Helios/Sol 455; Merkelbach 1984: 375 fig. 139; Selem 1980: 128–9 no. 89 pl. 24; CIMRM II, 1591; Matern 2002: 90, 113 n. 611, 226–7 G12.

72. Poetovio (Ptuj), Mithraeum III, RL 298.
In situ.
Marble.
3rd c. AD.
Fragment of a tauroctony-relief. In the upper left-hand corner bust of Sol, bare-headed, *chlamys*, above the heads of four horses.
LIMC Helios/Sol 380; CIMRM II, 1599 fig. 409; Selem 1980: 136–7 no. 99 pl. 26.

73. Plate 52.6
Poetovio (Ptuj), Mithraeum III, RL 299.
In situ.
Marble.
3rd c. AD.
Fragment of a tauroctony-relief. Among the various Mithraic scenes depicted: Sol kneeling before Mithras; Sol (?) and Mithras shaking hands; and Mithras ascending the *quadriga* behind Sol, radiate (nine rays), nude but for a *chlamys*, whip in his right hand.
LIMC Helios/Sol 254; Merkelbach 1984: 373 fig. 137; Selem 1980: no. 97 pl. 26; CIMRM II, 1579.
Image: © Photo documentation Regional Museum Ptuj-Ormož.

74. Plate 10.3
Ptuj, Pokrajinski Muzej Ptuj Ormož RL 707
Poetovio (Ptuj), Mithraeum IV.
Marble.
First half 3rd c. AD.
Fragment of a relief depicting the upper part of Sol, frontal, radiate (nine rays), billowing *chlamys* and *chiton*, raised right hand, under an arch.
LIMC Helios/Sol 124; Matern 2002: 125, 240 I51.
Image: © Photo documentation Regional Museum Ptuj-Ormož.

75. Plate 57.1
Zagreb, Museum 16.
Dolnoj Plemenšćini (Pregrade).
Marble.

Late 3rd-early 4th c. AD?

Tauroctony. In the upper right-hand corner Sol, radiate; upper left-hand corner Luna (crescent moon).

LIMC Helios/Sol 368; CIMRM II, 1468 fig. 373. Note the inversion of the placement of Sol and Luna. There is a raven on the border next to the bust of Luna.

Image: Lupa.at/22367 photograph Ortolf Harl.

76. Plate 58.1

Split, Archaeological Museum 413 D.

Salona (Split).

Marble.

3rd c. AD.

Roundel. In central tondo: tauroctony. On the circular band around it: Saturn (above the head of Mithras) reclining, between the busts of Sol (left), radiate (five rays) and Luna (right). Below Sol a snail and a crab, below Luna a crocodile and a dolphin; at the bottom a crater between two snakes.

LIMC Helios/Sol 383; Merkelbach 1984: 380 fig. 146; CIMRM II, 1861.

Image: © Archaeological Museum, Split.

77. Zagreb, Museum 32 (lost).

Siscia.

Marble.

3rd c. AD.

Open-work relief. In the centre the tauroctony within a circular wreath of corn-ears. Above, the flanking Sol and Luna are lost, but some Mithraic scenes are preserved. Other such scenes are preserved below, including Mithras crowning Sol, Sol and Mithras dining, and Mithras ascending the *quadriga* behind Sol.

LIMC Helios/Sol 254; Merkelbach 1984: 370–1 fig. 134; CIMRM II, 1475.

78. Belgrade.

Viminacium (Kostolac).

Marble.

Second half 3rd c. AD (Clauss 1992, 216).

Tauroctony. In the upper left-hand corner bust of Sol, bare-headed (?), right hand raised (?) Next to the heads of four horses; in the upper right-hand corner bust of Luna next to two horses.

LIMC Helios/Sol 380; CIMRM II, 2216 fig. 612.

79.   Plate 57.2
      Sofia, National Archaeological Museum.
      Golema Kutlovica (Lom distr.).
      White marble.
      3rd c. AD.
      Tauroctony. In the upper left hand corner Sol, radiate, *chlamys*, with
      overly large raised right hand; in the upper right hand corner Luna.
      Between them seven altars and seven cypresses, most missing. According
      to the LIMC Sol wears a tunica manicata, but I do not see this.
      LIMC Helios/Sol 376; Merkelbach 1984: 391 fig. 162; CIMRM II, 2237.
      Image: © Sofia Archaeological Museum / Krassimir Georgiev.

80.   Plate 59.1
      Sofia, National Archaeological Museum.
      Roustchouk (Sexantaprista).
      Marble.
      3rd c. AD.
      Tauroctony, above which two panels, with the bust of Sol in the left hand
      panel, to the left of a scene with Mithras, accompanied by a second fig-
      ure, shooting at a third figure in a cave. In the right hand panel a bull in a
      small boat, bust of Luna, and a three-legged table below Luna. Below the
      tauroctony a register consisting of one panel with two scenes: 1. Mithras
      placing his hand on the head of Sol; 6. Sol handing Mithras up onto his
      chariot with one horse jumping to the right, where Oceanus reclines.
      LIMC Helios/Sol 368; CIMRM II, 2272 fig. 632.
      Image: © Sofia Archaeological Museum / Krassimir Georgiev.

81.   Sétif (Algeria), Museum.
      Sitifis (Sétif).
      Stone.
      AD 299 (Clauss 1992, 250).
      Tauroctony. In the upper right-hand corner head of Sol, radiate (four
      rays); in the upper left-hand corner head of Luna.
      LIMC Helios/Sol 376; CIMRM I, 148/9 fig. 43.

82.   Bolzano, Museo Archeologico I/654.
      Mauls.
      Limestone.
      3rd–4th c. AD (Clauss 1992, 126 n. 4).
      Tauroctony. In the upper left-hand corner frontal bust of Sol, radiate (nine
      rays, of which one extends to Mithras), *chlamys*; in the upper right-hand

corner Luna. On the two lateral borders various Mithraic scenes, including (all on right-hand border): Sol and Mithras shaking hands; Sol and Mithras dining; Mithras ascending the *quadriga* behind Sol.
LIMC Helios/Sol 247; Merkelbach 1984: 368–9 fig. 132; CIMRM II, 1400, fig. 360.
Image: arachne.dainst.org/entity/3076804.

83. Plate 59.2
Rome, Musei Capitolini 1205.
Rome, Mithraeum at Piazza Dante.
Marble.
4th c. AD.
Tauroctony. In the upper left-hand corner, frontal bust of Sol, radiate (7? rays, of which one extending down to Mithras), preceded by bust of Lucifer; in the upper right-hand corner busts of Luna preceded by Hesperus.
LIMC Helios-Sol 368; Merkelbach 1984: 303 fig. 47; CIMRM I, 350–1; on the reading of the inscription cf. Clauss 1992, 26.
Image: arachne.dainst.org/entity/935071.

84. Plate 12.2
Rome, Musei Capitolini 2326.
Rome, P.za Dante, Mithraeum.
Marble.
4th c. AD.
Relief; Sol, depicted from the waste upwards, frontal, radiate nimbus (seven rays), long, wavy hair, *chlamys* and *chiton*, right hand raised, globe and whip in his left hand.
LIMC Helios/Sol 36; Merkelbach 1984: 303 fig. 49; CIMRM I, 354; Matern 2002: 106 n. 593, 131 n. 702, 146 n. 806, 263 B130; on the inscription cf. Clauss 1992, 26.
Image: Arachne Mal654-11_40818.jpg; arachne.dainst.org/entity/156676

85. Jajce, Bosnia.
In situ.
Niche cut into the wall of the cult room.
4th. c. AD (Vermaseren).
Tauroctony. In the upper left-hand corner bust of Sol (*chlamys*, radiate?) above Cautopates below and to the left, with a niche for a lamp above his head. In upper right-hand corner bust of Luna above Cautes with niche for a lamp above his head.

Merkelbach 1984: 380 fig. 147; CIMRM II, 267, 1902; for date cf. 266–7, no. 1901 (with ref).

86.   Plate 60.1
      Paris, Louvre AO 22255 (ex Collection de Clercq).
      Sidon (Saida), Mithraeum.
      Parian marble.
      Second half 4th c. AD. According to Clauss (1992, 242–3), the only available chronological information for this Mithraeum comes from inscriptions (CIMRM I, 76, 78/9, 84/5) which should be dated in AD 389. In his opinion, the Mithraeum was founded during the "pagan Renaissance" of the late fourth c. AD by Flavius Gerontius, presumably a high-ranking aristocrat, who imported the various cult-objects from Rome. This date was first proposed by E. Will (Syria 27 1950, 261–269), and is also accepted by Vermaseren. Gundel's date for the relief (ca. AD 188) is based on the assumption that the dates provided by the aforementioned inscriptions were based on the Seleucid calendar.
      Tauroctony with signs of the zodiac loosely spaced in an oval around the main scene. In the four corners busts of the four seasons in high relief in tondi. Next to the upper seasons, also in tondi in high relief, the busts of Luna (left) and Sol (right), *chlamys*; Sol's tondo is radiate. Note the inversion of the placement of Sol and Luna.
      LIMC Helios/Sol 375; Gundel 1992: 113–4 fig. 53, 229–32 no. 77; CIMRM I, 75.
      Image: © RMN-Grand Palais / Franck Raux / Art Resource, NY ART525103.

87.   Naples, Museo Nazionale 6747.
      Posilippo.
      Marble.
      Second half 4th c. AD (Clauss 1992, 52–3); 3rd c. AD (LIMC).
      Tauroctony-relief. In the upper left-hand corner bust of Sol, *chlamys*, radiate (six or seven vertical rays, points connected by a horizontal band); upper right-hand corner bust of Luna. Inscription: omnipotenti deo mitrhae appivs / clavdivs tarronivs dexter v(ir) c(larissimus) dicat.
      LIMC Helios/Sol 376; CIMRM I, 174–5, fig. 49.

88.   Trento, Museo Nazionale.
      Sanzeno.
      Marble.
      Undated.

Lateral fragment of a two-sided relief. On one side the tauroctony was depicted, of which only the left edge, including a small bust of Sol, radiate, survives. To the left of this main scene, five minor scenes survive, including (second from bottom) Sol, nude, radiate nimbus, standing next to bearded figure, capite velato (Saturn?). On the other side there was, apparently, only a main scene of which the right side survives. Preserved are part of a bull, a snake, a boar, a cypress, and Cautes.

LIMC Helios/Sol 247; CIMRM I 723, figures 1989.

89. Budapest, National Museum 120.1862.
    Alcšut.
    Marble.
    Undated.
    Tauroctony. Bust of Sol in upper left-hand corner, bust of Luna in upper right-hand corner. Above and below the main panel seven Mithraic scenes, including (below): Sol crowned by Mithras; Sol and Mithras dining; Mithras ascending the *quadriga* behind Sol.
    LIMC Helios/Sol 244; 252; 368; Merkelbach 1984 378–9, fig. 144; CIMRM II, 1740.

90. Plate 54.1
    Cluj-Napoca, National History Museum of Transylvania v 31806 (MIC 11).
    Micia.
    Limestone.
    Undated.
    Tauroctony. In the upper left-hand corner, bust of Sol, radiate (six rays), in the upper right-hand corner Luna.
    CIMRM II, 2025; Merkelbach 1984: 387 fig. 155.
    Image: courtesy National History Museum of Transylvania.

91. Plate 61.1
    Plovdiv, archaeological Museum. 2102.
    Kurtowo-Konare.
    Marble.
    Undated.
    Tauroctony. In the upper left-hand corner, frontal bust of Sol, and in right-hand corner Luna.
    CIMRM II, 2338; Merkelbach 1984: 392 fig. 164.
    Image: photograph courtesy Plovdiv Archaeological Museum, Elena Filadska.

92.   Plate 61.2
      Damascus, National Museum.
      Secia (Sî), near Damascus.
      Basalt.
      Undated.
      Tauroctony. In the upper left-hand corner bust of Sol, radiate nimbus; in
      the upper right-hand corner bust of Luna. Note that the snake is incor-
      rectly depicted as joining the scorpion rather than the dog.
      LIMC Helios/Sol 368; Merkelbach 1984: 282 fig. 22; CIMRM I, 88.
      Image: in the public domain (after American Journal of Archaeology 22
      (1918: p. 63)).

93.   Damascus, National Museum.
      Sî.
      Basalt.
      Undated.
      Fragment of a tauroctony, hacked out in the rock. Upper left-hand corner,
      bust of Sol, radiate nimbus.
      CIMRM I, 89; LIMC Helios/Sol 368.

94.   Plate 62.1
      Damascus, National Museum.
      Arsha-Wa-Koibar.
      Basalt?
      Undated.
      Tauroctony. In the upper left-hand corner, bust of Sol, radiate (three rays);
      in the upper right-hand corner Luna.
      CIMRM I, 71.
      Image: photograph in the public domain.

95.   Carthage, Museum?
      Carthage.
      Unknown.
      Undated.
      Tauroctony relief.
      CIMRM I, 119.

96.   Cairo, Archaeological Museum 7259.
      Memphis, Mithraeum.
      Limestone.

Undated.
Tauroctony. In the upper left-hand corner bust of Sol, in upper right-hand
corner Luna.
CIMRM I, 92.

97. Cairo, Archaeological Museum 85747.
Hermoupolis Magna.
Limestone.
Undated.
Tauroctony framed by an arch resting on two Corinthian pilasters. In the
upper left-hand corner above the arch, bust of Sol, radiate nimbus. In
the upper right hand corner bust of Luna. Immediately below the arch,
a third bust, bearded, looks down on the tauroctony. This is presumably
either Saturn or Caelus. CIMRM I, 91 (description accurate, but the photo
(fig. 34) is of a different relief); Boschung 2015: 223 fig.

98. Rome, Musei Capitolini.
Rome at the Via di S. Giovanni Lanza.
Marble.
Undated.
Tauroctony. In the upper left-hand corner, bust of Sol, radiate (five rays),
and in the upper right-hand corner bust of Luna.
LIMC Helios/Sol 376; CIMRM 357, figure 102.

99. Vatican, Sala degli Animali 149.
unknown.
marble.
undated.
Tauroctony. In the upper left-hand corner Sol in a *quadriga*, radiate; in
the upper right hand corner Luna in a *biga*.
LIMC Helios/Sol 380; CIMRM 554, figure 158.

100. Plate 61.3
Vatican, Cortile del Belvedere.
Unknown.
Marble.
Undated.
Tauroctony. In the upper left-hand corner, frontal bust of Sol, radiate
nimbus (six rays); in the upper right hand corner bust of Luna with a
four-pointed star above each point of the upturned crescent.

LIMC Helios/Sol 373; CIMRM 546, figure 154.
Image: drawing in the public domain, after Cumont 1899: 210 fig. 38.

101. Plate 61.4
Verona, Museum
Anzio.
Marble.
2nd c. AD.
Tauroctony. In the upper left-hand corner bust of Sol, radiate; upper right, bust of Luna.
Modonesi 1995, 83–84, no. 90.
Image: Arachne FA4826-01_55795.jpg; arachne.dainst.org/entity/435679.

102. Plate 62.2
Mannheim, Reiss-Engelhorn-Museum.
Ladenburg.
Sandstone.
Undated.
Mithras relief. Next to the tauroctony, Sol, standing, nude but for a *chlamys*, right hand raised and holding whip; with his left hand Sol holds the tail of the bull. Behind Sol, a lion jumps to the left. Below his feet are seven small altars. Mithras himself is bare-headed. In the upper right-hand corner a raven facing Mithras. Below the bull and the altars, the dedicant (?) places a jar on an altar next to a kantharos, with to either side a snake.
CIMRM II, 1274 fig. 334; Matern 2002: 106, 232 I12.
Image: © Reiss-Engelhorn-Museen Mannheim, Carolin Breckle.

103. Plates 63.1, 63.2
Stuttgart, Landesmuseum Württemberg, R89.Mun.sol & R89.Nub.luna.
Mundelsheim, villa rustica.
Sandstone.
2nd c. AD.
Votive altar for Sol, found together with an altar for Luna in the cellar of the villa, which served as a Mithraeum. Bust of Sol, *chlamys*, radiate with seven large, cut-out rays. On the altar for Luna the crescent is similarly cut out.
Planck, Ein römisches Mithräum bei Mundelsheim, Kreis Ludwigsburg, in: Arch. Ausgr. in. B-W 1989, 177–83.
Image: © Landesmuseum Württemberg, P. Frankenstein / H. Zwietasch; Bildarchiv 109373 & 109376.

104. Obernburg, Römermuseum inv. R 1937, 11.
     Obernburg, Kapellengasse.
     Red sandstone.
     Late 2nd c. AD.
     Frontal bust of Sol, radiate nimbus (eleven rays), *chlamys*. Found in
     1839, separate from a Mithraic inscription, which is, however, thought to
     belong to it.
     CSIR Deutschland II, 13, pp. 122–3 no. 191. For an image see: http://lupa
     .at/23722.

105. Warsaw, National Museum 198788.
     Acquired in Rome; reported to have arrived in Rome from Macerata,
     Marche region.
     Marble.
     1st c. AD (Greiffenhagen, cited by CSIR) or 2nd–3rd c. AD (CSIR).
     Tauroctony. Mithras killing the bull, face frontal, phrygian cap, radiate,
     (6 long, thin rays), cautopates to the left, Cautes on the right; dog, snake,
     and scorpion are also depicted. In the upper left corner, raven (but no
     Sol!); in the upper right corner an inscription (no Luna): [i]nvicto pro-
     pitio / sal(vius) novanio / [l]vcianvs / d(onum) p(osuit). The relief is a
     pastiche of different pieces. The missing first letters of the inscription
     (I of invicto and the L of Lucanius) show that the inscription is not in the
     correct place. The radiate Mithras is also exceptional.
     CSIR Pologne III, 1, pp. 41–2, pl 17.

106. Inveresk, Scotland
     Inveresk
     Sandstone, probably local.
     Mid 2nd c. AD.
     Votive altar for Sol, found in a Mithraeum in which it had been purpose-
     fully buried. On the upper moulding four small female busts (Seasons)
     above the dedicatory inscription: soli c(aius) cas(sius) fl(a ...). In the main
     field, within a tondo, frontal head of Sol, long wavy hair, six pointed rays.
     The back behind the head was hollowed out, and the rays, pupils, and
     mouth were pierced to allow light to shine through from a light source
     placed in the space at the back. An iron fitting behind the nose may have
     served to hang up instruments for sound effects as well. Found together
     with an altar dedicated to Mithras with only an inscription on the front,
     a griffin and a pan on the left side, and a lyre, a plectrum and a jug on the
     right side. Cf C2j.1.
     Hunter et al. 2016.

107. Plate 64.1
New York, Metropolitan Museum of Art 1997.145.3.
Unknown.
Bronze.
Second half 2nd c. AD; modern(?).
Tauroctony relief; upper left corner, bust of Sol, draped, radiate (thirteen rays); upper right, Luna on crescent. Authentic? Mithras is not look-ing back at Sol; Cautes, Cautopates, raven and extended ray from Sol to Mithras are all missing. The direction of Mithras' gaze and head has few parallels in Mithraic art.
Oliver 2000, 688 no. 11.
Image: courtesy Metropolitan Museum of Art.

108. St Petersburg, Hermitage.
Rome
Marble
Undated
Part of a tauroctony, with perhaps just the remains of Sol's *quadriga* vis-ible in the upper left corner above a raven. The relief is not complete as it lacks Luna, Cautes and Cautopates, but the manner in which it is currently presented makes it impossible to see what is original, and what is not.
CIMRM 603.

109. Plate 63.3
Tulln, Römermuseum 414.
Tulln.
Marble.
3rd c. AD.
Tauroctony. Busts of Sol and Luna in the upper corners, without any attri-butes (no rays, no crescent).
Lupa 5775.
Image: © Römermuseum Tulln.

110. Plate 64.2
Wiener Neustadt, Stadtmuseum 1285.
Winzendorf.
Limestone.
Undated.

Fragment of a tauroctony. Bust of Sol in upper left hand corner.
CSIR Österreich 1,5 (Scarbantia) 2; Lupa 6031.
Image: Lupa.at/6031 Photograph Ortolf Harl.

111. Plate 64.3
Bad Deutsch-Altenburg, private collection.
Carnuntum.
Sandstone.
Undated.
Tauroctony; heads of Sol and Luna in the upper corners.
Lupa 7989.
Image: Lupa.at/7989 Photograph Ortolf Harl.

112. Plate 65.1
Rozanec, Crnomelj, Slovenia.
In situ.
Limestone.
Undated.
Tauroctony relief carved into the naked rock of a cave. In the upper corners, busts of Sol, radiate, and Luna.
Lupa 9207.
Images: 112 and 112a in the public domain.

113. Plate 65.2
Cologne, Römisch-Germanisches Museum.
Cologne.
Marble.
2nd c. AD.
Tauroctony, with in the upper left corner the bust of Sol, radiate (seven rays, of which one extended). Upper right corner broken away.
Image: Arachne FA-S7626-01_94860.jpg; arachne.dainst.org/entity/152328.

114. Rome, Villa Doria Pamphilj, Casino Belrespiro.
Unknown.
Marble.
Second half 2nd c. AD.
Tauroctony, with in the upper left corner Sol, radiate, right hand raised, in his *quadriga* heading right, and in the upper right corner, Luna in her *biga* of oxen heading right.
Arachne 601483.

115.   Plate 66.2
        Alba Iulia, National Museum of the Union 203/11.
        Apulum.
        Sandstone.
        Undated.
        Tauroctony; in the upper left hand corner bust of Sol, radiate, one ray
        extended to Mithras; in the upper right hand corner Luna.
        CIMRM 1973.
        Image: courtesy National Museum of the Union, photograph author.

116.   Plate 66.1
        Alba Iulia, National Museum of the Union 209/1.
        Apulum.
        Marble.
        Undated.
        Tauroctony; in the upper left hand corner bust of Sol; in the upper right
        hand corner Luna.
        CIMRM 1975.
        Image: courtesy National Museum of the Union, photograph author.

117.   Plate 67.1
        Dunaújváros Intercisa Museum.
        Dunaújváros.
        Limestone.
        Undated.
        Tauroctony. In the upper left hand corner, bust of Sol, facing, radiate
        (seven rays), whip, with protomes of four horses; in the upper right hand
        corner bust of Luna right, behind the protomes of two horses.
        Visy 2008, 73 fig. 39.
        Image: © Intercisa Museum.

118.   Plate 66.3
        Cluj-Napoca, National History Museum of Transylvania V.1135.
        Potaissa.
        Marble.
        Undated.
        Tauroctony scene with a bust of Sol, not radiate, in the upper left corner
        and a bust of Luna in the upper right. At the top centre, a small lion's
        head.

CIMRM II, 2198.
Image: © National History Museum of Transylvania.

119. Plate 66.4
Cluj-Napoca, National History Museum of Transylvania V.1101.
Potaissa.
Marble.
Undated.
Tauroctony scene with a bust of Sol, *chlamys*, not radiate, in the upper left corner. The corresponding bust of Luna has been lost.
CIMRM 1924, 1925; CIL III, 6255.
Image: © National History Museum of Transylvania.

120. Cluj-Napoca, National History Museum of Transylvania v.15812.
Hida.
Limestone.
Undated.
Tauroctony scene in an aedicula framed with twisted columns. In the tympanum, from left to right: a lion walking right; a bust of Sol, *chlamys*, whip, head not preserved; a bust of Luna, and a bird facing left.
LIMC Helios/Sol 326; Csabo 2012.

121. Plate 67.2
Cluj-Napoca, National History Museum of Transylvania L. 48.
Micia.
Limestone.
Undated.
Tauroctony scene; in the upper left hand corner a bust of Sol, not radiate. The right half of the relief has been lost (including Luna).
CIMRM 2018
Image: © National History Museum of Transylvania.

122. Formello, Nuovo Museo dell'Agro Veientano inv. 143672.
Veii.
Marble.
Mid 2nd c. AD.
Tauroctony scene; in the upper left-hand corner Sol, radiate (?), nude but for a *chlamys*, in *quadriga* right; in the upper right-hand corner, Luna descends in her *biga*, right.
Fusco & Boitani 2015.

123.   Plate 68.2
Yale, Yale University Art Museum 1936.97.
Dura Europos.
Limestone.
AD 168.
Tauroctony relief: Note the inclusion of the dedicants.
Brody & Hoffman 2011: 212.
Image: photograph courtesy Yale University Art Museum.

124.   Plate 68.1
Amsterdam, Allard Pierson Museum 17.700.
Rome.
Rosso Antico.
3rd quarter of the 2nd c. AD.
Panel-shaped tauroctony relief of expensive rosso antico marble. In the upper left corner Sol in his *quadriga* in high relief heading right; in the right hand corner Luna in her *biga* heading right.
Dirven 2017.
Image: photograph Collectie Allard Pierson Museum, Amsterdam.

C2d. Jupiter Dolichenus

1.   Plate 69.1
Munich, Archäologische Staatssammlung 1985, 4472.
Dülük.
Bronze.
Ca. AD 50 (LIMC Zeus/Iuppiter Dolichenus; Hörig & Schwertheim 1987); 3rd c. AD (LIMC Helios/Sol).
Votive triangle; Jupiter Dolichenus standing right with axe in his raised right hand and a thunderbolt in his left hand. Below: the forntal busts of Luna (left) and Sol, radiate, right.
LIMC Helios/Sol 395; LIMC Zeus/Iuppiter Dolichenus 16; Hörig & Schwertheim 1987: 5.
Image: © Archäologische Staatssammlung München, Manfred Eberlein.

2.   Private collection.
Dülük.
Bronze.
Ca. AD 50 (LIMC Zeus/Iuppiter Dolichenus; Hörig & Schwertheim); 3rd c. AD (LIMC Helios/Sol).
Votive triangle; Jupiter Dolichenus, below, busts of Luna (left) and Sol (right), radiate (seven rays), *chlamys*.

LIMC Helios/Sol 396; LIMC Zeus/Iuppiter Dolichenus 15; Hörig & Schwertheim 1987: 6.

3. Plate 69.2
Wiesbaden, Stadtmuseum am Markt 6775.
Heddernheim.
Bronze.
Ca. AD 175.
Triangular plaque with arrowhead-like point. Top: frontal bust of Sol, tunica, seven rays. Centre: Jupiter Dolichenus, standing on the back of a bull, is crowned by a Victory flying above and to the right of him. Below: Juno Dolichena on a hind, between two bearded "mountain-gods" in military attire emerging from rocks and holding three leaves aloft in each hand; above the left-hand mountain god a bust of Sol, radiate nimbus (five rays), and above the right-hand one a bust of Luna.
Spätantike 543–4, no. 150; Huld-Zetsche 1994, 3, 48–50, 141; LIMC Zeus/Iuppiter Dolichenus 54; Hörig & Schwertheim 1987: 512.
Image: courtesy Museum Wiesbaden.

4. Plate 69.6
Vienna, Kunsthistorisches Museum M4.
Mauer an der Url.
Bronze.
Late 2nd c. AD.
Votive triangle surmounted by a winged Victory with palm-branch and wreath, and with a handle at the bottom. Four registers: in the top register and eagle; in the next, busts of Luna (right) and Sol (left), radiate (nine, possibly ten rays), whip; in the main register Jupiter Dolichenus and Juno Dolichena facing each other; in the lower register the two Dioscuri. On the other side, star above a hand holding a thunderbolt, between two peacocks and, below, two eagles.
LIMC Helios/Sol 332; LIMC Zeus/Iuppiter Dolichenus 51; Hörig & Schwertheim 1987: 294.
Image: © KHM Museumsverband.

5. Wiesbaden, Stadtmuseum am Markt 6776.
Heddernheim.
Bronze.
2nd–3rd c. AD.

Upper part of a triangular plaque. Preserved are a bust of Jupiter Dolichenus-Sarapis at the apex, below it the busts of Luna (left) and Sol (right), radiate (nine rays), whip, and three stars.
LIMC Helios/Sol 334; Hörig & Schwertheim 1987: 511.

6.   Plate 19.4
      Rome, Musei Capitolini 9750.
      Rome, Aventine, Dolichenum.
      Marble.
      3rd c. AD.
      Lower register: Jupiter Dolichenus and Juno Dolichena flank Isis and Sarapis; upper register: in the corners busts of Luna (right) and Sol (left), radiate (five rays), *chlamys*; between them the Dioscuri.
      LIMC Helios/Sol 364; LIMC Dioskouroi/Castores 84; LIMC Zeus/Iuppiter Dolichenus 47; Hörig & Schwertheim 1987: 386.
      Image: Arachne Mal626-09_39442,00.jpg; arachne.dainst.org/entity/6480871.

7.   Plate 71.1
      Corbridge, Corbridge Roman Site Museum.
      Corbridge.
      Sandstone.
      3rd c. AD.
      Frieze, originally thought to have depicted Sol and Luna, the Dioscuri, and Apollo and Diana flanking Jupiter Dolichenus; only Sol, one of the Dioscuri and Apollo remain. Sol, beardless, radiate, tunica, right hand raised, rides a winged horse right.
      LIMC Helios/Sol 367; Speidel 1978, 33–4, 43 fig. 4.; CSIR Great Britain I.1, 18–9 no. 52, pl. 15; Matern 2002: 261 B112.

8.   Plate 71.2
      Klagenfurt, Landesmuseum Kärnten 132.
      Waisenberg.
      Limestone.
      Early 3rd c. AD.
      Aedicula-shaped votive stele. In tympanum an eagle, in the acroteria frontal head of Sol (left), radiate (9? rays) and head of Luna (right). In the main field Jupiter Dolichenus (left) and Juno Dolichena.
      LIMC Helios/Sol 358; LIMC Zeus/Iuppiter Dolichenus 45; Hörig & Schwertheim 1987: 347.
      Image: courtesy Landesmuseum Kärnten, Klagenfurt.

9.   Plate 70.6
     Vienna, Kunsthistorisches Museum M5.
     Mauer an der Url.
     Bronze, silver- and gold-plated.
     First half 3rd c. AD.
     Votive triangle with a handle at the bottom. Five registers: in the top
     register an eagle; in the next, busts of Luna (right) and Sol (left), radiate
     (four, possibly five rays); in the third register a *quadriga* with two horses
     to the left and two to the right, with two charioteers, a woman leaning
     towards the right and holding the two right-hand horses by the reins, and
     a man, bare-headed, nude but for a *chlamys* billowing out behind him,
     springing towards the left behind the two other horses; the woman holds
     an attribute in her left hand, possibly a whip (I do not see how it could
     be a double axe-cf. Spätantike 546, also clearly hesitant on this identi-
     fication), the man a small staff (or whip?) in his right hand. In the next
     register Jupiter Dolichenus and Juno Dolichena to either side of an altar;
     in the lowest register, Victory on a globe above an altar, between Jupiter
     and Juno Dolichenus, each with a military standard behind them. It is dif-
     ficult to determine whether the two figures in the "split" *quadriga* are Sol
     and Luna, as the LIMC suggests; they lack defining attributes (pace LIMC,
     Sol definitely does not have a nimbus nor does he hold a whip in his left
     hand).
     LIMC Helios/Sol 331 (description of Sol erroneous; with ref.); Spätantike,
     546–548; Noll 1983.
     Image: © KHM Museumsverband.

10. Szentes Museum, Hungary.
     Potaissa (Turda).
     Bronze.
     3rd c. AD.
     Upper part of a two-sided votive triangle. Side A: at the apex an eagle,
     below it the busts of Luna (right) and Sol (left), radiate (four rays); Side B:
     mirror image of side A.
     LIMC Helios/Sol 333; Hörig & Schwertheim 1987: 142.

11. Plates 69.3, 69.4
     Budapest, National Museum 10.1951.106–7.
     Dunakömlöd-Lussonium.
     Bronze.
     Severan.

Two-sided votive triangle. Side a: busts of Sol (left), radiate, *chlamys*, and Luna above Jupiter Dolichenus on the back of a bull, being crowned by a Victory; in the lower corners busts of Hercules (left) and Minerva (right). Side b: at the apex an eagle, below which the busts of Sol (left), radiate, *chlamys*, whip, and Luna; in the main register Jupiter Dolichenus and Juno Dolichena facing each other; in the lowest register Jupiter Dolichenus in a decorated shrine between the Castores (?).

LIMC Helios/Sol 330; LIMC Zeus/Iuppiter Dolichenus 50 (side b), 58 (side a); Hörig & Schwertheim 1987: 2012.

Image: photograph of the upper part of side B, © Hungarian National Museum.

12.   Veliko Tarnovo, Archaeological Museum.
       Unknown, possibly Novae.
       Bronze.
       First half of the third c. AD.
       Triangular incised plaque, originally with an object on the upper point (statuette of Victory?), now broken off. In the upper register bust of Luna (left) and Sol (right), radiate. In the main register Jupiter Dolichenus (left), facing inwards, standing on the back of a bull. Above and to the right of him a flying Victory in the act of crowning him. To the right, Juno Dolichena on a cow. Between Jupiter and Juno a burning altar. According to Najdenova, the figures in the lower corners are again Jupiter Dolichenus (left) and Jupiter Dolichenus (right).
       Najdenova 1993; LIMC Zeus/Iuppiter Dolichenus 48; Hörig & Schwertheim 1987: 80.

13.   Plates 70.1–70.5
       Munich, Archäologische Staatssammlung inv. 1998.2161.
       Unknown.
       Bronze.
       2nd–3rd c. AD.
       Votive triangle in four registers (all images in high relief, unless indicated otherwise). At the top, an eagle; in the second register, Hercules, Minerva and Dionysus; in the third, largest register, Jupiter on Bull facing Juno on deer, between them a military standard; to the left of the top of the standard, incised, bust of Sol, radiate (seven or eight rays), *chlamys*, and to the right bust of Luna with crescent behind her shoulders; in the fourth register, a bearded figure by a burning altar, flanked by two eagle standards,

with to the right and left two bearded "mountain gods" standing behind, or emerging from a three-stepped base, each holding a branch (cf. C2d.3), each base flanked by two protomes of bulls.

Wamser et al. 2000: 197, 177a.

Images: 13, 13a, 13b, 13c, and 13d © Archäologische Staatssammlung München, Manfred Eberlein.

14. Art Market. Note: this object cannot be documented prior to 1992, and is therefore considered an undocumented artifact which cannot be ethically sold or traded (AIA code of ethics).

Unknown.

Bronze.

3rd c. AD.

Restored from many fragments. Votive triangle in four registers. In the top register an eagle with a wreath; in the next register the frontal busts of Sol, left, radiate (six rays), *chlamys*, and Luna, right, separated by a burning altar; in the main register, Jupiter Dolichenus and Juno Dolichena, both on the backs of bulls, separated by a burning altar; in the lower register the Dioscuri approach a burning altar from both sides, each leading a horse.

Christie's, London antiquities sale 5524, April 28, 2004, lot 129; Artemis gallery, New York, 2019 no. 143608.

C2e. Jupiter-Giant Pillars

1. Plate 72.1

Mainz, Mittelrheinisches Landesmuseum S137.

Mainz.

Limestone.

AD 57–67. Publius Sulpicius Scribonius Proculus was governor of Germania Inferior until his death in AD 67. It is not known in which year he was appointed governor.

Jupiter-Giant pillar, found in 1904/5, shattered into 2000 pieces. In WWII the pillar suffered further damage. It consists of a base, an intermediate socle, a column with five sculpted drums, the capital and the statue on top (the latter almost wholly lost). On the rectangular base: Jupiter, Fortuna and Minerva, Hercules, Mercurius and Salus; on the rectangular intermediate socle: inscription, Dioscure, Apollo, Dioscure; on each of the five column-drums four gods except the top drum which has three: a. Mars, Victory, Neptune, Diana; b. Amazon-like woman (Honos?, personification?), Vulcan, Amazon-like woman (Virtus?, Roma?), Ceres; c. four goddesses, none identified with certainty (suggested identifications: Venus, Vesta, Proserpina, Pax; Aequitas, Gallia, Italia, Pax); d. Genius, Lar, Liber, Lar; e. Juno, Sol, radiate nimbus (eleven rays), *chlamys*, whip, in *quadriga*, and Luna in *biga*. Inscription: i(ovi) o(ptimo) m(aximo) pro [sa]l(ute) [nero-][nis] clau[d]i caesaris au[g](usti) imp(eratoris) canaba[rii] publice p(ublio) sulpicio scribonio proculo leg[(ato)] aug(usti) p[r(o) p]r(aetore) cura et impensa q(uinti) iuli prisci et q(uinti) iuli aucti.

LIMC Helios/Sol 363; Bauchhenß-Noelke 1981, 162–3 nos. 272–275; Bauchhenß 1984 (with extensive bibliography); Matern 2002: 66, 70 n. 444, 90 n. 527, 218 Q67 (with refs.).

Image: © GDKE-Landesmuseum Mainz; photograph Ursula Rudischer.

2.   Plate 72.2
      Mainz, Mittelrheinisches Landesmuseum S992.
      Mainz.
      Limestone.
      Last quarter 1st c. AD.
      Rectangular block of a Jupiter-giant pillar, inscription on the front, full-length figures of Fortuna on the right, Luna on the back, and Sol, radiate nimbus (seven rays), nude but for a *chlamys*, whip in right hand, staff in left, on the left hand side. The inscription is a dedication by the inhabitants of a new vicus of Mainz.

      LIMC Helios/Sol 256; Bauchhenß-Noelke 1981: 167–8 no. 292 pl. 33.1; CSIR II,3, 32–3 no. 21, pls. 30–33; Matern 2002: 88–9, 90 n. 527, 174 n. 957, 225 G2.

      Image: © GDKE-Landesmuseum Mainz; photograph Ursula Rudischer.

3.   Auxerre, Musée Lapidaire.
      Auxerre.
      Limestone.
      2nd c. AD.
      Capital with busts of four deities on the sides: Mercury, female deity, Sol/Apollo with torch and *chlamys* (head largely destroyed), Mars. Discovered at the same time as the statue of Jupiter on horseback (Espérandieu IV, 2885), and therefore believed te have been the capital of a Jupiter-Giant pillar.

      LIMC Helios/Sol 264; von Mercklin 1962: 179 no. 433 figs. 841–3; Sol fig. 841, right.

4.   Darmstadt, Hessisches Landesmuseum A1956:796.
      Butzbach.
      Sandstone.
      Ca. AD 200 (found in a well with material dating to ca. AD 230).
      Jupiter-giant pillar with cylindrical block depicting the seven planetary
      deities full figure. Sol is nude but for a clumsily portrayed *chlamys* over
      his left arm, radiate (nine rays), with a whip in his right hand and a globe
      in his left
      CSIR Deutschland 2.12, 93–4, nos. 177–80, pls. 66–71 (Sol: no. 178, pl. 68).
      CSIR Deutschland II, 12, p. 94 no. 178, pl. 68.

5.   Jagsthausen, Schloß Neuenstein, Hohenlohe Museum.
      Jagsthausen.
      Sandstone.
      170–250.
      Cylindrical block of a Jupiter-giant pillar depicting the planetary deities,
      full figure, in niches. Sol has a radiate nimbus, is nude but for a *chlamys*,
      and holds a whip in his right hand, a patera in his left hand.
      LIMC Helios/Sol 282; Bauchhenß-Noelke 1981: 149 no. 229; Matern 2002:
      92, 228 G22.

6.   Plate 72.3
      Karlsruhe, Badisches Landesmuseum C20.
      Pforzheim-Brötzingen.
      Sandstone.
      2nd–3rd c. AD.
      One of three Viergöttersteine removed in 1818 from the wall of the ceme-
      tery of Brötzingen. On this block: a goddess too poorly preserved to iden-
      tify with certainty, but possibly Luna; Vulcan; Sol, nimbus, nude but for a
      chlamys, right hand raised, whip in left hand; Venus.
      LIMC Helios/Sol 257; Bauchhenß-Noelke 1981: 205 no. 427.
      Image: © Badisches Landesmuseum Karlsruhe.

7.   Plates 72.4, 72.5
      Mannheim, Reiss-Museum Inv. Baumann 16.
      Neckarelz.
      Sandstone.
      late 2nd to First half 3rd c. AD.
      Cylindrical block of a Jupiter-giant pillar depicting the planetary deities,
      full figure, in niches. Sol has a radiate nimbus, is nude but for a *chlamys*,
      and holds his right hand raised to his head.

LIMC Helios/Sol 282; Bauchhenß-Noelke 1981: 195 no. 394; Matern 2002: 106, 232–3 I13.
Images: 7 and 7a © Reiss-Engelhorn-Museen Mannheim, Patricia Pfaff.

8.   Plate 72.6
      Speyer, Historisches Museum der Pfalz Inv. A6.
      Godramstein.
      Sandstone.
      2nd–3rd c. AD.
      Rectangular block of a Jupiter-giant pillar; on the front an inscription, on the sides and the back two pairs and a trio of planetary deities respectively. Sol has a radiate nimbus.
      LIMC Helios/Sol 278; Bauchhenß-Noelke 1981: 137 no. 192.
      Image: Lupa.at/26498 photograph Ortolf Harl.

9.   Plates 73.1–73.3
      Stuttgart, Landesmuseum Württemberg RL 56.8.
      Stuttgart-Plieningen.
      Sandstone.
      2nd–3rd c. AD.
      Cylindrical block (of a Jupiter-giant pillar?) depicting a number of deities in niches. Sol, nimbus (no rays?) is nude but for a *chlamys*. His raised right arm and lower left arm are missing.
      Matern 2002: 106, 146 n. 806, 234 I21, fig. 44.
      Images: 9, 9a, and 9b © Landesmuseum Württemberg, Ortolf Harl.

10.   Plates 73.4–73.7
      Stuttgart, Landesmuseum Württemberg RL 391.
      Stetten am Heuchelberg.
      Sandstone.
      Late 2nd–First half 3rd c. AD.
      Cylindrical block of a Jupiter-giant pillar, depicting Sol, Luna, Venus, Juno (?), Neptune, Mercury, and an unidentified goddess (Fortuna?, Rosmerta?).
      LIMC Helios/Sol 262; Bauchhenß-Noelke 1981: 228 no. 498 pl. 46.1; Matern 2002: 106, 146 n. 806, 234 I20, fig. 43 (appears to identify this, incorrectly, as a Wochengötterstein).
      Images: 10, 10a, 10b, and 10c © Landesmuseum Württemberg, Ortolf Harl.

11. Bonn, Rheinisches Landesmuseum D 1004–1005.
Environs of Rommerskirchen.
Sandstone.
2nd quarter 3rd c. AD.
Fragments of a rectangular pilaster supporting a Jupiter-giant group. On each side a number of registers in which deities are represented full-figure. Registers I and III are completely preserved, register II only partially. It cannot be determined how many registers the pilaster originally had. Register I: Mercury, Mars, Virtus and Vulcan; register II: Minerva, Victoria, Neptune and an unidentified goddess, possibly Fortuna; register III: Juno, Luna, Hercules and Sol, radiate (seven rays), nude but for a *chlamys*, globe in left hand, whip in lowered right hand. According to Noelke (followed by Matern) Sol also wears a Phrygian cap, but from the photographs at my disposal I believe that he has a "wreath-coiffure".
LIMC Helios/Sol 259; Bauchhenß-Noelke 1981: 475–6 no. 175 pl. 92.4; Bauchhenß 1984: 331 fig. 4; Matern 2002: 90, 226 G10; Noelke 2010: 230 fig. 81a, 285.

12. Darmstadt, Hessisches Landesmuseum A1924.24.
Dieburg.
Sandstone.
Ca. AD 225.
Part of a Jupiter-giant pillar consisting of a rectangular Viergötterstein and a cylindrical segment with the planetary deities. Sol, among the planetary deities, is poorly preserved (head and lower arms lost). He is nude, but for a *chlamys*.
LIMC Helios/Sol 282; Bauchhenß-Noelke 1981: 114 no. 111; CSIR Deutschland II, 13, p. 151 no. 264.

13. Plate 72.7
Kassel, Hessisches Landesmuseum SK 53.
Mainz.
Sandstone.
Ca. AD 220–230.
Cylindrical socle of a Jupiter-giant pillar depicting the busts of the seven planetary deities and, in an eighth field, the full-length figure of a Genius. Sol is radiate (five rays), wears a *chlamys* and has a whip by his left shoulder.

LIMC Helios/Sol 281; Bauchhenß-Noelke 1981: 175–6 no. 317; CSIR II,3 59–60 no. 59.
Image: courtesy Hessisches Landesmuseum Kassel.

14.   Plates 72.8, 72.9
       Mainz, Mittelrheinisches Landesmuseum S657 [26249].
       Mainz Kastell.
       Sandstone.
       Ca. AD 240.
       Part of a Jupiter-giant pillar consisting of a rectangular Viergötterstein and an octagonal block with busts of the planetary deities on 7 sides and an inscription on the eighth. Sol is radiate (seven rays), *chlamys*.
       Inscription: in / h(onorem) / d(omus) / d(ivinae)
       LIMC Helios/Sol 280; Bauchhenß-Noelke 1981: 182–3 no. 355–6; CSIR II,3 48–9 no. 43.
       Images: 14 and 14a © GDKE-Landesmuseum Mainz photograph Ursula Rudischer.

15.   Plate 73.8
       Mannheim, Reiss-Museum Inv. Haug 1.
       Kirchheim a/d Eck.
       Sandstone.
       3rd c. AD.
       Rectangular block of a Jupiter-giant pillar: inscription on the front, back lost, sides partially preserved with Luna in *biga* (?) on one side, Sol, bare-headed, *chlamys*, whip in raised right hand, in *quadriga*, on the other side.
       LIMC Helios/Sol 263; Espérandieu VIII, 67–8 no. 5982 Bauchhenß-Noelke 1981: 152 no. 237; Matern 2002: 67, 218 Q66 (with refs.).
       Image: Reiss-Engelhorn-Museen Mannheim, Archäologische Denkmalpflege und Sammlungen.

16.   Stuttgart, Landesmuseum Württemberg RL 201.
       Stuttgart-Bad Cannstatt.
       Sandstone.
       3rd c. AD.
       Hexagonal block of a Jupiter-giant pillar, with six of the seven planetary deities (Saturn not represented); Sol, radiate, holds a whip (?) in his lowered left hand, right hand raised. Found together with a pillar and an altar on which Saturn is represented
       LIMC Helios/Sol 279; Bauchhenß-Noelke 1981: 234 no. 527.

17. Plates 74.1, 74.2
    Metz.
    Havange, Canton Audun-le-Roman.
    Limestone.
    Undated.
    Octagonal block of a Jupiter-giant pillar, depicting the planetary deities
    on seven sides and an inscription to Jupiter on the eighth. Sol, radiate,
    nude but for a *chlamys*, holds his right hand raised to his head.
    LIMC Helios/Sol 280. Espérandieu Recueil V, 446–7 no. 4414; Duval 1953:
    268.
    Image: photograph after Robert 1873, 37 pl. 3.

18. Frankfurt a.M., Archäologisches Museum α7108.
    Nida (Frankfurt-Heddernheim).
    Sandstone.
    Undated.
    Jupiter-giant pillar consisting of a Viergötterstein, an octagonal block
    with the planetary deities (busts), a pillar, a capital, and a crowning relief
    depicting Jupiter and Juno. The busts of the planetary deities are exe-
    cuted with little detail.
    Bauchhenß-Noelke 1981: 126–7 no. 156

19. Formerly Hanau, Hist. Museum der Stadt Hanau (destroyed in WWII).
    Butterstadt.
    Sandstone.
    First half 3rd c. AD.
    Remains of two Jupiter-giant pillars which stood next to each other: two
    Viergöttersteine, one octagonal block with planetary deities, one pillar,
    two capitals, and one horseman-giant group; it is not certain which sec-
    tions belong together. On the octagonal block the planetary deities are
    depicted as busts on 7 sides (Sol with nimbus), while Victoria is repre-
    sented full-figure on the eighth side.
    Espérandieu Germanie 72; Duval 1953: 287; Bauchhenß-Noelke 1981: 110,
    no. 95; CSIR Deutschland 2.12, 145–6, pl. 122 (Sol not visible).

20. Plate 73.9
    Karlsruhe, Badisches Landesmuseum C28.
    Pforzheim.
    Sandstone.
    Undated.

Hexagonal block on which the planetary deities are depicted (Venus and Jupiter together on one side). Sol is nude, holds a whip across his breast; his head is largely missing, but appears to have been radiate. Found together with various fragments of at least two Jupiter-giant pillars.
Bauchhenß-Noelke 1981: 204 no. 422.
Image: © Badisches Landesmuseum, Karlsruhe.

21.   Speyer, Historisches Museum der Pfalz A77.
      Ransweiler.
      Sandstone.
      Undated.
      Fragment of a Viergötterstein of a Jupiter-giant pillar, depicting (full-length): Mercury, Fortuna, an unidentifiable figure, and Sol, radiate (?) nimbus, whip in right hand.
      LIMC Helios/Sol 260; Bauchhenß-Noelke 1981: 209 no. 436.

22.   Speyer, Historisches Museum der Pfalz A71.
      Altrip, reused in the wall of the late-Roman castellum; the pillar originally may have stood in Ladenburg (Lopodunum).
      Sandstone.
      Undated.
      Rectangular block of a Jupiter-giant pillar. On the front: inscription; on the sides and back two pairs and a trio of planetary deities (busts) respectively. Sol is radiate (seven rays) and has a whip.
      LIMC Helios/Sol 278; Bauchhenß-Noelke 1981: 87 no. 7.

23.   Stuttgart, Landesmuseum Württemberg RL 269.
      Stuttgart-Zazenhausen.
      Sandstone.
      2nd–3rd c. AD.
      Cylindrical block of a Jupiter-giant pillar with the seven planetary deities, full-figure, in six niches formed by pillars carrying arches (Jupiter and Venus together); Sol is radiate, nude but for a *chlamys*, with a whip in his lowered right hand.
      Bauchhenß-Noelke 1981: 235 no. 531.

24.   Stuttgart, Landesmuseum Württemberg RL 209.
      Benningen.
      Sandstone.
      Undated.

Block of a Jupiter-giant pillar in the shape of a very irregular octagon. On seven sides the planetary deities are depicted, full-figure, in niches. In small panels below each deity: Erotes. The planetary deities are all preserved; Sol, much worn, is nude and holds an unidentifiable object in his right hand. The representation or inscription on the eighth side is lost.
Bauchhenß-Noelke 1981: 103 no. 70.

25. Stuttgart, Landesmuseum Württemberg RL 241.
Neckarteilfingen.
Sandstone.
Undated.
Octagonal block of a Jupiter-giant pillar, with the seven planetary deities and a giant (all full-figure). Sol, head lost, nude, torch (?) in raised right hand.
LIMC Helios/Sol 279; Bauchhenß-Noelke 1981: 195–6 no. 395.

26. Plate 74.3
Wiesbaden, Stadtmuseum am Markt 382.
Frankfurt-Heddernheim (Nida).
Sandstone.
Undated.
Octagonal block of a Jupiter-giant pillar, depicting the seven planetary deities and Fortuna, all full-figure. Sol, radiate, nude but for a *chlamys*, holds a whip in his right hand and may have held a globe in his left. (Description of Sol based on a photograph kindly provided to me by the museum).
LIMC Helios/Sol 280; Bauchhenß-Noelke 1981: 130 no. 171, pl. 18.1; Matern 2002: 106, 234 I22
Image: courtesy Stadtmuseum Wiesbaden.

27. Stuttgart, Landesmuseum Württemberg RL 218a & b.
Rottenburg.
Sandstone.
Undated.
Two fragments of an octagonal block of a Jupiter-giant pillar. Of the planetary deities, Sol, Luna and Venus are preserved.
Haug & Sixt 1914, 249 No. 138

28. Heidelberg, Kurpfälzisches Museum SG261/1.
Heidelberg-Neuenheim (excavated Spring 2007).

Sandstone.

Mid 2nd c. AD.

Jupiter-giant pillar consisting of a stepped base, a Viergötterstein (Juno, Minerva, Mercury and Mars), a second rectangular socle with busts of the planetary deities on three sides and an inscription on the fourth, an undecorated column, and a statue of Jupiter on horseback atop the capital.

Schmitt (ed.), Archäologische Ausgrabungen in Baden Württemberg 2007, Theiss 2008 (non vidi); Ludwig et al. 2010.

29.   Plate 76.1
      Tongeren, Gallo-Roman Museum.
      Tongeren, Vrijthof.
      Sandstone.
      Ca. AD 200.
      Drum of the shaft of a Jupiter column; Sol, nude bur for a *chlamys*, radiate (nine rays), whip in right hand, leaning against his right shoulder, long staff in left hand.
      Noelke 2010, 243 fig. 92b, 31920.
      Image: released by the municipality of Tongeren, 2010.

30.   Jülich, Museum Inv. 1368.
      Jülich.
      Sandstone.
      AD 200–225.
      Part of a four-sided pilaster in multiple registers, decorated with deities; Mercury, Mars, Apollo and Venus formed one register, Sol is the only surviving figure of another. Sol is radiate, nude but for a *chlamys*, globe in left hand, right arm broken off.
      Noelke 2010, 233 fig. 83e, 345–7 cat. 313.

31.   Bonn, Landesmuseum inv. D1330.
      Sinthern.
      Limestone.
      AD 200.
      Upper part of a four-sided pilaster with reliefs in multiple registers. Only Sol and Hercules survive. Sol is nude but for a *chlamys*, has a radiate nimbus, and, possibly, a globe in his left hand.
      Noelke 2010, 349–50 cat.320, fig. 50.

32.   Speyer, Historisches Museum der Pfalz A70.
      Godramstein.

Sandstone.

Undated.

Block (of a Jupiter-giant pillar) in the form of an irregular octagon, one side mutilated. Preserved are six of the seven planetary deities; Venus and the representation on the eighth side are lost. Sol is preserved only in outline.

LIMC Helios/Sol 278; Bauchhenß-Noelke 1981: 137 no. 193 (with lit.)

C2f. So-Called "Danubian Riders"

1.   Plate 17.1

Columbia, University of Missouri, Museum of Art and Archaeology 90.5.

Unknown (Pannonia or Dacia).

Lead.

3rd c. AD.

Two columns supporting an arch frame a complex scene in four registers. In the two upper corners a snake. In the upper register under the arch, Sol in frontal *quadriga* (two horses jumping to either side), right hand raised, *chlamys*, radiate (seven rays) globe and whip in left hand. In the next register, twin horsemen facing inwards flank a woman variously interpreted as goddess or priestess, frontal, holding a cloth in front of her; there is a fish below the left hand horseman, and behind him a solder with helmet and spear; a prostrate nude man lies below the right hand horseman, and behind there is a woman/goddess with right hand raised to her mouth. In the third, largest register a semi-circular couch with three diners and table, on which a dish with a fish. Two nude figures approach the diners from the right. To the left an animal-headed figure stands to the left of a tree from which the (headless?) skin of an animal is being hung by a second figure. In the lowest register, a crater (centre) stands between a lion (left) and a snake (right). In the right-hand corner a cock, in the left hand corner a three-legged table bearing a fish.

Lane 1993–4: 60–1 fig. 5.

Image: Museum of Art and Archaeology University of Missouri-Columbia, Weinberg Fund.

2.   Budapest, National Museum.

Intercisa.

Lead.

3rd c. AD.

Identical with previous.

Tudor 1969 I: 72 no. 123.

3.   Dörögdpuszta (now lost?).
      Dörögdpuszta.
      Lead.
      3rd c. AD.
      Identical with previous.
      Tudor 1969 I: 93 no. 165.

4.   Kaposvár, Museum.
      Magyar Egres, Somogy District, Hungary.
      Lead.
      3rd c. AD.
      Identical with previous.
      Tudor 1969 I: 72 no. 124.

5.   Pečs Museum.
      Lugo Florentia, Dunaszekcšo, Baranjo district, Hungary.
      Lead.
      3rd c. AD.
      Identical with previous.
      Tudor 1969 I: 75–6 no. 130.

6.   Székesfehérvár, Szent István Király Múzeum 9888.
      Gorsium-Herculia, Tác-Fövenypuszta.
      Lead.
      3rd c. AD.
      Identical with previous.
      Tudor 1969 I: 93 no. 166.

7.   Belgrade, National Museum.
      Singidunum (Moesia Superior).
      Lead.
      3rd c. AD.
      Identical with previous.
      Tudor 1969 I: 30 no. 51; Matern 2002: 53, 125, 241–2 I62.1.

8.   Belgrade, National Museum.
      Singidunum (Moesia Superior).
      Lead.
      3rd c. AD.
      Identical with previous.
      Tudor 1969 I: 31 no. 52; Matern 2002: 53, 125, 241–2 I62.1.

9. Belgrade, National Museum.
    Horreum Margi (Kuprija).
    Lead.
    3rd. c. AD.
    Identical with previous.
    Tudor 1969 I: 35 no. 60.

10. Zagreb, Archaeological Museum.
    Bassiana (Petrovći, Ruma district).
    Lead.
    3rd c. AD.
    Identical with previous.
    Tudor 1969 I: 77–8 no. 133; Matern 2002: 53, 125, 241–2 I62.4.

11. Vienna, Kunsthistorisches Museum.
    Unknown.
    Lead.
    3rd c. AD.
    Identical with previous.
    Tudor 1969 I: 93 no. 164.

12. Plate 75.1
    Northampton (Mass.), Smith College Museum of Art SC 1961.26.
    Hungary?
    Lead.
    3rd c. AD.
    Identical with previous.
    Tudor 1969 I: 105 no. 186; Matern 2002: 53, 125, 241–2 I62.3.
    Image: Five Colleges and Historic Deerfield Museum Consortium.

13. Belgrade, National Museum.
    Horreum Margi (Kuprija).
    Lead.
    3rd. c. AD.
    Identical with previous.
    Tudor 1969 I: 35 no. 61.

14. Sarajevo, Museum.
    Han Compagnie-Vitez.
    Lead.
    3rd c. AD.

Identical with previous.
Tudor 1969 I: 68 no. 117.

15.   Plate 75.2
       Mainz, Römisch-germanisches Zentralmuseum o.34585.
       Ilok.
       Lead.
       3rd c. AD.
       Rectangular plaque; the scenes are framed by two columns supporting
       an arch. In the corners above the arch: two snakes. Directly under the
       arch, Sol in frontal chariot (two horses to the right, two to the left), *chla-
       mys*, tunica, radiate (seven rays), right hand raised, globe and whip in left
       hand. Below Sol three registers: in the first, frontal goddess/woman in
       the centre, holding a cloth in front of her, between two horsemen facing
       inwards; behind the left-hand horseman a soldier (helmet, shield, spear)
       and behind the right-hand one a woman holding her hand to her mouth.
       Below the left hand horseman a fish, below the right-hand one a prostrate
       man. In the next register three men sit on a semicircular couch behind
       a round table with draped table-cloth; on the table a fish; two nude men
       approach from the right, at the left a tree on which a man is hanging a
       headless carcas; behind him an anthropomorph figure with a ram's head.
       In the bottom register (from left to right) a three-legged table with a fish
       on it, a lion, a kantharos, a snake, and a cock.
       LIMC Helios/Sol 231; Tudor 1969 I: 38–9 no. 68.
       Image: © GDKE-Landesmuseum Mainz photograph Ursula Rudischer.

16.   Budapest, Museum
       Carnacum (Sotin), Vukovar district.
       Lead.
       3rd c. AD.
       Identical with previous.
       Tudor 1969 I: 82–3 no. 141.

17.   Budapest, National Museum.
       Pannonia.
       Lead.
       3rd c. AD.
       Identical with previous.
       Tudor 1969 I: 94 no. 168.

18. Szegszárd, Museum.
    Tüskepuszta, Tolna district, Hungary.
    Lead.
    3rd c. AD.
    Identical with previous.
    Tudor 1969 I: 83 no. 142.

19. Zombor, Dr. Imre Frey collection.
    Ad Militare, Batina.
    Lead.
    3rd c. AD.
    Identical with previous.
    Tudor 1969 I: 76 no. 131.

20. Belgrade, National Museum.
    Sabać.
    Lead.
    3rd c. AD.
    Identical with previous.
    Tudor 1969 I: 83 no. 144.

21. Belgrade, National Museum.
    Nakučani (Pannonia Inferior).
    Lead.
    3rd c. AD.
    Identical with previous.
    LIMC Heros Equitans 411 (with refs.).

22. Belgrade, National Museum.
    Ušće (Moesia Superior).
    Lead.
    3rd c. AD.
    Identical with previous.
    LIMC Heros Equitans 412 (with refs.).

23. Zagreb, Archaeological Museum.
    Teutoburgium (Dalj, Osijek district).
    Lead.
    3rd c. AD.

Identical with previous.
Tudor 1969 I: 76 no. 132; Matern 2002: 53, 125, 241–2 I62.4.

24.   Zagreb, Archaeological Museum.
      Bassiana (Petrovći, Ruma district).
      Lead.
      3rd c. AD.
      Identical with previous.
      Tudor 1969 I: 78 no. 134.

25.   Zagreb, Archaeological Museum.
      Burgenae (Novi Banovci, Stara Pazova district).
      Lead.
      3rd c. AD.
      Identical with previous.
      Tudor 1969 I: 83 no. 143.

26.   Zagreb, Archaeological Museum.
      Unknown.
      Lead.
      3rd c. AD.
      Identical with previous.
      Tudor 1969 I: 93 no. 163.

27.   Plate 75.3
      New York, Metropolitan Museum of Art 21.88.175.
      Acquired in Rome.
      Lead.
      3rd c. AD.
      Identical with previous.
      Tudor 1969 I: 105 no. 185; Weitzmann 1979, 196–7 no. 176; Matern 2002: 53,
      125, 131 n. 702, 241–2 I62.2.
      Image: Metropolitan Museum of Art New York, Rogers Fund, 1921.

28.   Plate 75.4
      Columbia, University of Missouri, Museum of Art and Archaeology 90.4.
      Unknown (Pannonia or Dacia).
      Lead.
      3rd c. AD.

Two columns supporting an arch frame a complex scene in four registers. In the two upper corners a snake. In the upper register under the arch, Sol in frontal *quadriga* (two horses jumping to either side), right hand raised, *chlamys*, head and left hand missing. In the next register, twin horseman facing inwards flank a goddess/woman, frontal, holding a cloth in front of her; 2 stars; a fish below the right hand horseman, and behind him a woman/goddess with raised right hand; a prostrate nude man below the left hand horseman, and behind a solder with helmet and spear. In the third, largest register a semi-circular couch with three diners and table, on which a dish with a fish. Two nude figures approach the diners from the right. To the left an animal-headed figure stands to the left of a tree from which the (headless?) skin of an animal is being hung by a second figure. In the lowest register, a crater (centre) stands between a lion (right) and a snake (left), with a small amphora hanging above and behind each animal. In the right-hand corner a cock, in the left hand corner a three-legged table bearing a fish.
Lane 1993–4: 59–60 fig. 4. Mackintosh 1997 (identical relief in private British collection).
Image: Museum of Art and Archaeology University of Missouri-Columbia, Weinberg Fund.

29. Budapest, National Museum.
     Sirmium.
     Lead.
     3rd c. AD.
     Identical with previous.
     Tudor 1969 I: 75 no. 118.

30. Budapest, Museum of Fine Arts.
     Lugio-Florentia (Dunaszekcsö), Baranya district, Hungary.
     Lead.
     3rd c. AD.
     Identical with previous.
     Tudor 1969 I: 75 no. 129.

31. Budapest, National Museum.
     Pannonia.
     Lead.
     3rd c. AD.

Identical with previous.
Tudor 1969 I: 94 no. 167.

32.   Belgrade, National Museum.
      Region of Singidunum (Moesia Superior).
      Lead.
      3rd c. AD.
      Identical with previous.
      Tudor 1969 I: 31 no. 54.

33.   Zagreb, Archaeological Museum.
      Pannonia.
      Lead.
      3rd c. AD.
      Identical with previous.
      Tudor 1969 I: 74 no. 127; Matern 2002: 53, 125, 241–2 I62.4.

34.   Plate 75.5
      Cluj, National History Museum of Transylvania V 1097.
      Dacia.
      Lead.
      3rd c. AD.
      Identical with previous.
      Tudor 1969 I: 17 no. 30.
      Image: © National History Museum of Transylvania.

35.   Sarajevo, Museum.
      Halapić (Glamoć district, Dalmatia).
      Lead.
      3rd c. AD.
      Identical with previous.
      Tudor 1969 I: 67–8 no. 116.

36.   Budapest, National Museum.
      Čalma, Sremska Mitrovića district.
      Lead.
      3rd c. AD.
      Aedicula-shaped plaque with curved pediment and two acroteria. In
      pediment: fish. In main field at the top a crater between two snakes and a
      bust of Luna in the left-hand corner and bust of Sol, radiate, in right-hand

corner. Below the crater a woman standing on (above?, behind?) a table or single-legged pedestal, between two horsemen. Below each horse a prostrate man; behind the horsemen, left, a man, and right a woman holding her hand to her mouth. Below (left to right): three-legged table with two cups and a round object, a candelabrum, a dagger, a man skinning a ram hanging from a tree, a kantharos below three balls (loaves? fruit?) and a cock above a ram's head.
Tudor 1969 I: 82 no. 138.

37. Budapest, National Museum.
Pannonia.
Lead.
3rd c. AD.
Identical with previous.
Tudor 1969 I: 94 no. 169.

38. Budapest, National Museum.
Pannonia.
Lead.
3rd c. AD.
Identical with previous.
Tudor 1969 I: 94 no. 170.

39. Zagreb, Archaeological Museum.
Cibalae (Vinkovci).
Lead.
3rd c. AD.
Identical with previous.
Tudor 1969 I: 80–1 no. 137.

40. Sremska Mitrovica, Archaeological Museum.
Mačvanska Mitrovica (Pannonia Inferior).
Lead.
3rd c. AD.
Identical with previous.
LIMC Heros Equitans 430 (with refs.).

41. Plate 75.6
Columbia, University of Missouri, Museum of Art and Archaeology 90.2.
Unknown (Pannonia or Dacia).

Lead.

3rd c. AD.

Roundel. At the top, standing woman holding her hand to her mouth, between busts of Sol (left), radiate (seven rays) and Luna (right). Below, a woman between two horsemen; beneath the horses two prostrate men; to the left a cock, to the right an attendant. Under the prostrate men (from left to right): a kantharos, a candelabrum, a man skinning a ram hanging from a tree and a lion.

Lane 1993–4, 58–9 fig. 2.

Image: Museum of Art and Archaeology University of Missouri-Columbia, Weinberg Fund.

42.   Mačva, National Museum.
      Prnjavor.
      Lead.
      Second half 3rd–early 4th c. AD.
      Identical with previous.
      Krunić 1994/5, 166 fig. 3.

43.   Zagreb, Archaeological Museum.
      Unknown.
      Lead.
      3rd c. AD.
      Identical with previous.
      Tudor 1969 I: 92 no. 162.

44.   Budapest, National Museum.
      Pannonia.
      Lead.
      3rd c. AD.
      Identical with previous.
      Tudor 1969 I: 94 no. 171.

45.   Belgrade, National Museum.
      Obrenovac (Moesia Superior).
      Lead.
      3rd c. AD.
      Identical with previous.
      LIMC Heros Equitans 435.

46. Zagreb, Archaeological Museum.
    Popinč (Stara Pazova district).
    Lead.
    3rd c. AD.
    Roundel. In the centre a goddess/woman holding out her apron behind
    a three-legged table bearing a fish. Two snakes, two stars, Sol and Luna
    flank her head; below these, also flanking the central woman, two horse-
    men trampling two men underfoot. The head and shoulders of a male
    attendant are visible behind the right-hand one. In the exergue a kan-
    tharos between a cock and a ram above three rings.
    Tudor 1969 I: 82 no. 140.

47. Plate 77.5
    Columbia, University of Missouri, Museum of Art and Archaeology 90.1.
    Unknown, probably Pannonia or Dacia.
    Lead.
    3rd c. AD.
    Identical with previous.
    Lane 1993–4, 57–8 fig. 1.
    Image: Museum of Art and Archaeology University of Missouri-Columbia,
    Weinberg Fund.

48. Zagreb, Archaeological Museum.
    Unknown.
    Lead.
    3rd c. AD.
    Fragment of a roundel, identical with previous.
    Tudor 1969 I: 81–2 no. 139.

49. Unknown.
    Pannonia.
    Lead.
    3rd c. AD.
    Identical with previous.
    Tudor 1969 I: 94 no. 172.

50. Belgrade, National Museum.
    Landolje (Moesia Superior).
    Lead.

3rd c. AD.
Identical with previous.
LIMC Heros Equitans 413 (with refs.).

51.   Plate 77.6
       Columbia, University of Missouri, Museum of Art and Archaeology 90.6.
       Unknown (Pannonia or Dacia).
       Lead.
       3rd c. AD.
       Aedicula-shaped plaque with small rounded tympanum and two large
       acroteria. In tympanum Sol in frontal *quadriga* (two horses to the left,
       two to the right), radiate (7? rays), *chlamys* and *chiton*, right hand raised,
       globe and whip in left hand. Left-hand acroterium: male bust with torch
       and star above his head (Sol?); right-hand acroterium: female bust with
       crescent (Luna). Three registers below the pediment, framed by two spi-
       ral columns with snakes emerging from the capitals. In the upper register:
       frontal goddess/woman between two horseman, the left-hand one tram-
       pling a prostrate man underfoot, the right-hand one a fish. The woman
       holds out her apron; two stars and two lamps to either side of her head.
       An armed soldier stands behind the left-hand horseman, a woman hold-
       ing her hand to her mouth behind the right-hand one. In the central reg-
       ister a woman and two men dine at a table bearing a fish; from the right
       the table is being approached by three nude youths, to the left a man is
       skinning a ram hanging from a tree, with behind him a man with a ram's
       head. In the lower register (from left to right): a three-legged table with a
       fish, a torch, a kantharos in the centre between a lion (left) and a snake
       (right), a cock and an unidentifiable object.
       LIMC Helios/Sol 394 (under this number, Letta refers to Tudor 1969
       "passim" for further examples of Sol and Luna as flanking deities in
       Danube-rider reliefs); Lane 1993–4, 61–2 fig. 6.
       Image: Museum of Art and Archaeology University of Missouri-Columbia,
       Weinberg Fund.

52.   Szegszárd, Museum.
       Öcsény, Tolna district, Hungary.
       Lead.
       3rd c. AD.
       Identical with previous.
       Tudor 1969 I: 80 no. 136.

53. Belgrade, National Museum.
     Beljin (Moesia Inferior).
     Lead.
     3rd c. AD.
     Identical with previous.
     LIMC Heros Equitans 416 (with refs.).

54. Zagreb, Archaeological Museum.
     Divos (Stremska Mitrovića district).
     Lead.
     3rd c. AD.
     Identical with previous.
     Tudor 1969 I: 79–80 no. 135; Matern 2002: 53, 125, 241–2 I62.4.

55. Plate 77.1
     Sofia, National Archaeological Museum 7025.
     Gabare (Bêla Slatina district, Bulgaria).
     Lead.
     3rd c. AD.
     In the centre of the upper register, an eagle holding a wreath in its talons
     perches above a small, horizontal column with capitals at either end; to
     its left a raven, and in the corner a bust of Luna; to its right a cock and a
     bust of Sol, radiate, with whip. The upper register is separated from the
     main scene below it by two arches, springing outwards from each end
     of the small horizontal column to two vertical columns which frame
     the central scene. Below either arch a horseman, facing inwards, both
     crowned by a Victory; behind each horseman a woman with her hand
     to her mouth. In the centre, below the horizontal column, a frontal god-
     dess/woman holding each horse by the bridle. Below her a three-legged
     table with a fish, flanked to the left by a lion and an unclear, heart-shaped
     object, and to the right by a bull and a candelabrum-like vertical object.
     A thin line defines the lower register, with (from left to right) a tree, a
     dagger or sword, three candelabra (?) on three-legged pedestals, a large
     crater between two snakes, three rings with a dot in the middle below
     three triangles, a ram's head (?) above four oblique lines, and a tree.
     LIMC Heros Equitans 439; Tudor 1969 I: 43 no. 75.
     Image: © Sofia Archaeological Museum / Krassimir Georgiev.

56. Pleven Regional Historical Museum.
     Oescus (Gigen).

Lead.

3rd c. AD.

Fragment of a plaque, identical with previous.

Tudor 1969 I: 43 no. 74.

57.   Bucharest, Dr. S. Stefanescu collection.

Romula.

Lead.

3rd c. AD.

Identical with previous.

Tudor 1969 I: 20–1 no. 36.

58.   Zagreb, Archaeological Museum.

Sirmium (Stremska Mitrovića).

Lead.

3rd c. AD.

Aedicula-shaped plaque with small rounded tympanum between two acroteria. In the tympanum a fish and four stars. A roundel encompasses the main scene, leaving open the four corners with four busts (winds or seasons); within the roundel at the top a woman holding her hand to her mouth between busts of Luna (right) and Sol (left), radiate (five rays). Behind Sol a three-legged table bearing three objects, behind Luna a jug and an indistinct object. In the centre of the main field a goddess/woman and to either side a horseman, each trampling a prostrate man underfoot. Behind the left-hand horseman an attendant, behind the right-hand one four rings and a lamp. Below: a cock, a man skinning a ram hanging from a tree, a candelabrum and an indistinct object.

LIMC Heros Equitans 433; Tudor 1969 I: 72–3 no. 125.

59.   Plate 77.2

Split, Archaeological Museum H4975.

Bigeste (Humac).

Lead.

3rd c. AD.

Identical with previous.

Tudor 1969 I: 67 no. 115.

Image: © Archaeological Museum, Split.

60.   Belgrade, National Museum.

Jalovik.

Lead.

Second half 3rd c.–early 4th c. AD.
Identical with previous.
Krunić 1994/5: 165 fig. 2.

60a. Bucharest, National Museum.
      Sucidava.
      Lead.
      First half 3rd c. AD.
      Aedicula-shaped plaque. In the tympanum, busts of Luna (left) and Sol
      (right), radiate, between two serpents. In the main field a woman between
      two horsemen, of whom the left-hand one is trampling a man underfoot.
      In the next register (from left to right): three altars, a three-legged table
      with a fish, three rings on a low table and above them three triangular
      objects. In the lowest register, from left to right: a table with three rings, a
      candelabrum, a lion, a cock, a kantharos, a raven and a bull.
      LIMC Heros Equitans 422; Tudor 1969 I: 24–5 no. 42.

61.   Bucharest, National Museum.
      Orlea, (near Sucidava).
      Lead.
      3rd c. AD.
      Identical with previous.
      Tudor 1969 I: 25 no. 43.

62.   Turnu Severin (Rumania), Porţile de Fier Museum.
      Drobeta.
      Lead.
      3rd c. AD.
      Fragment, identical with previous.
      Tudor 1969 II: 12–13 no. 206.

63.   Pleven, Regional Historical Museum.
      Oescus (Gigen).
      Lead.
      3rd c. AD.
      Aedicula-shaped plaque. In the tympanum, Sol (left), radiate, and Luna
      (right), between two peacocks in the corners. The tympanum is separated
      from the main scene by a narrow register with (from left to right) a bull,
      an eagle, a cock, and a lion (or possibly a dog?). The main scene has a god-
      dess/woman (polos) between two horsemen (whose horses she holds by
      the reins), behind whom are two female figures dressed like the central

goddess/woman. Below the central goddess/woman a three-legged table, perhaps bearing a fish. Below each horseman a snake facing inwards, head just above the table. Below the left hand snake an indistinguishable object, a prostrate nude man facing inwards, a fish or dolphin facing inwards and a crater (?); similar figures, but without the indistinguishable object, below the right hand figure. In the lower register (from left to right) a horse (?), three altars with three rings, a three-legged table with a fish, a crater, a ram, and an unidentifiable vertical object.
Tudor 1969 I: 41–2 no. 72.

64. Turnu Severin (Rumania), Porţile de Fier Museum.
Romula.
Lead.
3rd c. AD.
Identical with previous.
LIMC Heros Equitans 419; Tudor 1969 I: 20 no. 35.

65. Óbud, Aquincum Museum.
Aquincum.
Lead.
3rd c. AD.
Roundel; at the top, centre, a standing woman holding her hand to her mouth, above a star; she is flanked left by the bust of Luna and a cock and right by the bust of Sol, radiate (five rays) and a ram's head. In the main field below two horsemen facing inward, above two prostrate men; the woman who normally stands between them is missing; behind the horsemen various objects. Below, from left to right: a lion, three circles below him, a man skinning a ram hanging from a tree, a star and a ram.
Tudor 1969 I: 70–1 no. 120.

66. Formerly Salaško (Croatia), now lost.
Salaško.
Lead.
3rd. c. AD.
Identical with previous.
Tudor 1969 I: 71 nr 121.

67. Plate 77.3
Berlin, Staatliche Museen FR 2008b.
Rome or environs of Rome.

Bronze.

2nd–3rd c. AD.

Bronze plaque. In the upper corners, busts of Sol (left), radiate, *chlamys*, and Luna (right), each accompanied by a star. They are separated from the main field by two snakes who rise up from two cypresses which frame the main scene, and with their heads facing inwards form a kind of arch. Between the snakes' heads, at the top centre, a lion's head, frontal. In the main scene, a horseman rides to the right over a man lying prostrate, face downwards. Behind him a bearded man with a ram's head in his raised right hand and a man's head in his left hand. Facing the horse a woman; behind her a bearded man; above her head a rectangular object (grid-iron? cista?). Below the prostrate man (from left to right): a lamp above a ram, a bull, a three-legged table with a fish below the woman, and a crater above a raven.

LIMC Heros Equitans 361; Tudor 1969 I: 97 no. 174.

Image: © Staatliche Museen zu Berlin.

68.   Terracina, Museo Archeologico.

Terracina.

Limestone.

3rd c. AD.

Relief in two registers; in the upper register a woman behind a three-legged table between two horsemen; below each horse a prostrate, nude man; above: frontal bust of Luna and a bust of Sol, radiate, *chlamys*, to either side. In the lower register (from left to right): an altar, a ram, a cock.

LIMC Helios/Sol 225; Tudor 1969 I: 98–9 no. 176.

Image: arachne.dainst.org/entity/778887.

69.   Pleven Regional Historical Museum.

Oescus (Gigen).

Lead.

3rd c. AD.

Fragment of a plaque; two columns (right hand column missing) support an arch. Above and to the right of the arch, bust of Luna, to the left (lost) Sol. Upper register under arch lost. Main register: two horsemen flanking a goddess/woman (lost); two prostrate, nude men under the horsemen. Various other attributes. Lower register almost completely lost.

Tudor 1969 I: 43 no. 73.

70.   Vacat (now C2v.3).

71.   Razgrad (Bulgaria), Regional Historical Museum.
      Ezerče.
      Marble.
      3rd c. AD.
      Slightly oval roundel. In the centre, goddess/woman behind a table with
      an object (fish?) on it. Above her, busts of Sol and Luna. The goddess/
      woman stands between two horseman, facing inwards. Below the horses
      two figures (prostrate men? One fish and one man?). In the exergue,
      two snakes, heads facing inwards, and below them (from left to right), a
      cock (?), a ram's head (?), an altar with a fish, a column (?) and a lion (?).
      Tudor 1969 I: 31 no. 86.

72.   Plate 77.4
      Sofia, National Archaeological Museum 2994.
      Novae.
      Lead.
      3rd c. AD.
      Aedicula-shaped plaque. In the apex an eagle with a wreath in its beak,
      two stars, and a dagger or sword. Slightly lower to the left Sol, radiate
      (seven rays), whip, with a lamp (?) next to him. To the right Luna and
      a snake; a second snake between Sol and Luna. In the main field a god-
      dess/woman stands in the centre behind a three-legged table with a fish
      on it. Flanking her are two horsemen facing inwards. The right-hand one
      is crowned by a small Victory and behind him a goddess/woman stands
      with her hand to her mouth. A goddess (?) with a spear stands behind the
      other horseman. Two prostrate men lie under the horses. At the bottom
      (from left to right): a lion, a kantharos, an altar, a cock, and a ram.
      LIMC Heros Equitans 428; Tudor 1969 I: 49–50 no. 83.
      Image: © Sofia Archaeological Museum / Krassimir Georgiev.

73.   Plate 78.3
      Sofia, National Archaeological Museum 4924.
      Almus (Lom, Bulgaria).
      Marble.
      3rd c. AD.
      In top corners, Luna (left) and Sol (right), radiate, *chlamys*. In centre of
      the main field, frontal goddess/woman, almost disappearing behind two
      horseman, facing inwards, flanking her. Behind each horse a woman,
      below each a prostrate man. A snake above each horse's head. In the
      lower register (from left to right): three candelabra, three loaves, three

apples, a ram, a three-legged table with a fish and a dagger or sword, a cock, a lion and a bow (?).
LIMC Heros Equitans 414; Tudor 1969 I: 40 no. 71.
Image: © Sofia Archaeological Museum / Krassimir Georgiev.

74. Sofia, National Archaeological Museum.
Biala Čercova (Pavlikeni district).
Marble.
3rd c. AD.
Plaque; main figure is a single horseman facing right above a prostrate man being attacked by a lion. Behind the horseman a woman holding her hand to her mouth. Lower right hand corner contains a three-legged table with three loaves and a fish, behind which stands a frontal goddess/ woman. Above her head a platter with three objects. In top right hand corner a female bust, possibly Luna. To the left of the bust a disc and two crosses. A second disc, possibly Sol, behind the head of the horseman.
Tudor 1969 I: 47 no. 79.

75. Plate 78.1
Sofia, National Archaeological Museum 6027.
Rebro (Breznik distr.).
Lead.
3rd c. AD.
Aedicula-shaped plaque. In tympanum: eagle. Main field: Two horsemen, facing inwards, flank a frontal goddess/woman who is holding the reins of the horses. Behind the left hand horse a woman holding her hand to her mouth, behind the right hand horse a man. At the edges, two snakes rearing upwards towards two busts in the upper corners: Luna (left) and Sol (right), radiate (seven rays). Below each horse a prostrate, nude man. In the lower register (from left to right): a candelabrum, seven round objects (pieces of fruit or loaves of bread?), a lion, a three-legged table bearing a fish, with a ram's head below the table, a bird, a gridiron, a quadruped, a nude man.
LIMC Heros Equitans 427; Tudor 1969 I: 48–9 no. 81.
Image: © Sofia Archaeological Museum / Krassimir Georgiev.

76. Sofia, National Archaeological Museum.
Sapaneva Bania (Stanke Dimitrov distr.).
Marble.
3rd c. AD.

Roundel (fragment): in the centre a goddess/woman behind a three-legged table bearing a fish. She stands between two horsemen, with above their heads traces of two busts, probably Sol and Luna. Below each horse a prostrate man. In the lower register (most of which is lost) a part of a snake can be made out.
Tudor 1969 I: 61–2 no. 105.

77. Lost (formerly Varna Museum).
      Varna.
      Marble.
      3rd c. AD.
      Rectangular plaque, only the upper left hand corner is preserved. Along the top three busts: Sol, with whip (?) in the corner, and at a short distance to the right a male bust (bearded, according to Tudor, but this is not clear from the sketch) and a female bust; below, the upper part of one horseman and the head of his horse, facing inwards, are preserved, as well as the head of the central goddess/woman.
      Tudor 1969 I: 54 no. 92.

78. Budapest, National Museum.
      Potaissa.
      Marble.
      2nd–3rd c. AD.
      Plaque with relief-decoration in three registers. Upper register: Sol (left), *chlamys*, and Luna (right) in the corners; two snakes rearing up to a kantharos in the centre. Main register: in the centre a horseman riding to the right over a prostrate man; behind him two attendants; in front of him two women, the second of whom holds her hand to her mouth, and a man. Lower register (from left to right): left corner missing; in centre a man holds something over an altar; at the right a seated man holds an object towards a three-legged table on which another object is lying.
      LIMC Heros Equitans 362; Tudor 1969 I: 5–6 no. 9.

79. Budapest, National Museum 2b.
      Area of Dacia Superior.
      Marble.
      3rd c. AD.
      Plaque with relief decoration in three registers; in the upper register traces of three busts (including Sol and Luna?); in the main register (partially

preserved) a goddess/woman behind a three-legged table between two horsemen; in the lower register (partially preserved) three men.
Tudor 1969 I: 15–16 no. 28.

80.   Budapest, National Museum 4959.
      Kápolna (District Heves, Hungary).
      Marble.
      3rd c. AD.
      Roundel; at the top the busts of Sol and Luna above two horsemen to either side of a goddess/woman behind a table. Below each horse a prostrate man. In the lower register various indistinct objects, including a woman raising her hand to her mouth.
      Tudor 1969 I: 69–70 no. 119.

81.   Belgrade, National Museum.
      Belgrade.
      Lead.
      Late 2nd–mid 3rd c. AD (Found in a closed well in conjunction with pottery dating from the late 2nd to mid 3rd c. AD).
      Relief in two registers. Above, in the centre, a goddess/woman holds the horses of two flanking horsemen by their bridles; below the right-hand horse a prostrate man, below the left-hand one a fish, behind the left-hand horse a woman holding her hand to her mouth. In the lower register a large number of objects, animals and figures: in the centre a man with Phrygian cap, whip behind his right shoulder, left hand raised; to the right a kantharos and a man skinning a ram hanging from a tree; to the left a three-legged table, a cock, a lion, two candelabrums, a dog, a pair of horns, a star, a crescent and an unclear object. Two upright snakes, bending inwards near the top, border the scenes; at the top, between the snakes' heads, a sphere between an eagle and a cock. In the upper corners beyond the snakes, the busts of Sol (left) with radiate nimbus and Luna (right). Despite the Phrygian cap, Krunić identifies the central figure on the lower register as Sol.
      Krunić 1994/5, 164 fig. 1 (description in English on p. 172).

82.   Belgrade, National Museum II/1562.
      Danube-valley.
      Lead.
      3rd c. AD.

Aedicula-shaped plaque; in upper corners above the pediment two flying Victoriae; in the tympanum, busts of Sol and Luna to either side of
an eagle (?); in the main field a goddess/woman between two horsemen; in the lower register a crater, a cock (?) and other objects, now
indistinguishable.
Tudor 1969 II: 14–5 no. 210; Iskra-Janošić 1966, p. 65 no. 1 pl IV/2.

83.   Belgrade, National Museum.
      Belgrade (Singidunum, Moesia Superior).
      Marble.
      3rd c. AD.
      Rectangular plaque with relief-decoration in three registers. Upper regis-
      ter: in centre bust of a woman between the busts of two bearded, hooded
      men; next two bearded men holding a fish (an altar by the left-hand one),
      next busts of Sol (left, almost completely lost) and Luna. Main register:
      a goddess/woman behind a three-legged table bearing a fish, between
      two horsemen and two attendants (left: Victory; right: male figure); below
      each horse a prostrate male. Lower register (from left to right): a cock
      above an unidentified object, a woman holding her hand to her mouth
      with a second round object at her feet, two men holding the skin of a ram
      in front of a third man, three vessels above a ram.
      LIMC Heros Equitans 426; Tudor 1969 I: 30 no. 50.

84.   Belgrade, National Museum.
      Viminacium (Kostolač).
      Lead.
      3rd c. AD.
      Roundel with relief in four registers. Upper register: eagle between two
      snakes and busts of Sol (left) and Luna (right); main register: woman,
      holding out her apron, behind a three-legged table (?); two stars (?) beside
      her head; she stands between two horsemen trampling two prostrate
      men underfoot; in a narrow band below the main register three rings, a
      three-legged table, and a small house with gabled roof; in the lower regis-
      ter various figures, almost all too damaged to be recognizable.
      LIMC Heros Equitans 423; Tudor 1969 I: 32–3 no. 56.

85.   Belgrade, National Museum.
      Paračin.
      Marble.

2nd–3rd c. AD.

Round-topped relief-plaque. In the main field a horseman riding right over a prostrate man who is being attacked by a lion; to the right three women, one behind the horse and two next to it, of whom one raises her hand to her mouth; in the upper left-hand corner bust of Sol, in the right-hand corner bust of Luna. In the lower register (from left to right): a ram's head, a gridiron or spiral column, a three-legged table bearing a fish and three round objects, an eagle, a star and a snake (?).

LIMC Heros Equitans 367; Tudor 1969 I: 36–7 no. 64.

86. Niš, Museum.
Mediana (Brzi Brod).
Marble.
2nd–3rd c. AD.

Round topped plaque. At the top, busts of Sol and Luna, below whom a horseman is riding to the right over a prostrate man who is being attacked by a lion. To the right of the horseman a goddess/woman behind a three-legged table on which a fish is lying; behind the horseman a goddess/woman holding her hand to her mouth and-above-a Victory. In the lower register unclear objects.

LIMC Heros Equitans 359; Tudor 1969 I: 34 no. 59.

87. Sremska Mitrovica, Museum.
Kuzmin (Pannonia Inf.).
Lead.
3rd c. AD.

Roundel; within two encircling snakes, scenes in three registers. At the top, busts of Sol (right, radiate, seven rays) and Luna. Main register, a frontal goddess/woman above a 3-legged table, approached from either side by a horseman trampling a prostrate figure underfoot. There is a kantharos behind the left-hand horseman, and a goddess/woman raising her hand to her mouth behind the right-hand one. In the lower register, from left to right, a candelabrum, a man disembowelling an animal, a tree, a lion, and a bird.

LIMC Heros Equitans 418

88. Lost.
Viminacium.
Bronze (reportedly).

3rd c. AD.
Roundel. Above busts of Sol, radiate, and Luna to either side of a goddess/
woman holding her hand to her mouth; behind Sol a bird, behind Luna
a three-legged table. In the main field a goddess/woman between two
horsemen trampling two prostrate men; behind the left-hand horseman
an amphora and a ram's head, behind the right-hand one an amphora (?)
and a cock. Below (from left to right): a lion, a vessel, a man skinning a
ram hanging from a tree, a candelabrum and a ram.
LIMC Heros Equitans 432; Tudor 1969 I: 33 no. 57

89.   Sinj (Croatia), Franciscan Church Museum.
       Aequum (Čitluk).
       Marble.
       3rd c. AD.
       Plaque in three registers. Upper register: vessel between two snakes, two
       stars and two busts (Sol and Luna, although they lack defining attributes).
       Main register: a goddess/woman standing in the centre between two
       horsemen trampling two prostrate men underfoot; behind each horse-
       man an attendant; behind the head of each horseman a star, to either
       side of the head of the woman a crescent; lower register: various objects.
       Tudor 1969 I: 66 no. 113.

90.   Plate 78.4
       Split, Archaeological Museum D 215.
       Salonae (Split).
       Marble.
       3rd c. AD (Tudor), 2nd–3rd c. AD (LIMC).
       Rectangular plaque with relief in three registers. Upper register: eagle
       between two snakes and two busts (Sol and Luna, although defining
       attributes cannot be made out); to the left of the left-hand bust a bird.
       Main register: a horseman riding to the right, trampling a prostrate man
       underfoot; behind him a goddess/woman holding her hand to her mouth,
       in front of a column; in front of him a woman holding out her apron in a
       pouch attended by a man. Lower register: various objects.
       Tudor 1969 I: 63 no. 107. LIMC Heros Equitans 364.
       Image: © Archaeological Museum, Split.

91.   Split, Archaeological Museum.
       Unknown.

Marble.

3rd c. AD.

Upper part of a round-topped plaque. In the upper register an eagle between two busts (Sol and Luna) and two indeterminate objects. Only the upper part of the main register is preserved, depicting a goddess/woman between two horsemen; behind the left-hand one a woman, behind the right-hand one a man and a woman.

Tudor 1969 I: 65–6 no. 112.

92. Plate 78.2

Columbia, University of Missouri, Museum of Art and Archaeology 90.3.

Pannonia or Dacia.

Lead.

3rd c. AD.

Aedicula-shaped plaque with small rounded tympanum (acroteria at the corners missing). In the tympanum a fish between four stars. A roundel encompasses the main scene, leaving open the four corners with four busts (winds or seasons) of which only two survive; within the roundel at the top a goddess/woman holding her hand to her mouth between busts of Luna (right) and Sol (left), radiate (probably five or six rays, almost certainly not seven). Behind Sol a three-legged table bearing three objects, behind Luna a lion with its forepaws on a vessel. In the centre of the main field a goddess/woman between two horsemen trampling two prostrate men underfoot; behind the left-hand horseman an attendant, behind the right-hand one a cock, two bases and a raven. Below: an animal, a kantharos, a cup, a candelabrum on a pedestal, a man skinning a ram hanging from a tree, and three rings.

Lane 1993–4, 59 fig. 3.

Image: Museum of Art and Archaeology, University of Missouri-Columbia, Weinberg Fund

93. Klagenfurt, Landesmuseum Kärnten.

Virunum (Zollfeld).

Copper.

3rd c. AD.

Rectangular plaque with relief-decoration in two registers. In the upper register a goddess/woman stands in the centre holding a piece of cloth in front of her, between two horsemen, of whom the left-hand one is trampling a prostrate man underfoot. Behind the horses two upright snakes,

bending inwards, heads facing each other to either side of the central woman's head. In the upper corners busts of Sol (left), radiate, and Luna (right). In the lower register (from left to right): a man skinning a ram hanging from a tree, a goddess/woman holding her hand to her mouth, a three-legged table bearing three fruit (?), a loaf (?) and a crescent-shaped object, with two amphorae between the legs of the table, a fish, a dagger, a cock, a vessel, a lion, and a man with a ram's head.
Tudor 1969 I: 95 no. 631.

94. Alba Julia, Muzeul Unirii.
Dark marble.
3rd c. AD.
Rectangular plaque. In the upper corners busts of Sol (left), radiate, and Luna (right). In the centre frontal standing goddess/woman behind a three-legged table bearing a fish; she stands between two horsemen trampling two prostrate men underfoot.
Tudor 1969 I: 4 no. 6.

95. Lost; plaster copies in Alba Julia, Muzeul Unirii & Rome, Museo di Gessi.
Dacia.
Marble.
3rd c. AD.
Roundel, divided into three registers. Upper register: veiled female bust between two hooded male busts. To the left, a three-legged table with a fish, two attendants and in the corner a small bust (Sol); to the right a man holding a fish and a bust (Luna). In the main field a goddess/woman behind a three-legged table bearing a fish, between two horsemen, each with a male attendant and each trampling a prostrate man underfoot. In the lower register (from left to right) a goddess/woman holding her hand to her mouth, two men holding a skin of a ram in front of a person (woman?), and a bull below a ram.
Tudor 1969 I: 2–3 no. 3.

96. Formerly Dr. Lestyán Jozséf collection, lost in WWII.
Unknown.
Marble.
3rd c. AD.
Rectangular plaque. In the upper half a goddess/woman stands between two horsemen trampling two men underfoot; Tudor assumes that busts

of Sol and Luna were in the upper corners, but this is not visible on the drawing. Below, a three-legged table at the centre bearing a fish, next to which stands a goddess/woman holding her hand to her mouth. At each side a man; various other, unidentifiable objects.
Tudor 1969 I: 4–5 no. 7.

97. Bucharest, G. Niţulescu archaeological collection.
Romula (Tudor); found in the Teslui river (LIMC).
Lead.
3rd c. AD.
Rectangular plaque, decorated in four registers. Top register: an eagle in the centre between two male busts, two figures carrying vessels and the busts of Luna (right) and Sol (left), radiate (5 double rays), whip. In the main register a goddess/woman stands in the centre behind a three-legged table bearing a fish. She stands between two horsemen, each trampling a prostrate man underfoot. Above the horses two stars and two snakes. In the next register (from left to right): a ram's head, a bull, a crater between two snakes, a lion and a dagger. In the lowest register (from left to right): three rings, three candelabra, and a branch.
LIMC Heros Equitans 417; Tudor 1969 I: 21–2 no. 37.

98. Bucharest, National Museum.
Danube, near Sucidava.
Terracotta.
3rd c. AD.
Aedicula-shaped applique, much worn. Above the pediment a raven between two busts (Sol and Luna); in the pediment three busts, between two snakes. Below, a goddess/woman behind a three-legged table bearing a fish, between two horsemen. Below the horsemen, next to the table, to the left three altars above a crater and an indistinguishable object, and to the right a lamp, an amphora (?) and a snake curled around a tree.
Tudor 1969 I: 23–4 no. 41.

99. Bucharest, National Museum.
Orlea (near Sucidava).
Lead.
3rd c. AD.

Roundel, very poorly preserved; most of the decoration impossible to make out. In the upper register to the left the radiate head of Sol is still visible.

Tudor 1969 I: 25–6 no. 44.

100. Formerly Bucharest, National Museum, now lost.
      Dacia inferior.
      Lead.
      3rd c. AD.
      Roundel. Above: frontal busts of Sol (left), radiate (six rays), and Luna with an upright snake between them; to the left an animal skin, an eagle and a dagger; to the right a goddess/woman holding her hand to her mouth. Below Sol and Luna a goddess/woman behind a three-legged table, between two horsemen, each trampling a prostrate man underfoot; each horseman is crowned by a Victory. In the exergue (from left to right): a lion, a kantharos above a cock, an unidentifiable object, a ram, a second unidentifiable object.
      LIMC Heros Equitans 431; Tudor 1969 I: p. 28 no. 48.

101. Bucharest, National Museum.
      Castelu, Constanţa district.
      Marble.
      3rd c. AD.
      Rectangular plaque. In the centre a goddess/woman behind a three-legged table with a fish on it, between two horsemen, trampling two prostrate men (?) underfoot. In the upper corners, two busts (Sol and Luna).
      LIMC Heros Equitans 415; Tudor 1969 I: 56 no. 97.

102. Bucharest, City Museum 6273/1949 & 444/1957.
      Moesia Inferior.
      Marble.
      3rd c. AD.
      Fragment of a plaque. Preserved are a goddess/woman standing behind a table, two horses' heads and the busts of Luna (right) and Sol (left) with balteus, to either side of the woman's head.
      Tudor 1969 I: 58–9 no. 101.

103. Călăraşi Museum.
      Durostorum (Silistra).

Marble.

3rd c. AD.

Fragment of a roundel; what remain are the upper part of a right-hand horseman and a bust of Sol in front of him.

Tudor 1969 II: 21 no. 229.

104. Plate 79.4

Cluj, National History Museum of Transylvania V. 19648.

Potaissa (Turda).

Marble.

3rd c. AD.

Two fragments of a rectangular plaque divided into three registers. Upper register (complete): crater between two snakes, two hooded male busts, and the busts of Luna (left) and Sol (right). Of the main register only the upper part is preserved, showing a goddess/woman between two horsemen. Of the lower register only the left-hand corner remains, with a spiral pillar, a cock and a ram (not depicted).

Tudor 1969 I: 7 no. 11.

Image: © National History Museum of Transylvania

105. Plate 79.3

Cluj, National History Museum of Transylvania.

Brucla (Aiud).

Marble.

3rd c. AD.

Large fragment of an (unfinished?) round-topped plaque. In the centre a goddess/woman, two busts (Sol and Luna) to either side of her head, between two horsemen; of the left-hand one enough is preserved to also reveal a prostrate man below him. In the lower register a bird, a large altar, and a man.

Tudor 1969 I: 11–2 no. 20.

Image: © National History Museum of Transylvania

106. Cluj, National History Museum of Transylvania.

Dacia Superior.

Marble.

3rd c. AD.

Roundel. In the centre a goddess/woman behind a three-legged table; to the left and right above her head two busts (Sol and Luna). She stands between two horsemen, the right-hand one accompanied by a lion, the left-hand one trampling a prostrate man underfoot and followed by an attendant. In the lower register a cock, three men with a ram, and a crater, all below two snakes.

LIMC Heros Equitans 421; Tudor 1969 I: 15 no. 27.

107. Deva, Museum.
Sarmizegetusa.
Marble.
3rd c. AD.
Upper left-hand corner of a rectangular plaque. In the upper register an egg-shaped vessel between two snakes, flanked to the left by a bust (Luna, according to Tudor). Only the top of the next register is preserved, show-ing (from left to right): the heads of two attendants, a horseman, a horse, and a woman. The plaque can have depicted only one horseman.
Tudor 1969 I: 9 no. 15.

108. Deva, Museum.
Sarmizegetusa.
Marble.
3rd c. AD.
Upper part of a rectangular plaque. In the centre of the upper register an eagle above the bust of a woman between the busts of two hooded men, two standing men each holding some object, and two busts in the corners (Sol, very worn, and Luna). Only the upper portion of the main register remains, with a goddess/woman in the centre between two horsemen, each followed by an attendant.
Tudor 1969 I: 12 no. 19.

109. Galaţi, History Museum.
Barboşi (Galaţi district), Romania.
Marble.
3rd c. AD.
Roughly aedicula-shaped plaque, originally serving a different function but reused as Danube-rider relief. In the apex of the tympanum an eagle above the bust of a woman between the busts of two hooded men and of Sol (left) and Luna (right). In the main field a goddess/woman behind a three-legged table between two horsemen, each trampling a prostrate man underfoot and each followed by an attendant goddess/woman hold-ing her hand to her mouth.
LIMC Heros Equitans 429; Tudor 1969 I: 57 no. 99.

110.   Lugoj, Museum of History, Ethnography, and Art.
       Tibiscum (Jupa), Romania.
       Marble.
       3rd c. AD.
       Upper left-hand corner of a rectangular plaque. In the top register (from
       left to right) the bust of Sol, *chlamys*, on a base, the legs of a person, and
       the remains of two draped busts. In the main register the preserved fig-
       ures are (from left to right) a female attendant, a horseman below a snake,
       and a goddess/woman behind a three-legged table bearing a fish.
       Tudor 1969 I: 11–2 no. 22.

111.   Lost
       Porolissum (Moigrad).
       Marble.
       3rd c. AD.
       Upper right-hand corner of a plaque, preserving a horseman riding to the
       left; in fromt of him a bust, possibly Sol.
       Tudor 1969 I: 5 no. 8.

112.   Lost.
       Potaissa (Turda).
       Marble.
       3rd c. AD.
       Upper right-hand corner of a plaque. In the upper register two snakes
       to either side of an egg-shaped vessel; to the right in the corner a bust,
       probably Sol, possibly Luna. In the main field (from left to right) head an
       forelegs of the horse of the single horseman, a goddess/woman, a second
       goddess/woman holding her hand to her mouth, and a male attendant at
       the right-hand edge.
       Tudor 1969 I: 6–7 no. 10.

113.   Lost (formerly collection of Count Joseph v. Kemény).
       Potaissa (Turda).
       Marble.
       3rd c. AD.
       Rectangular plaque; only two, inaccurate, descriptions survive. Upper
       register: bust of a woman between the busts of two hooded men, and
       the busts of Sol and Luna. Main register: goddess/woman behind a three-
       legged table with a fish, between two horsemen each trampling a pros-
       trate man underfoot. In the lower register various figures and objects.
       Tudor 1969, 8–9 no. 12.

114. Lost (formerly collection of Count Joseph v. Kemény).
      Potaissa (Turda).
      Marble.
      3rd c. AD.
      Roundel; only two, inaccurate, descriptions survive.
      Tudor 1969, 9 no. 13.

115. Lost (formerly collection of Count Joseph v. Kemény).
      Potaissa (Turda).
      Marble.
      3rd c. AD.
      Roundel; only two, inaccurate, descriptions survive.
      Tudor 1969, 9–10 no. 14.

116. Lost.
      Sarmizegetusa
      Stone.
      3rd c. AD.
      Right-hand part of a rectangular plaque in three registers. Upper register:
      in the right-hand corner a bust, probably Luna; next to her a ring (accord-
      ing to Tudor the back part a rearing snake). In the main register (from
      left to right): a single horseman, partially preserved, riding to the right
      and trampling a prostrate figure underfoot, and three figures. In the lower
      register two figures and a three-legged table.
      Tudor 1969 I: 9–10 no. 16.

117. Sibiu, Brukenthal museum.
      Apulum.
      Marble.
      3rd c. AD.
      Round-topped plaque, broken at the left. Upper border: two snakes.
      Main field: a horseman trampling a prostrate man underfoot; behind
      him an attendant, in front of him two women on a pedestal, the first
      one holding out an apron, the second holding her hand to her mouth.
      Above them a snake entwining a tree and a bust of Sol. In the lower
      register: a lion, a ram, a three-legged table bearing a fish, a crater with
      three drinking horns, a cock, a spiral column, and an unidentifiable
      object.
      Tudor 1969 I: no. 1.

118. Sighişoara, Museum.
Sarmizagetusa or environs.
Marble.
2nd–3rd c. AD.
Round-topped plaque, lower right-hand corner missing. At the top, an eagle between two busts (Sol and Luna). In the main field: a goddess/woman in the centre, seated, behind a three-legged table with a fish, between two horsemen, each trampling a prostrate man underfoot, of whom the left-hand one is attacked by a lion. In the lower register, from left to right: a bird, an animal, a person holding his/her hand to the mouth, and a group of three persons.
LIMC Heros Equitans 436; Tudor 1969 I: 10–1 no. 18.

119. Timişoara, Museum.
Pojejena.
Marble.
3rd c. AD.
Rectangular plaque, lower right-hand corner missing. In the centre a sketchily rendered figure behind a one-legged table. Above her head two busts (Sol and Luna). She stands between two horsemen, each trampling an even more sketchily rendered prostrate man underfoot. In the lower register, the cursory representations (from left to right) of: a cock, a crater below a ram's head, three figures and a ram.
Tudor 1969 I: 14 no. 25.

120. Timişoara, Museum.
Tibiscum, Roman camp, building B.
Marble.
2nd–3rd c. AD.
Round-topped rectangular plaque, broken into seven pieces. Three registers; in the upper register: bust of a woman between two male, hooded busts and the busts of Sol and Luna in the corners (heads damaged). In the main register a single horseman trampling a prostrate man. Behind him stands a male attendant, in front of him a woman and a man. In the lower register (from left to right): a spiral column, a vessel below a cock, a three-legged table between two men, and two bases.
LIMC Heros Equitans 200; Tudor 1969 II: 9 no. 200.

121. Private collection; clay copy in Timişoara, Museum.
Tibiscum.

Marble.

3rd c. AD.

Rectangular plaque. Three registers: in the upper register; an egg-shaped vessel between two snakes and the busts of Sol and Luna in the corners. In the main register a single horseman trampling a prostrate man. Behind him stands two male attendants, in front of him a woman with open arms, a second woman with her hand to her mouth and a man. In the lower register (from left to right): a bird, a man dragging a ram towards an altar, a seated man below three conical vessels, an unidentified object, and a three-legged table with a ram's head.

Tudor 1969 II: 11 no. 203.

122. Timişoara, Museum.

Tibiscum, civilian settlement, apsidal building.

Marble.

3rd c. AD.

Rectangular plaque, right corners broken. Three registers; in the upper register: bust of a woman between two male, hooded busts and the busts of Sol and Luna in the corners (damaged). In the main register two horsemen, each trampling a prostrate man, flank a goddess/woman with two snakes to either side of her head. In the lower register (from left to right): a spiral column on a base, a crater below a cock, a three-legged table with a fish, and below a vessel a four-legged table between two men, and an animal's head (damaged).

Tudor 1969 II: 11–2 no. 204.

123. Turnu Severin (Rumania), Porţile de Fier Museum.

Romula.

Lead.

3rd c. AD.

Rectangular plaque. The lateral borders are formed by two spiral columns from which spring two arches. Outside the arches two bearded busts in the corners, holding a horn to the mouth (the one at the left very damaged) and an eagle in the centre. Within the arches the busts of Luna (right-hand arch) and Sol (left-hand arch), radiate, whip (? Tudor describes this as a bow and quiver; I cannot make this out from the picture). Between them, below the joint of the two arches, a vessel between two snakes. Below this vessel, in the main field, a woman above a horizontal dagger, between two horsemen, each trampling a prostrate figure underfoot. Behind the left-hand one a soldier, behind the right-hand one

a male attendant. In the next register (from left to right): a lion, a kantharos, a three-legged table with a fish, a person holding his hand above
an altar, and a temple-like building with three pillars and a beamed roof,
within which several round objects. In the lowest register (from left to
right): a dog, three men, three rings below three lamps on three bases, a
candelabrum (three candelabra?) and a ram's head.
Tudor 1969 I: 19–20 no. 34.

124. Turnu Severin (Rumania), Porţile de Fier Museum.
Drobeta.
Marble.
3rd c. AD.
Roundel. In the centre a goddess/woman behind a table. Above her head
two busts (Sol and Luna). She stands between two horsemen, the right-
hand one accompanied by an attendant. Only two heads are preserved in
the lower register.
Tudor 1969 II: 12 no. 205.

125. Plate 79.5
Ptuj, Pokrajinski Muzej Ptuj Ormož RL 465.
Poetovio (Ptuj), sacellum of a private house.
Marble.
3rd c. AD.
Rectangular plaque. In the upper corners two busts, Sol (left, broken) and
Luna. In the main register a goddess/woman in a niche standing behind
a three-legged table; two snakes by her head. She stands between two
horsemen each trampling a prostrate man underfoot. In the next register
a crater between a lion and a fish. In the lower register (from left to right):
three men (the middle one with a ram's mask), a candelabrum, a three-
legged table with a round object, a woman stretching her hand to the
table, and a man skinning a ram hanging from a tree.
Found in a complex-partially excavated-consisting of over 14 rectangular rooms in two parallel rows, some rooms with antechambers. Rooms
A-B and E-P revealed no finds "out of the ordinary", but rooms C and D
revealed primarily sacred objects (reliefs, fragments of statues, altars).
The excavators interpret these two rooms as a small shrine in a private
complex. The finds were poorly preserved and fragmentary. The inscriptions on the three altars (one bilingual) do not preserve the names of the
deities to whom they were dedicated. Four fragmentary Danube Rider
Cult reliefs (identified as Kabirenreliefs) were found, as well as reliefs,

statues, and inscriptions related to Liber-Bacchus, Silvanus, Venus, Aesculapius and Hygieia, a Nutrix, and many otherwise unidentifiable fragments. The state of the finds suggests to the excavators that they were purposefully destroyed. The origin of the site is placed in the last decades of the 2nd c. AD. The bilingual altar was dedicated by an Επίτροπος Σεβαστοῦ (procurator Augusti) pro salute sua filiaeque et coniugis. Two inscriptions from Mithraeum I at Ptuj mention the imperial procurator C. Antonius Rufus. A large number of tile stamps were found, but not dated by the excavators. Various small finds (lamps, terra sigillata) should also be datable.

LIMC Heros Equitans 420; Tudor 1969 I: 89 no. 155; Abramić 1914, 94–5, fig. 70.

Image: © Pokrajinski Muzej Ptuj Ormož.

126. Nitra, Museum of the Archaeological Institute of the Slovak Academy.
      Transylvania?
      Marble.
      2nd–3rd c. AD.
      Rectangular plaque. Upper register: round object between two snakes; a bust in each corner (Sol and Luna). In the main register a horseman trampling a collapsing man underfoot; behind him an attendant; in front of him a goddess/woman holding her hand to her mouth and a man. In the lower register (from left to right): a bird, a three-legged table with a fish, a standing figure, a seated figure holding an object, and a standing figure.
      LIMC Heros Equitans 363; Tudor 1969 I: 104 no. 183.

127. Private collection, Czech or Slovak republic.
      Unknown.
      Marble.
      3rd c. AD.
      Round-topped rectangular plaque. Two busts (Sol and Luna) at the top, above a goddess/woman behind a three-legged table with a fish; she stands between two horsemen, each trampling a prostrate man underfoot, while the left-hand one is apparently also being attacked by an animal. The items in the lower register are hardly recognizable.
      Tudor 1969 I: 88–9 no. 154.

128. Present location unknown, formerly Bulgaria, private collection.
      Dimum (Beleni), Bulgaria.

Marble.

3rd c. AD.

Round-topped plaque. In the centre, behind a three-legged table bearing a fish, a goddess/woman (hardly visible) between two horsemen trampling two prostrate men underfoot. Above: two busts (Sol and Luna). In the lower register (from left to right): spiral column, two men holding something in front of a third man, and a cock above a round object. Tudor 1969, 45 no. 76.

129. Plate 80.1

Private collection; drawing in the Royal Library, Windsor: Dal Pozzo-Albani Drawings II, Fol. 30, 8285

Unknown.

Marble.

3rd c. AD.

Rectangular relief in three registers; top: bust of Sol in the left corner and bust of Luna in the right corner, both on bases; next to them two men in Phrygian caps, the one next to Sol holding a fish, the one next to Luna a sceptre; in the centre an eagle above the bust of a woman between the busts of two bearded men with Phrygian caps. Main field: Two horsemen, facing inwards, to either side of a frontal goddess/woman who is holding the reins of the horses. In front of her a three-legged table bearing a fish. Below the left-hand horse a prostrate man, next to the right-hand one a running dog. Behind each horseman an attendant, above each a snake. Lower register: in the centre a man with two attendants holding up a skin. To the left a standing goddess/woman holding her hand to her mouth; behind her indistinguishable objects. To the right a ram and a bull lying on the ground.

Tudor 1969 I: 103–4 no. 182.

Image: Royal Collection Trust / © Her Majesty Queen Elizabeth II 2018.

130. Plate 79.2

Rome? (formerly Museo Kircheriano inv. 9629, present whereabouts unknown).

Unknown. According to Abramić it had long been in the Kircher collection.

Limestone.

3rd c. AD.

Relief in two registers; main register: frontal goddess/woman in centre behind a three-legged table with a fish, her head between the busts of Sol

and Luna. She is approached from each side by a horseman, each trampling a prostrate man underfoot. Lower register (from left to right): spiral column (most missing), candelabrum, woman, table bearing a round object, quadruped.
Tudor 1969 I: 98 no. 175; Abramić 1914: 144–5, fig. 130.
Image: after Abramić 1914: fig. 130.

131.   Zagreb, Archaeological Museum.
Sirmium (Stremska Mitrovića).
Unknown (Pannonia or Dacia).
Lead.
3rd c. AD.
Identical with C2f.92.
LIMC Heros Equitans 434; Tudor 1969 I, 73–4 no. 126.

132.   Plate 79.1
Dunaújváros, Intercisa Museum 5964.
Dunaújváros.
Marble.
Undated.
Small roundel, two registers, carving very indistinct. Upper register, two riders approach a woman behind a three-legged table. Busts of Sol and Luna-both barely visible-to either side of her head. Lower register, a person and indistinguishable objects.
Ubi erat lupa 11058.
Image: Lupa.at/11058 photograph Ortolf Harl.

133.   Mosonmagyar-óvár, Hansági Múzeum, Inv. No. 2006.7.1.
Lébény-Barátföldpuszta, Gyõr-Moson-Sopron county, Hungary
Lead.
Mid 3rd c. AD.
Rectangular plaque with relief decoration in two registers. In the upper register a priestess or goddess stands frontal in the centre, approached by a rider from either side. Below the left-hand rider is a prostrate man, below the right-hand one a fish. In the upper left corner the frontal bust of Luna, in the upper righ corner the bust of Sol, radiate (five? rays), wearing a *chlamys*. Both corners are separated from the main scene by a diagonally placed snake. Along the top, an inscription consisting of the single word domino. In the lower register a jumble of ritual objects and symbols.
Szabó 2018: 27–54.

134. Budapest, Hungarian National Museum Inv. MNM RR 2010.5.1.
Unknown.
Marble.
Mid 2nd c. AD.
An aedicula-shaped plaque with relief decoration in four registers. In the tympanum, frontal bust of Sol, radiate (five triangular rays) and wearing a *chlamys* (?). In the next register a priestess or goddess in the centre, approached by a horseman from either side. Above each horse's head a star. Below the left-hand horseman lies a prostrate man, below the right-hand one a fish. In the third register a woman and two companions stand closely together behind a table or barrel. To the right, two nude male figures. To the left, one male figure standing by a tree from which an animal is hanging. In the bottom register, from left to right, a table with a fish on top, possibly a loaf of bread (?), a snake, a crater, a lion and a rooster.
Szabó 2018: 55–76.

C2g. Hosios kai Dikaios

1. Afyon, Archaeological Museum.
Unknown.
Limestone.
2nd c. AD.
Votive altar with partially preserved dedicatory inscription to Hosios. On left side, bust of Sol, radiate, *chlamys*; on the right side bust of Hercules; on the rear, 5 ears of corn.
Ricl 1992: 98–9 no. 5, pl 10.

2. Eskişehir Archaeological Museum A83–81.
Karikos.
Marble.
2nd c. AD.
Votive relief. In tympanum draped bust of Sol (?). Ricl proposes that the bust is that of Hosios kai Dikaios, which appears likely.
Matern 2002: 28 n. 211, 34 n. 263, 182 n. 991, 254 B64; Ricl 1992: 97–8 no. 3 pl. 9.

3. Afyon, Archaeological Museum.
Unknown.
Marble.
2nd–3rd c. AD.

Altar with an inscription to Hosios and Dikaios. On the front, bust of Diana; on the right side, Hercules; left side, bust of Sol, radiate (seven rays), *chlamys*, globe below the bust.
Matern 2002: 176 n. 963, 177 n. 972, 182 n. 991, 253 B59, fig. 76 (incorrect ref. to Ricl).

4.   Eskişehir, Archaeological Museum.
        Başara village, Han district, Eskişehir.
        Limestone.
        2nd–3rd c. AD.
        Altar with an inscription to Hosios and Dikaios. Within the inscription, a carefully executed but badly damaged bust of Sol, draped, radiate.
        Şahin & Uzunoğlu 2021: 79–81.

5.   Eskişehir Archaeological Museum inv. 4199.
        Dorylaeum.
        Marble.
        2nd–3rd c. AD.
        In the tympanum, Cybele. Below: Sol in *quadriga* to the right and bust (of a woman?).
        Ricl 1991: 15 nr 27, pl. 6

6.   Istanbul, Archaeology Museum 748.
        Dorylaeum.
        Marble.
        Early 3rd c. AD.
        On a stele, Sol on a *quadriga* (two wheels) with four small horses jumping up to the right. Above him: three deities. At the top, a deity with dog. Below, dedicatory inscription to Hosios and Dikaios.
        Matern 2002: 67, 217–8 Q64; Ricl 1991: 10–11 no. 20 pl. 3.

7.   Istanbul, Archaeology Museum 4481.
        Inönü.
        Marble.
        3rd c. AD.
        Naiskos framed by pilasters, with a dedication to the Mother of gods, Phoebus, Mên, Hosios, Dikaios and others. Sol, dressed in a short *chiton* and *chlamys*, on a *quadriga* right, radiate (12? Rays), whip in right hand, reins in left Above Sol is Zeus Brontos, below him are Mên and Dionysus.
        Matern 2002: 67, 218 Q65; Ricl 1991: 13–14 nr 25 pl. 5.

8. Kütahya, Archaeological Museum.
   Yaylababa village.
   Marble.
   3rd c. AD.
   Fragment of a stele; in tympanum: bust of Sol, radiate nimbus; below, figures of Hosios and Dikaios.
   Matern 2002: 182 n. 991, 254 B67; Ricl 1991: 24 no. 47, pl. 9; cf. nr. 49, pl. 10.

9. Paris, Louvre Ma 4289.
   Eski.
   Marble.
   3rd c. AD.
   Zeus Chryseos standing in a column-framed niche, bust of Sol, (radiate nimbus, seven rays) atop the left column, Luna atop the right column. In the lower right corner, bust of Hosios (?) on a stepped pedestal. Dedicated by Aurelios Chrestos (inscription).
   Matern 2002: 182 n. 991, 254 B68; Ricl 1991: 25 nr 49, pl. 10.

10. Eskişehir Archaeological Museum A65–67.
    Dorylaeum.
    Marble.
    Undated.
    Altar dedicated to Hosios and Dikaios. On one side, bust of Sol, radiate (five rays), *chlamys*, on a globe; on the other sides, Apollo Lykaios above a wolf, a bust defaced with a cross, and a figure with a set of scales (Dikaios).
    Matern 2002: 182 n. 991, 254 B63; Ricl 1991: 11 no. 21 pl. 4.

11. Paris, Louvre MA 4288.
    Dorylaeum.
    Marble.
    3rd c. AD.
    The main field is divided into two registers. Hosios and Dikaios stand in the middle of the upper register, with to the left a radiate (?) figure on horseback, and to the right a female bust. In the lower register Hermes, Herakles and yoked oxen. In the tympanon above, frontal busts of Zeus (centre), Sol (left) and Luna (right).
    LIMC Hosios and Dikaios 9.

C2h. Saturnus

1. Constantine, Musée National Cirta.
   Castellum Tidditanorum (Tiddis).
   Stone.
   Late 1st–early 2nd c. AD.
   Facade of a temple; in the tympanum: Tanit. Below: bust of Sol (left) and (probably) Luna (right).
   Leglay 1966: 42 no. 12.

2. Thala, reused as threshold in a house.
   Thala.
   Stone.
   Late 1st–early 2nd c. AD.
   Fragment of a stele. Three registers remain, each divided into small compartments. Above, centre, two cornucopiae, flanked, in a tondo to the right, by a bust of Sol, radiate ("rayons étoilés"). The corresponding tondo with Luna to the left is lost. In the next register two sphinxes and a dolphin. In the main register, below, the two dedicants (man and woman).
   Leglay 1961: 302–303

3. Constantine, Musée National Cirta.
   Castellum Tidditanorum (Tiddis).
   Stone.
   Early 2nd c. AD.
   Upper left-hand corner crescent; upper right-hand corner bust of Sol; below: niche with dedicant. Under the niche a bull.
   Leglay 1966: 44 no. 20.

4. Constantine, Musée National Cirta.
   Castellum Tidditanorum (Tiddis).
   Stone.
   Early 2nd c. AD.
   Upper left-hand corner crescent; upper right-hand corner bust of Sol; between them a wreath and a Tanit-sign. Below: arch with dedicant.
   Leglay 1966: 45 no. 22.

5. Constantine, Musée National Cirta.
   Castellum Tidditanorum (Tiddis).
   Stone.
   Early 2nd c. AD.

Upper left-hand corner crescent; upper right-hand corner bust of Sol; between them a wreath and a Tanit-sign. Below: arch with dedicant (very similar to C2h.7).
Leglay 1966: 45 no. 23

6.   Plate 81.3
     Constantine, Musée National Cirta.
     Castellum Tidditanorum (Tiddis).
     Stone.
     Early 2nd c. AD.
     Facade of a temple with two pillars supporting an architrave and frieze; on the frieze: Bust of Sol in the centre between crescent and rose (left) and a schematic Tanit and wreath (right).
     Leglay 1966: 43–4 no. 18.
     Image: drawing after Leglay 1966: no. 18, © Anna Hijmans.

7.   Constantine, Musée National Cirta.
     Castellum Tidditanorum (Tiddis).
     Stone.
     Early 2nd c. AD.
     Stele in the form of a temple-facade; of the upper part only a bust (of Sol?) and a crescent survive; below: dedicant and bull.
     Leglay 1966: 45–6 no. 24.

8.   Constantine, Musée National Cirta.
     Castellum Tidditanorum (Tiddis).
     Stone.
     Early 2nd c. AD.
     Stele in the form of a temple-facade; on the architrave various symbols, including the bust of Sol, radiate (?) right, and a crescent moon (left).
     Leglay 1966: 46 no. 25.

9.   Plates 21.1, 81.4
     Djemila, Museum.
     Djemila.
     Stone.
     Mid 2nd c. AD.
     Stele in four registers. In the upper register, large bust of Saturn between two small standing Genii; in the next register the busts of the 7 planetary deities, running from Saturn (left) to Venus; according to Leglay, the

bust of Saturn is actually the head of a lion, an animal which can some-times represent Saturn. In the third register two dedicants, one man, one woman, to either side of an altar; in the lowest register a bull led by a small figure, and a woman carrying other offerings. Leglay refers to a similar representation of the planetary deities on a stele discovered at Rapidum (Masqueray, Sour-Djouab) and reported in 1913, but subsequently lost.
Leglay 1966: 211–213 no. 7 pl. xxxiii,2
Image: drawing after Leglay 1966 pl. xxxiii,2 © Anna Hijmans.

10.   Timgad, Museum Inv. 4.
       Timgad.
       Limestone.
       First half of the 2nd c. AD.
       Above: bust of Saturn between the busts of Luna (left) and Sol (right), radiate, whip. In the main niche below two dedicants, a woman and a man, to either side of an altar bearing a ram. Below this, two rams.
       Leglay 1966: 135 no. 8.

11.   Plate 82.1
       Timgad, Museum Inv. 23.
       Timgad.
       Limestone.
       Second half 2nd c. AD.
       Above: bust of Saturn between the busts of Luna (right) and Sol (left), radiate (seven rays). In the main niche below, dedicant by an altar. Below this, a ram and a bull.
       Leglay 1966: 144 no. 33, pl. xxviii,3.
       Image: drawing after Leglay 1966 pl. xxviii,3 © Anna Hijmans.

12.   Timgad, Museum Inv. 24.
       Timgad.
       Stone.
       Second half 2nd c. AD.
       Above: bust of Saturn between the busts of Luna (right) and Sol (left). In the main niche below, dedicant (in this case a woman) by an altar. Below this, a ram and a bull.
       Leglay 1966: 144 no. 34.

13.   Plate 82.2
       Timgad, Museum Inv. 36.

Timgad, Thermes des Philadelphes.
Limestone.
First half 2nd c. AD.
Above: bust of Sol (sic), *chlamys*, between the busts of Luna (right) and Saturn (left). In the main niche below, dedicant between two Genii. Below this a small man leading a ram.
Leglay 1966: 134–5 no. 7, pl. xxvii,4.
Image: drawing after Leglay 1966 pl. xxvii,4 © Anna Hijmans.

14. Plate 82.3
Timgad, Museum Inv. 35.
Lambafundi (Henchir Touchine).
Limestone.
2nd c. AD.
Above: reclining Saturn between the busts of Luna (right) and Sol (left), radiate. In the main niche below, dedicant beside an altar. Below this, a bull.
Leglay 1966: 120–1 no. 6, pl. xxv,7.
Image: drawing after Leglay 1966 pl. xxv,7 © Anna Hijmans.

15. Timgad, Museum Inv. 45.
Timgad, environs of the Thermes des Philadelphes.
Limestone.
2nd c. AD.
Above: bust of Saturnus between the busts of Luna and Sol. In the main niche below, dedicant, with a ram behind him.
Leglay 1966: 141–2 no. 26.

16. Timgad, Museum Inv. 74.
Timgad.
Limestone.
2nd c. AD.
Above: a bird. In the main niche below, the dedicant by an altar; in the upper corners the busts of Saturnus (left) and, perhaps, Sol (right).
Leglay 1966: 140–1 no. 24, pl. xxvii,9.

17. Tunis, Bardo Museum.
Djebel Bou-Kournein.
Stone.
AD 139–145.

Fragment of a stele, preserving only a bust of Sol, radiate, in the upper left-hand corner and part of the inscription.
Leglay 1961: 37 no. 1.

18. Tunis, Bardo Museum.
Djebel Bou-Kournein.
Stone.
AD 166, December 13.
Stele, broken into various pieces. At the top, bust of Saturn within a tympanum, with the busts of Luna (right) and Sol (left, lost) outside it. Below: inscription.
Leglay 1961: 37 no. 1.

19. Tunis, Bardo Museum.
Djebel Bou-Kournein.
Marble.
February 18 or April 20, 182 AD.
In tympanum, Saturn, between Sol (left), radiate, whip, and Luna (right).
Catalogue Musée Alaoui C 651–5; Toutain, 1892: 21 no. 13 pl. 1 fig. 3.

20. Constantine, Musée National Cirta.
Mechta-Nahar.
Stone.
2nd–3rd c. AD.
Saturn, flanked to the leftt by bust of Sol (bust of Luna to the right lost).
Leglay 1966: 21 no. 3.

21. Constantine, Musée National Cirta.
Castellum Tidditanorum (Tiddis).
Stone.
2nd–3rd c. AD.
Stele in the form of a temple-facade; in the tympanum a crescent between a lozenge (left) and a star (right); in the spandrels bust of Sol (left) and sign of Tanit (right). Below, in the central rectangular niche the dedicant.
Leglay 1966: 48–9 no. 29.

22. Constantine, Musée National Cirta.
Castellum Tidditanorum (Tiddis).
Stone.
2nd–3rd c. AD.

Stele in the form of a temple-facade; in the tympanum a tanit-sign between a two-pointed crown and a rose; in the spandrels bust of Sol (left), radiate, and a crescent (right). Below, in the "entrance" of the temple the dedicant.
Leglay 1966: 49–50 no. 31.

23. Constantine, Musée National Cirta.
Castellum Tidditanorum (Tiddis).
Stone.
2nd–3rd c. AD.
Stele in the form of a temple-facade; above the pediment bust of Sol (left) and an unidentifiable bust (right); in the tympanum a tanit-sign flanked to either side by a two-pointed crown. Below, in the "entrance" of the temple, two dedicants.
Leglay 1966: 50 no. 32.

24. Constantine, Musée National Cirta.
Castellum Tidditanorum (Tiddis).
Stone.
2nd–3rd c. AD.
Stele in the form of a temple-facade; above the pediment a palm and a two-pointed crown (left) and a damaged symbol, either a crescent or a Tanit (right); in the tympanum a bust of Sol, radiate. Below, in a vaulted niche, the dedicant.
Leglay 1966: 50 no. 33.

25. Constantine, Musée National Cirta?
Castellum Tidditanorum (Tiddis).
Stone.
2nd–3rd c. AD.
Stele in the form of a temple-facade; above the pediment a crescent surmounted by a disc (left) and a bust of Sol, radiate, with a Tanit (right); in the tympanum a bust of Saturnus. Below, in a vaulted niche, two women holding a ram by a horn.
Leglay 1966: 49 no. 30.

26. Lambèse, Museum.
Lambaesis.
Stone.
2nd–early 3rd c. AD.

In tympanum bust of Saturnus between two damaged busts, presumably Sol and Luna.
Leglay 1966: 85 no. 6.

27. Lambèse, Museum.
    Lambaesis.
    Limestone.
    2nd–3rd c. AD.
    Heavily damaged stele. In tympanum traces of the bust of Saturnus between the damaged busts of, presumably, Sol and Luna. In a niche below, a man and a woman.
    Leglay 1966: 86 no. 11.

28. Lambèse, Museum Inv. 13.
    Lambaesis.
    Limestone.
    2nd–3rd c. AD.
    Stele in three registers. Upper register: the bust of Saturnus between the busts of Sol (left), radiate nimbus (8? rays), *chlamys* and whip, and Luna (right). In a niche below, a dedicant by an altar. In the lower register a sacrificial animal.
    Leglay 1966: 87 no. 13, pl. xxiii,2; Sintes & Rebahi 2003, 160 no. 66.

29. Lambèse, Museum.
    Lambaesis.
    Limestone.
    2nd–3rd c. AD.
    Stele in the form of a temple-facade. Pediment: bust of Saturnus between the busts of Sol (right) and Luna (left). In a niche below, a priest or dedicant. In the lower register a sacrificial animal.
    Leglay 1966: 87 no. 14.

30. Lambèse, Museum.
    Lambaesis.
    Limestone.
    2nd–early 3rd c. AD.
    Rectangular stele of which only the upper part is preserved. Above: bust of Saturnus between the busts of Sol (right) and Luna (left). In a niche below, a dedicant.
    Leglay 1966: 88 no. 15.

31. Lambèse, Museum.
    Lambaesis.
    Limestone.
    2nd–3rd c. AD.
    At the top: bust of Saturnus between the damaged busts of Sol and Luna.
    Below, between two pillars, the dedicant by an altar.
    Leglay 1966: 89 no. 17.

32. Lambèse, Museum.
    Lambaesis.
    Limestone.
    2nd–early 3rd c. AD.
    At the top: bust of Saturnus between the traces of two busts of which
    Luna (left) is still recognizable; the other is not, but must be Sol. Below, in
    a niche, the dedicant by ram on an altar. Below the niche two dolphins.
    Leglay 1966: 89 no. 18.

33. Plate 82.4
    Lambèse, Museum.
    Lambaesis.
    Limestone.
    2nd–early 3rd c. AD.
    At the top: bust of Saturnus between the busts of Luna (right) and Sol
    (left), radiate. Below, in a niche, the dedicant. Below the niche a ram.
    Leglay 1966: 89–90 no. 19, pl. xxiv,1.
    Image: drawing after Leglay 1966: pl. xxiv.1, © Anna Hijmans.

34. Lambèse, Museum.
    Lambaesis.
    Limestone.
    2nd–early 3rd c. AD.
    Upper part of a stele. At the top: bust of Saturnus between two busts of
    which that of Sol (left) is still recognizable. Below, in the entrance of the
    temple the dedicant by an altar.
    Leglay 1966: 90 no. 20.

35. Lambèse, Museum.
    Lambaesis.
    Limestone.
    2nd–3rd c. AD

Upper part of a stele. At the top: bust of Saturnus between the busts of Luna (right) and Sol (left). Below, the dedicant (head only survives). Leglay 1966: 90 no. 21.

36. Lambèse, Museum.
     Lambaesis.
     Limestone.
     2nd–3rd c. AD.
     Upper part of a stele. At the top: bust of Saturnus between the worn busts of Luna and Sol. Below, the dedicant (head only survives).
     Leglay 1966: 90 no. 22.

37. Lambèse, Museum.
     Lambaesis.
     Limestone.
     2nd–3rd c. AD.
     Upper part of a stele. At the top: bust of Saturnus between the busts of Luna (left) and Sol (right). Below, the dedicant (head only survives).
     Leglay 1966: 90–1 no. 23.

38. Lambèse, Museum.
     Lambaesis.
     Limestone.
     2nd–3rd c. AD.
     At the top: bust of Saturnus between the profile busts of Luna (left) and Sol (right). Below, in a niche, the dedicant by an altar on which lies a ram.
     Leglay 1966: 91 no. 26.

39. Lambèse, Museum.
     Lambaesis.
     Limestone.
     2nd–3rd c. AD.
     Upper part of a stele. At the top: bust of Saturnus between the busts of Luna (right) and Sol (left). Below, the dedicant (head only survives).
     Leglay 1966: 92 no. 27.

40. Lambèse, Museum.
     Lambaesis.
     Limestone.
     2nd–3rd c. AD.

Upper part of a stele. At the top: garland; below it three small niches with bust of Saturnus between the busts of Luna (right) and Sol (left), radiate. Below, the dedicants, man and woman.
Leglay 1966: 92 no. 28.

41. Lambèse, Museum.
    Lambaesis.
    Limestone.
    2nd–3rd c. AD.
    At the top: bust of Saturnus between the busts of Luna (right) and Sol (left). Below, in the main register, the dedicant. In the lowest register a ram.
    Leglay 1966: 92 no. 29.

42. Plate 83.1
    Lambèse, Museum.
    Lambaesis.
    Limestone.
    2nd–3rd c. AD.
    At the top: bust of Saturnus between busts of Luna (right) and Sol (left), radiate, whip behind left shoulder. Below, the dedicant. The lower part of the stele is broken off.
    Leglay 1966: 92–3 no. 30, pl. xxiv.2.
    Image: drawing after Leglay 1966: pl. xxiv.2, © Anna Hijmans.

43. Lambèse, Museum.
    Lambaesis.
    Limestone.
    2nd–3rd c. AD.
    At the top: bust of Saturnus between the busts of Luna (left) and Sol (right), radiate, whip behind his right shoulder. Below, in a niche, the dedicant by an altar on which lies a ram.
    Leglay 1966: 93 no. 31.

44. Lambèse, Museum.
    Lambaesis.
    Limestone.
    2nd–3rd c. AD.
    At the top: bust of Saturnus within the tympanum, between two busts, difficult to identify, outside the pediment (Sol & Luna). Below, in the

entrance of the temple, the dedicant. Below the dedicant in a separate niche a ram.

Leglay 1966: 93 no. 33.

45.   Lambèse, Museum.
       Lambaesis.
       Limestone.
       2nd–3rd c. AD.
       At the top: three busts, difficult to identify; probably Saturnus, Sol & Luna. Below, in a niche, the dedicant, possibly a priestess. Below the dedicant in a separate niche a ram.
       Leglay 1966: 93–4 no. 34.

46.   Lambèse, Museum.
       Lambaesis.
       Limestone.
       2nd–3rd c. AD.
       At the top: bust of Saturnus between the busts of Sol (left) and Luna (right). Below, in a niche, the dedicant by an altar.
       Leglay 1966: 94 no. 35.

47.   Plate 81.1
       Lambèse, Museum.
       Lambaesis.
       Limestone.
       2nd–early 3rd c. AD.
       At the top, bust of Saturn, between the busts of Luna (right) and Sol (left), radiate (five rays), *chlamys*. Below, in a niche: dedicant. Below the niche, a ram.
       LIMC Helios/Sol 356; R. Cagnat, Musée de Lambèse, pl. IV,9.
       Image: photograph after Cagnat (in the public domain).

48.   Timgad, Museum Inv. 11.
       Timgad.
       Limestone.
       2nd–early 3rd c. AD.
       Above: bust of Saturn between the busts of Luna (right) and Sol (left), radiate, whip. In the main niche below, dedicant by an altar. Below this, a ram.
       Leglay 1966: 143 no. 30.

49. Plate 83.2
     Timgad, Museum Inv. 33.
     Lambafundi (Henchir Touchine).
     Limestone.
     Late 2nd–3rd c. AD.
     Above: bust of Saturn between the busts of Luna (left) and Sol (right), radiate (6? rays). In the main niche below, two dedicants, man and woman. Below this, a ram.
     Leglay 1966: 119–20 no. 4, pl. xxv,5.
     Image: drawing after Leglay 1966: pl. xxv.5, © Anna Hijmans.

50. Plate 83.3
     Timgad, Museum Inv. 36.
     Lambafundi (Henchir Touchine).
     Limestone.
     2nd–early 3rd c. AD.
     Above: bust of Saturn between the busts of Luna (left) and Sol (right). In the main niche below, dedicant by an altar. Below this, two kneeling Telamones. On the horizontal upper face of this altar two nude men, one next to a double axe, the other with raised arms.
     Leglay 1966: 118–9 no. 3, pl. xxv,34.
     Image: drawing after Leglay 1966: pl. xxv.3, © Anna Hijmans.

51. Timgad, Museum Inv. 68.
     Timgad.
     Limestone.
     2nd–early 3rd c. AD.
     Above: bust of Saturnus between the busts of Luna (left) and Sol (right), radiate. In the main niche below, the dedicant by an altar. Below: a ram.
     Leglay 1966: 143 no. 31.

52. Plate 83.4
     Tunis, Bardo.
     Haidra.
     Limestone.
     2nd–3rd c. AD.

In the upper register, bust of Saturn between the busts of Luna (right) and Sol (left), radiate nimbus. Below, the two dedicants (man and woman). Leglay 1961: 330 no. 13, pl. xii.6.
Image: drawing after Leglay 1961: pl. xii.6, © Anna Hijmans.

53. Sour El Ghozlane (formerly Aumale), Place Publique inv. no. 53.
Sour El Ghozlane.
Stone.
3rd c. AD.
Upper register: bust of Saturn, capite velato, between a bust of Luna (right) and Sol (left), radiate. Below Saturn a lion devouring a hare. In the main register two dedicants, a man and a woman, to either side of an altar.
Leglay 1966: 309 no. 3

54. Djemila, Museum.
Djemila.
Stone.
Mid 3rd c. AD.
Stele in three registers. In the upper register, large bust of Saturn between two slightly smaller busts, of Luna (right) and Sol (left), *chlamys* and *chiton*, whip in right hand; in the next register two dedicants, one man, one woman, to either side of an altar; in the lowest register a bull and two persons.
Leglay 1966: 227 no. 31 pl. xxxiv.4.

55. Plate 84.1
Fedj-Mzala?
Diana Veteranorum (Zana).
Limestone.
3rd c. AD.
In the tympanum: bust of Saturnus between the busts of Sol (left), radiate, and Luna (right). In the main niche, dedicant.
Leglay 1966: 77–8 no. 4, pl. xxxi.4.
Image: drawing after Leglay 1966: pl. xxxi.4, © Anna Hijmans.

56. Ksar-Toual-Zammel (Vicus Maracitanus).
In situ.
Stone.

3rd c. AD.

Stele, fragment. Two registers survive; in the upper register, reclining Saturnus. In the lower register, the dedicant (in this case a woman); in the upper corners of this register the busts of Sol (right), radiate nimbus, and Luna (left).

Leglay 1961: 236 no. 5.

57. Ksar-Toual-Zammel.
In situ.
Stone.
3rd c. AD.
In the tympanum, two doves face a palm branch. In the next register bust of Saturnus between busts of Luna (left) and Sol (right), radiate. In the main register below, the dedicant.
Leglay 1961: 236–7 no. 6.

58. Plate 84.2
Lambèse, Museum.
Lambaesis.
Limestone.
Early 3rd c. AD.
Stele in the form of a temple-facade. At the top: bust of Saturnus between the busts of Sol (left), radiate and Luna (right). In a niche below, a priest or more probably (according to Leglay) a priestess. Below his/her feet a ram.
Leglay 1966: 88–9 no. 16, pl. xxiii,3
Image: drawing after Leglay 1966: pl. xxiii.3, © Anna Hijmans.

59. Plate 81.2
Lambèse, Museum.
Lambaesis.
Limestone.
3rd c. AD.
Upper part of a round-topped stele. At the top: bust of Saturnus between the busts of Luna (right) and Sol (left). Below, the two dedicants (man and woman) to either side of an altar.
LIMC Helios/Sol 356; Leglay 1966: 91 no. 24; Cagnat, Musée de Lambèse pl. IV.8.
Image: photograph after Cagnat, loc. cit., (in the public domain).

60.   Plate 85.1
       Lambèse, Museum.
       Lambaesis.
       Limestone.
       3rd c. AD.
       At the top: bust of Saturnus within the tympanum, between the busts of
       Luna (left) and Sol (right), radiate (six rays) outside the pediment. Below,
       in the entrance of the temple the dedicant by an altar. Below the dedicant
       in a separate niche a ram.
       LIMC Helios/Sol 357; Leglay 1966: 86–7 no. 12; Cagnat, Musée de Lambèse,
       1895: pl. 4.7.
       Image: photograph after Cagnat loc. cit. (in the public domain).

61.   Lambèse, Museum.
       Lambaesis.
       Limestone.
       3rd c. AD.
       At the top: bust of Saturnus between the busts of Luna (left) and Sol
       (right). Below, in a niche, the dedicant by an altar. Below his feet a ram.
       Leglay 1966: 91 no. 25.

62.   Plate 85.3
       Sétif, Archaeological Museum (formerly: Jardin Emir Abdelkader).
       Sétif.
       Stone.
       Early 3rd c. AD.
       Four registers. At the top, within a tympanum, a rosette with a garland
       around it, between two doves. Below, between two double pillars, the
       busts of Saturn (centre), Luna (right) and Sol (left), radiate (seven rays).
       Below these, under an arch, the dedicant by an altar. In the lowest regis-
       ter, a large altar between two sacrificial bulls.
       Leglay 1966:, 281–2 no. 32 pl. xxxviii, 3.
       Image: drawing after Leglay 1966: pl. xxxviii.3, © Anna Hijmans.

63.   Sétif, Archaeological Museum (formerly: Jardin Emir Abdelkader).
       Sétif.
       Stone.
       Second half of the 3rd c. AD.

At the top: bust of Saturnus within the tympanum between the busts of Sol (left), radiate and Luna (right) outside the pediment. Below: two standing dedicants and the bust of a third person above them. In the lowest register two rams facing each other.

Leglay 1966: 283 no. 36

64. Plate 84.4

Tébessa, Museum.

Henchir Rohban.

Limestone.

3rd c. AD (LIMC).

In the upper, round-topped niche Saturnus (right) and Ops-Caelestis (left) seated on thrones between rams and bulls respectively. In a separate niche below, a frontal lion's head between the busts of Luna (left) and Sol (right), radiate (seven rays), *chlamys*. Below this an inscription.

LIMC Helios/Sol 324; Leglay 1961: 352–4 no. 47.

Image: photograph after Gsell, Musée de Tébessa, 1902: pl. 1.2 (in the public domain).

65. Plate 85.2

Timgad, Museum Inv. 1.

Timgad.

Limestone.

Early 3rd c. AD.

Rectangular stele in three registers. In the upper register, Saturn, enthroned, is flanked by two persons each standing by a horse. At first glance these are the Dioscuri, but the right-hand one is clearly a woman (she is dressed in a short *himation* girded just below her breasts), while the left-hand one is a nude male, suggesting that the two are actually conflations of the Dioscuri and Sol & Luna. In the large central niche: dedicant. In the lower register, a bull between two funerary Erotes leaning on inversed torches.

Leglay 1966: 149–51 no. 46, pl. xxviii,6.

Image: drawing after Leglay 1966: pl. xxviii.6, © Anna Hijmans.

66. Plate 85.4

Timgad, Museum Inv. 13.

Timgad.

Limestone.

3rd c. AD.

Above: reclining Saturn between the standing Luna (right) and standing Sol (left), radiate, tunica, trousers (or long *chiton*?). In the main niche below, dedicant by an altar. Below this, a ram and a bull.

Leglay 1966: 152 no. 47, pl. xxviii,7.

Image: drawing after Leglay 1966: pl. xxviii.7, © Anna Hijmans.

67. Timgad, Museum Inv. 34.

Lambafundi (Henchir Touchine).

Limestone.

3rd c. AD.

Above: reclining Saturn between the busts of Luna (left) and Sol (right). In the main niche below, dedicant beside a ram.

Leglay 1966: 120 no. 5, pl. xxv,6.

Image: Wikimedia commons, https://commons.wikimedia.org/wiki/File: Estelas_funerarias_Timgad_03.jpg. Photograph by LBM1948, available under CC-BY-SA-4.0 license.

68. Timgad, Museum Inv. 45.

Timgad, Capitolium.

Limestone.

Second half 3rd c. AD.

Above: bust of Saturnus between the busts of Luna (right) and Sol (left), radiate. In the main niche below, dedicant. Below, a bull.

Leglay 1966: 153–4 no. 53.

69. Timgad, Museum Inv. 69.

Timgad.

Limestone.

Second half 3rd c. AD.

Above: reclining Saturnus between the busts of Luna (right) and Sol (left), whip. In the main niche below, the dedicant by an altar. Below: a ram and a bull.

Leglay 1966: 152 no. 48.

70. Timgad, Museum Inv. 78.

Timgad.

Limestone.

3rd c. AD.

Above: reclining Saturn, leaning on the bust of Sol (right); the corresponding bust of Luna has virtually disappeared. In the main niche, two dedicants (man and woman) embracing.

Leglay 1966: 152 no. 49.

71. Timgad, Museum.
    Timgad.
    Limestone.
    Early 3rd c. AD.
    Upper register of stele, Saturnus enthroned between Sol, nude but for a *chlamys* and radiate (seven rays) and Luna. They are each holding one horse as if they were the Dioscuri.
    LIMC Saturnus 82.

72. Tunis.
    El-Ayaïda (Tunisia).
    Sandstone.
    November 8th, 323 AD.
    Round-topped stele in three registers. In the upper register Saturn enthroned with sceptre and harpe; above the harpe frontal head of Sol, radiate nimbus (nine rays). In the middle register a man by an altar leading a ram. In the lower register, an inscription.
    Leglay 1988, 209–211 no. 31; LIMC Saturnus 88.

73. Lost.
    Masqueray/Sour-Djouab (Rapidum).
    Stone.
    Undated.
    At the top: triangle between busts of Sol and Luna. Below: sacrificial bull.
    Leglay 1966: 312 no. 7.

74. Skikda, Museum.
    Lambaesis.
    Sandstone.
    Undated.
    In the tympanum, bust of Saturn between the busts of Sol (left) and Luna (right). Below: dedicant.
    Leglay 1966: 94 no. 36.

75.   Tébessa, Museum.
       Henchir Rohban.
       Limestone.
       Undated.
       In the tympanum, bust of Saturnus. Below the tympanum, an arch, with a
       bust (of Sol?) in the left-hand corner above the arch; no bust has survived
       in the right-hand corner. Under the arch the dedicant. On the arch five
       holes, probably to fasten stars.
       Leglay 1961: 340 no. 13.

76.   Plate 86.1
       Tébessa, Museum.
       Henchir Rohban.
       Stone.
       Undated.
       Above, the bust of Saturn between the busts of Luna (right) and Sol (left,
       largely destroyed). Below, in a niche, two dedicants, a man and a woman,
       embracing each other.
       LIMC Helios/Sol 356; Leglay 1961: 339–40 no. 12, pl. xiii,1; S. Gsell, Musée
       de Tébessa 1902, 19 pl. I,3 (not I,2 as Leglay states).
       Image: photograph after Gsell loc. Cit. (in the public domain).

77.   Tébessa, Museum.
       Henchir Rohban.
       Limestone.
       Undated.
       In the tympanum a palm branch. Below: large bust of Saturn between the
       smaller busts of Luna (left) and Sol (right); each bust in a separate rectan-
       gular field. In the main register below this, representing an entrance, the
       dedicant (only his head survives).
       Leglay 1961: 341 no. 15.

78.   Tébessa, Museum.
       Henchir Rohban.
       Stone.
       Undated.
       In the tympanum a radiate bust (Sol) surrounded by a garland. Below:
       bust of Saturn between the busts of Luna (right) and Sol (left); each bust
       in a separate rectangular field. In the main register below (of which only
       the top survives), the dedicant.
       Leglay 1961: 342–3 no. 24.

79. Tébessa, Museum.
    Henchir Rohban.
    Limestone.
    Undated.
    In the tympanum bust of Sol, radiate (eleven rays). Below, the dedicant by an altar.
    LIMC Helios/Sol 221; Leglay 1961: 343 no. 26.

80. Tébessa, Museum.
    Henchir Rohban.
    Limestone.
    Undated.
    Upper part of a stele. At the top, bust of Saturnus between the busts of Luna (left) and Sol (right), radiate. Below: dedicant.
    Leglay 1961: 345 no. 29.

81. Tébessa, Museum.
    Henchir Majel.
    Limestone.
    Undated.
    Rectangular stele. Above, large bust of Saturnus between the smaller busts of Sol (right), radiate, and Luna (left). Below, a bull, two rams and an inscription.
    Leglay 1961: 354–5 no. 48, pl. xiii,3

82. Plate 86.2
    Tébessa, Museum.
    Henchir Majel.
    Stone.
    Undated.
    Worn, rectangular stele in five registers. Above, in a large central niche, Saturn enthroned between the busts of Sol (left), radiate (five rays), *chlamys*, above four frontal horses and Luna (right) above an animal next to an altar. Below Sol and Luna the two Dioscuri on horseback; together with two bulls below them they flank the dedicant, seated below Saturnus with a ram at his feet. Below this, seven women bearing large baskets with pine-cones on their heads. At the bottom: inscription.
    LIMC Helios/Sol 356; Leglay 1961: 355 no. 49; Gsell, Musée de Tébessa pl. 1.6.
    Image: photograph after Gsell, loc. cit. (in the public domain).

83.   Formerly Tébessa, private collection; now lost.
       Henchir-El-Hamacha.
       Stone.
       Too worn to be dated.
       Above, in a large central niche, Saturn, between the busts of Sol, above
       four frontal horses (three survive) and Luna. Below Sol and Luna the two
       Dioscuri on horseback; together with two bulls and two rams below them
       they flank the dedicant, seated below Saturnus. Below this, seven pine
       cones (six survive).
       Leglay 1961: 357 no. 52.

84.   Formerly Tébessa, private collection; now lost.
       Henchir-El-Hamacha.
       Stone.
       Too worn to be dated.
       Upper part of a rectangular stele. At the top: six pine cones between the
       busts of Sol and Luna; four frontal horses below the bust of Sol. In the
       central niche below, the seated dedicant between the Dioscuri and by
       two bulls. The rest of the stele is lost.
       Leglay 1961: 357 no. 53

85.   Plate 84.3
       Timgad, Museum Inv. 9.
       Timgad.
       Stone.
       Undated.
       Above: bust of Saturn between the busts of Luna (right) and Sol (left),
       whip. In the main niche below, dedicant between two Genii. Below this,
       a ram.
       Leglay 1966: 141 no. 25.
       Image: Wikimedia, photograph by LBM1948. https://upload.wikimedia
       .org/wikipedia/commons/3/3b/Estelas_funerarias_Timgad_03.jpg, detail.

86.   Timgad, Museum Inv. 45.
       Timgad.
       Limestone.
       Undated.
       Above: bust of Saturnus between the busts of Luna (right) and Sol (left),

radiate. In the main niche below, two dedicants (only their heads are preserved).
Leglay 1966: 142 no. 27.

87.   Timgad, Museum. Inv. 89.
      Timgad.
      Limestone.
      Too poorly preserved to be datable.
      Above: bust of Saturn, between the bust of Sol (right), whip, and a small standing person (left), perhaps with crescent (Luna?). In the main niche, two dedicants (man and woman).
      Leglay 1966: 154 no. 54.

88.   Timgad, Museum Inv. 130.
      Timgad.
      Limestone.
      Not dated.
      Fragment of a stele, preserving part of the upper register with bust of Luna at the right. Corresponding bust of Sol at the left, lost.
      Leglay 1966: 155 no. 63.

89.   Unknown.
      Bordj-Douimes.
      Stone.
      Undated.
      In the tympanum: bust of Sol. Below: inscription.
      Leglay 1961: 269 no. 12.

90.   Carthage, Museum.
      Djebel Bou-Kournein.
      Marble.
      Undated.
      Stele. At the top, bust of Saturn within a tympanum, with the busts of Luna (right) and Sol (left), radiate (four rays), whip, outside it. Below: inscription. At the bottom, a bull led by a man (only the head of the latter survives) and a ram
      Leglay 1961: 63–4 no. 115.

91.   Tunis, Bardo Museum.
       Djebel Bou-Kournein.
       Marble.
       Undated.
       Stele. In the middle, Saturnus, between the busts of Luna (right) and Sol
       (left), whip. Below: inscription.
       Leglay 1961: 67 no. 141. Toutain 1892, 53–4 no. 160, pl. 1.2.

92.   Tunis, Bardo Museum.
       Djebel Bou-Kournein.
       Marble.
       Undated.
       Stele. In the middle, Saturnus, between the busts of Luna (right, but
       largely broken away) and Sol (left), radiate, whip. Below: inscription.
       Leglay 1961: 67–8 no. 151. Toutain 1892, 56 no. 179.

93.   Tunis, Bardo Museum.
       Djebel Bou-Kournein.
       Marble.
       Undated.
       Stele, fragment: only the harpe of Saturnus and the head of Sol survive,
       plus a fragment of the inscription.
       Leglay 1961: 72 no. 207.

94.   Kairouan, Tunisia.
       Henchir-es-Srira.
       Stone.
       Undated.
       Stele, triangular top. At the top, symbols related to Saturnus. In the main
       register below: head of Sol, radiate, surrounded by palms. In the register
       below: altar, two rams and two goats.
       Leglay 1961: 317–8 no. 30.

95.   Ksar-Toual-Zammel.
       In situ.
       Stone.
       Undated.
       The tympanum is lost. In the next register bust of Saturnus between
       busts of Luna (right) and Sol (left), radiate. In the main register below,
       the dedicant.
       Leglay 1961: 237 no. 7.

96. Ksar-Toual-Zammel.
    In situ.
    Stone.
    Undated.
    In the tympanum, two doves face a palm branch. In the next register
    Saturnus on his throne between the standing Dioscuri (dressed in tunica
    or short *chiton*) and two standing figures in the corners, dressed in long
    robes; the right-hand one lacks attributes but the left-hand one may be
    Sol as he is radiate. His body is largely chipped away and as a result other
    identifying attributes may have been lost. The main register below is
    almost completely lost.
    Leglay 1961: 237–8 no. 8.

97. Ksar-Toual-Zammel
    In situ.
    Stone.
    Undated.
    In the tympanum, two doves face a palm branch. In the next register bust
    of Saturnus between busts of Luna and Sol. In the register below, a bull.
    Leglay 1961: 238 no. 10.

98. Private collection?
    Oued-Laya, near Sousse.
    Stone.
    Undated.
    In the tympanum, pine-cone between busts of Sol and Luna.
    Leglay 1961: 257 no. 2.

99. Sousse, Museum.
    Sousse.
    Stone.
    undated.
    Stele, unfinished, later used as sarcophagus-lid. Above, pine-cone. Below,
    triangular, Tanit-like figure between Sol and Luna.
    Leglay 1961: 257 no. 10.

100. Aïn Drinn, Aïn Boubenana road, reused in the wall of a fountain by a
     farm-house (near Lambaesis).
     Lambaesis.
     Stone.
     Undated.

At the top: bust of Saturn between the busts of Sol and Luna. Below, the dedicant by an altar, and below, left, a frontal ram.
Leglay 1971, 142 no. 14, fig. 14; Leglay 1988, 215 no. 41.

101. Lambaesis, Museum.
Aïn Drinn, Aïn Boubenana road, same farm-house as previous.
Stone.
Undated.
At the top: bust of Saturn between the busts of Sol and Luna. Below, the dedicant by a ram.
Leglay 1971, 145 no. 16, fig. 16; Leglay 1988, 215 no. 43, fig. 15.

102. Modern village at Lambaesis, reused in a wall.
Lambaesis.
Stone.
Undated.
Above: three small niches with busts, Saturnus in the centre, Sol and Luna to either side. Below, niche with dedicant. Lower part of stele apparently missing.
Leglay 1971, 145 no. 18, fig. 18; Leglay 1988, 216 no. 45.

103. Formerly Modern village at Lambaesis, garden of the prison director.
Lambaesis.
Stone.
Undated.
Above: bust of Saturnus in the centre, Sol, radiate, and Luna to either side. Below, niche with two dedicants.
Leglay 1971, 147 no. 21, fig. 21; Leglay 1988, 216 no. 48.

104. Lambaesis, Museum.
Lambaesis.
Limestone.
Undated.
In the upper register a bust of Saturn between the frontal busts of Sol, radiate (eleven rays), *chlamys* covering one shoulder, and Luna with a crescent above her head. In a large niche below, framed by two square pilasters with unadorned capitals, the dedicant is standing by a burning altar. Below the groundline, two crouching telamones support the pilasters; between them an animal, possibly a ram.
Leglay 1988.

105. Plate 87.1
Tunis, Bardo.
Lambaesis.
Limestone.
Undated.
At the top: bust of Saturnus between the busts of Luna (right) and Sol (left). Below, in the main register, the dedicant bringing sacrifice on a burning altar. In the lowest register a ram.
Lupa 24495.
Image: Lupa.at/24495 photograph Andreas Schmidt-Colinet.

C2ha. Saturnus-Sol Represented by a Symbol (Selection)

1. Constantine, Mus. National Cirta.
Castellum Tidditanorum (Tiddis).
Stone.
1st c. AD.
Tanit between a crescent (left) and a flower (right): Luna and Sol?
Leglay 1966: 38 no. 4.

2. Henchir R'Mel, Henchir Djal region
In situ?
Limestone.
1st c. AD.
Votive stele. In the tympanum: crescent surmounted by a radiate disc and between two palms. In main niche: the dedicant, and below a ram. Very sketchy sculpture.
Leglay 1988, 202 no. 15.

3. El-Afareg (Tunisia).
In situ?
Limestone.
Late 1st-early 2nd c. AD.
Stele in three registers; in the upper register a crescent surmounted by a rayed disc and between various objects. In the main register, inscription. Below: ram.
Leglay 1988, 205–7 no. 26; Mahjoubi 1967, 149–50 no. 3 pl. 3. Cf. C2ha.7.

4. Lambèse, Museum.
Lambaesis.
Limestone.

2nd–3rd c. AD.

Upper part of a stele. At the top, bust of Saturnus; below, three symbols: harp (Saturnus) flanked to the right by a crescent (Luna) and to the left by a whip (Sol). In a niche below: dedicant.

Leglay 1966: 93 no. 32.

5.   Lambèse, Museum.

       Lambaesis.

       Limestone.

       2nd–3rd c. AD.

       At the top: bust of Saturnus between two rosettes in place of Sol and Luna. Below, in a niche, the dedicant. In the lowest register, a ram.

       Leglay 1966: 94 no. 37.

6.   Tébessa, Museum.

       Henchir Rohban.

       Limestone.

       Undated.

       In the tympanum a palm-tree flanked by two birds (probably doves). Under the arch below, the dedicant (only her head survives); a star (left) and a crescent (right), symbolizing Sol and Luna?

       Leglay 1961: 343 no. 25.

7.   Modern village at Lambaesis, reused in a wall.

       Lambaesis.

       Stone.

       Undated.

       Niche with dedicant. Below, a ram; in the upper corners outside the niche: whip (Sol) and crescent (Luna).

       Leglay 1971, 145 no. 17, fig. 17; Leglay 1988, 215–6 no. 44.

8.   Formerly Batna (Algeria), now lost.

       Lambaesis.

       Stone

       Undated

       Above: crescent surmounted by a star and between two roses; according to Leglay these symbols represent Saturnus, Sol and Luna. Below: niche with dedicant.

       Leglay 1971, 147 no. 23, fig. 23; Leglay 1988, 217 no. 50.

C2i. Planetary Deities, Alone

1. Palmyra, temple of Bel, N.-thalamos.
   In situ.
   Stone.
   AD 32.
   Ceiling-relief: bust of Jupiter in the centre, surrounded by the six other planetary deities in arbitrary order (above Jupiter's head: Mars, followed anti-clockwise by Sol, Mercury, Saturn, Venus and Luna), within a zodiac circle.
   LIMC Helios in per. or. 15; Gundel 1992, no. 44.

2. Ostia, Museo 625.
   Ostia.
   Marble.
   3rd c. AD.
   Two fragments of a frieze decorated with busts; Sol, Luna, Mars are preserved on the one, Jupiter and Venus on the other.
   LIMC Helios/Sol 277; Becatti Ostia II pl. xxxviii.

3. Unknown.
   Auxerre?
   Limestone.
   3rd c. AD.
   Relief with the busts of the seven planetary deities, from Saturn to Venus.
   LIMC Planetae 15; LIMC Helios/Sol 277; Espérandieu Recueil IX, 7155; Duval 1953: 287.

4. Plates 8.2, 88.1
   Abbotsford House, Scotland (near Melrose).
   Voreda (Roman fort near Penrith).
   Stone.
   3rd c. AD.
   Five small, apparently unfinished reliefs depicting five of the seven planetary deities: Venus, Mars, Mercury, Jupiter and Sol, nude but for a *chlamys*, right hand raised, whip in left hand, not radiate.
   Reinach identifies Mars as Hercules, but this is incorrect as he has a shield, no lion skin, and appears to be holding a spear, unfinished but definitely too long to be a club. Reinach also mistakenly states that all

five reliefs were on one base. Matern follows Reinach. The reliefs were acquired by Sir Walter Scott and are incorporated in a garden wall.

LIMC Helios/Sol 261; Matern 2002: 106, 234 I23, fig. 46; Reinach RR II 528. Image: courtesy of Abbotsford House.

5.   Mannheim, Museum.
      Neckarau.
      Sandstone.
      Undated.
      Fragment of a pillar (Jupiter-giant monument?) with a niche in which the bust of Sol, radiate, *chlamys*, is preserved, between two other busts, almost completely broken away.
      Espérandieu, Germanie 435; Duval 1953, 287; LIMC Helios/Sol 277.

6.   Châtillon-sur-Seine Musée.
      Auxois à Magny-Lambert.
      Undated.
      Stone.
      Rectangular block with dedicatory inscription to Rosmerta and Mercurius. Below the inscription, busts of the planetary deities. Sol, second from the left, is largely destroyed, but six rays are still clearly visible.
      Espérandieu III, 2336; Duval 1989, 329.

7.   Rome, Museo Nazionale Romano, Terme di Diocleziano.
      Rome, ancient villa at Morena by the Via Anagnina, between the seventh and eighth mile of the ancient Via Latina, excavated in 2010–2011.
      2nd or early 3rd c. AD.
      Square base of a fountain from the impluvium of the villa. Each side consists of a central shell above a flight of six steps, with to either side an aedicula with one of the planetary deities: Sol and Luna; Mars and Mercury; Jupiter and Juno, Saturn and Caelus (?).
      Unpublished.

C2ia. Planetary Deities, with Others

1.   Plate 86.3
      Leiden, National Museum of Antiquities HAA3.
      Acquired in 1823 in Tunisia and said to be from the environs of ancient Vacca and Sicca Veneria.
      Limestone.
      2nd c. AD.

Fragment of a relief dedicated to Saturnus: planetary deities, running from Saturn (left) to Venus (right); Sol, radiate nimbus, is nude and holds a whip.
Halbertsma 1995, 1667.
Image: National Museum of Antiquities, Leiden.

2. Épinal, Museum.
   Soulosse.
   Limestone.
   2nd–3rd c. AD.
   Altar; front: standing, bearded male figure in a niche, holding a staff in his right hand and an unidentifiable attribute in his lowered left hand. Below him in two rows the seven busts of the planetary deities, their individual features and attributes no longer distinguishable.
   Espérandieu, Recueil VI, 4848.

3. Vienne.
   Vienne.
   Limestone.
   Ca. AD 200.
   Octagonal altar (?) With busts of the seven planetary deities (heads defaced) and of Septimius Severus. Sol has a *chlamys*, perhaps a whip behind his right shoulder, and long wavy hair. Whether he was radiate can no longer be ascertained Below the busts of Jupiter and Venus (?), dedicatory inscription to Jupiter Optimus Maximus.
   Espérandieu, Recueil I, 412; Duval 1953, 287; Lusnia 2004, 526, 529 fig. 11 (Sol and Luna on right hand photograph).

4. Plate 21.3
   Wiesbaden, Stadtmuseum am Markt 237.
   Heddernheim.
   Sandstone.
   2nd–3rd c. AD.
   In the main field, Minerva, Vulcan and Mercury; above: planetary deities, from Saturn (left) to Venus (right); Sol is radiate (seven rays) and wears a *chlamys*.
   LIMC Helios/Sol 285; F. Brommer 1973, 10. n. 49 pl. 44; Huld-Zetsche 1994, 161 fig. 67.
   Image: courtesy Stadtmuseum Wiesbaden.

5.   Épinal, Museum.
      Frémifontaine.
      Reddish sandstone.
      3rd c. AD.
      Triangular stele with two rows of busts, three above, seven below; the
      busts are uniformly executed and lack distinguishing characteristics,
      making it impossible to determine whether the lower seven are the plan-
      etary deities, as Espérandieu tentatively puts forward.
      Espérandieu, Recueil VI, 4784

6.   Frankfurt a.M., Archäologisches Museum X 2511.
      Heddernheim.
      Sandstone.
      Undated.
      Aedicula-shaped relief, damaged. In the main field, Minerva (? upper
      part of her body and head missing), Vulcan and Mercury. In a frieze above
      them, the busts of the planetary deities, running from Saturn (left, most
      missing) to Venus (right). In the tympanum, unidentified bust.
      Espérandieu, Germanie 98.

7.   Plate 88.2
      Fomerly Harisa, convent; current location unknown.
      Fikeh.
      Limestone.
      Undated.
      Octagonal altar depicting the planetary deities and Allat. Sol, nude but
      for a *chlamys*, radiate, whip in right hand, patera (?) in left hand. Next to
      Allat is Mercury, followed, from right to left, by the other planetary deities
      in order and ending with Mars. Jupiter, Mercury, and Venus are depicted
      in the guise of the Heliopolitan triad.
      Stern, Cal. 173–4 p. 32.3; Hajjar 1977, 149 no. 136 pls. 47–50; Matern 2002:
      92, 98, 228, G21; LIMC Planetae 8; LIMC Selene/Luna 28; Kropp 2010,
      fig. 13.
      Image: after Kropp 2010, fig. 13 (T. Weber).

      C2j. Apollo
1.   Plates 16.1, 16.2
      Newcastle-upon-Tyne, Great North Museum: Hancock. NEWMA 1956.341.A.
      Whitley Castle.
      Stone.

Second half 2nd c. AD. The coins dedicated on each of the four low pillars give a terminus post quem of ca. AD 150. The arguments used by Wright (1943, 38) to reject a 2nd c. date, namely that Mithraism was not prevalent in Northern Britain until the 3rd c. AD, is untenable, especially after the discovery of two second-century Mithraic altars at Inveresk.

Altar with relief sculpture on all four sides, originally set in a socket in a base supported by four low pillars (ca. 35 cms. high) with a dedicatory coin on top of each pillar. Front: Apollo with plectrum and cithara; right side: Sol, nude but for a *chlamys*, radiate, right hand raised, whip in left hand; back: Mithras between two torch bearers; left side: bearded man, clad in a tunic, with cup and jug, stands in front of a figure on a low platform; the dedicant offering to a local solar deity? Remnants of an inscription: D[e]o / Apo[lli]n[i] G(aius) / [. 6.]ius / [...] / [..] coh(ortis) [II] Ne[r(viorum)] /[...].

LIMC Helios/Sol 265; Wright 1943.

Image: photograph after RIB 1198, courtesy Great North Museum. Pencil drawing by Phoebe Hijmans.

For additional images see RIB 1198.

2.   Afyon, Mus E 1920 4423.
      Çavdarlı.
      Marble (?)
      Undated.
      Votive stele dedicated to Apollo and depicting a bust of Sol, long wavy hair, radiate.
      Matern 2002: 253 B58.

      C2k. Artemis
1.   Veria, Museum 249.
      Stenimachos.
      Marble.
      2nd–3rd c. AD.
      Votive stele depicting Artemis; in tympanum heads of Sol (left), radiate, and Luna (right).
      LIMC Helios 304; Chatzopoulos et al. 2015: 200–201.

      C2l. Asclepius
1.   Tenos, Museum A340.
      Tenos.
      White marble.

1st c. BC.

Man lying on a couch by a three-legged table; at his feet to the left: Hermes; by his arm to the right: herm and woman on pedestals; above the woman: bust of Sol, radiate, left; above Hermes: crescent.

LIMC Helios 302.

2.   Plovdiv, Archaeological Museum 1021.

Plovdiv.

Marble.

2nd c. AD.

Gods of the Asclepius-family, between busts of Sol and Luna on high pedestals.

LIMC Helios 298; LIMC Asklepios in Thracia 22 (both with the same, uninformative, reference).

C2m. Athena

1.   Ma'lûla (Syria).

In situ.

Rock.

Undated.

In the face of the rock, a section has been smoothed, and two shallow adjacent niches have been carved. Bust of Sol, radiate (thirteen rays) in the left-hand niche; bust of Athena in the other.

LIMC Helios in per. or. 40.

C2n. Dioscuri

1.   Plate 89.1

Paris, Louvre MA 746.

Larissa.

Marble.

2nd c. BC.

Votive naiskos dedicated to the Dioscuri. In the tympanum, the upper body of Helios, radiate (24 rays), draped, between the frontal protomes of four horses, two jumping to the left and two to the right.

LIMC Helios 83; Hamiaux: 1998, 179 no. 198; Matern 2002: 51, 208–9, Q8.

Image: © RMN-Grand Palais / Art Resource, NY ART519304; photograph Hervé Lewandowski.

C20. Genius

1. Plate 89.4
   Rome, Museo Nazionale Romano 78197.
   Rome, Scala Santa.
   Marble.
   AD 160–180.
   Votive relief. On the left-hand side frontal bust of Sol, radiate (five rays), long wavy hair, *chlamys*; next to him bust of an older, bearded man, cloaked; the lower right hand corner of the relief is missing and with it, perhaps, the man's left hand and/or attribute. Above his left shoulder a small profile bust of Luna facing Sol. To the right of the bearded man, inscription: soli invicto / pro salute imp(eratorum) / et genio n(umeri) eq(uitum) sing(ularium) / eorum, m(arcus) ulp(ius) / chresimus sace[r(dos)] / iovis doliche[ni] / v(otum) s(olvit) l(ibens) l(aetus) [m(erito)]. As now preserved, the bearded man is identified either as Jupiter Dolichenus, as the Genius Equitum Singularium or as the priest Marcus Ulpius Chresimus, all three mentioned in the inscription. Each identification is possible, although the iconography is very uncommon for Jupiter Dolichenus, and the man would definitely have to have held an attribute in his left hand appropriate to Dolichenus. In view of the dedication (to Sol and the Genius) the figure seems most likely to me to be the Genius; we should also keep in mind however that the form of the relief, broken at the right just beyond the inscription, with two figures to the left of it, implies that there were also two figures to the right of the inscription, now lost.
   LIMC Helios/Sol 404; Speidel 1978, 15–6 no. 17; Schraudolph 1993, 237 L149; Matern 2002: 42, n. 328, 171, 257 B82.
   Image: photograph courtesy DAIR MAL397-04_40710.01.

C2p. Isis & Sarapis

1. Bursa, Museum 1679.
   Bursa.
   Marble.
   Roman imperial ?
   Upper part of an aedicula-shaped stele; in the tympanum small frontal bust of Sol, radiate, *chlamys*; below: busts of Isis and Sarapis.
   LIMC Helios 303.

C2q. Jupiter

1.   Cambridge, Fitzwilliam Museum 182.1902.
      Beyşehr (Lyaconia).
      limestone.
      3rd c. AD.
      Votive altar for Zeus and Helios. On the right, bust of Zeus; on the left,
      bust of Helios, radiate nimbus (seven rays).
      Matern 2002: 182 n. 991, 253–4 B62; Budde & Nicholls 1964, 76–7 no. 124
      pl. 41.

2.   Plate 89.3
      Lost.
      Rome.
      Marble.
      Undated.
      Three fragments of a relief. In the centre, Jupiter standing on a base, eagle
      by his side, faced by an orant. To one side, above: Sol, nude but for a *chla-
      mys*, radiate, whip, on a *quadriga* right, and below: Luna on a *biga* left. On
      the fragment with Sol: dedit m(arcus) modius [agatho] / sancto domino /
      invicto Mithrae / iussu eius libens / dedit
      CIMRM I, 332–3; MMM II, 234–5 no. 71bis, b, and fig. 66.
      Image: pencil drawing by Phoebe Hijmans.

3.   Plate 89.2
      Rome, Fondazione Dino ed Ernesta Santarelli inv. E.D'O.339.
      Unknown.
      Marble.
      Undated.
      Small votive aedicula depicting Jupiter holding a long staff in his left
      hand and an eagle in his right hand. In the tympanum, frontal bust of Sol,
      radiate (ten rays).
      Unpublished.
      Image: courtesy Fondazione Dino ed Ernesta Santarelli.

C2r. Malakbel

1.   Plate 90.1
      Rome, Musei Capitolini S 107.
      Rome, Giardini Mattei.
      Marble.
      Second half 1st c. AD.

Altar with two inscriptions and relief-decoration on four sides. Side A: frontal bust of Sol, radiate nimbus (seven rays), fairly long curly hair, *chlamys*, above an eagle with outstretched wings; inscription: soli sanctissimo sacrum / ti(berius) claudius felix et / claudia helpis et / ti(iberius) claudius alypus fil(ius) eorum / votum solverunt libens merito / calbienses de coh(orte) III. Side B: Sol (?), bare-headed, dressed in *chlamys*, tunica and trousers, whip in his right hand, stepping into a chariot drawn by griffins; behind him, a winged Victory holding a crown above his head; inscription (Palmyrene): "This is the altar (which) Tiberius Claudius Felix and the Palmyrenes offered to Malakbel and the Gods of Palmyra. To their gods, Peace!" (translation according to Teixidor 1979: 47). Side C: a cypress, with a ribbon at the top and a small boy carrying a sheep on his shoulders emerging from the branches just to the right of the top. Side D: Saturnus, bearded, capite velato, holding a harpé in his right hand. For Bust of Sol above an eagle with outstretched wings cf. C2a.4 in the Vatican.

LIMC Helios in. per. or. 54; Teixidor 1979: 47–8 (dating the monument in the 3rd c. AD); Simon 1962: 765 (dating the monument mid 1st c. AD); Dirven 1999: 175–180, pl. XXI; Matern 2002: 37 n. 289, 41 n. 321, 66, 170, 173, 256 B80, fig. 82. Fowlkes-Childs 2016, 203–211.

Image: Arachne Mal626-01_16369,08.jpg; arachne.dainst.org/entity/ 2236444.

C2s. Mercurius

1.   Plate 90.2
      Beirut, National Museum 2607.
      Bted'i.
      Limestone.
      Roman Imperial.
      Small votive altar with fragmentary dedicatory inscription and damaged relief decoration. On the front, bust of Mercurius Heliopolitanus. On the left side, bust of Sol, radiate (seven rays), *chlamys*, whip. On the right side, bust of Luna.
      Hajjar 1977: 144–147 no. 131, pls. 44–5; Aliquot 2009: 244–5; Kropp 2010: 67.
      Image: sketch after dawing by C. de la Chaussée, BMB 1 (1937): 93 fig. 4.

C2sbis. Nemesis

1.   Plate 90.3
      Zagreb, Archaeological Museum.
      Scitarjevo/Andautonia (?)

Limestone.

AD 86–90.

Votive relief on the back of an older inscription. The votive is dedicated to Nemesis Regina by L. Funisolanus, who was governor of Moesia Superior between AD 86 and 90. Nemesis stands below an arch, dressed in a short *chiton*, diadem in her hair. She holds a whip (?) In her right hand, a rectangular shield on her left arm, and emerging above the are a torch, palm branch, and trident. Above the arch, left, frontal bust of Sol, not radiate, *chlamys*, and right bust of Luna with upturned crescent behind her shoulders.

CIL III, 4008 & 4013; Brunsmid 1905, 65 no. 125; Kremer 2015: 269–70 fig. 7; Lupa 5739; Hornum 2015; 175–6 no. 38, pl. 27.

Image: Lupa.at/5739 Photograph Ortolf Harl.

C2t. Sabazius

1.   Plate 90.4

Tirana, Archaeological Museum 20.

Shalesi, Elbasani district.

Bronze.

2nd–3rd c. AD.

Votive plaque. In the tympanum, Luna (left) and Sol (right, radiate, thirteen rays, *chlamys*, left hand holding horse lying in the right hand corner facing him, right arm disappears under his *chlamys*) flank a Sabazius-hand on a staff held by Luna; she also holds a horse, lying in the left hand corner facing her. In the main field: Sabazius enthroned, surrounded by a large number of gods and attributes.

LIMC Helios/Sol 335; Albanien. Schätze aus dem Land der Skipetaren (exhibition catalogue 1988): 402 n. 319.

Image (tympanum only): drawing © Zoë Hijmans.

2.   Plate 91.1

Plovdiv, Arch, Museum 3079

Plovdiv

Marble

3rd c. AD (LIMC)

Votive relief in two registers. Above: Sabazius, bearded, short *chiton* and *chlamys*, phrygian cap, pine cone in raised left hand, sceptre in right hand, resting left foot on the badly worn head or skull of a ram (?); in the upper left-hand corner worn bust of Luna above Pan (?) and full-figure of Hermes; in the upper right-hand corner very worn bust of Sol, above

Fortuna-Tyche and Daphne (LIMC). In lower register bearded Heros Equitans holding a pine-cone (?) in his raised right hand. In the left-hand corner a bust (Sol?, Luna?), to the right two women, below the horse a dog attacking a boar, below the women a ram.

LIMC Heros Equitans 564 (with refs.).

Image: photograph courtesy Plovdiv Archaeological Museum, Elena Filadska.

3. Plate 91.3
Lost?
Rome.
Bronze.
2nd–3rd c. AD?

Bronze votive plaque. In the upper corners, outside the aedicula, the Dioscuri stand facing inwards, each holding a horse by its bridle. In the tympanum, frontal *quadriga* with Sol (?). In main field: Sabazius surrounded by animals and objects; in the upper corners the busts of Luna (left) and Sol (right), radiate (seven or eight rays). Between them and Sabazius the caps of the two Dioscuri

Daremberg-Saglio VIII, 929–930, fig. 5983.

Image after Daremberg-Saglio loc. cit.

C2u. Silvanus

1. Plate 91.4
Rome, Musei Capitolini NCE 2668.
Rome.
Greek marble.
1st–early 2nd c. AD.

Votive relief; above, from left to right, the busts of Sol, radiate (nine rays), Luna, and Silvanus; below, inscription: soli lunae silvano / et genio cellae / groesianae / m(arcus) scanianus / zosa ex viso / posuit.

LIMC Helios/Sol 403; CIL VI 706; CIL VI.1 Im. 40–41 no. 12; Schraudolph 1993, 204 G16, pl. 21; Matern 2002: 28 n. 215, 256–7 B81 (error in inscription).

Image: drawing © Zoë Hijmans.

C2v. Other or Unknown Deity

1. Chesterholm, Museum.
Vindolanda (Chesterholm).
Sandstone.
2nd–3rd c. AD.

Aedicula-shaped relief: frontal, standing male figure, bearded, lowered
right hand holding an unidentified object (damaged) above a rectangular
block upon which something is standing (? Also damaged), a globe (?)
in the crook of his left arm; in lower right-hand corner a figure in Roman
armor, head lost, cloak (?) over his left arm, holding a spear in his right
hand (? arm lost). Above, in two niches flanking the head of the main figure, busts of Sol (left), five rays, and Luna (right) respectively. Birley identifies the central figure as Maponus (a Celtic god associated with Apollo).
Bauchhenss (LIMC Apollon/Apollo 610) rejects this identification.
Birley 1986, 57 fig. 3; LIMC Apollon/Apollo 610.

2.   Plate 17.2
     Speyer, Historisches Museum der Pfalz.
     Speyer.
     Sandstone.
     Undated.
     Round-topped aedicula-relief with Nantosuelta standing, frontal, with a
     long staff in her right hand, topped with a model of a round hut. In the
     pediment, frontal head of Sol, radiate nimbus (nine rays), whip to the left.
     Vilvorder & de Beenhouwer 2008.
     Image: Lupa.at/25707 Photograph Ortolf Harl.

3.   Plate 92.1
     Plovdiv Archaeological. Museum 2103.
     Plovdiv.
     Marble.
     First half 3rd c. AD.
     Round-topped votive relief. Three-headed rider galloping right towards
     altar with two figures. Behind the horse a standing figure, below: Cerberus
     attacking boar. Upper left corner bust of Luna (?), upper right Sol (?).
     Both busts lack clear distinguishing characteristics.
     LIMC Heros Equitans 580.
     Image: © Archaeological Museum, Plovdiv / Elena Filadska.

4.   Plate 91.2
     Aleppo, Archaeological Museum.
     Manbij (Hierapolis).
     Basalt.
     2nd–3rd c. AD.

Round-topped stele depicting an unknown, male god wearing a palu-
damentum over armour and long trousers, and holding a long, snake-
entwined staff upright next to him with his right hand. At his feet to
either side a lion, looking back and up towards the deity, To either side of
his head the busts of Luna, right and Sol, left. Sol wears a *chlamys* and is
radiate (nine rays).
Blömer 2014: 312–313, Pl. 92.2.
Image: photograph after Blömer 2014: 312.

C2w. Multiple Deities

1. Cairo, Egyptian Museum 26.6.20 no. 5.
   Unknown.
   Gypsum.
   1st c. BC.
   Within a naiskos, Cybele seated on a throne between standing Hermes
   (left) and a goddess with a torch (right). In the tympanum, two reclining
   lions. Above the pediment at the apex frontal face of Sol ("Sonnengesicht"),
   radiate nimbus (21 or 22 rays) between three Corybantes on each side.
   LIMC Helios 301.

2. Damascus, National Museum.
   Palmyra.
   Limestone.
   AD 119.
   Bust of Sol, radiate nimbus, in upper right corner; corresponding corner
   on the left broken away. Below, a group of three gods and a goddess.
   LIMC Helios in per. or. 31.

3. Plate 94.5
   Vatican, Museo Gregoriano Profano 1186.
   Rome, Celio.
   Marble.
   Second half 2nd c.–early 3rd c. AD.
   "Ara Casali", relief depicting the discovery of the adultery of Mars and
   Venus. In centre inscription surrounded by a wreath; above the wreath
   to the left Sol, radiate, nude but for a *chlamys*, in a *quadriga*; to the right
   Vulcan, looking downwards. Below: Mars and Venus in bed.
   LIMC Helios/Sol 185; LIMC Ares/Mars. Matern 2002: 188–9, 282 K30.
   Image: Arachne FA3638-09_19547.jpg; arachne.dainst.org/entity/447794.

4.   Lost.
      Oinoanda.
      Local rock.
      2nd–3rd c. AD.
      A complex tentatively identified as a fountain, with a range of reliefs and
      dedicatory inscriptions, four of which were recorded before they disap-
      peared in the late 1960s and early 1970s. The reliefs depict the Dioscuri on
      horseback flanking an unidentified woman, Mercurius, Jupiter, and Sol,
      radiate (nine rays), *chlamys*. The Dioscuri form the central image imme-
      diately above the arch of the presumed basin of the fountain, with the
      bust of Sol immediately to the right of them, still above the arch. There
      was space for a companion figure (Luna?) to the left of the Dioscuri, but
      there is no trace of such a figure. Standing full-figure to the right of Sol
      is Mercurius, followed on the right by a bust of Jupiter. To the left of the
      arch, possible similar figures did not survive. Each figure has an identify-
      ing inscription. Below Sol: Ἡλίῳ Μίθρᾳ.
      Matern 2002: 262 B120; Milner & Smith 1994, 70–76 nr 4, pls. XV–XVI.

5.   Plates 93.1–93.3
      Rome, Musei Capitolini 1250.
      Rome, Esquiline, in a wall with numerous other reliefs as spolia, near the
      church of S. Eusebio (Piazza Manfredo Fanti).
      Luna marble.
      AD 246.
      Aedicula-shaped relief, with scenes on the front and on each side. Front:
      Jupiter, standing, between Mars and Nemesis; left side: Victory; right side:
      Sol standing, bare-headed (no rays), nude but for a *chlamys*, right hand
      raised, whip in left hand; behind Sol, very damaged remains of a horse (?)
      or, more likely, four protomes of horses (cf. C2c.72). Inscription: i(ovi)
      o(ptimo) m(aximo) et marti et nemesi [et] soli et victoriae et omnibus /
      diis patriensibus civ(es) ex prov(incia) belgica aug(usta) viromandu /
      oru(m) milites iul(ius) iustus coh(ortis) I praet(orianae) c(enturiae)
      albani et / firm(us) maternianus coh(ortis) x praet(orianae) philippi-
      anarum / c(enturiae) artem[on]is v(otum) s(olvit) l(ibens) m(erito). For
      Sol and Victoria as the Dii Militares cf. Arch of Constantine. The same
      Belgians also dedicated C2w.6 below.
      LIMC Helios/Sol 93; Matern 2002: 29 n. 218, 42 n. 325, 90 n. 526, 105–6, 108,
      113, 233 I17, fig. 45; LIMC Nemesis 289. Colling 2010: 220–231.
      Images: 5, 5a, and 5b Arachne Mal1736-05_16595,00.jpg, Mal1736-04
      _16595,06.jpg, and Mal1736-11_16595,10.jpg; arachne.dainst.org/entity/
      6407973

6. Plate 93.4
   Rome, Musei Capitolini 1510.
   Rome, Esquiline.
   Luna marble.
   AD 238–244.
   Votive relief in two registers; upper register: Jupiter, between Mars (left) and Sol, of whom only the head (since lost), raised right hand, and left foot have been preserved; lower register (from left to right): Apollo, Mercury, Diana and Hercules. Inscription: diis [san]ctis patrie[nsi]bus / [i(ovi) o(ptimo)] m(aximo) et invict[o ap]ollini mercurio dianae h[erc] uli marti // ex provincia belgica [aug(usta) cives ?] veromand(uorum) / iul(ius) iustus mil(es) coh(ortis) I praet(oriae) p[iae vindic]is gordianae / val[erii] et / firmius mater[nianus mil(es) coh(ortis)] x pr[aet(oriae)] piae vindi[cis gordianae] da[...
   Note that the commonly given reading of et between Invicto and Apollini is incorrect. There is not enough space for the two extra letters, and from Hülsen's (1893: 263) sketch of the different pieces which make up this monument, it is clear that when it was first found, the O of invicto and the A of Apollini were both still visible and, more importantly, were both on the same fragment with no break between them. Apollo Invictus is rare, but not unique; cf. CIL 6, 36764; CIL 10, 123.
   Hülsen 1893; Matern 2002: 29, 42 n. 325, 106, 233 I16; Colling 2010: 220–231. Photograph adapted from Hülsen 1893 pl. x. Note the head of Sol (since lost).

7. Kütahya, Museum.
   Kusura, near Aezani.
   Marble.
   3rd c. AD.
   Altar with busts of Zeus, Hera (?), Meter Theon, Helios, radiate nimbus, draped, and Mên.
   Matern 2002: 182 n. 991, 254 B69.

8. Kütahya, Museum.
   Kusura, near Aezani.
   Marble.
   3rd c. AD.
   Altar with busts of Zeus (?), Meter Theon, Helios, radiate, draped, and Mên.
   Matern 2002: 182 n. 991, 254–5 B70.

9.   Kütahya, Museum.
      Kusura, near Aezani.
      Marble.
      3rd c. AD.
      Altar with busts of Zeus(?), Meter Theon, Helios, radiate nimbus, draped,
      and Mên.
      Matern 2002: 182 n. 991, 255 B71.

10.   Plate 19.3
      Paris, Louvre MA 4288.
      Eskişehir.
      Marble.
      3rd c. AD.
      Votive stele. In upper register bust of Zeus in niche, with small busts of
      Sol (left), radiate nimbus (eight rays), *chlamys*, and Luna to either side of
      the niche. In lower register, two rows of figures: in upper row from left to
      right an axe-wielding horseman riding right, two standing figures holding
      hands, and bust of a woman; below, Hercules, Mercurius, two bulls.
      Ricl 1991: 13 no. 24, pl. 3; Matern 2002: 256 B78.
      Image: © Musée du Louvre, Dist. RMN-Grand Palais / Thierry Ollivier /
      Art Resource, NY: ART559883.

11.   Plate 92.2
      Stuttgart, Landesmuseum Württemberg RL 401.
      Marbach.
      Sandstone.
      Undated.
      Relief, with in the center large figure of Mercurius, between other deities
      in two registers. Upper register left: Luna, Jupiter, and two unidentified
      female figures; right: Fortuna, Sol, radiate, and Silvanus. Lower register
      left: Dioscure and Mars (?); right: Dioscure and Hercules.
      Espérandieu 1931, 437 no. 695
      Image: © Landesmuseum Württemberg, Ortolf Harl.

12.   Ljubljana, National Museum L92.
      Crnomelj, probably Loka.
      Limestone
      Undated.
      Votive altar with reliefs on three sides. On the front, the Capitoline Triad.
      On the left side three women, possibly the Matres. On the right side, Sol

and Luna to either side of a male figure, possibly Apollo. Sol, radiate, drives a *quadriga*.

Šašel Kos 1997: 135; Ubi Erat Lupa 3795.
Images: Lupa.at/3795.

13. Tata, Museum.
Tata.
Limestone.
Undated.
Rectangular pilaster with niches with deities in three registers, alternated with rectangular reliefs. Top: rectangular reliefs with garland, bucrania and eagle (all four sides); first register: Fall of Phaethon (now lost) on the front, right side Vulcan, left side Apollo with griffin and tripod, rear Juno. Rectangular reliefs between first and second register: lost (front); animals (? right); genii carrying garlands (left); peacock (rear); second register: Sol (front); Venus (right); Silvanus (left); Minerva (rear); rectangular reliefs between second and third register: animals (? Front); genii carrying garlands (right); lost (left); reclining figure (rear); lower register: Luna, walking to right, with torch (front); Mars (right); Diana (left); Victory (rear); below: lost (front); weapons (right); animal (? Left); two winged horses (rear).

Barkóczi 1944 46, Taf. LVIII, 1–3; Lupa 6703.
Images: Lupa.at/6703.

14. Unknown.
Hierapolis in Phrygia.
Limestone.
Undated.
Stele honouring an association for the organization of a festival. In tympanum, Jupiter, between Fortuna and Mercurius, Sol (in *quadriga*) and-presumably-Luna (*biga* of oxes).

Ramsay 1927: 195 fig 1; Matern 2002: 222 Q96a.

15. Unknown.
Hierapolis in Phrygia.
Limestone.
Undated.
Stele honouring an association for the organization of a festival. In tympanum, Jupiter, between Fortuna and Mercurius, Sol (in *quadriga*) and, presumably, Luna (*biga* of oxes).

Ramsay 1927: 195 fig. 2; Matern 2002: 222 Q96b.

16.   Unknown.
       Zeune.
       Limestone (?)
       Undated.
       Altar with, on one side, a bust of Sol, radiate nimbus, *chlamys*. Luna is on
       another side, and Cybele on the third.
       Ramsay 1927: 278–80 fig 8; Matern 2002: 258 B92.

17.   Plate 94.3
       Vienna, Kunsthistorisches Museum I 350.
       Carthage.
       Limestone.
       Undated.
       Votive stele to Dea Caelestis of the so-called Ghorfa-stele type. Above:
       Dea Caelestis crowned with crescent and rosette, between busts of /Sol,
       radiate, and Luna. Also between Dionysus and Venus. Below: aedicula
       with bearded bust in tympanum and standing togatus between the col-
       umns. Bottom, sacrificial scene with two figures, bull and altar.
       Eingartner 2003: 602 fig. 2.
       Image: Lupa.at/9703, courtesy KHM Museumsverband.

18.   Plate 94.2
       Vienna, Kunsthistorisches Museum I 354.
       Carthage.
       Limestone.
       Undated.
       Votive stele to Dea Caelestis of the so-called Ghorfa-stele type. Above: Dea
       Caelestis crowned with crescent and rosette, between busts of Sol, radi-
       ate, and Luna. Also between Dionysus and Venus. Below: aedicula with
       bearded bust in tympanum and seated togatus between the columns.
       Eingartner 2003: 602.
       Cf. Tunis, Bardo Museum inv. cb 964, 966, 970–974.
       Image: Lupa.at/9704, courtesy KHM Museumsverband.

19.   Plate 94.1
       Tunis, Bardo.
       Maktar?
       Limestone.
       Undated.
       At top, Caelestis flanked by Sol and Luna. Various other deities and fig-
       ures below.

Lupa 24423.
Image: Lupa.at/24423, photograph Andreas Schmidt-Colinet.

20. Sbeitla, Sufetula Museum 68.
Sbeitla.
Limestone.
Undated.
Fragment of a stele, top and bottom broken off. Near the top, facing bust of Sol, radiate nimbus (eight rays), face completely lost, to the left of two central figures of whom only the legs survive; nothing remains of Luna on the right. Below them, seven deities (not planetary), from left to right: Neptune (?), an unidentified clothed male deity (?) with a sheaf of wheat, an unidentified clothed female deity (?) carrying a small basket, a clothed female deity (?) with a plough, identified as Ceres, an unidentified nude male deity (?), Mercurius, and a seated deity, thought to be Jupiter, but largely destroyed.
Lupa 23982.
Images: lupa.at/23982.

C2x. Emperor

1. Vatican, Cortile del Belvedere 1115.
Rome.
Marble.
12–2 BC.
Altar of the Lares Augusti, decorated on all four sides; on one side: apotheose of Caesar or Agrippa; above to the right Caelus, to the left *quadriga* of Sol (only the horses remain).
LIMC Helios/Sol 168; Matern 2002: 55, 216 Q54 (with refs.); Zanker 1969.

2. Plate 4.5
Munich, Glyptothek 553.
Unknown.
Marble.
AD 87.
Altar, presumably for Sol and the Genius of Domitian. Bust of Sol, radiate (seven rays, of which two lost), above a snake.
Inscription: [soli invic]to et / [6] / [a]bascantus Imp(eratoris) / [[[domitiani]]] caesaris / aug(usti) germanici ser(vus) / euporianus / aram [l(ocus)] d(atus) d(ecreto) d(ecurionum) / dedicavitque IIII k(alendas) iun(ias) / [[[imp(eratore) domitiano]]] aug(usto) germ(anico) XIII co(n)s(ule). If the emendation [Soli Invic]to is correct, this would be the

oldest accurately dated case of invictus as epithet for Sol. An alternative reading could be [soli augus]to, but the Clauss/Slaby epigraphic database lists only nine instances of soli augusto (compared to 236 for soli invicto), none of which have a firm or even likely date in the first century AD. Given that a Greek named Anicetus was already closely involved in the cult of Sol in Rome in the latter part of the first century AD (see pp. 824–826), the use of Invictus – the Latin for ἀνίκητος/Anicetus – as epithet of Sol at this time seems almost a certainty, and the emendation Soli invicto is therefore the most likely to be correct.

Matern 2002: 171, 182 n. 998, 255 B74, fig. 78.

Image: Staatliche Antikensammlungen und Glyptothek, Munich; photograph by Renate Kühling.

C3. Funerary Reliefs
C3a. Sarcophagi with Mythological Scenes
C3a1. Phaethon

1. Plate 94.4
    Florence, Uffizi 181.
    Rome.
    Marble.
    Ca. AD 170.
    Sarcophagus relief depicting the Phaethon-myth. At the right-hand end, Sol, nude but for a *chlamys*, stands receiving Phaethon. In the centre the fall of Phaethon witnessed by Sol and others.
    LIMC Phaethon I, 9; LIMC Helios/Sol 174; Matern 2002: 186, 278 K5.
    Image by Sailko, CC BY 3.0, https://commons.wikimedia.org/w/index.php?curid=90611163.

2. Vatican, Museo Chiaramonti 1965.
    Unknown.
    Marble.
    AD 170–180.
    Fragment of the lid of a sarcophagus; Phaethon facing a seated Sol, radiate (seven rays), half nude but for a garment draped over his knees and waist, whip in left hand. To the left, a standing female figure; to the right, a Wind-god in the guise of a winged putto.
    LIMC Helios/Sol 452; LIMC Phaethon I, 8; Amelung 1903: I, 394–5 no. 130, pl. 42; Matern 2002: 186, 280 K15.

3. Kyoto, Greece and Rome Museum (Previously in Okayama, Kurashiki Ninagawa Museum).
    Unknown (produced in Rome).

Marble.

Ca. AD 180.

Sarcophagus relief depicting the myth of Phaethon. Sol, seated, head lost, nude but for a *chlamys*, receives Phaethon; behind Sol, Luna. On the short sides: the Dioscuri.

LIMC Phaethon I, 6; Matern 2002: 186, 279 K10; Zanker & Ewald 2004: 87 fig. 69.

4. Liverpool, Merseyside County Museum (formerly Ince Blundell Hall). Tivoli.

Parian marble.

AD 190–200.

Sarcophagus relief depicting the Phaethon myth. Sol, radiate, nude but for a *chlamys*, is seated slightly left of centre and receives Phaethon (lost); to the right the four winds bring the four horses of the chariot.

LIMC Helios/Sol 177; LIMC Phaethon I, 7; ASR 3.3, 412–7 pl. 108; Matern 2002: 186, 279 K8.

5. Florence, Museo dell'Opera del Duomo.

Rome.

Marble.

AD 190–200.

Sarcophagus relief depicting the Phaethon-myth. At the right-hand end, Sol, nude but for a *chlamys*, stands receiving Phaethon. In the centre the fall of Phaethon witnessed by Sol and many others.

LIMC Phaethon I, 11; Matern 2002: 186, 278 K6.

6. Plate 95.1

Copenhagen, Ny Carlsberg Glyptotek 847.

Ostia.

Marble.

Late 2nd c. AD.

Sarcophagus depicting the fall of Phaethon; left: Sol, seated, right hand raised, nude except for some cloth (not fastened as a *chlamys*) over his left shoulder, and perhaps radiate (holes for rays (?) visible) facing Phaethon, standing, right hand raised, nude but for a *chlamys*, probably radiate (holes for rays (?) visible); nearby the four Horae, the winds holding the horses of Sol, and Aurora. In the centre: Fall of Phaethon. Right: mourning Sol, approached by Hermes.

LIMC Phaethon I, 19 (with ref); LIMC Helios/Sol 175; ASR 3.3 417–8 no. 336; Matern 2002: 186, 278–9 K7.

Image: © Ny Carlsberg Glyptotek, Copenhagen; Photograph: Ole Haupt.

7.   Nepi, Cathedral.
      Unknown.
      Marble.
      First half 3rd c. AD.
      Sarcophagus-relief depicting the fall of Phaethon, much damaged. At the
      right: seated Sol receives Phaethon; left of centre Sol (?) seen on the back,
      observing the fall of Phaethon. On the left-hand short side, Sol in *quad-
      riga*; on the right-hand short side, Luna in *biga*.
      LIMC Helios/Sol 178, 347a; Matern 2002: 186, 279 K9.

8.   Plate 96.1
      Verona, Museo Lapidario Maffeiano 28703.
      Unknown.
      Marble.
      AD 225–250.
      Right half of a sarcophagus-relief depicting the fall of Phaethon; upper
      right-hand corner Sol, standing, radiate (seven rays), nude but for a *chla-
      mys*, receives Phaethon.
      LIMC Helios/Sol 176; LIMC Phaethon I, 13; Matern 2002: 186, 280 K19.
      Image: Courtesy Museo Maffeiano.

9.   Plate 96.2
      St. Petersburg, Hermitage A985.
      Unknown.
      Marble.
      2nd quarter 3rd c. AD.
      Fragment of a sarcophagus depicting the fall of Phaethon. To the left, Sol,
      dressed only in a *chlamys*.
      Matern 2002: 186, 279 K12.
      Image: courtesy Hermitage, St. Petersburg.

10.   Benevento, Museo del Sannio.
      Unknown.
      Marble.
      Ca. AD 250.
      Fragment of a sarcophagus depicting the Phaethon-myth. Preserved are:
      seated Sol (head lost) receiving Phaethon (upper corner left); Sol (nude,
      chlamys, no rays) observing Phaethon's fall.
      LIMC Phaethon I, 17; Matern 2002: 186, 277 K1.

11. Paris, Louvre MA 1017.
    Rome.
    Marble.
    Late 3rd c. AD.
    Sarcophagus relief depicting Phaethon-myth. In the upper left-hand corner, Sol (head restored), seated, nude but for a *chlamys*, cornucopia, receives Phaethon. In the centre, fall of Phaethon.
    LIMC Phaethon I, 16; ASR 3.3 418–20 no. 337; Matern 2002: 186, 279 K11.

12. Plates 97.1, 97.2
    Rome, Villa Borghese, Giardino del Lago. (removed in 1994).
    Unknown.
    Marble.
    Ca. AD 300.
    Sarcophagus-relief depicting the fall of Phaethon; in the upper left-hand corner, Sol, seated, head lost, nude but for a *chlamys*, torch in right hand, cornucopia in left hand, receives Phaethon. In the centre, Phaethon's fall, observed from the left by Sol. On the left short side, much more cursorily executed: Sol, radiate (seven rays), nude but for a *chlamys*, torch in right hand, reins in left hand, in *quadriga* (Oceanus (?) below), and on the right short side, Luna in *biga*, (Tellus (?) below).
    LIMC Helios/Sol 179, 347b; LIMC Phaethon I, 15; Matern 2002: 186, 280 K16; ASR 3.3, 338. Cf. Phaethon sarcophagus in Ostia, Arachne 604955.
    Image: Arachne Mal2725-05_41136; arachne.dainst.org/entity/1098262. https://arachne.dainst.org/entity/6580430, photographer Cesare Faraglia.

13. Rome, Villa Borghese.
    Unknown.
    Marble.
    Ca. AD 300.
    Sarcophagus-relief depicting the fall of Phaethon; in upper left-hand corner Sol, seated, nude but for a *chlamys*, receives Phaethon. In the centre, Phaethon's fall, observed from the left by Sol.
    LIMC Helios/Sol 179; LIMC Phaethon I, 18; Matern 2002: 186, 280 K17.

C3a2 Endymion

1. Plates 98.1, 98.2
   New York, Metropolitan Museum of Art 47.100.4.
   Ostia.
   Marble.

AD 190–210.

Sarcophagus-relief depicting the myth of Endymion; on one short side Luna, on the other Sol, radiate (six rays), nude but for a *chlamys*, whip in right hand, reins in left hand, stepping onto a *quadriga*, horses jumping forwards, Lucifer with torch flying above the horses, Oceanus below them.

LIMC Helios/Sol 343; Matern 2002: 73–4, 189, 223 Q101.

Image: courtesy Metropolitan Museum of Art, New York.

2.   Rome, Villa Doria Pamphilj, Casino Belrespiro.

Unknown.

Marble.

First half 3rd c. AD.

Sarcophagus-relief depicting the myth of Endymion. In the upper left-hand corner Sol, head lost, nude but for a *chlamys* in a *quadriga*; upper right-hand corner Luna in a *biga*.

LIMC Helios/Sol 344; Matern 2002: 189, 283 K34.

3.   Rome, S. Paolo fuori le Mura.

Unknown.

Marble.

Ca. AD 220–250.

Sarcophagus-relief depicting the myth of Endymion. In the upper left-hand corner Sol, *chlamys* and *chiton*, in a *quadriga*, all very heavily damaged, riding left (sic!). On the right half, Luna views Endymion and in the centre Venus (?) or Luna (repeated) rides off to the left, but there is no corresponding small Luna in the right corner. As Sichtermann puts it (ASR p. 150): "Konventionell ist an diesem [Sarkophag] also nur wenig".

LIMC Helios/Sol 165; ASR 12.2, 149–150 no. 98; Matern 2002: 189, 283 K35.

4.   Plate 99.1

Cliveden.

Rome.

Marble.

Ca. 225–250.

Sarcophagus relief depicting the Endymion-myth; in the upper left-hand corner, Sol in *quadriga*, preceded by Lucifer; in the right-hand corner, Luna in *biga* with Hesperus

LIMC Helios/Sol 345; Robert 1900, 82–4, pl. 7d; ASR 12.2, 145–6 no. 95; Matern 2002: 189, 282 K32.

Image: photograph courtesy Arachne FA1056-07_4812,01; arachne.dainst
.org/entity/1065025

5.   Plate 99.2
     Woburn Abbey.
     Frascati.
     Marble.
     Ca. AD 250.
     Sarcophagus-relief depicting the myth of Endymion; along the upper
     border, just left of centre the tiny figure of Sol, nude but for a *chlamys*,
     right hand raised, globe in left hand, in a *quadriga* right; near the upper
     right-hand corner Luna in a *biga* to the right.
     LIMC Helios/Sol 345; ASR 12.2, 143–5 no. 94; Matern 2002: 189, 283 K36.
     Image: Arachne FA1113-11_31930.jpg; arachne.dainst.org/entity/163904.

6.   Rome, Catacombs of Domitilla.
     Rome.
     Marble.
     Ca. AD 300.
     Damaged sarcophagus depicting the Endymion myth. In the upper right
     corner, scant remains of Sol in a *quadriga*. In upper left corner: Luna in
     biga, preceded by Hesperus.
     Matern 2002: 189, 282–3 K33.

          C3a3 Mars and Venus
1.   Plate 100.2
     Grottaferrata, Abbey.
     Unknown.
     Marble.
     Ca. AD 160.
     Sarcophagus relief depicting the adultery of Venus and Mars; left: wed-
     ding of Vulcan and Venus; left of centre: Jupiter on throne and Apollo
     behind him, hear of the adultery from Vulcan and Sol, radiate, *chlamys*,
     chiton, whip; right of centre: Mars and Venus trapped in bed, Hypnos (?)
     and Mercury.
     LIMC Helios/Sol 186; Matern 2002: 188–9, 282 K29; Ambrogi 2008: 141-147.
     Images: courtesy Abbazia di Grottaferrata.

2.   Amalfi, Chiostro del Paradiso.
     Unknown.

Marble.
Antonine.
Sarcophagus depicting the adultery of Mars and Venus. Sol, nude but for a *chlamys*, head damaged, is radiate.
Matern 2002: 188–9. 282 K28.

3.   Rome, Palazzo Altemps, formerly Rome, Palazzo Albani del Drago.
Unknown.
Marble.
Antonine.
Sarcophagus depicting the adultery of Mars and Venus. Sol, head lost, is nude but for a *chlamys*.
Matern 2002: 188–9. 282 K31.

C3a4 Prometheus

1.   Plate 100.1
Paris, Louvre MA 339.
Arles.
Marble.
Ca. AD 240.
Sarcophagus-relief depicting the myth of Prometheus. In the upper left-hand corner in the background, bust of Sol, radiate, raised right hand, between Minerva and Prometheus. To the right of centre, next to Poseidon's trident, bust of Luna with crescent.
LIMC Helios/Sol 164; ASR 3.3, 444–6 no. 356; Matern 2002: 283, K38.
Image: © RMN-Grand Palais / Art Resource, NY, ART415095; photograph Hervé Lewandowski.

2.   Rome, Musei Capitolini 329.
Unknown.
Marble.
AD 220–240, possibly later.
Sarcophagus-relief of a child's sarcophagus, depicting the myth of Prometheus; near the upper left-hand corner, Sol, bare-headed, dressed in *chlamys* and long *chiton*, right hand raised, in *quadriga*, behind him Oceanus. Near the right-hand corner, Luna in *biga*.
LIMC Helios/Sol 346; Matern 2002: 189, 283 K39.

3.   Plate 20.1
Naples, Museo Nazionale 6705.
Pozzuoli.

Marble.

Ca. AD 300.

Sarcophagus-relief depicting the Prometheus myth. In the upper right-hand corner Sol in a *quadriga*, radiate nimbus, nude but for a *chlamys*, right hand raised, facing left; in left-hand corner Luna in *biga* facing right. LIMC Helios/Sol 347; Matern 2002: 189, 283 K37.

Images: photograph by Jebulon, in the public domain by CCO 1.0 license.

C3a5. Ariadne

1. Naples, Museo Nazionale 144995.

Auletta.

Marble.

Towards the end of the 3rd c. AD.

Sarcophagus depicting Ariadne asleep, surrounded by harvesting erotes. In the upper left hand corner Sol in *quadriga* right with Lucifer (all very poorly preserved) and in the upper right hand corner an even less well preserved depiction of Luna in her *biga*. On the two short sides: seasons. ASR 4.3, 403–4 no. 229, pl. 247.2.

C3a6. Meleager

1. Rome, Villa Albani.

Unknown.

Marble.

Ca. AD 170.

Sarcophagus-relief depicting the death of Meleager; right half: Meleager on his death-bed; at the foot of his bed his shield, with frontal bust of Sol, radiate (nine rays), *chlamys*. The shield is a prominent feature of sarcophagi of this type. Normally it is decorated with a gorgoneion. LIMC Helios/Sol 4; ASR 12.6, 119–20 no. 114, fig. 8; Bol 1994: 423–424 cat. 530, pl. 256–260.

C3a7. Judgement of Paris

1. Rome, Villa Medici.

Unknown.

Marble.

Second half 2nd c. AD.

Sarcophagus-relief depicting the judgment of Paris; Sol, whip, in *quadriga*, present at the return of the goddesses on the Olympus. Further to the right: Luna. LIMC Helios/Sol 166; Gundel 1992, 257–60 no. 187; Matern 2002: 189, 284 K42.

C3a8. Protesilaos

1.   Plate 99.3
Naples, S. Chiara.
S. Felice, near Teano.
Marble.
Ca. AD 160–170.
Sarcophagus-relief depicting the Protesilaos-myth; the scene is framed
by Luna, standing at the left end of the sarcophagus, and Sol, radiate,
nude but for a *chlamys*, right hand raised, left hand and attribute broken
off, standing at the right end of the relief. Sol and Luna are both depicted
as full-length figures.
LIMC Helios/Sol 342; Matern 2002: 74, 105, 147–8, 173 n. 953, 187 n. 1033,
189, 233 I14, fig. 40.
Image: photograph author.

C3a9. Rhea Silvia

1.   Plate 99.4
Rome, Palazzo Mattei.
Unknown.
Marble.
First half 3rd c. AD.
Sarcophagus-relief depicting the myth of Mars and Rhea Silvia; upper
left-hand corner: Sol in *quadriga*, radiate, *chlamys* and *chiton*, whip (?
largely restored), preceded by Lucifer and a wind-god.
LIMC Helios/Sol 163; LIMC Ares/Mars 401; Matern 2002: 189, 284 K40.
Image: photograph author.

C3b. Non-Mythological Sarcophagi
C3b1. Sol, Luna, and the Capitoline Triad

1.   Mantua, Palazzo Ducale 186.
Unknown.
Marble.
Ca. AD 160–180.
Lid of a sarcophagus; Capitoline triad and Fortuna between the Dioscuri
and Sol (left) on *quadriga*, radiate (seven rays), nude but for a *chlamys*,
whip in raised right hand, preceded by Lucifer, Oceanus below the
horses, and Luna (right) in *biga* preceded by Hesperus. On the connection between this type of lid and wedding-sarcophagi, cf. Wrede 2001:
28. He argues that the lid echoes the facade of the temple of Capitoline

Jupiter, which had Sol and Luna flanking the triad with Fortuna added. On the pediment of the temple, cf. Simon 1990: 114–118.

LIMC Helios/Sol 350; LIMC Athena/Minerva 283; LIMC Dioskouroi/ Castores 78; ASR 1.3, 202 no. 33, pl. 51.1; Matern 2002: 74, 222 Q100.

2. Plate 101.3
   Rome, Villa Borghese 89.
   Unknown.
   Marble.
   Ca. AD 170–180.
   Lid of a sarcophagus, heavily restored. At the left side, Sol ascends on his *quadriga*, whip in his right hand, reins in his left; Oceanus reclines below the chariot. In the centre, the Capitoline triad, between the Dioscuri. To the right, Luna descends in her *biga*, preceded by Vesper.
   ASR 1.3, 221 no. 95, pl. 51.2; LIMC Helios/Sol 350; Matern 2002: 75, 224 Q109.
   Image: courtesy of the Villa Borghese.

3. Plates 101.1, 101.2
   St. Petersburg, Hermitage A433.
   Monticelli (Tivoli).
   Marble.
   Ca. AD 180.
   Lid of a sarcophagus: On the right, Luna descends in her *biga*, preceded by Vesper, and on the left, (Sol), nude but for a *chlamys*, radiate (four rays), whip in his right hand, reins in the left, ascends in his *quadriga*, preceded by Lucifer and above Oceanus. They flank the three Parcae (left) and the Capitoline triad of Minerva, Jupiter and Juno (right). The main frieze depicts the married couple bringing sacrifice.
   LIMC Helios/Sol 351; ASR 1.3, 232–3 no. 137, pl. 51.3, 57.2; Matern 2002: 74, 223 Q103.
   Image: courtesy Hermitage, S. Petersburg.

4. Plates 102.1, 102.2
   Rome, S. Lorenzo fuori le Mura.
   Unknown.
   Marble.
   AD 180–190.
   Lid of a sarcophagus; Luna on *biga* (right) descending to the right, a winged female figure flying towards her from the upper right hand corner,

holding a large cloth in both hands. On the left side, Sol (damaged), nude but for a *chlamys*, whip in right hand, ascending on a *quadriga* over reclining Oceanus and preceded by a winged female figure (damaged). They flank two female and one male figure together with the Dioscuri. The three central figures are not the Capitoline triad because neither of the two women can be identified as Minerva. The left-hand woman stands between a bird (not a peacock) and a basket with fruit. The nude bearded male in the centre, damaged, has no surviving attributes. Between him and the woman to the right is a small animal, possibly a dog. Both women are similarly dressed. The main relief shows a sacrificial scene from the left side to the centre. In the centre a ram, an altar (or basket?) with fruit, and two attendants in front of a tabula ansata carried by four columns. On the right, husband, capite velato, and on the left, wife with incense burner. Next to her and approaching the centre from the left are a woman bearing a garland, an idealized youth, and Fortuna with turreted crown and cornucopiae. On the right portion of the frieze, the wedding of the deceased (dextrarum iunctio, Concordia between them) with attendants.

LIMC Helios/Sol 352; ASR 1.3, 224–5 no. 113, pl. 51.6, 65.1; Matern 2002: 75, 223 Q105.

Image: Arachne Fitt68-40-12_205039,02.jpg; D-DAI-ROM-7003_205039,13.jpg; arachne.dainst.org/entity/957370.

5.   Vatican, Museo Pio Clementino, Gabinetto delle Maschere, 800.
      Unknown.
      Marble.
      AD 180–190.
      Fragment of the lid of a sarcophagus; at the left end Sol (head restored) in a *quadriga*, nude but for a *chlamys*, whip in right hand, reins in left hand; below the front hooves of the horses: Oceanus; to the right of him one of the Dioscuri with a horse, then Jupiter, Juno, Minerva, and Fortuna; to the right of Fortuna a trace of the hindquarters of a horse, no doubt belonging to the second of the Dioscuri, while Luna in *biga* would have completed the scene.
      LIMC Helios/Sol 350; Amelung 1908 677–9 no. 426 pl. 78; ASR 1.3, 238 no. 154, pl. 51.4; Matern 2002: 75, 224 Q108.

6.   Plate 103.2
      Vatican, Museo Pio Clementino, Gabinetto delle Maschere 798.
      Unknown.

Marble.

AD 180–190.

Fragment of the lid of a sarcophagus; at the left end Sol, no rays, in a *quadriga*, nude but for a *chlamys*, whip in right hand, reins in left hand, preceded by Lucifer; below the front hooves of the horses: Oceanus or possibly Tellus, above whom one of the Dioscuri with a horse, and to the right of whom Caelus with his cloak billowing out over his head; to the right follow Minerva, Jupiter, Juno, and Fortuna.

LIMC Helios/Sol 350; LIMC Ouranos 7; Amelung 1908, 688–90 no. 430; ASR 1.3, 238 no. 155, pl. 51.5; Matern 2002: 75, 224 Q107.

Image: in the public domain.

7. Palermo, Museo Nazionale.
    Unknown.
    Marble.
    2nd c. AD

    Fragment of the lid of a sarcophagus; at the left end *quadriga* of Sol, preceded by Lucifer; below, Oceanus; to the right, Minerva.

    Matern 2002: 75, 223 Q102 (with refs.).

C3b2. Sol and Luna as Corner Masks of Sarcophagus Lids

1. Plates 26.7, 103.1, 104.1
    Paris, Louvre MA1335.
    St-Médard d'Eyrans.
    Marble.
    Ca. AD 225–250.

    Lid of an Endymion-sarcophagus; on the left-hand corner head/mask of Sol (thirteen rays), on the right-hand corner head of Luna.

    LIMC Helios/Sol 348; Matern 2002: 263 B129; Espérandieu II, 214–17 no. 1240; ASR 12.2, 126–7 no. 72.

    Image: © RMN-Grand Palais / Art Resource, NY; ART559881. Photograph: Hervé Lewandowski.

2. Plate 104.2
    Cambridge, Fitzwilliam Museum GR 48.1850.
    Acquired in Italy.
    Marble.
    Late 3rd–early 4th c. AD.

    Right front corner of a sarcophagus lid; head of Sol, long curly hair, radiate (four rays survive).

Budde & Nicholls 1964: 104–5 no. 164, pl. 47; Matern 2002: 259 B96.
Image: photograph courtesy Fitzwilliam Museum, CC BY-NC-ND licence.

3. Vatican, Museo Chiaramonti.
   Unknown.
   Marble.
   Late 3rd or 4th c. AD.
   Lid of a sarcophagus; on left-hand corner, head of Sol, radiate (four rays),
   on right-hand corner head of Luna.
   LIMC Helios/Sol 348; Himmelmann 1973: 31–34, pl. 36b (right half, Luna)
   and 55a (left half, Sol).

4. Plates 104.3, 104.4
   Avignon, Musée Calvet.
   Avignon.
   Marble.
   Ca. AD 300.
   Two fragments of a sarcophagus-lid, later reused for an inscription. On
   the right-hand corner, head of Sol, curly hair, four rays; on the left-hand
   corner, head of Luna.
   LIMC Helios/Sol 348; ASR 1.2, 144 no. 7
   Image: courtesy Calvet Museum.

5. Vatican, Museo Pio Cristiano.
   Unknown.
   Marble.
   2nd quarter 4th. c. AD.
   Fragment of the lid of a sarcophagus; left-hand corner, head of Sol, radi-
   ate (four rays remaining of originally 9 or 11); to the right, two scenes with
   Christ and one other, framed by trees. Rest broken off.
   Bovini & Brandenburg 1967: 102–3 no. 165, pl. 35 (with refs).

6. Rome, Palazzo Corsini.
   Rome, cemetery of S. Urbano.
   Marble.
   AD 310–320.
   Lid of sarcophagus; left corner bust of Sol, long curly hair, radiate; right
   corner Luna.
   Wrede 2001: 127–8 no. 21, pl. 19.1 (lid) and 19.2 (sarcophagus); Matern
   2002: 259 B103

C3b3. Sol and Luna on other Non-Mythological Sarcophagi

1.   Velletri, Museo Civico.
     Velletri.
     Marble.
     AD 140–150.
     Sarcophagus-relief with scenes from the underworld in two registers;
     above these: Caelus under an arch, between Sol, radiate (five rays), *chla-mys*, globe in left hand, whip in right, and Luna (each in a tympanum),
     two tritons under arches, and two eagles in tympanums.
     LIMC Helios/Sol 349; Matern 2002: 51 n. 376, 172, 260 B105.

2.   Rome, Museo Nazionale 124712.
     Rome, Via Aurelia.
     Marble.
     Ca. AD 180.
     Unfinished column sarcophagus with four arcades. In the two outer
     arcades: Dioscuri. In the two central arcades, the deceased couple, left
     in dextrarum iunctio (husband left, wife right) with Concordia and
     Hymenaeus; right bringing sacrifice on a burning altar (wife left, husband
     right) with two male figures in the background and a small cupido next to
     the wife. On the left short side of the sarcophagus Sol in rising *quadriga*,
     on the right short side Luna in rising *biga*, both executed very sketchily or
     unfinished.
     ASR 1.3, 218 no. 87, pl. 56.3, 58.5–6.

3.   Plate 102.3
     Pisa, Camposanto A6 Int.
     Unknown.
     Marble.
     AD 190–200.
     Sarcophagus relief. Strigilated sarcophagus with, on the left corner, a
     woman and attendant sacrificing; on the right corner a man and a cupid;
     in the centre two pillars connected by an arch, framing Amor and Psyche;
     above the capital of the left-hand pillar Sol in *quadriga* right, moving
     upward, above the right-hand pillar Luna in *biga* descending right.
     ASR 1.3, 207 no. 51, pl. 56.4 & 62.3 (with refs.).
     Image: Archivio Fotografico Opera del Duomo di Pisa.

4.   Plate 105.1
     Rome, Museo Nazionale, Terme di Diocleziano.
     Rome, Via Belluzzo, tomb D.

Marble.

Ca. AD 250.

Strigilated sarcophagus with two tondi. In the left-hand tondo, bust of Sol, radiate (five rays), *chlamys* and *chiton*, overly large raised right hand, whip in left In the right-hand tondo, Luna.

Matern 2002: 240 I54; Cianfriglia 1986: 130, figs. 589.

Image: © Museo Nazionale Romano, Terme di Diocleziano.

5.   Unknown.

Ağır Taş (Pisidia).

Limestone.

3rd c. AD.

Lid of a sarcophagus decorated with a gorgoneion between two winged Victories. In the left hand corner, frontal bust of Luna. In the right hand corner, frontal bust of Sol, radiate (nine rays).

Matern 2002: 260 B106.

C3b4. Sol (without Luna) on other Non-Mythological Sarcophagi

1.   Plate 105.2

Brignoles, Musée des Comtes de Provence

La Gayolle.

Marble.

2nd c. AD. The sarcophagus was reused in the 6th c. AD (inscription).

On the sarcophagus, from left to right: frontal bust of Sol in the upper left corner above the right arm of an angler. Sol, radiate nimbus (five rays), wears a *chlamys*. Next to Sol an angler standing, followed by three sheep and an anchor, below a bush with a bird facing right towards a standing female orant. A sheep emerges from behind the orant heading right, in front of a tree. In the centre (damaged) a seated philosopher with a pupil or orant. To the right of the latter a shepherd bearing a sheep on his shoulders and at the far right a bearded figure variously interpreted as Hades, the personification of a mountain, some deity, or the like.

Espérandieu I, p. 40–1 no. 40; Wilpert 1929/36: I, 7, 131 pl. 1.3; Wallraff 2001: 159–60, fig. 15; Matern 2002: 178 n. 976, 258 B93.

Image: © Musée des Comtes de Provence, Brignoles

2.   Vatican, Museo Pio Cristiano 119.

Vatican.

Marble.

290–300.

Sarcophagus-relief depicting various scenes from Scripture, of which the main one is the story of Jonah. Above the sails of the ship from which Jonah is thrown: bust of Sol, radiate nimbus, *chlamys*.
Wilpert 1929–32: I, 17, 26, 32, 109, 140, pl. 9.3; Bovini & Brandenburg 1967: 30–32 no. 35, pl. 11; Wallraff 2001, 160.

C3c. Stelai

1. Current location unknown?
   Eivili (Turkey).
   Marble.
   Late Hellenistic?
   Funerary relief. Head of Sol next to a man holding a lowered torch.
   LIMC Helios 306. Pfuhl/Möbius 123 no. 339.

2. Ankara, Archaeological Museum.
   Cotiaeum.
   Marble.
   Late Hellenistic?
   Funerary relief: small bust of Sol, radiate (?) nimbus, above busts of deceased couple.
   LIMC Helios 307.

3. Plate 106.1
   Vienna, Kunsthistorisches Museum I 1082. (formerly Battaglia Terme, Villa del Cataio).
   Unknown.
   Marble.
   1st c. BC (probably).
   Greek funerary relief; upper left-hand corner star and bust of Luna; upper right-hand corner bust of Sol, radiate (nine rays), *chlamys*, whip. Main field: horseman riding towards an altar; behind him a servant and two other figures.
   Dütschke 1882: 264–5 no. 671; LIMC Helios 305; LIMC Heros Equitans 358; Matern 2002: 169, 250 B43.
   Image: © KHM-Museumsverband, Wien.

4. Plate 106.2
   Bourges, Museum.
   Alléan.
   Limestone.

2nd c. AD.
Funerary stele. Portrait of a bearded man (head and upper body) holding a child in his right arm. In the tympanum, frontal bust of Sol, radiate, in a *quadriga*, two horses to the left, two to the right. Whip to the right of Sol.
Inscription: di(is) man(ibus) m(emoriae) priscini
Espérandieu II, 1510; LIMC Helios/Sol 219; Matern 2002: 215 Q49, fig. 8.
Image: © Museum, Bourges.

5. Current location unkown.
   Troad.
   Marble.
   2nd c. AD.
   Two pairs of horsemen below a bust of Sol, radiate.
   LIMC Helios 308; Matern 2002: 182 n. 991, 258–9 B95

6. Bursa, Museum 100.
   Bursa.
   Marble.
   2nd c. AD.
   Funerary relief. At the top, a *quadriga* right, above two busts. Below: bust of Helios between the Dioscuri.
   LIMC Helios 309; Matern 2002: 182 n. 991, 258 B94.

7. Plate 106.3
   Gaziantep, Museum 1749.
   Nisip.
   Limestone.
   Mid 2nd c. AD.
   Stele. Bust of Sol, radiate nimbus (nine rays), *chlamys*.
   Matern 2002: 177 n. 972, 182 n. 991, 259 B99.
   Image: Courtesy museum Gaziantep; photograph author.

8. Plate 107.1
   Langres, Museum 119.
   Langres, Citadel.
   Limestone.
   3rd c. AD.
   Upper part of a funerary stele; in the tympanum, bust of a man (the deceased?); on the acroteria the busts of Sol (right), radiate (five rays), *chlamys* (?), and Luna (left). Below the tympanum an inscription:

d(iis) m(anibus) pubilici(i) sarasi / et liberorum / eiius (sic) p(ublicius) sacrovirus / m(onumentum) p(osuit)
LIMC Helios/Sol 359; Matern 2002: 255 B72.
Image: © Musées de Langres-Photograph Caroline Lenoir.

9.   Munich, Glyptothek.
Asia Minor.
Marble.
3rd c. AD.
In lower field busts of a man and a women. In the upper field, triple Hecate between two goddesses (Demeter and Persephone?). Bust of Sol, radiate (five rays) rises up above the poloi (decorated with crescents) of triple Hecate.
LIMC Helios 310; Matern 2002: 182 n. 991, 259 B102.

10.   Hasanköy, Museum.
Akmoneia.
Marble.
3rd c. AD.
Fragment of an aedicula-shaped funerary relief. In the tympanum, bust of Mên; above the left-hand acroterion, bust of Sol, radiate, above the right-hand one bust of Luna.
LIMC Helios 313 (with lit.); Matern 2002: 182 n. 991, 259 B100.

11.   Plate 106.4
Istanbul, Archaeological Museum 5.
Cotiaeum.
Marble.
3rd c. AD.
Aedicula-shaped funerary relief; in the tympanum an eagle, below this Hecate triformis between Mên and a youth with a double axe; above the heads of Hecate, bust of Sol (?), radiate nimbus, above a crescent. Below the register with Hecate: busts of deceased couple.
LIMC Helios 311; Matern 2002: 182 n. 991, 185 n. 1020, 259 B101.
Image: D-DAI-IST-70-80_80557,01.jpg; arachne.dainst.org/entity/124233.

12.   Uşak, Museum.
Cotiaeum.
Marble.
3rd c. AD?

Funerary stele. Triple Hecate between two men; above her head, very shallow crescent below a bust of Sol, radiate. Below: busts of man and woman (the deceased).
LIMC Helios 312; Matern 2002: 182 n. 991, 260 B104.

13.   Sens, Museum.
Sens.
Stone.
Undated.
Fragment of a funerary relief with a beardless male bust on the left border of a deep niche, below which is a small radiate head of Sol.
Espérandieu IV, 42 no. 2825 (with ref. but no picture).

14.   Side, Museum 1631.
Unknown.
Marble.
Undated.
In the tympanum of a stele, bust of Sol, radiate nimbus (twelve rays), draped.
Matern 2002: 101 n. 578, 177 n. 972, 182 n. 991, 262–3 B126.

15.   Plate 108.1
Clermont-Ferrand, Musée Bargoin.
Gallo-Roman necropolis in the De la Liève district, Clermont-Ferrand.
Domite.
Second half of the 2nd c. AD.
Upper part of an aedicula-shaped funerary stele. In the tympanum, bust of Sol, radiate (five rays), *chlamys*; the bust is set slightly off-centre, and it may be that a whip was depicted in the space to the left of him, but there are no actual traces of this. Below, the stele is broken just below the head of a man in a niche.
Romeuf & Romeuf 1971.
Image: sketch after Romouf & Romeuf fig. 1.

C3d. Funerary Buildings or Monuments

1.   Plate 107.2
Vatican, Museo Gregoriano Profano Sezione X, inv. 10022.
Rome, Via Casilina, tomb of the Haterii.
Marble.
Ca. AD 100–125.

Fragments of a relief depicting the rape of Proserpina. In the upper part, to the right of a woman capite velato, Sol (?) in *quadriga*; only the torso of Sol and the hindquarters of the horses are preserved, but for Sinn & Freyberger (1996: 60) the identity of Sol is "zweifelsfrei".
Sinn & Freyberger 1996: 59–63 no. 7, pls. 1719.1, esp. pl. 18.1; Matern 2002: 189, 284 K43.
Image: photograph author.

2.   Plate 107.3
Igel, in situ.
Sandstone.
2nd c. AD.
Large funerary monument. In the N. tympanum, a frontal bust of Sol, radiate tent-like nimbus (eleven rays), *chlamys*, in frontal *quadriga* (protomes of two horses to the left, two to the right). In the S. tympanum: bust of Luna above the protomes of two bulls.
LIMC Helios/Sol 220; Matern 2002: 215 Q51 (with refs.).
Image: courtesy Landesmuseum Trier.

C3e. Other
1.   Cadenet.
In situ?
Local rock.
Undated.
Fragment of a relief cut into the face of a cliff, apparently in connection with a funerary monument; preserved are the busts of Sol and Luna.
LIMC Helios/Sol 305.

2.   Sicca Veneria (El Khef), Tunisia.
Sicca Veneria.
Stone.
Undated.
Funerary altar (?). In a niche, two men (only the upper part preserved). Above (from left to right): bust of Luna (facing left), Lucifer (facing left), full-figure, with torch, an eight-pointed star, and bust of Sol (facing left), radiate (six or seven rays).
LIMC Helios/Sol 360.

3.   Plate 109.1
Maarrat al-Nu'man, Museum.

Khirbat Bābūlīn (Syria).

Chalky marl.

Mid 3rd c. AD.

Section of a series of reliefs, illegally hacked out of an underground chamber tomb after it was discovered in 1985 during terracing work. Sol, radiate (seventeen rays), wearing a long, sleeved *chiton* and *chlamys*, stands in a frontal split chariot with his right hand raised, and holds a torch in his left hand. Two horses are jumping to the left, and two to the right, granting full view on the front of his 'chariot,' actually a rather stylized palmette, arranged much like a fan; no wheels. There is a parallel relief of Luna in a closely similar chariot, drawn by two bulls.

Chéhadeh & Griesheimer 1998.

Image: courtesy of the Maarrat al-Nu'man, Museum.

C3f. Funerary Altar

1. Plates 108.2, 108.3

    Paris, Louvre 1443.

    Rome.

    Marble.

    Last quarter 1st c. AD.

    Funerary altar of Julia Victorina, portrayed on one side with radiate crown and on the other with crescent moon. D(is) M(anibus) / Iuliae Victorinae / quae vix(it) ann(os) X mens(es) V / C(aius) Iulius Saturninus et / Lucilia Procula parentes / filiae dulcissimae fecerunt.

    LIMC Helios/Sol 454.

    Image: © RMN-Grand Palais / Hervé Lewandowski / Art Resource, NY, ART179237

2. Adamclisi, Museum 20460.

    Independenta.

    Limestone.

    Undated.

    Altar without inscription. On the upper moulding, above a garland hanging between two bulls' heads, small frontal bust of Sol, radiate nimbus (12? rays), *chlamys*.

    Covacef 2002: 225 n. 202; Lupa 21309.

    Image: Lupa.at/21309 (February 1, 2019).

C4. Other Reliefs or Reliefs of Unknown Function

1. Capua, Museo Campano.

    Capua.

Terracotta.

4th c. BC.

Oscan "Iovila" with frontal face of Sol, long wavy hair, completely surrounded by rays. On the reverse a sketch, incised, of a sacrificial animal. Inscription, repeated on each side: kluvatiium / pumperias pustm[-.

LIMC Helios/Sol 41; Franchi de Bellis 1981: 87–9 no. 2 fig. 2; Zavaroni 2006; Sampaolo 2016.

2. Brindisi, Museo Archeologico Provinciale 656.

Apulia.

Terracotta.

1st c. BC (Gundel); late Hellenistic (LIMC Semele); 3rd c. AD (LIMC Helios).

Large disc with 11 signs of the zodiac along the edge (libra missing). In the centre a figure in a *quadriga* led by Hermes and surrounded by a variety of figures and symbols, including the busts of Sol (above left) with a radiate nimbus and Luna (above right).

LIMC Helios 299; LIMC Semele 23; LIMC Dioskouroi 237; Gundel 1992: 237 no. 95, cf. 260–2 no. 192.

3. Venice, Museo Archeologico Nazionale 163.

Rome.

Marble.

AD 50–75.

Three-sided candelabrum. On the base, on all three sides, upper body of Sol, emerging from vegetation. He wears a *chiton* and is radiate (eight rays).

Matern 2002: 263 B132.

4. Plates 109.2, 109.3

Museu Nacional Arqueològic de Tarragona 45405.

Tarragona, Roman Villa.

Marble.

Last quarter 1st–1st quarter 2nd c. AD (on sculptural and stylistic grounds, cf. Koppel 1992: 141).

Fragmentarily preserved rectangular shield of a statue. In the upper part, Sol ascends a *quadriga* to the right. Sol, radiate, is nude but for a *chlamys*, holds the reins in his left hand and a whip (?) in his right hand. A small, winged nude figure flies above the horses before him. Oceanus reclines below the chariot. In the centre of the shield: head of Medusa. In the lower part, Luna rides her *biga* to the left. Tellus reclines below her.

Matern 2002: 75–6, 224–5 Q111, fig. 20 (with refs.); Koppel 1992.
Image: © MNAT/ R. Cornadó.

5.   Rome, Museo Torlonia 375.
       Rome, Villa dei Quintili.
       Marble.
       2nd c. AD.
       Charioteer riding left in a *quadriga*; stylized waves below the horses. The
       identification of the charioteer as Sol cannot be certain. His head, neck,
       part of his upper body, and left arm with folds of his toga are all modern
       restorations. As restored, his clothing (toga, no *chlamys*) is incompatible
       with Sol, but it is not impossible that he originally was dressed in a *chi-
       ton*. This is certainly the impression one gets from the vertical folds of
       clothing behind the outer horse's tail which-taken alone-would suggest
       a *chiton*. Furthermore the waves below the horses imply a deity, and Sol
       would be a logical candidate.
       Matern 2002: 65, 85, 218–9 Q70.

6.   Plate 111.1
       Avenches (Switzerland), Musée Romain SA/201.
       Aventicum (Avenches).
       Limestone.
       2nd c. AD.
       Fragment of a relief, depicting the frontal head of Sol, very long curly hair,
       radiate (over thirteen rays).
       LIMC Helios/Sol 3; Bossert 1998: 84–5 no. 38, pls. 30–31; Matern 2002: 263
       B127.
       Image: © AVENTICVM-Site et Musée romains d'Avenches.

7.   Plate 110.1
       Rouen, Musée Métropolitain R.91.173.
       Lillebonne.
       Limestone.
       2nd c. AD.
       Stele; bust of Sol, *chlamys*, radiate nimbus (seven rays). Discovered in
       1864 in a Roman villa. Suggestions, based on this relief, that the villa con-
       tained a Mithraeum are possible, but by no means certain. In the vicinity
       were a bust of a bearded figure (Poirel fig. 3) and a fragment of drapery,
       neither of which can be securely linked to a Mithraic context.
       LIMC Helios/Sol 28; Walters 1974: 124–5 no. 52, pl. 27; Poirel 1999; Matern
       2002: 178 n. 976, 257 B85 (incorrect number of rays).
       Image: © Musée-Métropole-Rouen-Normandie-Cliché Yohann Deslandes.

8. Plates 9.4, 110.4
   Cologne, Römisch-germanisches Museum 442.
   Cologne, Neumarkt (sw corner).
   Limestone.
   3rd quarter of the 2nd c. AD.
   Pilaster with reliefs on three sides in three registers; lower part of the botton register lost. Lower register: Mars, Venus, Fortuna; central register: Victory, Vulcan, Sol, radiate nimbus (9? rays), nude but for a *chlamys*, whip in right hand; upper register: Juno, Ceres, Minerva.
   LIMC Helios/Sol 258; Bauchhenß-Noelke 1981: 472–3 no. 172; Matern 2002: 89, 174 n. 957, 225 G1.
   Image: © Rheinisches Bildarchiv 022 381.

9. Plate 110.2
   Trier, Rheinisches Landesmuseum 1882.
   Trier, "near the baths".
   Limestone.
   2nd c. AD.
   Base; front: lion, snake in tree, crater; right side: bust of Sol emerging from leaves, radiate nimbus, *chlamys*; left side: Luna; rear: two cypresses.
   LIMC Helios/Sol 325; Merkelbach 1984: 338 fig. 94a (descriptions inverted); Matern 2002: 258 B87 (inaccurate references).
   Image: © GDKE/Rheinisches Landesmuseum Trier; photo: Th. Zühmer.

10. Plate 110.3
    Brooklyn, Brooklyn Museum 62.148.
    Behnesa (Oxyrrhynchos).
    Marble.
    2nd c. AD.
    Pediment (?) fragment consisting of a 3/4 bust of Sol, long wavy hair, radiate nimbus (seven rays), and *chiton* fastened at both shoulders.
    LIMC Helios 286; Matern 2002: 57, 174, 261–2 B118.
    Image: Brooklyn Museum, Charles Edwin Wilbour Fund, cc-by.

11. Hatra, Area II, room 18.
    In situ.
    Graffito on stone.
    2nd c. AD?
    Busts of Luna (right) and Sol (left), radiate (14? rays), within a zodiac circle (order of the signs unconventional, some signs lost or not executed?).
    Gundel 1992, 228 no. 70.

12.   Khirbet Abû Dûhûr.
In situ.
Rock.
August, AD 147.
Grafitto of a temple; in the tympanum radiate head between eagles.
LIMC Helios in per. or. 30; Langner 2001, no. 1245.

13.   Plate III.2
St.-Germain-en-Laye, Musée d'Archéologie Nationale 70062.
Entrains.
Sandstone.
2nd–3rd c. AD.
Relief, discovered in context with various Mithraic reliefs, depicting Sol on a frontal *quadriga*; the upper part of the relief, including the head of Sol is lost. In front of the *quadriga*: a krater and a snake. Next to Sol, above the two right hand horses, a bust (head lost), unidentifiable.
LIMC Helios/Sol 306; Espérandieu III, 258–9 no. 2273; CIMRM I, 942, fig. 233; Matern 2002: 214 Q41 (with incorrect current location).
Image: © Musée d'Archéologie Nationale, St.-Germain-en-Laye.

14.   Frankfurt a.M., Archäologisches Museum X8382 (destroyed in WWII).
Heddernheim.
Sandstone.
2nd–3rd c. AD. Found in a well together with a similar relief of Luna (or perhaps a male, Celtic moon-god) and the remains of two Jupiter-pillars, one of which bears a dedication dated March 13th 240, thus giving a terminus post quem for the burial.
Bust of Sol (?) or more likely a local, Celtic solar god in view of the strange object in his right hand; radiate, five rays.
LIMC Helios/Sol 33; Huld-Zetsche 1994: 45, 164 fig. 79

15.   Novae, depot.
Novae, sector 9, square 3, no. 155.
Stone.
2nd–3rd c. AD?
Fragment of a relief, showing part of a face (left eye) and one large ray (?) consisting of 6 lines; interpreted as the face of the Sun and connected with the cult of Mithras by the excavators.
LIMC Helios/Sol 6.

16. Plate 111.3
    Private collection, on loan to Metropolitan Museum of Art, New York (L.1993.85).
    Unknown.
    Marble.
    2nd–3rd c. AD; 1st c. AD (E. Moormann, pers. com.).
    Body of a cithara, decorated in relief. In the centre, frontal bust of Sol, radiate (seven rays), above the protomes of four horses. To the left, part of a Marsyas-scene, depicting the Scythian sharpening the blade for the flaying of Marsyas. Marsyas himself, to the right, is lost. The cithara presumably formed part of a colossal marble statue of Apollo.
    Unpublished.
    Image: photograph courtesy Metropolitan Museum of Art, New York, L36573/4438; with permission.

17. Épinal, Museum.
    Escles.
    Sandstone.
    3rd c. AD.
    Apex of the tympanum of a stele, frontal face of Sol, radiate (twelve rays).
    LIMC Helios/Sol 221; Espérandieu VI, 146 no. 4793; Matern 2002: 259 B98.

18. Plate 111.4
    Brussels, Royal Museums of Fine Arts B 206c.
    Virton.
    Limestone.
    3rd c. AD.
    Sol in *quadriga* (head of 4th horse missing) right, radiate nimbus (seven rays), nude but for *chlamys*, whip in right hand, reins (?) in left. Face of Sol damaged. Right side of relief damaged.
    LIMC Helios/Sol 142; Matern 2002: 66, 217 Q62.
    Image: © Royal Museums, Brussels, 4592.

19. Plate 6.3
    Corbridge, Corbridge Roman Site Museum.
    Corbridge.
    Stone.
    3rd c. AD.
    Plaque with frontal bust of Sol, radiate nimbus.

LIMC Helios/Sol 32.
Image: courtesy Roman Site Museum, Corbridge.

20.   New York, Art Market.
       Unkown.
       Basalt.
       3rd c. AD.
       Bust of Sol, radiate nimbus (eleven rays), *chlamys*.
       Matern 2002 263 B128.

21.   Plates 111.5
       Rome, Forum Romanum.
       In situ.
       Marble.
       November 20th, 303.
       Decennalia-base. Constantius Chlorus in the act of bringing sacrifice, in
       the presence of various gods; at the right Roma "velificans" with a frontal
       bust of Sol, radiate (nine rays) decorating her mantle. Gundel (1992, 305
       no. 363) suggests that Roma's billowing mantle may symbolize a "bildlose
       Zodiakos". In the 16th c. there were still traces visible of a female bust next
       to Sol; cf. Wrede 1981a: 122 n. 78.
       LIMC Helios/Sol 223; Wrede 1981a: 122; Kalas 2015: 34–42; Matern 2002:
       263 B131.
       Image: Photograph author.

22.   Plates 112.1, 112.2
       Paris, Bibliothèque Nationale de France, Cabinet des Médailles 57.86.
       Unknown.
       Marble.
       4th c. AD.
       Hexagonal plaque decorated in low relief. To the left, Cybele is seated on
       her throne between two lions (lion on the left broken away completely).
       On the apex of the throne: decorative element consisting of a small fron-
       tal head of Sol, radiate. Behind Cybele a dancing girl with cymbals, nim-
       bate, and next to her a dancing Corybant. To the right, Attis seated on a
       rock, supported by a Corybant.
       LIMC Helios/Sol 224 (with refs.); DA I 2, 1689 fig. 2250.
       Image: © BNF-Cabinet des Médailles.

23. Xanten, Museum, lost (destroyed in WWII).
    Xanten.
    Limestone.
    Undated.
    Stele; in tympanum frontal bust of Sol, radiate (seven rays); below, an illegible inscription.
    LIMC Helios/Sol 222; Espérandieu Recueil IX, 6591.

24. Athens, National Archaeological Museum Kar. 608.
    Unknown.
    Bronze.
    Undated.
    Bronze plaque; on the left-hand side two zones, the one above the other, with Helios-busts in one zone and Cybele-busts in the other. On the right-hand side four pairs of Cybele-busts.
    LIMC Helios 317.

25. As-Suwayda, Museum.
    'Aïn Zeman.
    Basalt.
    Undated.
    Rectangular cippus; on one side eagle and thunderbolt, on the other side bust of Sol, radiate nimbus, *chlamys*, above the bust of Luna (?).
    LIMC Helios in per. or. 5.

26. As-Suwayda, Museum.
    Si'â.
    Basalt.
    Undated.
    Fragment of a relief consisting of the head of a beardless youth with short, stylized curls and the remnants of a headdress interpreted as being a radiate nimbus.
    LIMC Helios in per. or. 37.

27. As-Suwayda, Museum.
    Si'â.
    Basalt.
    Undated.
    Bust of Helios, radiate nimbus (ten rays), draped.
    LIMC Helios in per. or. 22.

28. Plate 112.3
     Escolives-Sainte-Camille, Museum.
     Escolives-Sainte-Camille.
     Limestone.
     2nd c. AD.
     Bust of Sol, radiate nimbus (thirteen rays), *chlamys*, in a niche.
     Lupa 25729.
     Image: Lupa.at/25729 photograph Ortolf Harl.

29. Plates 113.1, 113.2
     Burgos, Church of S. Maria en Quintanilla de las Viñas.
     In situ.
     6th c. AD? or late 7th–early 8th c. AD (CSIR, tentatively).
     Limestone.
     Two lintels supporting an arch. On one lintel, imago clipeata of Sol, radi-
     ate (nine rays), long-haired, clean shaven. Inscription s // ol. Two angels
     carry the clipeus. On the upper border, a dedicatory inscription: (h)oc
     exiguum exigua off(ert) Δ(= d?)o(mina?) flammola votum d(?)(eo) (This
     small vow the unworthy (exigua) lady Flammola offers to God). The final
     D is not much more than a line extending from the top of the M, and may
     be spurious. The CSIR reads Δ(e)o instead of Δo(mina) and votum as the
     final word. On the other lintel, similar depiction of Luna with crescent;
     inscription lu // na. Luna appears to have a short beard.
     CSIR España II, 2, pp. 114–132 no. C8, pp. 355–6, pl. LVII.
     Image: photographs courtesy J. Lendering.

30. Plate 112.4
     München Staatliche Antikensammlungen und Glyptothek 557.
     Unknown.
     Marble.
     2nd–3rd c. AD.
     Facing bust of Sol, *chlamys*, long wavy hair, *anastole*, with holes for at
     least ten rays.
     Fendt & Knauß 2012, 314 fig. 21.13 cat. 382.
     Image: Staatliche Antikensammlungen und Glyptothek, photograph
     Renate Kühling.

31. Plate 112.5
     Apamea, Syria.
     Apamea.

Roman Imperial.
Marble.
Bust of Helios, radiate nimbus (nine rays), *chlamys*.
Unpublished?
Image: photograph courtesy J. Lendering.

32. Manisa, Museum inv. 6398.
Unknown.
Marble.
2nd c. AD.
Heavily damaged votive (?) altar with images on four sides. Front: dancing Maenad; left side: bust of Sol, radiate (nine rays) above a lion and
an unidentified animal; rear: female figure with polos and crescent; right
side: a deer attacked by a feline predator.
Malay 1994: 66–7, 161, pl. 22; Matern 2002: 255, B73.

33. Unknown.
Avdan-Teşvikiye.
Tufo.
Undated
Bust of Sol above a globe, on a cylindrical altar; next to Sol a female bust,
possibly Luna.
Matern 2002: 258, B90; Haspels 1971: 167, 200, fig. 283.

C5. Not or Probably Not Sol (Selection)

1. Plate 4.3
Delos, Museum A2915–2917.
Delos, Maison de Fourni.
Marble.
Hellenistic.
Fragment of a relief, showing the head and shoulders of Apollo-Helios,
radiate (seven rays), *chlamys*, quiver.
LIMC Helios 139; Marcadé 1973: 357–360.
Image: photograph after Plassart 1916: fig.20.

2. Delphi, Museum 9449.
Delphi, Hermeion-terrace.
Marble.
Early Hellenistic.

Fragment of a relief; head of Apollo-Helios, radiate, laurel wreath, cithara; Hermes.

LIMC Apollon 475.

3.   Istanbul, Archaeology Museum 36552.
      Troy.
      Terracotta.
      Late 2nd–1st c. BC.
      Helios-Apollo in *quadriga* to left, *chlamys*, *chiton*, impossible to make out whether he was radiate or bare-headed (relief broken at top of head), with a cithara in his hands. Mirror Image of the famous metope from Troy, now in Berlin, depicting Helios/Apollo.
      LIMC Helios 383; Thompson 1963: 143 no. 297.

4.   Damascus, National Museum C7939.
      Unknown, possibly environs of Homs.
      Basalt.
      AD 30/1.
      Male bust (face hacked away), radiate nimbus and crescent, *chlamys*, armor; in upper right-hand corner a snake (corresponding left-hand corner missing). Below the bust: seven small male busts, the three at the left facing right, the four at the right facing left. Below these, inscription dedicating the relief Ἡλίῳ θεῷ μεγίστῳ. The seven busts, as far as I can make out from the photograph in the LIMC, are all male, and have no specific attributes distinguishing the one from the other. The suggestion that they represent the planetary deities thus seems improbable.
      LIMC Helios 385; LIMC Helios in per. or. 60 (with lit.).

5.   Palmyra, Museum.
      Palmyra.
      Limestone.
      1st c. AD.
      Octagonal altar, three sides of which were originally decorated with standing deities, one of which is still preserved: standing deity, radiate (9? rays), *chlamys*, armor, lance.
      LIMC Helios in per. or. 44.

6.   Palmyra, Museum 6534 (B 1734).
      Sanctuary of Nabû.
      Limestone.

1st c. AD.

Fragment of a niche: bust of a deity, radiate nimbus (thirteen rays), *chlamys*, armor, between two eagles.

LIMC Helios in per. or. 17.

7. Palmyra, Museum 6850.
Palmyra, Temple of Ba'alshamin.
Limestone.
First half 1st c. AD.
Lintel: bust of a deity, radiate nimbus (27 rays), *chlamys*, armor, beside an eagle.
LIMC Helios in per. or. 1a.

8. Palmyra Museum 7955 (2226 B).
Palmyra, temple of Nabû.
Limestone.
2nd c. AD.
Fragment of a relief ("medallion"): bust of a deity, radiate nimbus (24 rays), *chlamys*, armor.
LIMC Helios in per. or. 35.

9. Palmyra, Museum 7971 (2232 B).
Palmyra, temple of Nabû.
Marble.
2nd c. AD.
Stele: deity, radiate nimbus, *chlamys*, armor, lance.
LIMC Helios in per. or. 46.

10. Plate 114.1
Berlin, Staatliche Museen, Ägyptisches Museum 10314.
Fayum.
Terracotta.
2nd c. AD?
Bust of a beardless man, long curly hair, radiate nimbus (six rays) with at the top a disc between two plumes and horns, *chlamys*, right hand raised, crocodile in left hand; to be identified as Souchos.
LIMC Souchos 25.
See also Cairo, Eg. Mus. CG 26902, LIMC Souchos 24.
Image: © Foto: Ägyptisches Museum und Papyrussammlung der Staatlichen Museen zu Berlin-Preußischer Kulturbesitz; photographer unknown.

11.   Cairo, Egyptian Museum CG 27569 (JE 30001).
       unknown.
       Limestone.
       3rd c. AD.
       Throning figure with staff, radiate nimbus, interpreted as "Caracalla-Sol",
       with soldiers standing around.
       LIMC Helios/Sol 428.

12.   Plate 114.2
       New Haven, Yale University Museum 1938:5312.
       Dura Europos.
       Limestone.
       AD 228/9.
       Standing Nemesis and a dedicant by an altar; between them a male bust
       (face hacked away), radiate nimbus, *chlamys*, armor.
       LIMC Helios in per. or. 3.
       Image: photograph courtesy Yale University Art Museum.

13.   Damascus, National Museum 5216.
       Khirbet Wadi Suwân.
       Limestone.
       Undated.
       Allat (left) and dedicant (right), by an altar, flank a sun-god, radiate
       nimbus (15? rays), right hand raised, torch in left hand, *chlamys*, richly
       decorated sleeved *chiton* with an elaborate belt. The presence of Allat
       suggests that this is Shamash, but this would then be the only case in
       which Shamash is depicted unarmed.
       LIMC Helios in per. or. 41a (with refs.).

14.   Damascus, National Museum.
       Khirbet Wadi Suwân.
       Limestone.
       Undated.
       Standing god, radiate nimbus, dressed in *chlamys* and Roman armor,
       holding an upright spear in his right hand (legs, left hand, and face lost);
       to the left: Allat.
       LIMC Helios in per. or. 42.

15.   Present location unknown.
       Mashara (Golan).
       Stone.

Undated.
Radiate bust on a crescent accompanied by bearded god and Luna.
LIMC Helios in per. or. 24.

16. Present location unknown.
Palmyra.
Stone.
Undated.
Fragment of a relief depicting a male deity, radiate, *chlamys*, armor.
LIMC Helios in per. or. 45.

17. Antioch.
Unknown.
Stone.
Undated.
Altar of the Heliopolitan triad; among the figures represented: radiate god on a chariot drawn by two griffons.
LIMC Helios in per. or. 55.

18. Plate 114.3
Châtillon-sur-Seine, Museum.
Essarois.
Limestone.
Undated.
Fragment of a votive relief; in the pediment, frontal bust, radiate (four of seven rays surviving), winged, of Apollo Vindonnus, a Gallo-Roman deity with a temple at Essarois. Inscription: [deo apollini vind]onno et fontibus / [...... p]risci (filius) v(otum) s(olvit) l(ibens) m(erito).
Espérandieu IV, 354–5 nr 3414.
Image: © Museum, Châtillon-sur-Seine; photographer unknown.

19. Lost.
Galilea.
Limestone.
Undated.
Frontal bust of Sol above a chariot drawn by two eagles.
LIMC Helios in. per. or. 38.

20. Ferzol, near Baalbek.
In situ.
Natural rock.

Undated.

Radiate horseman by a date-palm, accompanied by a nude Genius.

LIMC Helios in per. or. 50.

D. Mosaics and Opus Sectile

D1. Sol and Zodiac

D1a. Sol Alone, with Zodiac

1. Plate 114.4

    Bonn, Rheinisches Landesmuseum 31.184–185.

    Münster-Sarmsheim.

    Polychrome tessellae.

    3rd c. AD.

    Sol, radiate nimbus (nine rays), nude but for *chlamys*, whip in right hand, in *quadriga* with four rearing horses (two to the left, two to the right), within a zodiac circle (some signs missing).

    LIMC Helios/Sol 291; Gundel 1992: 234 no. 84; Krueger 1973; Matern 2002: 53, 214 Q40.

    Image: photograph Arachne D-DAI-ROM-64_704; arachne.dainst.org/entity/660827.

2. Plates 12.1, 115.1, 115.2

    Hammath-Tiberias, Synagogue.

    In situ.

    Polychrome tessellae.

    4th century AD (terminus ante quem AD 395).

    Synagogue floor with three panels. Central panel depicts Sol, radiate nimbus (seven rays), sleeved *chiton* and *chlamys*, right hand raised, globe in left hand, in frontal *quadriga* within zodiac circle; busts of the seasons in corners.

    LIMC Helios/Sol 292; Gundel 1992: 236 no. 91. On the date: Magness 2005: 813.

    Image D1a.2a: Wikimedia Commons, photograph Bukvoed, CC-BY3.0; https://commons.wikimedia.org/wiki/File:Hamat-Tiberias-132.jpg (February 1, 2019).

    Image D1a.2b: Wikimedia Commons, photograph ניר ר, CC-BY-SA4.0; https://commons.wikimedia.org/wiki/Category:Hamat_Tiberias_mosaic (February 1, 2019).

3. Plate 120.2

    Astypalaia, Maltezana, Tallaras Baths.

    In situ.

    Polychrome tessellae.

4th–5th c. AD?
Bust of Sol, draped, radiate crown, right hand raised, globe in left hand within a zodiac circle set in a square with the busts of the four seasons in the four corners.
Jacoby 2001.

4. Huseifa, Synagogue.
    In situ?
    Polychrome tessellae.
    c. 5th c. AD.
    Synagogue floor, very poorly preserved, with two panels. The main (eastern) panel preserves traces of a zodiac circle, possibly around a depiction of Sol in frontal *quadriga*.
    LIMC Helios/Sol 292; Gundel 1992: 236 no. 89.

5. Plate 116.1
    Sepphoris, synagogue.
    In situ.
    Polychrome tessellae.
    Early 5th c. AD (Weiss); 6th c. AD (Ma'oz 2015).
    Elaborate synagogue floor. Main panel: zodiac circle around a frontal chariot bearing a radiate disc (eight rays) atop a post; crescent moon and star in field. In the corners the four seasons (busts). For a similar depiction of the sun as a star in a chariot, cf. an altar in Berlin, Antikensammlung AvP VII 420, from Pergamon, date uncertain.
    Weiss & Netzer 1996 (esp. 26–29); Weiss 2005: 55–161, 225–262; Ma'oz 2015.
    Image: sketch drawing © Zoë Hijmans.

6. Plate 117.1
    Beth Alpha, Synagogue.
    In situ.
    Polychrome tessellae.
    6th c. AD.
    Synagogue floor with three panels. Central panel depicts Sol, radiate (six rays) in frontal *quadriga* (stars and crescent in field) within zodiac circle; busts of the seasons in the four corners.
    LIMC Helios/Sol 292; Gundel 1992: 234–6 no. 87.
    Image: Wikimedia Commons, photograph Anatavital, CC-BY-SA3.0; https://commons.wikimedia.org/wiki/File:Beth_Alfa_Synagogue_Mosaic_13.JPG.

7.   Naʾaran (Ain Douq), Synagogue.
      In situ?
      Polychrome tessellae.
      c. 6th c. AD.
      Synagogue floor, poorly preserved (images apparently wilfully destroyed).
      The main preserves traces of 9 of the 12 zodiac signs in a circle around a
      depiction of Sol, radiate (about eleven rays) in frontal *quadriga*. In the
      four corners: busts of the seasons.
      LIMC Helios/Sol 292; Gundel 1992: 236 no. 88.

8.   Huqoq, Synagogue.
      In situ.
      Polychrome tessellae.
      Early 5th c. AD.
      Partially preserved mosaic floor in the main nave of the synagogue,
      consisting of five panels depicting (from N. to S.): Noah's Ark; Egyptian
      soldiers drowning in the Red Sea; Sol within a circle of medallions con-
      taining signs of the Zodiac. Of Sol only the four (!)-wheeled *quadriga*,
      most of the four horses (two jumping to the left, two to the right, with
      the inner horses looking inward) a crescent slightly to the left of the
      chariot, some stars and two long rays are perserved. Whether the sun was
      depicted in his Graeco-roman anthropomorph guise, or as a disc atop a
      pole, as in Sepphoris, can no longer be ascertained.
      Magness et al. 2018: 106–111.

      D1b. Sol and Luna, with Zodiac or similar

1.   Sparta.
      In situ.
      Polychrome tessellae.
      Shortly after AD 325.
      Frontal busts of Luna (upturned crescent behind her shoulders) and Sol
      (not radiate) within zodiac circle; the four Winds in the corners.
      Gundel 1992: 234 no. 85; Panayotopoulou, 1998: 117 fig. 10.2; LIMC
      Helios 290.

2.   Plate 118.2
      Beit She'an, Monastery of St. Mary.
      In situ.

Polychrome tessellae.

Late 6th c. AD.

Frontal busts of Sol, radiate (seven rays), *chiton* and *chlamys*, torch, and Luna (upturned crescent on head and torch), within a circle of full-figure personifications of the 12 months.

LIMC Helios/Sol 401.

Image: in the public domain.

D2. Planetary Deities

1. Plate 118.1

    Itálica, Casa del Planetario, oecus.

    In situ.

    Polychrome tessellae.

    Second half 2nd c. AD.

    Planetary deities. The bust of Sol has a radiate nimbus with twelve rays.

    Matern 2002: 266 B154; Durán 1993: 73–5, 337 no. 13 pl. 18.

    Image: © 123RF 21751635 / J.R. Pizarro.

2. Itálica, private collection.

    Itálica.

    Polychrome tessellae.

    2nd c. AD.

    Four panels of a mosaic depicting busts of the planetary deities. Fully preserved are Sol, radiate (seven rays), *chlamys*, whip, and Luna; Saturn (falx) is partially preserved as is a fourth bust, probably female and therefore Venus.

    Blanco Freijero 1978: 36–7 no. 12; Matern 2002: 174 n. 957, 266 B155.

3. Tunis, Bardo Museum A 10.

    Bir Chana, villa, oecus.

    Polychrome tessellae.

    2nd c. AD.

    In the centre, geometrical group of seven hexagonal panels with the planetary deities (Saturn in centre), around which various panels with animals and the twelve signs of the zodiac are grouped. The mosaic as a whole is also hexagonal.

    LIMC Helios/Sol 273; Gundel 1992: 144 fig. 62; 266 no. 210; Matern 2002: 174 n. 957, 266 B158.

4.   Plate 119.1
     Boscéaz (Orbe, Switzerland), Roman villa.
     in situ.
     Polychrome tessellae.
     AD 200–225.
     Octagonal panel with Sol, radiate (eleven rays), nude but for a *chlamys*,
     whip in right hand, reins in raised left hand, in *quadriga* right The other
     octagons contain the planetary deities, of whom Venus occupies the cen-
     tral octagon in the room, as well as Narcissus, Ganymede, and groups of
     Nereids and Tritons
     LIMC Helios/Sol 272; Dunbabin 1999: 79 fig. 82, pl. 11; Matern 2002: 66,
     217 Q61.
     Image: photograph courtesy J. Lendring.

5.   Lost.
     Sainte-Colombe, Isère, Roman villa.
     Polychrome Tessellae.
     Undated.
     Celestial globe surrounded by the seven planetary deities, only two of
     whom survived when the mosaic was uncovered. They are full-figure and
     difficult to identify from the drawings, but one may be Sol.
     Artaud [nd] pl. XXII; Blanchet & Lafaye 1909: 46 no. 203; Blanchet 1913: 111;
     Duval 1953: 290; Lancha 1977: 179–82 pls. 989.

          D3. Sol and Seasons
1.   Plate 119.2
     Silin (near Leptis Magna), Roman villa.
     In situ.
     Polychrome tessellae.
     3rd–4th c. AD?
     Sol, radiate nimbus (eleven rays), nude but for a *chlamys*, whip over
     shoulder in right hand, reins in left hand emerging in the sky with his
     quadriga right, preceded by a winged Lucifer (?) with a double aulos,
     above the main scene (Horae with Aion).
     LIMC Helios/Sol 199; Gundel 1992: 302 no. 351.
     Image: photograph courtesy J. Lendering.

2.   Plate 119.3
     El Jem, Museum.

El Jem/Thysdrus, House of Silenus.

Polychrome tessellae.

Late 3rd–early 4th c. AD.

Busts of Sol (nimbate, *chlamys*), Luna, and seasons around central panel with bearded Aion.

LIMC Helios/Sol 400; LIMC Aion 4.

Image: Wikimedia commons / Maciej Szczepanczyk CC-BY2.5.

D4. Phaethon

1. Sens, Museum.

   Sens.

   Polychrome tessellae.

   2nd c. AD.

   Mosaic, partially damaged, depicting the myth of Phaethon; Sol, nude, on horseback, whip in right hand, tames the runaway horses of his *quadriga*. In the corners the four seasons.

   LIMC Helios/Sol 171; Matern 2002: 186, 280 K18.

2. Plate 119.4

   El Jem, Museum.

   Bararus/Henchir Rougga.

   Polychrome tessellae.

   Late 2nd–early 3rd c. AD.

   Fall of Phaethon and other scenes of Phaethon myth, including Sol, seated on a throne, nude but for a *chlamys*, radiate (twelve rays), right hand raised, torch in his left hand.

   LIMC Phaethon I, 2bis; Slim 2003.

   Image: photograph courtesy Zaher Kammoun.

D5. Other Mosaics with Sol

1. Plate 120.1

   Mérida, Casa del Mitreo.

   In situ.

   Polychrome tessellae.

   Mid 2nd c. AD.

   Large cosmological mosaic, partially destroyed, with a range of mainly cosmic personifications. Fairly high to the left: Sol, radiate nimbus (eleven rays), long *chiton* and *chlamys*, whip in right hand, on *quadriga* right, identified as ORIENS. Luna is depicted on the right in her *biga*.

LIMC Helios/Sol 341; Quet 1981; Alföldi-Rosenbaum 1993; Alvarez Martinez 1996; idem 2017: 37–41; Del Hoyo 2001; Matern 2002: 218, Q68.
Image: photograph at https://sites.google.com/site/domusdelmitreo/ in the public domain CC BY-NC-SA.

2.   Private Collection.
      Environs of Urfa.
      Polychrome tessellae.
      Late 2nd c. AD.
      Three fragments of a mosaic. Upper right hand corner: Sol, radiate nimbus (twelve rays), *chlamys*. Damaged.
      LIMC Helios/Sol 451; Matern 2002: 174 n. 957, 266 B153.

3.   Fig. 9.1–9.5, pp. 984–987.
      Vatican Necropolis, Mausoleum M.
      In situ.
      Polychrome tessellae.
      First half 3rd c. AD.
      In ceiling, Sol in frontal *quadriga*, all four horses rearing to the left? (the two left-hand horses destroyed by a hole in the ceiling), radiate (seven rays), dressed in *chlamys* and *chiton*, right hand raised, globe in left hand.
      Perler 1953; Toynbee & Ward-Perkins 1956; Huskinson 1974: 78–80; Hijmans 2000: 984–5 fig 9.1, 9.2.
      Image: photograph © Fabbrica di S. Pietro.

4.   Plate 8.1
      Rome, Museo Nazionale Romano 258548.
      Rome, Mithraeum of S. Prisca, niche behind the Tauroctony scene. The background of the niche was painted blue and green, suggesting the sky.
      Opus sectile, polychrome marbles.
      Ca. AD 200–250.
      Head of Sol, tilted, three-quarters frontal, slightly opened lips (lips lost, but the surviving space suggests this), upward gaze, grooved forehead, long curly hair. A typical Sol of the "Alexander"-type, unmistakably Sol in its original context.
      La Regina 1998: 254–5 (with refs.).
      Image: © 123RF 72350459 / Kosubo.

5. Palermo, Museum 2286.
    Palermo, Piazza della Vittoria, House A, room 2.
    Polychrome tessellae.
    3rd c AD.
    Large mosaic with numerous scenes; frontal bust of Sol, radiate (eleven rays).
    Boeselager 1983, 175–83, fig. 123.

6. Plate 122.1
    Sparta, Museum 11583.
    Sparta, from a building of unknown function.
    Polychrome tessellae.
    After AD 267.
    Bust of Sol, radiate, twelve rays. Other panels of this large mosaic floor depicted Hemera (day), Nyx (night), hunting scenes, poets, and in the central panel the Muses.
    LIMC Helios 134; Gundel 1992, 299 no. 337.1; Panayotopoulou 1998, 117; Dunbabin 1999, 215–6; Matern 2002: 172, 174 n. 957, 266 B156, fig. 89.
    Image: photograph courtesy J. Lendering.

7. Plate 119.5
    Tunis, Bardo Museum A 109 ter.
    Uthina, Villa of the Laberii.
    Polychrome tessellae.
    3rd c. AD.
    Bust of Sol, radiate nimbus (seven rays), *chlamys*.
    LIMC Helios/Sol 26; Matern 2002: 174 n. 957, 266 B 157.
    Image: after Gauckler 1896: fig. 6.

8. Paphos, House of Aion.
    In situ.
    Polychrome stone tessellae.
    Mid 4th c. AD.
    Mosaic floor with five panels. In the large, central panel, Victory of Kassiopeia over Nereids; in this scene, next to Aion, bust of Sol (partially destroyed) with nimbus (no rays?), *chlamys*, whip in left hand, right hand stretched downward to the left shoulder of Victory (winged, nimbate,

palm branch in left hand, raising a wreath above Kassiopeia with her right hand). By the bust of Sol: ΗΛΙ[...]. Daszewski (1985, 42–3) suggests that Luna may also have been depicted but has been completely destroyed.

Daszewski 1985: 403.

9. Plate 121.2
    El Jem, Museum.
    El Jem (Thysdrus), house A, terrain of Jilani Guirat.
    Polychrome tessellae.
    Late 2nd c. AD.
    One of a series of mosaic panels depicting divine couples. Sol, radiate nimbus (6? rays), nude but for a *chlamys* fastened over his right shoulder and hanging over his left shoulder, whip in his left hand, leads a woman, tentatively identified as Cyrene, clasping her left wrist with his right hand. The woman is identified as Cyrene on the assumption that the male is Apollo, but in another panel, Apollo, pursuing Daphne, is not radiate or nimbate, but has a wreath in his hair and appears to be carrying a bow, while a quiver can be made out immediately behind his head. Thus although both are nude except for a *chlamys*, Apollo and Sol are carefully differentiated from each other iconographically.
    Foucher 1960, 39–41.
    Image: photograph courtesy Zaher Kammoun.

10. Plate 121.1
    Qasr el-Lebia, Byzantine church (remains).
    Qasr Libya Museum.
    polychrome tessellae.
    AD 539.
    Sol, nude, radiate, holding rudder atop a globe in his right hand, standing on the lighthouse of Alexandria.
    Daumas & Matthieu 1987, 46.
    Image: in the public domain.

11. Plate 119.6
    Tetouan, Museum.
    Lixus, House of Helios.
    Polychrome tessellae.
    3rd c. AD.

Floor mosaic depicting Sol, radiate (probably seven rays), nude but for a *chlamys*, reins in left hand, right arm and hand destroyed, in a frontal split *quadriga* (only two horses remain). In the upper and lower right corners the heads of two of the four wind-gods. Only the right half of the mosaic survives.

Qninba 2012.

Image: photograph courtesy J. Lendering.

E. Wall-Paintings and Stucco Decoration
E1. Sol Alone
E1a. Sol, Standing Full-Figure

1. Plate 3.1

Naples, Museo Nazionale 9819. The inv. no. 8819, found in many publications, is incorrect.

Pompeii VI 7,20, atrium.

Fresco.

Ca. AD 69–79.

Sol standing, radiate nimbus (seven rays), nude but for a *chlamys*, whip in his lowered right hand, large globe in his left hand. The atrium also contained paintings of the seasons: PPM IV, 451.

LIMC Helios/Sol 90; Gundel 1992: 43 fig. 15, 294 no. 309; Matern 2002: 89–91, 98, 115, 226 G8, fig. 24.

Image: photograph © National Archaeological Museum of Naples.

2. Plate 122.2

Pompeii VI 7,23.

In situ.

Fresco.

Ca. AD 69–79.

Sol standing, radiate nimbus (seven rays), nude but for a *chlamys*, whip in his lowered right hand, large globe in his left hand.

Gundel 1992, 294 no. 310; LIMC Helios/Sol 91; Matern 2002: 90, 226 G9; Anguissola 2012.

Image: © Ministero per i Beni e le Attività Culturali; with permission.

E1b. Bust/Head of Sol

1. Plate 122.3

Delos, House 16.

In situ.

Terracotta disc, painted.

1st c. BC.

Painting on a terracotta tondo for insertion in frescoes on the outside wall of the house; frontal bust of Sol, radiate (at least 12 rays); damaged. The excavators identified 8 layers of decoration on the outside wall of this house. The disc was in use during the last three phases, apparently with a different painting each phase. The painting of Sol is the first (oldest) layer.

LIMC Helios 133; EADelos IX, pp. 45–46, 127 no. 23, pl. XXII; LIMC Apollon 473; Matern 2002: 168, 251 B48.

Image: photograph after Plassart 1916: fig.19.

2.   Destroyed.

Tivoli, Villa Adriana, Latin library.

Fresco.

2nd quarter 2nd c. AD.

Bust of Helios, radiate (twelve rays), *chlamys*.

Matern 2002: 266 B152.

E1c. Sol in Chariot

1.   Vatican necropolis, Mausoleum B.

In situ.

Fresco.

Ca. AD 125.

In the central tondo of the cross vault, Sol, nimbus (outline only; head and, possibly, rays have disappeared) in *quadriga* three-quarters frontal, moving right, whip in raised right hand, dressed in red *chlamys* and, possibly, a darker, sleeved *chiton*; in each of the four vaults: tondo with season.

Mielsch & von Hesberg 1986: 23–6, 36, Fig 19 & color plate 3.

2.   Plate 14.1

Destroyed in the early 18th c.

Rome, Vigna Moroni (one of 92 mausolea along the urban section of the Via Appia explored by Ficoroni between 1705 and 1710).

Fresco.

2nd–3rd c. AD.

In the vault, Sol, radiate, in a frontal split *quadriga*, dressed in long *chiton* (yellow in the watercolour on which this engraving is based) and *chlamys* (red), right hand raised, reins in his left hand.

Ficoroni 1732: 35–9; Cumont 1923: 65–80.

Image: after Ficoroni 1732. The print in Ficoroni's book is a mirror image; cf. the sketch from the Corsini collection currently in the Istituto Centrale per la Grafica (130183, cf. Arachne 1238921 and Xenia Antiqua 9 (2000), 143, cat. 82). For the watercolour see Cod. Vat. Cappon.285 29r.

E2. Sol and Luna

1. Rome, Museo Nazionale Romano 1174, E.
   Rome, Villa Farnesina.
   Fresco.
   Ca. 20 BC.
   Sol and Luna depicted as statues on bases. Sol, frontal, moving right, is nimbate and wears a tunica, boots or high-laced sandals. He holds a whip in his right hand and a staff in his left hand (both difficult to make out). The iconography of this figure is not canonical for Sol at all, and his identity is therefore not certain. There can be no doubt, however, that his counterpart is Luna.
   LIMC Helios/Sol 302; MusNazRom II, 1, 284–5 pl. 171.

2. Plate 123.1
   Destroyed.
   Pompeii IX 7,20.
   Fresco.
   Mid 1st c. AD.
   Two Lares flank Fortuna with cornucopia next to a burning altar. Two garlands above, and above the garlands the frontal busts of Luna (left) and Sol, radiate, whip.
   PPM IX p. 825–6; Trendelenburg 1871: 199–200; Matern 2002: 265 B149.
   Image: after a nineteenth century engraving by La Volpe, in the public domain; cf. PPM loc. cit.

3. Destroyed.
   Pompeii IX 7,19.
   Fresco.
   Mid 1st c. AD.
   Ala, rear wall: tondi with the head of Diana, wreath of leaves, two javelins, tunic, and Sol, radiate nimbus with, reportedly, blue rays, whip, tunic.
   LIMC Helios/Sol 302.

E3. Sol and Some or All Planetary Deities

1. Plate 122.4
   Naples, Museo Nazionale 9519.
   Pompeii, VI 17, Ins. Occ.
   Fresco.
   Mid 1st c. AD.
   Tondi with busts of the 7 planetary deities; Sol, radiate nimbus, *chlamys*, whip. Found in April 1760 in a "yellow room" together with tondi with personifications of months, seasons, etc.
   Long 1992; LIMC Helios/Sol 270; Matern 2002: 168 n. 934, 265 B150.
   Image: engraving of 1750, after Long 1992, 478.

2. Plate 11.1
   Pompeii VII 4,48, Casa della caccia antica, cubiculum 14.
   In situ.
   Fresco.
   AD 71–79 (Impressions of Vespasianic coins in the stucco give a terminus post quem of AD 71).
   On N.-wall, from right to left: tondo with bust of Sol, radiate (eleven rays), *chlamys*, whip; panel with Venus, fishing; tondo with bust of Mercury. On W.-wall (now in Naples, inv. 9549) panel: Danae and the golden rain (Jupiter). On S. wall (from right to left): tondo with bust of Luna; panel with Leda and the swan (Jupiter); tondo (only partially preserved) with bust of bearded male with staff, probably Jupiter (Saturn? But a staff is not a normal attribute for Saturn) – ergo: six of the seven planetary deities are present. Only Mars is missing.
   Matern 2002: 168 n. 934, 266 B151; Allison & Sear 2002: 35–38, figs. 168, 176.
   Image: Photograph author.

3. Pompeii IX 7,1-Officina Quactiliaria.
   In situ.
   Fresco.
   First half 1st c. AD.
   Bust of Sol, radiate (seven rays), along with busts of Luna, Mercurius, and Jupiter. There is no space for additional busts.
   LIMC Helios/Sol 271; Matern 2002: 168 n. 934, 265 B148; PPM IX, 768–773.

4. Tivoli, Villa Adriana.
   in situ or destroyed.
   Stucco.

First half 2nd c. AD.

Stucco ceiling decoration with Sol in *quadriga* in a central circle around which are grouped the planetary deities and the signs of the zodiac.

Lancha 1977, 181, quoting N. Ponce, Arabesques antiques des bains de Livie et de la villa hadrienne, Paris 1838, pl. IX.

Image: http://arachne.uni-koeln.de/item/buchseite/201775 (February 1, 2019).

E4. Sol in Mythological Scenes
E4a. Daedalus and Icarus

1. Pompeii I 7,7 triclinium (b), East wall.
   In situ.
   Fresco.
   Third style.
   Fall of Icarus. Sol in upper left-hand corner in *quadriga* to the right, long *chiton* (?) and *chlamys*. Very faded.
   Von Blanckenhagen 1968: 110 no. 5; LIMC Helios/Sol 182; PPM 1, 594–5 figs. 10–11; Matern 2002: 187–8, 281 K23.

2. Pompeii I 10,7 oecus (9), West wall.
   In situ.
   Fresco.
   Suggested dates range from Claudian to Vespasianic.
   Fall of Icarus. Sol in upper centre, heading right. Very faded.
   Von Blanckenhagen 1968: 110, no. 7; PPM II 420, fig. 29; Matern 2002: 187–8, 281 K 24.

3. Lost.
   Pompeii V 2,10.
   Fresco.
   Early 1st c. AD (third style).
   Fall of Icarus. Above: Sol, radiate, in radiate *quadriga*.
   Von Blanckenhagen 1968: 110–111 no. 6; PPM III 839, fig. 19; Matern 2002: 187–8, 281 K 25

4. Pompeii V 5,3.
   In situ.
   Fresco.

Early 1st c. AD (third style).

Fall of Icarus. Sol in upper left-hand corner. Very faded already at time of excavation (1897).

Von Blanckenhagen 1968: 112–3 no. 9; PPM III 1072, fig. 6; Matern 2002: 187–8, 281 K26.

E4b. Phaethon

1. Rome, Museo Nazionale Romano 1069.

   Rome, Villa Farnesina.

   Stucco.

   28 BC (Moormann).

   Panel depicting Sol on his throne facing left towards Phaethon and his old pedagogue.

   LIMC Helios/Sol 172; LIMC Apollon/Apollo 418; LIMC Phaethon I, 23; Matern 2002: 186, 279–80 K14; Moormann 2008.

E5. Mithras

1. Plate 123.2

   Capua, Mithraeum.

   In situ.

   Fresco.

   Mid 2nd c. AD (Clauss 1992: 51).

   Tauroctony; Sol, radiate (eleven rays), *chlamys*, whip, and Luna in chariots in the upper corners.

   LIMC Helios/Sol 340.

   Image: Photograph in the public domain.

2. Rome, Mithraeum Barberini.

   In situ.

   Fresco.

   2nd–3rd c. AD (Merkelbach); 2nd c. AD (Gundel).

   Tauroctony; Sol, radiate, in upper left-hand corner above zodiac; to either side various Mithraic scenes; on the right, scenes with Sol/Heliodromus: 1. crowning of Sol; 3. Mithras and Sol to either side of burning altar; 5. banquet; 6. Mithras and Sol on *quadriga* (scenes numbered in accordance with LIMC Helios/Sol pp. 608–9).

   LIMC Helios/Sol 242, 245a, 253a, 271a, 340a; Gundel 1992: 262 no. 194.

3. Rome, Mithraeum of S. Prisca.

   in situ.

Fresco.

Ca. AD 200.

Sol and Mithras at their banquet. Sol has long blond curly hair, a radiate nimbus (probably more than seven rays), wears a *chiton* (?) and *chlamys*, holds a globe in his left hand, and has raised his right hand. Mithras is nimbate, without rays.

LIMC Helios/Sol 248.

4.   Plate 123.3

New Haven, Yale University Art Museum.

Dura Europos.

3rd c. AD

Two tauroctonies, both with Sol (in the larger one, only his rays are preserved); various Mithraic scenes, including: 5. the crowning of Sol by Mithras, and Mithras and Sol dining.

LIMC Helios/Sol 243; Merkelbach 1984: 274–5 fig. 15; CIMRM I, 34–42.

Image: photograph courtesy Yale University Art Museum.

5.   Lost.

Rome.

Fresco.

Undated.

Tauroctony; Sol and Luna. The iconography of Mithras, if correctly rendered, is exceptional as he does not wear a pileus (Turcan 2001: n. 37).

LIMC Helios/Sol 340; CIMRM I, 337 fig. 94.

6.   Marino, Mithraeum.

In situ.

Fresco.

2nd–3rd c. AD.

Tauroctony. In the upper left-hand corner, bust of Sol with a radiate nimbus, one ray extending to Mithras. In the upper right-hand corner bust of Luna, nimbate. Below Sol and Luna are two rows of four minor scenes in black frames.

Vermaseren 1982.

E6. Sol in Biblical Scenes

1.   Rome, Catacomb of Via Latina, cubiculum B, right-hand arcosolium.

In situ.

Fresco.

First half 4th c. AD.

Joseph's dream: below, two figures each lying on a bed; four trees (?) and some greenery by the left-hand bed, nine yellow sheaves of corn (three upright and six lying) above the right-hand bed; in the upper left-hand corner busts of Sol, frontal, radiate, and Luna (also frontal, crescent).

Ferrua 1991: 78, fig. 51.

E7. Various Scenes with Sol

1. Vatican, Bibliotheca Apostolica.
    Via Appia.
    Stucco relief.
    1st c. BC.
    Fragment of a tondo with various combat-scenes grouped around a central clipeus with a frontal head of Sol, radiate (about 30 rays).
    LIMC Helios/Sol 6 (with refs.); Matern 2002: 252 B55; Richter 1958: 374–5, pls. 94.34, 95.357.

2. Pompeii IX 5,2-House of Achilles.
    In situ (very faded, February 1993).
    Fourth style.
    Upper part of a panel; Sol, radiate (6? rays) standing next to another standing figure. The rest of the panel is lost.
    WP 252.

E8. Not or Probably Not Sol

1. Naples, Museo Nazionale sala 88 (no inv. no.).
    Pompeii V 4.13.
    1st c. AD.
    Scene depicting origin-myth of Rome. Above: Mars descending from the sky towards Rhea Silvia. Below: she-wolf, Romulus and Remus, observed by Mercurius and a woman, as well as other scenes connected with the story. In upper left-hand corner Luna in *biga* (often misidentified as Sol).
    LIMC Helios/Sol 162 (refers to Luna as Sol, in *quadriga* rather than *biga*); LIMC Ares/Mars 391 (with refs.); Matern 2002: 189, 284 K41 (professes uncertainty as to whether Sol or Luna is depicted).

2. Lost
    Rome, Theatre of Pompey.
    Sail-cloth, painted.
    AD 66.
    Velarium, used in the theatre at the occasion of Tiridates' visit to Rome. Nero driving a chariot and surrounded by golden stars. Often interpreted

as Nero depicted as Sol and driving a *quadriga* among the stars, but the brief mention in Cassius Dio lacks detail (e.g. number of horses, dress of Nero, whether he is radiate) so that the interpretation lacks evidence.

Cass. Dio 63, 6. 2; LIMC Helios/Sol 426 (with refs.); Bergmann 1998: 181.

3. Naples, Museo Nazionale 9245.
   Pompeii IX 6,4–5 room d.
   Fresco.
   Early 1st c. AD.
   Fall of Icarus. Sol not depicted.
   Von Blanckenhagen 1968: 109 no. 3.
   LIMC Helios/Sol 183 (following Schefold 1957, 72q) confuses this painting with E4a.3.

4. Plates 123.4, 123.5
   Lost.
   Rome, Domus Aurea, Room 33.
   Fresco.
   AD 64–68.
   In the centre a male figure with radiate nimbus, nude but for cloak draped over left shoulder and right leg, seated on a throne on a dais below a canopy. To either side four standing women (Horae?); before the dais stand a male figure, nude but for a *chlamys* (left) facing a woman dressed in a *chiton* (right). This mythical scene, now lost, formed the centrepiece of the ceiling of decoration of room 30. It is known to us only through imperfect, 18th century copies. The suggestion that the central figure is Sol, and the youth before him is Phaethon, is rejected by Moormann (1998: 700). He proposes to identify the central figure as Dionysus, but if the scene is a Sternenstreit, he could be Apollo (cf. Hijmans 1994).
   LIMC Helios/Sol 170 (with refs.); LIMC Apollon/Apollo 419 (with refs.); LIMC Phaethon I, 1 (with refs.). Moormann 1998: 692 fig. 3, 700; Matern 2002: 186, 279 K13.
   Images: a. Anonymous drawing published by Robert 1897: 407; b. Anonymous drawing published by Robert 1907: 406.

F. Decorated Plates and Vessels
F1. Terracotta
F1a. Calenian Ware

1. Berlin, Staatliche Museen, Antikensammlung F 793.
   Unknown, produced in Cales.
   Terracotta.

275-200 BC. For the date of Calenian ware, cf. Pedroni 2001: 144–147.
Head of Sol within a medallion.
LIMC Helios/Sol 8.

2.　　Plate 124.2
　　　Heidelberg, University Antikenmuseum R27.
　　　Unknown, produced in Cales.
　　　Terracotta.
　　　275–200 BC.
　　　Around the central omphalos identical scene repeated five times, of a
　　　head (of Sol?) framed by two horses' protomes, one jumping to the left,
　　　the other to the right. Only very partially preserved; of one head the lower
　　　half remains, the other four have disappeared completely. Identification
　　　as Sol doubtful.
　　　LIMC Helios/Sol 131.
　　　Image: courtesy Antikenmuseum, Heidelberg University.

3.　　Plate 124.3
　　　Göttingen, Originalsammlung des Archäologischen Instituts 90.
　　　Unknown, produced in Cales.
　　　Terracotta.
　　　275–200 BC.
　　　Frontal head of Sol, radiate, above the protomes of two horses, one jump-
　　　ing to the left, the other to the right.
　　　Pagenstecher 1909: 22 no. 1a, pl. 6; LIMC Helios/Sol 131.
　　　Image: photograph courtesy D. Graepler, Göttingen University.

4.　　Karlsruhe, Kat. (Winnefeld) 705.
　　　Unknown, produced in Cales.
　　　Terracotta.
　　　275–200 BC.
　　　Frontal head of Sol (?), radiate (?) framed by the protomes of two horses,
　　　one jumping left, the other right.
　　　Pagenstecher 1909: 22 no. 1b; Matern 2002: 55, 215 Q52; LIMC Helios/
　　　Sol 131.

5.　　Paris, Louvre 277.
　　　Unknown, produced in Cales.
　　　Terracotta.

275–200 BC.

Frontal head of Sol (?), radiate (?) framed by the protomes of two horses, one jumping left, the other right.

LIMC Helios/Sol 131; Pagenstecher 1909: 22 no. 1c.

6. Paris, Louvre (De Witte 1350).
    Vulci.
    Terracotta.
    275–200 BC.
    Group, repeated five times around the omphalos, consisting of head of Sol between two horses' protomes and two heads of Dioscuri.
    LIMC Helios/Sol 266.

7. Sèvres, National Museum.
    Unknown, produced in Cales.
    Terracotta.
    275–200 BC.
    Group, repeated five times around the omphalos, consisting of frontal head of Sol, radiate (six rays) between two horses' protomes and two heads of Dioscuri.
    LIMC Helios/Sol 131.

8. London, British Museum.
    Unknown, produced in Cales.
    Terracotta.
    275–200 BC.
    Bust of Sol, radiate, above the protomes of two horses, one jumping left, one right
    LIMC Helios/Sol 130; cf. Pagenstecher 1909: 22. Note: probably refers to a guttus (BM 1824,0501.50) with a depiction of Eos.

9. Naples, ex collection Castellani.
    Unknown, produced in Cales.
    Terracotta.
    275–200 BC.
    Group consisting of two heads of Dioscuri flanking bust of Sol between protomes of two horses, repeated six times around the omphalos of a patera.
    LIMC Helios/Sol 266.

10.   Cracow, Czartoryski Museum.
        Unknown, produced in Cales.
        Terracotta.
        275–200 BC.
        Group consisting inter alia of bust of Sol between protomes of two horses,
        repeated four times around the omphalos of a patera.
        LIMC Helios/Sol 131.

11.   Plate 124.1
        London, British Museum GR 1928,0117.71.
        Unknown, produced in Cales.
        Terracotta.
        275–200 BC.
        Frontal bust of Sol, radiate, five rays, above the protomes of two horses,
        one to either side, repeated six times around the omphalos of a patera,
        and alternating with back to back busts of the Dioscuri wearing Persian
        caps. Inscribed: lucius canoleios l. f. fecit calenos.
        Roberts 1997: 188–193; LIMC Helios/Sol 130; Pagenstecher 1909: 76 no. 115.
        Image: photograph © Trustees of the British Museum.

12.   Unknown.
        Unknown, produced in Cales.
        Terracotta.
        275–200 BC.
        Frontal head of Sol, radiate, above the protomes of two horses, one jump-
        ing left, the other right.
        Pagenstecher 1909: 22 no. 1d.

13.   Private Collection.
        Unknown, produced in Cales.
        Terracotta.
        275–200 BC.
        Frontal bust of Sol, radiate (eleven rays), *chlamys*, within zodiac circle, on
        upturned crescent with two stars.
        LIMC Helios/Sol 296; Gundel 1992: 237–8 no. 97.

14.   Berlin?
        Unknown, produced in Cales.
        Terracotta.

First half 3rd c. BC (Pedroni 2001: 64 & 152).
Bust of Apollo-Sol, radiate (twelve rays), *chiton*, *chlamys*, lyre.
Pagenstecher 1909: 22 no. 2a.

15. Plate 125.1
Göttingen, Originalsammlung des Archäologischen Instituts 87.
Unknown, produced in Cales.
Terracotta.
First half 3rd c. BC.
Bust of Apollo-Sol, radiate (twelve rays), *chiton*, *chlamys*, lyre.
Pagenstecher 1909: 23 no. 2b.
Image: photograph courtesy D. Graepler, Göttingen University.

16. Plate 125.2
London, British Museum 1873,0820.444.
Unknown, produced in Cales.
Terracotta.
First half 3rd c. BC.
Bust of Apollo-Sol, radiate (twelve rays), *chiton*, *chlamys*, lyre.
Pagenstecher 1909: 23 no. 2c.
Image: drawing after Pagenstecher, loc. cit.

17. St. Petersburg, Hermitage.
Unknown, produced in Cales.
Terracotta.
First half 3rd c. BC.
Bust of Apollo-Sol, radiate (twelve rays), *chiton*, *chlamys*, lyre.
Pagenstecher 1909: 23 no. 2d.

18. Heidelberg University, Antikenmuseum R18.
Athens.
Terracotta.
Mid 3rd c. AD.
Head of Sol within a radiate medallion.
LIMC Helios 128; LIMC Helios/Sol 7; Matern 2002: 251 B50.

F1b. Other Wares
1. Boston, Museum of Fine Arts 98.828.
Unknown (produced in Italy).

Terracotta.

Ca. 20 BC–AD 10.

Mould for Arretine-ware bowl, depicting Phaethon-myth. Sol (?), nude, not radiate, on horseback catching the reins of the runaway horses. On the identification of the horseback rider as Sol, cf. Hartwig 1899 (with an accurate drawing of the mould, pl. IV). Problematic is the presence of six horses: two making off to the right, their loose reins caught by the figure identified as Sol; one horse next to the one ridden by Sol; one horse jumping away to the left with the shafts of the carriage; and finally the hind legs of a horse going to the left, visible behind Sol's horse (which is headed to the right); these legs must belong to a sixth horse because they are too far removed from the other horse heading left, but the missing sherd here has left a gap in the image that is too large to allow a clear reconstruction of this part of the image. Given that Sol's solar chariot was invariably a *quadriga*, the presence of two additional horses must be explained. Hartwig (1899: 487) suggests that Sol took along an extra horse ("Beipferd"). Another possibility is that not Sol but the Dioscuri were depicted, with the second Dioscure lost in the gap of the mould (although it is not immediately clear to me how we should then reconstruct the missing part). A third proposal, that the chariot was drawn by six horses and the rider is Phaethon in a desperate final attempt to corral the runaway horses before he is brought down, strikes me as very unlikely (cf. Hartwig 1899: 482–3).

LIMC Helios/Sol 181; Matern 2002: 186, 278 K3; Hartwig 1899.

2.   Plate 126.1

Cologne, Römisch-Germanisches Museum 58289.

Cologne.

Terracotta.

2nd c. AD.

Kantharos decorated with Mithraic figures, including Sol, standing, nude but for a *chlamys*, radiate (five rays), globe in left hand, right hand above a burning altar; Sol stands between Cautes and Cautopates.

LIMC Helios/Sol 457.

Image: drawing © Anna Hijmans.

3.   Cologne, Römisch-Germanisches Museum 58270.

Cologne.

Terracotta.

2nd c. AD.

Kantharos decorated with Mithraic figures, including Sol, standing, nude but for a *chlamys*, radiate (five rays), globe in left hand, right hand above a burning altar; Sol stands between Cautes and Cautopates.
LIMC Helios/Sol 457.

4. Cologne, Römisch-Germanisches Museum 58273.
Cologne.
Terracotta.
2nd c. AD.
Kantharos decorated with Mithraic figures, including Sol, standing, nude but for a *chlamys*, radiate (five rays), globe in left hand, right hand above a burning altar; Sol stands between Cautes and Cautopates.
LIMC Helios/Sol 457.

5. Plate 126.4
Heidelberg University, Antikenmuseum 64/1.
Asia Minor.
Terracotta.
2nd. c. AD?
Fragment of a bowl; frontal head of Sol, radiate between a bull (?) and a lion.
LIMC Helios/Sol 7; Matern 2002: 265 B145; LIMC Helios 155 (incorrect inv. no.).
Image: courtesy Antikenmuseum, Heidelberg University.

6. Craiova, Muzeul Oltenei.
Locusteni.
Terracotta.
2nd–3rd c. AD.
Vase-applique; Sol, nude, radiate (?), right hand raised, reins in left hand, on *quadriga* left.
LIMC Helios/Sol 151

7. Trier, Rheinisches Landesmuseum 33.513.
Trier?
Terracotta.
3rd c. AD.
Vase with two large vertical handles, decorated on the shoulder with relief busts of the seven planetary deities; only traces of Sol survive.
LIMC Planetae 32.

8.   Plates 126.2, 126.3
      Cologne, Römisch-Germanisches Museum 3022.
      Cologne, corner of Luxemburger and Hochstadenstrasse.
      Terracotta.
      4th c. AD.
      Squat white-ground amphora; on shoulder incised frontal busts of Saturn,
      Sol, and Luna; Sol is radiate (eight rays) and holds a whip in his left hand.
      La Baume 1964: 83–4 fig. 67.
      Image: © Rheinisches Bildarchiv Cologne, rba_mf051199.

9.   Plate 125.3
      Trier, Rheinische Landesmuseum 05.228.
      Trier (necropolis of S. Mathias).
      Terracotta (Terra Sigillata).
      Undated.
      Sol and Mithras at banquet with 2 servants, lion, krater with snake, cock
      and raven.
      LIMC Helios/Sol 253; CIMRM I, 988; Merkelbach 1984: 338 fig. 93.
      Image: © GDKE/Rheinisches Landesmuseum Trier, photograph: Th.
      Zühmer.

10.   Rheinzabern, Terra Sigillata Museum.
      Unknown.
      Terracotta (Terra Sigillata).
      Undated.
      Radiate head of Sol (7? rays).
      LIMC Helios/Sol 14.
      See C1ca.14.

11.   Lyon, Musée et Théâtres romains.
      Environs of Lyon.
      Terracotta.
      Undated.
      Fragment of pottery decorated in relief. Visible are the wheel and most of
      the horses of a chariot jumping up to the right over stylized clouds, with
      Tellus below. Identification with Sol by analogy with coins, medallions,
      and a phalera. Cf. K9.10.
      Wuilleumier 1952: 151 no. 284 pl. 7; Bergmann 1998: 248 fig. 4.

12. Lost?
Mainz.
Black glazed terracotta.
4th c. AD.
Cup inscribed: accipe m[e si]tie(n)s et trade sodali. The busts of the planetary deities run from left to right above the inscription, beginning with Saturn.
Maas 1902, 161 with fig. 12a.

13. Amsterdam, Allard Pierson Museum NR 2806.
Central Italy.
Light red terracotta.
Last quarter of the 1st c. BC–1st quarter of the 1st c. AD.
Central medallion of a dish depicting the facing head of Sol, radiate (twelve rays) above a very thin lunar crescent, within a circle on which the signs of the zodiac are depicted.
Pagenstecher "Nachtrag", JdI 1912: 70.

F2. Stone

1. Cologne, Römisch-Germanisches Museum Kl 626.
Probably acquired in Tunisia by the former owner.
Marble.
3rd c. AD.
Votive patera, decorated in relief with Saturn on a throne within an aedicula, between two sphinxes. Outside the aedicula, to either side, Sol (left), standing, radiate, nude but for a *chlamys*, globe in right hand, and Luna (right).
LIMC Saturnus 75.

F3. Bronze

1. Naples, Museo Nazionale 75091.
Unknown.
Bronze.
1st–2nd c. AD.
Eight-sided vat, with on seven sides the planetary deities. Sol is standing, wears a *chiton* and *chlamys*, and holds a whip.
LIMC Planetae 12.

2. Plate 129.1
   Augst, Römermuseum 21.78.
   Augst, near temple.
   Bronze.
   Mid 3rd c. AD.
   Cult vessel (incense burner?) depicting the planetary deities (standing figures); Sol is radiate (seven rays), nude but for a *chlamys*, holds a whip in his right hand and a globe (or patera?) in his left hand above a burning altar.
   LIMC Helios/Sol 276; Matern 2002: 92, 228 G20; Staehelin 1948: 568, fig. 175; Duval 1953: 290.
   Image: © Augusta Raurica.

3. Berlin, Staatliche Museen 15/69.
   Syria or Palestine?
   Bronze.
   Late 6th c. AD.
   Censer with six New Testament scenes. Flanking the crucifixion: busts of Sol and Luna.
   Weitzmann 1979, 626 no. 563.

4. Lyon, Musée et Théâtres romains BR 207.
   Gap.
   Bronze, silver-plated.
   Undated, hybrid (probably modern) assembly of various ancient elements of varying date.
   Hexagonal vase with swing-handle. The shoulder consists of a flat hexagonal plaque with a large hole in the centre, around which six of the seven planetary deities are arranged (Saturn to Jupiter).
   Duval 1953: 289; Boucher & Tassinari 1976: 148–151 no. 192.

5. Boston, Museum of Fine Arts 65.9.
   Syria/Palestine.
   Bronze.
   7th c. AD (?)
   Censer with five New Testament scenes. Flanking the crucifixion: busts of Sol and Luna (very rudimentary, barely visible).
   Unpublished?
   Image: https://www.mfa.org/collections/object/censer-55014 (February 1, 2019).

F4. Silver

1. Plate 14.4
   St. Petersburg, Hermitage Π 1838.25.
   Kertsch.
   Silver.
   3rd c. BC.
   Cup, with on the inside a depiction of Helios on 3/4 *quadriga*, radiate (nine rays), long-sleeved *chiton* and *chlamys*, whip in raised right hand.
   Gorbunova & Saverkina 1975: no. 99. Matern 2002: 61, 67, 80 n. 487, 213 Q35.
   Image: photograph courtesy Hermitage Museum, St. Petersburg.

2. Plates 127.1–127.3
   Paris, Louvre Bj 1969.
   Boscoreale.
   Gilded silver.
   Late 1st c. BC to first half 1st c. AD.
   Patera, with in the emblema the bust of a woman with elephant headdress (probably personification of Africa); her cornucopia is decorated in the upper register with a bust of Sol, draped, radiate (nine rays); in middle register eagle; in lower register caps of Dioscuri crowned by stars.
   LIMC Helios/Sol 329; LIMC Aigyptos 10; Matern 2002: 264 B138.
   Image: © RMN-Grand Palais / Hervé Lewandowski / Art Resource, NY.

3. Plates 128.1, 128.2
   Milan, Museo Archeologico 18901.
   Parabiago.
   Silver.
   Controversial, but usually dated 4th c. AD.
   Above the main scene (Attis & Cybele), on the left Sol, radiate, right hand raised, nude but for a *chlamys*, in *quadriga* to the right, preceded by Phosphoros, and on the right Luna, descending in *biga* (bulls), preceded by Hesperus.
   LIMC Helios/Sol 397; Gundel 1992, 260 no. 190.
   Image: courtsey of the Museo Archeologico, Milan.

4. Plate 129.2
   Lost.
   Wettingen.
   Silver.

Undated.

Planetary deities incised on a silver ladle. Sol, radiate (six rays), dressed in *chiton* and *chlamys*, holds a whip in his raised right arm. On a low, squat base next to him, a globe.

Matern 2002: 90, 118 n. 637, 227 G13, fig. 23; LIMC Planetae 13; Staehelin 1948: 568, fig. 174; Duval 1953: 289–90; Simonett 1946: 11–13, pl. 4, 11.

Image: drawing of 1635, preserved as part of the manuscript *Eigentlicher Abriß der Heidnischen Silbernen Blatten, So Anno 1634 zu Wettingen Under der Erden gefunden worden*, currently preserved in the Archaeological Museum in Zurich; cf. Simonett 1946: pl. 4.11.

5.   Art Market. Note: this object cannot be documented prior to 1970, and is therefore considered an undocumented artifact which cannot be ethically sold or traded (AIA code of ethics).

Unknown.

Silver.

3rd c. AD?

A shallow bowl richly decorated with hammered images. In the centre, a male figure in a sleeveless tunic approaches a burning altar from the left, holding a goat firmly by a horn with his left hand and carrying fruit and other objects in the crook of his right arm. Beyond the altar, atop a high podium reached by a long staircase, is a distyle temple with Minerva, fully armed, gazing down from the porch. In the centre, above the altar scene, a large figure of Sol, radiate nimbus, nude but for a *chlamys*, right hand raised and holding a globe in his left hand, appears above some thin clouds in a facing *quadriga*, the inner horses facing inwards, the outer jumping outwards. At the left a tree.

Christie's auction 2364, New York, December 9, 2010, lot 196.

6.   Art Market. Note: this object cannot be documented prior to 1970, and is therefore considered an undocumented artifact which cannot be ethically sold or traded (AIA code of ethics).

Unknown.

Silver and gilded silver.

3rd or 4th c. AD (or modern?).

A deep silver bowl, with at the bottom a roundel with a facing bust of Sol, radiate (ten rays), wearing what appears to be a sleeveless tunic fastened over each shoulder. Sol has long wavy hair, brushed back, and ending in two tresses which curve out and down ornamentally to fill the empty space above the shoulders. Sol's hair and tunic are gilded. The tunic is not characteristic for Sol, and the rays appear to be truncated.

Artemis Gallery, New York, 2019; no. 146607.

F5. Glass

1. Cologne, Römisch-Germanisches Museum 1002.
Cologne-Braunsfeld.
Glass.
AD 320–340.
Profile bust of Sol, left, radiate (twelve rays), *chlamys*, whip, in central medallion surrounded by circus-scene with four racing chariots.
LIMC Helios/Sol 198; Matern 2002: 265 B146.

G. Lamps
G1. Terracotta Lamps, Decoration on Body
G1a. Head/Bust of Sol

1. Copenhagen, National Museum 859.
Pompeii.
Terracotta.
ca. AD 50.
Frontal bust of Sol, eight rays (hole where ninth ray would be).
LIMC Helios/Sol 45; Matern 2002: 181, 267 B170b.

2. Plate 131.1
London, British Musum 1856,1226.411.
Pozzuoli.
Terracotta.
Ca. AD 40–80.
Frontal bust of Sol, radiate (eight rays).
LIMC Helios/Sol 44; Bailey 1975: Q1009; Matern 2002: 181, 268 B173a.
Image: photograph © Trustees of the British Museum.

3. Altino?
Altino, deposit of lamps midway between ustrinum and mausoleum.
Terracotta.
First half 1st c. AD.
Frontal bust of Sol.
Marcello 1956, 100–103 no. 9, pl. VIII; Ianovitz 1972: 60.

4. Verona, Archaeological Museum.
Verona.
Terracotta.
1st c. AD.
Bust of Sol, radiate, left.
LIMC Helios/Sol 77; Ianovitz 1972: 80 (with refs.).

5.   Bordeaux, Musée d'Aquitaine 60.8.559.
      Bordeaux, Terre Nègre Cemetery (discovered in 1863).
      Terracotta.
      1st c. AD.
      Frontal bust of Sol, radiate (five rays).
      A. Ziéglé, pers. comm. (unpublished).

6.   Mérida, Archaeological Museum CE06520.
      Mérida
      Terracotta
      Early 1st c. AD
      Frontal bust of Sol, radiate (ten rays) on thin upturned crescent.
      LIMC Helios/Sol 57; Matern 2002: 181, 271 B199.

7–9. Mérida, Archaeological Museum CE00930.
      Mérida, theatre.
      Terracotta.
      Early 1st c. AD.
      3/4 bust of Sol, radiate, whip. Gil Farrés (1948: 103 n. 1) mentions a second,
      similar lamp in the same collection as well as two from Villafranca de los
      Barros and one from Troia. All lamps are described as "Mithraic" (despite
      the early date for the Merida lamp) and as depicting a bust of Sol, radiate,
      whip in right hand.
      LIMC Helios/Sol 42; Gil Farrés 1948: 103–4 nos. 1–4; Matern 2002: 181, 272
      B212.

10.   Plate 131.8
      Seville, Archaeological Museum ROD2219.
      Unknown.
      Terracotta.
      2nd–3rd c. AD.
      Frontal bust of Sol, radiate (nine rays), *chlamys*, whip by right shoulder.
      Fernández Chicarro Y De Dios 1956: 100, 208, figs. 55.11 & 64.8.
      Image: courtesy Archaeological Museum, Seville.

11.   Oszöny, Museum.
      Brigetio.
      Terracotta.
      Early 1st c. AD.

Bust of Sol, radiate nimbus, *chlamys*.
LIMC Helios/Sol 43.

12. Prague University, Institute of Classical Archaeology 574/57.
M. Teplice.
Terracotta.
AD 30–60.
Frontal bust of Sol, radiate (five rays).
Marsa 1972, 115 no. 117 pl. IV.

13. Corinth, Museum 740.
Corinth.
Terracotta.
1st c. AD.
Frontal head of Sol, radiate.
Broneer: 1930, 180 no. 489; Matern 2002: 181, 270–1 B196a.

14. Plate 132.1
Boston, Museum of Fine Arts 72.224.
Cyprus.
Terracotta.
1st c. AD.
Frontal bust of Sol, radiate (ten rays).
Unpublished.
Image: © Museum of Fine Arts, Boston. Museum purchase with funds donated by subscription.

15. Copenhagen National Museum ABc 425.
Mysia?
Terracotta.
Second half 1st c. AD.
Bust of Sol facing left, *chlamys*, seven rays.
LIMC Helios/Sol 76; Matern 2002: 181, 272 B211.

16. Carthage, Museum 46.46.
Carthage.
Terracotta.
Last quarter 1st c. AD.
Frontal bust of Sol, radiate (nine rays).
Deneuve 1969: 108, no. 282; Matern 2002: 181, 267 B168a.

17.   Carthage, Museum 46.249.
       Carthage.
       Terracotta.
       Last quarter 1st c. AD.
       Frontal bust of Sol, radiate (five rays).
       Deneuve 1969: 150, no. 581; Matern 2002: 181, 267 B168b.

18.   Carthage, Museum 46.402.
       Carthage.
       Terracotta.
       Last quarter 1st c. AD.
       Frontal bust of Sol, radiate (seven rays).
       Deneuve 1969: 166, no. 705; Matern 2002: 181, 267 B168c.

19.   Sabratha, Museum 111.
       Sabratha, Byzantine Gate road.
       Terracotta.
       1st c. AD.
       Frontal bust of Sol, radiate (seven rays), *chlamys*.
       LIMC Helios/Sol 55; Joly 1974, 106 no. 76, pl. 7; Matern 2002: 181, 268 B177.

20.   Sabratha, Museum 342.
       Sabratha, excavations near theatre.
       Terracotta.
       1st c. AD?
       Frontal bust of Sol, radiate, *chlamys*.
       Joly 1974: no. 77.

21.   Unknown.
       Thamusida.
       Terracotta.
       Third quarter 1st c.–1st quarter 2nd c AD.
       Bust of Sol, radiate (10? rays) above crescent.
       Ponsich 1961: 89 no. 125; Matern 2002: 272 B206.

22.   Bologna, Museo Civico archeologico 6065.
       Unknown.
       Terracotta.
       1st c. AD.

Bust of Sol, radiate (five rays).
Matern 2002: 181, 267 B161.

23. Plate 131.2
Boston Museum of Fine Arts 01.8371. Bequest of Mrs. Arthur Croft-the
Gardner Brewer Collection.
Unknown.
Terracotta.
Late 1st c. AD.
Bust of Sol, radiate, twelve rays.
Unpublished.
Image: photograph © Museum of Fine Arts, Boston.

24. Budapest, National Museum 51.845.
Unknown.
Terracotta.
1st c. AD.
Frontal bust of Sol, radiate (five rays).
Matern 2002: 181, 267 B162.

25. Plate 133.1
Copenhagen, National Museum 5301.
Unknown.
Terracotta.
Second half 1st c. AD.
Frontal face surrounded by a radiate nimbus (Sonnengesicht).
LIMC Helios 9 (with incorrect inv. no.); LIMC Helios/Sol 45 (in this entry
Letta also lists Copenhagen National Museum 1245 as a lamp with a bust
of Sol, but this lamp actually has a rather nice frontal face of a bearded
satyr).
Image: photograph © Nationalmuseet Antiksamlingen, Copenhagen,
photograph no. D 1091, with permission.

26. Hannover, Kestner Museum 952.
Unknown.
Terracotta.
AD 30–100.
Bust of Sol between two dolphins.
Matern 2002: 167 B166b.

27.   Karlsruhe, Badisches Landesmuseum.
       Unknown.
       Terracotta.
       AD 25–50.
       Frontal bust of Sol, radiate (eight rays).
       Derksen 1978: 235–236, pl. 102 no. 4; LIMC Helios/Sol 44; Matern 2002: 181,
       267 B167.

28.   London, British Museum 1814,0704.105.
       Unknown.
       Terracotta.
       Second half 1st c. AD.
       Miniature mould-made lamp; frontal bust of Sol, radiate (seven rays)
       above globe.
       LIMC Helios/Sol 47; Bailey 1975: Q1096; Matern 2002: 181, 272 B207.

29.   Plate 133.2
       Prague, National Museum Inv. 2533.
       Unknown.
       Terracotta.
       AD 50–75.
       Frontal bust of Sol, radiate (five rays).
       Haken 1958: 58 no. 53.
       Image: courtesy National Museum, Prague.

30.   Rome, Museo Nazionale Romano.
       Unknown.
       Terracotta.
       AD 25–50.
       Frontal bust of Sol, radiate (nine rays), on upturned crescent with a star
       on each point.
       Derksen 1978: 236, pl 103.6; LIMC Helios/Sol 58; Matern 2002: 181, 271
       B200a.

31.   Rome, Museo Nazionale Romano.
       Unknown.
       Terracotta.
       Second half 1st c. AD.
       Frontal bust of Sol, radiate (five rays).

Derksen 1978: 236, pl. 102.5; LIMC Helios/Sol 46; Matern 2002: 181, 268 B176a.

32. Warsaw, Archaeological Museum 147887.
     Unknown.
     Terracotta.
     1st c. AD?.
     Only the seven rays of Sol survive.
     Matern 2002: 268 B179a.

33. Warsaw, Arch. Museum 147057.
     Unknown.
     Terracotta.
     1st c. AD?
     Bust of Sol over crescent, nine rays.
     Matern 2002: 268–9 B179b.

34. Plate 132.3
     Bordeaux, Musée d'Aquitaine 60.8.266.
     Rome, Baths of Diocletian.
     Terracotta.
     Last quarter 1st c.–first half 2nd c. AD.
     Frontal bust of Sol, radiate (five rays).
     LIMC Helios/Sol 46.
     Image: courtesy Musée d'Aquitaine, Bordeaux, photograph no. 76300,
     © Museum.

35. Camarina, Archaeological Museum.
     Camarina.
     Terracotta.
     1st–2nd c. AD.
     Frontal bust of Sol.
     Matern 2002: 181, 267 B163.

36. Florence, Archaeological Museum 1237.
     Found locally.
     Terracotta.
     1st–2nd c. AD.
     Bust of Sol.
     Unpublished.

37.   Florence, Archaeological Museum 2500 (case 6).
      S. Alessandro.
      Terracotta.
      1st–2nd c. AD.
      Bust of Sol.
      Unpublished.

38.   Hannover, Kestner Museum 1010.
      Unknown.
      Terracotta.
      AD 90–140.
      Frontal bust of Sol, radiate (five rays).
      Matern 2002: 267 B166c.

39.   Ripon College, Clark Collection EC.53.86.
      Unknown.
      Terracotta.
      1st–2nd c. AD.
      Frontal bust of Sol, radiate (five rays).
      Unpublished.
      Image: http://www.ripon.edu/external/clark/lamp4.html (February 1 2019).

40.   Jerusalem, Hebrew University 6058.
      Unknown (acquired in Beirut).
      Terracotta.
      1st–3rd c. AD.
      Frontal bust of Sol, radiate (ten rays), *chlamys*, on thin upturned crescent.
      Rosenthal & Sivan 1978: no. 347.

41.   Jerusalem, Hebrew University 6057.
      Unknown (acquired in Beirut).
      Terracotta.
      1st–3rd c. AD.
      Frontal face of Sol (?), surrounded by petal-like rays (9).
      Rosenthal & Sivan 1978: 88 no. 357

42.   Jerusalem, Hebrew University 6064.
      Unknown (acquired in Beirut).
      Terracotta.
      1st–3rd c. AD.

Frontal bust of Sol, radiate (10? rays), *chlamys*, on thin upturned crescent.
Rosenthal & Sivan 1978: 86 no. 348.

43. Plate 132.2
Brussels, Royal Museums of Fine Arts R 602 bis.
Unknown.
Terracotta.
AD 90–140.
Bust of Sol.
LIMC Helios/Sol 46.
Image: courtesy of the Royal Museums of Fine Arts, Brussels.

44. Montreal, McGill University 6292 / 02684.5.
Unknown.
Terracotta.
Late 1st–first half 2nd c. AD.
Frontal bust of Sol, radiate (five rays).
Zoitopoúlou & Fossey 1992, 99 no. 32.

45. Paris, Bibliothèque Nationale de France, Cabinet des Médailles 52.3870.
Unknown.
Terracotta.
Late 1st–early 2nd c. AD.
Frontal bust of Sol, radiate (five rays).
Matern 2002: 181, 268 B174.

46. Lodi, Museo Civico 243.
Lodivecchio.
Terracotta.
Early 2nd c. AD.
Frontal bust of Sol, radiate (five rays).
Cuomo di Caprio & Santoro Bianchi 1983: 138–9 no. 30 pl. III; Matern
2002: 181, 268 B172.

47. Albi, Musée Saint-Raymond 27.005.
Montans.
Terracotta.
Late 1st–mid 2nd c. AD.
Bust of Sol, radiate (five rays).
Bergès 1989: 70 no. 228.

48.   Plate 131.3
      London, British Museum 1898,1122.1.
      Reputedly found in a tomb at Cape de Tenes (near Cherchel), produced
      in Central Italy.
      Terracotta.
      First half 2nd c. AD.
      Frontal bust of Sol, radiate (five rays).
      LIMC Helios/Sol 46; Bailey 1975: Q1281; Matern 2002: 181, 268 B173b.
      Image: photograph © Trustees of the British Museum.

49.   Plate 131.4
      Bordeaux, Musée d'Aquitaine 60.8.555.
      Bordeaux, Terre Nègre Cemetery, discovered in 1863.
      Terracotta.
      First half 2nd c. AD.
      Frontal bust of Sol, radiate (five rays). On base, inscription: c(ai) oppi
      res(titui).
      A. Ziéglé, pers. comm.; CIL XIII 10001, 235A.
      Image: © Musée d'Aquitaine, Bordeaux; courtesy A. Ziéglé.

50.   Plate 133.3
      London, British Museum 1867,1122.236.
      Ephesus (produced locally).
      Terracotta.
      1st quarter 2nd c. AD.
      Frontal bust of Sol, radiate (six rays).
      Bailey 1975: Q3067; Matern 2002: 181, 268 B173d.
      Image: photograph © Trustees of the British Museum.

51.   Freiburg, art market.
      Unknown.
      Terracotta.
      2nd c. AD.
      Frontal bust of Sol, draped, seven rays, over crescent. Inscription:
      c mar ev.
      Matern 2002: 181, 267 B165; Galerie C. Puhze, Kunst der Antike Katalog 8,
      26 no. 271. Matern (2002, 270) lists the same lamp under B191 referring
      to the same catalogue and page, but no. 171. This number (on a different
      page) is a depiction of a fish.

52. Freiburg, Art Market.
    Unknown.
    Terracotta.
    2nd c. AD.
    Profile bust of Sol.
    Matern 2002: 270 B210.

53. Plate 133.4
    Berlin, Staatliche Museen, Antikensammlung TC 8217/106.
    Rome.
    Terracotta.
    2nd–3rd c. AD.
    3/4 bust of Sol with long, "radiate" hair.
    LIMC Helios/Sol 51; Heres 1972, 72 no. 441; Matern 2002: 181, 272 B209.
    Image: © Staatliche Musen, Berlin

54. Catania, Ursino Castle Museum MC 6227.
    Mozia.
    Terracotta.
    2nd–3rd c. AD.
    Frontal bust of Sol, five rays.
    Matern 2002: 181, 267 B164.

55. Plate 131.6
    London, British Museum 1905,0520.154.
    Herpes, Charente, reputedly from a Merovingian (!) cemetery.
    Terracotta.
    Ca. AD 150–250.
    Frontal bust of Sol, radiate (seven rays), whip. Found together with a
    lamp of Luna (Q1668).
    Bailey 1975 vol. III, 175, Q1669; Matern 2002: 181, 268 B173c.
    Image: available under CC BY-NC-SA 4.0 license. Trustees of the British
    Museum.

56. Cologne, Römisch-Germanisches Museum 1805.
    Environs of Cologne.
    Terracotta.
    2nd–3rd c. AD.
    Frontal bust of Sol.

Matern 2002: 181, 267 B169; a second (?) lamp with the same inventory number is listed by Matern 2002: B195.
Image: https://www.kulturelles-erbe-koeln.de/documents/obj/05711845 (February 1, 2019).

57.   Caracal, Museum 5793.
      Romula.
      Terracotta.
      2nd–3rd c. AD.
      Frontal bust of Sol, radiate (seven rays), *chlamys*.
      LIMC Helios/Sol 52; Matern 2002: 181, 270 B188.

58.   Jerusalem?
      Nabratein, Field 4, Roman house.
      Terracotta.
      Late 2nd–early 3rd c. AD (stratified date).
      Sol with globe in right hand.
      IEJ 31 (1981): 109–110.

59.   Unknown.
      Jerusalem.
      Terracotta.
      2nd–3rd c. AD.
      Bust of Sol above crescent.
      Matern 2002: 272 B204a.

60.   Unknown.
      Jerusalem.
      Terracotta.
      2nd–3rd c. AD.
      Bust of Sol above crescent.
      Matern 2002: 272 B204b.

61.   Unknown.
      Sebaste (Samaria)
      Terracotta
      2nd–3rd c. AD
      Bust of Sol above crescent.
      Matern 2002: 272 B205

62. Rabat, Archaeological Museum?
Banasa.
Terracotta.
Mid 1st c.–first quarter 2nd c. AD.
Bust of Sol, radiate (seven rays), *chlamys*, above globe.
Ponsich 1961: 96 no. 227; Matern 2002: 272 B208.

63. Catania, Museo Civico MC 6227.
Unknown.
Terracotta.
2nd–3rd c. AD.
Frontal bust of Sol, radiate (five rays), *chlamys*.
LIMC Helios 53.

64. Rome, Museo Nazionale Romano.
Unknown.
Terracotta.
Late 2nd–early 3rd c. AD.
Frontal bust of Sol, radiate (six rays), long-sleeved tunica and *chlamys*,
overly large raised right hand, globe in left hand in front of breast, whip
behind left shoulder.
Derksen 1978: 237–239, pl. 104.8; LIMC Helios/Sol 50; Matern 2002: 181,
268 B176b.

65. Plate 135.1
Portland, the Portland Art Museum 26.147.
Unknown.
Terracotta.
2nd–3rd c. AD.
Frontal bust of Sol, radiate (seven rays), *chlamys*.
LIMC Helios/Sol 48; Matern 2002: 181, 272 B213.
Image: courtesy the Portland Art Museum, Sally Lewis Collection.

66. Art Market.
Unknown.
Terracotta.
2nd–3rd c. AD.
Frontal bust of Sol, radiate (seven rays), *chlamys*.
Ancient and Oriental Antiquities (www. Antiquities.co.uk), autumn 2007.

67.   Delphi, Museum.
      Delphi.
      Terracotta.
      3rd c. AD.
      Frontal bust of Sol above crescent.
      LIMC Helios 159; Matern 2002: 270 B190.

68.   Unknown.
      Dura Europos.
      Terracotta.
      Mid 3rd c. AD.
      Frontal bust of Sol, radiate (seven rays), *chlamys*. Damaged.
      Dura IV, 111.

69.   Private collection.
      North Africa.
      Terracotta.
      3rd c. AD.
      Frontal bust of Sol, radiate (seven rays), *chlamys*, whip.
      Derksen 1978: 232–4, pl. 100–1; LIMC Helios/Sol 49; Matern 2002: 181, 266
      B159.

70.   Carthage, Museum 46.556.
      Carthage.
      Terracotta.
      Late 3rd–early 4th c. AD.
      Frontal bust of Sol, radiate (six rays), *chlamys*, raised right hand, whip
      behind left shoulder.
      Deneuve 1969: no. 1131; LIMC Helios/Sol 54.

71.   Athens, Agora museum L1792.
      Agora.
      Terracotta.
      Second half 5th–early 6th c. AD.
      Frontal head of Sol, radiate (9? rays).
      LIMC Helios 159; Perlzweig 1961: no. 2368; Matern 2002: 181, 266–7 B160a.

72.   Athens, Agora museum L1119.
      Agora.
      Terracotta.
      Second half 5th–early 6th c. AD.

Frontal head of Sol, radiate (9? rays).
Perlzweig 1961: 172 no. 2367; Matern 2002: 181, 266–7 B160b.

73–93.   Plates 131.5, 131.7, 132.4, 132.6, 133.5, 133.6, 133.7, 133.8
Corinth, Museum L 540–L 560.
Corinth.
Terracotta.
5th–6th c. AD (Broneer); Roman Imperial (Matern).
Frontal head of Sol, radiate (ten to twelve rays).
LIMC Helios 160b; Broneer 1930: 251–3 no. 1148–1168; Matern 2002: 181, 270–1 B196b-v.
Images: photographs of G1a.73 (L 540), G1a.77 (L 544), G1a.80 (L 547), G1a.81 (L 548), G1a.84 (L 551), G1a.85 (L 552), G1a.91 (L 558), and G1a.92 (L 559) all courtesy American School of Classical Studies, Athens.

94.   Plate 133.9
Corinth, Museum L 740.
Corinth.
Roman Imperial.
Terracotta.
Frontal head of Sol, radiate (twelve (?) rays, nine visible), damaged.
Broneer 1930: 253.
Image: photograph courtesy American School of Classical Studies, Athens.

95.   Delphi, Museum.
Delphi.
Terracotta.
5th–6th c. AD.
Frontal bust of Sol, radiate.
LIMC Helios 160c

96.   Volos, Museum?
Phthiotic Thebes.
Terracotta.
5th–6th c. AD.
Frontal bust of Sol, radiate.
ADelt 38 (1983), 2.1 p. 225 & pl. 94.

97–107.   Athens, Agora Museum L1319 (= Perlzweig 2371), L1374 (= Perlzweig 2376), L1405 (= Perlzweig 2876; mould for a lamp), L1549 (= Perlzweig

2372), L3384 (= Perlzweig 2373), L3480 (= Perlzweig 2374), L3546 (= Perlzweig 2375), L3681 (= Perlzweig 2369), L4277 (= Perlzweig 2370)
Agora.
Terracotta.
6th c. AD.
Frontal head of Sol, radiate (ca. nine rays).
Perlzweig 1961: 173 nos. 2369–2376 & 196 no. 2876; Matern 2002: 181, 266–7 B160c–g.
For (very small) images see ACSC.net (February 1, 2019).

108. Athens, National Archaeological Museum 2535.
Phyle, Parnitha, Cave of Pan.
Terracotta.
6th c. AD.
Frontal head of Sol, radiate (seven rays).
Karivieri 1996: 160.

109. Athens, National Archaeological Museum 2536.
Phyle, Parnitha, Cave of Pan.
Terracotta.
6th c. AD.
Frontal head of Sol, radiate.
Karivieri 1996: 160.

110. Tunis, Bardo CMA 1424.
Carthage.
Terracotta.
Late antique.
Frontal bust of Sol, *chlamys*.
Matern 2002: 268 B178.

111–9. Ostia, Museum 2485, 2676, 2741–3, 4410, 4460, 4712.
Ostia.
Terracotta.
Undated.
Bust of Sol.
Floriani Squarciapino 1962: 69 n. 1.

120. Ostia, Museum 2777.
Ostia.

Terracotta.
Undated.
Bust of Sol on upturned crescent with two stars.
Floriani Squarciapino 1962: 69 n. 1.

121. Porto, University Natural History and Science Museum.
Gulpilhares.
Terracotta.
Undated.
Bust of Sol, *chlamys*, *chiton*, radiate (?), both arms raised.
Matern 2002: 181, 268 B175.

122. Private collection.
Romula.
Terracotta.
Undated.
Frontal bust of Sol, radiate (seven rays). Worn.
LIMC Helios/Sol 52; Matern 2002: 181, 270 B189.

123. Adana, Museum?
Tarsus.
Terracotta.
Undated.
A total of eight lamps, mostly fragments, from the same mould. Frontal
bust of Sol, radiate (nine rays).
Matern 2002: 269 B180.

124. Unknown.
Dora (Phoenicia).
Terracotta.
Undated.
Bust of Sol above crescent.
Matern 2002: 272 B203.

125. Unknown.
Eleutheropolis (Beit Guvrin).
Terracotta.
Undated.
Bust of Sol above crescent.
Matern 2002: 272 B202.

126. Ann Arbor, University of Michigan, Kelsey Museum 0000.00.0480.
     Italy.
     Terracotta.
     Undated.
     Bust of Sol.
     Shier 1978: 39 no. 365.

127. Constantine, Museum.
     Unknown.
     Terracotta.
     Undated.
     Frontal bust of Sol, radiate (twelve rays), *chlamys*, on upturned crescent
     with a star on each point.
     Doublet & Gauckler 1892: 105 no. 2, pl. XI; Bussière 2000: 251 no. 66.

128. Plate 135.2
     Copenhagen, National Museum ABc 855.
     Unknown.
     Terracotta.
     Undated.
     Frontal bust of Sol, five rays.
     LIMC Helios/Sol 45.
     Image: photograph © Nationalmuseet Antiksamlingen, Copenhagen,
     no. 01091, with permission.

129. Damascus, Museum 5240.
     Unknown.
     Terracotta.
     Undated.
     Bust of Sol, radiate.
     Abdul-Hak & Abdul-Hak 1951: 95 no. 37.

130. Plate 130.1
     Heidelberg University, Antikenmuseum La 170.
     Unknown.
     Terracotta.
     Undated.
     Frontal bust of Sol, radiate (eight rays), on upturned crescent with a star
     on each point.
     LIMC Helios/Sol 55.

Image: © Antikenmuseum der Universität Heidelberg, photograph: Hubert Vögele.

131. Plate 131.9
Karlsruhe, Badisches Landesmuseum B 708.
Unknown.
Terracotta.
Undated.
Frontal bust of Sol, radiate (five rays).
LIMC Helios/Sol 55.
Image: © Badisches Landesmuseum, Karlsruhe.

132. Plate 135.3
Leiden, Rijksmuseum van Oudheden Brants 1173.
Greece.
3rd–5th c. AD.
Bust of Sol, radiate (nine rays).
Brants 1913, p. 67; Matern 2002: 268 B171.
Image: © National Museum of Antiquities, Leiden; photograph R.J. Looman.

133. Plate 134.1
Munich, Antikensammlung 1145 WAF.
Unknown.
Terracotta.
Undated.
Frontal bust of Sol, radiate (six rays).
LIMC Helios/Sol 55.
Image: Staatliche Antikensammlungen und Glyptothek, Munich; photograph by Renate Kühling.

134. Plate 134.2
Munich, Antikensammlung 1330 WAF.
Unknown.
Terracotta.
Undated.
Frontal bust of Sol, radiate (11 rays).
LIMC Helios/Sol 55.
Image: Staatliche Antikensammlungen und Glyptothek München; photo by Renate Kühling.

135. Plate 134.3
      Mozia, Whitaker Museum MOW 685.
      Lilybaeum (Marsala) Necropolis.
      Terracotta.
      2nd–3rd c. AD.
      Frontal bust of Sol, five rays.
      LIMC Helios/Sol 57.
      Image: © Whitaker Museum, Mozia.

136. Plate 134.4
      Munich, Antikensammlung 8578 (neue Inv.).
      Unknown.
      Terracotta.
      Undated.
      Frontal bust of Sol, radiate.
      LIMC Helios/Sol 55.
      Image: Staatliche Antikensammlungen und Glyptothek München; photo
      by Renate Kühling.

137. Oxford, Ashmolean Museum C 164.
      Unknown.
      Terracotta.
      Undated.
      Frontal bust of Sol.
      LIMC Helios/Sol 48.

138. Sao Paolo, University 64/9.2.
      Unknown.
      Terracotta.
      Unknown.
      Bust of Sol.
      LIMC Helios/Sol 55.

139. Seville, Palacio Lebrija.
      Unknown.
      Terracotta.
      Undated.
      Bust of Sol, radiate (ten rays) over crescent.
      Lopez Rodriguez 1981: 111 no. 89; Matern 2002: 271 B197a.

140. Seville, Palacio Lebrija.
Unknown.
Terracotta.
Mid 1st–early 2nd c. (Dressel 15).
Bust of Sol, radiate (ten rays) over crescent.
Lopez Rodriguez 1981: 111 no. 90; Matern 2002: 271 B197b.

141. Vienna, Kunsthistorisches Museum 6764.
Unknown.
Terracotta.
Undated.
Head of Sol, radiate nimbus, above crescent.
Matern 2002: 271 B201.

142. Art market.
Unknown.
Terracotta.
Undated.
Frontal bust of Sol, radiate (five rays).
Kricheldorf Auktion XII, 1962: 19 no. 126.

143. Art market.
Unknown.
Terracotta.
Undated.
Frontal bust of Sol, radiate (seven rays).
Kricheldorf Auktion XII, 1962: 19 nr 127.

144. Plate 132.5
Arles, Musée Départemental Arles Antique RAL.1976.15.
Arles, Rochefleur (Alyscamps necropolis), cremation tomb E.
Terracotta.
1st c. AD.
Bust of Sol.
Robin Petitot 2000: 73 no. 242; Heijmans e.a. 2012: 1924.
Image: photograph courtesy Musée Départemental Arles Antique.

145. Arles, Musée Départemental Arles Antique FAN.1991.2047.
Arles.
Terracotta.
1st c.–early 2nd c. AD.

Bust of Sol, five rays.
Robin Petitot 2003: 60 no. 121.

146. Art Market. Note: this object cannot be documented prior to 1970, and is therefore considered an undocumented artifact which cannot be ethically sold or traded (AIA code of ethics).
Unknown.
Terracotta.
3rd c. AD.
Bust of Sol, *chlamys*, radiate (six rays).
Alte Roemer Ancient Art and Antiquities Gallery AR2786.

147. Plate 132.7
Art Market.
Archaeological Gallery, Israel, 2006; Export License n° 2920.
Terracotta.
2nd c. AD.
Bust of Sol, draped, radiate (eight rays), above a thin crescent.
Ifergan galleries, Malaga, reference r37104.
Image: photograph courtesy Ifergan galleries.

148. Plate 135.4
Rouen, Musée Métropole R.94.374.
Unknown.
Undated.
Bust of Sol, six rays.
Unpublished.
Image: © Musée-Métropole-Rouen-Normandie-Cliché Yohann Deslandes.

149. Cologne, Römisch-Germanisches Museum 3082.
Environs of Cologne.
Terracotta.
2nd–3rd c. AD.
Frontal bust of Sol.
Rheinisches Bildarchiv Photo number RBA 121 711.
Image: https://www.kulturelles-erbe-koeln.de/documents/obj/05711844 (February 1, 2019).

150. Plate 135.5
Copenhagen, Thorvaldsens Museum. H1148.
Unknown.

Terracotta.
1st–2nd c. AD.
Fragment of a lamp (?) with the head of Sol, long wavy hair, in high relief.
Melander 2014: 88–89 no. X,3.
Image: © Thorvaldsens Museum, Copenhagen.

151. Plate 135.6
Copenhagen, Thorvaldsens Museum. H1149.
Unknown.
Terracotta.
AD 90–140.
Bust of Sol, radiate (five rays).
Melander 2014: 74–75 cat. VIII,8
Image: © Thorvaldsens Museum, Copenhagen.

152. Plate 134.5
Malibu, Getty Museum 83.AQ.377–485.
Asia Minor.
Terracotta.
AD 50–100 (Loeschke type III).
Head of Sol, radiate (twelve (?) rays) above an upturned crescent with a
star on each point.
Bussière & Wohl 2017, no. 153.
Image: Digital image courtesy of the Getty's Open Content Program.

153. Plate 134.6
Malibu, Getty Museum 83.AQ.377-133.
Asia Minor.
Terracotta.
AD 50–120 (Loeschke type V).
Head of Sol, radiate (twelve rays) above an upturned crescent with a star
on each point.
Bussière & Wohl 2017, no. 249.
Image: Digital image courtesy of the Getty's Open Content Program.

154. Mérida, Archaeological Museum CE10732.
Mérida.
Terracotta.
AD 75–175.
Bust of Sol, radiate (seven rays), whip behind right shoulder.
Rodríguez Martín 2002, 25, 69; LIMC Helios/Sol 57.

155.	Plate 134.7
	Leiden, Rijksmuseum van Oudheden Brants 833.
	Tunisia.
	Terracotta.
	1st–3rd c. AD.
	Bust of Sol, radiate (seven rays).
	Brants 1913: p. 46.
	Image: © National Museum of Antiquities, Leiden; photograph R.J. Looman.

156.	Plate 135.7
	Leiden, Rijksmuseum van Oudheden Brants 557.
	Tunisia.
	Terracotta.
	1st–3rd c. AD.
	Bust of Sol, radiate (seven rays).
	Brants 1913: p. 37.
	Image: © National Museum of Antiquities, Leiden; photograph R.J. Looman.

157.	Plate 135.8
	Leiden, Rijksmuseum van Oudheden Brants 768.
	Tunisia.
	Terracotta.
	1st–3rd c. AD.
	Bust of Sol, radiate (seven rays).
	Brants 1913: p. 43.
	Image: © National Museum of Antiquities, Leiden; photograph R.J. Looman.

158.	Plate 135.9
	Leiden, Rijksmuseum van Oudheden Brants 769.
	Tunisia.
	Terracotta.
	1st–3rd c. AD.
	Bust of Sol, radiate (seven rays).
	Brants 1913: p. 43.
	Image: © National Museum of Antiquities, Leiden; photograph R.J. Looman.

159.	Plate 132.8
	Leiden, Rijksmuseum van Oudheden Brants 926.
	Tunisia.
	Terracotta.

1st–3rd c. AD.
Bust of Sol, radiate (five rays).
Brants 1913: p. 50.
Image: © National Museum of Antiquities, Leiden; photograph R.J. Looman.

160. Plate 136.3
Leiden, Rijksmuseum van Oudheden Brants 928.
Tunisia.
Terracotta.
1st–3rd c. AD.
Bust of Sol, radiate (five rays).
Brants 1913: p. 50.
Image: © National Museum of Antiquities, Leiden; photograph R.J. Looman.

161. Plate 132.9
Ptuj, Regional Museum of Ptuj-Ormož R 496.
Unknown.
Terracotta.
Undated.
Bust of Sol, radiate, above a crescent (?).
Unpublished?
Image: courtesy Regional Museum of Ptuj-Ormož.

162. Plate 134.8
Tarragona, Museum MNAT 4005.
Tarragona.
Terracotta.
Undated.
Bust of Sol, radiate, (ten rays), above a thin, upturned crescent.
Unpublished?
Image: © MNAT/R. Cornadó.

163. Plate 136.4
Lorca (Spain), Archaeological Museum.
Lorca, Avenida de Santa Clara.
Terracotta.
AD 80–120.

Lamp (type Loeschke 4) with a frontal bust of Sol, radiate (twelve rays), draped, above a crescent between two stars.
Artefacts.mom.fr Lmp 42337.

164. Private collection.
Tipasa (Algeria) Necropolis.
Terracotta.
AD 150–200.
Bust of Sol, radiate (six rays), *chlamys*.
Artefacts.mom.fr LMP-41568.1; Bussière 2000, no. 1907.

165. Private collection.
Acquired in Sbeitla (Tunisia).
Terracotta.
AD 150–200.
Bust of Sol, radiate, *chlamys*.
Artefacts.mom.fr LMP-41568.2; Bussière & Rivel 2012.

166. Copenhagen, National Museum Abc.417.
Unknown.
Terracotta.
Second half 1st c. AD.
Head of Sol, radiate nimbus.
LIMC Helios/Sol 9; Matern 2002: 267, 170a.

167. Plate 134.9
Harvard Art Museum 1977.216.3235, gift of Oric Bates.
Unknown.
Terracotta.
Undated.
Bust of Sol, radiate (nine rays).
Unpublished?
Image: photograph © President and Fellows Harvard College, with permission.

168. Ephesus, Museum.
Ephesus, Theatre.
Terracotta.
Latter part of the 2nd c. AD.

Bust of Sol, radiate (six rays).
Waldner 2017: 141, 206 K106, pl. 311 & 345.

169. Ploiesti, Prahova County History and Archaeology Museum.
Unknown, acquired in Bucharest in 1961.
Terracotta.
3rd c. AD (Loeschcke VIII),
Facing bust of Sol, radiate nimbus (6 rays), *chlamys* and whip.
Topoleanu 2012: 163 no. 97.

170. Louvain-la-Neuve, museum FM233.
Unknown.
Terracotta.
1st c. AD.
Bust of Sol, radiate (twelve rays), draped (tunic or *chlamys* fastened over both shoulders), above an upturned crescent. Beside each point of the crescent a star.
Wilmet 2003: 245–246 no. 8; Wilmet 2012: 348.

171. Saint-Germain-en-Laye, Museum 12517.
Unknown.
Terracotta.
1st c. AD.
Bust of Sol, radiate (ten rays), above an upturned crescent with a star on each point.
Bémont & Chew 2007: 71, 187 IT 43, 445 pl. 20.

172. Raqqada, museum?
Raqqada, Roman cemetery.
Terracotta.
2nd–3rd c. AD.
Bust of Sol, radiate, above an upturned crescent with a star above each point.
Ennabli 1973: 115, C6.

173. Seville, Palacio Lebrija.
Unknown.
Terracotta
Mid 1st–early 2nd c. AD.

Bust of Sol, long wavy hair, radiate (nine rays), damaged.
Lopez Rodriguez 1981: 114–115 no. 116.

174. Plate 136.1
London, British Museum 1898, 1122.1
Cap de Tenes, Algeria.
Terracotta.
AD 90–140.
Bust of Sol, radiate (five rays), long curly hair.
Image available under CC BY-NC-SA 4.0 license, Trustees of the British Museum.
Image: photograph © Trustees of the British Museum.

175. Rabat, Archaeological Museum?
Cotta.
Terracotta.
Last quarter 1st c. BC–third quarter 1st c. AD.
Fragment of a lamp depicting a bust of Sol, radiate.
Ponsich 1961: 86 no. 99, cf. 83 no. 59.

176. Rabat, Archaeological Museum?
Volubilis.
Terracotta.
Mid 1st c. AD–first quarter 2nd c. AD.
Bust of Sol, radiate (seven rays), *chlamys*, above a globe.
Ponsich 1961: 96 no. 221.

177. Rabat, Archaeological Museum?
Thamusida.
Terracotta.
Mid 1st c. AD–first quarter 2nd c. AD.
Bust of Sol, radiate (seven rays), *chlamys*, above a globe.
Ponsich 1961: 98 no. 242.

178. Rabat, Archaeological Museum?
Sala.
Terracotta.
Mid 1st c. AD–first quarter 2nd c. AD.
Bust of Sol, radiate (seven rays), *chlamys*, above a globe.
Ponsich 1961: 98 no. 248.

179. Rabat, Archaeological Museum?
    Tocolosida.
    Terracotta.
    Undated.
    Fragment of a lamp; bust of Sol, radiate (seven rays), *chlamys*.
    Ponsich 1961: 114 no. 452.

180. Rabat, Archaeological Museum?
    Cotta.
    Terracotta.
    Undated.
    Fragment of a lamp; bust of Sol, radiate (seven rays).
    Ponsich 1961: 115 no. 464.

181. Rabat, Archaeological Museum?
    Mogador.
    Terracotta.
    Undated.
    Fragment of a lamp; bust of Sol, radiate.
    Ponsich 1961: 116 no. 485.

182. Montauban, Ingres Museum.
    Unknown.
    Terracotta.
    Undated.
    Fragment of a lamp; bust of Sol, radiate.
    Ponsich 1963: 128 no. 127, pl. VIII.

183. Saint-Germain-en-Laye, Musée des Antiquités Nationales inv. 12407.
    Vaison.
    Terracotta.
    Late 1st–mid 2nd c. AD.
    Bust of Sol, radiate, five rays.
    Bonnet & Delplace 1983: 178 no. 11; Bémont & Chew 2007: 273 GA 187, 477
    pl. 52.

184. Nîmes, Musée de la Romanité Inv. 137.
    In the region of Orange.
    Terracotta.
    1st–early 2nd c. AD.
    Bust of Sol, radiate, five rays.
    Bonnet & Delplace 1983: 178 no. 12.

185. Cavaillon, Museum.
     Sannes, Gallo-Roman necropolis, tomb XV.
     Terracotta.
     Late 1st c. AD.
     Bust of Sol, radiate, five rays.
     Dumoulin 1958: 231, pl. 40.8; Bonnet & Delplace 1983: 178 no. 13.

186. Nicosia, Cyprus Museum D2546.
     Cyprus.
     Terracotta.
     Undated.
     Radiate bust of Sol.
     Oziol 1977: 156 no. 462.

187. Nicosia, Cyprus Museum 1935/X-II/3.
     Cyprus.
     Terracotta.
     Undated.
     Radiate bust of Sol.
     Oziol 1977: 185–6 no. 548.

188. Saint-Germain-en-Laye, Musée des Antiquités Nationales inv. 12408.
     Vaison?
     Terracotta.
     Second half 1st c.–first quarter 2nd c. AD.
     Bémont & Chew 2007: 235–6 GA30, 459 pl. 34.

189. Glanum, excavation depot 3780.
     Glanum.
     Terracotta.
     AD 90–150.
     Bust of Sol, radiate (five rays), *chlamys* (?).
     Bémont 2002: 186 no. 248, pl. 23.

190. Glanum, excavation depot 3972.
     Glanum.
     Terracotta.
     AD 90–150.
     Bust of Sol, radiate (five rays), *chlamys* (?).
     Bémont 2002: 186 no. 249, pl. 23.

191. Glanum, excavation depot 1700.
     Glanum.
     Terracotta.
     AD 90–150.
     Bust of Sol, radiate (five rays), *chlamys* (?).
     Bémont 2002: 186 no. 250, pl. 23.

192–7. Montans, depot Miq 75.FC.896; 75.FC.897; 75.FC.898; 75.FC.899; 75.FC.948.
     Montans.
     Terracotta.
     Late 1st–mid 2nd c. AD.
     Bust of Sol, radiate (five rays).
     Bergès 1989: 70 nos. 223–227, 91 fig. 41 (= 223).

     G1b. Sol in Quadriga
1.   Brugg, Vindonissa Museum B859.
     Vindonissa.
     Terracotta.
     1st c. AD.
     Man, nude, reins in both hands, on *biga* left The man is perhaps radiate (difficult to make out on photograph). Probably not Sol.
     LIMC Helios/Sol 152.

2.   Plate 136.5
     London, British Museum 1870,0709.45.
     Reportedly purchased in Alexandria.
     Terracotta.
     AD 150–250.
     Sol, standing in frontal chariot, two horses rearing up to the left, two to the right. Sol has a radiate nimbus (12? rays), is nude but for a *chlamys*, and has raised both hands.
     Bailey 1975: Q2076; Derksen 1978: 241, fig. 2; Matern 2002: 53, 214 Q44.
     Image: photograph © Trustees of the British Museum.

3.   Paris, Bibliothèque Nationale Froehner VII 586.
     Unknown, possibly Egypt.
     Terracotta.
     3rd c. AD.

Sol, standing in frontal chariot, two horses rearing up to the left, two to the right. Sol has a radiate nimbus (11? rays), is nude but for a *chlamys*, and has raised both hands. He is described as holding a whip in each hand, but I cannot make this out on the photograph available to me. Matern 2002: 53, 214 Q45.

4. Plate 138.1
Art Market. Note: this object cannot be documented prior to 1970, and is therefore considered an undocumented artifact which cannot be ethically sold or traded (AIA code of ethics).
Unknown.
Terracotta.
2nd c. AD?
Sol in a frontal *quadriga*, two horses rearing to the left, and two to the right. Sol is depicted as a draped bust with curly hair and seven rays.
Sold September 4, 2019, London, Timeline auctions lot 1070.

5. Plate 136.6
Paris, Louvre CP 4404
Italy.
Terracotta.
1st c. AD.
Sol, radiate (twelve rays) on a facing *biga*, one horse jumping to the left, and one to the right, Image: courtesy Louvre.

G1c. Sol and Luna

1. Berlin, Staatliche Museen, Antikensammlung TC 6002.
Unknown.
Terracotta.
Second half 1st–first half 2nd c. AD.
Frontal busts of Sol, radiate, on the left, and Luna, torch, on the right. The disc and the lamp do not belong together.
LIMC Helios/Sol 314; Heres 1972: 51–2 no. 233; Matern 2002: 181–2, 273 B224.1.

2. Plate 136.2
London, British Museum 1856,1226.401.
Pozzuoli (lamp-type North African).
Terracotta.
Second half 2nd c. AD.

Frontal busts of Sol (left), radiate (six rays), *chlamys* and long-sleeved *chiton*, globe in right hand, and Luna (right), with torch but no crescent, next to each other.
Derksen 1978: 239–41, fig. 1; LIMC Helios/Sol 314; Bailey 1975: Q1704; Matern 2002: 181–2, 273 B224.2.
Image: photograph © Trustees of the British Museum.

3. Patras, Museum 1473.
Patras, Od. Kanari 54 & Od. Korinthou.
Terracotta.
2nd c. AD?
Within a zodiac circle profile busts of Sol (radiate, four rays survive) and Luna next to each other.
LIMC Helios 325; Petropoulos 1978: 306–7 no. 4; Gundel 1992: 238 no. 100.1; Matern 2002: 181–2, 273 B222.

4. London, British Museum 1814,0704.50.
Produced in Central Italy.
Terracotta.
Ca. AD 175–225.
Very worn. Busts of Sol, radiate (four or five rays) and Luna facing each other.
LIMC Helios/Sol 313; Bailey 1975: Q1354; Matern 2002: 181–2, 273 B220. Previously registered as 1864,0617.22, according to the British Museum website (June 3, 2017). http://britishmuseum.org/research/collection_on line/collection_object_details.aspx?objectId=436028&partId=1&museum no=1964,0617.22&page=1 but Tran Tam Tinh (1984: 320 no. 9) lists that lamp as one decorated with Sol kissing Sarapis.

5. Plate 137.1
London, British Museum 1756,0101.589.
Produced in Central Italy.
Terracotta.
Ca AD 175–225.
Sol standing, radiate nimbus (seven rays), nude but for a *chlamys*, globe in right hand, whip in left hand, facing Luna (torch, crescent). The base is inscribed: saecvl: a reference to the Ludi Saeculares of AD 206? Cf. G19.3 below.
Bailey 1975: 349, Q 1343; LIMC Helios/Sol 312; Matern 2002: 91, 227 G19.
Image: photograph © Trustees of the British Museum.

6.   Oxford, Ashmolean Museum C150.
      Reported to be from Rome.
      Terracotta.
      2nd–3rd c. AD.
      Facing busts of Sol, radiate (seven rays), *chlamys*, sleeved *chiton*, globe in
      his right hand, and Luna.
      Derksen 1978: 239–241, pl. 104.9; LIMC Helios/Sol 314; Matern 2002: 181–2,
      273 B224.4.

7.   Ptuj, Pokrajinski Muzej Ptuj Ormož. G.B.10/I.Z.2796*.
      Ptuj.
      Terracotta.
      2nd–3rd c. AD.
      Frontal busts of Sol and Luna.
      LIMC Helios/Sol 315; Matern 2002: 273 B223.

8.   Plate 136.9
      London, British Museum 1986,1003.3.
      Egypt.
      Terracotta.
      2nd–3rd c. AD.
      Profile busts of Sol and Luna, facing each other. A swastika is inscribed in
      the base.
      Matern 2002: 273 B221; Bailey 1975: Q2052bis.
      Image: photograph © Trustees of the British Museum.

9.   Jerusalem, Museum of Prehistory 6202.
      Unknown.
      Terracotta.
      2nd–3rd c. AD.
      Busts of Sol and Luna, kissing.
      Matern 2002: 273 B218.

10.   Berlin, Staatliche Museen, Antikensammlung TC 891.
      Unknown.
      Terracotta.
      Early 3rd c. AD.
      Profile busts of Sol (right) and Luna (left) facing each other. Sol is radi-
      ate (four rays), Luna has an upturned crescent moon above her forehead;
      between their foreheads a star, below Sol a globe, below Luna a torch.
      LIMC Helios/Sol 313 (with refs); Matern 2002: 181–2, 273 B215, fig. 94.

11. Plate 137.3
    Athens, Benaki Museum 12204.
    Alexandria.
    Terracotta.
    4th c. AD.
    Busts of Sol, radiate with three indistinct rays (left) and Luna, crescent (right), facing each other.
    Matern 2002: 181–2, 272–3 B214a.
    Image: courtesy of the Benaki Museum, Dr. I. Papageorgiou; photograph author.

12. Plate 137.2
    Athens, Benaki Museum 12205.
    Alexandria.
    Terracotta.
    4th c. AD.
    Busts of Sol, radiate, five rays, and Luna, facing each other.
    Matern 2002: 181–2, 272–3 B214b.
    Image: courtesy of the Benaki Museum, Dr. I. Papageorgiou; photograph author.

13. Ostia, Museum 2299.
    Ostia.
    Terracotta.
    Undated.
    Busts of Sol and Luna.
    Floriani Squarciapino 1962, 69 n. 1.

14. Ostia, Museum 2415.
    Ostia.
    Terracotta.
    Undated.
    Busts of Sol and Luna.
    Floriani Squarciapino 1962, 69 n. 1.

15. Unknown.
    Syracuse.
    Terracotta.
    Undated.
    Busts of Sol and Luna.
    Matern 2002: 273–4 B224.6.

16.   Carthage, Museum 650.
       Carthage.
       Terracotta.
       Undated.
       Busts of Sol, radiate, *chlamys*, and Luna facing each other.
       LIMC Helios/Sol 314; Matern 2002: 181–2, 273 B219.

17.   Sabratha, Museum 862.
       Sabratha, Regio IV.
       Terracotta.
       Undated.
       Frontal busts of Sol, left, radiate (7? rays), long-sleeved *chiton* and *chla-mys*, globe in front of him in right hand, and Luna, right, upturned cres-cent behind shoulders, torch.
       Matern 2002: 181–2, 273–4 B224.5

18.   Plate 18.4
       Karlsruhe, Badisches Landesmuseum B 691.
       Unknown.
       Terracotta.
       Undated.
       Busts of Sol and Luna.
       LIMC Helios/Sol 314.
       Image: Courtesy Badisches Landesmuseum. Karlsruhe.

19.   Plate 136.7
       Mainz, Römisch-Germanisches Zentralmuseum O.36629.
       Unknown.
       Terracotta.
       Undated.
       Frontal busts of Sol (left) and Luna (right); Sol is radiate (five rays), wears a *chlamys* and-possibly-a long sleeved *chiton*, and holds a globe in his left hand before his breast.
       LIMC Helios/Sol 314; Matern 2002: 181–2, 273 B224.3.
       Image: photograph Ursula Rudischer, © GDKE-Landesmuseum Mainz

20.   Plate 136.8
       Munich, Antikensammlung 1248 WAF.
       Unknown.

Terracotta.
Undated.
Profile busts of Sol and Luna.
LIMC Helios/Sol 314.
Image: Staatliche Antikensammlungen und Glyptothek München; photograph Renate Kühling.

21. Montreal, Anawati CollectionNA-165.
Unknown.
Terracotta.
3rd–4th c. AD.
Busts of Sol, radiate crown (four or five rays), and Luna facing each other.
Djuric 1995: 38 no. C97.

22. Prague National Museum H10-6221.
Tunisia.
Terracotta.
Late 2nd–early 3rd c. AD
Profile busts of Sol (right), radiate (four? rays) and Luna (left), facing each other. Very worn, but the identity of Sol appears to be beyond doubt.
Svobodova 2006: 17 no. 96.

G1d. Sol, Luna and Capitoline Triad
1. Rome, Antiquarium Communale.
Rome.
Terracotta.
2nd–3rd c. AD.
Above: Capitoline triad, seated, between two Tritons (?) blowing their horns. Below, left, Sol, radiate, nude but for *chlamys*, right hand raised, in *quadriga* ascending to the right, and right, Luna in *biga*, descending to the right.
Derksen 1978: 241–244; LIMC Helios/Sol 392 (with refs.); Matern 2002: 70, 219 Q74.

2. Plate 138.2
Berlin, Staatliche Museen, Antikensammlung TC 871.
Unknown.
Terracotta.
2nd–early 3rd c. AD (Type Loeschke 7b).

Above: Capitoline triad, seated, between two Tritons (?) blowing their horns. Below, left, Sol, radiate, nude but for *chlamys*, right hand raised, in *quadriga* ascending to the right, and right, Luna in *biga*, descending to the right.

Heres 1972, 72 no. 440; Derksen 1978: 241–244, fig. 3; Matern 2002: 70, n. 444, 219 Q73.

Image: photograph © Staatliche Museen Berlin.

G1e. Sol and Sarapis

1. Plate 139.2
   Alexandria, Graeco-Roman Museum 8545.
   Alexandria.
   Terracotta.
   3rd c. AD.
   Frontal bust of Sarapis, embraced and kissed by Sol (profile bust) to the left of him.
   Tran Tam Tinh 1984: 319 no. 4. From the same mould: Alexandria, Museum 8969 and 5040; Tübingen, Arch. Inst. H.S./112039.
   Image: photograph Jean-Yves Empereur, with permission.

2. Alexandria, Graeco-Roman Museum 8546.
   Alexandria, Serapeum, subterranean passageways.
   Terracotta.
   3rd c. AD.
   Frontal bust of Sarapis, embraced and kissed by Sol (profile bust) to the left of him.
   Tran Tam Tinh 1984: 318 no. 1. From the same mould: Cairo, Egyptian Museum 26424 (disc only).

3. Plate 139.3
   Alexandria, Graeco-Roman Museum 8969.
   Alexandria.
   Terracotta.
   3rd c. AD.
   Frontal bust of Sarapis, embraced and kissed by Sol (profile bust) to the left of him.
   Tran Tam Tinh 1984: 319 no. 3. From the same mould: Alexandria, Museum 8545 and 5040; Tübingen, Arch. Inst. H.S./112039.
   Image: photograph Jean-Yves Empereur, with permission.

4.   Plate 140.1
      Alexandria, Graeco-Roman Museum 16333.
      Alexandria.
      Terracotta.
      3rd c. AD.
      Frontal bust of Sarapis, embraced and kissed by Sol (profile bust) to the
      left of him.
      Tran Tam Tinh 1984: 319 no. 5. From the same mould: London, BM EA
      49647; Münster, Arch. Museum d. Univ. inv. 458.
      Image: photograph Jean-Yves Empereur, with permission.

5.   Plates 15.2, 140.2
      Alexandria, Graeco-Roman Museum 29062.
      Alexandria.
      Terracotta.
      3rd c. AD.
      Frontal bust of Sarapis, embraced and kissed by Sol (profile bust) to the
      left of him.
      Tran Tam Tinh 1984: 319 no. 6.
      Image: photograph Jean-Yves Empereur, with permission.

6.   Alexandria, Graeco-Roman Museum 29073.
      Alexandria.
      Terracotta.
      3rd c. AD.
      Frontal bust of Sarapis, embraced and kissed by Sol (profile bust) to the
      left of him.
      Tran Tam Tinh 1984: 319 no. 7.

7.   Plate 140.3
      Alexandria, Graeco-Roman Museum 31801.
      Alexandria.
      Terracotta.
      3rd c. AD.
      Frontal bust of Sarapis, embraced and kissed by Sol (profile bust) to the
      left of him.
      Unpublished.
      Image: photograph by Dr. Merwatte Seif el-Din, with permission.

8. Plate 140.4
    Alexandria, Graeco-Roman Museum 31802.
    Alexandria.
    Terracotta.
    3rd c. AD.
    Frontal bust of Sarapis, embraced and kissed by Sol (profile bust) to the
    left of him.
    Unpublished.
    Image: photographs by Dr. Merwatte Seif el-Din, with permission.

9. Alexandria, Graeco-Roman Museum 31810.
    Alexandria.
    Terracotta.
    3rd c. AD.
    Frontal bust of Sarapis, embraced and kissed by Sol (profile bust) to the
    left of him.
    Unpublished.

10. Athens, Benaki Museum 11887.
    Egypt.
    Terracotta.
    3rd c. AD.
    Frontal bust of Sarapis, embraced and kissed by Sol (profile bust) to the
    left of him.
    Tran Tam Tinh 1984: 320 no. 14.

11. Athens, Benaki Museum 21028.
    Egypt.
    Terracotta.
    3rd c. AD.
    Frontal bust of Sarapis, embraced and kissed by Sol (profile bust) to the
    left of him.
    Tran Tam Tinh 1984: 320 no. 15.

12. Cairo, Egyptian Museum 2642.
    Alexandria?
    Terracotta.
    3rd c. AD.
    Frontal bust of Sarapis, embraced and kissed by Sol (profile bust) to the
    left of him.

Tran Tam Tinh 1984: 320 no. 10; Hornbostel 1973: fig. 242. From the same mould as Alexandria, Museum 8546.

13. Hannover, Kestner Museum 1932.252.
Egypt.
Terracotta.
3rd c. AD.
Frontal bust of Sarapis, embraced and kissed by Sol (profile bust) to the left of him.
Matern 2002: 181–2, 273 B217.

14. Vacat (= G1c.4).

15. London, British Museum 1877,1112.2.
Alexandria.
Terracotta.
AD 150–250.
Frontal bust of Sarapis, embraced and kissed by Sol (profile bust) to the left of him.
Tran Tam Tinh 1984: 319 no. 8; Bailey 1975: Q2049. From the same mould as Alexandria, Museum 16333 = G1e.4 and Münster, Arch. Museum Univ. 458 = G1e.16.

16. Münster, Archäologisches Museum der Universität 458.
Unknown, acquired in Egypt.
Terracotta.
3rd c. AD.
Frontal bust of Sarapis, embraced and kissed by Sol (profile bust) to the left of him.
Tran Tam Tinh 1984: 320 no. 11.

17. Nafplion, Archaeological Museum 459.
Egypt.
Terracotta.
3rd c. AD.
Frontal busts of Sol and Sarapis next to each other.
Cf. Tran Tam Tinh 1984: 320 n. 8.

18. Tübingen, Archäologisches Institut inv. 6975.
Unknown, acquired in Egypt.
Terracotta.

3rd c. AD.
Frontal bust of Sarapis, embraced and kissed by Sol (profile bust) to the
left of him.
Tran Tam Tinh 1984: 320 no. 12; Cahn-Klaiber 1977: 227, 233, 246, no. 331.

19.   Tübingen, Archäologisches Institut inv. H.S./112039.
        Alexandria.
        Terracotta.
        3rd c. AD.
        Frontal bust of Sarapis, embraced and kissed by Sol (profile bust) to the
        left of him.
        Tran Tam Tinh 1984: 320 no. 13; Cahn-Klaiber 1977: no. 350. Same mould
        as Alexandria, Museum 5040, 8969, and 8545.

20.   Alexandria, Graeco-Roman Museum 5040.
        Alexandria.
        Terracotta.
        3rd c. AD.
        Frontal bust of Sarapis, embraced and kissed by Sol (profile bust) to the
        left of him.
        Tran Tam Tinh 1984: 319 no. 2. From the same mould: Alexandria, Museum
        8969 and 8545; Tübingen, Arch. Inst. H.S./112039.

21.   Plate 139.1
        Neuchatel, private collection.
        Alexandria.
        Terracotta.
        2nd–3rd c. AD (Loeschke VIII).
        Frontal bust of Sarapis, embraced and kissed by Sol (profile bust) to the
        left of him.
        Artefacts.mom.fr Lmp-4377.
        Image: Photograph courtesy Artefacts.mom.fr.

22.   Berkeley, Phoebe Hearst Museum of Anthropology 8-9848.
        Italy.
        Terracotta.
        1st–2nd c. AD.
        Frontal bust of Sarapis, embraced and kissed by Sol (profile bust) to the
        left of him.
        Unpublished?

G1f. Planetary Deities

1. Unknown.
    Rome.
    Terracotta.
    Undated.
    Busts of the seven planetary deities.
    LIMC Saturnus 42.

G1g. Other

1. Hannover, Kestner Museum 950.
    Unknown.
    Terracotta.
    AD 40–100.
    Twelve busts of deities: Jupiter, Juno, Minerva, Luna, Mercurius, Mars, Sol, Neptune, Ceres, Vesta, Venus, Vulcan.
    Matern 2002: 267 B166a.

2. Plate 140.5
    London, British Museum 1980,1008.3
    Produced in Campania
    Terracotta.
    Second half 1st c. AD.
    Above an upturned crescent, scene consisting of profile head, right, of Sol, radiate (six rays), crowned from behind with a wreath by a small winged Victory in long *chiton*.
    Bailey 1975: 458, Q1227bis.
    Image: photograph © Trustees of the British Museum.

3. London British Museum 1756.0101.1093.
    Unknown; produced in Central Italy.
    Terracotta.
    Ca. AD 175–225.
    Rather worn, details difficult to discern. Shepherd clad in short tunica, carrying a sheep on his shoulder. In front of him: crescent. Behind him, bust of Sol, radiate (seven rays). Bailey identifies the indeterminate blobs by his feet as "several indeterminate animals, presumably part of his flock". The base is inscribed: saecvl: a reference to the Ludi Saeculares of AD 206? A similar lamp, also inscribed saecvl, is described by De Rossi 1870 (cf. Finney 1994, 132–5: figs. 5.4–6). This lamp is now in Berlin. Cf. G1c.5 above.
    LIMC Helios/Sol 391; Bailey 1975: 357–8, Q1370, pl. 80, figs. 48, 109.

G2. Terracotta Lamps, Decoration on Handle
G2a. Head/Bust of Sol

1.   Plate 142.1
     Berlin, Staatliche Museen, Antikensammlung TC 8760.
     Art market Italy, acquired in 1904; reputedly found in Boscotrecase.
     Terracotta.
     Mid 1st c. AD (Claudian).
     Handle, triangular, depicting a caduceus behind a cock walking right;
     lower left-hand corner frontal bust of Sol, twelve rays; lower right hand
     corner frontal bust of Luna with crescent moon above her forehead.
     On lamp bust facing left (of Sol?) on upturned crescent with a star on
     each point and a hand above his forehead. (Heres, followed by Matern,
     describes the bust as Luna).
     Heres 1972: 13 no. 5; Matern 2002: 181–2, 273 B216.
     Image: © Staatliche Museen zu Berlin; photographer unknown.

2.   Plate 140.7
     London, British Museum 1904,0204.495.
     Produced in Gaul.
     Terracotta.
     1st c. AD.
     Bust of Sol, radiate (22 rays), *chlamys*, above crescent.
     Bailey 1975: 163, Q1565; Matern 2002: 181, 269 B183b.
     Image: photograph © Trustees of the British Museum.

3.   London, British Museum 1980,1001.56 (formerly Victoria and Albert
     Museum).
     Salamis or Curium; produced on Cyprus.
     Terracotta.
     AD 40–100.
     Frontal bust of Sol, radiate (twelve rays), *chlamys*, on crescent.
     Bailey 1975: 306, Q2449; LIMC Helios/Sol 56; Matern 2002: 181, 269 B183a.
     Image: Artefact.mom.fr Lmp-41079.

4.   Plate 140.6
     Alexandria, Graeco-Roman museum 5095.
     Alexandria.
     Terracotta.
     1st c. AD?

Frontal bust of Sol, radiate (thirteen rays), *chlamys.*
Matern 2002: 174, 181, 269 B181.1b
Image: photograph Jean-Yves Empereur, with permission.

5. Alexandria, Graeco-Roman museum 6480.
Alexandria.
Terracotta.
1st c. AD?
Frontal bust of Sol, radiate (thirteen rays), *chlamys.*
Matern 2002: 174, 181, 269 B181.1a.

6. Plate 141.4
Athens, Benaki Museum 22239.
Alexandria.
Terracotta.
1st c. AD?
Frontal bust of Sol, radiate nimbus (thirteen rays) in front of crescent.
LIMC Helios 159; Matern 2002: 174, 181, 269 B181.2. LIMC, followed by
Matern, incorrectly gives Patras as the location of this lamp.
Image: courtesy of the Benaki Museum, Dr. I. Papageorgiou; photograph
author.

7. Berlin, Staatliche Museen, Antikensammlung 19384.
Darb Gase? Egypt.
Terracotta.
1st c. AD?
Frontal bust of Sol, radiate (thirteen rays), *chlamys.*
Matern 2002: 174, 181, 269 B181.3a.

8. Plate 143.1
St. Petersburg, Hermitage 62191.
Egypt.
Terracotta.
1st c. AD?
Frontal bust of Sol, radiate (thirteen rays), *chlamys,* in front of upturned
crescent.
Matern 2002: 174, 181, 269 B181.7.
Image: courtesy Hermitage Museum, St. Petersburg.

9.   Plate 140.8
      Frankfurt University, Archaeological Museum 23.
      From the old collection of the Italian numismatist Giovanni Dattari
      (Cairo), dissolved in 1912.
      Terracotta.
      Second half 1st c. AD.
      Frontal bust of Sol, radiate (thirteen rays), *chlamys*.
      Matern 2002: 174, 181, 269 B181.5.
      Image: photograph © Antikensammlung der Goethe Universität, Frank-
      furt am Main, Matthias Recke.

10.   London, British Museum 1960,0411.4.
      Unknown.
      Terracotta.
      Second half 1st c. AD.
      Frontal bust of Sol, radiate nimbus (thirteen rays), *chlamys*, in front of
      crescent.
      Bailey 1975: 238, Q1945; Matern 2002: 269, B181.6

11.   Magdalensburg, Museum 4679.
      Unknown.
      Terracotta.
      First half 1st c. AD.
      Triangular handle; frontal bust of Sol, radiate (twelve rays), *chlamys*,
      above crescent and volutes.
      Matern 2002: 181, 269 B184, fig. 91.

12.   Rome, Museo Nazionale Romano.
      Unknown.
      Terracotta.
      Augustan.
      Frontal bust of Sol, radiate (23 rays), *chlamys*, on upturned crescent.
      Derksen 1978: 236–237, pl. 103.7; LIMC Helios/Sol 56; Matern 2002: 181, 271
      B200b.

13.   Berlin, Staatliche Museen, Antikensammlung 8828/4.
      Acquired by C. Schmidt in Alexandria in 1907.
      Terracotta.
      Undated.

Handle in the shape of a crescent moon behind a frontal bust of Sol, radiate nimbus (thirteen rays), *chlamys*.

Heres 1972: 81 no. 504; Matern 2002: 174, 181, 269 B181.3b

14. Unknown.
    Canopus.
    Terracotta.
    Undated.
    Triangular handle; frontal bust of Sol, radiate, *chlamys*, above crescent moon and volutes.
    Matern 2002: 181, 269–70 B186.

15. Frankfurt a.M., Archäologisches Museum β561.
    Unknown.
    Terracotta.
    Undated.
    Triangular handle; frontal bust of Sol, radiate (nine rays), *chlamys*, above two cornucopiae.
    Matern 2002: 181, 269 B182.

16. Plate 140.9
    Munich, Antikensammlung 1363.
    Unknown.
    Terracotta.
    Undated.
    Triangular handle; frontal bust of Sol, radiate, *chlamys*, above crescent moon.
    Matern 2002: 181, 269–70 B185.
    Image: Staatliche Antikensammlungen und Glyptothek München; photo by Renate Kühling.

17. Tübingen, Archäologisches Institut.
    Unknown.
    Terracotta.
    Undated.
    Bust of Sol, radiate nimbus (thirteen rays), *chlamys*, on upturned crescent moon.
    Cahn-Klaiber 1977: 196 no. 203 (with refs.); Matern 2002: 174, 181, 269 B181.8.

18. Plate 141.1
    London, Petrie Museum UC 54435.
    Unknown.
    Terracotta.
    Undated.
    Crescent-shaped handle with draped bust of Sol, radiate nimbus (thirteen rays).
    Image: photograph courtesy The Petrie Museum of Egyptian Archaeology UCL under CC BY-NC-SA 3.0 license.

19. Plate 141.2
    London, Petrie Museum UC 54436.
    Ehnasya.
    Terracotta.
    Undated.
    Crescent-shaped handle with draped bust of Sol, radiate nimbus (9? rays).
    Petrie 1905: pl. 54 D1.
    Image: photograph courtesy The Petrie Museum of Egyptian Archaeology UCL under CC BY-NC-SA 3.0 license.

20. Plate 141.3
    Geneva, Musées d'art et d'histoire 12081; don Walther Fol, Genève (1871).
    Ascalon (Egypt).
    Terracotta.
    1st–2nd c.
    Frontal bust of Sol, radiate nimbus (twelve rays), crescent above, stars to either side.
    Chrzanovski 2011: 12 no. 5.
    Image: © Musées d'art et d'histoire, Geneva, photograph: Chaman ateliers multimédia.

21. Plate 6.1
    Athens, Benaki Museum.
    Egypt.
    Terracotta.
    Undated.
    Bust of Sol, radiate nimbus (nine rays), long wavy hair.
    Unpublished.
    Image courtesy of Benaki Museum, Dr. I. Papageorgiou; photograph author.

22. Plate 141.5
    Neuchatel, Private collection.
    Alexandria.
    Terracotta.
    AD 50–200.
    Crescent-shaped handle, bust of Sol, radiate (thirteen rays), *chlamys*, superimposed on the crescent.
    Artefacts.mom.fr LMP-4486.1
    Image: courtesy Artefacts (artefacts.mom.fr), Lmp-4486 (photo L. Chrzanovski).

23. Plate 141.6
    Neuchatel Private collection.
    Unknown.
    Terracotta.
    AD 50–200.
    Crescent-shaped handle, bust of Sol, radiate (thirteen rays), *chlamys*, superimposed on the crescent.
    Artefacts.mom.fr LMP-4486.2.
    Image: courtesy Artefacts (artefacts.mom.fr), Lmp-4486.2 (photo L.P. Cavaillé).

G2b. Sol, Luna & Isis

1. Marseille, Musée d'Archéologie Méditerranéenne.
   Marseille, Rue Belsunce.
   Terracotta.
   Undated.
   On handle, draped bust of Isis on a globe, between Sol (?) and a crescent.
   Froehner 1897: 219.

G3. Bronze Lamps, Decoration on Handle

1. Plate 4.2
   Lyon, Musée des Beaux Arts L 260.
   Unknown.
   Bronze.
   2nd c. AD.
   Handle crowned with a head of Sol, radiate (fourteen rays).
   LIMC Helios/Sol 11.
   Image: © Musée des Beaux Arts, Lyon.

2. Plate 143.2
    Paris, Louvre Collection de Clercq (formerly 111).
    Unknown.
    Bronze.
    2nd–3rd c. AD.
    Handle ends in a leaf-ornament from which Sol emerges; Sol is radiate
    (six rays), dressed in *chiton* and *chlamys*, has his right hand raised and
    holds a globe in his left hand.
    LIMC Helios/Sol 67; de Ridder 1905: 316 no. 519, pl. 61.2; Matern 2002: 117,
    239 I47. The location for this lamp given in LIMC is incorrect.
    Image: after De Ridder 1905 (in the public domain).

3. Cairo, Egyptian Museum 27841.
    Unknown.
    Bronze.
    Undated.
    Upper body of Sol, radiate, dressed in *chiton* and *chlamys*, right hand
    raised, globe in lowered left hand.
    LIMC Helios/Sol 67; Matern 2002: 117, 239 I45, fig. 54.

4. Plate 144.1
    Cairo, Egyptian Museum 27842.
    Unknown.
    Bronze.
    Undated.
    Upper body of Sol, radiate, dressed in *chiton* and *chlamys*, with whip in
    lowered left hand and torch in raised right hand.
    LIMC Helios/Sol 67; Reinach RépStat IV 61,8; Matern 2002: 97, 117 n. 635,
    228 G26, fig. 26.
    Image: courtesy of the Egyptian Museum, Cairo.

5. Cairo, Egyptian Museum.
    Unknown.
    Bronze.
    Undated.
    Upper body of Sol, radiate (seven rays), dressed in *chiton*, right hand
    raised, globe in lowered left hand.
    Matern 2002: 117, 239 I46.

6. Paris, Louvre (ex collection de Clercq).
    Lebanon, near Beirut.

Bronze.

Undated.

Handle ends in a bust of Sol?

De Ridder 1905, 309 no. 502.

7. Rome, Museo Nazionale Romano 67481.

Unknown.

Bronze.

1st c. AD (?).

Bilichne lamp with a handle in the form of a head of Sol, radiate (seven rays).

Conticello de' Spagnolis & De Carolis 1983, 17–18, 22–3 no. II.3.

8. Israel Antiquities Authority.

Caesarea, harbour.

Bronze.

Late 3rd–early 4th c. AD.

Handle of a bronze lamp in the form of a statuette of Sol emerging from a calyx; he is dressed in a long *chiton* and *chlamys*, radiate (seven rays, of which one is missing), right hand raised, globe on outstretched left hand.

Unpublished.

9. Plate 144.2

Budapest, Hungarian National Museum, Roman Collection, 78.1913.

Mór.

Bronze.

1st–2nd c. AD.

Handle of a lamp in the shape of an upturned crescent, supporting a bust of Jupiter. Below Jupiter, in front of the crescent, bust of Sol, radiate.

LIMC Helios/Sol 338.

Image: courtesy of the Hungarian National Museum.

G4. Bronze Lamps, Other

1. Plate 18.1

Florence, Archaeological Museum 1676.

Unknown.

Bronze.

2nd–3rd c. AD.

Handle of a lamp consisting of a bronze circular band, to which are attached two Tritons (the one on the right lost) flanking statuettes of Luna (right) and Sol (left), radiate (seven rays), right hand raised, *chlamys*, and

long-sleeved *chiton*, globe in left hand. Milani (1899) believes that statuette and lamp do not belong together, pointing out that the statuette was
attached to the lamp some time after 1704 (when they still had separate
inv. numbers) and before 1753 (when they were listed as a single object).
LIMC Helios/Sol 316; von Hesberg 1981, 1151 no. 45a; Milani 1899, 81–2;
Matern 2002: 117, 119, 176, 239 I44, fig. 56.
Image: courtesy of the Archaeological Museum, Florence.

H. Intaglios[21]

H1. Sol in *Quadriga* to Left
H1a. ... Nude but for Chlamys, Whip in Right Hand, Reins in Left hand
1.   Aquileia, Museo Nazionale 27463.
     Aquileia.
     Glass paste.
     Identification as Sol in *quadriga* very uncertain (according to Sena
     Chiesa it is not a *quadriga* at all, but one horse on undulating terrain).
     Sena Chiesa states that this is not a ringstone, but a decorative element,
     possibly connected with representations of the zodiac.
     50 BC–AD 50.
     Sena Chiesa 1966: no. 1070.

2.   Aquileia, Museo Nazionale 27561.
     Aquileia.
     Glass paste.
     Identification as Sol not certain

---

21   The catalogue section on intaglios is organized along slightly different lines. Each subsec-
     tion consists of iconographically closely similar images. Hence the description is given in
     the heading of each (sub)section and is applicable for each intaglio in that section. In the
     entries of the intaglios individually, Only additional information (if any) is given. Gems
     may be illustrated by a photograph of the actual stone, a photograph of an impression
     made from the actual stone, or both. In the descriptions, *left* and *right* refer to the gem-
     image, not the impression. If Sol is described as having his right arm raised, the impres-
     sion would depict him with his left arm raised. In the case of *cretule* the description refers
     to the gem that made the impression, not to the impression itself. The catalogue of inta-
     glios is divided into two parts, H and HA. Most intaglios are gathered under H, but those
     still set in ancient rings are presented separately in HA, using the same iconographic
     subdivisions. This is done for dating purposes. It is notoriously difficult to date intaglios
     accurately, the main criteria being style, cutting techniques and (to some extent) material
     and form. Ancient rings, on the other hand, can more often be dated with a reasonable
     degree of precision, based on type. Thus it is often possible to give an intaglio set in an
     ancient ring a probable *terminus ante quem* without relying on the engraving itself.

50 BC–AD 50.
Sena Chiesa 1966: 308 no. 867.

3. Plate 144.3
Göttingen, Originalsammlung des Archäologischen Instituts G.126.
Unknown.
Heliotrope, damaged.
Head of Sol very close to edge; no rays?
Late 1st c. AD (AGD).
AGD III, 130 no. 378.
Image: photograph courtesy Daniel Graepler, Originalsammlung des Archäologischen Instituts.

4. Plate 145.1
Paris, Bibliothèque Nationale de France, Cabinet des Médailles 58.1479.
Unknown.
Sard.
Late 1st–2nd c. AD.
Chabouillet 1858: 209 no. 1479.
Image: gem impression and photograph of the gem impression by author.

5. Aquileia, Museo Nazionale 25935.
Aquileia.
Green jasper.
Identification as Sol not certain.
2nd c. AD.
Sena Chiesa 1966: 308 no. 865.

6. Sa'd Collection.
Gadara, Decapolis (Umm Qeis).
Carnelian.
2nd c. AD (Henig).
Henig & Whiting 1987: 12 no. 63; Matern 2002: 67, 220 Q89.

7. Plate 146.1
Paris, Bibliothèque Nationale de France, Cabinet des Médailles 58.1479bis
Unknown
Green jasper
2nd c. AD
Chabouillet 1858: 1479bis.
Image: courtesy of the Bibliothèque Nationale de France.

8.   Aquileia, Museo Nazionale 25981.
         Aquileia.
         Green jasper, damaged.
         Identification as Sol not certain.
         Late 2nd–3rd c. AD.
         Sena Chiesa 1966: 308 no. 866.

9.   Aquileia, Museo Nazionale 26202.
         Aquileia.
         Black jasper.
         Identification as Sol not certain.
         Late 2nd–3rd c. AD.
         Sena Chiesa 1966: 308 no. 864.

10.   Plate 145.2
         Berlin, Staatliche Museen, Antikensammlung 8650.
         Unknown.
         Heliotrope, damaged.
         2nd–3rd c. AD?
         Furtwängler 1896: 8650.
         Image: gem impression and photograph of the gem impression by author.

11.   Plates 145.4, 145.5
         Copenhagen, Thorvaldsen Museum I 1619.
         Acquired in Rome.
         Green jasper, damaged.
         Star in field below forelegs of horses.
         2nd–3rd c. AD.
         LIMC Helios/Sol 145.
         Image: photograph and impression courtesy Thorvaldsen Museum, Copenhagen; photograph of the impression by author.

12.   Plate 145.3
         Princeton University Art Museum 64-38.
         Unknown.
         Heliotrope.
         2nd–3rd c. AD (Forbes).
         Forbes 1978: 55–6 no. 38.
         Image: photograph courtesy of the Art Museum, Princeton University.

13. Aquileia, Museo Nazionale 25969.
    Aquileia.
    Green jasper, damaged.
    Identification as Sol not certain.
    3rd c. AD.
    Sena Chiesa 1966: 308–9 no. 868

14. Private collection.
    Unknown.
    Heliotrope.
    Early 3rd c. AD (v.).
    Vollenweider 1984: 260 no. 447; Matern 2002: 67, 220 Q81.

15. Plate 145.6, 145.7
    Munich, Archäologische Staatssammlung 1971,1201.
    Mangolding.
    Green jasper.
    2nd–3rd c. AD.
    Unpublished?
    Image: Staatliche Antikensammlungen und Glyptothek München; photograph (front and back) by Renate Kühling.

H1b. ... Nude but for Chlamys, Whip in Left Hand, Reins in Right Hand

1. Plate 145.8
   Berlin, Staatliche Museen, Antikensammlung 6314.
   Unknown.
   Glass paste.
   1st c. AD.
   Furtwängler 1896: 6314.
   Image: impression and photograph of the impression by author.

2. Plate 145.9
   Berlin, Staatliche Museen, Antikensammlung 8160.
   Unknown.
   Nicolo.
   Late 1st–early 2nd c. AD.
   Furtwängler 1896: 8160; Matern 2002: 67, 219–20 Q76.
   Image: impression and photograph of the impression by author.

3.   Plate 145.10
      Munich, Archäologische Staatssammlung 1971,1201.
      Mangolding.
      Green jasper.
      2nd–3rd c. AD.
      AGD I-3, 84 no. 2649; Matern 2002: 67, 220 Q85. Platz-Horster 2018: 95
      no. 76.
      Image: Staatliche Antikensammlungen und Glyptothek München; pho-
      tograph by Renate Kühling.

4.   Plate 145.11
      Kassel, Staatliche Kunstsammlung 158.
      Unknown.
      Heliotrope.
      Inscribed IA (neg.).
      3rd c. AD (MK); 2nd c. AD (Matern).
      LIMC Helios/Sol 148; Matern 2002: 67, 220 Q82 (with refs.).
      Image: courtesy of the Staatliche Kunstsammlung, Kassel.

5.   Plate 145.12
      Vienna, Kunsthistorisches Museum XII 890.
      Unknown.
      Heliotrope.
      3rd c. AD.
      LIMC Helios/Sol 148; Matern 2002: 67, 220 Q88.
      Image: photograph © KHM-Museumsverband.

6.   Art Market.
      Unknown.
      Heliotrope.
      Undated.
      Basel, Münzen und Medaillen AG Sonderliste L (1969), no. 49.

7.   Private collection.
      Romula.
      Carnelian.
      Star above horses.
      Undated.
      Berciu & Petolescu 1976: 55 no. 60.

Hic. ... Nude but for a Chlamys, Right Hand Raised, Whip in Left Hand

1. Florence, Archaeological Museum inv. Migl. 1511.
   Unknown.
   Green jasper.
   Crescent and star in field.
   1st C. AD.
   Tondo & Vanni 1990: 172 no. 77 & 219 fig. 77.

2. Seville, Archaeological Museum.
   Itálica.
   Haematite.
   2nd c. AD.
   Lopez de la Orden 1990: 120–21 no. 50.

3. Museum of London
   30 Gresham Street, London, larger well (excavations of 2000–2001).
   Green Jasper
   AD 150–200 (terminus ante quem).
   Unpublished.
   The intaglio was found in the upper portion of the backfill of the well, which also contained pottery dated to AD 150–200.

4. Private collection.
   Gadara, Decapolis (Umm Qeis).
   Red jasper.
   2nd c. AD (Henig).
   Henig & Whiting 1987: 12 no. 64.

5. Private collection.
   Gadara, Decapolis (Umm Qeis).
   Green jasper.
   2nd c. AD (Henig).
   Henig & Whiting 1987: 12 no. 65.

6. Berlin, Staatliche Museen, Ägyptisches Museum 9833.
   Unknown.
   Plasma.

Reverse: Isis & Nephthys stand on a scarab with open wings and protect the remains of Osiris.

2nd c. AD.

Philipp 1986: 82–3, 113; CBd 2086; retrieved from: classics.mfab.hu/talis mans/cbd/2086 on 19-11-2017.

7. Munich, Staatliche Münzsammlung 2650.
Nijmegen? (formerly Smetius-collection; cf. Maaskant-Kleibrink 1986: 115 app. 31).
Heliotrope, damaged.
2nd–3rd c. AD.
LIMC Helios 35; Helios/Sol 149; Matern 2002: 126, 243–4 I66.10c.

8. Cardiff, National Museum of Wales, 81.79H/4.38 (stolen).
Caerleon, legionary fortress baths, frigidarium drain.
Heliotrope.
Stratified ante quem date of AD 150–230.
Zienkiewicz 1986: 134–5 no. 38, pl. 10; Matern 2002: 243 I66.3.

9. Plate 145.13
Nijmegen, Valkhof Museum BA VII 65f/G149.
Winseling (The Netherlands).
Red carnelian, damaged.
2nd–3rd c. AD.
Maaskant-Kleibrink 1986, 77 no. 149; Matern 2002: 126, 243–4 I66.11.
Image: courtesy Valkhof Museum.

10. Plates 145.14, 145.15
Columbia, University of Missouri, Museum of Art and Archaeology 68.317.
Unknown.
Heliotrope.
2nd–3rd c. AD (MK).
LIMC Helios/Sol 147; Matern 2002: 126, 243 I66.5.
Image: photograph and impression © Museum of Art and Archaeology, University of Missouri, Columbia; photograph of the impression by author.

11. Private collection.
Caesarea Maritima.
Heliotrope.

3rd c. AD (MK).
Hamburger 1968: 26 no. 21; Matern 2002: 126, 243 I66.6.

12.   Athens, National Numismatic Museum.
       Unknown.
       Green jasper.
       Later 3rd c. AD (MK).
       Svoronos 1913: 199.

13.   Plate 145.16
       Sofia, National Archaeological Museum 4090.
       Unknown.
       Green jasper.
       3rd c. AD (D.-M.).
       Dimitrova-Milcheva 1981: 91 no. 275; Matern 2002: 125, 242–3 I63.11b.
       Image: © Sofia Archaeological Museum / Krassimir Georgiev.

14.   Private collection.
       Romula.
       Heliotrope, damaged.
       Undated.
       Berciu & Petolescu 1976, 55 no. 61.

15.   Cambridge, Fitzwilliam Museum CM.52.1904.
       Unknown.
       Heliotrope.
       Undated.
       Matern 2002: 67, 220 Q79

16.   Private collection.
       Unknown.
       Greenish-black jasper.
       Seven stars, each with a vowel, in field. On edge, inscription: εκτωβεϲτρι-
       λαριτιαππ..λωνϲατραπερκ[.; on reverse, inscription (pos.?): ϲθομβαογηβαολ
       ϲθομβαλλακαμ ϲθομβληθαεαθιεμμενετηαρ
       Undated.
       Bonner 1950, 291 no. 228.

17.   Plate 14.2
       Cologne, University, Institut für Altertumskunde 33.

Unknown.
Red jasper.
In field: crescent, palm branch, wreath.
2nd c. AD.
Zwierlein-Diehl 1992, no. 33; CBd 1963; retrieved from: classics.mfab.hu/talismans/cbd/1963 on 19-11-2017.
Image: courtesy Institut für Altertumskunde, Cologne University.

18. Trieste, Civico museo di storia ed arte, Orto lapidario e Lapidario terges-
    tino 23356.
    Aquileia.
    Green jasper.
    3rd c. AD.
    Unpublished?

19. Plate 146.7
    Museum Carnuntinum Car-Ge-192 (17 912).
    Carnuntum.
    Carnelian.
    Undated.
    Dembski 2005, 92 no. 412.
    Image: Landessammlungen Niederösterreich, Archäologischer Park Car-
    nuntum (Photograph: Nicolas Gail).

Hd. ... Nude but for Chlamys, Right Hand Raised, Reins in Left Hand

1. Plates 146.2, 146.3
   Copenhagen, Thorvaldsen Museum I 624.
   Acquired in Rome.
   Glass paste, damaged.
   1st c. AD (MK).
   Fossing 1929: 590.
   Image: photograph and impression courtesy Thorvaldsen Museum; pho-
   tograph of impression by author.

2. Plates 146.4, 146.5
   Copenhagen, Thorvaldsen Museum I 625.
   Acquired in Rome.
   Glass paste, damaged, part missing.
   Identification as Sol uncertain.

1st c. AD.

Fossing 1929: 591.

Image: photograph and impression courtesy Thorvaldsen Museum; photograph of impression by author.

3. Private collection.
Castlesteads.
Heliotrope.
2nd c. AD (Henig).
Henig 1974: 13 no. 35.

4. Munich, Staatliche Münzsammlung 2651.
Unknown.
Dark green jasper.
2nd–3rd c. AD (MK).
AGD I-3, 84 no. 2651; Matern 2002: 126, 243–4 I66.10b.

5. Athens, National Numismatic Museum.
Unknown.
Jasper.
Early 3rd c. AD (MK).
Svoronos 1913: 198.

6. Plate 146.6
Leiden, National Museum of Antiquities GS-01116.
Unknown.
Dark green jasper.
Inscription on the reverse: αυολερθε/μεινωπιες/cιμουιθρι/μφ.
3rd c. AD (MK).
Maaskant-Kleibrink 1978: 1116.
Image: © National Museum of Antiquities, Leiden; photograph R.J. Looman.

> *Hιda ... Nude but for Chlamys, Right Hand Raised, Reins in Left Hand; a Star and the Bust of Luna on Upturned Crescent Above the Horses; a Snake Below and in Front of the Horses*

1. Naples, Museo Archeologico 27036/1191.
Unknown.
Heliotrope.

On the reverse: schematic ouroboros, two letters and a star.
3rd c. AD (SEH).
Pannuti 1994, no. 271; Cbd 43, retrieved from: classics.mfab.hu/talismans/
cbd/43 on 18-11-2017.

H1e. ... Nude but for Chlamys, Reins in Both Hands

1. Plate 146.8
    Sofia, National Archaeological Museum, Excavation Inv. 470.
    Oescus (excavations of 1948).
    Dark red carnelian.
    First half 2nd c. AD (D.M.); 1st-early 2nd c. AD (MK).
    Dimitrova-Milcheva 1981: 91 no. 276; Matern 2002: 67, 220 Q86.
    Image: © Sofia Archaeological Museum / Krassimir Georgiev.

2. Cambridge, Fitzwilliam Museum, Lewis Collection.
    Mons Pagus, bought at Smyrna in 1891.
    Red and yellow agate, mottled.
    3rd c. AD (Henig).
    Henig 1975: 16 no. 19; Matern 2002: 67, 220 Q78.

H1f. ... Nude but for Chlamys, Action and Attributes Indistinct

1–6. Tripoli?
    Cyrene.
    Cretula (clay impression).
    Identification as Sol uncertain.
    1st c. BC–1st c. AD.
    Maddoli 1963/4: 113 no. 694–99.

7. Bonn, Rheinisches Landesmuseum 14383 G73.
    Kastell Niederbieber.
    Onyx.
    2nd c. AD.
    Sol ascending his *quadriga*.
    Matern 2002: 243 I66.2.

8. Berlin, Staatliche Museen, Antikensammlung 7880.
    Unknown.
    Carnelian.
    Damaged; representation of Sol largely erased. On the reverse an eagle
    between two standards.

2nd–3rd c. AD.
Furtwängler 1896: 7880.

9.   Munich, Staatliche Münzsammlung 2648.
     Unknown.
     Reddish brown carnelian.
     Sol appears to be holding a branch or a wreath in his right hand.
     2nd–3rd c. AD.
     AGD I-3, 83 no. 2648; Matern 2002: 126, 243–4 I66.10a.

10–26. Berlin, Staatliche Museen, Antikensammlung, 4585–4601.
        Unknown.
        Three green, three green-and-white, four brown-and-white, one violet,
        one black, and five brown glass pastes.
        Non vidi: some or all may be Sol, or not.
        Mainly 50 BC–AD 50.
        Furtwängler 1896: 4585–4601.

27–38. Copenhagen, Thorvaldsen Museum.
        Acquired in Rome.
        One carnelian, eight brown, two yellow and one black glass paste.
        Non vidi. Some may be Sol, but unlikely in the case of 965, charioteer
        with wreath, and 972, charioteer with wreath and palm branch.
        Mainly 50 BC–AD 50.
        Fossing 1929: 964–975.

*H1fa. … Nude but for Chlamys, Action and Attributes Indistinct,
Surrounded by a Zodiac Circle*

1.   Unknown.
     Unknown.
     Chalcedony.
     undated.
     Lippert 1767: I, 194.

H1g. … Nude but for Chlamys, Left Hand Raised, Reins in Right Hand

1.   Plate 146.9
     Vienna, Kunsthistorisches Museum IX B 607.
     Aquileia.
     Dark green jasper, damaged.
     Difficult to say which hand is raised.

2nd–3rd c. AD (MK).
LIMC Helios/Sol 150; Matern 2002: 126, 243–4 I66.12.
Image: photograph © KHM-Museumsverband.

H1ga. ... *Above Luna in a Biga, Descending to the Left, Five Stars and a Crescent Below the Horses of Sol*

1. Plate 146.10
London, British Museum 1864,1127.38.
Unknown.
Heliotrope.
Inscription on the reverse.
1st–2nd x. AD.
Michel 2001: 244; CBd-642. Retrieved from: classics.mfab.hu/talismans/cbd/642 on 18-11-2017.
Image: drawing after classics.mfab.hu/talismans/cbd/642.

H1h. ... *Nude but for Chlamys, Torch in Right Hand, Reins in Left Hand*

1. Plate 146.11
Berlin, Staatliche Museen, Antikensammlung 2667.
Unknown.
Chalcedony.
Mid 1st–early 2nd c. AD (SEH).
Furtwängler 1896: 2667.
Image: Cornell University Gem Impressions Collection.

2. Unknown.
Unknown.
Red jasper.
Undated.
Lippert 1767: I.IV, 81 no. 191.

H1ha. ... *Nude but for a Chlamys, Torch in Left Hand, Reins in Right Hand, within a Zodiac*

1. Art market.
Unknown.
Amethyst.
Inscription σελευκος below chariot.
Early 1st c. AD.
Matern 2002: 67, 221 Q91.

H1i. ... Dressed in a Long Chiton and Chlamys, Right Hand Raised, Globe in Left Hand, Preceded by Lucifer, Looking Back, and Bearing Two Torches

1. Unknown.
    Unknown.
    Red Jasper.
    On edge: αυξονιεηιποδια; on reverse: λαχαρμαρ μαραφβα συντηρησον με αγηρατον.κεχαριτωμενην
    Undated.
    Carnegie 1908: 173 N51.

H1j. No Additional Description Available

1. Plate 146.12
    Bad Deutsch-Altenburg, Museum Carnuntinum Car-Ge-191 (18 043).
    Carnuntum.
    Heliotrope.
    Identification as Sol uncertain.
    Undated
    Dembski 2005, 92 no. 409.
    Image: Landessammlungen Niederösterreich, Archäologischer Park Carnuntum (Photograph: Nicolas Gail).

2. Private collection.
    Carnuntum.
    Brownish red jasper.
    Undated.
    Dembski 2005, 92 no. 410.

H2. Sol on Quadriga to Right
H2a. ... Nude but for Chlamys, Left Hand Raised, Whip in Right Hand

1. Plate 146.13
    Leiden, National Museum of Antiquities GS00578.
    Unknown (Thoms coll., i.e. probably acquired in Italy).
    Agate.
    Star and crescent under front hooves of horses; in exergue: EYTYXHC (inversed).
    1st c. AD.
    Maaskant-Kleibrink 1978: 231–2 no. 578.
    Image: © National Museum of Antiquities, Leiden; photograph R.J. Looman.

2.   Plate 146.14
     Cambridge, Fitzwilliam Museum CG 265.
     Unknown.
     Heliotrope.
     May equally well be that Sol is depicted with his right hand raised and the
     whip in his left hand.
     Second half 1st c. AD.
     Matern 2002: 243 I66.4.
     Image: photograph courtesy Fitzwilliam Museum, under CC BY-NC-ND
     licence.

3.   Verona, Museum 26106.
     Unknown.
     Dark orange carnelian.
     2nd–3rd c. AD.
     Sena Chiesa 2009: 43 no. 74.

       H2aa. ... To the Left of Sol, Diana with Bow and Quiver Looking Left
1.   Plate 146.15
     St. Petersburg, Hermitage ГР-22359.
     Unknown.
     Carnelian.
     2nd–3rd c. AD.
     http://www.hermitagemuseum.org/wps/portal/hermitage/digital-collec
     tion/18.+carved+stones/1069853 (accessed 12/12/2018).
     Image: courtesy Hermitage Museum, St. Petersburg.

       H2b. ... Nude but for Chlamys, Left Hand Raised, Reins in Right Hand
1.   Plate 147.1
     Berlin, Staatliche Museen, Antikensammlung 2668.
     Unknown.
     Carnelian.
     2nd–3rd c. AD (SEH).
     Furtwängler 1896: 2668.
     Image: Cornell University Gem Impressions Collection.

2.   Plate 147.2
     Berlin, Staatliche Museen, Ägyptisches Museum 10993.
     Rome?

Yellow jasper.

Reverse: αηικο/ηιαωυοη/ηωιαο/υ.

1st–2nd AD (Philipp) 2nd–3rd c. AD (MK).

Philipp 1986: 43–4, 33; Matern 2002: 126, 243 I66.1; CBd 2009; retrieved from: classics.mfab.hu/talismans/cbd/2009 on 19-11-2017.

Image: impression and photograph of impression by author

H2c. ... Nude but for Chlamys, Whip in Left Hand, Reins in Right Hand; Behind Him Winged Victory Holding a Wreath Above His Head

1. Plate 147.3

Copenhagen, National Museum 1568.

Unknown.

Heliotrope.

2nd–3rd c. AD (MK).

LIMC Helios/Sol 203; Matern 2002: 66–7, 220 Q84.

Image: impression courtesy National Museum, Copenhagen; photograph of impression by author.

H2ca. ... without the Winged Victory

1. Plate 147.4

Rome, Musei Capitolini 68/12m.

Santarelli collection.

Heliotrope.

3rd c. AD.

Gallottini 2012: 124 no. 180.

Image: courtesy Fondazione Dino ed Ernesta Santarelli.

2. Nîmes, Centre de documentation archéologique du Gard.

Nîmes.

Red jasper.

2nd c. AD.

Guiraud 2008: 96 no.1097.

H2d. ... Nude but for Chlamys, Reins in Both Hands

1. London, Guildhall Museum 19067.

London, Walbrook, Bucklersbury House site.

Heliotrope.

1st–2nd c. AD (Henig).

Henig 1978, 13 no. 34.

*H2e. … Dressed in Chiton and Chlamys, Reins in Left Hand,
Whip in Right*

1. Plate 147.5
    Rome, Musei Capitolini 47/96g.
    Santarelli collection.
    Citrine.
    A woman is depicted behind Sol. This gem is iconographically confusing. The beardless, radiate charioteer is Sol, but the struggling woman is typically Proserpina as she is snatched away by Pluto. The combination is unparalleled and, together with the less usual direction of Sol's *quadriga*, raises questions.
    1st–2nd c. AD; modern?
    Gallottini 2012, 125 no. 181.
    Image: courtesy Fondazione Dino ed Ernesta Santarelli.

H3. Sol on Frontal *Quadriga*, Two Horses Jumping to the Left, Two to the Right[22]

*H3a. … Nude but for a Chlamys, Right Hand Raised, Whip
in Left Hand*

1. Plate 147.6
    Paris, Bibliothèque Nationale de France, Cabinet des Médailles 58.1479ter.
    Unknown.
    Carnelian.
    Reverse: Portrait (?) bust of bearded male, right.
    1st–early 2nd c. AD; portrait on reverse modern.
    Chabouillet 1858: 1479ter.
    Image: impression and photograph of impression by author.

2. Plate 147.10
    Sofia, National Archaeological Museum 8091.
    Unknown.
    Chalcedony.
    2nd–3rd c. AD (DM).
    Dimitrova-Milcheva 1981: 90 no. 273; Matern 2002: 125, 242–3 I63.11a.
    Image: © Sofia Archaeological Museum / Krassimir Georgiev.

3. Plate 147.7
    Kassel, Staatliche Kunstsammlung Ge 157.

---

22   A configuration often described as a facing "split" *quadriga.*

Unknown.

Heliotrope, damaged.

Reverse and edge, inscriptions (pos.): σημεω/κοντευ/κεντευ/κηριδευ/αρυν[.]ω'Edge: λυκυνξκαν〚..]ρη.

2nd c. AD (AGD); quite possibly much later (MK)

Matern 2002: 125, 242 I63.7; LIMC Helios/Sol 126; AGD III, 157.

Image: impression courtesy Staatliche Kunstsammlung, Kassel; photograph of impression by author.

4. Plate 147.8

Vienna, Kunsthistorisches Museum IX B 608.

Acquired in Ragusa in 1829.

Sard.

Second half 2nd–first half 3rd c. AD.

Matern 2002: 125, 242–3 I63.12; AGWien III, 305–6 no. 2761.

Image: photograph © KHM-Museumsverband.

5. Munich, Staatliche Münzsammlung 2645.

Unknown.

Reddish orange carnelian.

3rd c. AD (AGD).

LIMC Helios/Sol 125. AGD I-3, 2645.

6. Plate 147.9

Harrow School Museum 1864.828.

Spalato (Split).

Octagonal flat translucent carnelian.

3rd c. AD (Middleton).

Middleton 1991: 55 no. 51.

Image: photograph courtesy Harrow School.

7. Munich, Archäologische Staatssammlung 1984.3522.

Yugoslavia.

Carnelian.

Second half 3rd c. AD (Z.) (possibly much earlier).

Zahlhaas 1985: 41 no. 44; Matern 2002: 125, 242 I63.9.

8. Private collection.

Unknown.

Carnelian.
Early 3rd c. AD (V.).
Vollenweider 1984,: no. 442; Matern 2002: 242,I63.4a.

9.   Unknown.
       Unknown.
       Red jasper.
       Undated.
       Carnegie 1908, 52–3 D1.

10.   Ann Arbor, Bonner collection 5.
       Unknown.
       Mottled jasper, green, yellow & red.
       Undated.
       LIMC Abraxas 37.
       Image: https://www.lib.umich.edu/special-collections-research-center/
       amulet-collection-group-4 (February 1, 2019).

11.   Private collection.
       Unknown.
       Heliotrope, damaged.
       Six stars; inscription (pos.): μιχαηλσαβα.[θρ]αφαηλ. Reverse: winged Vic-
       tory with wreath and palm-branch; inscription (pos.): ραχαηλαβρασαξ.
       Undated.
       LIMC Abraxas 36.

12.   Ann Arbor, University of Michigan, Special Collections.
       Unknown.
       Heliotrope.
       Reverse: anguipede.
       Undated.
       Bonner 1950: 174; CBd 1059, retrieved from: classics.mfab.hu/talismans/
       cbd/1059 on 19-11-2017.

13.   Plate 149.1
       Stuttgart, Landesmuseum Württemberg KK grün 896.
       Unknown.
       Carnelian.
       3rd c. AD.

Wentzel 1956: 29. See: http://www.museum-digital.de/bawue/pdf/pub
licinfo.php?oges=4826&lang=en (retrieved on October 8, 2017).
Image: photograph © Landesmuseum Württemberg, Hendrik Zwietasch.

14. Münster, University Archaeological Museum?
Unknown.
Carnelian.
2nd–3rd c. AD.
Stupperich 1986: 241–2 no. 27.

H3aa. ... within a Zodiac

1. Florence.
Unknown.
Onyx.
Undated.
Gundel 1992: 249 no. 156; Matern 2002: 54, 214 Q42.

H3b. ... Nude but for a Chlamys, Right Hand Raised

1. Art market, Medusa-art.com MA531.
Unknown.
Unknown stone, octagonal.
2nd–3rd c. AD.
Unpublished.

2. Plate 149.2
New York, Metropolitan Museum of Art 41.160.688.
Unknown.
Carnelian.
2nd–3rd c. AD.
CBd 1117, retrieved from: classics.mfab.hu/talismans/cbd/1117 on 19-11-
2017; otherwise unpublished (?)
Image: courtesy Metropolitan Museum of Art, New York.

H3c. ... Nude but for a Chlamys, Right Hand Raised, Reins in Left

1. Plate 149.4
New York, Metropolitan Museum of Art 81.6.173.
Unknown.
Yellowish Chalcedony.
1st–2nd c. AD (LIMC).

LIMC Helios 32; Matern 2002: 125, 242 I63.10.
Image: photograph courtesy Metropolitan Museum of Art, New York.

2. Private collection.
Unknown.
Carnelian.
2nd–3rd c. AD.
Sternberg AG, fixed price catalogue 10, 1998, no. 647.

3. Plate 149.3
Debrecen (Hungary), Déri Museum DF. R. XI. 10.
Ószönyi/Brigetium.
Translucent yellow carnelian, oval, flat.
3rd c. AD.
LIMC Helios/Sol 125 Matern 2002: 125, 242 I63.3.
Image: photograph © Déri Museum / Lajos Lakner.

4. Athens, National Numismatic Museum.
Unknown.
Jasper.
3rd–early 4th c. AD (MK).
Svoronos 1913: no. 197; Richter 1971: 33 no. 86; Matern 2002: 242, I63.2

5. Plate 149.5
Princeton University, Art Museum y19 40-375.
Unknown.
Mottled gray agate (burnt jasper?)
3rd–4th c. AD (Forbes).
Forbes 1978: 53–5 no. 37.
Image: Princeton University Art Museums collections online, December 9, 2023, https://artmuseum.princeton.edu/collections/objects/21610..

H3d. ... *Dressed in a Long Chiton and Chlamys, Right Hand Raised, Globe in Left*

1. Plate 14.3
London, 1772, 0315.492.
Unknown.
Red jasper.
Reverse: Head of city of Caesarea (l.), veiled, crowned with Mount Argaios; inscription:. (pos.): ευτ/υχι (left of head), βοχ/οντι (right of head).
3rd c. AD (Walters).

Walters 192: 179 no. 1663; Matern 2002: 125, 243 I64.2b
Image: photograph © Trustees of the British Museum.

H3da. ... Nude but for a Chlamys, Right Hand Raised, Globe in Left

1.   Plate 2.1
New York, Metropolitan Museum of Art 81.6.297.
Unknown.
Heliotrope, damaged.
Above Sol inscription (pos): ΑΒΛΑΝΑΘΑΝΑΛΒΑ; in exergue (pos.): ΤΥΞΕΥΙ
(or ΤΥΞΕΥΙ), with star below. Reverse: Mithras in the act of killing the
bull. Merkelbach's suggestion that in ΤΥΞΕΥΙ the Ξ be read as an inverted
E and the I as T (thus creating ΕΥΤ twice, once inverted and once positive) is ingenious (ΑΒΛΑΝΑΘΑΝΑΛΒΑ is a palindrome) but far-fetched
(both beta's in ΑΒΛΑΝΑΘΑΝΑΛΒΑ are pos.).
3rd c. AD (LIMC); 2nd c. AD (SEH).
LIMC Helios/Sol 128; CBd 1097, retrieved from: classics.mfab.hu/talis-
mans/cbd/1097 on 19-11-2017.
Merkelbach (1984: 394–5 fig. 168) gives an inaccurate description (Sol
definitely does not hold a whip in his right hand as M. states).

*H3e. ... Nude but for a Chlamys, Left Hand Raised, Whip and Reins in
Right Hand*

1.   Plates 149.6, 149.7
Copenhagen, Thorvaldsen Museum I 628.
Acquired in Rome.
Carnelian.
Small flying Victory crowning Sol from left, two letters to either side: I (or
inverted F?) V on the left, F (pos.) E (or I?) on the right. Reverse: Nereid on
sea-horse.
50 BC–50 AD (MK); 3rd c. AD (LIMC).
LIMC Helios/Sol 204; Matern 2002: 125, 243 I64.1.
Image: photograph and impression courtesy Thorvaldsen Museum; pho-
tograph of the impression by author.

2.   Unknown.
Egypt.
Carnelian.
1st–early 2nd c. AD (SEH).
El-Mohsen El-Khachab 1963, 154–5 no. 22, pl. XXV no. 21.

3. Aquileia, Museo Nazionale 25497.
Aquileia.
Green jasper.
2nd c. AD.
Sena Chiesa 1966: no. 87; Matern 2002: 125, 242 I63.1.

4. Private collection.
Unknown.
Dark red translucent glass paste.
Gesture and attribute of right hand difficult to make out.
Early 3rd c. AD (V.).
Vollenweider 1984: 258 no. 443; Matern 2002: 242, I63.4b.

5. Münster, University Archaeological Museum L GV 62.
Unknown.
Glass paste.
Late 1st c. BC–mid 1st c. AD. Taken together, the imperial cap-and-rim style and the material (glass paste) suggest a date of around the middle of the first c. AD for this intaglio.
Alvarez Bendezu 2015: 327 no. 85.

H3ea. ... Nude but for a Chlamys, Left Hand Raised

1. Plate 149.8
Boston, Museum of Fine Arts 1963.1524. Theodora Wilbour Fund in Memory of Zoë Wilbour.
Athens.
Carnelian.
2nd–4th c. AD (Vermeule).
Vermeule 1966a, 18–35.
Image: photograph © Museum of Fine Arts, Boston.

H3f. ... Gesture and Attributes Indistinguishable

1. Cologne, Römisch Germanisches Museum 62,61.
Xanten, chance find, before 1900.
Dark brown jasper, heavily damaged
Most of the body of Sol missing, but he appears to have left hand raised. Obverse: cock-headed, anguipede Abrasax with whip and shield. On shield (pos.) ιαω; along border (pos.) Κρεσκεντινιος Βενιγνος (Crescentinius Benignus). In exergue αβρασαξ/σαβαω
2nd–3rd c. AD (Krug).

Krug 1980, no. 47; Matern 2002: 125, 242 I63.8; Nagy, A.M. "Die Gemme des Crescentinius Benignus. Judaica auf kaiserzeitlichen Amuletten." In: R. Gross et al. (edd.), *Im Licht der Menora. Jüdisches Leben in der römischen Provinz*, Frankfurt am Main 2014, 331–343 & 454–478.

2. Unknown.
   Unknown.
   Banded onyx.
   Undated (modern?).
   Smith & Hutton 1908 no. 155.

   H3g. ... Dressed in a Long Chiton and Chlamys, Right Hand Raised, Whip in Left

1. Plate 149.9
   Paris, Bibliothèque Nationale de France, Cabinet des Médailles, Schlumberger 359.
   Unknown.
   Green jasper, damaged.
   Two stars to the left, crescent and star to the right of Sol's head; in exergue: I[.]ΑΒΡΑCΑΞ. Amulet, not a ring stone.
   2nd–3rd c. AD (MK).
   LIMC Helios/Sol 129.
   Image: impression and photograph of impression by author.

2. Ann Arbor, Kelsey Museum 1963.04.0016.
   Unknown.
   Heliotrope, damaged.
   Two stars to the left, two stars to the right, and two stars in the exergue. Inscription: μιχαηλσαβαη[λρ]αφαηλ. On reverse: winged Victory with wreath and palm branch: ραχαηλ αβρασαξ.
   2nd–3rd c. AD.
   Bonner 1950: 227; CBd 467, Retrieved from: classics.mfab.hu/talismans/cbd/467 on 18-11-2017.

   H4. Sol in Frontal or Three-Quarter *Quadriga*, Horses Next to Each Other
   H4a. ... Whip in Left Hand, Reins in Right Hand

1. Copenhagen, National Museum DFa 582.
   Unknown.
   Heliotrope.

2nd–3rd c. AD (MK).
LIMC Helios/Sol 146; Matern 2002: 67, 220 Q83.

2.   Oxford, Ashmolean, Evans sealing, sheet 17, L.
Dalmatia, either Aenona (Nona/Nin) or Epidaurum (Ragusa Vecchia).
Carnelian (impression of –), damaged.
2nd–3rd c. AD (Middleton).
Middleton 1991, 54–55 no. 50.

H4b. ... Left Hand Raised, Reins in Right Hand

1.   Private Collection.
Caesarea Maritima.
Heliotrope.
1st–2nd c. AD (MK).
Hamburger 1968, 26 no. 20; Matern 2002: 125, 242 I63.6.

2.   Plate 149.10
Hannover, Kestner Museum K878.
Unknown.
Carnelian, damaged.
2nd–3rd c. AD.
LIMC Helios/Sol 146; Matern 2002: 126, 243 I66.7.
Image: courtesy Kestner Museum, Hannover.

3.   Plate 149.12
Malibu, Getty Museum 82.AN.162.76.
Unknown.
Quartz.
Inscription ιαω on reverse.
2nd–3rd c. AD.
Thoresen 2011; CBd 2334; retrieved from: classics.mfab.hu/talismans/
cbd/2334 on 19-11-2017.
Image: Digital image courtesy of the Getty's Open Content Program.

H4c. ... Reins in Both Hands

1.   Plate 149.13
Berlin, Staatliche Museen, Antikensammlung 2666.
Unknown.
Chalcedony.

1st c. AD (SEH/MK).
Furtwängler 1896: 2666; LIMC Helios 34; Matern 2002: 215 Q47.
Image: impression and photograph of impression by author.

H4d. ... Gesture and Attributes Indistinguishable

1. Aquileia, Museo Nazionale 48591.
   Aquileia.
   Haematite.
   On the photograph the head of Sol (with four or five rays) is vaguely visible above the heads of the two central horses. Sena Chiesa omits this in her description.
   1st c. AD (Sena Chiesa).
   Sena Chiesa 1966: no. 1071.

2. Tripoli?
   Cyrene.
   Cretula.
   The auriga is clearly visible but the impression is too indistinct to determine whether he is Sol.
   75 BC–AD 113.
   Maddoli 1963/4, 113 no. 700.

H4da. ... Gesture and Attributes Indistinguishable, within Zodiac Circle

1. Unknown.
   Unknown.
   Onyx.
   On reverse Luna in *biga*.
   Undated.
   Lippert 1767, I, 192

2. London, British Museum 1872,0604.1408.
   Unknown.
   Heliotrope.
   Possibly right hand raised.
   1st–2nd century AD.
   Michel 2001, 245; CBd 643, retrieved from: classics.mfab.hu/talismans/cbd/643 on 18-11-2017.

H4e. ... Sceptre in Right Hand

1. Plate 149.14
    Berlin, Staatliche Museen, Antikensammlung 7198.
    Unknown.
    Sardonyx.
    First half 1st c. AD (MK).
    Furtwängler 1896: 7198; Matern 2002:67, 219 Q75; LIMC Helios/Sol 146.
    Image: impression and photograph of impression by author.

H4f. ... Nude but for Chlamys, Right Hand Raised, the Dioscuri on
Horseback to the Left and Right of the Quadriga, Facing Inwards

1. Plate 149.11
    Copenhagen, National Museum M38.
    Unknown.
    Glass paste.
    50 BC–AD 50 (MK).
    LIMC Helios/Sol 267.
    Image: courtesy of the National Museum, Copenhagen.

H4g. ... Whip in Right Hand

1. Aquileia, Museo Nazionale 25451.
    Aquileia.
    Dark carnelian.
    The very sketchily executed figure of Sol is described by Sena Chiesa as
    a star, which it closely resembles (vertical bar and X). However, the pres-
    ence of the whip (not described by Sena Chiesa, but clearly visible on the
    photograph), shows that the figure is Sol.
    2nd–3rd c. AD.
    Sena Chiesa 1966: no. 1072.

H4h. Apollo/Helios on Quadriga to Left, Nude but for Chlamys
Billowing Out Behind Him, Quiver Behind His Shoulder, Torch in
Either Hand. Below the Horses Lie Oceanus (?) and a Nymph (?)

1. Naples, Museo Nazionale 26806/248.
    Unknown.
    Carnelian, cracked.
    late 1st c. BC.
    LIMC Helios/Sol 144; Matern 2002: 61 n. 412, 67–8, 77, 97, 220–1 Q90
    (with refs.).

H5. Sol/Usil on Frontal *Triga*, Both Hands Raised, Possibly Bearing Unidentifiable Objects

H5a. ..., Sol Radiate

1. Paris, Bibliothèque Nationale de France, Cabinet des Médailles 58.1480.
Unknown.
Carnelian, scarab.
3rd c. BC? (MK) – a globolo style.
Chabouillet 1858: 1480.

2. Paris, Bibliothèque Nationale de France, Cabinet des Médailles 58.1482.
Unknown.
Carnelian, scarab.
3rd c. BC? (MK) – a globolo style.
Chabouillet 1858: 1482.

H5b. Sol Not Radiate

1. Plate 150.4
Paris, Bibliothèque Nationale de France, Cabinet des Médailles 58.1481.
Unknown.
Carnelian, scarab.
3rd c. BC? (MK) – a globolo style.
Chabouillet 1858: 1481.
https://medaillesetantiques.bnf.fr/ws/catalogue/app/collection/record/21278?vc=ePkH4LF7w1I9geonpBCEJmRDEwtDcJoK8wMALkUSeA$$
Image: courtesy of the Bibliothèque Nationale de France.

2. Paris, Bibliothèque Nationale de France, Cabinet des Médailles 58.1483.
Unknown.
Carnelian, scarab.
3rd c. BC? (MK) – a globolo style.
Chabouillet 1858: 1483.

H6. Sol, Standing

H6a. ... Nude but for Chlamys, Left Hand Raised, Whip in Right Hand

1. Plate 150.1
Vienna, Kunsthistorisches Museum XII 918.
Unknown.
Brownish orange translucent glass paste.
1st c. AD (SEH).
LIMC Helios/Sol 95; Matern 2002: 106–7, 235 I24.14c.
Image: photograph © KHM-Museumsverband

2.   Berlin, Staatliche Museen, Antikensammlung 3481.
      Unknown.
      Brownish violet translucent glass paste.
      1st c. AD.
      Furtwängler 1896: 3481.

3.   Plate 150.2
      Paris, Bibliothèque Nationale de France, Cabinet des Médailles,
      Froehner.2868.
      Unknown.
      Heliotrope.
      Two stars in front of Sol and two stars behind him. Reverse: αβρασαζ/ιαω.
      Late 1st–early 2nd c. AD (MK).
      LIMC Abrasax 336; LIMC Helios/Sol 101.
      Image: impression and photograph of impression by author.

4.   Aquileia, Museo Nazionale 26224.
      Aquileia.
      Jasper.
      2nd c. AD.
      Sena Chiesa 1966: no. 74; Matern 2002: 106–7, 234 I24.1b.

5.   Aquileia, Museo Nazionale 51921.
      Aquileia.
      Carnelian, damaged.
      2nd c. AD.
      Sena Chiesa 1966: no. 76; Matern 2002: 106–7, 234 I24.1d.

6.   Aquileia, Museo Nazionale 26218.
      Aquileia.
      Black jasper.
      2nd c. AD.
      Sena Chiesa 1966: no. 78; Matern 2002: 106–7, 234 I24.1f.

7.   Aquileia, Museo Nazionale 50806.
      Aquileia.
      Black jasper.
      2nd c. AD.
      Sena Chiesa 1966: no. 79; Matern 2002: 106–7, 234 I24.1g.

8. Aquileia, Museo Nazionale 25986.
    Aquileia.
    Black jasper.
    2nd c. AD.
    Sena Chiesa 1966: no. 83; Matern 2002: 106–7, 234 I24.1k.

9. Plate 150.3
    Malibu, Getty Museum 83.AN.353.2.
    Tunisia.
    Heliotrope.
    2nd c. AD.
    Spier 1992, 134 no. 366; Matern 2002: 106–7, 235 I24.8.
    Image: Digital image courtesy of the Getty's Open Content Program.

10. Plate 150.5
    Berlin, Staatliche Museen, Antikensammlung 8651.
    Unknown.
    Heliotrope.
    2nd c. AD (SEH).
    Furtwängler 1896: 8651.
    Image: Cornell University Gem Impressions Collection.

11. Plate 150.6
    Vienna, Kunsthistorisches Museum IX B 1524.
    Unknown.
    Heliotrope.
    2nd c. AD (MK).
    LIMC Helios/Sol 94; AGWien 165 no. 1260; Matern 2002: 106–7, 235
    I24.14a.
    Image: photograph © KHM Museumsveband.

12. Vienna, Kunsthistorisches Museum XII 1023.
    Unknown.
    Green jasper.
    2nd c. AD.
    AGWien III 306 no. 2763; Matern 2002: 106–7, 235 I24.14b.

13. Aquileia, Museo Nazionale 24829.
    Aquileia.
    Carnelian.

2nd–3rd c. AD.
Sena Chiesa 1966: no. 75; Matern 2002: 106–7, 234 I24.1c.

14. Aquileia, Museo Nazionale 25937.
    Aquileia.
    Jasper.
    Late 2nd–3rd c. AD.
    Sena Chiesa 1966: no. 77; Matern 2002: 106–7, 234 I24.1e.

15. Aquileia, Museo Nazionale 26204.
    Aquileia.
    Green jasper.
    2nd–3rd c. AD.
    Sena Chiesa 1966: no. 80; Matern 2002: 106–7, 234 I24.1h.

16. Udine, Museo Civico 1325/109.
    Aquileia?
    Heliotrope.
    2nd–3rd c. AD.
    Tomaselli 1993: 47 no. 13.

17. Cardiff, National Museum of Wales, 81.79H/4.36.
    Caerleon, legionary fortress baths, frigidarium drain.
    Heliotrope.
    Three horizontal lines on torso, which are difficult to interpret.
    Zienkiewicz believes they indicate a tunica, but there is no indication of
    a tunica below the waste. On the other hand, the lines would appear to be
    too uniform and linear to indicate musculature.
    Stratified ante quem date of ca. AD 150–230.
    Zienkiewicz 1986: 134 no. 36, pl. 10.

18. Utrecht, Rijksmuseum het Catharijneconvent (formerly Aartsbischop-
    pelijk Museum).
    Unknown.
    Glass paste imitating nicolo.
    The intaglio is part of the elaborate decoration of the cover of the Evan-
    gelistarium of St. Ansfridus.
    2nd–3rd c. AD? (SEH).
    Snijder 1932, 19, fig. 6.

19. Plates 150.7, 150.8
    Berlin, Staatliche Museen, Antikensammlung 8653.
    Unknown.
    Heliotrope.
    Inscription (neg.): ΣΙΔΟΝΙΑ ΧΕΡΕ.
    late 2nd–3rd c. AD (SEH/MK).
    Furtwängler 1896: 8653; Matern 2002: 106–7, 234 I24.2.
    Image: photograph courtesy Staatliche Museen, Berlin; impression and
    photograph of impression by author.

20. Plates 150.9–11
    Berlin, Staatliche Museen, Ägyptisches Museum 11928.
    Unknown.
    Red jasper.
    On reverse: ΙΨΠΡΟ & pictograms.
    2nd–3rd c. AD (Philipp); 2nd c. AD (MK/SEH).
    Philipp 1986: 44–5, 35; Matern 2002: 106–7, 234 I24.3; CBd 2011; retrieved
    from: classics.mfab.hu/talismans/cbd/2011 on 19-11-2017.
    Image: Photograph © Staatliche Museen Berlin, Ägyptisches Museum,
    Margarete Büsing; images of impressions (obv & rev.): Cornell University
    Gem Impressions Collection.

21. Cologne, Römisch Germanisches Museum 449.
    Unknown.
    Heliotrope.
    2nd–3rd c. AD (Krug).
    Krug 1980, 226 no. 294; Matern 2002: 106–7, 235 I24.6.

22. Cologne, Römisch Germanisches Museum 472.
    Unknown.
    Red jasper.
    Identification as Sol uncertain: attributes not clear.
    2nd–3rd c. AD (Krug).
    Krug 1980, 235 no. 347.

23. Munich, Staatliche Münzsammlung 2647.
    Environs of Nijmegen? (formerly Smetius-collection).
    Carnelian.
    2nd–3rd c. AD (MK).

LIMC Helios/Sol 95; LIMC Helios 329; AGD I-3, 83 no. 2647; Maaskant-Kleibrink 1986, 115 App.no. 39; Matern 2002: 106–7, 235 I24.9b.

24. Nürnberg, Germanisches Nationalmuseum SiSt 1626.
Unknown.
Heliotrope, damaged.
2nd–3rd c. AD (Weiß); 2nd c. AD (MK).
Weiß 1996: 78 no. 115.

25. Paris, Bibliothèque Nationale de France, Cabinet des Médailles 58.1478.
Unknown.
Agate.
Late 2nd–early 3rd c. AD.
Chabouillet 1858: 1478.

26. Aquileia, Museo Nazionale 25938.
Aquileia.
Green jasper.
3rd c. AD.
Sena Chiesa 1966: no. 73; Matern 2002: 106–7, 234 I24.1.

27. Aquileia, Museo Nazionale R.C.1122.
Aquileia.
Heliotrope.
3rd c. AD.
Sena Chiesa 1966: no. 85; Matern 2002: 106–7, 234 I24.1l.

28. Aquileia, Museo Nazionale 25987.
Aquileia.
Green jasper.
3rd c. AD.
Sena Chiesa 1966: no. 81; Matern 2002: 106–7, 234 I24.1i.

29. Aquileia, Museo Nazionale 25683.
Aquileia.
Jasper.
3rd c. AD.
Sena Chiesa 1966: no. 82; Matern 2002: 106–7, 234 I24.1j.

30. Udine, Museo Civico, 1326/7.
Aquileia?
Dark orange carnelian.
3rd c. AD.
Tomaselli 1993: 47–8 no. 14.

31. Narbonne, Palais des Archevêques 38.1.4.6.
Narbonne, sarcophagus of Marcia Donata.
Glass paste nicolo.
3rd c. AD (G.).
Guiraud 1988: 91 no. 45.

32. Narbonne, Palais des Archevêques 38.1.4.7.
Narbonne, sarcophagus of Marcia Donata.
Glass paste nicolo.
3rd c. AD (G.).
Guiraud 1988: 91 no. 45.

33. Tata, Kuny Domokos Museum K 2003.
Szöny (Brigetio).
green jasper.
First half 3rd c. AD.
Gesztelyi 2001:: 42 no.28.

34. Plate 151.1
Sofia, National Archaeological Museum 3740.
Pleven.
Dark green jasper.
3rd c. AD (D.-M.).
Dimitrova-Milcheva 1981: 91–2 no. 278; Matern 2002: 106–7, 235 I24.13a.
Image: © Sofia Archaeological Museum / Krassimir Georgiev.

35. Plate 151.2
Sofia, National Archaeological Museum 4015.
Lom district.
Heliotrope.
3rd c. AD (D.-M.).
Dimitrova-Milcheva 1981: 91 no. 277; Matern 2002: 106–7 I24.13b.
Image: © Sofia Archaeological Museum / Krassimir Georgiev.

36.   Plate 151.3
       Kassel, Staatliche Kunstsammlung 159.
       Unknown.
       Carnelian.
       Star and crescent in front of Sol.
       3rd c. AD (AGD); late 2nd–3rd (MK).
       LIMC Helios/Sol 100; Matern 2002: 106–7, 234 I24.5b.
       Image: impression courtesy Staatliche Kunstsammlung, Kassel; photo-
       graph impression by author.

37.   Plate 151.4
       Kassel, Staatliche Kunstsammlung 212.
       Unknown.
       Nicolo.
       A star to either side of Sol's feet. Reverse: ηρ (lig.) Anchor / εισνυς / χρε-
       στυς / γαβριε / ανανια / αμε
       3rd c. AD.
       LIMC Helios/Sol 99; Matern 2002: 106–7, 234 I24.5a.
       Image: impression courtesy Staatliche Kunstsammlung, Kassel; photo-
       graph impression by author.

38.   Munich, Staatliche Münzsammlung 2646.
       Unknown.
       Dark green jasper.
       Late 3rd c. AD (AGD).
       LIMC Helios/Sol 98 (refers incorrectly to AGD I-3 2642, but must mean
       this one); LIMC Helios 330; AGD I-3, 83 no. 2646; LIMC Helios 330;
       Matern 2002: 106–7, 235 I24.9a.

39.   Plate 151.5
       Princeton University Art Museum 40-221.
       Unknown.
       Red jasper.
       3rd c. AD (Forbes).
       Forbes 1978: 52–3 no. 35.
       Image: courtesy Art Museum, Princeton University.

40.   Plate 151.6
       Princeton University Art Museum 52-125.
       Unknown.

Heliotrope.
3rd c. AD (Forbes).
Forbes 1978: 53 no. 36.
Image: courtesy Art Museum, Princeton University.

41. Private collection.
Unknown.
Heliotrope.
3rd c. AD (v.).
Vollenweider 1984: 259–60 no. 446; Matern 2002: 106–7, 235 I24.7.

42. Rome, Musei Capitolini.
Esquiline.
Black jasper.
On reverse: A Ω.
Undated.
Righetti 1955: 10–11 no. 4, pl. I,2; Matern 2002: 106–7, 235 I24.12.

43. Gloucester City Museum
Ashel Barn, Kingscote, Gloucestershire.
Heliotrope.
Undated.
Henig 1978, 113 App.no. 47.

44. Münster, Landesmuseum.
Höxter.
Gemstone.
Roman intaglio reused in a medieval seal.
Undated.
Matern 2002: 106–7, 235 I24.11.

45. Plate 151.7
Bad Deutsch-Altenberg, Museum Carnuntinum Car-Ge-185 (17 792).
Carnuntum.
Carnelian.
2nd–3rd c. AD.
Dembski 2005: 91 no. 398.
Image: Landessammlungen Niederösterreich, Archäologischer Park Car-
nuntum (Photograph: Nicolas Gail).

46. Private Collection.
    Carnuntum.
    Green jasper.
    2nd–3rd c. AD.
    Dembski 2005: 91 no. 396.

47. Plate 151.8
    Bad Deutsch-Altenburg, Museum Carnuntinum Car-Ge-187 (18 002).
    Carnuntum.
    Heliotrope.
    2nd–3rd c. AD.
    Dembski 2005: 91 no. 398.
    Image: Landessammlungen Niederösterreich, Archäologischer Park Car-
    nuntum (photograph: Harald Wraunek).

48. Zalau, Museum 6/1958, no. 2.
    Porolissum.
    Green jasper.
    Undated.
    Teposu-Marinescu & Lako 1973: 9 no. 30, pl. II.

49. Ann Arbor, Bonner collection 30.
    Unknown.
    Chalcedony.
    Star and crescent in field; reverse: inscription αβρασα.
    Undated.
    LIMC Abraxas 34; CBd 1067, retrieved from: classics.mfab.hu/talismans/
    cbd/1067 on 19-11-2017.

50. Cambridge, Fitzwilliam Museum CM.82.1982 (A 66414).
    Unknown.
    Sard, damaged.
    Undated.
    Nicholls 1983: 23 no. 82.

51. Private collection.
    Unknown.
    Green jasper, damaged.
    Star and crescent in field and inscription αβρασαξ

Undated.
LIMC Abraxas 35.

52. Plate 151.9
Aachen, Suermondt-Ludwig-Museum (no inv. no.).
Unknown.
Green Jasper.
Undated.
Sporn 2009: 251 cat. 379; 295 pl.
Image: Arachne FA-S13081-02_130942,01.jpg; arachne.dainst.org/entity/
78856.

53. Belgrade, National Museum 1609/III.
Unknown.
Red jasper.
3rd c. AD.
Pilipović 2013: 601 no. 6.

54. Belgrade, National Museum 3969/III.
Veliko Gradište.
Dark orange translucent carnelian.
3rd c. AD.
Pilipović 2013: 602 no. 9.

55. Plate 151.10
Rome, Musei Capitolini 68/5m.
Santarelli collection.
Green jasper.
2nd c. AD.
Gallottini 2012: 124 no. 179.
Image: courtesy Fondazione Dino ed Ernesta Santarelli.

56. Plate 151.11
Stuttgart, Landesmuseum Württemberg KK grün 1078.
Unknown
Nicolo
1st–2nd c. AD.
http://www.museum-digital.de/bawue/pdf/publicinfo.php?oges=5433&
lang=en (retrieved 8 October 2017).
Image: photograph © Landesmuseum Württemberg, Hendrik Zwietasch.

57.   Plate 151.12
      Munich, Archäologische Staatssammlung 1990,3455i.
      Merkershausen.
      Glass paste nicolo.
      23rd c. AD.
      Platz-Horster 2018: 136 no. 115.
      Image: photograph © Archäologische Staatssammlung / Stefanie Friedrich.
      Platz Horster compares it to a gem found in a Merovingian tomb nearby
      and suggests the 6th c. AD as a possible date for this intaglio.

58.   Plate 151.13
      Harvard Art Museums 1952.71.67, Mrs. Charles B. Perkins, gift to the Fogg
      Art Museum.
      Unknown.
      Heliotrope.
      1st–2nd c. AD.
      LIMC Helios/Sol 95.
      Image: photograph © President and Fellows Harvard College.

59.   Munich, Staatliche Antikensammlungen und Glyptothek.
      Unknown.
      Heliotrope.
      Wünsche & Steinhart 2010: 38 no. 16.

60.   Schwäbisch Hall, Hällisch-Fränkisches Museum.
      Aalen.
      Agate.
      Undated.
      Luik 1994: 55–59.

61.   Sisak Municipal Museum.
      Sisak.
      Heliotrope.
      2nd–3rd c. AD.
      Kaić 2016: 25.

62.   Plate 151.14
      Debrecen, Déri Museum DF. R XI. 74.
      Ószönyi/Brigetium.
      Heliotrope, oval, flat.

3rd c. AD.
LIMC Helios/Sol 95.
Image: photograph © Déri Museum / Lajos Lakner.

63. Plate 151.15
Debrecen, Déri Museum DF. R. XI. 76.
Ószönyi/Brigetium.
Green jasper, oval, flat.
3rd c. AD.
LIMC Helios/Sol 95.
Image: photograph © Déri Museum / Lajos Lakner.

64. Châtillon-sur-Seine, archaeological museum.
Vertault.
Pale orange Jasper.
Late 2nd–Early 3rd c. AD.
Guiraud 1997: 44.

65. Eauze archaeological Museum 86580.
Eauze.
Glass paste Nicolo.
Mid 2nd c.–mid 3rd c. AD.
Guiraud 2008: 96 no. 1096.

66. Verona, Museum 26099.
Unknown.
Red carnelian.
2nd–3rd c. AD.
Sena Chiesa 2009: 43 no. 69.

67. Verona, Museum 26100.
Unknown.
Green Jasper.
2nd–3rd c. AD.
Sena Chiesa 2009: 43 no. 70.

68. Verona, Museum 26102.
Unknown.
Heliotrope.
2nd–3rd c. AD.
Sena Chiesa 2009: 43 no. 71.

69. Verona, Museum 26103.
     Unknown.
     Red jasper.
     2nd–3rd c. AD.
     Sena Chiesa 2009: 43 no. 72

70. Verona, Museum 26105.
     Unknown.
     Heliotrope?
     2nd–3rd c. AD.
     Sena Chiesa 2009: 43 no. 73.

H6aa. ... Nude but for Chlamys, Left Hand Raised, Whip in Right Hand, Next to a Burning Altar

1.   Munich, Staatliche Münzsammlung A.631.
     Unknown.
     Light pinkish glass paste.
     1st c. BC–1st c. AD (SEH/MK); 3rd c. AD (LIMC & AGD).
     LIMC Helios/Sol 97.

2.   Montauban, Ingres Museum.
     Environs of Montauban.
     Red jasper.
     1st–2nd c. AD.
     Guiraud 1988: 91 no. 48.

3.   Cardiff, National Museum of Wales.
     Caerleon, Monmouthshire.
     Heliotrope, damaged.
     2nd c. AD (found in a drain in context with material from ca. AD 130–230).
     Henig 1978, 12 no. 31; Matern 2002: 106–7, 164, 235 I25.4.

4.   Plates 152.1–3
     Berlin, Staatliche Museen, Antikensammlung 8652.
     Unknown.
     Heliotrope.
     Reverse: ABAPACƷ.
     2nd c. AD (SEH/MK).
     Furtwängler 1896: 8652, pl. 61; Matern 2002: 106–7, 164, 235 I25.1.

Image: photographs courtesy Staatliche Museen Berlin; impressions: Cornell University Gem Impressions Collection.

5. Plate 151.16
    Vienna, Kunsthistorisches Museum IX B 1200.
    Unknown.
    Carnelian.
    Letter ĸ (pos.) above altar; on reverse ABPACAЕ.
    2nd c. AD.
    AGWien III, 2208; Matern 2002: 106–7, 164, 236 I25.8.
    Image: photograph © KHM Museumsverein.

6. Plate 152.4
    Bologna, Museo Civico Archeologico Gl. 67.
    Unknown.
    Heliotrope, damaged.
    2nd–3rd c. AD.
    Mandrioli Bizzarri 1987: 90 no. 144; Matern 2002: 106–7, 164, 235 I25.2.
    Image: Courtesy of Museo Civico Archeologico-Photo Archive, Bologna.

7. Plate 152.5
    Braunschweig, Herzog Anton Ulrich Museum 42.
    Unknown.
    Heliotrope.
    Late 2nd–3rd c. AD (MK).
    LIMC Helios/Sol 96; Matern 2002: 106–7, 164, 235 I25.3.
    Image: Courtesy Herzog Anton Ulrich Museum, Braunschweig.

8. Ferrara, Museo Civico 10012.
    Unknown.
    Green jasper.
    3rd c. AD.
    Matern 2002: 106–7, 164, 235–6 I25.5.

9. Plates 152.6, 152.7
    Göttingen Originalsammlung des Archäologischen Instituts G.75.
    Unknown.
    Heliotrope.
    Late 3rd AD; 3rd c. (MK).

LIMC Helios/Sol 96; Matern 2002: 106–7, 164, 235 I25.6.

Image: photograph and impression courtesy of the Archaeological Institute, Göttingen University; photograph of impression by author.

10.   Munich, Staatliche Münzsammlung 2917.

Unknown.

Yellowish jasper-agate?

Reverse: ΟΡΒΛ/ΧΛΧΧ (neg.).

3rd–5th c. AD (AGD); 3rd c. AD (MK).

LIMC Helios/Sol 96.

11.   Bad Deutsch-Altenburg, Museum Carnuntinum Car-Ge-190 (17 944).

Carnuntum.

Carnelian.

3rd c. AD.

Dembski 2005, 92 no. 406.

12.   Berlin, Antikensammlung inv. 32.237.366.

Unknown.

Heliotrope.

On the other side a cock with a wreath in his beak, above a thunderbolt (Weiß; I cannot make it out on the photograph). Around the edge, in mirror image, αβρασαζ.

Weiß 2007: 319 no. 669.

> *H6ab. ... Nude but for Chlamys, Left Hand Raised, Whip in Right Hand, Standing on a Globe between Four Serpents*

1.   Unknown.

Afghanistan.

Heliotrope.

Inscription:)()(λαοκμαφοανν. Reverse: Abrasax with whip and shield. On shield: ιλιλνινε; in field ται ται. On edge: αεηιουω.

Undated.

Carnegie 1908, 172 no. N50.

> *H6ac. ... Nude but for Chlamys, Left Hand Raised, Whip in Right Hand, Standing to the Left of Nemesis Who Is Flanked on Her Right by Minerva*

1.   Plate 152.8

Leiden, National Museum of Antiquities GS-00981.

Unknown.

Dark red carnelian.

Seven stars and a crescent in the field.

2nd–3rd c. AD (MK).

Maaskant-Kleibrink 1978, 327 no. 981; Matern 2002: 106–7, 236 I28; LIMC Nemesis 199.

Image: © National Museum of Antiquities, Leiden; photograph R.J. Looman.

H6ad. ... Dressed in Short Chiton and Chlamys, Left Hand Raised, Whip in Right Hand, Next to a Burning Altar

1. Plate 152.9

   Berlin, Staatliche Museen, Antikensammlung 8654.

   Unknown.

   Heliotrope.

   1st–2nd c. AD (SEH).

   Furtwängler 1896: 8654.

   Image: photograph courtesy Staatliche Museen Berlin; impression and photograph of impression by author.

2. Edinburgh, National Museum of Scotland FRA 746.

   Newstead, Roxburghshire.

   Carnelian.

   Henig interprets the burning altar as a corn ear, followed, tentatively, by Matern.

   2nd c. AD (H.).

   Henig 1978: 12 no. 30; Matern 2002: 98, 170 n. 938, 240–1 I56.

H6b. ... Nude but for Chlamys, Right Hand Raised, Whip in Left Hand

1. Monistrol-sur-Loire, Dépôt de fouilles.

   Les Souils (Arlempdes, Haute-Loire).

   Green jasper.

   Possibly an altar in front of Sol.

   2nd c. AD (G.).

   Guiraud 1988: 91 no. 49.

2. Linares, Museum.

   Cástulo.

   Black jasper.

   Late 2nd–3rd c. AD.

   Lopez de la Orden 1990: 121–2 no. 52.

3.   Private collection.
        Gadara, Decapolis (Umm Qeis).
        Carnelian.
        Very poor carving; Sol may be dressed in a short *chiton*.
        3rd c. AD.
        Henig & Whiting 1987: 12 no. 67.

4.   Munich, Staatliche Münzsammlung 2911.
        Unknown.
        Green jasper, lower half missing.
        Thirteen stars in field; inscription (pos.) around: ..]ρηνα**βλαν[.. Reverse:
        Abrasax with whip and shield; inscr. (pos.) around: ..]EC*E**IA.
        3rd c. AD (AGD).
        LIMC Helios/Sol 102.

5.   Munich, Staatliche Münzsammlung 2658.
        Unknown.
        Black jasper, damaged.
        Stars (or letters?) in field; identification as Sol by no means certain.
        Reverse: two figures with raised arms; stars.
        5th c. AD (AGD).
        LIMC Helios/Sol 190; AGD I-3, no.2658.

6.   Plate 152.10
        Bad Deutsch-Altenburg, Museum Carnuntinum Car-Ge-188 (17 777).
        Carnuntum.
        Carnelian.
        3rd c. AD.
        Dembski 2005: 91 nr 400 ...
        Image: Landessammlungen Niederösterreich, Archäologischer Park Car-
        nuntum (Photograph: Harald Wraunek).

7.   Bucharest, National Museum of Antiquities 648 (formerly Cabinet
        Numismatique).
        Unknown.
        Green jasper.
        Undated.
        Gramatopol 1974: 60 no. 279.

8.   Belgrade, National Museum 1590/II
        Unknown.

Chalcedony.

3rd c. AD.

Pilipović 2013: 602 no. 7.

9. Vienna, Kunsthistorisches Museum AS IX.

Carnuntum.

Carnelian.

1st–2nd c. AD.

Dembski 2005: 91 no. 395.

10. Jerusalem, Hebrew University Institute of Archaeology?

Aelia Capitolina.

Carnelian.

2nd–3rd c. AD

Damaged object in front of Sol described as an ear of corn; possibly an altar?

Peleg 2003: 58, 65 no. 3.

H6ba. … Nude but for Chlamys, Right Hand Raised, Whip in Left Hand, Next to a Burning Altar

1. Athens, National Numismatic Museum.

Unknown.

Carnelian.

Late 2nd–early 3rd c. AD (MK).

Svoronos 1913: no. 196.

2. Bucharest, National Museum (formerly Cabinet Numismatique) 67.

Unknown.

Carnelian.

Undated.

Gramatopol 1974: 60 no. 280.

3. Plates 152.11, 152.12

London, British Museum 1869,1201.2 (OA.9740).

Unknown.

Heliotrope.

Inscription on the reverse.

3rd c. AD.

Michel 2001: 243; CBd 641, retrieved from: classics.mfab.hu/talismans/cbd/641 on 18-11-2017.

Image: photograph © Trustees of the British Museum. Sketch of reverse after Cbd 641.

4.   Newstead FRA746 (formerly Beazley collection M26).
       Unknown.
       Cornelian.
       Sol may be wearing a short *chiton* or tunic. Burning altar also interpreted as ears of corn.
       3rd c. AD.
       http://www.beazley.ox.ac.uk/record/8E68181C-D4C0-4F3A-A1FC-2B7B18 A56DC0.

> *H6bb. … Nude but for Chlamys, Right Hand Raised, Whip in Left Hand, Facing Standing Male Figure, Bearded, Dressed in Himation, Staff*

See HA6bb

> *H6bc. … Nude but for Chlamys, Right Hand Raised, Whip in Left Hand, Facing Jupiter, Seated, Staff and Thunderbolt. Between Them an Eagle, Looking up towards Jupiter*

1.   Munich, Staatliche Münzsammlung 2461.
       Unknown.
       Red jasper.
       3rd c. AD (AGD).
       LIMC Helios/Sol 234; Matern 2002: 110, 237 I38 (omits eagle).

> *H6bd. … Nude but for Chlamys, Right Hand Raised, Whip in Left Hand, Behind Juno (Diadem and Sceptre) Facing Jupiter, Seated, Draped, Staff. Between Them an Eagle, Looking up towards Jupiter; a Second Eagle Flies Above, in the Space between Juno and Jupiter; a Third Flies Above the Head of Jupiter. Mercurius Stands Behind Jupiter. Crescent and Star Above Head of Sol*

1.   Plates 152.13, 152.14
       Berlin, Staatliche Museen, Antikensammlung 2545.
       Unknown.
       Chalcedony.
       Inscribed ΔΟΜΕΤΙC in mirror image.
       2nd–3rd c. AD (SEH).
       LIMC Helios/Sol 332; Matern 2002: 106–7, 236 I27a.
       Image: photograph courtesy Staatliche Museen Berlin; impression: Cornell University Gem Impressions Collection.

H6be. ... Nude but for Chlamys, Right Hand Raised, Whip in Left Hand, Facing Standing Jupiter, Nude, Staff, Thunderbolt; between Them an Eagle Looking up towards Jupiter

1. Plates 152.15, 152.16
   Copenhagen, Thorvaldsen Museum I 677.
   Acquired in Rome.
   Plasma.
   Late 1st–early 2nd c. AD (MK).
   LIMC Helios/Sol 233; Matern 2002: 106–7, 236 I29.
   Image: photograph courtesy Thorvaldsen Museum; photograph of impression courtesy Cornell University gem impressions collection.

H6bf. ... Nude but for Chlamys, Right Hand Raised, Whip in Left Hand, Facing Seated Saturn, Bearded, capite velato, Staff and Harpe

1. Plate 153.2
   Copenhagen, National Museum 1457.
   Bought in Beirut.
   Jasper.
   Star and crescent in field.
   Late 2nd–3rd c. AD.
   LIMC Helios/Sol 235. Cf. Louvre Bn1209.
   Image: photograph of impression © National Museum, Copenhagen.

H6bg. ... Nude but for Chlamys, Right Hand Raised, Whip in Left Hand; Behind Him to the Right Victoria, Winged, Holds a Wreath Above His Head

1. Plate 153.1
   Sofia, National Archaeological Museum 4714.
   Unknown.
   Heliotrope.
   2nd–3rd c. AD (D.-M.).
   Dimitrova-Milcheva 1981: 43 no. 58.
   Image: © Sofia Archaeological Museum / Krassimir Georgiev.

H6bh. ... Nude but for Chlamys, Right Hand Raised, Whip in Left Hand, Stands to the Right of a Very Large Burning Altar (Star and Crescent Above). Opposite Him, on the Other Side of the Altar, a Nude Male Figure in the Act of Placing Something on the Altar (or Possibly Pouring a Libation from a Bowl)

1. Plate 153.3
   Berlin, Staatliche Museen, Antikensammlung, 8656.

Unknown.

Green jasper.

2nd–3rd c. AD (SEH/MK).

Furtwängler 1896: 8656; Matern 2002: 106–7, 236 I27b (Matern describes a different gem on p. 240, I 55 under the same inv. Number).

Image: Cornell University Gem Impressions Collection.

> *H6bi. … Standing on the Prow of a Boat with Six Other Figures (Three Fully Anthropomorph, Two Animal-Headed, One Head Missing, Identified by Delatte-Derchain as Hermes/Anubis, Anubis, Unidentified Fig., Sarapis, Anubis, and the Unidentified Pilot of the Ship) on Deck; the Scene Is Surrounded by an Ouroboros*

1. Plates 153.5, 153.6

Paris, Bibliothèque Nationale de France, Cabinet des Médailles, Schlumberger.390.

Unknown.

Heliotrope, damaged.

On reverse: Triple Hecate with torch stands next to burning altar which is being approached by three animal-headed figures, of whom the first is in the act of pouring a libation on the altar; inscriptions (pos.), above: ΤΑΡΒΑΘΑ/ΓΡΑΜΝΗΦΙΒΛΩ; below: ΧΝΗΜΕΩΠΕΡΩΜ/ΟΝΙΓΡΩ.

1st–2nd c. AD (SEH/MK).

LIMC Ouroboros 4; Delatte-Derchain 1964, 215–7 no. 294 (detailed description and interpretation); Matern 2002: 106–7, 236 I30.

Image: impression and photograph of impression by author.

> *H6bj. Sarapis on Throne, with Modius and Staff, Facing Right; in Front of Him Three-Headed Cerberus. Facing Sarapis Is Sol, Nude but for a Chlamys, Radiate (Five Rays), Left Hand Raised, Whip in Right Hand, Standing Left. In Field, Letters*

1. New York, American Numismatic Society 0000.999.33939.

Unknown.

Carnelian.

Undated.

CBd 1932; retrieved from: classics.mfab.hu/talismans/cbd/1932 on 19-11-2017.

> *H6c. … Dressed in Chiton and Chlamys, Left Hand Raised, Globe in Right Hand*

1. Private Collection.

Unknown.

Chalcedony, damaged.

According to Bonner, each of the seven rays ended in a vowel, although ιου are missing as the stone is chipped. Reverse: inscription (pos.): σεμ-σειλ/αμς [horizontal line with five upright bars] χιθ/ιαβλανα/θανλβαφ/ρηυχ.
Undated.
Smith & Hutton 1908: 255; Bonner 1950: 290–291 no. 223.

> *H6ca. ... Nude but for Chlamys, Left Hand Raised, Globe in Right Hand*

1. Plate 153.4
   Philadelphia, University of Pennsylvania Museum of Archaeology and Anthropology 29-128-867.
   Unknown.
   Chalcedony.
   Undated.
   Sommerville 1889, 722, 867, pl. 71.
   Image: photograph courtesy University of Pennsylvania Museum of Archaeology and Anthropology.

2. Plate 153.8
   New York, Metropolitan Museum of Art 95.15.56.
   Unknown.
   Hematite.
   On the reverse: ιαω.
   2nd–3rd c. AD (SEH).
   CBd 1139, retrieved from: classics.mfab.hu/talismans/cbd/1139 on 19-11-2017.
   Image: courtesy Metropolitan Museum of Art, New York.

> *H6cb. ... Nude but for Chlamys, Left Hand Raised, Globe in Right Hand, Next to a Burning Altar*

1. Rome, Museo Nazionale Romano.
   Rome.
   Heliotrope.
   Sol is leaning on a pillar.
   Undated.
   Righetti 1955: 11 no. 5 pl. I,3; Matern 2002: 106–7, 164, 236 I26, fig. 47.

> *H6cc. ... Nude but for Chlamys, Left Hand Raised, Globe in Right Hand within a Zodiac Circle*

1. Athens, National Numismatic Museum.
   Unknown.

Silex, damaged.

Star and crescent next to Sol's head. On bevelled edge inscription: αβλαθ..
αλβ ... On reverse: small Harpocrates with Isis or Aphrodite (only partially preserved) and snake (?).

Late 2nd–3rd c. AD (MK).

Gundel 1992: 249 no. 157.

> *H6d. ... Dressed in Chiton and Chlamys, Globe in Right Hand, Whip
> in Left Hand*

Vacat.

> *H6da. ..., Globe in Left Hand, Right Hand Raised*

1. Ann Arbor, University of Michigan Special Collections Library 31.
    Unknown.
    Chalcedony.
    Inscription on the reverse.
    2nd–3rd c. AD.
    Bonner 1950: 223; CBd 1068, retrieved from: classics.mfab.hu/talismans/
    cbd/1068 on 19-11-2017.

> *H6db. ... within a Zodiac Circle*

1. London, British Museum 1986,0501.113.
    Unknown.
    Hematite.
    Inscription on the reverse.
    3rd century AD.
    Michel 2001: 246; CBd 644, retrieved from: classics.mfab.hu/talismans/
    cbd/644 on 18-11-2017.

> *H6e. ... Nude but for Chlamys, Globe in Right Hand, Whip
> in Left Hand*

1. Cambridge, Fitzwilliam Museum, Lewis Collection.
    Unknown.
    Heliotrope.
    3rd–4th c. AD (Henig).
    Henig 1978: 16 no. 20.

2. Unknown.
    Romula.
    Red jasper.

Undated.
Berciu & Petolescu 1976: 54 no. 58.

3.   Vienna, Kunsthistorisches Museum AS IX.2678.
Carnuntum.
Dark brown jasper.
3rd–4th c. AD.
Dembski 2005: 91 no. 403.

*H6ea. ... Nude but for Chlamys, Globe in Left Hand, Whip
in Right Hand*

1.   Plate 153.9
Baltimore, Walters Art Museum 42.1157
Unknown, probably Rome; formerly in the collection of Thomas Howard,
earl of Arundel (1585–1646), then in the Marlborough collection.
Rock crystal.
2nd c. AD, gold setting 17th c.
Boardman et al. 2009: 128.
Image: photograph of impression courtesy the Walters Art Gallery,
Baltimore, under creative commons zero: no rights reserved-license.
Colour photo at http://www.beazley.ox.ac.uk/record/D1A4C0F4-6D1E
-44F3-B0F0-44745ED7217F.

*H6f. ... Nude but for Chlamys, Sceptre or Staff in Right Hand, Whip in
Left Hand*

1.   Berlin, Staatliche Museen, Antikensammlung 3482.
Unknown.
Violet glass paste, lower part missing, with flange (ergo never used).
50 BC–AD 50 (SEH/MK).
Furtwängler 1896: 3482; Matern 2002: 89, 93, 225 G3.

2.   Plate 153.7
Leiden, National Museum of Antiquities GS-00481.
Unknown.
Red carnelian.
1st–2nd c. AD.
Maaskant-Kleibrink 1978, 481; Matern 2002: 89, 225 G4.
Image: © National Museum of Antiquities, Leiden; photograph R.J.
Looman.

3.   New York, Metropolitan Museum of Art 81.6.172.
Unknown.
Heliotrope.
1st–2nd c. AD (LIMC).
LIMC Helios 331; Matern 2002: 89, 93, 226 G6, fig. 22.

4.   Plate 153.10
Hannover, Kestner Museum K485.
Unknown.
Heliotrope.
2nd c. AD (AGD).
LIMC Helios/Sol 103; AGD IV Hannover, 261–2 no. 1401; Matern 2002: 89,
226 G5.
Image: photograph © Kestner Museum, Hannover.

5.   Verona, Museum 26104.
Unknown.
Heliotrope.
Mid 1st to 2nd c. AD.
Sena Chiesa 2009: 43 no. 68.

> *H6fa. ... Nude but for Chlamys, Sceptre or Staff in Right Hand,*
> *Whip in Left Hand, Facing a Small Orant with Raised Arms, Dressed*
> *in Tunica*

1.   Plate 153.11
Vienna, Kunsthistorisches Museum XII 925.
Unknown.
Heliotrope, damaged.
2nd c. AD (Z.-D.).
LIMC Helios/Sol 190; AGWien, 166 no. 1262; Matern 2002: 89, 226 G7.
Image: photograph © KHM-Museumsverein.

> *H6g. ... Nude but for Chlamys, Sceptre in Right Hand, Burning Torch*
> *in Left Hand*

1.   Plate 153.12
Berlin, Staatliche Museen, Antikensammlung 8655.
Unknown.
Heliotrope.
2nd c. AD (SEH).
Furtwängler 1896: 8655; Matern 2002: 93, 96, 228 G24.

Image: photograph of impression courtesy Cornell University collection of gem impressions.

H6ga. ... Holding a Torch to His Right with Both Hands (No Sceptre)

1. Cambridge, Fitzwilliam Museum B324 (CM).
    Unknown.
    Heliotrope.
    1st c. AD.
    Henig 1994: 135; Matern 2002: 228, G25.

H6h. ... Nude, Right Hand Raised, Surrounded by Zodiac

1. Naples, Museo Archeologico 27159/1298.
    Unknown.
    Carnelian.
    Identification as Apollo-Sol very uncertain
    Modern? (SEH/MK).
    Pannuti 1994: no. 129.

H6i. ... Nude but for Chlamys, Left Hand Raised, Sceptre in Right Hand

1. Plate 153.13
    London, British Museum 1923,0401.194.
    Unknown.
    Heliotrope.
    First half 2nd c. AD (SEH).
    Walters 1926: 179 no. 1660.
    Image: courtesy trustees of the British Museum.

H6j. ... Right Hand Raised, Details Otherwise Indistinguishable

1. Saint-Marcel (Indre), Centre de Recherches Archéologiques.
    Saint-Marcel.
    Glass paste nicolo.
    Undated.
    Guiraud 1988: 91 no. 47.

H6k. ... Nude but for Chlamys, Two Torches, Facing Jupiter, Staff, Seated on Throne. Between Them an Eagle, Looking up at Jupiter

1. Nürnberg, Germanisches Nationalmuseum SiSt 1458.
    Unknown.
    Chalcedony.
    3rd c. AD (W.).
    Weiß 1996: 49 no. 1.

H6l. ... Nude but for Chlamys, Embracing Luna (Chiton) on the Right

1. Plate 153.14
    Berlin, Staatliche Museen, Ägyptisches Museum 10133.
    Unknown.
    Magnetite.
    Reverse: Inscription (pos.): αεη/ιου/ω.
    2nd c. AD (Philipp); 2nd–early 3rd c. AD (MK).
    Philipp 1986: 44, 34; CBd 2010; retrieved from: classics.mfab.hu/talis
    mans/cbd/2010 on 19-11-2017.
    Image: impression and photograph of impression by author.

*H6m. ... Nude but for Chlamys, Left Hand Raised, Details Otherwise
    Indistinguishable*

1. Private collection.
    Dragonby, Lincolnshire?
    Orange carnelian, damaged.
    Undated.
    Henig 1978: 12 no. 32.

*H6n. ... Nude but for Chlamys, Whip in Right Hand, Left Arm
    Hanging Downwards Above Altar*

1. Aquileia, Museo Nazionale 25938? (This inv. no. is given to two separate
    gems in Sena Chiesa's catalogue).
    Aquileia.
    Plasma.
    2nd c. AD.
    Sena Chiesa 1966: no. 84; Matern 2002: 98, 227 G16.

*H6o. ... Dressed in Short Chiton and Chlamys, Left Hand Raised,
    Whip in Right Hand*

1. Private Collection.
    Caesarea Maritima.
    Heliotrope, damaged.
    Next to right leg of Sol along the edge: AMI (pos.).
    2nd–3rd c. AD (MK).
    Hamburger 1968: 26 no. 19; Matern 2002: 241, I61.

2. Plate 153.15
    Göttingen Originalsammlung des Archäologischen Instituts G.76.

Unknown.
Green jasper.
Reverse: a crab (?) and a kettle or pot with handle above a globular pot with two handles.
Late 3rd c. AD; 2nd c. AD (MK).
LIMC Helios/Sol 95; Matern 2002: 106–7, 234 I24.4.
Image: photograph courtesy Archaeological Institute, Göttingen University.

3. Copenhagen, National Museum 1792.
    Unknown.
    Jasper.
    Short *chiton*?
    3rd–4th c. AD (MK).
    LIMC Helios/Sol 101; Matern 2002: 98, 241 I57.

4. Paris, Bibliothèque Nationale de France, Cabinet des Médailles, Froehner.2867.
    Unknown.
    Jasper.
    A star to either side of Sol. Reverse: ABPA/CAƷ.
    3rd–4th c. AD (MK).
    LIMC Abrasax 33a.

5. Private Collection.
    Petronell.
    Green jasper.
    Undated.
    Dembski 1969: 115 no. 219.

6. Private Collection.
    Carnuntum.
    Carnelian.
    Undated.
    Dembski 1969: 116 no. 221.

7. Gaziantep, museum 5946.58.01.
    Zeugma, Agora archives.
    Clay.
    Cretula. Sol dressed in military attire?

2nd–3rd c. AD.
Önal 2007: no. 34–35; CBd 1594; retrieved from: classics.mfab.hu/talismans/cbd/1594 on 19-11-2017.

H6p. Described as "Sol Standing, Radiate"
1. Ostia, Museum 4382.
    Ostia.
    Unknown.
    Undated.
    Floriani Squarciapino 1962: 69.

H6q. ... Nude but for a Chlamys, Left Hand Raised, Blazing Sword ("Flammenschwert") in Right Hand
1. Bad Deutsch-Altenburg, Museum. Carnuntinum 17 778.
    Carnuntum.
    Carnelian.
    3rd c. AD.
    Dembski 2005: 91, no. 404.

H6r. ... Nude but for a Chlamys, Right Hand Raised, Globe in Left Hand
1. Private collection.
    Carnuntum.
    Dark brown jasper.
    K A in field.
    Undated.
    Dembski 1969: 117 no. 225.

H6s. ... Nude but for a Chlamys, Right Hand Raised, Whip in Left Hand, Facing Luna, with Crescent, Velificans
1. Plate 155.1
    London, British Museum 1986,0501.124.
    Unknown.
    Magnetite.
    Vocabula on back.
    2nd c. AD.
    Michel 2001, 64; CBd 443, retrieved from: classics.mfab.hu/talismans/cbd/443 on 18-11-2017.
    Image: drawing after classics.mfab.hu/talismans/cbd/443.

> *H6t. ... Nude but for a Chlamys, Whip in Left Hand, Globe with*
> *Victory in Right Hand, Looking towards in the Centre, a Small*
> *Crescent Above Her Head, Velificans, Walking to the Left towards an*
> *Unidentified Male Figure*

1. Plate 155.2
   London, British Museum OA.9585
   Unknown
   Heliotrope
   Inscriptions on the obverse, reverse, and edge.
   3rd c. AD.
   Michel 2001: 65; CBd 444, Retrieved from: classics.mfab.hu/talismans/cbd/444 on 18-11-2017.
   Image: drawing after classics.mfab.hu/talismans/cbd/444.

> H7. Head or Bust of Sol, Radiate, Left

1. Munich, Staatliche Münzsammlung A2206.
   Acquired in Istanbul.
   Aquamarine (a very rarely-used stone in antiquity).
   3rd–1st c. BC (AGD).
   AGD I-1, 92–3 no. 524; Matern 2002: 169, 182, 252 B56.4a.

2. Munich, Staatliche Münzsammlung A2207.
   Unknown.
   Heliotrope.
   3rd–1st c. BC (AGD).
   AGD I-1, 93 no. 525; Matern 2002: 169, 182, 253 B56.4b.

3. Delos, Museum 74/665, 74/2719, 74/4095, 74/6553 & 74/9211.
   Delos, Maison des sceaux.
   Five cretule with impressions of the same intaglio.
   Late 2nd–early 1st c. BC (period of use).
   Boussac 1992: 111 no. Hλ 24.

4. Delos, Museum 74/588.
   Delos, Maison des sceaux.
   Cretula.
   Late 2nd–early 1st c. BC (period of use).
   Boussac 1992: 111 no. Hλ 25.

5.   Delos, Museum 74/8144.
        Delos, Maison des sceaux.
        Cretula.
        Late 2nd–early 1st c. BC (period of use).
        Boussac 1992: 112 no. Hλ 25 bis.

6.   Delos, Museum 74/6337.
        Delos, Maison des sceaux.
        Cretula.
        Late 2nd–early 1st c. BC (period of use).
        Boussac 1992: 112 no. Hλ 26.

7.   Delos, Museum 75/2845.
        Delos, Maison des sceaux.
        Cretula.
        Late 2nd–early 1st c. BC (period of use).
        Boussac 1992: 112 no. Hλ 27.

8.   Delos, Museum 75/3061.
        Delos, Maison des sceaux.
        Cretula.
        Late 2nd–early 1st c. BC (period of use).
        Boussac 1992: 112 no. Hλ 28.

9.   Delos, Museum 75/1873.
        Delos, Maison des sceaux.
        Cretula.
        Late 2nd–early 1st c. BC (period of use).
        Boussac 1992: 112 no. Hλ 29.

10.   Delos, Museum 74/1382.
        Delos, Maison des sceaux.
        Cretula.
        Late 2nd–early 1st c. BC (period of use).
        Boussac 1992: 112 no. Hλ 30.

11.   Delos, Museum 74/3330.
        Delos, Maison des sceaux.
        Cretula.

Late 2nd–early 1st c. BC (period of use).
Boussac 1992: 112 no. Hλ 31.

12. Delos, Museum 74/1202, 74/5926 & 74/6338.
Delos, Maison des sceaux.
Three cretule with impressions of the same intaglio.
Monogram below chin: M.
Late 2nd–early 1st c. BC (period of use).
Boussac 1992: 112 no. Hλ 32.

13. Delos, Museum 74/7698.
Delos, Maison des sceaux.
Cretula.
Late 2nd–early 1st c. BC (period of use).
Boussac 1992: 112 no. Hλ 33.

14. Delos, Museum 74/7751.
Delos, Maison des sceaux.
Cretula.
Late 2nd–early 1st c. BC (period of use).
Boussac 1992: 112 no. Hλ 34.

15. Delos, Museum 74/7680.
Delos, Maison des sceaux.
Cretula.
Late 2nd–early 1st c. BC (period of use).
Boussac 1992: 112 no. Hλ 35.

16. Delos, Museum 74/7617.
Delos, Maison des sceaux.
Cretula.
Late 2nd–early 1st c. BC (period of use).
Boussac 1992: 112 no. Hλ 36.

17. Delos, Museum 74/5168.
Delos, Maison des sceaux.
Cretula.
Late 2nd–early 1st c. BC (period of use).
Boussac 1992: 112 no. Hλ 37.

18.   Delos, Museum 74/303.
        Delos, Maison des sceaux.
        Cretula.
        Late 2nd–early 1st c. BC (period of use).
        Boussac 1992: 112 no. Hλ 38.

19.   Delos, Museum 74/7628.
        Delos, Maison des sceaux.
        Cretula.
        Late 2nd–early 1st c. BC (period of use).
        Boussac 1992: 112 no. Hλ 39.

20.   Delos, Museum 74/6347.
        Delos, Maison des sceaux.
        Cretula.
        Late 2nd–early 1st c. BC (period of use).
        Boussac 1992: 112 no. Hλ 40.

21.   Delos, Museum 74/1235.
        Delos, Maison des sceaux.
        Cretula.
        Late 2nd–early 1st c. BC (period of use).
        Boussac 1992: 112 no. Hλ 41.

22.   Delos, Museum 74/6345 & 74/6745.
        Delos, Maison des sceaux.
        Two cretule with impressions of the same intaglio.
        Late 2nd–early 1st c. BC (period of use).
        Boussac 1992: 113 no. Hλ 42.

23.   Delos, Museum 75/384.
        Delos, Maison des sceaux.
        Cretula.
        Late 2nd–early 1st c. BC (period of use).
        Boussac 1992: 113 no. Hλ 43.

24.   Delos, Museum 75/1796.
        Delos, Maison des sceaux.
        Cretula.
        Late 2nd–early 1st c. BC (period of use).
        Boussac 1992: 113 no. Hλ 44.

25. Delos, Museum 74/1045.
    Delos, Maison des sceaux.
    Cretula.
    Late 2nd–early 1st c. BC (period of use).
    Boussac 1992: 113 no. Hλ 45.

26. Delos, Museum 74/3245.
    Delos, Maison des sceaux.
    Cretula.
    Late 2nd–early 1st c. BC (period of use).
    Boussac 1992: 113 no. Hλ 46.

27. Delos, Museum 74/17.
    Delos, Maison des sceaux.
    Cretula.
    Late 2nd–early 1st c. BC (period of use).
    Boussac 1992: 113 no. Hλ 47.

28. Delos, Museum 75/3448.
    Delos, Maison des sceaux.
    Cretula.
    Late 2nd–early 1st c. BC (period of use).
    Boussac 1992: 113 no. Hλ 48.

29. Delos, Museum 74/1690.
    Delos, Maison des sceaux.
    Cretula.
    Late 2nd–early 1st c. BC (period of use).
    Boussac 1992: 114 no. Hλ 54.

30. Delos, Museum 75/807, 75/963 & 75/984.
    Delos, Maison des sceaux.
    Three cretule with impressions of the same intaglio.
    Late 2nd–early 1st c. BC (period of use).
    Boussac 1992: 114 no. Hλ 55.

31. Delos, Museum 75/2321 & 75/2441.
    Delos, Maison des sceaux.
    Two cretule with impressions of the same intaglio.
    Late 2nd–early 1st c. BC (period of use).
    Boussac 1992: 114 no. Hλ 56.

32. Delos, Museum 74/3847.
     Delos, Maison des sceaux.
     Cretula.
     Late 2nd–early 1st c. BC (period of use).
     Boussac 1992: 114 no. Hλ 57.

33. Delos, Museum 74/1587.
     Delos, Maison des sceaux.
     Cretula.
     Late 2nd–early 1st c. BC (period of use).
     Boussac 1992: 114 no. Hλ 58.

34. Delos, Museum 74/532 & 74/2297.
     Delos, Maison des sceaux.
     Two cretule with impressions of the same intaglio.
     Late 2nd–early 1st c. BC (period of use).
     Boussac 1992: 114 no. Hλ 59

35. Delos, Museum 74/8116.
     Delos, Maison des sceaux.
     Cretula.
     Late 2nd–early 1st c. BC (period of use).
     Boussac 1992: 114 no. Hλ 60.

36. Delos, Museum 74/6735.
     Delos, Maison des sceaux.
     Cretula.
     Late 2nd–early 1st c. BC (period of use).
     Boussac 1992: 114 no. Hλ 61.

37. Delos, Museum 74/6343.
     Delos, Maison des sceaux.
     Cretula.
     Late 2nd–early 1st c. BC (period of use).
     Boussac 1992: 114 no. Hλ 62.

38. Delos, Museum 74/6348.
     Delos, Maison des sceaux.
     Cretula.
     Late 2nd–early 1st c. BC (period of use).
     Boussac 1992: 115 no. Hλ 63.

39. Delos, Museum 87/71.
    Delos, Maison des sceaux.
    Cretula.
    Late 2nd–early 1st c. BC (period of use).
    Boussac 1992: 115 no. Hλ 64.

40. Delos, Museum 74/9311.
    Delos, Maison des sceaux.
    Cretula.
    Late 2nd–early 1st c. BC (period of use).
    Boussac 1992: 115 no. Hλ 65.

41. Delos, Museum 74/6344.
    Delos, Maison des sceaux.
    Cretula.
    With bow and quiver, according to Boussac, and therefore Helios-Apollo;
    difficult to discern on photograph.
    Late 2nd–early 1st c. BC (period of use).
    Boussac 1992: 115 no. Hλ 66.

42. Delos, Museum 74/3588 & 87/1227.
    Delos, Maison des sceaux.
    Two cretule with impressions of the same intaglio.
    With bow and quiver, according to Boussac, and therefore Helios-Apollo;
    difficult to discern on photograph.
    Late 2nd–early 1st c. BC (period of use).
    Boussac 1992: 115 no. Hλ 67.

43. Delos, Museum 74/9312.
    Delos, Maison des sceaux.
    Cretula.
    With bow and quiver, according to Boussac, and therefore Helios-Apollo;
    difficult to discern on photograph.
    Late 2nd–early 1st c. BC (period of use).
    Boussac 1992: 115 no. Hλ 68

44. Delos, Museum 87/258.
    Delos, Maison des sceaux.
    Cretula.
    With bow and quiver, according to Boussac, and therefore Helios-Apollo;
    difficult to discern on photograph.

late 2nd–early 1st c. BC (period of use).
Boussac 1992: 115 no. Hλ 69.

45. Delos, Museum 75/1100 & 75/1290.
Delos, Maison des sceaux.
Two cretule with impressions of the same intaglio.
With bow and quiver, according to Boussac, and therefore Helios-Apollo-
difficult to discern on photograph.
Late 2nd–early 1st c. BC (period of use).
Boussac 1992: 115 no. Hλ 70.

46. Delos, Museum 75/1184, 75/1520, 75/1526, 75/1821, 75/2222, 75/2430,
75/2438, 75/2671, 75/2856, 75/2942, 75/2988, 75/3127, 75/3188, 75/4028,
75/4029, 87/299, 87/453, 87/464, 87/524, 87/550, 87/1086 & 87/1149.
Delos, Maison des sceaux.
Twenty-two cretule with impressions of the same intaglio.
With bow and quiver, according to Boussac, and therefore Helios-Apollo-
difficult to discern on photograph.
Late 2nd–early 1st c. BC (period of use).
Boussac 1992: 116 no. Hλ 71.

47. Delos, Museum 74/3554.
Delos, Maison des sceaux.
Cretula.
Helios-Apollo, according to Boussac, because of hair-roll (chignon).
Late 2nd–early 1st c. BC (period of use).
Boussac 1992: 116 no. Hλ 72.

48. Delos, Museum 74/3514 & 74/8873 (2×).
Delos, Maison des sceaux.
Two cretule with a total of three impressions of the same intaglio.
Helios-Apollo, according to Boussac, because of hair-roll (chignon).
Late 2nd–early 1st c. BC (period of use).
Boussac 1992: 116 no. Hλ 73.

49. Delos, Museum 74/6335.
Delos, Maison des sceaux.
Cretula.
Helios-Apollo, according to Boussac, because of hair-roll (chignon).
Late 2nd–early 1st c. BC (period of use).
Boussac 1992: 116 no. Hλ 74.

50.   Delos, Museum 74/1470.
       Delos, Maison des sceaux.
       Cretula.
       Helios-Apollo, according to Boussac, because of hair-roll (chignon).
       Late 2nd–early 1st c. BC (period of use).
       Boussac 1992: 116 no. Hλ 75.

51.   Delos, Museum 74/6351.
       Delos, Maison des sceaux.
       Cretula.
       Helios-Apollo, according to Boussac, because of hair-roll (chignon).
       Late 2nd–early 1st c. BC (period of use).
       Boussac 1992: 116 no. Hλ 76.

52.   Delos, Museum 74/24, 74/608, 74/663, 74/1403, 74/2055, 74/2265, 74/3223,
       74/5934, 74/5951, 74/5952, 74/5953, 74/5954, 74/5955, 74/5956, 74/5957,
       74/5958, 74/6339, 74/6340, 74/6340 bis, 74/6548, 75/3380.
       Delos, Maison des sceaux.
       Twenty-one cretule with impressions of the same intaglio. Helios-Apollo,
       according to Boussac, because the radiate bust has a laurel wreath.
       Late 2nd–early 1st c. BC (period of use).
       Boussac 1992: 116–7 no. Hλ 77.

53.   Munich, Staatliche Münzsammlung, A2208.
       Unknown.
       Dark brown sard.
       1st c. BC.
       LIMC Helios/Sol 17; AGD I-3, 20 no. 2210; Matern 2002: 169, 182, 253 B56.4c.

54.   Nürnberg, Germanisches Nationalmuseum, SiSt 1681.
       Unknown.
       Brown to apple green plasma.
       1st c. BC (Weiß); 50 BC–AD 50 (MK).
       Weiß 1996: 78 no. 116.

55.   Unknown (glass paste copy in Würzburg, Martin von Wagner Museum).
       Unknown.
       Carnelian.
       Portrait? Z.-D. suggests the rays are part of a diadem with bands of the
       ribbon in the neck. This is difficult to make out clearly.

1st c. BC. Modern? (SEH/MK).
Zwierlein-Diehl 1986: 75 no. 71.

56. Unknown (glass paste copy in Würzburg, Martin von Wagner Museum).
     Unknown.
     Carnelian.
     Inscription (pos.): favstvs..
     Mid 1st c. BC.
     Zwierlein-Diehl 1986: 154–5 no. 330; Matern 2002: 182, 274–5 B233.12.

57. Plate 155.3
     Sofia, National Archaeological Museum 2301.
     Durostorum (Silistriu).
     Red carnelian.
     2nd–3rd c. AD (D.-M.); Imperial classicizing (stripy) style; wheel-style,
     50 BC–AD 50 (MK).
     Dimitrova-Milcheva 1981: 43 no. 57.
     Image: © Sofia Archaeological Museum / Krassimir Georgiev.

58. Plate 155.4
     Bonn, Akademisches Kunstmuseum der Universität, B174,15.
     Alexandria?
     Red jasper.
     1st c. BC (M.-E.); to first half 1st c. AD (MK).
     Mandel-Elzinga 1985: 253–4 no. 8.
     Image: courtesy of the Akademisches Kunstmuseum der Universität, Bonn.

59. Moscow, Pushkin Museum HC.1000.
     Neapolis (Crimea), necropolis.
     Greenish blue glass paste.
     2nd c. AD; 50 BC–AD 50 (MK/SEH).
     Finogenowa 1993: no. 76.

60. Oxford, Ashmolean Museum 1941.443.
     Unknown.
     Glass paste, imitating amethyst.
     1st c. BC (LIMC).
     LIMC Helios 145; Matern 2002: 169, 182, 253 B56.6.

61. Athens, National Numismatic Museum.
     Unknown.

Mottled carnelian.
Portrait?
30 BC–AD 30 (MK).
Svoronos 1913: 197.

62. Plates 155.5, 155.6
Berlin, Staatliche Museen, Antikensammlung 6315.
Unknown.
Yellowish brown glass paste.
Seven stars (one between each pair of rays) and a crescent in front of Sol's
forehead.
50 BC–AD 50 (SEH/MK).
Furtwängler 1896: 6315. This glass paste was taken from the same mould
as London, BM 3024 (H7.66), and a paste in Geneva (H7.64).
Image: impression and photograph of impression by author.

63. Berlin, Staatliche Museen, Antikensammlung 6316.
Unknown.
Glass paste, layered dark violet, white, light brown, imitating sardonyx,
damaged.
50 BC–AD 50 (SEH/MK).
Furtwängler 1896: 6316.

64. Plate 155.7
Geneva, Musées d'art et d'histoire MF 1593.
Unknown.
Yellow glass paste, damaged.
Seven stars (one between each pair of rays) and a crescent in front of Sol's
forehead.
First half 1st c. BC (V.); 50 BC–AD 50.
Vollenweider 1979: 87–8 no. 84; Matern 2002: 169, 182, 252 B56.2. This glass
paste was taken from the same mould as London, BM 3024 (H7.66), and
Berlin, Staatliche Museen, Antikensammlung 6315 (H7.62).
Image: © Musées d'art et d'histoire, Ville de Genève, photograph: Chaman
ateliers multimédia.

65. Plate 155.8
Kassel, Staatliche Kunstsammlung, Ge 113.
Unknown.
Sardonyx.
50 BC–AD 50 (MK); 3rd c. AD (LIMC).

LIMC Helios/Sol 72; AGD III, 223 no. 113; Matern 2002: 182, 274–5 B233.7. Image: impression courtesy Staatliche Kunstsammlung Kassel, photograph of impression by author.

66.   London, British Museum 1923,0401.627.
      Unknown.
      Glass paste imitating sard.
      Seven stars (one between each pair of rays) and a crescent in front of Sol's forehead.
      50 BC–AD 50 (SEH/MK).
      Walters 1926, 290 no. 3024. This glass paste was taken from the same mould as Berlin, Staatliche Museen, Antikensammlung 6315 (H7.62) and a paste in Geneva (H7.64).

67.   Munich, Staatliche Münzsammlung 3029.
      Unknown.
      Glass paste, violet, translucent.
      2nd c. AD (LIMC); 50 BC–AD 50 (MK).
      LIMC Helios/Sol 68; AGD I-3, 142 no. 3029.

68.   Munich, Staatliche Münzsammlung 3028.
      Unknown.
      Glass paste, red (imitating jasper?).
      2nd c. AD (LIMC); 50 BC–AD 50 (MK).
      LIMC Helios/Sol 68; AGD I-3, 141 no. 3028.

69.   Oxford, Ashmolean Museum 1941.606.
      Unknown.
      Glass paste.
      1st c. BC–1st c. AD.
      This gem is mentioned by Henig 1974: 12 under no. 28.

70.   Princeton University, Art Museum 52-155.
      Unknown.
      Red jasper.
      1st BC–1st c. AD.
      Forbes 1978: 57–8 no. 40.

71–8. Tripoli?
      Cyrene.
      Cretule (clay impressions), some damaged.

75 BC–AD 113.
Maddoli 1963/4: 99 no. 472, 474–480.

79. Plates 155.9, 155.10
Florence, Museo Archeologico 72441.
Luni.
Yellow glass paste.
Early 1st c. AD (S.C.).
Sena Chiesa 1978: 97–8, no. 94; Matern 2002: 169, 182, 252 B56.1b.
Image: courtesy of M. Cristina Guidotti, Museo Archeologico Nazionale di Firenze, © Archivio Fotografico Archeologico Polo Museale della Toscana.

80. Lyon, Musée et Théâtres romains.
Lyon.
Carnelian.
1st c. AD.
Guiraud 1988: 91–2 no. 50.
Found on the floor of a dwelling dating to the 1st–2nd c. AD (fouilles du Verbe Incarné).

81. Private collection.
Nanstallon, Cornwall.
Glass paste, light blue on black, imitating onyx.
1st c. AD (Henig).
Henig 1978: 110 App. 20.

82. Plate 155.11
Malibu, Getty Museum 84.AN.1.42.
Asia Minor.
Carnelian.
Identification as Helios/Sol doubtful. Inscription (neg.): CKY (reading upward).
1st c. AD (Spier).
Spier 1992, 101 no. 243; Matern 2002: 182, 274–5 B233.9.
Image: Digital image courtesy of the Getty's Open Content Program.

83. Plate 155.12
Berlin, Staatliche Museen, Antikensammlung 7201.
Unknown.
Carnelian.

Crescent above head, star below; inscription (neg.) CEƷ TIANOC.
1st c. AD (MK/SEH); poorly executed but not late.
Furtwängler 1896: 269, 7201; LIMC Helios/Sol 311; Matern 2002: 182, 276
B235b.
Image: impression and photograph of impression by author.

84.   Cambridge, Fitzwilliam Museum, Lewis Collection.
       Unknown.
       Carnelian.
       1st c. AD (Henig).
       Henig 1978: 16 no. 17.

85.   Plate 155.13
       Hannover, Kestner Museum K481.
       Unknown.
       Heliotrope.
       1st c. AD (MK); 2nd c. AD (AGD).
       LIMC Helios/Sol 69; AGD IV Hannover, 291 no. 1587; Matern 2002: 182, 275
       B233.6.
       Image: photograph © Kestner Museum, Hannover.

86.   Indiana University Art Museum, B.Y. Berry Collection.
       Unknown.
       Carnelian.
       1st c. AD? (SEH).
       Berry 1969: 40 no. 72.

87.   Plate 155.14
       Vienna, Kunsthistorisches Museum IX B 318.
       Unknown.
       Dark green heliotrope.
       2nd–3rd c. AD (Z.D.); 1st c. AD (SEH/MK) (but perhaps not ancient?).
       LIMC Helios/Sol 70; AGWien 166 no. 1264; Matern 2002: 182, 274–5
       B233.11b.
       Note that AGWien 963 has the same inventory number.
       Image: photograph © KHM-Museumsverband.

88.   Plate 155.15
       Vienna, Kunsthistorisches Museum IX B 606.
       Unknown.

Carnelian.

Inscription (pos) ηλι ος.

2nd c. AD (Z.D.); 1st c. AD (MK).

LIMC Helios/Sol 70; AGWien 166 no. 1263; Matern 2002: 182, 274–5 B233.11a.

Image: photograph © KHM-Museumsverband.

89. Cardiff, National Museum of Wales, 81.79H/4.8.
Caerleon, legionary fortress baths, frigidarium drain.
Pale orange carnelian.
Broken diagonally, lower part lost.
Stratified ante quem date of AD 85–110.
Zienkiewicz 1986: 130 nr 8, pl. 6.

90. Private collection.
Gadara, Decapolis (Umm Qeis).
Burnt carnelian.
1st–2nd c. AD.
Henig & Whiting 1987: 12 no. 61.

91. Plate 155.16
Princeton University, Art Museum 34–81.
Egypt.
Red jasper.
1st–2nd c. AD.
Forbes 1978: 57–8 no. 40.
Image: photograph courtesy Art Museum, Princeton.

92. Bari, Museo Archeologico 2025.
Unknown.
Orange carnelian.
2nd–3rd c. AD (T.); 1st–2nd c. AD (SEH/MK).
Tamma 1991: 69 no. 86.

93. Plate 156.1
Berlin, Staatliche Museen, Antikensammlung 7757.
Unknown.
Sardonyx.
1st–2nd c. AD (SEH/MK).
Furtwängler 1896: 7757.
Image: impression and photograph of impression by author.

94.   Nürnberg, Germanisches Nationalmuseum, SiSt 1680.
       Unknown.
       Red jasper.
       2nd c. AD (Weiß); 1st–early 2nd c. AD (SEH/MK).
       Weiß 1996: 78 no. 117.

95.   Plate 156.2
       Sofia, National Archaeological Museum 8052.
       Novae, chance find.
       Red carnelian.
       2nd c. AD (Dimitrova-Milcheva); imitation of late-Hellenistic types,
       either ancient or modern, impossible to date (MK).
       Dimitrova-Milcheva 1981: 84 no. 246.
       According to Dimitrova-Milcheva, "protectress of the city with corona
       muralis".
       Image: © Sofia Archaeological Museum / Krassimir Georgiev.

96.   Private collection.
       Gadara, Decapolis (Umm Qeis).
       Carnelian.
       2nd c. AD.
       Henig & Whiting 1987: 12 no. 60.

97.   Winchester, Hampshire.
       Winchester, early medieval grave (probably not intentionally placed in
       grave).
       Glass paste nicolo.
       2nd–3rd c. AD (Henig).
       Henig 1978: 12 no. 28.

98.   Plate 156.3
       Nijmegen, Museum Het Valkhof. XXVIII.18. C1/G119.
       Unknown.
       Heliotrope.
       2nd–early 3rd c. AD.
       Maaskant-Kleibrink 1986, 60 no. 119; Matern 2002: 182, 274–5 B233.10.
       Image: courtesy Museum Het Valkhof, Nijmegen.

99.   Plate 155.17
       Sofia, National Archaeological Museum 8035.
       Novae, chance find.

White jasper.

2nd–3rd c. AD (D.-M.); 1st c. AD (SEH/MK).

Dimitrova-Milcheva 1981: 43 no. 56.

Image: © Sofia Archaeological Museum / Krassimir Georgiev.

100. Copenhagen, National Museum 1458.

Unknown (acquired in Beirut).

Multicolored stone ("pietra screziata").

2nd–3rd c. AD (LIMC); 1st c. AD, if ancient (MK/SEH, but impossible to determine conclusively on basis of the photograph).

LIMC Helios/Sol 73; Matern 2002: 182, 274–5 B233.8.

101. Plate 156.5, 156.6

Geneva, Musées d'art et d'histoire C466.

Cruscilles, Haute-Savoie.

Glass paste nicolo.

3rd c. AD (context: found in a treasure buried in the middle of the 3rd c.).

Guiraud 1988: 92 no. 51.

Image: © Musées d'art et d'histoire, Ville de Genève, photograph: Flora Bevilacqua.

102. Hyères, Museum 45.134.

Hyères.

Lapis lazuli.

3rd c. AD (G.); modern (MK).

Guiraud 1988: 92 no. 53.

103. Rennes, Mus. de Bretagne?

Rennes.

Glass paste nicolo.

3rd c. AD.

Guiraud 1988: 92 no. 52 (Guiraud gives the inventory number as 2233, but F. Berretrot of the Musée de Bretagne informed me that this number is incorrect, and that he had been unable to locate the intaglio).

104. Belgrade, National Museum 942.

Unknown.

Chalcedony.

3rd c. AD (LIMC).

LIMC Helios 71.

105. Plates 156.7, 156.8
Geneva, Musées d'art et d'histoire 20892.
Unknown.
Carnelian.
Early 3rd c. AD (V.).
Vollenweider 1979: 255 no. 267; Matern 2002: 182, 275 B233.5a.
Image: © Musées d'art et d'histoire, Ville de Genève, photograph: Flora Bevilacqua.

106. Unknown.
Aldborough, Yorkshire.
Carnelian.
Undated.
Henig 1978: 12 no. 29.

107. Plate 156.4
Bad Deutsch-Altenburg, Museum Carnuntinum Car-Ge-310 (18 039).
Carnuntum.
Reddish brown carnelian.
Undated.
Dembski 1969: 201 no. 378.
Image: Landessammlungen Niederösterreich, Archäologischer Park Carnuntum (Photograph: Harald Wraunek).

108. Plate 156.9
Bad Deutsch-Altenburg, Museum Carnuntinum Car-Ge-311 (17 771).
Carnuntum.
Orange carnelian.
Undated.
Dembski 1969: 201 no. 379.
Image: Landessammlungen Niederösterreich, Archäologischer Park Carnuntum (Photograph: Nicolas Gail).

109. Zalau, Museum 30/195ş.
Porolissum.
Green paste.
Described as radiate, but rays not visible on illustration in catalogue.
Undated (50 BC–AD 50).
Teposu-Marinescu & Lako 1969: 9 no. 31, pl. II.

110. Zalau, Museum 408/1966.
     Porolissum.
     Pink jasper.
     Described as radiate, but rays not visible on illustration in catalogue.
     Undated.
     Teposu-Marinescu & Lako 1969: 9 no. 32, pl. II.

111. Private collection.
     Petronell.
     Rusty red jasper.
     Undated.
     Dembski 1969: 200–1 no. 377.

112. Private collection.
     Petronell.
     Reddish brown jasper.
     Undated.
     Dembski 1969: 201–2 no. 380.

113. Private collection.
     Carnuntum.
     Orange carnelian.
     Undated.
     Dembski 1969: 202 no. 381.

114. Private collection.
     Carnuntum.
     Dark orange carnelian.
     Undated.
     Dembski 1969: 202 no. 382.

115. Unknown.
     Unknown.
     Chalcedony.
     Carnegie's suggestion that this may be a portrait of Nero has no merit.
     Undated.
     Carnegie 1908: 53 D3.

116. Plate 156.10
     Bologna, Museo Civico Archeologico Gl. 162.

Unknown.

Green jasper.

3rd–4th c. AD (M.R.); modern (MK).

Mandrioli Bizzarri 1987: 124 no. 253; Matern 2002: 182, 274 B233.1b.

Image: Courtesy of Museo Civico Archeologico-Photo Archive, Bologna.

117. Plate 156.11

Bologna, Museo Civico Archeologico, Gl. 187.

Unknown.

Green jasper.

3rd–4th c. AD (M.R.); modern? (MK).

Mandrioli Bizzarri 1987, 124 no. 252; Matern 2002: 182, 274 B233.1a.

Image: Courtesy of Museo Civico Archeologico-Photo Archive, Bologna.

118. Ferrara, Museo Civico, RA 715.

Unknown.

Lapis lazuli.

3rd–4th c. AD; modern (SEH/MK).

D'Agostini 1989: 40 no. 59; Matern 2002: 182, 274–5 B233.4.

119. Geneva, Musées d'art et d'histoire.

Unknown.

Carnelian.

3rd–4th c. AD (V.); Renaissance (probably 16th c.) (MK).

Vollenweider 1979: 257–8 no. 269; Matern 2002: 182, 274–5 B223.5b.

120. Paris, Bibliothèque Nationale de France, Cabinet des Médailles, 58.1475.

Unknown.

Yellowish citrine (quartz).

Hellenistic (Vollenw.); Modern (SEH/MK). Treatment of hair (especially under the rays), eye, and stone-type bring us to classify this gem as modern.

Vollenweider 1995: 41.

121. Belgrade, City Museum 942.

Ritopek (Tricornium).

Orange translucent carnelian.

3rd c. AD.

Pilipović 2013: 601 no. 3.

122. Belgrade, National Museum 3393/III.
     Unknown.
     Glass paste.
     3rd c. AD.
     Pilipović 2013: 601 nr 4.

123. Belgrade, National Museum 3399/III.
     Unknown.
     Niccolo.
     3rd c. AD.
     Pilipović 2013: 601 no. 5.

124. Plate 156.12
     Private Collection.
     Xanten.
     Red jasper.
     2nd c. AD.
     Arachne 950058; Matern 2012: 275–6, B233.13b
     Image: Arachne FA-S12413_215206.jpg; arachne.dainst.org/entity/950058

125. Plate 156.13
     Stuttgart, Landesmuseum Württemberg KK grün 919.
     Unknown.
     Jasper.
     1st c. BC.
     http://www.museum-digital.de/bawue/pdf/publicinfo.php?oges=4846&
     lang=en (retrieved 8 October 2017).
     Image: photograph © Landesmuseum Württemberg, Hendrik Zwietasch.

126. Plate 156.14
     Stuttgart, Landesmuseum Württemberg KK grün 218.
     Unknown.
     Carnelian.
     Second half 1st c. BC.
     http://www.museum-digital.de/bawue/pdf/publicinfo.php?oges=3725&
     lang=en (retrieved 8 October 2017).
     Image: photograph © Landesmuseum Württemberg, Hendrik Zwietasch.

127. Plate 156.15
     Munich, Archäologische Staatssammlung 1974.3137.

Eining.
Red jasper.
2nd c. AD.
Platz-Horster 2018: 72 no. 54.
Image: photograph © Archäologische Staatssammlung / Stefanie Friedrich.

128.   Plate 156.16
       Bad Deutsch-Altenburg, Museum Carnuntinum Car-Ge-308 (18 113).
       Carnuntum.
       Carnelian.
       Undated.
       Image: Landessammlungen Niederösterreich, Archäologischer Park Car-
       nuntum (Photograph: Nicolas Gail).

129.   Bonn, Rheinisches Landesmuseum 2648 G110.
       Unknown.
       Carnelian.
       1st c. AD.
       Matern 2002: 274, B233.3a. Platz-Horster 1984: 109, 116 pl. 30.

130.   Private Collection.
       Xanten.
       50 BC–AD 50.
       Glass paste.
       Matern 2012: 275–6, B233.23a.

131.   Ankara, Erimtan museum 238.
       Anatolia.
       Dark sard. Fragment of an iron ring.
       2nd c, AD.
       Konuk & Arslan 2000: 82 no. 58.

132.   Munich, Staatliche Antikensammlungen und Glyptothek.
       Unknown.
       Sard.
       Wünsche & Steinhart believe this to be a portrait of the deified Antinoos.
       2nd c. AD
       Wünsche & Steinhart 2010: 85 no. 71.

133. Verona, Museum 27122.
     Unknown.
     Green jasper.
     2nd c. AD.
     Sena Chiesa 2009: 44 no. 77.

134. Verona, Museum 27123.
     Unknown.
     Red jasper.
     2nd c. AD.
     Sena Chiesa 2009: 44 no. 78.

135. Verona, Museum 27132.
     Unknown.
     Blue glass paste.
     1st c. AD.
     Sena Chiesa 2009: 43 no. 74.

136. Çorum, Archaeological Museum 5320.
     Uğulurdağ area.
     Red translucent carnelian (?).
     2nd–3rd c. AD (SEH).
     İbiş 2022: 95–6, fig. 48.

137. Çorum, Archaeological Museum 5320.
     Uğulurdağ area.
     Orange translucent glass.
     Late 1st c. BC–early 1st c. AD (SEH).
     İbiş 2022: 95–6, fig. 49.

H7a. …, Whip

1. Paris, Bibliothèque Nationale de France, Cabinet des Médailles, 1475a.
   Unknown.
   Carnelian.
   Possibly a portrait? The presence of the whip strongly suggests Sol is meant.
   1st c. BC (SEH).
   Unpublished.

2. Udine, Museo Civico, 63/827.
   Aquileia?
   Heliotrope.
   2nd–3rd c. AD (T.); 1st-2nd (SEH).
   Tomaselli 1993: 146 no. 360.

3. Unknown (Impression in Oxford, Ashmolean Museum, Evans sealing sheet 1,1).
   Aequum (Sitluk), Dalmatia.
   Unknown.
   1st–2nd c. AD (Middleton).
   Middleton 1991: 56 no. 53.

4. Florence, Museo Archeologico 1521.
   Unknown.
   Yellow jasper.
   2nd–3rd c. AD (1st c. AD?).
   Tondo & Vanni 1990: 174 no. 110, 208 fig. 110.

5. Plate 156.17
   Vienna, Kunsthistorisches Museum XII 886.
   Unknown.
   Red jasper.
   Second half 2nd–first half 3rd c. AD.
   AGWien III, 306 no. 2764; Matern 2002: 182, 274–5 B233.11d.
   Image: photograph © KHM-Museumsverband.

6. Plates 156.18, 156.19
   Geneva, Musées d'art et d'histoire, 20516.
   Unknown.
   Dark red jasper.
   270/80 AD (Vollenweider); 2nd–early 3rd c. AD (MK-see note Nijmegen 119).
   Vollenweider 1983: 187–8 no. 238; Matern 2002: 182, 275 B233.5c.
   Image: © Musées d'art et d'histoire, Ville de Genève, photograph: Flora Bevilacqua.

7. Cambridge, Fitzwilliam Museum, CM.39.1982.
   Carnelian.
   Undated; 1st c. AD?
   Nicholls 1983: 18–19 no. 51.

8.   Ankara, Erimtan Museum 239.
     Anatolia.
     Sard.
     Five rays.
     2nd c. AD.
     Konuk & Arslan 2000: 79 no. 55.

H7b. … on Upturned Crescent

1.   Unknown (sealing in Oxford, Ashmolean Museum, Evans sealing sheet 23).
     Salona, Dalmatia.
     Sard.
     2nd–1st c. BC (Middleton).
     Middleton 1991: 33–4 no. 2.

2.   Oxford, Ashmolean 1941, 557 (also Evans sealing, sheet 38).
     Scardona (Skradin), Dalmatia.
     Carnelian.
     1st c. BC–1st c. AD (Middleton).
     Middleton 1991: 55–6 no. 52.

3.   Plate 156.20
     Leiden, National Museum of Antiquities GS-00517.
     Unknown.
     Red carnelian.
     7 stars in field below crescent. Identified by Maaskant-Kleibrink as Selene/Luna; however, there can be no doubt that Sol is meant, as Selene is never depicted radiate, but always with a crescent in her hair. Cf. H7ba, where the whip further emphasizes that Sol, not Luna is meant.
     1st–2nd c. AD.
     Maaskant-Kleibrink 1978, 517.
     Image: © National Museum of Antiquities, Leiden; photograph R.J. Looman.

4.   Verona, Museum 27124.
     Unknown.
     Chalcedony.
     1st–2nd c. AD
     Sena Chiesa 2009: 43 no. 74.

H7ba. ... on Upturned Crescent, Whip

1. Plate 157.1
    Vienna, Kunsthistorisches Museum IX B 1460.
    Unknown.
    Carnelian, somewhat translucent.
    Star below crescent.
    1st–2nd c. AD (MK); 3rd c. AD (AGWien).
    LIMC Helios/Sol 75; AGWien, 166 no. 1265; Matern 2002: 182, 276 B239.
    Image: photograph © KHM-Museumsverband.

H7bb. ... on Upturned Crescent, between Two Eagles, Star on Each
Point of Crescent

1. Paris, Bibliothèque Nationale de France, Cabinet des Médailles 58.1477bis.
    Unknown.
    Lapis lazuli.
    1st–2nd c. AD? Dubious; could well be modern (MK).
    Chabouillet 1858: 1477bis.

H7bc. ... on Upturned Crescent, Star on Each Point of Crescent

1. Plates 157.2, 157.3
    Copenhagen, Thorvaldsen Museum I 213.
    Acquired in Rome.
    Green quartz.
    1st c. BC–early 1st c. AD (MK); 3rd c. AD (LIMC).
    LIMC Helios/Sol 74; Matern 2002: 182, 276 B238. LIMC and Matern give
    incorrect inv. number.
    Image: photograph and impression courtesy Thorvaldsen Museum,
    Copenhagen, photograph of impression by author.

2. Plate 157.4
    Berlin, Staatliche Museen, Antikensammlung 6317.
    Unknown.
    Yellowish brown glass paste.
    50 BC–AD 50 (SEH/MK).
    Furtwängler 1896: 6317.
    Image: impression and photograph of impression by author.

3. Munich, Staatliche Münzsammlung 2644.
    Unknown.
    Carnelian.

Early 2nd c. AD (AGD).
AGD I-3, 83 no. 2644.
Identified by the AGD as bust of Selene.

4. Plate 157.5
Berlin, ex Stosch coll. (glass paste in M. von Wagner Museum in Würz-burg).
Unknown.
Carnelian.
2nd–3rd c. AD (Z.-D.).
Zwierlein-Diehl 1986, 249 no. 746; Matern 2002: 182, 276 B241.
Image: courtesy of the M. von Wagner Museum, Würzburg.

5. Oxford, Ashmolean, 1892.1453.
Unknown.
Heliotrope.
Undated.
Unpublished; referred to by Middleton 1991 under no. 52.

H7c. ... Next to Upturned Crescent

1. Plates 18.5, 157.6
Berlin, Staatliche Museen, Antikensammlung, 7200.
Unknown.
Carnelian.
Inscriptions (neg.): SOL (under bust of Sol); LVNA (above crescent).
1st c. AD (SEH/MK); 3rd c. AD (LIMC).
LIMC Helios/Sol 311; Matern 2002: 182, 276 B235a.
Image: Cornell University Gem Impressions Collection.

H7d. ... Facing Bust of Luna

1. Paris, Bibliothèque Nationale de France, Cabinet des Médailles 58.1476 (glass paste copy in M. von Wagner Museum, Würzburg).
Unknown.
Yellow carnelian, translucent.
Three letters (neg.) between the busts: C Y M. Vollenweider & Avisseau-Broustet believe that the two busts are portraits, possibly of Antiochus IX and Cleopatra.
Late 2nd–early 1st c. BC (Vollenweider & Avisseau-Broustet); 50–25 BC (Z.-D.); 1st c. AD; the hair of Sol and Luna was reworked in modern times. (MK)

Vollenweider & Avisseau-Broustet 1995: 17 9 no. 189; Zwierlein-Diehl 1986: 119 no. 163.

Matern (2002: 182, 276 B240) catalogues only the paste in Würzburg.

2. Athens, National Numismatic Museum.
    Unknown.
    Pseudo-nicolo.
    1st c. AD (MK).
    Svoronos 1913: no. 200.

3. Hannover, Kestner Museum K1302.
    Unknown.
    Moss agate.
    Below busts, a lizard.
    2nd c. AD (AGD); 1st–2nd c. AD (SEH/MK)
    LIMC Helios/Sol 309; AGD IV Hannover, 310 no. 1709; Matern 2002: 182, 276 B236.

4. Oxford, Ashmolean 1910.778.
    Unknown.
    Mottled carnelian.
    Undated.
    Referred to by Middleton 1991, 56 no. 53.

5. Art Market.
    Unknown.
    Heliotrope.
    Sol with whip, Luna with a torch.
    2nd c, AD?
    Christie's Auction Antiquities 1561, London, October 1, 2014, lot 55.

H7e. ... Next to Bust of Luna

1. Copenhagen, National Museum 8577 (lost).
    Unknown.
    Heliotrope.
    3rd c. AD (LIMC); 1st–early 2nd c. if not modern (MK).
    LIMC Helios/Sol 310; Matern 2002: 182, 276 B237.

2. Gaziantep, Museum 5580.1.07.
    Zeugma, Agora Archives.

Clay.

Cretula, damaged.

1st–2nd c.

Önal 2010: no. 48; CBd 1593; retrieved from: classics.mfab.hu/talismans/ cbd/1593 on 19-11-2017.

H7f. ... Above Star and Scorpion

1. Plate 157.7

London, British Museum 1814,0704.1627.

Unknown.

Yellow jasper.

"Late Roman" (Walters); 1st–2nd c. AD (SEH).

Walters 1926, no. 1666.

Image: courtesy of the Trustees of the British Museum.

H7g. ... between Two Standards (?)

1. Plate 157.8

Vienna, Kunsthistorisches Museum IX B 1367.

Acquired in Vienna in 1837.

Red jasper.

1st–2nd c. AD.

AGWien III, 306 no. 2765; Matern 2002: 182, 274–5 B233.11c.

Image: photograph © KHM-Museumsverband.

H7h. ... Upturned Crescent Above Head

1. Delos, Museum 74/947.

Delos, Maison des sceaux.

Cretula.

Crescent difficult to see on photograph.

Late 2nd–early 1st c. BC (period of use).

Boussac 1992: 113 no. Hλ 49.

2. Delos, Museum 74/5875, 74/6294 & 74/6803.

Delos, Maison des sceaux.

Three cretule with impressions of the same intaglio.

Late 2nd–early 1st c. BC (period of use).

Boussac 1992: 113 no. Hλ 50.

3. Delos, Museum 74/6073.

Delos, Maison des sceaux.

Cretula.
Crescent uncertain.
Late 2nd–early 1st c. BC (period of use).
Boussac 1992: 113 no. Hλ 51.

4. Delos, Museum 74/2846.
Delos, Maison des sceaux.
Cretula.
Late 2nd–early 1st c. BC (period of use).
Boussac 1992: 113 no. Hλ 52.

5. Delos, Museum 74/1916.
Delos, Maison des sceaux.
Cretula.
Late 2nd–early 1st c. BC (period of use).
Boussac 1992: 113 no. Hλ 53.

H7i
See HA7i.

H7j. ... Surrounded by Four Quadrigas Running Counterclockwise
1. Berlin, Antikensammlung 32.237.387.
Unknown.
Brown sard.
Late 2nd–early 3rd c. AD.
Weiß 2007: 171 nr 164.

H8. Bust or Head of Sol, Radiate, to the Right
1. Poitiers, Mus. Sainte-Croix (Collection Bonsergent).
Environs of Poitiers.
Lapis lazuli.
3rd c. AD? Modern (MK).
Guiraud 1988: 92 no. 54.

2. Bucharest, National Museum of Antiquities 122/C.O (formerly Cabinet
Numismatique).
Unknown.
Reddish carnelian, translucent.
Portrait?

Undated.
Gramatopol 1974: 71 no. 416.

3. Bucharest, National Museum of antiquities 55 (formerly Cabinet Numismatique).
Red jasper.
An object in front of Sol, identified by Gramatopol as a cross, may be a whip (but difficult to make out from the photograph).
Undated.
Gramatopol 1974: 71 no. 411.

4. Art market, Medusa-art.com MA244.
Unknown.
Carnelian.
1st c. AD or (more probably) modern.
Unpublished.

5. Plate 157.9
Leiden Rijksmuseum van Oudheden GS 50081.
Turkey.
Clay (impression).
Undated.
Maaskant-Kleibrink 1971, no. 125.
Image: © National Museum of Antiquities, Leiden; photograph R.J. Looman.

6. Ankara, Erimtan museum 93.
Anatolia.
Yellow jasper.
2nd c. AD.
Konuk & Arslan 2000: 80 nr 56.

7. Unknown.
Unknown.
Jasper.
Around the bust: eleven stars and ΑΣΗΡΟΣ, ΙΦΗ, ΙΑΩΑΒΑΩΣ; on the bevelled edge: ΑΒΡΑΣΑΞ. Uncertain whether the drawing is based on the intaglio or its impression, so the direction of Sol's bust is unconfirmed.
Undated.
Mastrocinque 2003: 329 no. 280.

8.   Versailles, Service départemental de l'archéologie RPF 3082.2.
     Richebourg.
     Red jasper.
     Whip behind his far shoulder.
     2nd c. AD.
     Guiraud 2008: 96 no. 1098

H8a. ... Facing a Rabbit (?); 7 Stars
1.   Debrecen (Hungary), Déri Museum, DF. R. XI. 38.
     Ószönyi/Brigetium
     Green jasper, oval, flat.
     Reverse: a lion (?) jumps left; above, inscr. (pos.): ξρην (sic).
     3rd c. AD.
     LIMC Helios/Sol 188; CBd 1458; retrieved from: classics.mfab.hu/talis
     mans/cbd/1458 on 19-11-2017.

H8b. ... Facing Bust of Luna
1.   Plate 157.10
     Sofia, National Archaeological Museum 5159.
     Vratsa District.
     Dark brown jasper.
     2nd c. AD (D.-M.).
     Dimitrova-Milcheva 1981: 68 no. 168.
     Image: © Sofia Archaeological Museum / Krassimir Georgiev.

H8c. ... Facing Cock, Above Lion Walking to the Right
1.   Plate 157.11
     Berlin, Staatliche Museen, Ägyptisches Museum 12475.
     Unknown (acquired in Strasbourg).
     Heliotrope.
     Inscription (pos.): from above Sol's head along the edge: AIPHAAI.I; in
     front of Sol: N; Behind Sol, along the edge, downward: ΦPH; Reverse:
     inscription (pos.): AKPA/MAXA/MAPE/three symbols
     2nd–early 3rd c. AD (Philipp); 1st–2nd c. AD (MK).
     Philipp 1986: 43, 32; CBd 2008; retrieved from: classics.mfab.hu/talis
     mans/cbd/2008 on 19-11-2017.
     Image: impression and photograph of impression by author.

H8d. ... Back-to-Back with a Bust of Luna Above an Egg (?)
on a Pedestal

1. Unknown.
   Unknown.
   Unknown.
   On reverse: lion-headed snake.
   Undated.
   Mastrocinque 2003: 330–1 no. 286.

   H9. Frontal or Three-Quarters Bust or Head of Sol
1. Palermo, Museo Archeologico.
   Selinunte, Temple C.
   Cretula, clay impression, damaged.
   4th–early 3rd c. BC (Terminus ante quem of 250 BC).
   Salinas 1883: no. 492 (Type CLII).

2–23. Delos, Museum 74/6574, 74/9117, 74/728, 74/634, 74/1280, 74/6326, 74/1512, 75/2646, 74/3814, 74/6330, 74/5181, 74/6327, 74/1955, 74/6333, 74/6331, 74/6328, 74/4233, 74/2691, 74/3245, 74/6346, 74/6396, 87/463, 74/379, 74/1249, 74/3297, 74/2855, 75/1282.
   Delos, Maison des sceaux.
   27 cretule with impressions of 22 different intaglios.
   Late 2nd–early 1st c. BC (period of use).
   Boussac 1992: 108–111 nos. Hλ 1–22

24. Plate 157.12
    London, British Museum 1799,0521.24.
    Unknown.
    Carnelian.
    Hellenistic.
    Matern 2002: 169, 182, 252 B56.3; LIMC Helios 147.
    Image: photograph © Trustees of the British Museum.

25. Berlin, Staatliche Museen, Antikensammlung, 4851.
    Unknown.
    Black glass paste, banded white.
    1st c. BC (SEH/MK).
    Furtwängler 1896: 195, 4851; Matern 2002: 182, 276 B234.

26.   Plates 157.13, 157.14
       Copenhagen, Thorvaldsen Mus, I 622.
       Acquired in Rome.
       Sardonyx.
       Inscription (neg.): c ae s.
       3rd–1st c. BC (Thorvaldsens Museum); 50 BC–AD 50 (MK); 1st c. AD
       (LIMC).
       LIMC Helios/Sol 38; Matern 2002: 182, 274 B230.
       Image: Photograph and impression courtesy Thorvaldsen Museum,
       Copenhagen, photograph of impression by author.

27.   Udine, Museo Civico, 777/253.
       Aquileia?
       Greenish black jasper.
       Unfinished.
       1st c. BC–1st c. AD?
       Tomaselli 1993: 146 no. 359.

28.   Plate 157.15
       Berlin, Staatliche Museen, Antikensammlung, 2378.
       Unknown.
       Plasma.
       Late Hellenistic/50 BC–AD 50 (SEH).
       LIMC Helios 149; Matern 2002: 182, 274 B225
       Image: Cornell University Gem Impressions Collection.

29.   Plate 157.16
       Hannover, Kestner Museum K482.
       Unknown.
       Bright orange carnelian.
       1st c. BC–1st c. AD (MK); 2nd c. AD (AGD)
       LIMC Helios/Sol 39; AGD IV, Hannover, 291 no. 1588; Matern 2002: 182, 274
       B228.
       Image: photograph © Kestner Museum, Hannover.

30–32. Tripoli?
       Cyrene.
       Three cretule (clay impression), all damaged, of three different intaglios.
       75 BC–AD 113.
       Maddoli 1963/4: 99 no. 469–471.

33. Cambridge, Fitzwilliam Museum CG 506.
    Unknown.
    Heliotrope.
    3rd c. AD.
    Sol has seven rays; in field two stars and below the image (continuing up
    to the right) seven letters and signs. On the reverse: crescent and three
    stars. Note the repetition of the number seven in the number of rays,
    number of letters, and number of planets (five stars, a crescent, and Sol).
    Henig 1994: 230 no. 506; Matern 2002: 274 B226; CBd 116, classics.mfab.hu/
    talismans/cbd/116 on 18-11-2017.

34. Private collection.
    Carnuntum.
    Reddish brown jasper.
    Undated.
    Dembski 1969: 202 no. 383.

35. Plate 157.17
    St. Petersburg, Hermitage ГР-21630.
    Unknown.
    Rock crystal.
    1st c. AD.
    Matern 2002: 274 B232.
    Image: photograph courtesy Hermitage, St. Petersburg.

36. Unknown.
    Unknown.
    Reddish brown jasper.
    Undated.
    Frank Sternberg Auktion XXIV, 19–20 nov. 1990, no. 513.

37. Berlin, Staatliche Museen, Ägyptisches Museum 9847.
    Unknown.
    Lapis lazuli.
    Obverse: Anubis; inscription (pos.): .νοχαρριαμιοτιμιοβιουβαλ βηλ; bev-
    elled edge, inscription (pos.): ανοχαρβιαψυχναετβντκαιφρεα.
    1st c. AD (Philipp); modern (MK).
    Philipp 1986, 95 no. 141; CBd 224, retrieved from: classics.mfab.hu/talis
    mans/cbd/224 on 18-11-2017.

38. Copenhagen, National Museum, 234.
    Italy.
    Carnelian-onyx.
    Modern? (MK).
    LIMC Helios/Sol 40; Matern 2002: 182, 274 B231.

H9a. ... Surrounded by Rays

1. Paris, Bibliothèque Nationale de France, Cabinet des Médailles 58.1485.
   Unknown.
   Opal.
   Modern (SEH/MK).
   Chabouillet 1858: 1485.

H9b. ... within Zodiac Circle

1. Plate 157.18
   London, British Museum 1895,0621.5.
   Unknown.
   Garnet.
   Hellenistic.
   Gundel 1992: 152; LIMC H 324; Matern 2002: 182, 253 B57.2.
   Image: photograph © Trustees of the British Museum.

2. Plates 157.19, 157.20
   Geneva, Musées d'art et d'histoire, 20506.
   Unknown.
   Green agate.
   Late 2nd–early 1st c. BC (V.).
   Vollenweider 1983: 178–80 no. 228; Gundel 1992: 152.1; Matern 2002: 182, 274 B227.
   Image: © Musées d'art et d'histoire, Ville de Genève, photograph: Bettina Jacot-Descombes

H9c. ... on Upturned Crescent

1. Plate 158.1
   Florence, Museo Archeologico, 72440.
   Luni.
   Dark carnelian, damaged.
   A star on each point of the crescent.

Late 2nd–early 1st c. BC.
Sena Chiesa 1978: 98–9, no. 95; Matern 2002: 169, 182, 252 B56.1a.
Image: courtesy of M. Cristina Guidotti, Museo Archeologico Nazionale di
Firenze, © Archivio Fotografico Archeologico Polo Museale della Toscana.

2. Private collection.
   Gadara, Decapolis (Umm Qeis).
   Heliotrope.
   1st c. BC.
   Henig & Whiting 1987: 11 no. 59.

3. Unknown.
   Unknown.
   Garnet.
   Inscription (neg.) ΣIPA.
   Undated.
   Carnegie 1908: 53 no. D2.

4. Ankara, Erimtan museum 926.
   Anatolia.
   Brown jasper. In a fragment of an iron ring.
   A star on each point of the crescent.
   Konuk & Arslan 2000: 81 nr 57.

5. Unknown.
   Unknown.
   Carnelian.
   Above Sol a star; below him a serpent.
   Undated.
   Mastrocinque 2003: 329 no. 283.

6. Berlin, Antikensammlung 32.237.595.
   Unknown.
   Glass paste.
   An ouroboros is depicted below the crescent; a star above each point of
   the crescent.
   2nd c. AD.
   Weiß 2007: 171 no. 163.

H9d. ... Crowned by Two Victories

1.   Plate 158.2
Kassel, Staatliche Antikensammlung, Ge 114.
Unknown.
Carnelian, damaged.
50 BC–AD 50 (MK); 1st c. AD (AGD).
LIMC Helios/Sol 202; AGD III, 224 no. 114; Matern 2002: 182, 274 B229.
Image: impression courtesy Staatliche Antikensammlung; photograph of the impression by author.

H9e. ... between Profile Busts, Facing Inwards, of Saturn and Luna

1.   Unknown.
Unknown.
Chalcedony.
Seven stars in field.
1st–2nd c. AD (SEH).
Smith & Hutton 1908, no. 108.

H9f. ... Below an Upturned Crescent (the Crescent Is Independent of the Head)

1.   Delos, Museum 75/508.
Delos, Maison des sceaux.
Cretula.
Late 2nd–early 1st c. BC (period of use).
Boussac 1992: 111 no. Hλ 22.

H10. Sol as a Minor Figure
H10a. Above: Sol on Chariot to Left, Whip in Right Hand, Reins in Left Hand, Faced by Bust of Sarapis to Right; Below: Aesculapius (Right), Hygieia (Centre) and Isis. Five Stars and an Upturned Crescent

1.   Plate 158.3
Berlin, Staatliche Museen, Antikensammlung 2669.
Unknown.
Carnelian.
2nd c. AD (SEH).
Furtwängler 1896: 2669; LIMC Helios 85; Matern 2002: 67, 220 Q77.
There are 5 stars in the field, rather than 4 as stated by Furtwängler, the LIMC, and Matern.
Image: impression and photograph of impression by author.

H10b. Above: Fairly Large Frontal Bust of Sol between Isis and Harpocrates; Below: Characters/Letters

1. Plates 158.4, 158.5
Berlin, Staatliche Museen, Ägyptisches Museum 11933.
Unknown.
Lapis lazuli, damaged.
Reverse: palm branch (or cypress?) within a laurel or olive wreath.
1st c. AD (reworked in 18th/19th c.) (Philipp); modern (MK).
Philipp 1986: 42–3, 31; CBd 2007; retrieved from: classics.mfab.hu/talismans/cbd/2007 on 19-11-2017.
Image: impression and photograph of impression by author.

H10c. To the Right, in Front of a Column on a High Base, a Herm with Erect Phallus Protruding from the Table-Like Base Bearing a Bearded Head Facing Left. In Front of the Herm a Burning Altar; to the Left, Three Heads Facing Right, Next to Each Other; the Rear Head Bearded, the Other Two Clean-Shaven. Above the Heads, Bust of Sol, Radiate, Facing Right; Behind Sol a Cornucopiae, in Front of Sol, above the Altar, a Phallus. To the Right Above the Phallus, a Small Radiate Globe (Sun?, Star?), and Another Phallus Above the Herm. Behind the Column a Small Upturned Crescent

1. Plate 158.6
Berlin, Staatliche Museen, Antikensammlung, 3366.
Unknown.
Brown sard.
Modern? But in that case of exceptional quality. Perhaps Republican, but then very strange.
LIMC Helios 315.
Image: impression and photograph of impression by author.

H10d. Seated Cybele (?), Facing Right, between a Small Lion (?) and Holding a Wreath (?) and Staff (?); Facing Her, Fortuna with Modius, Cornucopiae and Rudder. Above, between Them, Frontal Bust of Sol on Upturned Crescent

1. Plate 158.7
Berlin, Staatliche Museen, Antikensammlung, 8626.
Unknown.
Red jasper, damaged.
2nd–3rd c. AD (SEH).

Furtwängler 1896: 8626.

One lion only, not two as described by Furtwängler.

Image: impression and photograph of impression by author.

H10e. Sarapis on Throne, with Modius and Staff, Facing Right; in Front of Him Three-Headed Cerberus. Sarapis Is Flanked to the Right by Bust of Sol Facing Left, and to the Left by Upturned Crescent with Two Stars

1. Plate 158.8
    Hannover, Kestner Museum K446.
    Unknown.
    Jasper.
    2nd–3rd c. AD (AGD); 2nd c. AD (SEH/MK).
    LIMC Helios/Sol 390.
    Image: photograph © Kestner Museum, Hannover.

H10f. Bust of Sol Facing Left Above an Eagle

1. Philadelphia, University of Pennsylvania Museum of Art and Anthropology 29-128-1632.
    Unknown.
    Carnelian. Set in a modern ring.
    Undated.
    Crescent and star to the left and right of the bust respectively.
    Berges 2002: 42, 155, pl. 31.

H10fa. ... between Two Army Standards

1. Munich, Staatliche Münzsammlung 2463.
    Unknown.
    Reddish orange carnelian.
    Sol may, according to AGD, be Zeus Ammon.
    3rd c. AD (AGD).
    AGD I-3, 60 no. 2463.

H10g. Two Busts of Dioscuri, Facing Each Other; Behind Each a Palm Branch. Between Them, Below, Frontal Bust of Sol with a Staff Above His Head and an Upturned Crescent at the Top

1. Munich, Staatliche Münzsammlung, A.1967.
    Unknown (acquired in Istanbul).
    Red carnelian, damaged.

Below: inscription (neg.): ΑΓΑΘΟΠΟΥΣ. For ἀγαθοπους, cf. the modern Greek concept of "lucky feet". A C. Iulius Agatopus was a goldsmith in Rome in the first century AD (CIL 3945).

1st c. AD (AGD); 50 BC–AD 50 (MK)

AGD I-3, 39 no. 2330.

> H1oh. *Large, Convex Stone, Empty but for a Very Small Bust of Sol on One Side and the Name* IΠΠΑΡΧΟΥ. *On the Bevelled Edge:* IΠΠΑΡ

1. Paris, Bibliothèque Nationale de France, Cabinet des Médailles 58.1484.
    Unknown.
    Agate.
    Late Hellenistic?
    Chabouillet 1858: 1484.
    Chabouillet omits the inscription on the edge.

> H1oi. *Two Fortunae (Each with Cornucopia) Facing Each Other, Clasping Hands Above a Modius; Above the Clasped Hands Small Bust of Sol to Left*

1. Plate 158.9
    Malibu, Getty Museum, 85.AN.370.72.
    Unknown.
    Dark brown agate.
    2nd c. AD (Spier).
    Spier 1992: 135 no. 368; Matern 2002: 182, 277 B246.
    Image courtesy Getty Museum.

> H1oia. *As Previous, but Head of Sol Facing, Above a Crescent, and a Griffin instead of a Modius Below the Clasped Hands; No Inscription*

1. Plates 19.2, 159.1
    Leiden, National Museum of Antiquities GS-00883.
    Unknown.
    Red carnelian.
    1st–2nd c. AD.
    Maaskant-Kleibrink 1978: 883.
    Image: © National Museum of Antiquities, Leiden; photograph R.J. Looman.

2. Plate 158.10
    Vienna, Kunsthistorisches Museum XII 912, 1677.
    Unknown.

Heliotrope.

The "griffin" (damaged) is identified by Zwierlein-Diehl as an owl, followed by Matern.

2nd c. AD.

AGWien III, 314 no. 2820; Matern 2002: 182, 277 B248c.

Image: photograph © KHM-Museumsverband.

H10ib. ... with two Fortunae, Each with Cornucopia, Clasping Hands
Above Inscription χαρά; Bust of Sol Above Their Clasped Hands

1. Berlin, Staatliche Museen, Antikensammlung, 8667.

Unknown.

Brown and green jasper.

2nd c. AD.

Furtwängler 1896: 8667

H10j. Above: Small Standing Figure of Mars (?) with Lance and
Armor, Facing Left, Opposite Bust of Sol, Facing Right, and Star.
Below: Eagle with Spread Wings Filling the Whole Lower Half
of the Stone

1. Bucharest, National Museum of Antiquities 565 (Formerly Cabinet Numismatique).

Unknown.

Red jasper.

Undated.

Gramatopol 1974, 68 no. 379.

H10k. Sol and the Planetary Deities

H10ka. Obverse: Sol, Jupiter, Luna and Mercury Together with Four
Signs of the Zodiac and a Star. Reverse: Saturn, Venus and Mars; a
Woman Reclining on a Couch and Two Signs of the Zodiac

1. Plate 158.11

Kassel, Staatliche Kunstsammlung, Ge 80.

Unknown.

Yellow jasper.

1st c. AD.

LIMC Helios/Sol 295; AGD III, 216 no. 80; Matern 2002: 182, 276–7 B244b.

Image: impression courtesy Staatliche Antikensammlung; photograph of the impression by author.

*H10kb. Bust of Sarapis Facing Left within Two Concentric Circles; in
the Inner Circle the Gods of the Days of the Week; in the Outer Circle:
Signs of the Zodiac*

1.   Plate 159.3
London, British Museum 1907,0717.1.
Egypt.
Amethyst.
1st–2nd c. AD (SEH).
Gundel 1992: 126 fig. 56b, 246 cat. no. 144; Walters 1926: 180 no. 1668.
Image: photograph © Trustees of the British Museum.

*H10l. At the Right, Victory, Winged, with Palm Branch (?) Holds up
a Wreath Behind a Radiate Bust of Sol Facing Left, Where Fortuna
Stands with Cornucopia and Rudder. Below Sol Inscription χαρά
(Neg.) Above Two Clasped Hands*

1.   Plate 159.2
London, British Museum 1923,0401.197.
Unknown.
Yellow jasper.
Above hands and below bust of Sol, inscription (neg.): XAP/A.
Second half 3rd c. AD (Walters); 2nd c. AD (SEH/MK).
LIMC Helios/Sol 205; Walters 1926, 1665.

*H10m. On a Nile-Ship Made of Reeds, Sarapis (Winged Scarab on
His Head) Is Seated in the Centre, Facing Left, on a Throne. He Holds
a Staff in His Left Hand, and with His Right Hand He Points to a
Human-Headed Scarab in Front of Him. Above the Scarab a Bust of
Sol, Radiate, Facing Sarapis. Behind the Throne of Sarapis Stands
Fortuna with Cornucopia, Holding the Rudder of the Ship. On the
Bow and Stern of the Ship the Heads of Osiris and Isis Respectively,
Both Facing Inwards*

1.   Formerly Hamburg, Skoluda Collection M129; current location unknown.
Unknown.
Heliotrope.
In field, inscriptions (pos.): ΙΑΛ ΔΑ (above); ΒΑΙΜ (below the ship).
On reverse: ΜΙΧΑΗΛ / ΓΑΒΡΙΗΛ / ϹΑΜΑΗΛ / ΡΑΦΡΙΗΛ.
2nd c. AD.
Sternberg, Auktion XXXIII (1997); CBd 1669; retrieved from: classics.mfab.
hu/talismans/cbd/1669 on 19-11-2017.

H10n. Above a Base Line, an Assembly of Deities: (from Right to Left) Seated Jupiter Holding a Globe Surmounted by a Victory, Mars, Minerva, Apollo, Diana, and Nemesis; Above Them Two Letters in Mirror Image: B (?) and F. Below the Line, Small Figure of Sol, Standing, Radiate (Four Rays), Nude but for a Chlamys, Right Hand Raised, Whip in Left, between a Crescent and Star. Note That Contrary to the Letters, the Image of Sol Is Not in Mirror Image

1. Gotha, Museum.
    Unknown.
    sardonyx.
    2nd–3rd c. AD.
    LIMC Nemesis 288.

H11. Busts of Sol and Luna as Minor Figures
H11a. ... in Depictions of the Mithraic Tauroctony

1. Plate 160.1
    Baltimore, Walters Art Gallery 42.1342.
    Nemea?
    Sard.
    Sol is in the wrong place and Luna is not visible (damage).
    1st c. AD (MK/SEH), probably Augustan.
    CIMRM II, 393 no. 2367.
    Image: photograph courtesy the Walters Art Gallery, Baltimore, under creative commons zero: no rights reserved-license.

2. Plate 58.2
    Paris, Bibliothèque Nationale de France, Cabinet des Médailles 58.2031.
    Unknown.
    Yellow chalcedony, damaged.
    Luna as crescent rather than as bust.
    2nd c. AD (LIMC); 1st c. AD (MK)
    LIMC Helios/Sol 384; CIMRM II, no. 2363
    Image: in the public domain: mithraeum.eu/monument/279.

3. Florence, Museo Archeologico 15110; also glass pastes in M. von Wagner Museum in Würzburg.
    Unknown.
    Heliotrope.
    Reverse: lion and spread out in field. Inscription: σημεα καντευ κοντευ κομτευ κηριδευ δαρυνκω λυκυνξ.

Late 1st–2nd c. AD (Z.-D.)
LIMC Helios/Sol 386.
For the inscription cf. H3a.3; Zwierlein-Diehl 1986: 246–7 no. 736; Mastrocinque 2003: 304–5 nr, 256.

4. Plate 160.3
Baltimore, Walters Art Gallery 42.868.
Unknown.
Haematite.
Reverse: Abrasax with shield and whip.
2nd–3rd c. AD (LIMC).
LIMC Helios/Sol 385; LIMC Abraxas 43.
Image: photograph courtesy the Walters Art Gallery, Baltimore, under CC zero: no rights reserved-license.

5. Udine, Museo Civico 1138/152.
Aquileia?
Carnelian.
3rd c. AD (LIMC); 2nd–3rd c. AD (SEH).
LIMC Helios/Sol 386; Ianovitz 1972: 30 fig. 2; Tomaselli 1993: 46–7 no. 12.

6. Bad Deutsch-Altenburg, Museum Carnuntinum.
Carnuntum.
Carnelian.
3rd c. AD.
LIMC Helios/Sol 385. Likely the same as H11a.8.

7. Plate 161.1
Vienna, Kunsthistorisches Museum IX 2599.
Kostolac (Viminacium), Yugoslavia (near Belgrade).
Dark red jasper.
3rd c. AD.
Zwierlein-Diehl 1979: 184 no. 1376.
Image: photograph © KHM-Museumsverband.

8. Plate 160.2
Bad Deutsch-Altenburg, Museum Carnuntinum Car-Ge-196 (17 752).
Carnuntum.
Rusty red jasper.
Undated.

Dembski 1969: 122 no. 233.
Image: Landessammlungen Niederösterreich, Archäologischer Park Carnuntum (Photograph: Nicolas Gail).

9.   Cairo, Egyptian Museum.
     Egypt.
     Jasper, chipped.
     Reverse: inscription (pos.): ΝΕΙΚΑ/ΡΟΠΛΗΞ/ΙΑW. On edge, inscription (pos.): ΑCWΝΙΗΛ.
     Undated.
     CIMRM II, 392 no. 2359; Barry 1906: 247–8 no. 9.

10. Unknown.
     Unknown.
     Sard.
     Undated.
     Carnegie 1908: 180–2 no. N63, cf. no. 64.

11. Plate 160.5
     Archäologische Staatssammlung Munich.
     Flintsbach, St. Peter's Abbey on the Madron.
     Heliotrope.
     2nd–3rd c. AD.
     Faraone 2013, 21, no. 18.
     Image: courtesy Archäologische Staatssammlung Munich.

12. Plate 160.4
     Berlin, Antikensammlung Inv. 32.237.416.
     Unknown.
     Heliotrope.
     2nd–3rd c. AD.
     Weiß 2007: 323 no. 676.
     Image: Cornell University Gem Impressions Collection.

H11b. … in Depictions of the Danube Riders

1.   Plates 159.5
     Paris, Bibliothèque Nationale de France, Cabinet des Médailles, reg.M.5992.
     Unknown.
     Haematite.
     Bust of Sol right, Luna left.
     3rd c. AD (SEH).

LIMC Helios/Sol 387; LIMC Heros Equitans 437; LIMC Nemesis 202; Mastrocinque & Duyrat 2014: 158 no. 423.
Image: courtesy of the Bibliothèque Nationale de France.

2. Plate 161.5
Paris, Bibliothèque Nationale de France, Cabinet des Médailles reg.M.6099.
Unknown.
Jasper.
Instead of busts of Sol and Luna only crescent and star are depicted.
3rd c. AD (SEH).
Tudor 1969: I, 106 no. 187; Mastrocinque & Duyrat 2014: 158 no. 422.
Image: courtesy of the Bibliothèque Nationale de France.

3. Lost; two impressions in Prague and Magdeburg, archives of Bishop Bruno of Olmütz, who used the inatglio as his seal in 1245–47.
Unknown.
Unknown.
3rd c. AD.
Tudor 1969: I, 113–4 no. 199.

4. Unknown.
Near East.
Chalcedony.
Reverse: walking lion with star and crescent; inscription (neg.) ΤΑΥΑΓϹ.
Undated.
Tudor 1969: I, 108 no. 191.

5. Perugia, Museo Etrusco-Romano.
Unknown.
Black jasper, damaged.
Reverse: Abrasax with shield and whip.
Undated.
Tudor 1969 II: 20 no. 228.

6. Unknown.
Unknown.
Unknown, damaged.
Reverse: lion & inscr. ΛΕWΝ.
Undated.
Tudor 1969: I, 109 no. 192.

7. Unknown.
Chalcedony.

Reverse: a crater, a bowl, two large stars, two serpents and two bows.
Undated.
Tudor 1969: I, 109–10 no. 193.

8. Unknown; drawing in German Arch. Inst., Rome.
Unknown.
Unknown.
Reverse: Triple Hecate and woman; below them prostrate, nude man.
Letters scattered in field haphazardly: Ι Ω Ε Ι Ι Ε Ν Ι Α Ι Ι Ζ Ζ Ζ Υ.
Undated.
LIMC Heros Equitans 438; Tudor 1969: I, 110–1 no. 194; LIMC Nemesis 203.

9. Plate 158.12
London, British Museum 1868,0811.2 (OA.9725).
Unknown.
Carnelian.
Reverse: male and female figure facing each other. In exergue: man skinning ram hanging from a tree.
2nd c. AD.
Michel 2001, 300; CBd 686, retrieved from: classics.mfab.hu/talismans/cbd/686 on 19-11-2017.
Image: drawing after classics.mfab.hu/talismans/cbd/686.

10. Plate 158.13
London, British Museum 1864,1127.5 (OA.9606).
Unknown.
Agate.
2nd–3rd c. AD.
Michel 2001, 301; CBd 687, retrieved from: classics.mfab.hu/talismans/cbd/687 on 19-11-2017.
Image: drawing after classics.mfab.hu/talismans/cbd/687.

11. Oxford, Ashmolean Museum 2003.103.
Unknown.
Heliotrope.
Reverse: Venus Victrix.
2nd c. AD.
Henig & MacGregor 2004: no. 13; CBd 1162, retrieved from: classics.mfab.hu/talismans/cbd/1162 on 19-11-2017.

HIIc. ... with Two Fortunae, Each with Cornucopia, Clasping Hands Above Inscription χαρά and Clasped Hands

1. Private collection.
   Gadara, Decapolis (Umm Qeis).
   Heliotrope.
   Inscription positive.
   1st–2nd c. AD (H.&W.).
   Henig & Whiting 1987, 16 no.119.

2. Plate 161.2
   Kassel, Staatliche Kunstsammlung, Ge 82.
   Unknown.
   Greenish red jasper, cracked.
   Inscription neg.
   2nd c. AD (AGD); 1st–2nd c. AD (SEH)
   AGD III, 217 no. 82.
   Image: impression courtesy of the Staatliche Kunstsammlung, Kassel; photograph of impression by author.

HIIca. ... with Two Fortunae, Each with Cornucopia, Clasping Hands Above a Tripod

1. Plate 161.3
   Berlin, Staatliche Museen, Antikensammlung 7167.
   Unknown.
   Milky white Chalcedony.
   2nd c. AD (SEH/MK).
   Furtwängler 1896: 7167; Matern 2002: 182, 276 B242.
   Image: Cornell University Gem Impressions Collection.

HIIcb. ... with Two Fortunae, Each with Cornucopia, Clasping Hands Above an Eagle

1. Plate 161.4
   Kassel, Staatliche Kunstsammlung, Ge 83.
   Unknown.
   Very dark green jasper.
   2nd–3rd c. AD.
   AGD III, 217 no. 83.
   Image: impression courtesy of the Staatliche Kunstsammlung, Kassel; photograph of impression by author.

Hɪɪcc. As Previous, but a Burning Altar instead of a Eagle Below the Clasped Hands; Rather Than Bust of Sol and Luna, a Star and a Crescent

1. Braunschweig, Herzog Anton Ulrich Museum.
   Unknown.
   Green jasper, damaged.
   3rd c. AD (AGD).
   AGD III, 38 no. 113.

Hɪɪd. ... with Winged Victory on the Right, Holding Palm Branch and Wreath, Facing Fortuna with Modius and Cornucopia on the Left; between Them Griffin Facing Fortuna

1. Plate 159.4
   Vienna, Kunsthistorisches Museum IX B 291.
   Unknown.
   Dark orange-red carnelian.
   Zwierlein-Diehl identifies the Fortuna as Sarapis, as does Matern.
   1st–2nd c. AD (MK).
   AGWien 152 no. 1198; Matern 2002: 182, 277 B248b.
   Image: photograph © KHM-Museumsverband.

Hɪɪda. ... with Winged Victory on the Right, Holding Palm Branch and Wreath, Facing Fortuna with Modius and Cornucopia on the Left; between Them Clasped Hands Holding Corn-Ear

1. Private Collection.
   Gadara, Decapolis (Umm Qeis).
   Blue glass paste.
   1st c. AD (H.&W.).
   Henig & Whiting 1987: 38 no. 399.

Hɪɪdb. ... with Winged Victory on the Right, Holding Palm Branch and Wreath, Facing Fortuna with Modius and Cornucopia on the Left; between Them Lion with One Paw on Head of Animal

1. Berlin, Staatliche Museen, Antikensammlung, 7173.
   Unknown.
   Light brown sard.
   2nd c. AD (SEH).
   Furtwängler 1896: 7173.

2. Plate 161.6
   Ann Arbor, University of Michigan, Special Collections Library 59.
   Unknown.

Haematite.

Identification of the right hand figure as Victory is uncertain. Fortuna appears to also holding a rudder.

3rd c. AD.

Bonner 1950, 240; CBd 1069, retrieved from: classics.mfab.hu/talismans/cbd/1069 on 19-11-2017.

Image: photograph in the public domain.

3.   Paris, Bibliothèque Nationale de France, Cabinet des Médailles, de Clercq 3462.

Unknown.

Blue glass paste.

Unclear whether there is anything under the lion's paw.

1st c. AD?

Mastrocinque 2014: 162 no. 434.

> *Hɪɪdc. ... with Winged Victory on the Right, Holding a Wreath, Facing Fortuna with Modius, Rudder and Cornucopia, Inscription χαρά and Clasped Hands*

1.   Plate 161.7

London, British Museum 1923,0401.628.

Unknown.

Black glass paste.

Late 3rd c. AD (Walters); 1st c. AD (SEH).

LIMC Helios/Sol 323; Walters 1926: 290, 3025.

Image: photograph © Trustees of the British Museum.

> *Hɪɪe. ... with Ephesian Artemis between Two Deer*

1.   Munich, Staatliche Münzsammlung A 1872.

Unknown.

Reddish orange carnelian.

1st c. AD (AGD).

AGD I-3, 30 no. 2277.

2.   Plates 19.1, 161.8

Leiden, National Museum of Antiquities GS-00673

Acquired at Isparta, Turkey, 1965

Dark brownish-red carnelian

1st–2nd c. AD

Maaskant-Kleibrink 1978, 673

Image: © National Museum of Antiquities, Leiden; photograph R.J. Looman.

3. Plate 161.9
   Hannover, Kestner Museum K97.
   Unknown.
   Dark orange carnelian, broken.
   2nd–3rd c. AD (AGD).
   LIMC Helios/Sol 389; Matern 2002: 182, 276 B243.
   Image: photograph © Kestner Museum, Hannover.

4. Copenhagen, Thorvaldsen Museum 647
   Acquired in Rome
   Carnelian
   Undated
   Fossing 1929: 231 no. 1707

5. New York, Metropolitan Museum of Art, 81.6.175.
   Unknown.
   Carnelian.
   Undated.
   LIMC Helios 316.

6. Paris, Bibliothèque Nationale de France, Cabinet des Médailles 58.1495
   Unknown
   Carnelian
   Undated
   Chabouillet 1858: 1495.

Hɪɪea. ... with Ephesian Artemis between Two Deer and two Nemeses of Smyrna

1. London, British Museum 1912,0311.2.
   Unknown.
   Sard.
   2nd c. AD (Walters); 1st–2nd c. AD (SEH).
   Walters 1926: 151 no. 1340; Matern 2002: 182, 277 B245b; LIMC Nemesis 196.

Hɪɪf. ... with Venus on Throne, 7 Stars

1. Plate 161.10
   Unknown (glass paste cast in M. von Wagner Museum, Würzburg).
   Unknown.
   Unknown.
   1st c. AD.

Zwierlein-Diehl 1986: 115 no. 332.
Image: Cornell University Gem Impressions Collection.

2. Plate 161.11
Vienna, Kunsthistorisches Museum IX B 635.
Unknown.
Sardonyx, yellowish to reddish brown.
2nd c. AD (AGWien); 1st–2nd c. AD (SEH).
LIMC Helios/Sol 388.
Image: photograph © KHM-Museumsverband.

Hng. ... with Venus Anadyomene, Herm (Pan), Two Stars, Crescent and Inscription

1. Munich, Staatliche Münzsammlung A. 1855.
Acquired in Rome.
Reddish orange carnelian, damaged.
Inscription: three letters remain, scattered in field: I O C.
1st c. BC (AGD); 2nd c. AD (MK).
LIMC Helios 314; AGD I-3 1855.

Hnh. ... above an Eagle and a Fish

1. London, British Museum OA.9558.
Unknown.
Amethyst.
On reverse anguipede Abrasax.
2nd–3rd c. AD.
Michel 2001: 485; CBd 843, retrieved from: classics.mfab.hu/talismans/cbd/843 on 19-11-2017.
The bust facing Sol is almost certainly Luna, not Jupiter.

Hni. ... to Either Side of Minerva Holding Victory on Outstretched Hand

1. Plate 161.12
Leiden RMO GS 50053.
Turkey.
Clay.
Undated.
Bust of Sol, lower left, damaged; Luna is depicted as a crescent.
Maaskant-Kleibrink 1971: no. 31.
Image: © National Museum of Antiquities, Leiden; photograph R.J. Looman.

H11j. Bust of Sol Only, Right, Next to an Eagle Holding a Wreath Above a Round Altar on Which a Rabbit Lies

1. Berlin, Antikensammlung Dressel Inv. 32.237.116.
    Rome.
    Dark brown sard.
    In field: ΔYEYTYCHEZ.
    1st c. AD.
    Weiß 2007: 253 no. 412.

H11k. Anchor with Bust of Sol on the Right, Facing Left, and on the Left Crescent and Star

1. Berlin, Antikensammlung inv. 32.237.443.
    Unknown.
    Sardonyx.
    1st c. AD.
    Weiß 2007: 298 no. 585.

H12. Sol Riding on Horseback
H12a. ... to Left, Right Hand Raised, Whip in Left Hand

1. Aquileia, Museo Nazionale, 25964.
    Aquileia.
    Black jasper.
    3rd c. AD.
    Sena Chiesa 1966: 86.

2. Reading Museum, Duke of Wellington collection, 03001.
    Silchester, Hampshire.
    Green prase with dark patches.
    3rd c. AD (H.); 2nd c. AD (SEH).
    Henig 1978: 12 no. 33.

3. Princeton University Art Museum 40-369.
    Unknown.
    Red jasper.
    No whip.
    3rd–4th c. AD.
    Forbes 1978: 56–7 no. 39.

4. Plate 162.1
    Leiden, National Museum of Antiquities GS-01133.
    Unknown.

Heliotrope.
In field, crescent and inscription (pos., letters scattered): IAW; on reverse, inscription (pos.): ΓΟΥC/CON.
Undated.
Maaskant-Kleibrink 1978: 1133.
Image: © National Museum of Antiquities, Leiden; photograph R.J. Looman.

5. Plate 162.2
Cologne, Cathedral, Dreikönigenschrein.
Acquired in Cologne in 1953.
Carnelian
Second half 2nd century AD
Zwierlein-Diehl 1998: 302 no. 194.
Image: Arachne FA21-15_133984.jpg; arachne.dainst.org/entity/66920

6. Plate 162.3
Cologne, Cathedral, Dreikönigenschrein.
Acquired in Cologne in 1953.
Carnelian.
Second half 2nd century to 3rd century AD.
Zwierlein-Diehl 1998: 301–2 no. 193.
Image: Arachne FA21-14_133983.jpg; arachne.dainst.org/entity/66919.

H12b. ... to Left, Reins in Right Hand, Lance in Left Hand, Spearing Lion Below Front Hooves of the Horse; under Horse Lies a Man

1. Plate 162.4
Leiden, National Museum of Antiquities 01134.
Unknown.
Haematite.
In field inscription (pos.): S T N E; on reverse: standing figure in long dress, lifting hand to mouth.
2nd–3rd c. AD. A connection with the Danube Rider cult seems likely.
Maaskant-Kleibrink 1978: 1134.
Image: © National Museum of Antiquities, Leiden; photograph R.J. Looman.

H12c. ... to Right, Left Hand Raised, Whip in Right Hand. Crocodile Below Horse

1. Plate 162.5
Sofia, National Archaeological Museum 8042.

Novae.

Light red carnelian.

Probably the Egyptian god Souchos, rather than Sol: cf C5.89.

2nd–3rd c. AD (D.-M.).

Dimitrova-Milcheva 1981: 90–1 no. 274; Matern 2002: 182, 277 B247.

Image: © Sofia Archaeological Museum / Krassimir Georgiev.

2.   Unknown.

Unknown.

Onyx.

No crocodile; in field Ιαω.

Undated.

Maastrocinque 2003: 330 no. 285.

*H12d. Side A, above: Sol in Frontal Quadriga, Radiate, Nude but
for a Chlamys, Right Hand Raised, Whip in Left Hand; Below: Sol,
Radiate, Nude but for a Chlamys, Whip in Left Hand, Riding a Horse
Left towards Mercurius. Side B, Above (from Left to Right): Luna
velificans, Woman with Veil, Nemesis with Wheel, Sol, Nude but for a
Chlamys, Radiate, Right Hand Raised, Whip in Left Hand, Advancing
Left; Below: Unidentifiable Figure or Object (Damaged) between Two
Lions Advancing Inwards*

1.   Plate 162.6

Private Collection.

Unknown.

Carnelian.

Undated.

Wagner & Boardman 2003: no. 569; CBd 1180; retrieved from: classics
.mfab.hu/talismans/cbd/1180 on 19-11-2017.

Image: drawing after classics.mfab.hu/talismans/cbd/1180.

H13. Sol, Seated

H13a. ... Facing Left, Right Hand Raised, Whip and Globe in Left Hand

1.   Copenhagen, National Museum 243.

Italy.

Heliotrope.

3rd c. AD (LIMC); modern?

LIMC Helios/Sol 161; Matern 2002: 186, 281 K21.

H13b. ... Facing Right, Whip in Right Hand
1.   Plate 15.4
Leiden, National Museum of Antiquities GS-00626.
Unknown.
Heliotrope.
1st–2nd c. AD.
Maaskant-Kleibrink 1978: 626; Matern 2002: 186, 280–1 K20.
Image: © National Museum of Antiquities, Leiden; photograph R.J. Looman.

H14. Sol on *Biga* to Left, Right Hand Raised, Whip in Left Hand
1.   Private collection.
Gadara, Decapolis (Umm Qeis).
Carnelian.
2nd c. AD (H.&W.).
Henig & Whiting 1987: 12 no. 62; Matern 2002: 126, 243–4 I66.13.

2.   Private collection.
Unknown.
Heliotrope.
2nd–3rd c. AD (V.).
Vollenweider 1984: 259 no. 445; Matern 2002: 67, 220 Q80.

H15. Sol with Animal
H15a. Frontal Bust of Sol on Neck of Bull, Right
1.   London, British Museum, 1814,0704.1409.
Unknown.
Garnet, broken.
Hellenistic?
Walters 1926: 238, no. 2345; Matern 2002: 182, 277 B245a.

H15b. Profile Bust of Sol between Horns of Bull Walking Left;
Upturned Crescent and Seven Stars in Field; Two Corn Ears in Front
of Bull
1.   Plate 162.10
Kassel, Staatliche Kunstsammlung, 194 (glass paste copy in M. von Wagner
Museum, Würzburg).
Unknown.
Carnelian.
2nd–4th (AGD); Second half 1st c. BC–first half 1st c. AD (Z.-D.); 1st–
2nd (MK).

LIMC Helios/Sol 390; Zwierlein-Diehl 1986: 232 no. 656; Matern 2002: 182, 276–7 B244a.

Image: impression courtesy of the Staatliche Kunstsammlung, Kassel; photograph of impression by author.

H15c. Profile Bust of Sol on Back of Lion Walking to Left

1. Aquileia, Museo Nazionale, 25713.
   Aquileia.
   Nicolo.
   1st–2nd c. AD.
   Sena Chiesa 1966: no. 1171.

2. Plate 162.7
   Malibu, Getty Museum 83.AN.437.53.
   Unknown.
   Magnetite.
   Below the lion, a prostrate man.
   2nd–4th c. AD.
   Michel 2004: nr 37; CBd 2349; retrieved from: classics.mfab.hu/talismans/cbd/2349 on 19-11-2017.

H15ca. Sol Riding on Lion to Right, Right Hand Raised

1. Ann Arbor, University of Michigan, Kelsey Museum of Archaeology 1963.04.0015.
   Unknown.
   Pyrites.
   Forepaw of lion on a skull (?) of an ox (?); a female worshipper (Bonner) stands facing Sol, her right hand raised. Inscription (pos.): ιαω (above); αβρασαξ (in exergue). On reverse: cock-headed anguipede with shield (inscribed ιαω) and whip.
   Undated.
   Bonner 1950: 226; CBd 1095, retrieved from: classics.mfab.hu/talismans/cbd/1095 on 19-11-2017.

2. Plate 162.11
   London, British Museum 1986,0501.74.
   Unknown.
   Hematite.
   Lion has a snake-headed tail. On reverse: inscription.
   3rd c. AD.

Michel 2001: 260; CBd 658, retrieved from: classics.mfab.hu/talismans/
cbd/658 on 18-11-2017.
Image: drawing after classics.mfab.hu/talismans/cbd/658.

3.   Plate 162.12
     London, British Museum 1874,0314.63.
     Unknown.
     Hematite.
     Below the lion a prostrate man; facing Sol a woman with her right hand
     raised to her mouth.
     3rd c. AD.
     Michel 2001: 282; CBd 668, retrieved from: classics.mfab.hu/talismans/
     cbd/668 on 19-11-2017.
     Image: drawing after classics.mfab.hu/talismans/cbd/668.

4.   Plate 162.13
     London, British Museum 1986,0501.73.
     Unknown.
     Hematite
     Lion has a snake-headed tail; right hand part of intaglio is missing. On
     reverse: inscription.
     3rd c. AD.
     Michel 2001: 283; CBd 669, retrieved from: classics.mfab.hu/talismans/
     cbd/669 on 19-11-2017.
     Image: drawing after classics.mfab.hu/talismans/cbd/669.

5.   Paris, Bibliothèque Nationale de France, Cabinet des Médailles
     Schlumberger.337.
     Unknown.
     Hematite.
     Undated.
     Mastrocinque 2014: no. 51.

6.   Paris, Bibliothèque Nationale de France, Cabinet des Médailles AA.Seyrig.11.
     Unknown.
     Hematite.
     Undated.
     Mastrocinque 2014: no. 53.

H15cb. Sol Standing on the Back of a Lion, Nude but for Chlamys,
Right Hand Raised, Torch in Left Hand; Below Lion, Recumbent Man

1.   Private Collection.
      Unknown.
      Red jasper?, damaged.
      Reverse: standing, snake-headed figure, star and crescent.
      Undated.
      Bonner 1950: 291 no. 225.

H15cc. As Previous, but Whip in Left Hand and No Figure Below the
Lion

1.   Paris, Bibliothèque Nationale de France, Cabinet des Médailles 58.2174A.
      Corbeny (Aisne).
      Jasper (heliotrope?).
      Inscription (pos.): ΝΟΦΗΡ ΑΒΛΑΝΑΘΑΝΑΛΒΑ; reverse: cock-headed
      anguipede (shield and whip) above Medusa-head; inscription (pos.):
      ΑΒΛΑΝΑΘΑ ΙΑΩ ΑΒΡΑΣΑ ΤΕ ΣΑΒΑΩ ΜΙΧΑΗ.
      Undated.
      Mastrocinque 2014: 121 no. 320.

2.   Paris, Bibliothèque Nationale de France, Cabinet des Médailles de
      Clercq.3458.
      Unknown.
      Heliotrope.
      Inscription (pos.): ΑΒΛΑΝΑΘΑΝΑΛΒΑ ΑΒΡΑΣΑΞ ΦΡΗ; reverse: inscription.
      Undated.
      Mastrocinque 2014: 18 no. 394.

H15cd. As Previous, but Globe in Left Hand

1.   London, British Museum 1880,0531.64.
      Unknown.
      Heliotrope.
      3rd c. AD.
      Michel 2001: 259; CBd 657, retrieved from: classics.mfab.hu/talismans/
      cbd/657 on 18-11-2017.

2.   Plates 162.8–9
      Stuttgart, Landesmuseum Württemberg KK grün 1090.
      Unknown.
      Heliotrope.

2nd–3rd c. AD.
http://www.museum-digital.de/bawue/pdf/publicinfo.php?oges=3435&
lang=en (retrieved October 8, 2017).
Image: photograph © Landesmuseum Württemberg, Hendrik Zwietasch.

3. Unknown.
    Egypt.
    Unknown.
    In front of Sol: four stars, a crescent, and φρη; along the edge: αλβλα αβρα-
    σαξ αβαλναμ.
    Undated.
    Mastrocinque 2003: 328 no. 279.

H16. Sol Standing, Staff in Left Hand, Wreath in Right Hand, on Top of Mount Argaios (Inscr.)

1. London, British Museum, 1867,0507.57.
    Unknown.
    Red jasper.
    In exergue, inscription (neg.): αργαιος.
    Unknown.
    Walters 1926: 179 no. 1662.

H16a. Bust of Sol, Radiate, Left, between Crescent (Left) and Star (Right), above Mount Argaios

1. Ankara, Erimtan museum 12.
    Anatolia.
    Red jasper.
    2nd c. AD.
    Konuk & Arslan 2000: 83 nr 59.

H17. Dubitanda
H17a. Hercules and Cerberus on the Right, Male Warrior, Radiate, with Lance and Armor, Grabbing an Opponent by the Hair on the Left

1. Munich, Staatliche Münzsammlung A.2003.
    Acquired in Rome.
    Plasma.
    "Sol" has boots and is wearing armor. Perhaps he is an oriental monarch
    with radiate crown?

Late 1st–early 2nd c. AD (style; plasma used only from Flavian period to ca. AD 120).
AGD I-3, 94 no. 2717.

2.   Plate 162.14
      Berlin, Staatliche Museen, Antikensammlung 6855.
      Unknown.
      Red jasper.
      Furtwängler notes that in this intaglio "Sol" is bearded, and may be Commodus.
      Undated.
      Furtwängler 1896: 6855.
      Image: photograph courtesy Staatliche Museen, Berlin.

H17b. Young Radiate Male Figure, Nude, Holding Caduceus and Surrounded by a Large Variety of Symbols; Magical Inscriptions

1.   Naples, Museo Archeologico, 27020/1175.
      Unknown.
      Jasper, damaged.
      For the inscriptions between the rays and on the reverse, see Pannuti or Cbd.
      Undated, probably modern.
      Pannuti 1994: 301–3 no. 269; CBd 2197; retrieved from: classics.mfab.hu/talismans/cbd/2197 on 19-11-2017.

H17c. Head of Beardless Youth Left, Radiate, Modius

1.   Tripoli?
      Cyrene.
      Cretula, (clay impression).
      Maddoli does not mention the "modius" visible in the photograph.
      75 BC–AD 113.
      Maddoli 1963/4: 99 no. 473.

2.   Aquileia, Museo Archeologico Naz., N 852.
      Aquileia.
      Red jasper.
      1st–2nd c. AD (O. e A.); 50 BC–AD 50 (MK).
      Ori e Argenti 1961, 150 no. 462.

3. Paris, Bibliothèque Nationale de France, Cabinet des Médailles, 58.1477.
Unknown.
Red jasper.
1st c. AD (MK).
Chabouillet 1858: 1477.

> *H17ca. Head of Beardless Youth Left, Radiate, Modius, Ram's Horns;*
> *Trident Encircled by Snake in Front of Him*

1. Hannover, Kestner Museum K483.
Unknown.
Red, opaque glass paste.
50 BC–AD 50 (SEH/MK); 2nd c. AD (AGD).
AGD IV, 290–1 no. 1583.

2. Vienna, Kunsthistorisches Museum IX B 318?
Unknown.
Light brownish violet glass paste.
Ram's horns, and a trident with a snake in front of the deity.
50 BC–AD 50 (MK); 50–150 AD (AGWien).
AGWien 89 no. 963. Note: AGWien no. 1264 has the same inventory
number.

> *H17d. Livia (Head and Upper Body Only) Holding a Cornucopia from*
> *Which Head of Augustus/Sol Emerges*

1. Plate 162.15
London, British Museum 1814,0704.1546.
Unknown.
Carnelian, damaged.
Early 1st c. AD (LIMC).
LIMC Helios/Sol 429.
Image: photograph © Trustees of the British Museum.

> *H17e. Standing Youth, Radiate, Nude but for Chlamys, Leaning with*
> *His Right Arm on a Column, Holding a Whip (?) or Rudder (?) in His*
> *Left Hand (Partially Damaged), Quiver (?) Behind Right Shoulder*

1. London, British Museum, 1923,0401.140.
Unknown.
Glass paste, imitating sard, damaged.
50 BC–AD 50.

Walters 1926: 139 no. 1219.
This would appear to be a radiate Apollo.

H18. Varia
H18a. Bust of Souchos Helios Right, Above Crocodile; He Is Radiate and Has a Small Raised Right Hand, and Faces Premamnes

1.   Florence, Museo Archeologico.
Unknown.
Jasper.
Undated.
LIMC Souchos 26.

H18b. Fragment of Intaglio, Consisting of Zodiac Circle (Partially Preserved) around Bust (Almost Wholly Destroyed)

1.   London, British Museum, 1889,0810.38.
Unknown.
Sard.
No secure indication of the presence of Sol.
Undated.
Walters 1926: 180 no. 1669.

H18c. Lion Crouching, Left; Behind Him a Tree with an Eagled on a Branch Holding a Wreath in His Beak; Inscription (Neg.) Ἥλιε

1.   Braunschweig, Museum, 290.
Unknown.
Carnelian, damaged.
3rd c. AD (AGD); 1st–2nd c. AD? (SEH).
AGD III, 54 no. 188.

H18d. Hybrid Figure of Sol (Both Arms Raised, Radiate) and Scarab with Outspread Wings

1.   Berlin, Staatliche Museen, Ägyptisches Museum 9876.
Unknown.
Plasma.
Reverse: inscription (pos.): συποσ/..λζζχπ/πποζιαιαιαδαθ/ιακινσηφαιωχ/ νημεωιαρβαθ/αγραμνηφι/βαωχ.
2nd c. AD (P.).
Philipp 1986: 84–5, 118.

HA. Intaglios in Ancient Rings
HA1. Sol in *Quadriga* to Left
HA1a. ... Nude but for Chlamys, Whip in Right Hand, Reins in Left Hand

1. Plate 148.1
Vienna, Kunsthistorisches Museum VI 1813.
Acquired in Budapest in 1873.
Heliotrope. Bronze ring of the 4th(?) c. AD. The stone does not fit well.
Second half 2nd–first half 3rd c. AD.
AGWien III, 306 no. 2762; Matern 2002: 67, 220 Q87.
Image: photograph © KHM-Museumsverband.

HA1b. ... Nude but for Chlamys, Whip in Left Hand, Reins in Right Hand

1. Basel, Museum, 3243.
Augst.
Green jasper. Silver ring, form Guiraud 3g.
3rd c. AD.
Henkel 1913: 61 no. 444.

HA1c. ... Nude but for Chlamys, Right Hand Raised, Whip in Left Hand

1. Plate 148.2
Saalburg Museum, P.641.
Saalburg.
Heliotrope. Iron ring, form not clear (cf. Henkel 1913: 172 no. 1895).
It may be that Sol has raised his left arm; difficult to make out on the photograph.
2nd–3rd c. AD (Krug).
Krug 1978: 499 no. 34.
Image: photograph © Römerkastell Saalburg, Peter Knierriem.

HA1d. ... Nude but for Chlamys, Right Hand Raised, Reins in Left Hand

1. Cologne, Römisch.-Germanisches Museum, 5260.
Cologne, Luxemburgerstrasse.
Heliotrope. Silver ring, form Guiraud 3g.
2nd–3rd c. AD (Krug); ring 3rd c. AD.
Krug 1980: 188 no. 75; Matern 2002: 126, 243 I66.8.

HA2. Sol in a *Quadriga* to the Right
HA2ca. ... Nude but for Chlamys, Whip in Left Hand, Reins in
Right Hand

1. Plate 148.3
   St. Petersburg, Hermitage ГР-28331.
   Unknown.
   Carnelian, set in an ornate gold ring.
   3rd c. AD.
   http://www.hermitagemuseum.org/wps/portal/hermitage/digital-collec
   tion/18.+carved+stones/1057079. Accessed 07/12/2018.
   Image: photograph courtesy Hermitage Museum, St. Petersburg.

HA3. Sol on Frontal *Quadriga*, Two Horses Jumping to the Left,
Two to the Right
HA3a. ... Nude but for Chlamys, Right Hand Raised, Whip in
Left Hand

1. Plates 148.4, 148.5
   Hamburg, Museum für Kunst und Gewerbe, KG 1967,17.
   Unknown.
   Heliotrope. Silver ring.
   First half 2nd c. AD (small grooves style) (MK); 2nd–3rd c. AD (LIMC);
   Matern 2002: 125, 242 I63.5; LIMC Helios/Sol 127; LIMC Helios 33.
   Image: photograph © Museum für Kunst und Gewerbe, Hamburg.

HA3c. ... Nude but for Chlamys, Right Hand Raised, Reins in
Left Hand

1. Plates 148.6, 148.7
   Copenhagen, Thorvaldsen Museum, I 1618.
   Acquired in Rome.
   Carnelian. Silver ring.
   3rd–4th c. (Fossing).
   LIMC Helios/Sol 125; Fossing 1929: 1686.
   Image: Photograph and impression courtesy Thorvaldsen Museum,
   Copenhagen, photograph of impression by author.

HA3e. ... Nude but for Chlamys, Left Hand Raised, Whip and Reins in
Right Hand

1. London, British Museum, 1923,0401.195.
   Unknown.
   Nicolo. Gold ring.

3rd c. AD (Walters).
Marshall 1908: 91 no. 534; Walters 1926: 1661; Matern 2002: 125, 243 I64.2a.

HA6. Sol, Standing
HA6a. ... Nude but for Chlamys, Left Hand Raised, Whip in Right Hand

1. Plate 154.1
   Vienna, Kunsthistorisches Museum VII B 367.
   Unknown.
   Red jasper. Gold ring.
   1st–early 2nd c. AD (MK); 2nd c. AD (AGWien).
   AGWien 165–6 no. 1261; LIMC Helios/Sol 95; Matern 2002: 110, 237–8 I39.
   LIMC (Helios Sol 94 & 95) confuses Vienna Inv. nos. IX B 1524 & VII B 367.
   Image: photograph © KHM-Museumsverband

2. London, British Museum, 1872,0604.344.
   Unknown.
   Heliotrope. Bronze ring, flat hoop expanding upwards.
   2nd c. AD (SEH/MK).
   Walters 1926: no. 1659; Marshall 1908: 1351.

3. Lyon, Musée et Théâtres romains.
   La Celle-en-Morvan.
   Glass paste nicolo. Ring, form Guiraud 2d.
   2nd–3rd c. AD.
   Guiraud 1988: 91 no. 43.

4. Munich, Archäologische Staatssammlung 1984.3513.
   Der-el Zor (Syria).
   Jasper. Gold ring.
   4th c. AD (Zahlhaas).
   Zahlhaas 1985: 37 no. 35; Matern 2002: 106–7, 235 I24.10.

5. Plate 154.2
   Munich, Archäologische Staatssammlung 1994,1634d.
   Michelfeld.
   Glass paste nicolo set in a bronze ring.
   First half 3rd c. AD (Guiraud type 2f).
   Platz-Horster 2018: 137 no. 116.
   Image: photograph © Archäologische Staatssammlung / Stefanie Friedrich.

6.   Plate 154.3
      Geneva, Musées D'art et d'histoire C0575.
      Unknown.
      Glass paste nicolo. Gold ring.
      2nd–3rd c. AD.
      Unpublished.
      Image: © Musées d'art et d'histoire, Ville de Genève, photograph: Bettina
      Jacot-Descombes.

      *HA6aa. ... Nude but for Chlamys, Left Hand Raised, Whip in Right
      Hand, Next to a Burning Altar*
1.   Private collection.
      Gadara, Decapolis (Umm Qeis).
      Heliotrope. Iron ring, fragment.
      Star and crescent by Sol's feet.
      2nd c. AD (H.&W.).
      Henig & Whiting 1987: 12 no. 66.

2.   London, British Museum, 1917,0501.493.
      Egypt.
      Nicolo, truncated cone. Gold ring, hoop thin below, expanding upwards,
      hollow and rounded without, a very sharp angle on either side.
      3rd c. AD (Walters).
      Walters 1926: 179, no. 1657 pl. 22; Marshall 1908: 84–5 no. 493; LIMC Helios/
      Sol 101; Matern 2002: 106–7, 164, 236 I25.7.

      *HA6ae. ... Nude but for Chlamys, Left Hand Raised, Whip in Right
      Hand, behind Jupiter, Standing, Nude, Spear in Right Hand, an Eagle
      in Front of Him*
1.   Private collection.
      Carnuntum.
      Carnelian. Iron ring, form X.
      2nd c. AD.
      Dembski 2005: 57 no. 43.

      HA6b. ... Nude but for Chlamys, Right Hand Raised, Whip in
      Left Hand
1.   Private collection.
      Province of Sevilla.
      Carnelian. Bronze ring, form unclear from photograph.

Late 2nd c. AD.
Lopez de la Orden, 121 no. 51.

2. Private Collection.
Türkenfeld.
Chalcedony. Gold ring.
2nd–3rd c. AD.
Henkel 1913, no. 423.

3. Berlin, Staatliche Museen, Antikensammlung, 7199.
Unknown.
Carnelian. Silver ring, form Guiraud 2d; Vollenweider 2618; Henig X.
2nd–3rd c. AD (ring type).
Furtwängler 1896: 7199.

4. Private collection.
Carnuntum.
Green Jasper. Bronze ring.
2nd–3rd c. AD.
Dembski 2005: 91 no. 402.

> *HA6bb. ... Nude but for Chlamys, Right Hand Raised, Whip in Left Hand, Facing Standing Male Figure, Bearded, Dressed in Himation, Staff*

1. London, British Museum, 1917,0501.1366.
Unknown.
Sard. Gilded bronze ring, rounded hoop expanding upwards.
Two stars and a crescent in field.
1st–2nd c. AD.
Walters 1926: 179 no. 1658; Marshall 1908: 1366.

> *HA6d. ... Dressed in Chiton and Chlamys, Globe in Right Hand, Whip in Left Hand*

1. Plate 154.4
Berlin, Staatliche Museen, Antikensammlung, 8161.
Friesdorf, near Bonn.
Nicolo. Ring, type Guiraud 2d; Vollenweider 2618; Henig X.
2nd c. AD (MK).
Henkel 1913: 414; Matern 90, 98, 227 G17.
Image: photograph courtesy Staatliche Museen, Berlin.

2.   Cologne, Römisch-Germanisches Museum, 1000.
     Cologne, Apostelkloster.
     Nicolo. Silver ring.
     2nd c. AD (Krug).
     Krug 1980: 183–4 no. 59; Matern 2002: 91, 98, 227 G18.

         HA7.   Head or Bust of Sol, Radiate, Left
1.   Paris, Bibliothèque Nationale de France, Cabinet des Médailles, de Clercq
     3065.
     Tortosa.
     Gray chalcedony. Ring ...
     1st c. BC.
     Vollenweider & Avisseau-Broustet 1995: 181–2 no. 196.

2.   Mainz, Museum, 349.
     Mainz.
     Unknown.
     50 BC–AD 50.
     Henkel 1913: 1442.

3.   Plates 154.5, 154.6
     Geneva, Musées d'art et d'histoire C.1703.
     Pompeii.
     Red jasper. Bronze ring.
     1st c. AD.
     Henkel 1913: 201–2 no. 2278.
     Image: © Musées d'art et d'histoire, Ville de Genève.

4.   Formerly Dumfries, Burgh Museum (stolen).
     Carzield, Dumfriesshire.
     Sard. Iron ring, Henig type II.
     1st c. AD (Henig).
     Henig 1978: 11–12 no. 27.

5.   Plates 154.7, 154.8
     Boston Museum of Fine Arts 1970.588; gift of Miss Gladys Clark.
     Unknown.
     Carnelian. Gold ring.
     2nd–3rd c. AD.

Morgan 1975/76: 45 no. 52.
Image: photograph © Museum of Fine Arts, Boston.

6. Cambridge, Fitzwilliam Museum, Lewis Collction Loan Ant.103.455.
Unknown.
Carnelian. Hollow gold ring.
2nd–3rd c. (Henig).
Henig 1978: 16 no. 18.

7. Sofia, National Archaeological Museum 4797.
Nikolaevo (Pleven distr.).
? (not given by D.-M.). Silver ring.
Undated.
Dimitrova-Milcheva 1981: 43 no. 59.

8. Plate 154.9
Bad Deutsch-Altenburg, Museum Carnuntinum Car-Ge-309 (20 517).
Carnuntum.
Carnelian. Bronze ring.
Undated.
Unpublished?
Image: Landessammlungen Niederösterreich, Archäologischer Park Carnuntum (photograph: Nicolas Gail).

9. Münster, University Archaeological Museum inv. 3370.
Unknown.
Glass paste. Iron ring, Henig type II; Guiraud type 2 a–c.
50 BC–AD 50.
Alvarez Bendezu 2015: 299 no. 10.

10. Münster, University Archaeological Museum inv. 3091.
Unknown.
Carnelian. Gold ring, Henig type I; Guiraud type 1b.
1st c. BC.
Alvarez Bendezu 2015: 298–9 no. 9.

HA7i. ... Torch before Bust

1. Ankara, Erimtan museum 249.
Anatolia.
Red jasper in gold ring (F2).

2nd–3rd c. AD.
Konuk & Arslan 2000: 84 no. 60.

HA9. Frontal Bust or Head of Sol
HA9b. ... within Zodiac Circle

1. Private Collection.
    Unknown.
    Carnelian. Gold ring, form: Cf. Henkel 118, 137, 182 (hellenistic-Roman and early imperial).
    Inscription (neg.): BAEDRO; only 11 signs of the zodiac.
    First half 1st c. BC.
    Vollenweider 1984: 122, no. 208; Matern 2002: 182, 253 B57.1.

HA10. Sol as Minor Figure
HA10n. ... above Abrasax; below a Crescent Moon

1. British museum 489.
    Unknown.
    Lapis lazuli. Gold ring, hoop thin below, expanding upwards, strongly projecting shoulders.
    2nd–3rd c. AD (Marshall). Intaglio quite possibly modern (non vidi) because of stone-type.
    Marshall 1907: 84, no. 489.

HA11. Sol and Luna as Minor Figures
HA11ca... . with two Fortunae, Each with Cornucopia, Facing Each Other; between Them: Griffin

1. Plate 154.10
    Vienna, Kunsthistorisches Museum VII A 146.
    Unknown.
    Brownish red carnelian.
    2nd c. AD (AGWien).
    LIMC Helios/Sol 323; Matern 2002: 182, 277 B248a.
    Image: photograph © KHM-Museumsverband.

HA12. Sol Riding on Horseback
HA12a. ... on Horseback to Left, Right Hand Raised, Whip in Left Hand

1. Leiden, National Museum of Antiquities(?), NS 28.
    Nijmegen.
    Carnelian. Silver ring.

3rd c. AD.
Henkel 1913, 63 no. 455.

I. Cameos
I1. Head or Bust of Sol
1. London, British Museum 1894,1128.3.
    Syria.
    Sardonyx.
    1st–2nd c. AD.
    Head of Sol (?) right, wearing a radiate, jewelled diadem.
    Walters 1926: 3650.

J. Jewellery, Costume (including Ependytes), Personal Ornaments
J1. Diadems
1. Vacat

2. Vacat (see K9.45)

3. Jerusalem, Israel Museum 76.63.50 (665).
    Nablus.
    Gold.
    1st–3rd c. AD.
    Head of Sol to either side of the 12 Gods.
    LIMC Helios/Sol 227; LIMC Dodekatheoi 58.

4. Izmir, Museum.
    Unknown.
    Gold.
    2nd–3rd c. AD.
    Two frontal busts of Sol, flanking 3 deities.
    LIMC Helios/Sol 228.

5. Cologne, Römisch-Germanisches Museum 74.383.
    Acquired in Aleppo, Art Market; reputedly from Laodicea.
    Gold.
    Second half 3rd c. AD (dated on dubious grounds).
    Diadem: in centre, bust of Sol, radiate (eleven rays) above four horses' protomes, between ten gods on the left and eight gods (from the same matrix) on the right.
    LIMC Helios/Sol 269; Long 1987: 320–22; Matern 2002: 56–7, 216 Q53.

6.   Plate 163.1
      Copenhagen, National Museum 4977.
      Rome.
      Bronze.
      3rd c. AD.
      Small, aedicula-shaped bronze plaque, which formed part of a diadem.
      In the tympanum, frontal chariot (two horses to the left, two to the right)
      of Sol, radiate, nude but for a *chlamys* billowing out behind him, whip in
      left hand, globe (?) in right hand; two stars in the corners. In the upper
      corners outside the tympanum the Dioscuri. In the main field, Sabazius
      standing, surrounded by a large array of cult objects and animals; in the
      upper right hand corner bust of Sol, radiate (ten rays), *chlamys*, and in the
      upper left hand corner bust of Luna.
      LIMC Helios/Sol 230 & 394a; LIMC Dioskouroi/Castores 51 (with lit.);
      Matern 2002: 53, 214 Q43 (incorrect inv. no.).
      Image: photograph © National Museum, Copenhagen.

7.   Unknown, formerly Goluchow collection.
      Unknown.
      Gold.
      Second half 3rd c. AD.
      Diadem: frontal radiate head of Sol between the 12 gods.
      LIMC Helios/Sol 269; Matern 2002: 263–4 B134.

          J2. Sol as Decorative Element of *Ependytes*
          J2a. Aphrodisian Aprodite
1.   Erlangen, Univ. I 505.
      Probably from Italy.
      Marble.
      2nd c. AD (LIMC); 3rd c. AD (Noelke).
      Fragment of a statuette; preserved is the torso from the neck down to
      slightly above the waist; on the *ependytes*: busts of Sol and Luna.
      LIMC Helios 293; LIMC Aphrodite (Aphrodisias) 15; Noelke 1983: 118–9 no.
      17 fig. 12.

2.   Munich, Antiquarium der Residenz.
      Rome.
      Marble.
      2nd c. AD (Noelke).

Statuette of Aphrodite of Aphrodisias; on *ependytes*: busts of Sol and Luna.

LIMC Aphrodite (Aphrodisias) 24 (with refs.); Noelke 1983: 121–2 no. 24.

3.   Vatican, Museo Gregoriano Etrusco 12185.
     Rome, Forum Romanum.
     Marble.
     Early 2nd c. AD.
     Aphrodite of Aphrodisias; on *ependytes* busts of Sol and Luna.
     LIMC Aphrodite (Aphrodisias) 29; Noelke 1983: 115 no. 1; Floriani Squarciapino 1959.

4.   Unknown.
     Ostia.
     Marble.
     Mid 2nd c. AD.
     Small statuette of Aphrodite of Aphrodisias; on *ependytes* busts of Sol and Luna.
     LIMC Aphrodite (Aphrodisias) 38; Noelke 1983: 122 no. 26, 123 fig. 16.

5.   Private collection.
     Split.
     Marble.
     Mid 2nd c. AD.
     Statuette of Aphrodite of Aphrodisias; on *ependytes* busts of Sol and Luna.
     LIMC Aphrodite (Aphrodisias) 33; Noelke 1983: 117 no. 11.

6.   Plate 163.2
     Aphrodisias (Geyre), depot.
     Aphrodisias, Bouleuterion.
     Marble.
     Mid 2nd c. AD.
     Damaged statue of Aphrodite of Aphrodisias. On *ependytes*: busts of Sol, radiate nimbus (eleven rays) and Luna.
     LIMC Aphrodite (Aphrodisias) 18; Noelke 1983: 129 no. 21.
     Image: photograph William Neusiedel; cc-by2.0; https://commons.wiki media.org/wiki/File:Afrodite_of_Aphrodisias_-_Cult_Image.jpg

7. Athens, National Archaeological Museum 1795 & 2147.
  Athens.
  Marble.
  2nd c. AD (and not BC, as mistakenly in LIMC).
  Two parts of a statue of Aphrodite of Aphrodisias (? not certain that
  the two fragments belong to the same statue); on *ependytes* busts of Sol
  and Luna.
  LIMC Helios 291; Noelke 1983: 121 no. 22; LIMC Aphrodite (Aphrodisias) 11.

8. Chicago, Smart Museum of Art 1967.114.413.
  Unknown.
  Marble.
  Mid 2nd c. AD.
  Headless statuette of Aphrodite of Aphrodisias; on *ependytes* busts of Sol
  and Luna.
  LIMC Aphrodite (Aphrodisias) 14; Noelke 1983: 118 no. 13.

9. Plate 163.3
  Bologna, Museo Civico Archeologico G 1078.
  Unknown.
  White Marble, with black marble hands and face.
  2nd–3rd c. AD.
  Aphrodite of Aphrodisias; on *ependytes*: frontal busts of Sol, radiate, on
  the right and Luna on the left.
  LIMC Aphrodite (Aphrodisias) 13; Noelke 1983: 116 no. 8.
  Image: Courtesy of Museo Civico Archeologico-Photo Archive, Bologna.

10. Plates 19.5, 163.4
  Naples, Museo Nazionale, Racc. Cumana. 10801.
  Rome.
  Marble.
  3rd c. AD (Noelke).
  Aphrodite of Aphrodisias; on *ependytes* busts of Sol and Luna.
  LIMC Aphrodite (Aphrodisias) 26; Noelke 1983: 123 no. 27.
  Image: photograph of a drawing by Pirro Ligorio (1512–1583).

11. Plate 164.1
  Rome, Musei Capitolini 2959.
  Rome.
  Marble.

3rd c. AD (Noelke).
Aphrodite of Aphrodisias; on *ependytes* busts of Sol and Luna.
LIMC Aphrodite (Aphrodisias) 31; Noelke 1983: 115 no. 2; Floriani
Squarciapino 1959: figs. 45.
Image: courtesy of the Musei Capitolini, Rome.

12. Cologne, Römisch-Germanisches Museum.
Italy?
Marble.
Undated.
Statuette of Aphrodite of Aphrodisias; on *ependytes* busts of Sol and
Luna.
LIMC Aphrodite (Aphrodisias) 20a.

13. Florence, Uffizi 490.
Unknown, possibly found locally.
Marble.
Undated.
Torso of a statuette of Aphrodite of Aphrodisias; on *ependytes* busts of Sol
and Luna.
LIMC Aphrodite (Aphrodisias) 17; Noelke 1983: 115–6 no. 5.

14. London, Sloane Museum M430.
Italy.
Marble.
Undated.
Upper part of the torso of a statue of Aphrodite of Aphrodisias. Below the
belt the tips of a few rays of Sol's radiate crown have been preserved.
LIMC Aphrodite (Aphrodisias) 22; Noelke 1983: 119–20 no. 19.

15. Napels, Museo Nazionale.
Rome.
Marble.
Undated.
Statue of Aphrodite of Aphrodisias; on *ependytes*: busts of Sol and Luna.
LIMC Aphrodite (Aphrodisias) 25; Noelke 1983: 115 no. 3.

16. Parma, Museum.
Parma.
Marble.

Undated.

Torso of a statuette of Aphrodite of Aphrodisias; on *ependytes* frontal busts of Sol (right), radiate nimbus, and Luna (left).

LIMC Aphrodite (Aphrodisias) 28; Noelke 1983: 116 no. 6.

17.   Rome, Museo Nazionale Romano 7873.
       Siena.
       Marble.
       Undated.
       Aphrodite of Aphrodisias; on *ependytes* busts of Sol and Luna.
       LIMC Aphrodite (Aphrodisias) 30; Noelke 1983: 116 no. 7, 117 figs. 1011.

18.   Unknown.
       Ariccia, near Rome.
       Marble.
       Undated.
       Statuette of Aphrodite of Aphrodisias; on *ependytes* busts of Sol and Luna.
       LIMC Aphrodite (Aphrodisias) 37; Noelke 1983: 115 no. 4.

19.   Aphrodisias (Geyre), depot 69/293.
       Aphrodisias.
       Marble.
       Undated.
       Fragment of a statue of Aphrodite of Aphrodisias. On *ependytes*: busts of Sol, radiate nimbus (eleven rays) and Luna.
       LIMC Aphrodite (Aphrodisias) 19; Noelke 1983: 129 no. 29.

20.   Ephesus (Selçuk), Museum W 66/158.
       Ephesus.
       Marble.
       Undated.
       Fragment of a statue of Aphrodite of Aphrodisias. On *ependytes*: busts of Sol, radiate nimbus and Luna.
       LIMC Aphrodite (Aphrodisias) 34 & 36; Noelke 1983: 118 no. 16.

21.   Istanbul, Archaeology Museum.
       Aphrodisias.
       Marble.
       1st c. AD?

Fragment of a relief depicting Aphrodite of Aphrodisias. On *ependytes*: busts of Sol, radiate nimbus, and Luna.
Mendel 1914: no. 516.

22. Plate 164.2
Baltimore, Walters Art Gallery.
Baalbek.
Bronze.
Undated.
Statuette of Aphrodite of Aphrodisias. On *ependytes*: busts of Sol, radiate nimbus, and Luna.
LIMC Aphrodite (Aphrodisias) 40; Noelke 1983: 117 no. 12.
Image: photograph courtesy the Walters Art Gallery, Baltimore, under CC zero: no rights reserved-license.

23. Plates 164.3, 164.4
Vienna, Kunsthistorisches Museum I 139.
Unknown.
Marble.
2nd c. AD.
Aphrodite of Aphrodisias; on *ependytes* busts of Sol and Luna.
LIMC Aphrodite (Aphrodisias) 35; Noelke 1983: 123 no. 28, fig. 17.
Image: photograph © KHM-Museumsverband.

24. Private Collection.
Unknown.
Marble.
Undated.
Headless statuette of Aphrodite of Aphrodisias; on *ependytes* busts of Sol and Luna.
LIMC Aphrodite (Aphrodisias) 27; Noelke 1983: 116–7 no. 10, figs. 2021.

25. Unknown, copy in Berlin.
Unknown.
Unknown (copy in bronze).
Unknown, possibly modern.
Aphrodite of Aphrodisias; busts of Sol and Luna on *ependytes*.
LIMC Aphrodite (Aphrodisias) 41 (with refs.); Noelke 1983: 122 (under no. 26).

26.   Aphrodisias, Museum 861.
       Aphrodisias, atrium house.
       Marble.
       Late 2nd–early 3rd c. AD.
       Headless bust of a person carrying a headless statuette of Aphrodite of
       Aphrodisias; busts of Sol and Luna on her *ependytes*.
       Smith 2006: 238–9, no. 127, pl. 95.

          J2b. Heliopolis, Jupiter
1.   Istanbul, Archaeology Museum 2570.
       Soukhné, Northeast of Palmyra.
       Limestone.
       2nd–3rd c. AD.
       Statuette of Jupiter Heliopolitanus. On the *ependytes*, inter alia,
       bust of Sol, radiate, and Luna (crescent) flanking the bust of Jupiter
       Heliopolitanus. According to Hajjar, the Palmyrene triad of Bel, Iarhibol,
       and Aglibol. Hajjar rejects the identification of the central bust as Jupiter
       Heliopolitanus on the grounds that it is unlikely that the *ependytes* of the
       god would be decorated with an image of the god.
       Mendel 1914: 613–616 no. 1404; Fleischer 1973: 328 H6, pl. 148 (with lit.);
       Hajjar 1977: 211–214 no. 186 pl. 70.

2.   Avignon, Musée Calvet 41.
       Marseille.
       Marble.
       Undated.
       Stele with depiction, in high relief, of Jupiter Heliopolitanus, his *epen-
       dytes* decorated with three groups of two busts-all worn and damaged-
       separated vertically by a herm. Hajjar recognizes the planetary deities in
       the busts and herm, with Sol (left) and Luna (right) at the top to either
       side of the bust of Mercury surmounting the herm.
       Hajjar 1977: 349–352 no. 284 pl. 105.

3.   Beirut, National Museum 3279.
       Apamea.
       Limestone.
       Undated.
       Rectangular base for a column. On the base a relief depiction of Jupiter
       Heliopolitanus, with on the *ependytes* two busts, badly worn but almost
       certainly Sol and Luna (Hajjar).
       Hajjar 1977: 197–8 no. 172, pl. 65.

4. Berlin, Staatliche Museen VA 3360.
   Kafr Yasin (between Beirut and Byblos).
   Bronze.
   Undated.
   Statuette of Jupiter Heliopolitanus. His *ependytes* is decorated at the top
   with the busts of Sol, radiate (left), and Luna (right).
   Hajjar 1977: 264–6 no. 226, pl. 85.

5. Lost (formerly Graz, Joanneum).
   Unknown.
   Bronze.
   Undated.
   Statuette of Jupiter Heliopolitanus. On the *ependytes*, busts of Sol (l.)
   radiate, and Luna.
   Hajjar 1977: 409–11 no. 313, pl. 124.

6. Plate 165.1
   Paris, Louvre AO 11.446.
   Lebanon, Beka'a region.
   Bronze.
   Undated.
   Statuette of Jupiter Heliopolitanus. On the *ependytes* two busts, without
   distinguishing attributes but nonetheless "without doubt" Sol and Luna
   (Hajjar) above a bearded bust of Saturnus.
   Hajjar 1977: 172–5 no. 153, pls 578.
   Image: photograph © Musée du Louvre, Dist. RMN-Grand Palais / Thierry
   Ollivier / Art Resource ART556062.

7. Plate 165.2
   Paris, Louvre AO 11.451.
   Beirut.
   gilded bronze.
   Undated.
   Statuette of Jupiter Heliopolitanus. On *ependytes*, upper register, busts of
   Sol (l.) with long, wavy hair (no rays?), and Luna (r.); in the next register,
   three standing figures identified as Zeus between Ares and Hermes, and
   in the third register standing figure of Tyche.
   Hajjar 1977: 236–239 no. 208, pls.789.
   Image: photograph © Musée du Louvre, Dist. RMN-Grand Palais / Thierry
   Ollivier / Art Resource, NY: ART559884.

8.   Plate 165.3
     Paris, Louvre AO 19.534.
     Baalbek?
     Bronze.
     Undated.
     Statuette of Jupiter Heliopolitanus. On his *ependytes*, the busts of the
     seven planetary deities: from top to bottom, Sol (left), long hair, radiate,
     and Luna (right); Mars (left) and Mercury (right); Jupiter (left) and Venus
     (right-Hajjar suggests Juno, who can sometimes replace Venus); Saturnus.
     Hajjar 1977: 274–284 no. 232, pls. 889.
     Image: photograph © RMN-Grand Palais / Art Resource, NY: ART185185.

9.   Plate 166.1
     Paris, Louvre AO 22267.
     Lebanon.
     Bronze.
     Undated.
     Statuette of Jupiter Heliopolitanus. On his *ependytes*, at the top, the
     busts of Sol (draped, long hair, not radiate) and Luna, followed below by
     the busts of the other planetary deities: first Saturnus (left) and Jupiter
     (right); .next Mars (left) and Venus (right), and finally Mercury. On the
     back, an eagle, a solar disc, and the busts of Neptune, Ceres/Demeter,
     Minerva, Diana, and Hercules. Together with the seven planetary deities,
     these are the gods connected with the twelve signs of the zodiac.
     Hajjar 1977: 284–6 no. 233 pls. 901.
     Image: photograph © Musée du Louvre, Dist. RMN-Grand Palais / Thierry
     Ollivier / Art Resource, NY: ART559886.

10. Plates 17.3, 165.4
     Paris, Louvre AO 22268.
     Phoenicia.
     bronze.
     Not dated.
     Statuette, damaged, of Jupiter Heliopolitanus. On his breast: bust of Sol,
     radiate.
     Hajjar 1977: 234.
     Image: photograph © Musée du Louvre, Dist. RMN-Grand Palais / Thierry
     Ollivier / Art Resource, NY: ART559885

11. Plate 167.1
Rome, Fondazione Dino ed Ernesta Santarelli inv. E.D'O.1.
Unknown.
Marble.
Undated.
Part of a statuette of Jupiter Heliopolitanus; head, arms, and lower part of
the legs missing. On the *ependytes*, at the top, busts of Sol (left) and Luna
(right). In the next register, Jupiter flanked by Mars (left) and Mercury (?).
Three additional figures in the lower register.
Unpublished.
Image: courtesy Fondazione Dino ed Ernesta Santarelli.

J2c. Myra, Artemis Eleuthera

1. Myra, Theatre.
In situ.
Limestone.
After AD 141, when the theatre was restored after being destroyed by an
earthquake.
Relief of Artemis Eleuthera: on her *ependytes* bust of Sol, radiate, and
crescent. This is the only representation of Artemis Eleuthera which is
sufficiently well preserved to give an idea of the iconography of the main
cult statue. It appears to confirm that Sol and Luna were included on the
decoration of the *ependytes*.
LIMC Artemis Eleuthera 2; LIMC Helios 292.

J2d. Hecate

1. Plates 167.2–5
Sibiu, Bruckenthal Museum 43444.
Ocna Mures.
Marble.
2nd c. AD.
Statuette of triple Hecate, two dressed in *chiton*, one in *ependytes*. On
ependytes: frontal bust of Sol, radiate (seven? rays).
LIMC Helios/Sol 217.
Images: Lupa.at/17500

J2e. Other

1. Art Market, New York.
Unknown.

Bronze.

Undated.

Two figures, one male and one female, wearing a common *ependytes*, on which are depicted, inter alia, the planetary deities (Sol, Mars, Mercury and Saturn on the front, Luna, Venus and Jupiter on the back) and a nude youth on the front holding a zodiac circle which encircles the statuette.

Hecht 1989: no. 22.

2.   Rome, Soprintendenza Speciale per il Colosseo, il Museo Nazionale Romano e l'Area Archeologica di Roma, inv. 592065.

Rome, N.E. slopes of the Palatine.

Marble

First half 3rd c. AD

Small, headless statuette of a figure dressed in an *ependytes*, decorated on the breast with a frontal bust of Sol, radiate (more than eight rays). A full-figured Luna in high relief adorns the lower part of the *ependytes*, down to the feet. Tentatively identified as a statuette of Apollo of Hierapolis.

Papini 2015.

J3. Other Decorative Elements of Statues and Statuettes

1.   Plates 168.1, 168.2

Brussels, Royal Museums of Fine Arts.

Unknown.

Marble.

1st–2nd c. AD.

Portrait of a young, clean-shaven man. Above his forehead a disc bearing a face within a full circle of rays (Sonnengesicht); very worn.

LIMC Helios/Sol 5.

Image: photograph © Royal Museums of Fine Arts.

2.   Lost.

Southern France.

Silver.

2nd–3rd c. AD.

Pantheistic, winged Tutela, with cornucopia, rudder, wheel, and mural crown with Isiac emblem; to either side of the crown, busts of Sol and Luna.

LIMC Helios/Sol 339; Boucher 1976: 150 n.262.

3. Plate 21.2
    London, British Museum 1824,0424.1.
    Mâcon.
    Gilded silver.
    Ca. AD 150–220.
    Pantheistic Tutela, with patera, two cornucopiae topped with the busts of
    Sol and Luna, and above her head the two Dioscuri and the seven plan-
    etary deities.
    LIMC Dodekatheoi 54 (with references); LIMC Helios/Sol 289.
    Image: photograph © Trustees of the British Museum.

4. Lost.
    Montpellier.
    Bronze.
    Undated.
    Busts of the seven planetary deities, beginning with Saturn (l.), on a cres-
    cent. Duval suggests it may be part of a statuette comparable to the one
    from Mâcon in the British Museum (J3.3).
    Montfaucon 1722: Suppl. I, 37–8, pl XVII.1 (identifies the crescent as a
    ship); Duval 1953: 289.

    J4. Rings
1. Plate 168.3
    London, British Museum 1917,0501.268.
    Tarsus.
    Gold.
    Second half 3rd AD.
    Massive, hexagonal gold ring; in relief, facing busts of Sol and Sarapis.
    Marshall 1908: 47 no. 268.
    Found in 1863 as part of the "Trésor de Tarse" (cf. Longpérier 1868). A coin
    of Gordian of AD 243 gives the terminus post quem. The name Gerontius
    on one of the rings in the treasure (Marshall 1908: no. 188) was common
    in the 4th c., but not in the 3rd.
    Image: photograph © Trustees of the British Museum.

2. London, British Museum 1872,0604.319.
    Unknown.
    Gold.
    3rd–4th c. (?)

Three plain rings, fastened together by two small rings surmounted by small rectangular plaques with engraved design; on the one: two facing busts, the right-hand one radiate, possibly Sol, the left-hand one unidentifiable. On the other: radiate profile head of Sol on the left, facing right, crescent above star.
Marshall 1908: 983.

3. London, British Museum 1917,0503.1143.
Byblos.
Silver.
Undated.
Ring ending in two facing snakes' heads holding a small, hexagonal (partially broken) plate with frontal bust of Sol (radiate) in relief.
Marshall 1908: 1143.

4. Gaziantep, Kamer Işsever collection inv. G-043.
Unknown.
Silver and gold.
Undated.
Frontal bust of Sol on a small gold disc set into a silver ring.
Artefacts.mom.fr BAG-4075

5. Gaziantep, Kamer Işsever collection, inv. G-042
Unknown.
Bronze.
2nd–3rd c. AD.
Medallion-like bezel supported by a ring with two snake heads. In the bezel, busts of Sol, right, radiate, and an unknown deity.
Artefacts.mom.fr BAG-4074.

6. Art Market. Note: this object cannot be documented prior to 1995, and is therefore considered an undocumented artifact (no documentation prior to 1970) which cannot be ethically sold or traded (AIA code of ethics).
Unknown.
Silver and gold.
Undated.
Silver fingerring with a gilded bezel depicting the profile bust of Sol, right, radiate (seven rays) and long wavy hair.
Christie's Ancient Jewelry auction 2375, New York, December 9 2010, lot 434.

J5. Earrings

1. Paris, Louvre BJ 272 & 273.
Bolsena.
Gold.
325–275 BC (Louvre). Second quarter of the 3rd c. BC (Nicolini).
Head of Sol, radiate (seven rays) behind the frontal protomes of four horses. They appear to be resting on the centre of an upturned lunula (rather than a small ship, as Nicolini would have it). The points are surmounted by odd "palmettes", but Nicolini points out that these are a modern restoration, and should therefore be ignored. In my opinion the two points of the lunula were probably originally surmounted by two stars. To either side of the crescent and slightly below it are two winged Victories, each carrying a large trophy. Sol reportedly raises his right hand on one of the earrings, but I have not been able to confirm this with the images available to me. According to Matern Sol may be holding a whip. Nicolini's rather precise date is predicated on the assumption that the crescent is a boat, and that these earrings represent the final phase of a "boat-earring" type that was popular in the fifth and fourth centuries BC. LIMC Helios 87; Nicolini 2001: 6–8, 10, 29–30 (with good images); Matern 2002: 208, Q6.

J6. Bracelets

1. Plate 168.6
Formerly the De Witte collection. Current location uncertain; apparently donated by De Witte to the Cabinet des Médailles.
Syria.
Gold.
Roman Imperial.
Bracelet with the busts of Tyche and the seven planetary deities, their names inscribed in Greek, starting with Kronos.
LIMC Planetae 17.
Image: drawing after de Witte 1877 pl, 8.

J7. Pendants

1. London, British Museum 1983,1108.52.
Unknown.
Blue glass.
4th c. AD.
Small pendant with a loop at the top. In the round field a depiction of Sol, radiate (?), right hand raised, reins in lowered left hand, *chlamys*

billowing out behind his left shoulder, on a frontal *quadriga*, two horses jumping inwards, two outwards. I cannot make out whether Sol is dressed in a *chiton* or nude.
Entwistle & Finney 2013: 3.

2.　　Plate 168.4
　　　London, British Museum 1983,1108.53.
　　　Unknown.
　　　Amber glass.
　　　4th c. AD.
　　　Small pendant with a loop at the top. In the round field a depiction of Sol, radiate (?), right hand raised, reins in lowered left hand, dressed in a *chiton* and *chlamys* billowing out behind his left shoulder, on a frontal *quadriga*, two horses jumping inwards, to outwards.
　　　Entwistle & Finney 2013: 5.
　　　Image: photograph © Trustees of the British Museum.

3.　　Budapest, Museum of Fine Arts 93.27 A.
　　　Unknown.
　　　Gold.
　　　2nd–3rd c. AD.
　　　Frontal bust of Sol, radiate (five rays), draped.
　　　http://www.szepmuveszeti.hu/adatlap_eng/gold_pendant_with_bust_of
　　　_3873 accessed November 21, 2017.

K. Minor Objects
K1. Appliques

1.　　Plate 168.5
　　　Copenhagen, National Museum.
　　　Agersbøl.
　　　Silver.
　　　1st c. AD.
　　　Frontal face surrounded by rays (Sonnengesicht).
　　　LIMC Helios/Sol 10.
　　　Image: photograph © National Museum, Copenhagen.

2.　　Art market.
　　　Syria.
　　　Terracotta.

1st–2nd c. AD.

Star-shaped applique with bust of Sol, radiate (seven rays), *chlamys*, possibly a quiver.

Matern 2002: 265 B143.

3.   Vaison-La-Romaine, Musée Municipale.
Vaison, Maison au Dauphin, lararium.
Bronze.
2nd c. AD.
Bust of Sol, radiate (five rays).
Goudineau 1979: 30, 167, pl. 3; Rolland 1965: 79 no. 127; LIMC Helios/Sol 66.

4.   Plate 169.1
Avenches, Musée Romain 1912/5521.
Avenches.
Bronze.
2nd–3rd c. AD.
Bust of Sol, radiate (8? rays, of which 5 preserved).
LIMC Helios/Sol 65; Matern 2002: 247, B21.
Image: photograph © AVENTICVM-Site et Musée romains d'Avenches.

5.   Plate 177.6
Székesfehérvár, Szent István Király Múzeum 75.37.2.
Adony, Dolichenum.
Bronze.
2nd–3rd c. AD.
Bust of Sol, radiate (seven rays), *chlamys*.
LIMC Helios/Sol 59; Fitz 1998: 96 no. 161.
Image: courtesy of the Szent István Király Múzeum.

6.   Paris, Bibliothèque Nationale de France, Cabinet des Médailles 118.
Rimat, near Saïda, Syria.
Bronze.
2nd–3rd c.
Bust of Sol, radiate.
Babelon & Blanchet 1895: 55 no. 118; Matern 2002: 182, 249 B34; Fani 2016; Mattusch 2016.

7.   Plate 169.2
Kassel, Staatliche Kunstsammlung Br. 132.
Unknown.

2nd–3rd c. AD.
Bronze.
Bust of Sol, radiate (five rays).
LIMC Helios/Sol 66; Bieber 1915: 307 pl. 49.
Image: photograph © Staatliche Kunstsammlung, Kassel.

8.   Paris, Bibliothèque Nationale de France, Cabinet des Médailles 116.
      Unknown.
      Bronze.
      2nd–3rd c.
      Bust of Sol, radiate (six rays), whip by right shoulder.
      Babelon & Blanchet 1895: 54 no. 116; Matern 2002: 172, 182, 249 B32.

9.   Plate 170.1
      Paris, Bibliothèque Nationale de France, Cabinet des Médailles 119.
      Unknown.
      Bronze.
      2nd–3rd c.
      Bust of Sol, radiate (five rays).
      Babelon-Blanchet 56 no. 119; Matern 2002: 182, 249 B35.
      Image: drawing after Babelon-Blanchet loc. cit., in the public domain

10.   Plate 170.2
      Paris, Bibliothèque Nationale de France, Cabinet des Médailles 120.
      Unknown.
      Bronze.
      2nd–3rd c.
      Bust of Sol, radiate (seven rays), the tops of the rays connected to each
      other by a semi-circular band.
      Babelon-Blanchet 56 no. 120; Matern 2002: 182, 249 B36.
      Image: drawing after Babelon-Blanchet loc. cit., in the public domain

11.   Plate 169.3
      Paris, Louvre Br 523.
      Unknown.
      Bronze.
      2nd–3rd c. AD.
      Bust of Sol, radiate (five rays).

LIMC Helios/Sol 66.
Image: photograph © Musée du Louvre.

12.   Plates 170.6, 170.7
       St.-Germain-en-Laye, Musée d'Archéologie nationale MAN 12843.
       Châlons-sur-Marne.
       Bronze.
       3rd c. AD (?)
       Bronze medallion of a phalera; head of Medusa within double concentric
       circle, between two maritime creatures (?-only their tails survive), below
       frontal head of Sol, radiate (seven rays) within a wreath.
       Schauenburg 1955: 33–4 fig. 18; LIMC Helios/Sol 207.
       Image: photograph © Musée d'Archéologie nationale.

13.   Belgrade, National Museum 2706/III.
       Podunavlje? Moesia Superior, precise findspot unknown.
       Bronze.
       3rd c. AD.
       Bust of Sol, radiate (seven rays decorated with small incised circles), eyes,
       nose and mouth incised.
       Veličković 1972: 180–1 no. 120.

14.   Bucharest, National Museum.
       Romula.
       Terracotta.
       3rd c. AD.
       Vase-appliqué; Sol, nude (?) but for a *chlamys*, head damaged, right hand
       raised, whip in left hand, on *quadriga* right within a partially preserved
       zodiac circle.
       LIMC Helios/Sol 297; Gundel 1992: 237 no. 96.1; Matern 2002: 243 I65;
       Filip 2021: 93–4, 118 fig. 19.

15.   Plate 169.4
       Budapest, National Museum 43.1933.96.
       Brigetio (Dolichenum).
       Bronze.
       Early 3rd c. AD.
       Bust of Sol, radiate (five rays). Found together with a slightly larger bust
       of Luna (5 cm and 8.5 cm high respectively), inv. 43.1933.95 (Ratimorská

& Minaroviech 2009: 120 fig. 3) and other objects, including a Victory on a globe.

LIMC Helios/Sol 66; Jucker 1961: 184 fig. 29; Hörig & Schwertheim 1987: 247 pl. 48; Ratimorská & Minaroviech 2009: 120 fig. 4, 126, 130 no. 10.

Image: photograph © National Museum, Budapest.

16.   Plate 170.3
       Brescia, Museum?
       Brescia.
       Bronze.
       Undated.
       Bust of Sol.
       Dütschke 1880: 148, d; Museo Bresciano vol. 1 (1838) pl. LII; LIMC Helios/ Sol 66; Jucker 1961: 185 n.1. Not in: Stella 1987.
       Image: drawing by M. Hijmans after Museo Bresciano 1838: pl. LII.

17.   Plates 169.5, 169.6
       Besançon, Musée des Beaux-Arts et d'Archéologie 852.2.7.
       Besançon, "le champ noir."
       Bronze.
       Undated.
       Bust of Sol, radiate (five rays).
       LIMC Helios/Sol 66; Lebel 1961: no. 165.
       Image: photograph © Musée des Beaux-Arts et d'Archéologie / J.-M. Dubois.

17a.   Lebel (see K1.17) refers to a second appliqué, taken from a cast of the first. Jacques-Marie Dubois of the museum in Besançon informs me that this is a copy dating from the 18th or 19th c. (inv. A 478).

18.   Plate 169.7
       Besançon, Musée des Beaux-Arts et d'Archéologie 859.9.3.
       Sournay (Haute-Saône).
       Bronze.
       Undated.
       Bust of Sol, radiate (five rays, now lost).
       Lebel 1961: no. 164. Lebel gives an incorrect inv. no. The cast he mentions under no. 290 (p. 77) is not a Dioscure, but actually an 18th or 19th c. cast of this appliqué.
       Image: photograph © Musée des Beaux-Arts et d'Archéologie / J.-M. Dubois.

19. London, British Museum 1879,1130.1.
Palmyra.
Terracotta.
1st–2nd c. AD.
Medallion-like appliqué or a token; Atargatis or Allath seated, between two lions. On the left frontal bust of a woman (face worn), on the right frontal bust of male deity, radiate nimbus (ten rays), *chlamys*, armor, above a globe (?-not a star as commonly stated) and crescent.
LIMC Helios (in per. or.) 13; Rostovtzeff 1971: pl. 21.1.

20. Plate 169.8
Sofia, Archaeological Museum of the Bulgarian Academy 1228.
Unknown.
Bronze.
Undated.
Bust of Sol, radiate, five rays.
Matern 2002: 182, 249 B38a, fig. 71.
Image: © Sofia Archaeological Museum / Krassimir Georgiev.

21. Plate 169.9
Sofia, Archaeological Museum of the Bulgarian Academy 6234.
Unknown.
Bronze.
Undated.
Bust of Sol, radiate, five rays.
Matern 2002: 182, 249–50, B38b, fig. 72.
Image: © Sofia Archaeological Museum / Krassimir Georgiev.

22. Unknown.
Unknown.
Bronze.
Undated.
Mask of Sol, radiate.
Matern 2002: 264 B135.

23. Art Market.
Unknown.
Terracotta.
Undated.

Bust of Sol, *chlamys*.
Matern 2002: 265 B147.

24. Berlin, Staatliche Museen.
Aïn-Djoudj.
Lead.
Roman?
Four votive appliqués, originally crowning wooden shafts (Seyrig 1929: 339); radiate head above a disc. A single or double crescent almost encircles the disc from below.
LIMC Helios (in per. or.) 11b (with refs.).

25. Berlin, Staatliche Museen.
Aïn-Djoudj,
Lead,
Roman?
As previous, but instead of a disc crowned with a head the crescent is surmounted by a radiate bust of Sol.
LIMC Helios (in per. or.) 11b (with refs).

26. London, British Museum 1978,0102.17.
West Hill, Uley, Gloucestershire.
Bronze.
Roman Imperial.
Bust of Sol, radiate (seven rays, of which five survive), *chlamys* (?).
Woodward & Leach 1993: fig. 85.1.

27. Cologne, Römisch-Germanisches Museum 776.
Unknown.
Bronze.
2nd–3rd c. AD.
Frontal bust of Sol, radiate.
Rheinisches Bildarchiv RBA L 02 586/00A.
Image: https://www.kulturelles-erbe-koeln.de/documents/obj/05726658

28. Plate 4.1, 170.4
Mâcon, Museum 72-10 (13229).
Sainte-Colombe-les-Vienne.
Bronze.
Undated.

Bust of Sol, radiate (six rays).
Bigeard & Feugère 2011: 21–22 no. 8.
Image: courtesy Artefacts (artefacts.mom.fr) APM-4028.

29. Plate 169.10
Stuttgart, Landesmuseum Württemberg R 19901.
Unknown.
Silver.
3rd–4th c. AD.
Bust of Sol, radiate (seven rays, the central one accentuated), *chlamys*, emerging from foliage consisting of seven leaves.
Willburger 2007.
Image: photograph © Landesmuseum Württemberg, P. Frankenstein / H. Zwietasch.

30. Plate 169.11
Amsterdam, Allard Pierson Museum 08532.
Turkey.
Bronze.
Undated.
Head of Sol, radiate (five rays).
Unpublished.
Image: photograph courtesy Allard Pierson Museum, S.L.A. van der Linden.

31. Plate 170.5
Private Collection.
Sleaford, North Kesteven, Lincolnshire.
Bronze.
3rd c. AD.
Bust of Sol, radiate, eight rays.
Portable Antiquities Scheme LIN A65125 (2004): https://finds.org.uk/ database/artefacts/record/id/59788 (Accessed: November 11, 2017).
Image: photograph and sketch available under a CC BY-SA 4.0 license.

32. Plate 169.12
Private Collection.
Highnam, Tewkesbury, Gloucestershire. Bronze.
3rd c. AD.
Bust of Sol, radiate, five rays.

Portable Antiquities Scheme WAW-BC67D3 (2003): https://finds.org.uk/
database/artefacts/record/id/53142 (Accessed November 11, 2017).
Image: photograph and sketch available under a CC BY-SA 4.0 license.

33.　Private Collection.
　　　Kirkby La Thorpe, North Kesteven, Lincolnshire.
　　　Bronze.
　　　3rd c. AD.
　　　Bust of Sol, radiate nimbus, seven rays. Very worn.
　　　Portable Antiquities Scheme DENO-6AB7C3.

34.　Plate 170.8
　　　Toronto, Royal Ontario Museum 916.1.508.
　　　Al-Fayyum, Egypt.
　　　Bronze.
　　　3rd c. AD.
　　　Bust of Sol, radiate, nine rays.
　　　Unpublished?
　　　Image: courtesy of the Royal Ontario Museum.

35.　Plate 170.9
　　　Athens, Benaki Museum.
　　　Unknown.
　　　Gold.
　　　3rd–4th c. AD (?)
　　　Small, thin gold disc with hammered relief decoration depicting a frontal
　　　bust of Sol, radiate (twelve rays ending in small dots), *chlamys*, small pro-
　　　tomes of two horses (one frontal, in front of the neck of the other one, in
　　　profile) behind his right shoulder, and an indistinct image, possibly the
　　　protomes of two other small horses, above his left shoulder.
　　　Unpublished.
　　　Image courtesy of the Benaki Museum, Dr. I. Papageorgiou; photograph
　　　author.

36.　Saldaña, Museo Monográfico de la villa romana La Olmeda.
　　　Villa of La Olmeda (found in 1988).
　　　Bronze.
　　　2nd–3rd c. AD.
　　　Sol, radiate (seven rays), nude but for a *chlamys*, right hand raised, whip
　　　in left hand, with attachment pins at the back.
　　　Abásola 2013.

37. Plate 170.10
    Art Market. Note: this object cannot be documented prior to 1970, and is therefore considered an undocumented artifact which cannot be ethically possessed, sold or traded (AIA code of ethics).
    Unknown.
    Bronze.
    1st–2nd c. AD.
    Frontal bust of Sol with long wavy hair and a radiate crown (eight rays).
    Sotheby's New York, June 7 2012, lot 29.
    Image: photo courtesy Sotheby's New York.

38. Art Market.
    Istanbul.
    Bronze.
    1st–2nd c. AD.
    Frontal bust of Sol with long wavy hair and nine (?) stumps of rays.
    Christie's antiquities sale 2565, New York June 8, 2012, lot 206.

39. Art Market. Note: this object cannot be documented prior to 1970, and is therefore considered an undocumented artifact which cannot be ethically possessed, sold or traded (AIA code of ethics).
    Unknown.
    Bronze.
    3rd c. AD
    Fairly large bust of Sol, facing, radiate nimbus (nine rays), *chlamys*.
    Bonhams antiquities sale 23364, June 8, 2016, lot 169.

40. Florence, Museo Archeologico Nazionale inv. 129.
    Unknown.
    Bronze.
    Julio-Claudian.
    Bust of Sol, radiate (nine rays).
    Luberto 2015.

    K2. Armor and Harness
1. Naples, Museo Nazionale 5687.
    Herculaneum.
    Silver.
    Augustean (Künzl).

Part of a cingulum, consisting of a rectangular plate with representation of Othryades to which a large round boss is connected depicting Sol, radiate (seven rays), *chlamys* and long *chiton*, in a *quadriga* to the right, reins in the right, long whip in his left hand. Forms a pair with a mirror-image part, also depicting Othryades, with Luna on the boss in a *biga* to the left. Thought to have been used for the fastening of a pugio (Künzl 1977, 84 & n. 4), but that leaves the companion-element with Luna (on the right hip) without a function (swords in the early principate were carried with a shoulder-belt).
Künzl 1977; Ensoli 1995: 400 no. 6.17.2; Matern 2002: 65, 70 n. 444, 218 Q69.

2. Plate 172.1
Vatican, Braccio Nuovo.
Primaporta.
Marble.
Ca. 17 BC.
Statue of Augustus. On his breastplate, below Caelus, Sol, wearing a *chiton* and *chlamys*, drives his *quadriga* right, preceded by Luna (not in *biga*!) with torch disappearing behind winged Aurora carrying a jug. Below this, the main scene depicts the returning of legionary standards to a Roman (or Mars?) by the Parthians, with a seated, mourning woman to either side, representing conquered (or client) states. Below, reclining Tellus with cornucopia, between Apollo with lyre on griffin (left) and Diana on a stag (right) with torch (!) and quiver.
Zanker 1988: 188–192; LIMC Helios/Sol 167; Matern 2002: 56, 65, 219 Q71; Squire 2013b: 253.
Image: Photograph by Sailko, made available under CC BY-SA 3.0, https://commons.wikimedia.org/wiki/Category:Augustus_of_Prima_Porta#/media/File:Augusto_di_pirma_porta,_inv._2290,_02.JPG.

3. Plate 171.1, 171.2
Naples, Museo Nazionale 5014.
Pompeii.
Bronze.
mid 1st c. AD.
Statuette of a loricatus. Breastplate decorated with silver inlay depicting Sol, radiate, in frontal chariot above Tellus between two animals (Bull and Ram?-star signs?).

LIMC Helios/Sol 218; Matern 2002: 56, 216–7 Q58 (with refs.).

Image: nineteenth c. engraving by N. La Volpe, in the public domain.

4. Plate 22.1, 22.2

Vatican, Museo Gregoriano Profano 9948.

Caere.

Marble.

Mid 1st c. AD, possibly AD 39/41, possibly Neronian. The date of AD 39/41 is based on the find context, but as Boschung (2002: 88–9) argues, the find-context is not conclusive for the group of statues discovered in 1840, to which this one belongs, as they were found dumped in a well, and hence their original context is unknown. A Neronian date has also been suggested for our statue (cf. Boschung 2002: 89 n. 30, with refs.).

Statue of a loricatus; on breastplate: Sol, radiate (seven rays), *chlamys*, on frontal *quadriga* (two horses to the left, two to the right, heads of all horses facing outwards) emerging from the sea.

LIMC Helios/Sol 214 (incorrect ref. to Stemmer); Stemmer 1978: 96–7 no. VIIa2, pl. 65 1–2; Matern 2002: 55–6, 217 Q59 (with refs.); Kantorowicz 1963: 120–1 fig. 13.

Image: Arachne FA2303-10_21311,22.jpg arachne.dainst.org/entity/1935426.

5. Cartagena, Museum.

Cartagena.

Marble.

Tiberian.

Fragment of a statue of a loricatus with, on the breastplate, remains of a frontal *quadriga* of Sol.

Stemmer 1978: 97 no. VIIa3, pl. 65.3; Matern 2002: 55, 216 Q55.

6. Plates 171.3

Private collection. Sold by Sotheby's on June 11, 2010, lot 37.

Salona, in or near one of the twin temples in the NE corner of the Forum.

Marble.

Tiberian (Stemmer); Julio-Claudian (Maršić).

Statue of a loricatus; on breastplate: Sol, radiate (nine rays), *chlamys*, on frontal *quadriga* (2 horses to the left, two to the right, heads of inner horses facing inwards) emerging from the sea.

Stemmer 1978: 56 no. V 1, pl. 34, 1; Matern 2002: 56, 216 Q56; Kantorowicz 1963: 120–1, fig. 14; Maršić 2014.

7. Turin, Museum 313.
   Susa.
   Marble.
   Tiberian.
   Bust of a general; on breastplate, Sol, not radiate, in frontal chariot, two horses to the left, and two to the right.
   Stemmer 1978: 96 no. VIIa1; LIMC Helios/Sol 213; Matern 2002: 217 Q60; Kantorowicz 1963: 120, fig 12.

8. Lecce, Museo Provinciale 4598.
   Lecce (Theatre).
   Marble.
   Late 1st–mid 2nd c. AD.
   Torso of a loricatus; Sol, radiate (only 2 rays preserved), *chiton* and *chlamys*, in frontal *quadriga* emerging from waves (only two horses preserved). Below the waves 2 Nereids on kete.
   LIMC Helios/Sol 215; Matern 2002: 216, Q57.

9. Bagdad, Iraq Museum 5676.
   Hatra.
   Marble.
   2nd c. AD.
   Statue of Apollo/Nabu (? the identity of the headless statue is uncertain); on breastplate, bust of Sol.
   LIMC Helios 140; LIMC Helios (in per. or.) 9 (with refs.); Kaizer 2000, 2412.

10. Liverpool, Museum (formerly Ince Blundell Hall).
    Unknown.
    Marble.
    Trajanic and Hadrianic/Antoninian.
    Head of Trajan on a mailed bust of later date. On the shoulder straps of the breastplate: bust of Sol, radiate, *chlamys* (right) and Luna (left).
    LIMC Helios/Sol 366 (with refs.). LIMC's date for the bust (as opposed to the head) is too early.

11. Sofia, National Archaeological Museum.
    Toptschi.
    Silver-plated bronze foil.
    3rd c. AD.

Forehead piece of parade-harness of a horse, decorated with a frontal winged Victory raising a disc above her head depicting the face of Sol surrounded by rays (Sonnengesicht).
LIMC Helios/Sol 206.

12. Berlin, Staatliche Museen, Sammlung Lipperheide 86.
Jordan.
Bronze.
Early 3rd c. AD.
Fragment of a bronze helmet. On the front: two winged Victories holding a medallion with a portrait of a clean-shaven man; on the back, two depictions of Sol (?), nude but for a *chlamys*, both on a chariot, and both holding a spear in each hand. According to LIMC: Sol Oriens and Sol Occidens. According to Schauenburg (1955, 38), Sol and Neptunus.
LIMC Helios/Sol 226 (with refs.).

13. Plate 173.1
Vienna, Kunsthistorisches Museum VI 1673.
Nikyup (Bulgaria).
Bronze.
Undated.
Partially preserved head of Sol in relief, frontal, surrounded by rays (originally ca. 17), on a damaged helmet.
LIMC Helios/Sol 191 (with refs.).
Image: photograph © KHM-Museumsverband.

14. Plate 171.4
Belgrade, National Museum 4180/III
Ritopek
Bronze
2nd–3rd c. AD
Breastplate, decorated with the seven busts of the planetary deities. In the centre: Mars. On the left side (from top to bottom): Luna (heavily restored, but the tip of a crescent is still visible behind her right shoulder), Sol, damaged, with a whip behind his left shoulder, radiate (but the rays immediately above either shoulder are the only ones preserved), and Saturn (falx); on the right (from top to bottom): Mercury (wings), Jupiter (thunderbolt) and Venus (mirror). In the top corners: eagles. To either side of Mars: legionary standards. The identification of the busts given

by Popović is untenable, as all of the busts are clearly identified by their attributes as the planetary deities; cf. Pilipović 2014.
Popović 1993; Junkelman 1996: 71 fig. 145 & 98, P43; Pilipović 2014.

15.　Mainz, Römische-Germanisches Zentralmuseum O.42645.
　　　Unknown.
　　　Bronze.
　　　3rd c. AD.
　　　Breastplate decorated with a large image of Sol on a frontal *quadriga*, with two horses jumping to either side. Sol, nimbate (no rays?) is nude but for a *chlamys*, holds a whip in his raised right hand and the reins in his left hand. Below the chariot, the Roman she-wolf with twins, and in the two lower corners busts within wreaths.
　　　Künzl 2004.

16.　Plates 172.3, 172.4
　　　Berlin, Antikensammlung.
　　　Tell Um Hauran, Syria.
　　　Bronze.
　　　2nd c. AD.
　　　Decorated parade helmet. Along the sides, two *quadriga*e driven by bearded charioteers with billowing cloaks. On top, bust of Sol, radiate (twelve rays), long wavy hair.
　　　Antike Helme 1988: 327–364 (G. Waurick). Image: arachne.dainst.org/entity/2399007.

K2a. Military Standards

1.　Plate 172.2
　　　Hexham Abbey.
　　　Corbridge.
　　　Sandstone.
　　　Terminus ante quem: AD 98.
　　　Funerary stele for Flavinus, standard bearer of the ala Petriana. Flavinus, on horseback, carries a long pole diagonally by his side, srmounted by a round signum decorated with the frontal bust of Sol, radiate, five rays (of the original 7?) surviving. Inscription. Often interpreted as the radiate portrait of an emperor. Frontal radiate depictions of emperors are quite rare, making the interpretation of this image as Sol both more likely and more straightforward.

Matern 2002: 259 B97; RIB 1172.

Image: photograph by F.J. Haverfield, prior to 1919 (in the public domain).

K3. Decorative Elements of Chariots

1. Plates 173.3, 173.4

   Boston, Museum of Fine Arts 03.983. Francis Bartlett Donation of 1900.

   Unknown.

   Bronze.

   Ca. AD 200.

   Rein guide for a chariot, with an elaborate sculptural decoration depicting the battle of gods and giants. The gods are represented by Sol and Luna standing in a fortress with a large gate and corner towers. Luna, velificans, has a small crescent above her head. Sol, head lost, is nude but for a *chlamys*. He is repelling a snake-legged giant attacking the fortress from the left. Sol's weapon is difficult to make out but appears to be a staff, possibly a whip. The attacking giant rests on the left-hand loop of the rein guide which consists of the protome of a griffin emerging from leaves. Below the fortress is a second snake-legged giant. The right-hand loop of the rein guide, the giant on it, and most of the defender against this giant are lost. The identification of the headless male figure as Sol seems likely, but cannot be certain. There is no obvious candidate for the third defending deity, largely lost.

   Comstock & Vermeule 1971: no. 671.

   Image: photograph © Museum of Fine Arts, Boston.

2. Plate 173.2

   Lyon, Musée et Théâtres romains Br 29.

   Les-Roches-de-Condrieu (Isère).

   Bronze.

   2nd–3rd c. AD.

   Roughly rectangular plaque, possibly decorative element of a chariot? (or of a parade harness?). Head of Sol, radiate (six rays), between the busts of Diana (quiver) and Juno (?) above the main figures (Bacchus and Silenus).

   LIMC Helios/Sol 268; LIMC Dionysus/Bacchus (in per. occ.) 115 (with refs); Matern 2002: 264 B137.

   Image: photograph © Conseil Général du Rhone, Musée de la Civilisation Gallo-Romaine.

K4. Sundials

1.   Plate 174.1
     Berlin, Staatliche Museen, Antikensammlung SK 1048.
     Athens.
     Marble.
     1st–2nd c. AD.
     Block of marble, originally of an altar (?), reworked as a sundial. Below
     the concave sundial, frontal face with "radiate" waving hair: Sol?
     Conze 1891: 417 no. 1048.
     Image: photograph courtesy Staatliche Museen, Berlin.

K5. Parapegmata
K5a. ... Image of Sol Preserved

1.   Dura Europos EA 23.
     Dura Europos.
     Stucco.
     AD 164–215.
     Graffito, fragmentary, of parapegma. Preserved are the busts of all seven
     planetary deities; Sol is radiate (seven rays) and holds a whip. Three busts
     recur below, including bust of Sol, radiate (ten rays), whip, and Luna.
     LIMC Helios/Sol 274 (with refs.) and 302a; Lehoux 2007: 170 B.ii.

2.   Plate 175.1
     Muséoparc Alésia.
     Alésia.
     Bronze.
     3rd c. AD.
     Bronze disc with a hole in the centre, incised busts of the seven plane-
     tary deities arranged in a circle along the edge. Sol is radiate (seven rays),
     wears a *chlamys* and has a whip behind his right shoulder.
     LIMC Helios/Sol 275 (with refs.).
     Image: photograph © Archives du Palais du Roure, Fondation Flandreysy-
     Espérandieu (Fonds Espérandieu A12), Avignon / Rémy.

3.   Plate 174.2
     Trier, Rheinisches Landesmuseum S.T. 12014.
     Altbachtal.
     Terracotta.
     3rd quarter 3rd c. AD.

Upper left-hand part of a parapegma; preserved are the busts of Saturn, Sol (radiate, five rays), Luna, Mars and Mercurius in the upper register, and the upper part of a next register.
Meyboom 1978: 785; LIMC Helios/Sol 286; Lehoux 2007: 176 B.ix.
Image: photograph © Rheinisches Landesmuseum, Trier.

4. Lost, but known from early 19th c. drawings and a terracotta copy.
Rome, Domus Aurea room 21.
Graffito in stucco.
Undated.
Parapegma incised into the stucco of a wall. Above: busts of the planetary deities-from Saturn to Venus-with attributes; Sol, radiate (eight rays), whip behind right shoulder. Below: zodiac circle between two vertical rows of 15 holes numbered I–XXX consecutively.
LIMC Helios/Sol 274; Gundel 1992: 45 fig. 17, 228 no. 69; Lehoux 2007: 168–70 B.i.

5. Arlon, Musée Luxembourgeois GR/C 63.
Unknown.
Limestone.
Undated.
Fragment of a parapegma; preserved are the heads of Saturn (not Luna, as Espérandieu says) and Sol (radiate, five rays). There is a hole below each bust.
LIMC Helios/Sol 277; Espérandieu V 4016; Duval 1953: 287; Meyboom 1978: 785 (with refs.); Lehoux 2007: 177–8 B.xii.

6. Plate 174.3
Trier, Rheinisches Landesmus. S.T. 14726.
Unknown.
Terracotta.
Undated.
Mould of a parapegma depicting the seven planetary deities (from Saturn to Venus).
LIMC Helios/Sol 286 (with refs.); Lehoux 2007: 176–7 B.x.
Image: photograph © Rheinisches Landesmuseum, Trier.

K5b. ... Image of Sol Lost

1. Stuttgart, Landesmuseum Württemberg R171.55.
Rottweil.

Terracotta (Terra Sigillata, probably Rheinzabern production).
2nd–3rd c. AD (Gundel).
Two fragments of a parapegma. Reconstructed as consisting of a double row with signs of the zodiac (part of Gemini and Capricorn preserved), a single row of planetary deities (lower right-hand corner with Jupiter and Venus preserved), and a row of thirty holes along the bottom.
Gundel 1992: 216 no. 36 (with refs); Meyboom 1978: 785; LIMC Helios/ Sol 286; Lehoux 2007: 178–9 B.xiii.

2.   Épinal, Musée départemental d'Art ancien et contemporain.
        Soulosse.
        Limestone.
        Undated.
        Fragment of a parapegma; preserved are the busts of Mars, Mercury, Jupiter and Venus.
        Meyboom 1978: 785; Sadurska 1979: 74, 1:7; Lehoux 2007: 177 B.xi.

        K5c. ... No Images
1.   Baltimore, Johns Hopkins University Archaeological Collection 5384 a/b.
        Posilippo.
        Marble.
        1st c. BC.
        Fragment of a parapegma; preserved are holes with accompanying inscriptions for four planetary deities (Saturn to Mars); below a row of geographical names, also accompanied by holes romae capvae calatiae benev[...
        Meyboom 1978: 784 (with refs.); Sadurska 1979: 75, 1:11; Lehoux 2007: 174 B.viii.

2.   Naples, Museo Nazionale 4072.
        Unknown.
        Marble.
        Undated.
        Fragment of a parapegma; only a small part of the accompanying inscriptions are preserved: mer]cvri iovis v[eneris..
        Meyboom 1978: 786 & n. 22; Sadurska 1979: 75, 1:10; Lehoux 2007: 173 B.v.

3.   Augst, Römermuseum 68.8167.
        Augst.
        stone.

Undated.

Parapegma.

Sadurska 1979: 1, 14.

K6. Pyxides, Chests, and the Like

1. Budapest, National Museum 20.1902, 23.

   Császár.

   Bronze.

   3rd–4th c. AD.

   Bronze fittings of a chest, discovered in a tomb in 1902. The precise position of the elements of the fittings is not certain (for a reasonable proposal cf. Buschhausen 1971 pl. 86). The following figures were part of the overall scheme: A. An arcaded row of the planetary deities; Sol, second from the left, is radiate, nude but for a *chlamys*, holds a globe in his left hand and has his right hand raised (Buschhausen suggests that Sol holds a whip in his right hand, but I see no sign of this in the photograph). B. Four roundels, grouped two and two, with the Good Shepherd (above) and Daniel in the Lion's den (below) forming one group, and the Sermon on the Mount (?) (above) and the sacrifice of Isaac (below) forming the other group. C. Two groups of two arcaded figures, primarily dancing women; possibly the seasons, but Buschhausen rejects this and speaks of a thiasos.

   Buschhausen 1971: A69 (pp. 140–144), pls. 86–89, with lit.

2. Budapest, National Museum Inv. 64/1903 19, 20, 21, 23, 24 and Intercisa museum.

   Intercisa. The fittings currently in the National Museum in Budapest were discovered in 1903 in a tomb. This tomb was not fully excavated until 1961 when the additional fittings were discovered. These are currently in the Intercisa museum.

   Bronze.

   2nd quarter 4th c. AD.

   Bronze fittings of a box or chest. The fittings consisted of three vertical bands, one along each side and a slightly broader one in the middle, connected with a decorative lattice-work of bronze strips. The side-bands each consist of four rectangles each containing a standing figure. The top figure was attached to the front side of the lid, the other three to the actual chest. The central band, more poorly preserved, consisted of two rows of smaller, vertical figures (six survive) on the chest itself, and one large figure in a roundel on the corresponding part of the side of lid. The figures on the left side, from top to bottom, are: Mars, Mars, Sol, and Mars, and on the right they are Jupiter, Jupiter, Minerva (seated) and Sol. Identical figures are from the same matrix. Sol is standing, frontal, head facing right, radiate (?), nude but for a *chlamys*, right hand raised and a whip in his left hand. The whip has previously been taken for a caduceus, leading to the erroneous identification of this figure as Mercury. The central panel on the side of the lid consists of a large roundel with Orpheus; in the four corners are small roundels with the bust of Sol (upper left-hand corner), radiate, facing right; Luna (upper right-hand corner); Chi-Rho (lower left-hand corner), and eagle (lower right-hand corner). (Buschhausen (1971, 134) reverses the lower roundels.) The corresponding central band on the front of the box depicts Lazarus (upper left), Moses striking the rock (upper right), the Good Shepherd (middle left), the sacrifice of Isaac (middle right, rather unclear), Jonah (lower left), and the healing of the blind (lower right). Above the upper figures, the bottom portion of a second impression of the Orpheus roundel has been preserved.

Buschhausen 1971: A65 (pp. 132–136) and pls. 79–82, with lit.

3.　　Plate 176.1
　　　Munich, Staatliche Antikensammlung, Inv. no. 514.
　　　Athens, environs of the Parliament (former Royal Palace), discovered in a
　　　shallow grave.
　　　Silver.
　　　The tomb contained a small bronze coin of Constantius II, giving a terminus post quem of at least AD 324 for the tomb.
　　　A small, hexagonal silver pyxis with lid. On the six sides, busts in profile of six of the seven planetary deities: Luna, Mars, Mercury, Venus, Saturn, and Sol. Sol is radiate. Other finds from the tomb, now lost, are reported to have been an "elegant" silver vase and a silver sistrum.
　　　Buschhausen 1971: B2 (pp. 179–181), pl. 6, with refs.
　　　Image: © Staatliche Antikensammlungen und Glyptothek, Munich；
　　　Photograph Renate Kühling.

4.　　Budapest, National Museum.
　　　Csázár.
　　　Bronze.
　　　Roman Imperial.
　　　Bronze fitting for the front of a box or chest, decorated primarily with intercolumnar reliefs of deities. In the lower right hand corner Sol on a frontal chariot, two horses jumping left and two right. Sol is radiate

and has raised his right hand and holds a whip (?) in his left. The other figures are: top row Diana, Minerva, and Fortuna; flanking the keyhole Bacchus (?) and Victoria; below the keyhole Victoria, Diana, Minerva, and Fortuna (same moulds); bottom row Hercules and Cerynian Hind, Mars (or Minerva, from a different mould) and Sol.
Buschhausen 1971: A39 (pp. 83–86) and Pls. 42–44,with lit.

5.   Budapest, National Museum, 40/1903, 23.
      Intercisa.
      Bronze.
      Roman Imperial.
      The four fragments of bronze fitting listed under this inventory number are said to include one that preserves the head, nimbate, and upper body of Sol with traces of a whip.
      Buschhausen 1971: A97 (pp. 164–5), with lit.

6.   Budapest, National Museum.
      Intercisa.
      Bronze.
      Roman Imperial.
      Various fragments of bronze fittings of a chest. They include fragments of a tondo with Sol on a frontal chariot; preserved are Sol's head with radiate nimbus, traces of a whip, and the head of the most right-hand horse.
      Buschhausen 1971: A102 (pp. 167–8), pl. 101, with lit.

7.   Cairo, Museum Inv. 9037.
      Achmim?
      Bronze.
      Roman Imperial.
      Small wooden box covered with bronze fittings decorated in relief. On the front, these include the bust of Sol (top left), radiate, and the bust of Luna (top right) with crescent.
      Buschhausen 1971: A31 (pp. 69–72) and pl. 34, with lit.

8.   Mainz, Römisch-Germanisches Zentralmuseum Inv. o 4652.
      Intercisa.
      Bronze.
      Roman Imperial.
      Small rectangular bronze relief, used as the fitting of a chest. Preserved are four figures above a floral motif. They are (from left to right) Mars,

Sol, Dea Roma, and Jupiter. The figures iconographically closely resemble those of the chest from Intercisa described above (K6.2).
Buschhausen 1971: A94 (pp. 162–3), fig. 5 & pl 98, with lit.

9. Braunschweig, Herzog Anton Ulrich-Museum MA 59.
   Unknown, probably produced in Metz
   Ivory and copper.
   9th–10th c. AD.
   Small box with carved ivory panels on sides and gabled lid. The lid panel above a side-panel with scene of the crucifixion depicts two Victories and a Hand of God holding a wreath, between Sol (left) in *quadriga* going right, right hand raised, and Luna (right) in *biga*.
   Kunst des Mittelalters, Herzog Anton Ulrich-Museum Braunschweig, Braunschweig 1985: 5 figs. 34.

10. Plate 176.2
    Baltimore, Walters Art Museum 71.116.
    Unknown.
    Ivory and bone.
    4th–5th c. AD.
    Relief panel, originally attached to a pyxis? Upper register: Jupiter, seated, in centre, framed by Sol (left), radiate (six rays), torch in his right hand, depicted in frontal squatting (!) position, head turned right towards Jupiter, and Luna (right), in profile to the left. To the left of Sol, Victory and a soldier. To the right of Luna: Minerva, standing (statue?) and two women, nude, one walking towards Jupiter, the other standing to the right of Minerva. Lower register: burning altar in centre; from the right, three figures, one of whom is Mercurius, lead a sacrificial bull. Two male figures stand behind them. On the left, two women walk towards the altar carrying square boxes on their heads; the second woman is holding a child by the hand. To the left of them, three dancing women.
    Unpublished?
    Image: photograph courtesy the Walters Art Gallery, Baltimore, under creative commons zero: no rights reserved-license.

   K7. Weights
1. Plate 177.1
   Boston, Museum of Fine Arts 1972.79.
   Reputedly from Istanbul.
   Bronze.

Ad 150–250.

Bust of Sol, radiate (seven rays), *chlamys*, atop mount Argaios. At the foot of the mountain, a dish of fruit.

Matern 2002: 248 B23.

Image: Photograph © Museum of Fine Arts, Boston. John Michael Rodocanachi Fund.

2. Avignon, Mus. Calvet J 307G.

Unknown.

Bronze.

Undated (too heavily corroded).

Bust of Sol (?), radiate (five rays).

Rolland 1965: 163 no. 369.

K8. Mirrors

1. Plate 177.2

Boston, Museum of Fine Arts 95.72.

Cosenza.

Bronze.

3rd c. BC.

Bronze mirror with incised decoration. Profile head of Sol, left, within a radiate circle.

R. D. De Puma, CSE, USA 2, 19, 23, 25–26 (no. 4), 72–75, figs. 4a–d; Carpino 2003: 17, 108, n. 50; 28, 113, n. 118.

Image: Photograph © Museum of Fine Arts, Boston. Catharine Page Perkins Fund.

K9. Other

1. Plate 177.3

Boston, Museum of Fine Arts 97.318-97.323.

Eretria, tomb of the Erotes.

Terracotta, painted and gilded.

310-240 BC.

Small roundel in the shape of a round shield, frontal bust of Sol, radiate (thirteen rays). A number of similar/identical shields, both round and oblong, are reported to have come from the same tomb.

LIMC Helios 150–1; Matern 2002: 250 B42.

Image: Photograph © Museum of Fine Arts, Boston. Catharine Page Perkins Fund.

2.   St Petersburg, Hermitage Inv. N 1091/5070.
       Oxus, temple (Bactria/Tajikistan).
       Silver with traces of gilding.
       3rd c. BC.
       Silver foil with relief bust of Sol, frontal, radiate (twelve rays).
       Litvinsky 2000.

3.   Plate 177.4
       London, British Museum, 1824,0405.3.
       Paramythia (Epirus).
       Bronze.
       2nd c. BC.
       Decorative attachment; frontal head of Sol, radiate (seven rays).
       Walters 1899: 273.
       Image: photograph © Trustees of the British Museum.

4.   Plate 177.5
       Athens, Agora Museum SS 1183.
       Athens, Agora.
       Terracotta.
       2nd c. BC.
       Amphora stamp from Rhodes. Sol, radiate, in *chiton* and *chlamys*, on a
       quadriga to the right, whip in right hand, reins in left. Around the image:
       Λ[--]ινου [Επὶ ἱερ]ρέως Εὐκρατίδα
       Moreno 1995: 185 fig. 4.26.4; Matern 2002: 61–2, 213 Q37 (with lit. and ref-
       erences to similar stamps on Rhodes and Delos).
       Image: courtesy American School of Classical Studies, Athens.

5.   Istanbul, Archaeology Museum 356.
       Pergamum.
       Marble.
       2nd c. BC.
       Richly decorated support of a table; decoration includes a small head of
       Sol, radiate.
       Mendel 1912: 573–578 no. 251 (esp. p. 575); Matern 2002: 168, 252 B52.

6.   Rhodes, Museum.
       Rhodes.
       Terracotta.
       ca. 100 BC.

Amphora stamp; Sol standing, radiate.

LIMC Helios 333.

7. Athens Acropolis Museum 2526.
Athens, Theatre of Dionysus.
Marble.
1st c. BC–1st c. AD.
Stone sphere with relief-decoration and magical inscriptions. On one side: Helios on a throne holding a long three-pronged staff in his left hand and a whip (?) in his right hand; between a dog and a lion. On the other side a lion, a snake and inscriptions.
LIMC Helios 371; Follet 2012.

8. Plate 178.1
Chaironeia, Museum.
Livadhia.
Limestone.
Late 1st c. BC–early 1st c. AD (?)
Stone sphere with bust of Sol, radiate (eleven rays), on one side and bust of Luna on the other side.
LIMC Helios 295; Matern 2002: 91 n. 532, 168, 251 B47, fig. 74.
Image: photograph © Hellenic Ministry of Culture and Sport, Ephorate of Antiquities of Boeotia.

9. London, British Museum 1814,0704.1184.
Unknown.
Bronze.
1st–2nd c. AD ?
Small oval bronze disc with profile bust of Sol (r.), radiate, in relief.
Marshall 1908: nr 1643.

10. Plate 179.1
Vatican, Medagliere.
Rome, environs of Circus Maximus.
Bronze.
2nd c. AD.
Bronze disc or phalera. Within a zodiac circle, Sol in *quadriga* ascends right, reins in left hand, right hand lowered. The horses jump up over clouds above which Lucifer flies with torch. Below, Tellus. In exergue: inventori lucis soli invicto augusto.

Guarducci 1983; Bergmann 1998, 247–8 pl. 46.4; Matern 2002: 223, Q104.
Image: photograph after Bergmann 1998.

11.   Lausanne, Musée Romain de Vidy.
       Vidy
       Bronze.
       Ca. AD 100–150.
       Bronze disc depicting the fall of Icarus. Below the bust of Sol (radiate, six
       rays), flies Daedalus. Icarus, below, has fallen; to the left lies Oceanus.
       Bérard & Hofstetter 1979; LIMC Helios/Sol Matern 2002: 281, K27.

12.   Nancy, Museum.
       Grand.
       Ivory.
       Mid 2nd c. AD (terminus ante quem AD 170).
       Ivory diptych with engraved astrological figures. In centre: frontal busts
       of Sol and Luna (Sol is not radiate) within concentric circles containing
       the signs of the zodiac and related letters and images.
       Abry 1993; Gundel 1992: 232–3 no. 82.

13.   Vacat

14.   Belgrade, National Museum 645/II.
       Unknown.
       Gold.
       2nd–3rd c. AD.
       Trapezoidal piece of gold foil depicting Sol, nude but for a *chlamys*, radi-
       ate, right hand raised, globe and whip in left hand.
       Popović 1996, 194 no. 152.

15.   Plates 179.3, 179.4
       Paris, Louvre MA 540.
       Rome.
       Marble.
       2nd–3rd c. AD.
       "Tabula Bianchini"; fragments of a marble tablet engraved with astrologi-
       cal table; star signs in the centre, enclosed within concentric circles, con-
       taining astrological and planetary symbols and images, including Sol.
       LIMC Helios/Sol 294; Gundel 1992, 111 fig. 51; 226 no. 63.

Image: © RMN-Grand Palais / Art Resource, NY: ART150085. Photograph H. Lewandowski.

16. St.-Germain-en-Laye, Mus. Ant. Nat. MAN 52835.
Mathay.
Bronze.
2nd–3rd c. AD.
Rectangular fragment of a relief in bronze foil depicting 3 of the 7 planetary deities; Sol, not radiate, nude but for a *chlamys*, right hand raised, whip in left hand; Luna (small crescent above her forehead) and Mars.
LIMC Helios/Sol 287; Espérandieu VII, 37 no. 5289, Duval 1953: 287.

17. Brugg, Vindonissa Museum V80/1.73.
Windisch.
Bronze.
3rd c. AD.
Fragment of hammered bronze foil, decorated with three busts. Top: Sarapis above thunderbolt; center: Sol, radiate (eleven rays), *chiton* fastened over both shoulders, and four stars. Below, unidentifiable bust.
Kaufmann-Heinimann 1994: 105–6 pl. 71.

18. Eichstätt, Museum für Ur- und Frühgeschichte.
Pfünz, Dolichenum.
Bronze.
Severan.
Strip of bronze foil to which a medallion depicting the busts of Sol, radiate, and Luna, crescent, within a dotted circle is attached.
Hörig & Schwertheim 1987: 483.c

19. Kingscote, Gloucestershire.
Roman Villa.
Copper alloy.
Late 3rd c. AD.
Small cube matrix for hammered metal foil with scenes in intaglio on all six sides: 1. bust of Sol, radiate, right, inscribed: sol invictvs in mirror image; 2. Sol in frontal chariot, left hand raised, whip in right hand; 3. seated Roma; 4. Mars; 5. clasped hands; 6. hunting scene.
LIMC Helios/Sol 78; Henig 1977.

20. Plate 180.1
    Darmstadt, Hessisches Landesmuseum A 1956: 943,2.
    Butzbach.
    Silver, gilded.
    Ca. AD 250.
    Open worked rectangular decorative element: Sol, radiate (three rays),
    nude but for *chlamys*, right hand raised, whip (?) in left hand, ascending
    quadriga jumping to the right.
    LIMC Helios/Sol 153; Matern 2002: 66, 217 Q63 (with refs.); Pfahl 2006.
    Image: photograph © Hessisches Landesmuseum, Darmstadt.

21. Çanakkale, Museum 33-236.
    Troy.
    Marble.
    3rd c. AD.
    Small tablet decorated in relief; preserved is the breast of a man on which
    (lower right) is depicted a bust of Sol, radiate.
    LIMC Helios 156.

22. Cambridge, Fitzwilliam Museum
    Qanawat (Kanatha), Syria
    basalt
    3rd c. AD
    A shrine that originally supported a lamp; the shrine had reliefs on three
    sides and a door frame (open) on the fourth. On the right side, bust of Sol,
    radiate (nine rays), *chlamys* and on the left side a bust of Luna. On the
    rear an acanthus leaf and an inscription: Λύχνος Μαλειχάθιου.
    Budde & Nicholls 1964, 78–9 no. 126, pl. 42.
    Images: arachne.dainst.org/entity/1112631.

23. Plate 180.2
    Columbia, University of Missouri, Museum of Art and Archaeology 84.53
    Syria
    Bronze
    3rd c. AD?
    Globe on a square base-originally a Victory on the globe. On one side of
    base, incised busts of Sol, radiate (seven rays), *chlamys*, and Luna.
    Lane 1989/90.
    Image: photograph © Museum of Art and Archaeology, University of
    Missouri-Columbia. Weinberg Fund.

24. Private Collection.
    Caesarea Maritima.
    Wood.
    3rd c. AD?
    Part of a wooden object, found at Caesarea Maritima in the mid 1980s.
    Within a zodiac circle, a solar deity, radiate, *chlamys*, body armor,
    right hand raised, left arm lost. On other side, remnants of a personal
    horoscope.
    Ovadiah & Mucznik 1996.
    Not Sol, but Near Eastern solar deity. He is not wearing a cap, as Ovadiah
    & Mucznik believe.

25. Hamburg, Museum für Kunst und Gewerbe 1969.152.
    Unknown.
    Silver.
    3rd c. AD.
    Relief in silver foil. A goddess on horseback and a woman in a peplos
    between the busts of Jupiter (left) and Sol (right), with an eagle.
    Matern 2002: 264 B136.

26. London, British Museum 1857.1013.1.
    Italy (Rome?).
    Ivory.
    2nd quarter 4th c. AD.
    Diptych leaf depicting the apotheosis of an emperor. In the upper right-
    hand corner, behind a partial zodiac, bust of Sol, radiate.
    LIMC Helios/Sol 169; Gundel 1992: 140 fig. 59 & 260 no. 191.

27. Plates 181.1, 181.2
    Paris, Louvre OA 9062.
    Unknown.
    Ivory.
    Ca. AD 400.
    Diptych showing imperial priest as donor of animal games. Above the
    priest, on both leaves, busts of Sol (left) and Luna (right). Sol, radiate,
    chlamys, has five rays on the right-hand leaf; on the left-hand leaf the
    number of rays is indistinguishable.
    LIMC Helios/Sol 399.
    Image: photograph © Erich Lessing / Art Resource, NY, ART209125.

28.   Budapest, National Museum Inv. 64/190318.
       Intercisa.
       Silver.
       Roman Imperial.
       Silver relief of uncertain function, reused as a metal fitting with a key-
       hole. In the centre, a roundel with Sol on a frontal chariot, two horses
       to the left, and two to the right. Sol is radiate, has his right hand raised,
       holds a globe in his left, and is dressed in a *chiton* and billowing *chlamys*.
       In the background a crescent moon and three stars. The lower right-hand
       portion of the central scene is pierced by a large, horizontal keyhole.
       The central scene is between two Corinthian spiral columns, secondary
       additions that damage and partially cover four small roundels that origi-
       nally occupied the four corners around the central scene. The scenes in
       these four roundels are difficult to make out. Buschhausen identifies a
       leaf (upper left), a hand (lower left), a hippocamp (lower right); noth-
       ing can be made of the scene in the upper right-hand roundel. The left-
       hand column is set on a normal base, but the right-hand column rests
       on an inverted Corinthian capital. Above Sol and the pillars is a narrow
       frieze with hunting scenes between trees. One complete scene (winged
       putto and leopard) has been preserved (left), followed (right) by a scene
       with two animals (a lion and his prey) the latter of which was largely cut
       away when the relief was reused. Below Sol and the columns is a single,
       wavy vine. The fitting was fastened over the keyhole with Medusa-headed
       bosses.
       Buschhausen 1971: A14 (pp. 41–44) and Pl. 15, with lit.

29.   Vatican, Bibliotheca Apostolica Cod. Vat. Gr. 1291 fol. 9r.
       Manuscript illumination.
       9th c. copy of original of mid-3rd c. AD.
       Sol, radiate, wearing a *chiton* and *chlamys*, right hand raised, globe and
       whip in left hand, in frontal chariot in central tondo surrounded by five
       concentric rings with the hours (personified), their names (in Greek), the
       months (personified), their names, and the signs of the zodiac.
       LIMC Helios/Sol 293; Gundel 1992: 132, 318 no. 417, pl. 6.
       Image available at https://digi.vatlib.it/view/MSS_Vat.gr.1291 (December 4,
       2017).

30.   Vatican, Bibliotheca Apostolica Cod. Vat. Barb. Lat. 2154 (part B fo. 11r).
       Manuscript illumination.
       Codex calendar of AD 354; 9th c. copy of the original of the mid-4th c. AD.

Sol standing, radiate, *chiton* and *chlamys*, right hand raised, globe and whip in left hand.
LIMC Helios/Sol 92; Salzman 1991.
Image available at https://digi.vatlib.it/view/MSS_Barb.lat.2154.pt.B (December 4, 2017).

31. Ostia, Museum Inv. 4151–4157.
Ostia.
Bronze.
Undated.
Seven rectangular plaques, of which five each bear a sign of the zodiac and one depicts Sol, radiate, nude but for a *chlamys*, right hand raised, whip in left hand.
LIMC Helios/Sol 298; Gundel 1992: 264 no. 205; Matern 2002: 106, 233 I15.

32. Rome, Musei Capitolini 75.
Rome.
Marble, giallo antico.
Late 1st c. BC–1st c. AD.
Relief, fragment, with scenes from the shield of Achilles and text of Iliad 18, 483–557. Sol in his *quadriga* right is in the far left just under the inscription. Luna in her *biga* left is on the outer rim below, between two columns of text. An inscription in larger letters than the homeric text identifies this as the ασπις Αχιληος Θεοδωρ[ηος καθ' Ομηρον] or [ηος η τεχνη]. Squire (2012: 3–4) prefers the former. Columns of the Homeric text (the *ekphrasis* of the shield of Achilles) begin on the convex edge of the shield and continue on the back. Given its small size and the manner in which the text is presented, this shield is closely related to the Tabulae Iliacae.
Squire, M.J. 201, 1–30; LIMC Helios/Sol 405.

33. Private Collection.
"Eastern Mediterranean".
Gold.
Undated.
Gold foil reliefs from a tomb: 1. Decorative plaques of a headband depicting the 7 planetary deities; bust of Sol, radiate (seven rays), *chlamys*. 2. Relief of the head of Sol. 3. Relief of the head of Sol.
Matern 2002: 264 B141.

34.   Plates 181.3, 181.4
      Columbia, Univ. of Missouri, Museum of Art and Archaeology 90.7.
      Unknown.
      Bronze.
      Undated.
      Roundel: above, centre, bearded male bust velificans, below left, bust of
      Sol, radiate (four rays), *chlamys*, and right Luna on upturned crescent;
      7 stars in field.
      Unpublished.
      Image: photograph © Museum of Art and Archaeology, University of
      Missouri-Columbia. Weinberg Fund.

35.   Plate 182.1
      London, British Museum 1856,0701.33.
      Unknown.
      Bronze.
      Undated.
      Castration tongs, decorated with busts of various deities: left (from back
      to front): Tyche with mural crown, protome of a horse, Mercurius, Jupiter,
      Venus (?), Venus (?), goddess (Venus again?), protome of a bull, lion's
      head; right: goddess (?) behind protome of a horse, Mars, Luna, Sol (six
      rays), Saturn, bull, lion.
      Hobbs & Jackson 2010: 114 fig. 88; Glass & Watkin 1997, 375 & n. 12.
      Image: photograph © Trustees of the British Museum.

36.   Trier, Rheinisches Landesmuseum G 105.
      Unknown.
      Bronze.
      Undated.
      Bronze disc with scene in relief (rough, worn) depicting Sol (radiate?),
      nude (except for a *chlamys*?) in *quadriga* to the right above reclining
      Oceanus (left) and Tellus (right).
      LIMC Helios/Sol 154; Matern 2002: 72–3, 225 Q112.

-37. Private Collection.
      Unknown.
      Copper.
      Roman imperial.
      Oval disc, obverse convex, depicting the seven planetary deities and
      magical inscriptions. From left to right: Saturn, Jupiter, Mars, Sol, Venus,
      Mercurius, and Luna. Sol is in a frontal *quadriga*, two horses jumping to

the left, and two to the right. He holds a whip in his raised right hand. For the long magical inscription see Keil 1946, 136. The planets are depicted according to their distance from earth in the geocentric system.
LIMC Helios/Sol 236; Keil 1946.

38. Plate 179.2
London British Museum 1899,1201.2.
Pessinus.
Silver.
3rd c. AD.
Leaf disc in silver foil. On the disc, frontal bust of Sol, radiate (eleven rays), *chlamys*. Behind each shoulder the protome of a horse.
Walters 1921: no. 227.
Image: photograph © Trustees of the British Museum.

39. Plate 182.2
London British Museum 2003,0901.18.
Baldock, Ashwell, metal detector find.
Silver.
Undated.
A leaf-shaped votive (?) plaque depicting Roma seated on a pile of shields, facing left, helmeted, upright spear in left hand, statuette of Victory on her outstretched right hand. At the lower left, facing Roma, a small suppliant figure, damaged. Above the main scene a frontal bust of Sol, radiate (nine rays), draped, whip behind left shoulder. In the apex a small upturned crescent and star (?).
Unpublished.
Image: photograph © Trustees of the British Museum.

40. Plate 182.3
London, British Museum 1865,0720.33.
Corfu, Roman tomb.
Silver relief set in an ivory stud.
Undated.
Frontal bust of Sol, radiate (seven rays).
Walters 1921: 68.
Image: photograph © Trustees of the British Museum.

41. Plate 182.4
Berlin, Staatliche Museen, Antikensammlung Misc. 8170a & b.
Rome.

Gilded bronze.

1st c. AD (Matern).

Two aedicula-shaped bronze plaques, both damaged, connected by hinges; left-hand plaque: seated Sabazius surrounded by cult symbols, in tympanum eagle. Right-hand plaque: throning Cybele between Mercurius and Attis; in tympanum frontal head of Sol (seven rays) above *quadriga*, two horses' protomes jumping left, two to the right. A second set from the same mould also survives.

LIMC Helios/Sol 229; Vermaseren 1977: 82 no. 304; Matern 2002: 53, 56, 215 Q48.

Image: photograph courtesy Staatliche Museen, Berlin.

L. Coins and Medallions (Selection)[23]
L1. Coins of the Roman Republic

1.   Plates 183.1, 183.2

Anonymous

Uncia

Rome

217-215 BC

Obv.: facing bust of Sol, draped and radiate, on left a dot (signifies denomination).

Rev.: upturned crescent, two stars and an orb.

RRC 39/4; LIMC Helios/Sol 18.

Image ANS 1969.83.100 courtesy American Numismatic Society open database policy.

2.   Plate 183.3

M. Aburius

Denarius

---

23   The aim of this section is to give an impression of the main types of sol-images used on Roman coins (L1 and L2), medallions, including contorniates (L3) and Tesserae (L4). The bulk of this section is devoted to coins, and it should be noted that no account is taken of how common or rare coins are, and very little attempt has been made to extend the list beyond what is presented by the RIC. Furthermore, multiple issues of coins bearing the same type of image (but from different dies, with different obverses and other details) under the same emperor are generally listed under a single catalogue number. It must be stressed, therefore, that this list gives absolutely no indication of how common or uncommon specific coins depicting Sol were. No attempt has been made to incorporate Roman provincial coins. The medallions collected in section L3 also represent only those mentioned in a few of the most important corpora. The section on tesserae relies largely on a single source and does not come anywhere close to indicating the actual numbers of these overlooked items that have actually been excavated.

Rome

132 BC

Obv.: head of Roma, helmeted.

Rev.: Sol radiate, wearing *chiton* and *chlamys*, driving a *quadriga* right, holding whip in his raised right hand and reins in his left.

LIMC Helios/Sol 155; RRC 250/1.

Image: courtesy open access policy Yale University Art Gallery, 2001.87.676.

3. Plate 183.4

A. Manlius

Denarius

Rome

118–107 BC; 118 BC (Mattingly 1998, 156).

Obv.: head of Roma, helmeted.

Rev.: Sol radiate, wearing *chiton* (?), head turned right, standing in facing *quadriga*; on either side of the horses a star; an X on the left side of Sol, a crescent on the right; clouds or waves below the horses.

LIMC Helios/Sol 132; RRC 309/1.

Image: ANS 1944.100.648 courtesy American Numismatic Society open database policy.

4. Plates 183.9, 185.1

Cn. Cornelius Sisenna

Denarius

Rome

118-107 BC

Obv.: head of Roma, helmeted.

Rev.: Jupiter in *quadriga* right, holding thunderbolt in right hand and sceptre in left Above horses, radiate head of Sol facing Jupiter and a crescent. Star behind Jupiter and in front of horses. Below horses' hooves an anguipede giant with thunderbolt in right hand and left hand raised. It also appears as though there is a serpent (?) on right side of giant.

RRC 310/1.

Image: ANS 1944.100.712 courtesy American Numismatic Society open database policy.

5. Plates 7.2, 183.5, 183.6

Mn. Aquillius

Denarius

Rome

109 or 108 BC
Obv.: head of Sol right, radiate crown, X in front of neck.
Rev.: Luna in *biga* right, holding reins in both hands, crescent above her head, three stars above horses and one below.
LIMC Helios/Sol 319; RRC 303/7.
Image: courtesy open access policy Yale University Art Gallery, 2001.87.676.

6.   Plates 183.7, 183.8
       L. Lucretius Trio
       Denarius
       Rome
       76 BC
       Obv.: radiate head of Sol right.
       Rev.: upturned crescent and inscr. L(ucius) LUCRETI TRIO.
       LIMC Helios/Sol 320: RRC 390/1.
       Image: courtesy open access policy Yale University Art Gallery, 2001.87.1600.

7.   Plate 183.10
       C. Coelius Caldus
       Denarius
       Rome
       51 BC
       Obv.: head of C. Coelius Caldus, consul of 94 BC.
       Rev.. head of Sol right, radiate crown, behind neck a shield with thunderbolt, in front of neck a shield with star.
       RRC 437/1a–b; LIMC Helios/Sol 19.
       Image: ANS 1944.100.3250 courtesy American Numismatic Society open database policy.

8.   Plate 183.11
       Mn. Cordius
       Quinarius
       Rome
       46 BC
       Obv.: radiate head of Sol right.
       Rev.: eagle.
       RRC 463/4a–d.
       Image: https://numismatics.org/crro/id/rrc-463.4d made available under open database license.

9. Plates 183.13, 183.14
   L. Valerius Acisculus
   Denarius
   Rome
   45 BC
   Obv.: Radiate head of Sol right, behind his head is a pickaxe (acisculus).
   Rev.: Luna in a *biga* right, whip in left hand, crescent above her head.
   LIMC Helios/Sol 319; RRC 474/5.
   Image: courtesy open access policy Yale University Art Gallery, 2001.87.2093.

10. Plates 183.15, 183.16
    L. Mussidius Longus
    Denarius
    Rome
    42 BC
    Obv.: facing bust of Sol, draped and radiate.
    Rev.: shrine of Venus Cloacina.
    RRC 494/43a–b.
    Image: ANS 1937.158.328 courtesy American Numismatic Society open
    database policy.

11. Plates 183.17, 183.18
    P. Clodius
    Aureus and denarius
    Rome
    42 BC
    Obv.: radiate head of Sol right, quiver. Rev.: crescent and five stars.
    LIMC Helios/Sol 320; RRC 494/20a–b & 21.
    Image: courtesy open access policy Yale University Art Gallery, 2001.87.2113.

12. Plates 6.2, 183.12
    M. Antonius
    Denarius
    Moving with M. Antonius
    42 BC
    Obv.: bust of M. Antonius.
    Rev.: Within a distyle temple a facing bust of Sol, radiate nimbus and
    draped.
    RRC 496/1; LIMC Helios/Sol 21.
    Image: courtesy open access policy Yale University Art Gallery, 2001.87.2142.

13.   Plate 183.19
       M. Antonius
       Denarius
       Moving with M. Antonius
       42 BC
       Obv.: bust of M. Antonius, lituus.
       Rev.: radiate head of Sol right.
       RRC 496/2–3; LIMC Helios/Sol 22.
       Image: courtesy open access policy Yale University Art Gallery, 2001.87.2144.

14.   Plate 183.20
       M. Antonius
       Denarius
       Moving with M. Antonius
       38 BC
       Obv.: radiate head of Sol right.
       Rev.: M. Antony standing, capite velato, holding a lituus.
       RRC 533/2.
       Image: courtesy open access policy Yale University Art Gallery, 2001.87.2179.

       L2. Roman Imperial Coins[24]

Augustus, 27 BC–AD 14

1a.   Plates 7.1, 183.21–24
       L. Aquillius Florus
       Denarius
       Rome
       19 BC
       Obv.: head of Sol radiate, right.
       Rev.: a. Slow *quadriga* right.
       Image: ANS 1937.158.382 courtesy American Numismatic Society open
       database policy.

---

24   All images of Sol are on the reverse unless otherwise stated. The corresponding obverse
      image is a bust or head of the emperor unless otherwise stated. The issuing authority is
      the emperor, unless otherwise stated. One entry may cover multiple variants or issues. All
      dates are AD, unless otherwise stated.

1b.　As previous, but rev.: kneeling Parthian returning standard.
　　RIC 1 303 (a)–304 (b).
　　Image: ANS 1944.100.38319, courtesy American Numismatic Society open database policy.

Vespasian, 69–79

2.　Plates 184.1, 184.2
　　Denarius
　　Rome
　　74
　　Facing head of Sol, radiate.
　　LIMC Helios/Sol 410; RIC 2.1 689.
　　Image: Photo British Museum 1897,0305.82, © Trustees of the British Museum.

3.　Plate 184.3
　　Aureus
　　Rome
　　76
　　Obv. Bust of Titus or bust of Vespasian.
　　Rev. Aeternitas draped and veiled, standing left, holding head of Sol in right and head of Luna in left extended over a lighted altar which sits at her feet.
　　LIMC Helios/Sol 336; RIC 2.1 838, 839, 856, 866, 867.
　　Image: photograph ANS 1954.256.9 courtesy American Numismatic Society open database policy.

4.　Plate 184.5
　　Denarius
　　Rome
　　79
　　Radiate figure, probably Augustus (and definitely not Sol) standing facing on rostral column, holding a long spear or staff with his right hand and possibly a parazonium in his left hand (although it may be a fold of his cloak).
　　RIC 2.1 1064–66 (each with a different obverse bust).
　　Image: photograph ANS 1944.100.39947 courtesy American Numismatic Society open database policy.

Titus, 79–81

5. Plate 184.6
Aureus and denarius.
Rome
79
As L2.4.
RIC 2.1 45 (aureus). Similar, but with differing obverse busts: 9, 27, 44 (aurei) and 10, 28, 46 and 47 (denarii).
Image: photograph of British Museum 1995,0716.1 available on the Online Coins of the Roman Empire Database under the open database policy.[25]

6. Plate 184.4
Aureus
Rome
76
Obv. Bust of Titus or bust of Vespasian.
Rev. Aeternitas draped and veiled, standing left, holding head of Sol in right and head of Luna in left extended over a lighted altar which sits at her feet.
RIC 2.1 Vespasian 856, 866, 867.
Image: photograph of British Museum R.10334, available at OCRE under ODbL.

Domitian, 81–96

7. Plate 184.7
As, Dupondius
Rome
85
As L2.3
RIC II.1 297a, 366, 375, 376, 411,
Image: photograph of a coin in a private collection.

Trajan, 98–117

8. Plates 184.9, 184.10
Denarius
Rome

---

25 Henceforth abbreviated as OCRE.

112 (Komnick 2001)
As L1.6 (76 BC), re-issued by Trajan (restored coin).
LIMC Helios/Sol 320; RIC II 785.
Image: photograph of British Museum 1841, 0726.1230, © Trustees of the British Museum.

9. Denarius
Rome
112 (Komnick 2001)
As L1.9 (49 BC), re-issued by Trajan (restored coin).
LIMC Helios/Sol 319; RIC II 803.

10. Plate 184.8
Denarius
Rome
103–117
Aeternitas draped and veiled, standing, holding head of Sol on right and head of Luna on left hand
RIC II 91–92 (103–111), 229 (111), 241–242 (112–117).
Image: photograph of ANS 1944.100.43565 courtesy American Numismatic Society open database policy.

11. Plates 184.11, 195.1
Aureus, Denarius
Rome
114–117
Bust of Sol radiate and draped, right.
RIC II 326–330 (114), 341–342 (114–117); LIMC Helios/Sol 79.
Image: photograph of ANS 1958.214.16 courtesy American Numismatic Society open database policy.

Hadrian, 117–138

12. Plate 184.12
Aureus, Dupondius, quadrans
Rome and uncertain
117–128
As L2.11.

RIC II, 1.6, 20 (117), 43a–c (118), 145 (123, uncertain mint), all aurei, 661 (126–128), dupondius, BMCRE 3, 1860 (117–138; bust of Sol on obverse), quadrans.
LIMC Helios/Sol 80.
Image: photograph of ANS 1986.147.2 courtesy American Numismatic Society open database policy.

13.   Plate 184.13
       Aureus
       Rome
       125–128
       Sol, radiate, in *quadriga* right, holding reins in right hand.
       LIMC Helios/Sol 156; RIC II 167.
       Image: b/w photograph © Trustees of the British Museum.

14.   Plates 184.14, 195.2
       Aureus
       Rome
       125–128
       As L2.13 but *quadriga* left.
       RIC II 168.
       Image: photograph of Münzkabinett Wien ID61010, available on OCRE under the open database policy.

15.   Plates 184.15, 186.1
       Dupondius, Sestertius, Denarius
       Rome
       118–138
       As L2.10
       RIC II 38, 48 (118), 81 (119–125), 114–115 (119–122), 597a–d (119–121), 744 (134–138).
       Image: photograph of ANS 1944.100.45634, courtesy American Numismatic Society open database policy.

16.   Plates 184.16, 186.2, 195.4
       Aureus
       Rome
       134–138

Roma seated left on cuirass, holding heads of Sol and Luna and spear, behind shield. LIMC Helios/Sol 337; RIC II 263.
Image: photograph © Trustees of the British Museum.

Antoninus Pius, 138–161

17. Plate 184.21
    Aureus
    Rome
    141–161
    Obv.: Bust of Faustina.
    Rev.: Faustina standing in a *quadriga* left, holding a sceptre; the *quadriga* is being driven by a charioteer tentatively identified as Sol, bending forward towards the horses.
    RIC III 383a–c.
    No iconographic reason to identify the charioteer as Sol.
    Image: photograph © Trustees of the British Museum.

Commodus, 180–192

18. Plate 184.17
    Aureus
    Rome
    185
    Bust of Sol, radiate and draped, right.
    RIC III 119; LIMC Helios/Sol81.
    Image: photograph © Trustees of the British Museum.

Septimius Severus, 193–211

19. Plate 184.18
    Denarius
    Laodicea ad Mare and Rome
    196–208
    Sol, nude but for a *chlamys*, radiate, standing left, right hand raised and whip in left hand.
    LIMC Helios/Sol 104; Rome: RIC IV.1 101 (197), 115, 117, 742, 744, 749 (197–198), 217 (208); Laodicea: 489 (196–197), 492 (197).
    Image: photograph British Museum 1867,0101.748, © Trustees of the British Museum.

20.   Plate 184.19
      Aureus, Denarius
      Rome
      201–210
      Bust of Sol right, radiate, draped.
      RIC IV.1 282; LIMC Helios/Sol 82.
      Image: photograph coin in private collection.

21.   Plates 184.20, 195.5
      Aureus
      Rome
      197
      Sol standing in a *quadriga* rising up to the right, right hand raised and
      reins in left. Lucifer, with torch, flies ahead of the *quadriga*, above the
      horses; below and in front of the horses: clouds or rocky terrain and Tellus
      reclining right.
      LIMC Helios/Sol 157; RIC IV.1, 102.
      Image: courtesy open access policy Yale University Art Gallery,
      ILE2013.17.259.

-21a. Variant, whip in right hand.

Caracalla and Geta under Septimius Severus

22.   Plate 184.22
      As, dupondius, sestertius, denarius, aureus
      Rome
      199–210
      Obv.: Bust of Caracalla.
      Rev.: Male youth, nude except for cloak hanging loose over left shoulder,
      standing, head left, globe in right hand, spear in left.
      RIC IV.1 Caracalla 30a–b, 39a–40, 55a, 141, 407, 408a–b, 410, 412, 474.
      Image: photograph of ANS 1948.19.1546, courtesy American Numismatic
      Society open database policy.
      This male youth is usually described as Sol and said to be radiate, but
      he is not wearing a *chlamys*, a spear is not an attribute of Sol, and I do
      not know of any coin on which the supposed rays are actually visible.
      Therefore the identification as Sol should be rejected.

23. Plate 184.23
Aureus
Rome
203–210
Obv.: Bust of Geta or Caracalla.
Rev.: bust of Sol, radiate and draped, right. RIC IV.1 50 (Geta), 163 (Caracalla). LIMC Helios/Sol 83.
Image: in the public domain.

Geta, co-emperor 211

24. Denarius
Laodicea ad Mare
211
Sol, nude but for a *chlamys*, standing left, right hand and whip in left hand.
RIC IV.1 108.

Caracalla, 211–217

25. Plate 184.24
Denarius, antoninianus, aureus, gold multiple
Rome
214–216
Sol, nude but for a *chlamys*, radiate standing left, right hand raised, globe in left hand.
LIMC Helios/Sol 106; RIC IV.1 245, 264a–e, 281a–d.
Image: photograph of ANS 1944.100.51561, courtesy American Numismatic Society open database policy.

26. Plate 187.1
As, dupondius, sestertius, denarius, antoninianus, aureus
Rome
215–217
Sol, nude but for a *chlamys*, radiate, mounting *quadriga* left, right hand holding reins, whip in left hand.
LIMC Helios/Sol 158; RIC IV.1 265a–h, 282a–f, 294a, c 543a–b, 551, 556, 562, 566, 570.

Image: photograph of ANS 1944.100.51563, courtesy American Numismatic Society open database policy.

26a. Plate 187.2
      As L2.26, but with raised right arm, rather than holding reins.
      AD 217
      RIC IV.1 294B.
      Image: photograph of British Museum R12688, made available at OCRE under ODbL.

27.   Plate 187.3
      Denarius, antoninianus, aureus
      Rome
      217
      Sol, nude but for a *chlamys*, radiate, standing left, right hand raised, whip in left hand.
      LIMC Helios/Sol 105; RIC IV.1 293a–f.
      Image: photograph of ANS 1944.100.51572, courtesy American Numismatic Society open database policy.

28.   As
      Rome
      216
      As L2.22
      RIC IV.1 563.

Heliogabalus, 218–222

29.   Plate 187.4
      Aureus
      Antioch
      218–222
      Sol, nude but for a *chlamys*, radiate, walking right, holding a thunderbolt in raised right hand.
      LIMC Helios/Sol 118; RIC IV.2 198.
      Image: photograph © Trustees of the British Museum.

30.   Plate 187.5
      As, denarius
      Rome
      219–220

Sol, nude but for a *chlamys*, radiate, standing left, right hand raised, whip in left hand.

LIMC Helios/Sol 105; RIC IV.2 17a–b, 303.

Image: photograph of ANS 1944.100.51894, courtesy American Numismatic Society open database policy.

31. Plate 187.6

    As, dupondius, sestertius, denarius

    Rome

    218–222

    Sol, nude but for a *chlamys*, radiate, advancing left, right hand raised and whip in left hand; in field, star.

    LIMC Helios/Sol 119; RIC IV.2 28a–b, d, 40a–b, 41, 63, 289b–c, 300b, d, 301–302, 318b, d, 319, 320b, d.

    Image: photograph of ANS 1944.100.52303, courtesy American Numismatic Society open database policy.

32. Plate 187.7

    Denarius, aureus

    Rome

    221

    Sol, nude but for a *chlamys*, radiate, standing front, head turned right, right hand raised, whip in left hand; in field, star.

    RIC IV.2 37–38.

    Image: photograph of British Museum R.12695, made available at OCRE under ODbL.

33. Aureus

    Rome

    221

    As previous, but head turned left.

    RIC IV.2 39.

Severus Alexander, 222–235

34. Plate 187.8

    Denarius, Aureus

    Rome

    222, 230–231

    Sol, nude but for a *chlamys*, radiate, standing left, right hand raised, whip in left hand.

RIC IV.2 8, 100a–b,101a–b, 106.

Image: photograph of ANS 1944.100.52491, courtesy American Numismatic Society open database policy.

35. Plate 187.9

As, dupondius, sestertius

Rome

229–232

Sol, nude but for a *chlamys*, standing right, right hand raised, holding globe in left hand.

LIMC Helios/Sol 106; RIC IV.2 491, 503, 504, 515c–d, 516, 528c–d, 529, 530.

Image: photograph of ANS 1944.100.52611, courtesy American Numismatic Society open database policy.

36. Plate 187.10

As, dupondius, sestertius

Rome

230–232

Sol, nude but for a *chlamys*, standing front, head turned left, right hand raised and whip in left hand.

RIC IV.2 500–502, 511–513, 514f–g, 525b, d, 526, 527.

Image: photograph of ANS 1944.100.53272, courtesy American Numismatic Society open database policy.

37. Plate 187.11

As, dupondius, sestertius, quinarius, denarius, aureus

Rome

231–235

Sol, nude but for a *chlamys*, radiate, walking left, right hand raised, whip in left hand.

LIMC Helios/Sol 119; RIC IV.2 110b–c, 114c–d, 115a, c, 116, 119c–d, 120, 122–123, 125, 517, 531c–d, 532, 535b–d, f–g, 537b, d, 538c–d, 539f–g, 540b, d, 541c–d, 542f–g, 543c–d.

Image: photograph of ANS 1944.100.53274, courtesy American Numismatic Society open database policy.

38. Plate 187.12

Denarius

Rome

230

Sol, nude but for a *chlamys*, radiate, standing right, head turned left, right hand raised, globe in left hand.

RIC IV.2 102a–b.

Image: photograph of ANS 1948.19.1829, courtesy American Numismatic Society open database policy.

39. Plate 187.13
Quinarius, denarius, aureus
Rome
228–232
Sol, nude but for a *chlamys*, radiate, standing left, right hand raised and globe in left hand.

RIC IV.2 76, 109c–d, 111c–d, 112c–d, 113, 118.

Image: photograph of ANS 1944.100.52495, courtesy American Numismatic Society open database policy.

40. Denarius
Rome
232
Described as: "Sol, walking left, with rock (?)"

RIC IV.2 117.

Maximinus Thrax, 235–238

41. Denarius, sestertius
Rome and uncertain
235–238
Sol, radiate, nude but for a *chlamys*, standing left, right hand raised and whip in left hand.

RIC IV.2 101, 108.

Gordian III, 238–244

42. Antoninianus
Rome
239
Sol, nude but for a *chlamys*, radiate, standing left, right hand raised, globe in left hand.

RIC IV.3 31.

43.   Plate 187.14
      Antoninianus
      Antioch
      242–244
      As L2.42.
      RIC IV.3 213.
      Image: photograph of ANS 1923.151.40, courtesy American Numismatic
      Society open database policy.

44.   Plate 187.15
      Quinarius, denarius, antoninianus, aureus
      Antioch, Rome
      238–239 (Antioch); 241–243 (Rome)
      Sol, nude but for a *chlamys*, radiate, standing front, head left, right hand
      raised, globe in left hand.
      LIMC Helios/Sol 106; RIC IV.3 83, 97, 109, 111, 117 (Rome); 168 (Antioch).
      Image: photograph of ANS 1967.153.196, courtesy American Numismatic
      Society open database policy.

45.   Aureus
      Rome
      241–243
      Sol, standing front, head left, nude but for a *chlamys*, radiate, right hand
      raised, globe and whip in left hand.
      RIC IV.3 98.

46.   Aureus
      Rome
      241–243
      Sol, nude but for a *chlamys*, radiate, standing front, head left, globe in
      right hand, whip in left hand.
      RIC IV.3 98.

Philip I, 244–249

47.   Antoninianus
      Uncertain
      244–249
      Sol, nude but for a *chlamys*, radiate, standing front, head right, right hand
      raised, globe in left hand.
      RIC IV.3 90.

48. Antoninianus
    Rome
    244–249
    Sol, nude but for a *chlamys*, radiate, advancing left, right hand raised, whip in left hand.
    LIMC Helios/Sol 119; RIC IV.3 112.

49. Plate 187.16
    Antoninianus
    Rome
    246–247
    Obv.: bust of Philip II.
    Rev.: as L2.48.
    RIC IV.3 226.
    Image: photograph of ANS 1981.40.38, courtesy American Numismatic Society open database policy.

50. Antoninianus
    Antioch
    244–249
    Obv.: bust of Otacilia Severa.
    Rev.: Sol, nude but for a *chlamys*, radiate, standing left, right hand raised, globe in left hand.
    RIC IV.3 137

Valerian, co-ruler with Gallienus, 253–260

51. Plate 187.17
    Aureus, antoninianus
    Lugdunum, Rome
    257–258
    Sol, nude but for a *chlamys*, radiate, standing left, right hand raised, globe in left hand.
    RIC V.1 2 (Lugdunum), 106, 107 (Rome).
    Image: photograph of ANS 1944.100.27178: courtesy American Numismatic Society open database policy.

52. Plate 187.18
    Antoninianus
    Colonia Agrippinensis, Rome
    257–259

Sol, nude but for a *chlamys*, radiate, walking left, right hand raised, whip in left hand.

RIC V.1 10–13 (Lugdunum).

Image: photograph of the Digital Coin Collection of the University of Eichstätt 119, available on OCRE under ODbL.

53. Plate 187.19

As, dupondius, sestertius, quinarius, denarius, aureus

Rome

256–258

Sol, nude but for a *chlamys*, radiate, standing left, right hand raised, whip in left hand.

RIC V.1 46, 106, 107, 144, 148, 170, 187, 198.

Image: photograph of a coin in the Hardy Museum, University of Alberta, no inv. no.

54. Plate 187.20

Aureus, Antoninianus

Rome, Viminacium, Mediolanum

256–257

Sol, nude but for a *chlamys*, radiate, standing left, right hand raised, globe in left hand.

LIMC Helios/Sol 106; RIC V.1 47 (Rome), 211 (Viminacium), 228, 229, 232 (Mediolanum).

Image: photograph of ANS 1944.100.27220, courtesy American Numismatic Society open database policy.

55. Plate 187.21

Antoninianus

Rome

256

Sol, nude but for a *chlamys*, radiate, walking left, whip in right hand, right hand raised.

RIC V.1 142.

Image: photograph of a coin in the Hardy Museum, University of Alberta, no inv. no.

Saloninus (Caesar under Gallienus) 257–260

56. Antoninianus

Rome

257
Sol, nude but for a *chlamys*, radiate, standing left, holding a whip.
RIC V.1 24

Gallienus (joint reign) 253–260

57. Plate 187.22
Aureus, antoninianus, sestertius
Rome, Mediolanum
257–258
Sol, nude but for a *chlamys*, radiate, standing left, right hand raised, globe in left hand.
RIC V.1 86, 154, 229 (Rome), 302, 303, 373, 387, 388 (Mediolanum).
Image: photograph courtesy Gallienus.net.

58. Antoninianus
Rome
257–258
Sol, nude but for a *chlamys*, radiate, walking left, right hand raised, globe in left hand.
RIC V.1 154

59. Plate 187.23
Antoninianus, as
Rome
257–258
Sol, nude but for a *chlamys*, radiate, standing left, right hand raised, whip in left hand.
LIMC Helios/Sol 105; RIC V.1 106, 154, 273.
Image: photograph of ANS 1975.27.2, courtesy American Numismatic Society open database policy.

60. Plate 187.24
Antoninianus
Rome
255–257
Sol, nude but for a *chlamys*, radiate, walking left, right hand raised, whip in left hand.
RIC V.1 117, 119–121, 154.
Image: photograph courtesy Gallienus.net.

61. Sestertius
     Rome
     257–8
     Sol, nude but for a *chlamys*, radiate, walking left, right hand raised, left hand covered.
     RIC V.1 230

Gallienus 260–268

62. Plate 188.1
     Aureus, quinarius aureus, antoninianus, denarius.
     Rome, Mediolanum, Asia
     260–268
     Sol, nude but for a *chlamys*, radiate, standing left, right hand raised, globe in left hand.
     RIC V.1 24, 99, 119, 160, 251, 340, 348 (Rome), 465–466 (Mediolanum), 611, 620, 629, 630 (Asia).
     Image: photograph of ANS 1984.67.3198, courtesy American Numismatic Society open database policy.

63. Plate 188.2
     Aureus, quinarius aureus, antoninianus.
     Rome, Mediolanum, Asia.
     260–268
     Sol, nude but for a *chlamys*, radiate, standing left, right hand raised, whip in left hand.
     RIC V.1 62 (Rome), 448, 451, 494–496 (Mediolanum), 640, 658 (Asia).
     Image: photograph of ANS 1944.100.30365, courtesy American Numismatic Society open database policy.

64. Plate 188.3
     Aureus, antoninianus, denarius
     Rome, Asia
     260–268
     Sol, nude but for a *chlamys*, radiate, walking left, right hand raised, whip in left hand.
     RIC V.1 62, 248–250, 354 (Rome), 639 (Asia).
     Image: photograph of ANS 1944.100.30232, courtesy American Numismatic Society open database policy.

65. Antoninianus.
    Siscia
    260–268
    Sol, nude but for a *chlamys*, radiate, standing right, right hand raised, globe in left hand.
    RIC V.1 555.

66. Antoninianus.
    Rome
    260–268
    Sol, nude but for a *chlamys*, radiate, walking right, right hand raised, whip in left hand.
    RIC V.1 286.

67. Quinarius aureus.
    Rome
    260–268
    Sol, nude but for a *chlamys*, radiate, standing or walking left, whip in right, palm branch in left hand.
    RIC V.1 113, 114.

68. Antoninianus.
    Mediolanum
    260–268
    Sol, nude but for a *chlamys*, radiate, in *quadriga* left.
    RIC V.1 497–498.

69. Antoninianus.
    Rome
    260–268
    Obv.: bust of Salonina on crescent.
    Rev.: Sol, nude but for a *chlamys*, radiate, standing left, right hand raised, globe in left hand.
    RIC V.1 Salonina (2) 18.

Regalianus, usurper in Austria 260

70. Plate 188.4
    Antoninianus

Carnuntum

260

Sol, nude but for a *chlamys*, radiate, standing front, head right, right hand raised, whip in left hand.

LIMC Helios/Sol 105; RIC V.2 67.

Image: photograph courtesy Museum Carnuntum, Bad Deutsch Altenburg.

Macrianus Minor, usurper 260–261

71. Plate 188.5

Antoninianus.

Antioch.

260–261.

Sol, nude but for a *chlamys*, radiate, standing left, right hand raised, globe in left hand.

LIMC Helios/Sol 106; RIC V.2 12.

Image: photograph of ANS 1944.100.30782, courtesy American Numismatic Society open database policy.

Quietus, brother of Macrianus Minor, 260–261

72. Plate 188.6

Antoninianus

Antioch

260–261

Sol, nude but for a *chlamys*, radiate, standing left, right hand raised, globe in left hand.

RIC V.2 10

Image: photograph of ANS 1995.11.1823, courtesy American Numismatic Society open database policy.

Postumus, usurper in Gaul, 260–269

73. Plate 188.7

Aureus, antoninianus

Lugdunum, Colonia Agrippinensis

260–269

Sol, nude but for a *chlamys*, radiate, walking left, right hand raised, whip in left hand.

LIMC Helios/Sol 119; RIC V.2 31, 77 (Lugdunum), 316 (Colonia Agrippinensis).
Image: photograph of ANS 1995.11.1087, courtesy American Numismatic Society open database policy.

74. Plate 188.8
Aureus, Sestertius
Lugdunum
260–269
Sol, nude but for a *chlamys*, radiate, in *quadriga* left, right hand raised, whip in left hand.
LIMC Helios/Sol 158; RIC V.2 152; Rheinisches Bildarchiv rba_c007710.
Image: photograph courtesy R. Kuenker.

75. Plates 188.9, 196.1
Aureus, denarius
Colonia Agrippinensis
260–269
Jugate busts of Sol, radiate, draped, right, and Luna, with crescent in hair, draped, right, on crescent.
LIMC Helios/Sol 320a; RIC V.2 260, 336.
Image: photograph courtesy Sixbid.com, auction 327, lot 139.

76. Plate 188.10
Antoninianus
Colonia Agrippinensis
260–269
Bust of Sol, radiate, draped, right.
RIC V.2 317; LIMC Helios/Sol 84.
Image: photograph of ANS 1944.100.30992, courtesy American Numismatic Society open database policy.

76a. Plates 188.11, 196.2
Aureus.
Colonia Agrippinensis.
Autumn 261.
Three busts of Sol in a row; the central bust is frontal; the two lateral busts are profile, facing each other.
LIMC Helios/Sol 444; Woods 2012.
Image: in the public domain.

Claudius II Gothicus, 268–270

77. Plate 188.12
     Antoninianus
     Rome, Mediolanum, Cyzicus.
     268–270
     Sol, nude but for a *chlamys*, radiate, standing left, right hand raised, globe
     in left hand.
     LIMC Helios/Sol 106; RIC V.1 16–7, 76–8, 115–116 (Rome), 153–5 (Mediola-
     num), 270 (Cyzicus, consecration series).
     Image: photograph courtesy Ph. Gysen.

78. Plate 188.13
     Antoninianus
     Rome, Mediolanum, Antioch
     268–270
     Sol, nude but for a *chlamys*, radiate, standing left, right hand raised, whip
     in left hand.
     LIMC Helios/Sol 105; RIC V.1 78 (Rome), 155 (Mediolanum), 221 (Antioch).
     Image: photograph courtesy Ph. Gysen.

79. Plate 188.14
     Antoninianus
     Cyzicus
     270
     Sol, nude but for a *chlamys*, radiate, walking left, right hand raised, whip
     in left hand.
     RIC V.1 281 (consecration series).
     Image: photograph courtesy Ph. Gysen.

80. Plates 188.15, 196.5
     Antoninianus
     Antioch
     268–270
     Luna standing left, holding torch, facing Sol, nude but for a *chlamys*, radi-
     ate, standing right, right hand raised, whip in left hand.
     LIMC Helios/Sol 321; RIC V.1 198.
     Image: in the public domain.

Quintillus, brother of Claudius II Gothicus, 270

81. Plate 188.16
Quinarius, Antoninianus.
Rome.
270.
Sol, nude but for a *chlamys*, radiate, standing left, right hand raised, globe
in left hand.
LIMC Helios/Sol 106; RIC V.1 7, 40.
Image: photograph of ANS 1944.100.32705, courtesy American Numismatic Society open database policy.

82. Antoninianus
Mediolanum
270
Sol, nude but for a *chlamys*, radiate, running left, right hand raised and
whip in left hand; in field left, star.
RIC V.1 244 no. 56.

Victorinus, usurper in Gaul, 268–271

83. Plate 188.17
Aureus, antoninianus
Colonia Agrippinensis
268–271
Sol, nude but for a *chlamys*, radiate, walking left, right hand raised, whip
in left hand.
LIMC Helios/Sol 119; RIC V.2 97, 112–5.
Image: photograph of ANS 1944.100.30890, courtesy American Numismatic Society open database policy.

84. Aureus
Unknown (Southern Gaul)
268–271
Obv.: jugate busts of Victorinus, laureate, left, and Sol, radiate, left.
Rev.: Pegasus, Hercules, wild boar, and Jupiter respectively.
RIC V.2, 12, 13, 21, 25

85.   Aureus
      Unknown mint in Southern Gaul.
      268–271
      Bust of Sol, radiate, right, facing bust of Diana, holding bow.
      RIC V.2 33.

86.   Plate 188.18
      Aureus
      Colonia Agrippinensis.
      268–271
      Bust of Sol, radiate, right
      RIC V.2 96; LIMC Helios/Sol 85.
      Image: photograph of British Museum 1864,1128.142, made available at
      OCRE under OdbL.

Aurelian, 270–275

87.   Plates 188.21, 188.22. 190.3, 190.4
      Double Aurelianus
      Serdica
      April–November 274
      Obv.: Male bust right, *chlamys* and cuirass, longish hair. SOL DOMINVS
      IMPERI(i) ROMANI.
      Rev.: Aurelian, capite velato, standing left, holding a patera in his right
      hand over a burning altar, and a sceptre in his left hand.
      RIC V.1 319; LIMC Helios/Sol 86.
      The obverse bust, widely identified as Sol on the basis of the legend, is an
      ambiguous image. The uncharacteristically long hair is suggestive of Sol,
      but the lack of rays and the hint of a cuirass on the right shoulder both
      suggest that this cannot be Sol. The coin is very rare.
      Image: Roma Numismatics ltd., auction VII lot 1232; photograph courtesy
      Roma Numismatics ltd.

-87a. Double Aurelianus
      Serdica
      April–November 274
      Obv.: radiate bust of Sol, right, *chlamys*, longish hair. SOL DOM(inus)
      IMP(erii) ROMANI.

Rev.: Aurelian, military attire, standing left, holding a patera in his right hand over a burning altar, and a sceptre in his left hand.

RIC V online, temporary number 2665, http://www.ric.mom.fr/en/coin/2665 (July 28, 2017).

Only one known, in a private collection. The radiate crown (without lemnisci) unequivocally identifies the obverse bust as Sol. There is no hint of a cuirass on the right shoulder.

88. Double Aurelianus
     Serdica
     April–November 274.
     Obv,: bust of Sol, radiate, right, above the protomes of four horses, right. SOL DOM(inus) IMP(erii) ROMANI
     Rev.: Aurelian, capite velato, standing left, holding a patera in his right hand over a burning altar, and a sceptre in his left hand.
     RIC V.1 320.

89. Plates 7.3, 188.23, 190.2
     Double Aurelianus
     Serdica
     April–November 274.
     Obv,: facing bust of Sol, radiate (seven rays), above the protomes of four horses, two jumping right, two left. SOL DOM(inus) IMP(erii) ROMANI
     Rev.: Aurelian, military attire, standing left, holding a patera in his right hand over a burning altar, and a sceptre in his left hand.
     LIMC Helios/Sol 133; RIC V.1 321.
     Image: Private Collection. Photograph courtesy S. Estiot.

90. Plate 188.19
     Aureus, antoninianus, denarius.
     Rome, Mediolanum, Siscia, Antioch, Cyzicus.
     270–275
     Sol, nude but for a *chlamys*, radiate, standing frontal or left, head left, right hand raised, globe in left hand.
     LIMC Helios/Sol 106; RIC V.1 18, 20, 44, 54, 67 (Rome), 136 (Mediolanum), 188 (Siscia), 371, 374, 375, 387 (Antioch), 397 (unknown); RIC V online temporary number 2951 (Cyzicus).
     Image: photograph of ANS 1944.100.32737, courtesy American Numismatic Society open database policy.

91.   Plate 188.20
      Aureus, Antoninianus
      Mediolanum, Siscia, Serdica, Antioch. Unknown
      270–275
      As L2.90, but with one captive.
      LIMC Helios/Sol 192; LIMC Helios/Sol 194; RIC V.1 135 (Mediolanum),
      185, 246–250, 257 (Siscia), 276, 277 (Serdica), 372, 373 (Antioch), 390
      (unknown).
      Image: photograph of ANS 1948.19.923, courtesy American Numismatic
      Society open database policy.

92.   Plate 188.24
      Aureus, antoninianus.
      Rome, Siscia, Serdica.
      272–275
      As L2.90 but between two captives.
      LIMC Helios/Sol 195RIC V.1 17 (Rome), 187, 251–3 (Siscia), 278–81, 307–11
      (Serdica).
      Image: photograph courtesy Ph. Gysen.

93.   Plate 189.1
      Antoninianus
      Siscia
      271–272
      Sol, nude but for a *chlamys*, radiate, standing or walking left, right hand
      raised, whip in left hand.
      RIC V.1 230.
      Image: photograph courtesy Ph. Gysen.

94.   Plate 189.2
      Antoninianus.
      Rome, Mediolanum, Siscia, Ticinum, Cyzicus, unknown mint.
      272–275
      Sol, nude but for a *chlamys*, radiate, walking left between two captives,
      right hand raised, globe in left hand.
      LIMC Helios/Sol 196; RIC V.1 61, 62 (Rome), 137, 150 (Mediolanum), 151, 154
      (Ticinum), 254 (Siscia), 263–25 (Cyzicus), 413–9 (unknown).
      Image: photograph of ANS 1944.100.32741. courtesy American Numis-
      matic Society open database policy.

95. Plate 189.3
    Antoninianus
    Antioch
    270–275
    As L2.94, but with one captive.
    RIC V.1 384.
    Image: photograph courtesy Ph. Gysen.

96. Plate 189.4
    Antoninianus
    Serdica
    April–November 274
    Sol, standing left, nude but for a *chlamys*, whip in left hand and extending a globe with his right hand to Jupiter, standing right. Between them, a captive.
    Image: photograph courtesy Ph. Gysen.

97. Plate 189.5
    Antoninianus
    Rome, Cyzicus, Antioch
    273–275
    Sol, nude but for a *chlamys*, radiate, standing or walking right, with a spear, sceptre or vexillum in his right hand, one captive.
    RIC V.1 65 (Rome), 367, RIC temp. 2999 (Cyzicus), 383 (Antioch).
    Image: photograph of ANS 1944.100.32918 courtesy American Numismatic Society open database policy.

98. Plates 189.6, 198.1
    Antoninianus
    Rome, Cyzicus
    273–274
    Sol, nude but for a *chlamys*, radiate, standing front, head left, right hand raised, globe in left hand, two captives.
    RIC V.1 63 (Rome), 361 (Cyzicus).
    Image: photograph courtesy Ph. Gysen.

99. Denarius
    Rome
    273–274

As L2.98, but with one captive.
RIC V.1 66.

100. Plate 189.7
Antoninianus
Serdica, Cyzicus
273
Emperor standing right, receiving globe from Sol, nude but for a *chlamys*, radiate, standing left, whip in left hand, captive between them.
LIMC Helios/Sol 417; RIC V.1 274–5, 283, 312–7 (Serdica), 353 (Cyzicus).

101. Plates 189.8, 198.2
Antoninianus
Serdica, Siscia
273–274
As L2.100, but without captive.
RIC V.1 282; http://www.ric.mom.fr/fr/coin/2268.
Image: in the public domain.

102. Plate 189.9
Antoninianus
Lugdunum
274–275
Sol, nude but for a *chlamys*, radiate, walking left, right hand raised, whip in left hand
LIMC Helios/Sol 119; RIC V.1 6, 7.
Image: photograph courtesy Ph. Gysen.

103. Plate 189.10
Aureus, antoninianus
Siscia, Antioch
275
As L2.102, with two captives.
RIC V.1 255 (Siscia); Estiot 165 (Antioch).
Image: photograph courtesy Ph. Gysen.

104. Plates 189.11, 200.2
Aureus, antoninianus
Rome, Ticinum, Siscia, Serdica
274–275

Fides, standing right, holding two military standards, facing Sol, nude but for a *chlamys*, radiate, standing left, right hand raised, globe in left hand. RIC V.1 19 (Rome), 152–3 (Ticinum), 189, 256 (Siscia), 284–5 (Serdica). Image: photograph courtesy Ph. Gysen.

105. Plates 189.13, 189.14
Antoninianus
Ticinum
270–275
Obv.: bust of Severina
Rev.: as L2.104.
LIMC Helios/Sol 209; RIC V.1 Severina 9.
Image: photograph courtesy Ph. Gysen.

106. Plate 189.12
Denarius, sestertius, as
Rome
274
Sol, nude but for a *chlamys*, radiate, right hand raised, globe in left hand, on *quadriga* left.
RIC V.1 77, 79–82.
Image: photograph courtesy Ph. Gysen.

107. Plate 189.15
Denarius
Rome
274
As l2.106, but whip instead of globe.
Estiot 13, 14.
Image: in the public domain.

108. Sestertius
Rome
274
Sol, nude but for a *chlamys*, radiate, right hand raised, globe and whip in left hand, on facing, split *quadriga*.
RIC V.1 78.

109. Plate 189.16
Antoninianus

Serdica

274

Hercules, standing right, receiving globe from Sol, nude but for a *chlamys*, radiate, standing left, whip in left hand, captive between them

RIC V.1 318.

Image: photograph courtesy Ph. Gysen.

110.   Plate 189.17

Antoninianus

Cyzicus

275

As L2.109, but Mars Invictus instead of Hercules.

LIMC Helios/Sol 237; RIC V.1 358–9.

Image: photograph of ANS 1956.163.220, courtesy American Numismatic Society open database policy.

111.   Plates 189.18, 200.3

Antoninianus

Cyzicus

275

As L2.110, but no captive.

RIC V.1 357.

Image: photograph courtesy Ph. Gysen.

112.   Plate 189.19

Antoninianus

Rome

275

Sol, nude but for a *chlamys*, radiate, walking right, laurel branch in right hand, bow in left hand, captive.

LIMC Helios/Sol 193; RIC V.1 64.

Image: photograph courtesy Ph. Gysen.

113.   Plate 189.20

Sestertius

Rome

275

Emperor and empress clasping hands, bust of Sol, radiate, above hands.

LIMC Helios/Sol 421; RIC V.1 75–6, 80.

Image: photograph of ANS 1944.100.32990 courtesy American Numismatic Society open database policy.

113a. Aureus, Aurelianus
Ticinum
274–275
Obv.: bust of Severina.
Reverse: as L2.113.
RIC V.1 Severina 9, 10; Estiot 78.

Vabalathus, Palmyra, 267–272

114. Plate 189.21
Antoninianus
Unknown mint
March–May 272
Sol, nude but for a *chlamys*, radiate, standing right, looking left, right hand raised, globe in left hand.
RIC V.2, 2; RIC online temp no. 3115.
Photo: courtesy Roma Numismatics ltd. https://www.acsearch.info/search.html?id=5576880.

Tetricus I, usurper in Gaul, 271–274

115. Antoninianus
Colonia Agrippensis or Southern Gallic mint.
271–274
Sol, nude but for a *chlamys*, radiate, standing right.
RIC V.2 64.

116. Plate 189.22
Antoninianus
Colonia Agrippensis or Southern Gallic mint.
271–274
Sol, nude but for a *chlamys*, radiate, walking left, right hand raised and whip in left hand.
LIMC Helios/Sol 105; RIC V.2 54, 82–84, 98, 162, 163, 183, 234, 246.
Image: photograph of ANS 1984.67.966, courtesy American Numismatic Society open database policy.

117. Antoninianus
Colonia Agrippensis or Southern Gallic mint.
271–274

As L2.116, but with a globe.

RIC V.2 99, 182, 245.

Tacitus, 275–276

118.　Plate 189.23

　　　Antoninianus

　　　Siscia, Serdica

　　　275–276

　　　Providentia standing right, with two ensigns, facing Sol, nude but for a *chlamys*, radiate, standing left, right hand raised, globe in left hand.

　　　LIMC Helios/Sol 209; RIC V.1 52, 53 (Gaul), 193–197 (Serdica).

　　　Image: photograph courtesy Ph. Gysen.

119.　Plate 189.24

　　　Aureus

　　　Antioch, Cyzicus

　　　November/December 275

　　　Sol, nude but for a *chlamys*, right hand raised, whip in left hand, riding a *quadriga* left.

　　　www.ric.mom.fr temp. no. 4005 (Cyzicus), no. 4052.(Antioch).

　　　Image: photograoh courtesy Sincona AG; https://www.acsearch.info/search.html?id=4452919.

119a.　Plate 191.1

　　　Aureus

　　　Antioch

　　　276

　　　Sol, nude but for a *chlamys*, standing frontal, head left, right hand raised, globe in left hand.

　　　www.ric.mom.fr temp. no. 4084.

　　　Image: photograph courtesy Fritz Rudolph Künker GMBH; https://www.acsearch.info/search.html?id=4840530

Florian, 276

120.　Plate 191.2

　　　Antoninianus

　　　Lugdunum

　　　July, 276

Sol, nude but for a *chlamys*, radiate, running left, right hand raised, whip in left hand.

RIC V.1 79.

Image: photograph courtesy Numismatik Naumann; https://www.ac search.info/search.html?id=2114482

121. As
Rome
276
Sol, nude but for a *chlamys*, radiate, walking left, right hand raised, whip in left hand.

RIC V.1 52.

May be Pax, with scepter and branch (cf. RIC V.1 51; www.ric.mom.fr temp no. 4256 & 4257).

122. Plate 191.3
Aureus
Rome, Cyzicus
July–August 276
Sol, nude but for a *chlamys*, radiate, in *quadriga* left, right hand raised, whip in left hand.

RIC V.1 17–18 (Rome), 114–115 (Cyzicus).

Image: photograph courtesy Numismatica Ars Classica; https://www.ac search.info/search.html?id=4954227

123. Plates 191.4, 200.5
Antoninianus
Serdica, Siscia
July–August 276
Fides or Providentia standing right, with two ensigns, facing Sol, nude but for a *chlamys*, radiate, standing left, right hand raised, left holding globe.

LIMC Helios/Sol 208; RIC V.1 110–113.

Image: photograph courtesy Ph. Gysen.

Probus, 276–282

124. Plate 191.5
Aureus, Antoninianus
Lugdunum, Rome, Ticinum, Cyzicus, Antioch
276–282

Sol, nude but for a *chlamys*, radiate, standing front, head left, right hand raised, globe in left hand.
LIMC Helios/Sol 106; RIC V.2 3 (Lugdunum), 134–5, 168 (Rome), 309, 347–53 (Ticinum), 891 (Cyzicus), 915 (Antioch).
Image: photograph courtesy Ph. Gysen.

125. Aureus, Antoninianus
Lugdunum, Ticinum, Siscia
276–282
Sol, nude but for a *chlamys*, radiate, standing left, right hand raised, globe in left hand.
RIC V.2 21, 22 (Lugdunum), 392, 589–90 (Ticinum), 669–72 (Siscia).

126. Plate 191.6
Antoninianus
Lugdunum
276–282
Sol, nude but for a *chlamys*, radiate, walking left, right hand raised, globe in left hand, two captives.
RIC V.2 44.
Image: photograph courtesy Ph. Gysen.

127. Plate 191.7
Antoninianus, as
Rome, Siscia
276–282
Sol, nude but for a *chlamys*, radiate, walking left, right hand raised, whip in left hand.
LIMC Helios/Sol 119; RIC V.2 293, 294 (Rome), 673, 700 (Siscia).
Image: photograph courtesy Ph. Gysen.

127a. Plate 191.7a
Antoninianus
Lugdunum
276–282
Sol, nude but for a *chlamys*, radiate, standing right, branch in right hand, bow in left hand.
RIC V.2 45

Image: photograph of ANS 1944.100.33094, courtesy American Numismatic Society open database policy.

128. Antoninianus
      Serdica
      276–282
      Sol, nude but for a *chlamys*, radiate, walking right, right hand raised.
      RIC V.2 835.

129. Plate 191.8
      Aureus, antoninianus
      Rome, Ticinum, Siscia, Cyzicus
      276–282
      Sol, nude but for a *chlamys*, head frontal, radiate, in frontal split *quadriga*, right hand raised, globe and whip in left hand.
      LIMC Helios/Sol 134; RIC V.2 204–5 (Rome), 311, 418–20 (Ticinum), 776–82 (Siscia), 911 (Cyzicus).
      Image: photograph courtesy Ph. Gysen.

129a. Plate 191.9
      Antoninianus
      Serdica
      276–282
      As L2.129, but no globe.
      RIC V.2 861–74.
      Image: photograph courtesy Ph. Gysen.

129b. Plates 191.10, 198.3
      As L2.129, but head left.
      Image: photograph courtesy Ph. Gysen

129c. Plate 191.11
      As L2.129a, but head left.
      Image: photograph courtesy Ph. Gysen.

129d. As L2.129, but head left and no whip.

130. Antoninianus
      Rome, Ticinum
      276–282

Sol, nude but for a *chlamys*, radiate, on a *quadriga* left, globe in right hand, whip in left hand.

RIC V.2 199 (Rome), 421–2 (Ticinum).

131.   Plate 191.13
       Antoninianus, quinarius
       Rome
       276–282
       As L2. 130, but right hand raised, globe and whip in left hand.
       RIC V.2 200–3, 206–8, 267.
       Image: photograph of ANS 1974.136.75 courtesy American Numismatic Society open database policy.

132.   Plate 191.12
       Antoninianus
       Siscia
       276–282
       As L2.131, but no globe.
       RIC V.2 767–775.
       Image: photograph courtesy Ph. Gysen.

133.   Plate 191.14
       Aureus
       Rome, Siscia, Serdica
       276–282
       Bust of Sol, radiate, right.
       RIC V.2 138 (Rome), 597 (Siscia), 829 (Serdica); LIMC Helios/Sol 87.
       Image: photograph courtesy Ph. Gysen.

134.   Antoninianus
       Rome
       276–282
       Bust of Sol, radiate, left.
       RIC V.2 209; LIMC Helios/Sol 87

135.   Plates 191.15, 198.4
       Antoninianus
       Ticinum
       276–282

Sol, nude but for a *chlamys*, radiate, standing in a hexastyle temple.
RIC V.2 354, 414–7, 536–8.
Image: photograph courtesy Ph. Gysen.

136.   Plate 191.16
Antoninianus
Lugdunum, Ticinum
276–282
Concordia, standing right, two ensigns, facing Sol, nude but for a *chlamys*,
radiate, standing left, right hand raised, globe in left hand.
RIC V.2 23 (Lugdunum), 323–4, 343, 344 (Ticinum).
Image: photograph courtesy Ph. Gysen.

137.   Plate 191.17
Antoninianus
Ticinum
276–282
Emperor left, treading on a captive and being crowned by Sol, nude but
for a *chlamys*, radiate, standing left behind the emperor, whip in left
hand.
RIC V.2, 404–6, 456.
Image: photograph courtesy Ph. Gysen.

138.   Plate 191.18
Aureus
Siscia, Serdica.
276–282
Obv.: jugate busts of emperor and Sol, radiate, left.
Rev.: Securitas seated left.
LIMC Helios/Sol 412; RIC V.2 596 (Siscia), 829 (Serdica).
Image courtesy Heritage Auctions; https://www.acsearch.info/search
.html?id=5570605.

139.   Plate 191.19
Antoninianus
Serdica
276–282
Providentia, two ensigns, facing Sol, nude but for a *chlamys*, radiate,
standing left, right hand raised, globe in left hand.

LIMC Helios/Sol 209; RIC V.2 844–50.
Image: photograph of ANS 1948.19.1001, courtesy American Numismatic Society open database policy.

Carus, 282–283

140. Plate 191.20
     Antoninianus.
     Rome.
     282–283.
     Sol, nude but for a *chlamys*, radiate, walking left, right hand raised, whip in left hand.
     LIMC Helios/Sol 119; RIC V.2 35–6.
     Image: photograph of ANS 1944.100.36337, courtesy American Numismatic Society open database policy.

141. Plates 191.21, 197.1
     Uncertain
     Siscia
     282–283
     Obv.: Bust of emperor, radiate, cuirassed, left, facing bust of Sol, radiate, draped, right. DEO ET DOMINO CARO AUG or DEO ET DOMINO CARO INVIC(to) AUG(usto).
     LIMC Helios/Sol 411; RIC V.2 99.
     Image: photograph © Trustees of the British Museum.

142. Antoninianus
     Lugdunum
     282–283
     Obv.: bust of Numerian.
     Rev.: bust of Sol, radiate, right.
     RIC V.2 355.

143. Aureus
     Antioch
     282–283
     Obv.: bust of Numerian.
     Rev.: Sol, nude but for a *chlamys*, radiate, standing left, right hand raised, globe in left hand.
     RIC V.2 373.

An unpublished variant (whip instead of globe) was sold at auction on December 5th, 2002, by Numismatica Ars Classica, https://www.ac search.info/search.html?id=117615 (March 20, 2017).

Carinus, 283–285

144. Antoninianus
 Rome
 283–285
 Sol, nude but for a *chlamys*, radiate, standing or walking right or left, right hand raised, whip or globe in left hand.
 RIC V.2 262.

145. Plate 191.22
 Aureus
 Siscia
 283–285
 Obv.: bust of Carinus.
 Rev.: Sol, nude but for a *chlamys*, radiate, standing front, head left, right hand raised, globe in left hand.
 RIC V.2 310.
 Image: photograph of ANS 1967.153.200, courtesy American Numismatic Society open database policy.

146. Aureus, denarius
 Lugdunum, Siscia
 283–285
 Obv.: bust of Numerian.
 Rev.: Sol, nude but for a *chlamys*, radiate, standing left, right hand raised, globe in left hand.
 RIC V.2 381, 428–9 (Lugdunum), 454 (Siscia).

147. Plate 191.23
 Antoninianus
 Rome
 283–285
 Obv.: bust of Numerian.
 Rev.: Sol, nude but for a *chlamys*, radiate, walking left, right hand raised, globe in left hand.
 RIC V.2 411–2

Image: photograph of ANS 1948.19.1015, courtesy American Numismatic Society open database policy.

Diocletian, 284–305

148. Plate 192.1
     Quinarius
     Rome
     286
     Obv.: Jugate busts of emperor, laureate and cuirassed, with spear and shield, and Sol radiate, holding whip.
     LIMC Helios/Sol 412; RIC V.2 189.
     Image: photograph © Trustees of the British Museum.

149. Plate 192.2
     Aureus, antoninianus
     Rome, Cyzicus, Carthage, Siscia.
     284–294
     Sol, nude but for a *chlamys*, radiate, standing left, right hand raised, globe in left hand.
     RIC V.2 174 (Rome), 302 (Cyzicus); RIC VI Carthage 9, Siscia 30
     Image: photograph courtesy of CNG coins auction Triton VIII lot 1215 (Jan. 2005).

150. Plate 192.3
     Antoninianus
     Trier
     285
     As L2.149, with captive.
     RIC V.2, 206–207.
     Image: photograph courtesy Vauctions, auction 246 lot 79.

151. Plate 192.4
     Antoninianus
     Lugdunum
     284–294
     As L2.149 but whip instead of globe.
     RIC V.2 60
     Image: photograph courtesy of the American Numismatic Society open database policy.

152. Plate 192.5
     Aureus, antoninianus
     Rome, Ticinum
     284–294
     As L2.151, but Sol walking left.
     LIMC Helios/Sol 119; RIC V.2 147–8 (Rome), 206–7 (Ticinum).
     Image: photograph of ANS 1970.15.153, courtesy American Numismatic
     Society open database policy.

Carausius, Britain, 286/7–293

153. Plate 192.6
     Antoninianus
     Londinium
     286–293
     Sol, nude but for a *chlamys*, radiate, standing front, head left, right hand
     raised, globe in left hand.
     RIC V.2 29.
     Image: photograph courtesy Numismatica Ars Classica auction 87, lot 347.

154. Plate 192.7
     Antoninianus
     Londinium
     286–293
     Sol, nude but for a *chlamys*, radiate, walking left, right hand raised, globe
     in left hand.
     RIC V.2 30, 95.
     Image: photograph courtesy Roma Numismatics auction 13 lot 1100.

155. Plate 192.8
     Antoninianus
     Londinium, unknown mint
     286–293
     Sol, nude but for a *chlamys*, radiate, walking left, right hand raised, whip
     in left hand.
     RIC V.2 96 (Londinium), 807, 871 (unknown).
     Image: photograph courtesy CNG electronic auction 204 lot 211

156. Antoninianus
     Camulodunum, unknown mint
     286–293

Sol, nude but for a *chlamys*, radiate, standing or walking left, right hand raised, globe or whip in left hand.

RIC V.2 294–7 (Camulodunum), 473, 569–70, 611, 869–70 (unknown mint).

157. Antoninianus
     Camulodunum
     286–293
     Sol, nude but for a *chlamys*, radiate, standing or walking left, right hand raised, globe or whip in left hand, two captives.
     RIC V.2 298.

158. Antoninianus
     Camulodunum
     286–293
     Sol, nude but for a *chlamys*, radiate, standing or walking left, right hand raised, globe or whip in left hand, one captive.
     RIC V.2 299.

159. Antoninianus
     Unknown mint
     286–293
     Sol, nude but for a *chlamys*, radiate, walking right, right hand raised, whip in left hand.
     RIC V.2 868.

160. Antoninianus
     Camulodunum, unknown mint
     286–293
     Sol, nude but for a *chlamys*, radiate, walking right, right hand raised, whip in left hand, two captives.
     RIC V.2 407.

161. Antoninianus
     Londinium, Camulodunum, unknown mint
     286–293
     Sol, nude but for a *chlamys*, radiate, in *quadriga* left.
     LIMC Helios/Sol 158; RIC V.2 179 (Londinium), 408–9 (Camulodunum), 806 (unknown mint).

162. Plate 192.9
    Antoninianus
    Londinium, unknown mint
    286–293
    Bust of Sol, radiate, right.
    RIC V.2 97 (Londinium), 872–4 (unknown mint).
    Image: photograph of a coin in a private collection, by author.

163. Antoninianus
    Camulodunum, unknown mint
    286–293
    Obv.: Busts of Emperor and Sol, raised right hand and whip, jugate right.
    Rev.: Providentia.
    RIC V.2 233–4, 304, 341, 527, 788 (Camulodunum), 1044 (unknown mint).

163a. Plates 192.10, 196.4
    Antoninanus
    Camulodunum?
    291–292
    Obv.: Jugate busts of Sol, radiate, whip in right hand, and Carausius left
    Rev.: Providentia
    Image: photograph courtesy Lanz Auction 100, lot 473, http://www.lanz
    auctions.com/showcoin.php?no=918534527.

164. Antoninianus
    Camulodunum
    286–293
    Providentia standing right, holding two ensigns, facing Sol, nude but for a
    chlamys, radiate, standing left, right hand raised, globe in left hand.
    RIC V.2 380, 434.

Allectus, Britain, 293–296/7

165. Plate 192.11
    Aureus, antoninianus
    Londinium, Camulodunum

293–297
Sol, nude but for a *chlamys*, radiate, standing left, right hand raised, left holding globe or whip.
LIMC Helios/Sol 195; RIC V.2 4, 26–7 (Londinium), 84 (Camulodunum).
Image: photograph Münzkabinett Berlin made available at OCRE under OdbL.

165a. As L2.145, but between two captives seated at his feet.

Constantius I Chlorus, Caesar 293–305, joint emperor 305–306

166. Antoninianus
     Lugdunum
     295
     Sol, nude but for a *chlamys*, radiate, standing left, right hand raised, globe in left hand, one captive.
     RIC V 116–117.

167. Half aureus
     Siscia
     294–305
     As L2.166, but without captive
     RIC VI 30.

168. Plate 192.12
     Aureus, antoninianus
     Lugdunum, Siscia
     294–305
     Sol standing left, right hand raised, whip in left hand. RIC V.2 631 (Lugdunum), 28, 31 (Siscia).
     Image: photograph of ANS 1944.100.38405, courtesy American Numismatic Society open database policy.

Maximianus, 286–305 and 307–308

169. Plate 192.13
     Antoninianus
     Lugdunum
     287–293

Sol, nude but for a *chlamys*, radiate, walking left, right hand raised, globe in left hand, between two captives.

RIC V.2 394a.

Image: photograph of ANS 1984.146.175, courtesy American Numismatic Society open database policy.

170. Antoninianus
Trier
295–296
Sol, nude but for a *chlamys*, radiate, standing left, right hand raised, globe in left hand holding globe; at foot, captive.
LIMC Helios/Sol 192; RIC V.2 472–4.

171. Aureus
Trier, Antioch
295–305
Bust of Sol radiate and draped right.
RIC VI 83 (Treveri), 26 (Antioch); LIMC Helios/Sol 88.

172. Plate 192.14
Aureus, half solidus
Siscia
302–305
Sol, nude but for a *chlamys*, radiate, standing left, right hand raised, whip in left hand.
LIMC Helios/Sol 105; RIC VI 28b, 31b.
Image: photograph courtesy Ph. Gysen.

Galerius Maximianus, Caesar 293–305, emperor 305–311

173. Plate 192.15
Aureus
Nicomedia
294
Sol, nude but for a *chlamys*, radiate, standing left, right hand raised, globe and whip in left hand.
RIC VI 7.
Image: photograph Leu Numismatik, auction 1 lot 373.

174. Plate 192.16
     Aureus, Antoninianus
     Lugdunum, Alexandria
     294–296
     Sol, nude but for a *chlamys*, radiate, walking left, right hand raised, globe
     in left hand; sometimes one or two captives.
     LIMC Helios/Sol 174; RIC V.2 682–3, 685 (Lugdunum); RIC VI 2
     (Alexandria).
     Image: photograph courtesy of the American Numismatic Society open
     database policy.

175. Antoninianus
     Treveri
     295
     Sol, nude but for a *chlamys*, radiate, standing left, right hand raised, globe
     in left hand, captive.
     LIMC Helios/Sol 192; RIC V.2 694.

176. Plate 192.17
     Antoninianus
     Lugdunum
     295
     Sol, nude but for a *chlamys*, radiate, standing left, right hand raised, whip
     in left hand. RIC V.2 684
     Image: photograph of ANS 1944.100.38048, courtesy American Numis-
     matic Society open database policy.

176a. Plate 192.18
      Aureus
      Trier
      295–305
      Bust of Sol, radiate, right.
      RIC VI Treviri 83.
      Cf. L2.171.
      Image: in the public domain.

177. Plate 192.19
     Follis
     Antioch

310
Sol radiate, in long robe, standing, head left, right hand raised, globe in left hand, in facing split *quadriga*
LIMC Helios/Sol 136; RIC VI 144, 145a.

177a. Plate 192.20
Bronze
Antioch
310
Sol, radiate, in long robe, right hand raised, globe in left hand, standing in *quadriga* left.
RIC VI Antioch 142.
Image: in the public domain.

177b. Plate 192.21
Bronze
Trier
310
Sol, radiate, in long robe, right hand raised, whip in left hand, standing in frontal *quadriga* at rest.
Image: photograph courtesy Numismatica Ars Classica auction 72, lot 1706.

Severus II, 306–307

178. Plates 192.22, 199.6
Aureus
Treveri
305–307
Sol, nude but for a *chlamys*, radiate, standing front, head left, right hand raised, globe in left hand.
LIMC Helios/Sol 106; RIC VI 616, 630a–32.
Image: photograph of ANS 1944.100.5960, courtesy American Numismatic Society open database policy.

Maximinus II Daia, Caesar 305–309/310, joint emperor 310–313

179. Plate 192.23
Aureus
Nicomedia, Ticinum

305–308, 312–313
Sol, nude but for a *chlamys*, radiate, standing front or right, head right, right hand raised, whip and globe in left hand.
LIMC Helios/Sol 107; RIC VI 35–6, 43, 46 (Nicomedia), 134 (Ticinum).
Image: in the public domain.

180. Aureus, follis
Siscia, Londinium
308–309, 312–313
Sol, nude but for a *chlamys*, radiate, standing left, right hand raised, whip and globe in left hand.
RIC VI 192, 193 (Siscia), 244 (Londinium).

180a. Plate 192.24
Bronze
Londinium
310–312
As L2.180, but holding globe in right hand and whip in left hand.
RIC VI Londinium 146b
Image: photograph of ANS 1984.146.1208, courtesy American Numismatic Society open database policy.

181. Plate 193.1
Follis
Antioch
310
Sol radiate, in long robe, head left, right hand raised, left hand holding globe, in facing split *quadriga*
LIMC Helios/Sol 137; RIC VI 140–2, 144–45b.
Image: photograph of ANS 1944.100.1881, courtesy American Numismatic Society open database policy.

182 and 182a. Plates 193.2, 193.3, 199.1, 199.2
Aureus, follis
Heraclea, Nicomedia, Cyzicus, Antioch, Alexandria.
Sol radiate, standing left in long robe, right hand raised, left hand holding head of Sarapis.
LIMC Helios/Sol 238; RIC VI 78 (Heraclea), 73, 77 (Nicomedia), 92, 98–9, 106, 110 (Cyzicus), 154, 159, 167–8 (Antioch), 94a, 96, 132 (Alexandria).

The bust held by Sol sometimes, as here, resembles a woman (Isis?) more than Sarapis, but perhaps not too much should be made of that as the bust on coin L2.182a rather closely resembles Darth Vader.

Images: L2.182 and L2.182a, photographs of ANS 1984.146.946 and ANS 1948.19.128 respectively, both courtesy American Numismatic Society open database policy.

183. Plates 193.4, 199.3
    Aureus
    Antioch
    311–313
    Sol radiate, standing left in long robe, right hand raised, left hand holding Victoriola.
    LIMC Helios/Sol 111; RIC VI 160
    Image: photograph courtesy Gorny & Mosch auction 249 lot 932.

184. Plate 193.5
    Base silver
    Treveri
    312
    Sol, radiate, naked to waist, standing with head left in facing *quadriga*, right hand raised, globe and whip in left hand.
    RIC VI 826.
    Image: photograph of ANS 1944.100.6010, courtesy American Numismatic Society open database policy.

185. Plates 193.6, 193.7
    Follis
    Rome, Treveri, Ticinum, Alexandria
    312–313
    Sol, nude but for a *chlamys*, radiate, standing left, right hand raised, globe in left hand.
    RIC VI, 322b, 323b, 327b-330b, 370, 373, 375 (Rome), 84a, 86a, 88, 90a, 92a (Ostia), 630, 631, 866b (Treveri), 127 (Ticinum).
    Image L2.185: photograph of ANS 1944.100.5961, courtesy American Numismatic Society open database policy; L2.185a: ANS 1948.19.128, courtesy American Numismatic Society open database policy.

186. Plate 193.8

As L2.185, but Sol standing right.

RIC VI, 335b-338b (Rome), 130, 131b (Ticinum).

Image: photograph of ANS 1984.146.2030, courtesy American Numismatic Society open database policy.

187. Plates 190.1, 193.9

As L2.185, with captive

RIC VI, 341 (Rome), 142 (Aquileia).

Image: photograph of ANS 1944.100.5689, courtesy American Numismatic Society open database policy.

188. As L2.187, but Sol walking right.

RIC VI, 344 (Rome).

189. Plate 193.10

Follis

Antioch

312

Genius standing left, nude but for a *chlamys*, holding head of Sol and Cornucopiae.

LIMC Helios/Sol 422; RIC VI 164.

Image: photograph courtesy Solidus Numismatik auction 27, lot 625.

Licinius, 308–324

190. Aureus

Siscia

307–308

Sol, nude but for a *chlamys*, radiate, standing left, right hand raised, globe and whip in left in left hand.

LIMC Helios/Sol 108; RIC VI 191.

191. Follis

Antioch

310

Sol radiate and in long robe, right hand raised, standing in *quadriga* galloping right.

LIMC Helios/Sol 159; CIL VI 143.

191a. Plate 193.11
As 191, but *quadriga* left.
Image: photograph courtesy of the Classical Numismatic Group, mail bid sale 72, lot 1768.

192. Aureus
Siscia
311–313
Sol, nude but for a *chlamys*, radiate, standing left, right hand raised, whip and globe in left hand.
RIC VI 217; RIC VII 14.

193. Plate 193.12
Aes
Rome, Londinium, Ticinum, Arelate, Ostia, Siscia
312–316
Sol, nude but for a *chlamys*, radiate, standing left or right, right hand raised, globe in left hand.
LIMC Helios/Sol 106; RIC VI 121c (Londinium), 131c (Ticinum), 320, 322c, 323c, 328c, 329c, 335c-8c (Rome), 84b, 86b, 90b, 92b (Ostia); RIC VII 19–20, 35, 48–9, 53, 60–1, 79–80, 96–8 (Londinium), 4, 9–10, 17, 22, 46, 69 (Ticinum), 21–4, 29–30, 32, 35–6, 38, 42–3 (Rome), 3–4, 17–8, 42–3, 46–7, 59–61, 67–8, 74, 76–7, 82–3, 86–8, 91, 94–5, 147–8, 153–5 (Arelate), 38 (Siscia).
Image: photograph of ANS 1944.100.3058, courtesy American Numismatic Society open database policy.

193a. As L2.193 with one prisoner
RIC VI 143 (Aquileia).

194. Plates 193.13, 199.5
Bronze
Cyzicus, Antioch
312
Sol, radiate, standing wearing a long robe, right hand raised, bust of Sarapis in his left hand.
LIMC Helios/Sol 238; RIC VI 98 (Cyzicus), 167a, 168 (Antioch).
Image: private collection, photograph author.

194a. Plate 194.14
Bronze
Antioch
AD 312
Genius standing facing, head left, holding the head of Sol on his right
hand, a corucopia in his left.
RIC Antioch 164a.
Image: photograph courtesy Agora auctions sale 65 lot 228.

195. Plate 193.15
Aes
Londinium
310–312
Sol, nude but for a *chlamys*, radiate, standing left, globe in right hand,
whip in left hand.
RIC VI 146c.
Image: ANS 1947.97.14, courtesy American Numismatic Society open
database policy.

196. Aes
Ticinum
312–313
Sol, nude but for a *chlamys*, radiate, standing right, right hand raised,
whip and globe in left hand.
RIC VI 135b.

197. Plate 193.16
Aes
Londinium
316
Sol, radiate, dressed in *chiton* and *chlamys*, standing in facing *quadriga*,
raising right hand and holding globe and whip in left hand
RIC VII 83
Image: photograph courtesy Classical Numismatic Group mail bid sale
62, lot 1065.

198. Plate 193.17
Aes
Thessalonica

319
Plan of Roman camp, Sol standing in the middle, nude but for a *chlamys*,
radiate, right hand raised, globe in left hand.
RIC VII 68.
Image: photograph courtesy Spink auction 3014, lot 208.

Constantine I, 306–337

199. Plate 193.18
Aes
Alexandria, Londinium, Treveri, Rome, Ticinum, Ostia, Arelate, Lugdu-
num, Serdica, Siscia, Aquileia.
308–318
Sol, nude but for a *chlamys*, radiate, standing left (sometimes right), right
hand raised, globe in left hand.
LIMC Helios/Sol 106; RIC VI 97 (Alexandria), 113–5, 120–32, 193, 234–40,
279–87; RIC VII 5–18, 27–9, 32–4, 43–7, 54–9, 62–3, 68–78, 88–95, 99–102,
106–12, 119–20, 124–6, 137–41, 148–51, 164–5, 169–70 (Londinium); RIC
VI 865–76, 898–900; RIC VII 39–47, 70–6, 92–107, 127–35, 157–62, 164–7
(Treveri); RIC VI 316–40, 368–77; RIC VII 1, 2, 5, 18–20, 27–8, 31, 33–4, 37,
39–41, 56–8, 78–80, 97, 136 (Rome); RIC VI 127–33, 137–8; RIC VII 1–3,
7–8, 14–6, 20–1, 43–5, 61–4, 67–9 (Ticinum); RIC VI 83–92 (Ostia); RIC
VII 14–21, 35–47, 50–8, 62–6, 71–3, 75, 79–81, 84–5, 89–90, 92–3, 96–105,
108–12, 136–9, 144–6, 149–52, 164–5, 169–70, 180, 184 (Arelate), 1–9, 15–25,
30–47, 51–62 (Lugdunum), 4 (Serdica), 31–5 (Siscia).
Image: photograph of ANS 1984.146.1229, courtesy American Numismatic
Society open database policy.

200 Plate 193.19
Aes
Rome
316
As L2.199, with Victory on globe
LIMC Helios/Sol 110; RIC VII 45, 48–50.
Image: photograph of ANS 1944.100.6242, courtesy American Numismatic
Society open database policy.

201. Plate 193.20
Solidus, aes

Treveri, Rome, Aquileia, Thessalonica

313–315

As L2.199, with captive.

LIMC Helios/Sol 192; RIC VII 51–55 (Rome), 48 (Treveri), RIC VI 144, 145, RIC VII 1, 2 (Aquileia), 8, 9 (Thessalonica).

Image: photograph of ANS 1933.999.201, courtesy American Numismatic Society open database policy.

202. Aes

Rome, Lugdunum

312–315

As L2. 199, whip instead of globe.

RIC VI 313–315 (Rome); RIC VII 26 (Lugdunum).

203. Plate 193.21

Aes

Londinium, Ticinum

312–313, 316

As L2.199, but whip and globe in left hand.

RIC VI 243; RIC VII 62 (Londinium); RIC VI 134–6 (Ticinum).

Image: photograph of ANS 1984.146.1832, courtesy American Numismatic Society open database policy.

204. Solidus

Siscia

317

As L2.203, captive

RIC VII 24–5.

205. Plate 193.22

Aes

Londinium

307–312

Sol, nude but for a *chlamys*, radiate, standing left, globe in right hand, whip in left hand.

RIC VI 101–2, 146–92.

Image: photograph of ANS 1984.146.1209, courtesy American Numismatic Society open database policy.

206. Aes
     Londinium
     310
     Sol, nude but for a *chlamys*, radiate, standing left whip in right hand,
     globe in left hand.
     LIMC Helios/Sol 109; RIC VI 116, 128.

207. Plate 193.23
     Aes
     Lugdunum, Rome, Aquileia
     309–310, 317–318
     Sol, nude but for a *chlamys*, radiate, walking left, right hand raised, whip
     in left hand.
     RIC VI 312 (Lugdunum); RIC VII 59, 80 (Rome), 14 (Aquileia).
     Image: British Museum 1927,0616.581 courtesy OCRE open database
     policy.

208. Aes
     Lugdunum
     314–315
     As L2.207, but globe instead of whip.
     RIC VII 27

209. Aes
     Ostia
     312
     As L2.208, captive.
     RIC VI 93.

210. Plate 193.24
     Aes
     Lugdunum, Ticinum
     308–313
     As L2.199, but standing front.
     RIC VI 307–11 (Lugdunum), 133 (Ticinum).
     Image: photograph of ANS 1984.146.347, courtesy American Numismatic
     Society open database policy.

211.　Plates 194.1, 198.6
　　　Solidus
　　　Ticinum
　　　312–313
　　　Sol, dressed in *chiton* and *chlamys*, radiate, right hand raised, in frontal *quadriga*; behind him, Victory with wreath in right hand, palm in left.
　　　RIC VI 113.
　　　Image: British Museum 1896,0608.97. Photograph © Trustees of the British Museum.

212.　Plate 194.2
　　　Aes
　　　Londinium
　　　316
　　　Sol, radiate, dressed in *chiton* and *chlamys*, right hand raised, globe and whip in left hand, standing in frontal *quadriga*.
　　　LIMC Helios/Sol 138; RIC VII 81–84.
　　　Image: photograph of ANS 1944.100.6010, courtesy American Numismatic Society open database policy.

213.　Plate 194.3
　　　Aes
　　　Treveri
　　　310–313
　　　Bust of Sol, radiate, right.
　　　RIC VI 886–95.
　　　Image: photograph of ANS 1984.146.1381, courtesy American Numismatic Society open database policy.

214.　Plates 194.4, 200.6
　　　Solidus
　　　Ticinum, Thessalonica, Arelate, Aquileia, Antioch, Sirmium.
　　　316–317, 320–321, 324–325.
　　　Sol, nude but for a *chlamys*, radiate, standing right, presenting Victory on a globe to the emperor, standing left, between them a captive.
　　　LIMC Helios/Sol 418; 419; RIC VII 56, 108 (Ticinum), 10 (Thessalonica), 114 (Arelate), 35 (Aquileia), 49 (Antioch), 8 (Sirmium).
　　　Image: photograph of ANS 1944.100.9594, courtesy American Numismatic Society open database policy.

215. Plates 194.5, 200.7
     Solidus, multiple
     Sirmium, Ticinum
     320–321
     Sol, nude but for a *chlamys*, radiate, standing right, crowning emperor.
     LIMC Helios/Sol 415; RIC VII 21, 22 (Sirmium), 98–9 (Ticinum).
     Image: photograph Münzkabinett Berlin made available at OCRE under
     the open database policy.

216. Plates 194.6, 200.1
     Solidus
     Sirmium
     322
     As L2.215 but standing left.
     RIC VII 31.
     Image: photograph courtesy Numismatica Ars Classica Auction 24 lot 277,
     5 December 2002.

217. Plates 194.7, 194.8
     Aes
     Nicomedia, Antioch
     312
     Sol standing left, radiate, dressed in a long *chiton*, right hand raised, bust
     of Sarapis in his left hand.
     RIC VI 73c, 77c (Nicomedia), 154d, 167c (Antioch).
     Images: photograph of 217: ANS 1944.100.4477; 217a: ANS 1944.100.4477,
     both courtesy American Numismatic Society open database policy.
     On the identity of the bust on Sol's left hand, cf. L2.182.

218. Solidus
     Ticinum
     315
     Jugate busts of the emperor and Sol, radiate, left.
     LIMC Helios/Sol 413; RIC VII 32, 53.
     See Plate 202.2 for an image.

219. Plates 194.9, 198.5
     Aes
     Thessalonica

319
Sol, nude but for a *chlamys*, radiate, right hand raised, globe in left hand, standing on a schematic army camp.
LIMC Helios/Sol 97; RIC VII 66–7.
Image: photograph by anonymous of a coin in a private collection; in the public domain.

Constantine II, Caesar 317–337, emperor 337–340

220. Plate 194.10
    Aes
    Londinium, Treveri, Arelate, Siscia, Thessalonica.
    317–318
    Sol, nude but for a *chlamys*, radiate, standing left (sometimes right), right hand raised, globe in left hand.
    LIMC Helios/Sol 106; Helios/Sol 192; RIC VII 104, 117–8, 123, 131, 145–7, 153 (Londinium), 107, 137, 148–9 (officina B), 153–5, 163, 168, 172–4, 179–81; 183 (Treveri), 104–5, 118–9, 140–1, 156–8, 166, 171, 181–2 (Arelate), 36–7 (Siscia), 23 Thessalonica.
    Image: photograph of ANS 1984.146.1473, courtesy American Numismatic Society open database policy.

221. Plate 194.11
    Aes
    Treveri, Aquileia, Rome, Arelate
    316–318
    As L2.220, but walking and whip and globe in left hand.
    RIC VII 125, 126, 147, 149 (officina A) (Treveri), 19 (Aquileia), 85, 98, 130 (Rome), 122 (Arelate).
    Image: photograph of ANS 1984.146.1456, courtesy American Numismatic Society open database policy.

222. Aes.
    Ticinum, Aquileia, Rome.
    316–318.
    As L2.220, but walking and whip in left hand.
    LIMC Helios/Sol 119; RIC VII 66, 80–1 (Ticinum), 15–8, 20 (Aquileia), 84, 129 (Rome).

223. Plate 194.12
     Aes
     Arelate
     317
     As L2.220, but walking
     LIMC Helios/Sol 120; RIC VII 120–2.
     Image: photograph of ANS 1944.100.11194, courtesy American Numismatic
     Society open database policy.

224. Plate 194.13
     Aes
     Thessalonica
     319
     Sol, nude but for a *chlamys*, radiate, right hand raised, globe in left hand,
     standing on a schematic army camp.
     LIMC Helios/Sol 197; RIC VII 71.
     Image: photograph of ANS 1984.146.894, courtesy American Numismatic
     Society open database policy.

Crispus, Caesar 317–326

225. Plate 194.14
     Aes
     Londinium, Treveri
     317–318
     Sol, nude but for a *chlamys*, radiate, standing left, right hand raised, globe
     in left hand.
     LIMC Helios/Sol 106; RIC VII 103, 113–6; 121–3, 127–30, 142–4, 152 (London),
     106, 136, 146–52, 156, 175–8, 182 (Trier).
     Image: photograph of ANS 1984.146.1245, courtesy American Numismatic
     Society open database policy.

226. Plate 194.15
     Aes
     Thessalonica
     319
     Sol, nude but for a *chlamys*, radiate, right hand raised, globe in left hand,
     standing on a schematic army camp.
     LIMC Helios/Sol 197; RIC VII 69.

Image: photograph courtesy Classical Numismatic Group electronic auction 325 lot 655.

227. Plate 194.16
      Aes
      Treveri, Rome, Ticinum
      316
      Sol, nude but for a *chlamys*, radiate, walking left, right hand raised, whip in left hand
      RIC VII 124 (Treveri), 81–3 (Rome), 79 (Ticinum).
      Image: photograph of ANS 1947.97.38, courtesy American Numismatic Society open database policy.

228. Aureus
      Nicomedia
      319
      Sol, dressed in *chiton* and *chlamys*, radiate, standing left, right hand raised, globe in left hand.
      LIMC Helios/Sol 112; RIC VII 22.

Licinius II, Caesar 317–324

229. Aes.
      Siscia.
      317.
      Sol, nude but for a *chlamys*, radiate, standing left, right hand raised, globe in left hand.
      RIC VII, 38.

230. Plate 194.17
      Aes
      Thessalonica
      319
      Sol, nude but for a *chlamys*, radiate, right hand raised, globe in left hand, standing on a schematic army camp.
      LIMC Helios/Sol 197; RIC VII 70.
      Image: photograph of ANS 1984.146.894, courtesy American Numismatic Society open database policy.

L3. Contorniates and Medallions

1. Plate 201.20
   Bronze medallion
   Unknown
   1st c. BC–1st c. AD
   Malibu, Getty Museum 71.AC.373.
   Bust of Sol, radiate (seven rays), draped.
   Unpublished.
   Image: Digital image courtesy of the Getty's Open Content Program.

2. Bronze medallion
   Rome (?)
   117–138
   Obv.: Bust of Hadrian.
   Rev.: Bust of Sol, radiate, r.
   Gnecchi 1912, vol. III, p. 23 no. 126.

3. Plate 201.1
   Bronze medallion
   Rome
   AD 136–138
   Obv.: bust of L. Aelius, left.
   Rev.: Sol in *quadriga* right.
   Gnecchi 1912: vol. II p. 9 Aelius 2, pl. 42.8.
   Image: after Gnecchi, in the public domain.

4. Plate 201.2
   Bronze medallion
   Rome
   145–147
   Obv.: Bust of Antoninus Pius.
   Rev.: Sol standing in a *quadriga* rising up to the right, whip in right hand and reins in left, Lucifer, with torch, flies ahead of the *quadriga*, above the horses; below and in front of the horses: clouds and Tellus reclining left.
   Gnecchi (1912), vol. II p. 16, Antoninus Pius 67, pl. 50.6; LIMC Helios/Sol 157; Bergmann 1998, pl. 46.1.
   Image: after Gnecchi, in the public domain.

5. Plate 201.3
    Bronze medallion
    Rome
    AD 156–161
    Obv.: bust of Faustina, left.
    Rev.: Sol in *quadriga* left in front of Luna in *biga* right above Tellus (right) and Oceanus (left).
    Gnecchi 1912: vol. II, p. 41 Faustina 23, pl. 68.8.
    Image: after Gnecchi, in the public domain.

6. Bronze medallion
    Nicaea
    161–180
    Obv.: Bust of Marcus Aurelius.
    Rev.: Sol standing in a *quadriga* rising up to the right, whip in right hand and reins in left, Lucifer, with torch, flies ahead of the *quadriga*, above the horses; below and in front of the horses: clouds and Tellus reclining left.
    RPC IV, 5913 (temporary); Bergmann 1998, pl 46.5. Image at RPC online: https://rpc.ashmus.ox.ac.uk/coin/184933

7. Plate 201.4
    Bronze medallion
    Rome
    190–191
    Obv.: Bust of Commodus.
    Rev.: Sol standing in a *quadriga* rising up to the right, whip in right hand and reins in left, Lucifer, with torch, flies ahead of the *quadriga*, above the horses; below and in front of the horses: clouds and Tellus reclining left.
    LIMC Helios/Sol 299; Gnecchi (1912) vol. II., p.52 Commodus 3, pl. 78.3; Bergmann 1998, pl. 46.23.
    Image: after Gnecchi, in the public domain.

8. Tübingen University, Department of Archaeology coin collection inv. v 376/2a.
    Acquired in Paris, 1895
    Copper and brass
    AD 190–191
    Bimetal medallion with on the obverse a bust of Commodus and on the reverse Sol, radiate, nude but for a *chlamys*, standing in his chariot

holding the reins in his left hand and a whip in his right had, ascending to the right; below lies Tellus (difficult to make out).
Krmnicek 2016: 12 no. 3.

9. Gold medallion
Rome
AD 215
Obv.: Bust of Caracalla right.
Rev.: Sol in *quadriga* left.
Gnecchi 1912: vol. 1, p. 4 Caracalla 2, pl. 1.4.
See L2.26.

10. Plate 201.5
Silver medallion, gilded
Rome
238–244
Obv.: Bust of Gordian III.
Rev.: Gordian standing left, holding scepter in his left hand, shakes hands with Sol with his right hand. Sol, radiate (nude but for a *chlamys*, stands facing Gordian, holding a globe in his left hand. Between them a soldier and two captives. Gordian is crowned by Roma; behind Sol, a soldier with spear and vexillum; three standards in central space behind Sol and Gordian
Gnecchi 1912, vol. I, p. 48 no. 11; on the medallions of Gordian III cf. Bardin 2014.
For a bronze medallion with the same reverse, cf. Gnecchi 1912: II, 93 Gordian 56, pl. 106.8; LIMC Helios/Sol 416.
Image: after Gnecchi, in the public domain.

11. Plate 201.6
Copper alloy medallion
Rome
238–244
Obv.: Bust of Gordian III
Rev.: Emperor standing left, pouring libation on an altar with his right hand and holding a spear or staff in his left hand. A Victory stands behind the emperor and crowns him with a wreath. In the middle of the medallion, Sol (iconographic details unclear) in facing *quadriga* with two horses to the left and two to the right, the inner horses with their heads

turned inward, the outer with their heads outward. Under the chariot: two river-gods, identified as the Tigris and the Euphrates; behind: standards. LIMC Helios/Sol 420; Gnecchi 1912, Vol. II, p.89 no. 24.
Image: after Gnecchi, in the public domain.

12. Plate 201.7
Bronze medallion, gold-plated
Siscia
266–267
Bust of Gallienus with lion skin of Hercules.
Bust of Sol, radiate, right.
Unpublished.
Image: photograph courtesy Solidus Numismatik, auction March 25, 2017, lot 335.

13. Bronze medallion
Rome?
268–270
Obv.: Bust of Claudius Gothicus.
Rev.: Sol standing, right hand raised, globe in left hand.
Gnecchi 1912 vol. III, p. 64 nos. 1515.

14. Plate 201.8
Bronze medallion.
Cyzicus.
268–270.
Obv.: Bust of Claudius Gothicus.
Rev.: Sol standing in a *quadriga* rising up to the right, whip in right hand and reins in left, Lucifer, with torch, flies ahead of the *quadriga*, above the horses; below and in front of the horses: clouds or rocky terrain and Tellus reclining left.
Unpublished.
Image: photograph courtesy Ira & Larry Goldberg Coins & Collectibles, Inc. Auction 70, lot 3377.

15. Plate 201.9
Bronze medallion
Rome
276

Obv.: Bust of Tacitus.

Rev,: Sol in *quadriga* left, nude but for a *chlamys*, right hand raised, globe in left hand.

www.ric.mom.fr temp no. 3524; Gnecchi 1912: vol. II, p. 114 Tacitus 8, pl. 118.7.

Image: after Gnecchi, in the public domain.

16. Plate 201.10
Bronze medallion.
Unknown
AD 271.
Obv.: bust of Tetricus II, right.
Rev.: Sol in *quadriga* left, holding a whip in his raised right hand.
LIMC Helios/Sol 158; Gnecchi 1912: vol. II, p. 112 Tetricus Filius 1, pl. 116.10.
Image: after Gnecchi, in the public domain.

17. Plate 201.11
Bronze medallion.
Rome?
Ad 270–275.
Obv.: bust of Aurelian, right.
Rev.: Sol in *quadriga* left, right hand raised, globe in left hand.
LIMC Helios/Sol 158; Gnecchi 1912: vol. II, p.113 Aurelian 2, pl. 117 nos. 910.
Image: after Gnecchi, in the public domain.
Cf. L2.106.

18. Bronze medallion.
Rome?
AD 270–275.
Obv.: bust of Aurelian, left.
Rev.: Sol in frontal chariot, right hand raised, whip.
Gnecchi 1912: vol. II, p. 113 Aurelian 3.
Cf. L2.108.

19. Plate 201.12
Copper alloy medallion
Rome
281
Obv.: jugate busts of Probus and Sol.

Rev.: Fides handing globe to Probus.
Gnecchi 1912 vol. II, p. 116 Probus 11, pl. 119.7.
Image: after Gnecchi, in the public domain.

20.   Copper alloy medallion
       Rome
       281
       Obv.: jugate busts of Probus and Sol.
       Rev.: Probus in frontal *quadriga*, crowned by Victory.
       Gnecchi 1912 vol. II, p. 117 Probus 14.

21.   Plate 201.13
       Copper alloy medallion, plated in gilt silver.
       Rome.
       281.
       Obv.: jugate busts of Probus and Sol right.
       Rev.: three Monetae.
       Gnecchi 1912 vol. II, p. 119 Probus 32, pl. 121.1 and 2.
       Image: photograph © Trustees of the British Museum.
       Cf. similar medallion with jugate busts of Probus and Sol left. Gnecchi
       1912 vol. II, p. 119 Probus 33, pl. 121.3.

22.   Plate 201.14
       Bronze medallion.
       Rome?
       AD 281.
       Obv.: bust of Probus, left.
       Rev.: Sol in frontal chariot, right hand raised, whip.
       Gnecchi 1912: vol. II, p. 119 Probus 38, pl. 121.7.
       Image: after Gnecchi, in the public domain.

23.   Plate 201.15
       Bronze medallion
       Rome?
       AD 281.
       Obv.: bust of Probus, left.
       Rev.: Sol in *quadriga* left, preceded by a female figure.
       LIMC Helios/Sol 158; Gnecchi 1912: vol. II, p. 120 Probus 41, pl. 121.8.
       Image: after Gnecchi, in the public domain.

24. Plate 201.16
    Bronze medallion
    Unknown
    AD 283
    Obv.: bust of Carinus, right.
    Rev.: Carinus, left, and Numerianus, right, stand facing each other; Carinus is crowned by Hercules, Numerianus by Sol.
    Gnecchi 1912: vol. II, p. 121–2 Carinus 8, pl. 122.9.
    Image: after Gnecchi, in the public domain.

25. Plate 201.17
    Gold medallion
    Rome
    283–285
    Obv.: bust of Carinus.
    Rev.: Carus, draped, cuirassed, standing right, holding sceptre in right hand and handing Victory over to Carinus; crowning Carus, Sol, nude but for a *chlamys*, radiate; crowning Carinus, Hercules.
    LIMC Helios/Sol 414; Gnecchi 1912, vol. I, p. 10 Carinus 1.
    Image: after Gnecchi, in the public domain.

26. Plate 202.1
    Harvard Art Museum 2001.185, David M. Robinson Fund.
    Unkown.
    Bronze.
    1st–3rd c. AD.
    Frontal bust of Sol, radiate (twelve rays), draped; above his shoulders the caps of the Dioscuri surmounted by a star.
    https://www.harvardartmuseums.org/tour/ancient-mediterranean-and-near-eastern-bronzes-at-the-harvard-art-museums (continuously updated collection catalogue)
    Image: photograph © President and Fellows Harvard College, with permission.

27. Plate 201.18
    Berlin, Münzkabinett, Staatliche Museen zu Berlin 1907/230.
    Abukir.
    3rd c. AD

Gold medallion. Obv.: Bust of Alexander the Great with lance and shield. On the shield, Tellus flanked by the profile busts of Sol (left) and Luna (right) below five signs of the zodiac.
Dahmen 2008, 526–7, pl. 102; LIMC Helios/Sol 406.
Image: photograph © Münzkabinett, Staatliche Museen zu Berlin.
Identical medallion in Baltimore, Walters Art Museum 59.1.

28.   Gold medallion
      Siscia
      317
      Obv.: frontal bust of Constantine, nimbate, right hand raised, globe in left hand.
      Rev.: Sol, standing frontal, head left, nude but for a *chlamys*, radiate (five rays), right hand raised, globe and whip in his left hand; at his feet a captive.
      RIC 25 (Siscia).

29.   Gold medallion
      Unknown
      305–311
      Obv.: Bust of Maximian
      Rev.: Bust of Sol, radiate, right.
      Gnecchi 1912, vol. I, p. 14 Maximian 3.

30.   Plates 201.19, 202.2
      Gold medallion (nine solidus multiple)
      Ticinum
      313
      Obv.: Jugate busts of Sol (radiate) and Constantine (laureate), above the shield of Constantine, on which Sol is depicted in a frontal split chariot, with two horses jumping to the left over Tellus, and two to the right over Oceanus. Sol is nude but for a *chlamys*, radiate, his right arm raised and a whip in his left hand.
      Rev.: Constantine on horseback.
      Gnecchi 1912, vol. I, p. 16 no. 16. Hostein 2012.
      Image: photograph by Marie-Lan Nguyen, in the public domain, File: Constantin 1er multiple d'or 39,79 g.jpg (February 1, 2019).

31.   Gold medallion
      Sirmium

320–321
Obv.: Bust of Constantine.
Rev.: Constantine, with lance and globe, crowned by Sol, nude but for a *chlamys*, radiate.

32. Gold medallion
Sirmium
321
Obv.: Bust of Constantine II.
Rev.: Constantine II (or Constantine?) with lance and globe, crowned by Sol.
Gnecchi 1912, vol. I, p. 25 no. 14.

33. Bronze contorniate
Rome
AD 355–395 or 423
Obv.: Trajan
Rev.: Vulcan and the shield of Aeneas, decorated with a zodiac and the busts of Sol and Luna.
Alföldi 1976, 131–2 nr 391 (reverse 30); LIMC Helios/Sol 407.

34. Copper alloy contorniate
Rome
Late 4th–5th c. AD
Obv.: Bust of Alexander.
Rev.: Sol in facing *quadriga*, right hand raised, globe in left hand.
Mittag 1999, reverse die 12; Alföldi 1976, 58.; LIMC Helios/Sol 139

35. Copper alloy contorniate
Rome
Late 4th–5th c. AD
Obv.: Bust of Sallust.
Rev.: As previous, crocodile below.
Mittag 1999, reverse die 13. Alföldi 1976, 107.6; LIMC Helios/Sol 140.

L4. Tesserae (Small Selection)
1. Plate 194.18
Lead Tessera.
Arles, Musée Départemental RHO.2009.10.483.
Found near Arles.

Undated.
Obv.: bust of a youth.
Rev.: Sol in frontal *quadriga*.
Arles, Musée Départemental Arles Antique RAL. 76.00.93.
Artefacts.mom.fr TES-4087.
Image: courtesy of the Musée Départemental Arles antique.

2.   Rome.
     Lead.
     Undated.
     Obv.:Eagle on thunderbolt.
     Rev.: bust of Sol, radiate, right.
     Rostowzew 1903: no. 268

3.   Rome.
     Lead.
     Undated.
     Obv.: Soldier or Mars.
     Rev.: bust of Sol, radiate, left.
     Rostowzew 1903: no. 189

4.   Rome.
     Lead.
     Undated.
     Obv.: athlete.
     Rev.: bust of Sol, radiate, right.
     Rostowzew 1903: no. 754.

5.   Rome.
     Lead.
     Undated.
     Obv.: horse.
     Rev.: bust of Sol, radiate, right.
     Rostowzew 1903: no. 755.

6.   Rome.
     Lead.
     Undated.
     Obv.: horse, running.
     Rev.: bust of Sol, radiate, right.
     Rostowzew 1903: no. 756

7.   Rome.
        Lead.
        Undated.
        Obv.: horse, protome.
        Rev.: bust of Sol, radiate, right.
        Rostowzew 1903: no. 757.

8.   Rome.
        Lead.
        Undated.
        Obv.: horse.
        Rev.: bust of Sol, radiate, right.
        Rostowzew 1903: no. 829.

9.   Rome.
        Lead.
        Undated.
        Obv.: club or torch.
        Rev.: bust of Sol, radiate, right.
        Rostowzew 1903: no. 1216

10.   Rome.
        Lead.
        Undated.
        Obv.: indistinct letters
        Rev.: bust of Sol, radiate, left.
        Rostowzew 1903: no. 1277

11.   Rome.
        Lead.
        Undated.
        Obv.: M SCA
        Rev.: bust of Sol, radiate, right.
        Rostowzew 1903: no. 1314.

12.   Rome.
        Lead.
        Undated.
        Obv.: Hecate triformis.
        Rev.: bust of Sol, radiate, right.
        Rostowzew 1903: no. 2461

13.   Rome.
       Lead.
       Undated.
       Obv.: bust of Sol, radiate, right.
       Rev.: Bull.
       Rostowzew 1903: no. 3021.

14.   Rome.
       Lead.
       Undated.
       Obv.: bust of Sol, radiate, right.
       Rev.: Centaur.
       Rostowzew 1903: no. 3022.

15.   Rome.
       Lead.
       Undated.
       Obv.: bust of Sol, radiate, right.
       Rev.:
       Rostowzew 1903: no. 3023.

16.   Rome.
       Lead.
       Undated.
       Obv.: bust of Sol, radiate, right.
       Rev.: rooster.
       Rostowzew 1903: no. 3024.

17.   Rome.
       Lead.
       Undated.
       Obv.: bust of Sol, radiate, right.
       Rev.: two clubs.
       Rostowzew 1903: no. 3025.

18.   Rome.
       Lead.
       Undated.
       Obv.: bust of Sol, radiate, right.
       Rev.: Cargo ship under sail left, below crescent.
       Rostowzew 1903: no. 3026.

19.　Rome.
　　　Lead.
　　　Undated.
　　　Obv.: bust of Sol, radiate, right.
　　　Rev.: phallus.
　　　Rostowzew 1903: no. 3027.

20.　Rome.
　　　Lead.
　　　Undated.
　　　Obv.: bust of Sol, radiate, right.
　　　Rev.: clasped hands.
　　　Rostowzew 1903: no. 3028.

21.　Rome.
　　　Lead.
　　　Undated.
　　　Obv.: bust of Sol, radiate, right.
　　　Rev.: palm.
　　　Rostowzew 1903: no. 3029.

22.　Rome.
　　　Lead.
　　　Undated.
　　　Obv.: bust of Sol, radiate, right.
　　　Rev.: crown.
　　　Rostowzew 1903: no. 3030

23.　Rome.
　　　Lead.
　　　Undated.
　　　Obv.: bust of Sol, radiate, right.
　　　Rev.: ?
　　　Rostowzew 1903: no. 3031.

24.　Rome.
　　　Lead.
　　　Undated.
　　　Obv.: bust of Sol, radiate, right.
　　　Rev.: ARC
　　　Rostowzew 1903: no. 3032.

25. Rome.
     Lead.
     Undated.
     Obv.: bust of Sol, radiate, right.
     Rev.: CLA
     Rostowzew 1903: no. 3033

26. Rome.
     Lead.
     Undated.
     Obv.: bust of Sol, radiate, right.
     Rev.: EV RB
     Rostowzew 1903: no. 3034.

27. Rome.
     Lead.
     Undated.
     Obv.: bust of Sol, radiate, right.
     Rev.: F
     Rostowzew 1903: no. 3035.

28. Rome.
     Lead.
     Undated.
     Obv.: bust of Sol, radiate, right.
     Rev.: HER
     Rostowzew 1903: no. 3036.

29. Rome.
     Lead.
     Undated.
     Obv.: bust of Sol, radiate, right.
     Rev.: PAP
     Rostowzew 1903: no. 3037.

30. Rome.
     Lead.
     Undated.

Obv.: bust of Sol, radiate, right.
Rev.: SFA
Rostowzew 1903: no. 3038.

-31. Rome.
Lead.
Undated.
Obv.: bust of Sol, radiate, right.
Rev.: IIII
Rostowzew 1903: no. 3039.

32. Athens.
Lead.
3rd c. AD.
Obv.: Sol, radate, in split *quadriga*, whip in right hand, reins in left hand.
Rev.: -
Lang and Crosby 1964: 119, L311.

33. Athens.
Lead.
3rd c. AD.
Obv.: Sol, radate, in split *quadriga*, whip in right hand, reins in left hand.
Rev.: Luna in a *biga* of bulls.
Lang and Crosby 1964: 119, L312.

34. Athens.
Undated.
3rd c. AD.
Obv.: bust of Sol, radiate, right.
Rev.: -
Lang and Crosby 1964: 119, L311.

35. Athens.
Lead.
Undated.
Obv.: bust of Sol, radate, left.
Rev.: indistinct.
Lang and Crosby 1964: 119, L313.

36.   Rome.
      Lead.
      Undated.
      Obv.: PRIMI/CAESAR/SERVI
      Rev.: facing bust of Sol, radiate.
      Rostowzew 1903: 1471.

37.   Rome.
      Lead.
      Undated.
      Obv.: Hercules (and the Hesperides?).
      Rev.: facing bust of Sol, radiate.
      Rostowzew 1903: 2536.

38.   Rome.
      Lead.
      Undated.
      Obv.: facing bust of Sol, radiate.
      Rev.: Bust of Luna.
      Rostowzew 1903: 3003.

39.   Rome.
      Lead.
      Undated.
      Obv.: Sol, radiate, nude but for a *chlamys*, standing left, whip in left hand,
      right hand raised.
      Rev.: Fortuna, standing left.
      Rostowzew 1903: 3002.

40.   Rome.
      Lead.
      Undated.
      Obv.: facing bust of Sol, radiate.
      Rev.: crescent.
      Rostowzew 1903: 3004.

41.   Rome.
      Lead.
      Undated.

Obv.: facing bust of Sol, radiate.
Rev.: crescent and stars.
Rostowzew 1903: 3005.

42. Rome.
Lead.
Undated.
Obv.: facing bust of Sol, radiate.
Rev.: crescent in a circle of ten stars.
Rostowzew 1903: 3006.

43. Rome.
Lead.
Undated.
Obv.: facing bust of Sol, radiate.
Rev.: Victory standing right.
Rostowzew 1903: 3007.

44. Rome.
Lead.
Undated.
Obv.: facing bust of Sol, radiate.
Rev.: APP/PAA.
Rostowzew 1903: 3008.

45. Rome.
Lead.
Undated.
Obv.: facing bust of Sol, radiate.
Rev.: C or crescent.
Rostowzew 1903: 3009.

46. Rome.
Lead.
Undated.
Obv.:Sol, radiate, nude but for a *chlamys*, standing left, whip in left hand, globe in right hand.
Rev.: Victory.
Rostowzew 1903: 3001

47. Rome.
     Lead.
     Undated.
     Obv.: bust of sol, radiate, right.
     Rev.: bust of Luna, right.
     Rostowzew 1903: 3010.

48. Rome.
     Lead.
     Undated.
     Obv.: bust of sol, radiate, right.
     Rev.: bust of Luna, right.
     Rostowzew 1903: 3011.

49. Rome.
     Lead.
     Undated.
     Obv.: bust of sol, radiate, right.
     Rev.: crescent.
     Rostowzew 1903: 3012.

50. Rome.
     Lead.
     Undated.
     Obv.: bust of sol, radiate, right.
     Rev.: crescent.
     Rostowzew 1903: 3013.

51. Rome.
     Lead.
     Undated.
     Obv.: bust of sol, radiate, right.
     Rev.: crescent.
     Rostowzew 1903: 3014.

52. Rome.
     Lead.
     Undated.
     Obv.: bust of sol, radiate, right.
     Rev.: crescent.
     Rostowzew 1903: 3015.

53.   Rome.
      Lead.
      Undated.
      Obv.: bust of sol, radiate, right.
      Rev.: Victory standing right.
      Rostowzew 1903: 3016.

54.   Rome.
      Lead.
      Undated.
      Obv.: bust of sol, radiate, right.
      Rev.: Victory standing.
      Rostowzew 1903: 3017.

55.   Rome.
      Lead.
      Undated.
      Obv.: bust of sol, radiate, right.
      Rev.: Fortuna standing left.
      Rostowzew 1903: 3018.

56.   Rome.
      Lead.
      Undated.
      Obv.: bust of sol, radiate, right.
      Rev.: Spes standing.
      Rostowzew 1903: 3019.

57.   Rome.
      Lead.
      Undated.
      Obv.: bust of sol, radiate, right.
      Rev.: bust of Sarapis.
      Rostowzew 1903: 3020.

58.   Athens, Agora museum IL 171.
      Athens, Agora.
      Lead.
      Roman Imperial.

Obv.: Sol, head left, radiate, right hand raised (? described as holding a whip, but I cannot make this out in the photograph), *chlamys* (?) in facing split *quadriga*.
Rev.: Luna in *biga*.
Agora X, 119 no. L 312.

59.   Athens, Agora museum IL 370.
      Athens, Agora.
      Lead sealing.
      Roman Imperial.
      Obv.: Sol, radiate (seven rays) in facing split *quadriga*.
      Rev.: blank.
      Agora X, 119 no. L 311a.

60.   Athens, Agora museum IL 380.
      Athens, Agora.
      Lead sealing.
      Roman Imperial.
      Obv.: Sol, radiate, in facing split *quadriga*.
      Rev.: blank.
      Agora X, 119 no. L 311.

61.   Plate 194.19
      Athens, Agora museum IL 409.
      Athens, Agora.
      Lead sealing.
      Roman Imperial.
      Obv.: Sol, radiate (?), holding a whip(?) in his raised right hand, and reins (?) in his left hand, nude (?) but for a *chlamys*, in facing split *quadriga*.
      Rev.: blank.
      Agora X, 119 no. L 311.
      Image: Agora Image 2017.12.0052; Giannis Tzitzos.

62.   Athens, Agora museum IL 508.
      Athens, Agora.
      Lead.
      Roman Imperial.
      Obv.: Sol, radiate, right hand raised (? described as holding a whip, but I cannot make this out in the photograph), *chlamys* in facing split *quadriga*.

Rev. Luna in *biga*.
Agora x, 119 no. L 312.

63. Plate 194.20
Athens, Agora museum IL 520.
Athens, Agora.
Lead sealing.
Roman Imperial.
Obv.: Sol, radiate (seven rays), right hand raised, reins (?) in his left hand, nude (?) but for a *chlamys*, in facing split *quadriga*.
Rev.: blank.
Agora x, 119 no. L 311.
Image: Agora Image 2017.12.0144; Giannis Tzitzos.

64. Plates 194.21, 194.22
Athens, Agora museum IL 525.
Athens, Agora.
Lead.
Late Roman.
Obv.: Sol, radiate, nude (?) but for a *chlamys*, right hand raised, reins in left hand, in facing split *quadriga*.
Rev. Luna in *biga* of oxen.
Agora x, 119 no. L 312.
Images: Obv. Agora Image 2017.12.0140; rev. Agora Image: 2017.12.0141; Giannis Tzitzos.

65. Athens, Agora museum IL 1036.
Athens, Agora.
Lead.
Late Roman.
Obv.: Sol in facing split *quadriga*.
Rev.: blank.
Agora x, 119 no. L 311.
Images: Obv. Agora Image 2017.12.0243; rev. Agora Image: 2017.12.0244; Giannis Tzitzos.

66. Plates 194.23, 194.24
Athens, Agora museum IL 1240.
Athens, Agora.

Lead.

Late Roman.

Obv.: Sol, radiate (seven rays), nude (?) but for a *chlamys*, right hand raised, reins in left hand, in facing split *quadriga*.

Rev. Luna in *biga* of oxen.

Agora X, 119 no. L 312.

Images: Obv. Agora Image 2017.12.0243; rev. Agora Image: 2017.12.0244; Giannis Tzitzos.

67.   Athens, Agora museum IL 1338.

Athens, Agora.

Lead sealing.

Roman Imperial.

Obv.: Sol, radiate (seven? rays), right hand raised, reins (?) in his left hand, nude (?) but for a *chlamys*, in facing split *quadriga*.

Rev.: blank.

Agora X, 119 no. L 311.

68.   Plates 201.21, 201.22

Athens, Agora museum IL 1339.

Athens, Agora.

Lead.

Late Roman.

Obv.: Sol, radiate (?), nude (?) but for a *chlamys*, right hand raised, reins in left hand, in facing split *quadriga*.

Rev. Luna in *biga* of oxen.

Agora X, 119 no. L 312.

Images: Obv. Agora Image 2017.12.0291; rev. Agora Image: 2017.12.0292; Giannis Tzitzos.

69–74. Athens, Agora Museum IL 365, IL 379, IL 405, IL 449, IL 455 and IL 658.

Athens, Agora.

Lead.

Roman Imperial to late Roman.

Obv.: Sol in facing split *quadriga*.

Rev.: Luna in *biga*.

Agora X, 119 no. L 312.

4   Discussion

A1

The catalogue lists 33 surviving full scale sculptures (complete statues and busts), of which two are probably not Sol. Of the other 31, eight are of the Sol standing type, and 23 are heads or busts. The catalogue also lists a somewhat random selection of lost statues of Sol of all three basic image types (charioteer, standing figure, and bust). These show that all three image types of Sol are attested in full length sculpture. Most dates are based on stylistic considerations, but some are derived from context. A number of the lost sculptures have precise dates given in the surviving inscriptions. Overall, the dates are unremarkable.

A1a. Identification as Sol Probable

Only eight full-length statues have survived that can be identified as Sol, and only one of which the identification is completely certain, namely the recently discovered Sol-statue from Perge (A1a.8). This statue, probably Severan in date, is fully congruent with all aspects of Sol's standard iconography. The only open question concerns the attribute he held in his left hand. A globe seems the most likely.[26] Papini (2002) makes a persuasive case that the Antonine statue in the Palazzo Barberini (A1a.1) and a closely related statue of similar date in a private collection in France (A1a.2) both represent Sol. They depict him in the standard image type of a youth, nude but for a *chlamys*, holding a whip in his right hand. Both statues, however, have heads that were added later, and therefore an alternative identity cannot be excluded, the more so as their original context is not known.[27] In effect, the identification hinges on the whip. Papini points out that there are no nude figures other than Sol for whom a whip is a standard attribute in Roman art. By the same argument a limestone statue in Stuttgart (A1a.4) is probably Sol, although it too is quite damaged (lower legs, right arm, face and part of its head are missing), so that again we can only rely on the whip he carries in his left hand to identify him as Sol.

That the statue in Copenhagen (A1a.5) represents Sol is widely accepted, and more than likely correct. This statue was either made or set up by Flavius Chryseros of Aphrodisias. It was found in 1885 in a highly fragmented state

---

26   Kara 2015, p. XIX, fig. 13.

27   Cf. Papini 2002: 96. Both statues come from old collections, and both were found no later than the 17th century, probably in Mithraeum. Papini (2002: 99) writes that he could imagine them as part of the decoration of a Mithraeum, given their slightly reduced size and fairly superficial execution, but emphasizes that he has not found any concrete evidence for their actual provenance.

on the Esquiline hill in Rome, where its pieces had been reused as building material in a wall together with numerous fragments of other statues.[28] A total of ten heads, many body fragments, and a number of signed bases were found at the time.[29] Out of these fragments four statues a satyr with the infant Dionysus, Poseidon, Zeus and Sol were reconstructed. They were acquired by Carl Jacobsen for the Glyptothek in Copenhagen together with a head of Herakles from the same group. The other fragments were dispersed and their whereabouts is unknown.[30]

The Copenhagen statue has all the hallmarks of Sol: a young man, nude but for a *chlamys*, raised right hand, his beardless face framed with rich curly hair. The stone, radiate nimbus has no direct parallels,[31] but other attempts to portray Sol three-dimensionally with nimbus and rays exist.[32] There is a problem, however, insofar as the image type Sol is never accompanied by only one horse as is apparently the case here.[33] Even so, if the missing attribute in his left hand

---

28   Moltesen 2000.

29   C.L. Visconti reports on the discovery in various installments in *BCom* 14 (1886) under the sections headed "Trovamento di oggetti d'arte e di antichità figurata": pp. 234–6, 297–8 (mentioning the ten heads and listing 9), 314–323 (inscriptions), 339–341, 359–60 (on the restoration of the statue of Neptune).

30   LIMC Helios/Sol 461, referring to *EA* 170, suggests that the group included a second head of sol, closely similar to the Copenhagen head. This is incorrect, as the photo in *EA* shows the Copenhagen head itself, before the statue was restored. Based on Visconti's report in *BullComm* (*supra* n. 20) the missing heads are: head of Juno, idealized bust of a youth (Paris?), portrait bust of a woman (heavily damaged), and the head of a beardless male (so much damaged as to be hardly recognizable). The head of Cupid mentioned by Visconti is probably the head of the infant Dionysus. Cf. Floriani Squarciapino 1943: 42–3.

31   This radiate nimbus has generally been described as a radiate mural crown, following Visconti (*supra* n. 20), who actually described the head as a Cybele with mural crown following the incorrect restoration of the rays as turrets when the statue was reassembled. Now that these turrets have been removed together with the other restorations, the fact that this is a radiate nimbus is obvious. It is interesting to note that while the nose is not yet restored on the photograph *EA* 170, the turrets *are* present. This presumably shows that the restoration was in progress when the photograph was taken.

32   Cf. a marble bust in Venice (A3.2) and one in the Prado (A3.11) for stone nimbi with metal rays; for triangular stone rays cf. a bust in Sevilla (A3.17).

33   Matern (2002: 113) disagrees with me on this point, but the only other example she gives of Sol with a single horse is on a small relief in Rome (C2w.5). What Matern identifies as the protome of one horse by the right leg of Sol is in fact a portion of the relief that is so badly damaged that virtually nothing remains of the horse except for a fringe of manes. I have looked closely at this relief on various occasions and the damage is simply too extensive to admit any certainty about the number of horses originally depicted; there may well have been two or even four staggered horses' heads rather than the single head postulated by Matern. The relatively high position of the surviving fringe of manes relative to Sol's leg supports this (cf. C2c.72). Matern also refers to a statue in Paris (Louvre

was a globe or a whip, this would clinch the identification as Sol. But as the attribute is missing, we cannot be certain, the more so because Squarciapino (1943, 38) emphasizes that the fragments of the statues were put together "senza molta scrupolosità tanto che è dubbia la pertinenza delle teste ai tronchi e delle statue stesse ai plinti cui furono ravvicinate".[34] This could mean, of course, that the protome of a horse which currently acts as a support for this statue was originally part of a different one. Perhaps the head of a youth, tentatively identified by Visconti as Paris (*supra* n. 20) was actually one of the Dioscuri, and the horse was a support for his statue. As it is, we cannot take for granted that the current combination of iconographic elements in this statue is accurate, and hence cannot be certain that it is, indeed, Sol.

The context in which the statue was found also does not help us. Although it seems likely that all the fragments found together on the Esquiline hill near the Sette Sale cistern belonged to a group of statues from a single location, this need not mean that they stood together as part of one iconographic program or group.[35] Thus we cannot hazard any serious guess as to the original iconographic or programmatic context of the statue, which could otherwise have helped in confirming its identity.[36]

There is one potential parallel for the statue in Copenhagen, but it is equally problematic. The North Carolina Museum of Art houses a statue of a youth, rather dubiously identified as Caracalla in the guise of Sol, supported by a single horse, nude but for a *chlamys*, and wearing the remnants of a crown that may have been quite similar to the one of the Copenhagen statue (A1b.2). Here the rays were not sculpted in relief on the side, however, but are presumed to

---

MA 74; Matern 2002: G32, fig. 28) with two horses by his right leg, which she identifies as Sol but I do not. Her identification of this figure is based solely on seven small holes in the head which may have held rays. Unfortunately, the original attributes he held are lost and his clothing (short *chiton*) is most uncommon for Sol, so that this statue cannot be securely identified. In any case, one must also account for the fact that there are *two* horses here, suggesting that – for whatever reason – just one would not do. In general the presence of a single horse suggests the person accompanied by the horse was its rider, while more than one horse is needed to imply a chariot.

34   Matern (2002: 113) points out that in the case of this particular statue the head and torso do appear to belong together.

35   Visconti (*supra* n. 20, p. 298), clearly considers the female portrait bust – now lost – to be different (and later) in style. Even so, it seems too much to suggest – as Kiilerich & Torp (1994: 310) do – that it is pure chance that brought these statues together, and that they need not even have come from the same building. It is much more likely, as they themselves suggest further on (p. 314), that the statues adorned a rich, late antique villa on the Esquiline.

36   Kiilerich & Torp 1994: 113–4; cf. Moltesen 2000: 128–9.

have consisted of twelve metal spikes set on top along the edge.[37] I have argued elsewhere that it is more likely a statue of Castor (Hijmans 1994; cf. chapter 6). The single horse, the youthfulness, the *chlamys*, the right arm stretched out to hold a spear, and the traces on the left arm of a *parazonium* all point in this direction. Taken in isolation, this identification cannot be confirmed, but if the statue was originally set up as one of a pair, the identification would be beyond doubt.[38]

Lack of sufficient data makes it equally impossible to securely identify the other potential statues of Sol. The colossal marble statue in Berlin (A1a.7) lacks attributes (the present ones are modern restorations), but an inscription on the base reads Διι Ἡλι[...], which has suggested the identification as Sol. This is all but confirmed by its companion statue of Luna, and together they may have enhanced the monumental entrance to a temple of Sarapis. The statue of Apollo from Silahtarağa (A1a.6) is probably Sol, as Kiilerich and Torp (1994: 314–316) believe, but his identity hinges on his missing hands, as well as on the separately made, and now also missing, headdress. This may well have been a radiate crown or nimbus of some sort, but something completely different, such as a Parthian cap of Attis, cannot be excluded. If the statue represents Sol, it can be linked to the Selene found in the same cache, and together with the Artemis and Heracles is an interesting example of the manner in which the elite of late Roman times remained interested in pagan themes, decorating their homes with such statues.[39]

Finally, excavations in 1955 at Henchir Tounga (ancient Cincari) in Tunisia revealed a statue which may be Sol. This statue was found near a building which was originally the frigidarium of a bath-complex, but was subsequently transformed into a *Septizodium*, i.e. a monument dedicated to the planetary gods.[40] It was found together with fragments of two other statues, one of Mars and one of Saturn. The statue is of a youth, nude but for a *chlamys*, with fairly long, wavy hair. His right arm and right leg are missing, as are his left arm below the elbow and his left leg below the knee. Thus attributes such as a

---

37   Only the twelve holes remain, and we cannot be certain that they contained rays.

38   Naturally, given the right setting and attributes, this statue could be of Sol. My argument is simply that the attributes of a Dioscure best fit the lost elements of the statue.

39   Longfellow (2016) offers an extensive discussion of the manner in which this group had been set up, and argues cogently for a fourth century date (especially pp. 74–77). Note, however, that she relies somewhat on parallels with the Esquiline group now in Copenhagen (including A1a.5), whose fourth century date has recently been challenged by Attanasio (2015).

40   Picard 1961. Septizodia are often conceived of as fountains but Picard (1961: 93) points out that there is no firm evidence for hydraulic works in any of the surviving septizodia. Cf. Duval & Lamare 2012: 87–109 (http://mefra.revues.org/198).

whip or globe, which could have clinched the identification, are lacking. As it is, the statue taken in isolation cannot be firmly identified. The context, however, makes its identity as Sol likely. The nature of the monument in its second phase, dominated by seven niches quite probably meant to contain seven statues, is virtually confirmed by the discovery nearby of a fragmentary inscription on which by chance only the word *septidonium* (*sic*) was preserved.[41] This, together with the discovery of three of the seven planetary gods (Saturn, Sol and Mars) suggest that the statue under discussion is indeed Sol. However, the excavation has been insufficiently documented, and it is impossible to verify Picard's claim that the inscription, the statues, and the second phase of the frigidarium can indeed be considered contemporaneous.[42]

A1b. Identification as Sol Possible, but Uncertain

Various other statues have more or less tentatively been identified as Sol in the past, but in all cases the identification remains possible at best, though not necessarily probable. Two torsi of nude youths with a *balteus* decorated with signs of the zodiac can serve as an example.[43] Both are sometimes deemed remains of statues of Sol, but there are no parallels for Sol with such a *balteus*, and all the attributes one would expect with Sol are either absent (e.g. the *chlamys*) or lost. Hence there is no reason to identify the two as Sol, the more so because there is a good case to be made for identifying these torsi as *Annus* or *Eniautos*, a young man, nude, with a zodiac as his main attribute.[44] This too, however, is obviously no more than a hypothesis.

Radiate statues of Apollo, with quiver, are sometimes equated with Sol. They certainly represent the Olympian Apollo in his solar guise, but fall outside the scope of this study, and have hence mostly been excluded from the catalogue. An example of such a statue is the Apollo in Civitavecchia thought by Langlotz (1975/6) to be a copy of the colossal statue of Helios on Rhodes. It is in every respect closer to Apollo than Helios, as he has none of the iconographic elements typical of latter. Langlotz' suggestion that this is a copy of the Colossus of Rhodes can be no more than hypothetical, as we lack sufficient data on the appearance of the original.

---

41   Picard 1961: 90 fig. 8; Duval & Lamare 2012: 81–86 (http://mefra.revues.org/198).
42   Until recently, the only publication of these excavations was that of Picard (1961). An article with further details was promised (Duval & Cintas 1976: 856 n. 1), but did not appear until 2012 (Duval & Lamare 2012). It incorporated material from the archive of J. Cintas (primarily photographical), but does not adduce new evidence.
43   LIMC Helios/Sol 301; LIMC Helios 335.
44   On Annus/Eniautos cf. Zuntz 1991: 37–45 (with references); LIMC Annus, commentary (p. 800).

This brings us lastly to the terracotta statue (torso and head; A1b.1), about two-thirds of life-size, which formed part of the decoration of the temple "dello Scasato" at Falerii Veteres (Civita Castellana). According to Ensoli (1995, 400) this is not Apollo-as has generally been thought-but probably Helios. She claims that the figure "... è fortemente influenzata dai ritratti di Alessandro (...)", and especially of Alexander-Helios (comparing it specifically with the Capitoline bust A3.4). In view of the early date of this statue (late 4th–early 3rd c. BC) this is surprising. On the problem of Alexander-Helios, see chapter four.

There are other examples of statues that at one point or another were deemed to represent Sol, usually because they were radiate. But because Sol is not the only deity to emit divine light, rays alone can never be considered adequate grounds to identify a figure as Sol.

A2. Full Statues, Lost

We have literary references to a number of statues of Sol, ranging from Vespasian's transformation of Nero's Colossus to the various *quadrigae solis* on temples in Rome and elsewhere-not to mention the famous Hellenistic statue of Helios on Rhodes. The iconography of these statues is unknown and the selection of lost statues discussed below is not comprehensive.

The most famous sculptural depiction of Helios in a *quadriga* was the statue group by Lysippos set up by Rhodes either on Rhodes itself or in Delphi. As for Roman statues, there were *quadriga*e of Sol on the roof of the temple of Apollo Palatinus (A2a.1) and possibly on the roof of the temple of Sol in the Circus Maximus (A2a.2) as well as on the Lechaion gate at Corinth (A2a.3), to name a few. The tradition of placing statues on the roofs of temples is an Italic one, and if Ensoli (1995: 400) is right in her interpretation of the terracotta statue from Falerii Veteres (A1b.1), there is an early precedent for placing Sol on the roof of a temple in Città Castellana.[45]

Cult statues of Sol are attested for the temple of Elagabal at Emesa (A2b.3), in the temple of Helios at Isthmia (A2b2) and in the temple of Sol in Rome built by Aurelian (A2b.4), to name a few of the most important examples. Licinnius stipulated an annual burning of incense on November 18th for a cult statue of Sol according an inscription from Mahmudia in Romania, dating to ca. AD 320 (A2b.5).[46] In other cases statues of Sol together with Luna are recorded in sanctuaries of other deities (A2c.1–3), as are statues of Sol in larger groups

---

45   For an even earlier antefix with the Etruscan Usil, cf. LIMC Helios/Usil 14.
46   Cf. an inscription from Como recording the building of a *templum solis* – with cult statue? – by T. Flavius Postumius Titianus during the reign of Diocletian; AE 1948: 202.

(A2e). At various locations statues of Sol as one of the planetary deities may be assumed (A2d).

As to the iconography of these *quadrigae* and statues, we have no clue, with the exception of the Colossus of Nero, on which see chapter 6. They serve to confirm, however, that statues of Sol were not overly rare, could be found throughout the Roman Empire, and could date to almost any period.

A2f. Assimilations of the Emperor with Sol
As I argue in chapter 7, the statues of the emperor as Sol are probably misinterpretations, and depict either the emperor or Sol, but not the two conflated.

A3. Heads/Busts of Sol
The catalogue lists 23 life-size or over life-size busts of Sol, almost all made of marble. The list is certainly incomplete, and more problematically, almost certainly gives a somewhat skewed impression of the nature and iconography of busts of Sol. The problem is that such busts are among the more difficult representations of Sol to recognize with certainty. The issue is straightforward. Reducing Sol to a bust obviously limits the scope for identifying attributes, particularly in the case of sculpture in the round.[47] Basically, the only available identifying characteristics are clean-shaven youth, longish hair, and rays (with or without nimbus), but none of these are sufficient to identify a bust conclusively as Sol (as we have seen in chapter two). Common sense suggests that the one remaining characteristic attribute of Sol-rays-gains additional significance under these circumstances, making it likely that in the eyes of a Roman viewer the default identity of a bust of a beardless youth with longish wavy hair and rays would be Sol. But rays are not indispensable. There are examples of busts without any visible trace of rays which almost certainly represented Sol in view of their find context, and there are busts with rays that are clearly portraits, not Sol.

To begin with the former: a bust from a Mithraeum depicting a beardless, bare-headed youth is likely to depict Sol, even if it lacks rays.[48] Context, therefore, or a removable metal radiate crown, can have been a decisive factor for a Roman viewer in identifying such busts, and that leaves us empty-handed when dealing with the numerous busts of unknown provenance depicting idealized youths with long wavy hair. Even the (presumed) presence of rays does not resolve the question. In most such cases only holes have survived, and we

---

47   In the case of two-dimensional representations, it is still fairly easy to include, for instance, a whip behind Sol's shoulder (cf. e.g. E3.1, E3.2).

48   Cf. A3.8.

cannot be certain what was fastened onto the head with these holes.[49] We cannot exclude the possibility that they served to fasten some other object such as a metal wreath, perhaps, or something more elaborate covering the head (cf. A3.6). And even if it is safe to assume that in most cases the holes held rays, this still leaves us with a number of radiate portrait busts which clearly depict a human individual rather than Sol.[50] These have in common that the rays do not emerge directly from the head, but are fastened into a clearly articulated band encircling the head just above the ears. This emphasizes the physical reality of the depicted object with its spiky "rays", as opposed to the intangibility of light emanating directly from the head. Together with the distinct portrait features, this physical reality of their radiate "crown" clearly sets these busts apart from busts of Sol: they depict the portrayed person not "as Sol" but as radiate "in a manner different from Sol."

Of the busts listed in this section of the catalogue, most can be identified as Helios/Sol with reasonable certainty. Two busts have a nimbus with holes for rays (A3.2 & A3.11), two have triangular stone rays (A3.17 & A3.19), two have no rays (cat.A3.1 & A3.8) and the rest have holes for rays drilled directly into the head.

An "Alexander-Helios" (A3.12), found in the Agora in Athens, and originally described by Shear (1971) as a portrait of Alexander, is now widely accepted to be an image of Sol.[51] Frantz (1988: 37) very tentatively links this bust, which she believes was salvaged by its later owners from the Herulian rubble, with a bust of Luna discovered in the vicinity. Both, she feels, may have come from a Mithraeum destroyed by the Herulians.[52]

The much weathered bust of the late first or early second c. AD found in the Villa of Maxentius at Rome (A3.5), has holes (for rays?) set directly in its head, but with its short hair and gaunt appearance is more like a portrait than a bust of Sol. Its poor preservation may be the distorting factor here, and makes it impossible to arrive at any firm conclusions about this bust.

B

The iconography of almost all the full figure statuettes and busts/heads in this section follows the established norms for Sol. Some statuettes may have

---

49   In only two cases the actual rays – of marble rather than bronze – have survived.

50   Clear portraits – with holes for rays – include a bust (of a priest of Sol?) of the early 3rd c. AD in Paris (Louvre Ma 4710), a bust of Severus Alexander in the Museum of Costanza (Bergmann 1998: 280–1 pl. 55.2), a bust of Gordian III in Florence, Palazzo Medici-Riccardi Inv. GFN 16340 (Bergmann 1998: 279 pl. 55.1), and a bust of Gallienus in Copenhagen (Bergmann 1998: 281 pl. 55.3). Cf. also A3.5.

51   Nielsen 1993: 140; Frantz 1988: 37, 41; LIMC Helios 175.

52   On Alexander and Sol cf. chapter 4, pp. 135–142.

been of the image type Sol, but cannot be securely identified due to the loss of potentially defining attributes. A number have attributes that deviate from the norm. Strictly speaking these do do not belong here but I have nonetheless included a few to serve as examples of the problems that arise when the iconographic criteria for images of Sol are not fully taken into account. A head found in Romula (B4b.1), for example, which may or may not have belonged to a fairly large statuette, represents a beardless male with long hair in a wreath-coiffure and five evenly spaced holes which may have held rays. The back of the head is worked down to half a sphere, apparently so that it could be covered by something else. Tudor assumed that is was a metal nimbus,[53] but there are various other possibilities such as the conical cap of the Dioscuri or the Parthian cap of Mithras. Without certainty about the nature of the (metal) covering of the head, its identity must remain open.

The bust in Boston (B4b.2) most likely does not depict Sol. The many-pointed crown is not really radiate, and it has no parallels in depictions of the image type Sol. The prominent uraeus on the front of the crown confirms that this is a very different type of head-dress. Given that this head was originally part of a statuette, we can assume that further iconographic characteristics may have helped identify this as a very different figure.

The Copenhagen statuette (B4a.5), discovered in Denmark in the 19th century, is an enigma. How this statuette, according to some a posthumous portrait of Constantine with radiate crown and jewel, ended up in Jutland is difficult enough to explain (Viking contacts with Byzantium?). The iconography itself is also hard to understand. Stutzinger believes that the statuette is a copy or adaptation of a famous statue of Constantine,[54] but the original can certainly not have been the statue on the porphyry column in Constantinople (cf. A2f.1), as Stutzinger, quoting Mackenprang, believes. There was definitely no space for a *quadriga* on that column, and there can be little doubt that the Copenhagen-statuette was a *quadriga*tus. Poulsen's (1993) suggestion, that the statue represents Theoderic in the guise of (a famous statue of) Constantine is interesting, but as Poulsen himself points out it is no more than an hypothesis and one that requires a rather later date for the statuette than it is generally given. Bergmann argues that the statuette is simply a late 4th or early 5th c. AD representation of Sol. She sees no clear portrait features and explains the straight hair as a late antique, stylized rendition of Sol's long hair, pointing out that it is markedly longer than the hair of the 4th c. emperors. Bergmann also points out that there are no parallels or precedents for depicting the emperor in the clothing of a charioteer. On the other hand she acknowledges that there

---

53   Quoted by Berciu & Petolescu 1976: 43 n. 31.
54   *Spätantike* 507–8 no. 114

are also no parallels for Sol with a jewel on the front of his radiate crown.[55]
In short, there is no consensus on this statue, and all we can conclude, then,
as far as this study is concerned, is that we have here a late statue, possibly a
portrait of a ruler, in an iconography that reminds one of the image type Sol as
charioteer. But bearing in mind that both hands (with a wide range of potential
attributes) are missing, it seems best not to make too much of this.[56]

The statuette in Sion (B4a.3) is strange, and I hesitate to designate it as Sol,
as the gesture towards the head by the right hand has no parallel, I cannot
make out the whip he is reported to hold in his left hand, and the strange "radiate nimbus" could almost be a feather headdress of some first nations peoples
in N. America. It is possible that this statuette/appliqué and the statuette of

---

55   Bergmann 1998: 287–9; Wallraff (2001: 134 n. 41) feels that the statuette does not need to
      be the emperor *or* Sol, but does not explicitly address Bergmann's reservations about an
      imperial identity of the statuette.

56   Some have suggested that this statuette is a copy of a statue that was paraded in the hip-
      podrome of Constantinople at the opening of the chariot races. There is no evidence to
      support this, and good reason to doubt any connection. We know little with certainty
      about this statue, apparently made of gilded wood. Our sources provide quite confusing
      information, identifying it alternately as Constantine, Helios, and a female charioteer (full
      sources in Preger 1901: 166–9). It stood on a chariot and, depending on the source, bore
      a "Tyche" or a "running statuette". Given that the Tyche of Constantinople was depicted
      seated on a throne, Preger suggests that the statuette was actually a Nike rather than
      Tyche, although the sources that identify the statuette at all are unanimous in identifying
      it as the latter. Preger concludes that the statue depicted Constantine in the long *chiton* of
      Sol (that long garment leading to it later being mistaken for a woman), bearing a running
      Nike. This is ingenious, but as Bergmann points out that emperors were not depicted in
      the garb of charioteers. Iconographically a statue of Constantine in a long *chiton* as chari-
      oteer on a chariot and bearing a Tyche or Nike would be quite bizarre, and to postulate an
      iconographically unparalleled statue simply to make sense of clearly confused sources is
      not sound methodology. Alternatively one could, with equal lack of evidence but perhaps
      greater probability, suggest the following: 1. Under Constantine, a statue of Sol – patron
      deity of the circus – was a prominent part of the opening parade at circus games, as it
      was in Rome. 2. At some point – sooner rather than later – the statue of Sol was dropped
      from the parade. 3. At the time of Malalas (Preger 1901: 466), a gilded wooden statue of
      Constantine bearing a Tyche was driven around the hippodrome in a ceremony that
      Malalas believed dated back to the time of Constantine. 4. At the time of our later sources
      (Preger 1901: 467–8) this statue was also no longer paraded and, in a somewhat garbled
      and conflated form, the two Constantinian traditions (the parading of a statue of Sol and
      of a gilded wooden statue of Constantine) had become attached to at least one, but prob-
      ably more than one ancient statue in Constantinople (the female charioteer reportedly
      stood in the Neolaia, the statue of Helios on the Milion). As a hypothesis this is no more
      amenable to proof than Preger's unparalleled statue of Constantine in Sol's *chiton* and
      our sources are too confused and unreliable to allow any firm conclusions. Under these
      circumstances, any attempt to link the statue in Copenhagen to this (which?) lost statue
      in Constantinople inevitably leads to circular arguments.

Venus with which it was found are two of the seven planetary gods, but with five of the seven lost, this suggestion remains to be proven.

The statuette from Boscoreale (B4a.1), identified as Sol by the LIMC and as Alexander-Helios by the Walters Art Museum, is almost certainly not Sol (nor Alexander). It is much more likely to be a Dioscure, as Hill (1949: 29 no. 51) suggests.

Unfortunately very little is known of the find contexts of most statuettes of Sol. It seems certain that the *typum Solis* (B5.1) stood somewhere in Augst, but the inscribed bronze plate of its base was discovered in the 1850s on the pole of a farmers cart to which it had been nailed.[57] Likewise very little is known of the vaulted, underground room in Rimat, Syria, where a bust of Sol, an applique of Sol and a statuette of a kriophoros were discovered in 1847 (B2.10, K1.6). The Ordona statuette (B1.5) was found in the courtyard of the villa, its stratification not fully clear, and its context suggesting that it is more of a stray find than that we should take it as an indication that some object or monument stood in the courtyard with which this statuette was connected. The bust from Carnuntum (B2.8) is, unfortunately, an illegal, stray find. Thus only the rather anomalous chariot from Mithraeum 7 in Stockstadt comes from a clear, but hardly revealing, context. Thus all that really emerges from the known provenances is that statuettes and small busts of Sol occur in most parts of the empire, ranging from Syria, Rhodes and Bulgaria to Italy, Austria, Switzerland, Germany and France.

Matern devotes a significant section of her study to the bronze statuettes of Sol with a raised right hand, a schema which she terms the "invictus" type. Among these she recognizes a main type and a subordinate type, and she contends that the similarities among the statuettes of the main type are so striking that they must depend on a single original. That original, she believes, may have been none other than the Colossus of Rhodes.[58] Intriguing though this hypothesis is, the evidence for it is too meagre. Matern bases her argument primarily on what she considers to be the "erstaunlich wenige Abweichungen beim Standmotiv, der Armhaltung oder der Blickrichtung",[59] but to my mind these are not nearly as striking as Matern would have it. In the 12 statuettes of her "main type"[60] the direction of the gaze varies between left (e.g. B1.2, B1.19), straight ahead (e.g. B1.17, B1.18), and right (e.g. B4a.4), and can be down (e.g.

---

57   Von Fellenberg 1860: 74–76.
58   Matern 2002: 99–108, 147–164.
59   Matern 2002: 147.
60   Matern assigns B1.1, B1.6–7, B1.10, B1.12, B1.14, B1.17–19, B4a.2, and B4a.4 to her "main type", to which we can add B1.2.

B1.14, B1.19), level (e.g. B1.15, B1.17), or up (B1.7); the right hand can be raised
to shoulder height with the palm horizontal, facing down (e.g. B1.18, B1.19), or
with the fingers as high as the crown of the head and the palm vertical, facing
outwards (e.g. B1.7), and with a nearly straight arm (e.g. B1.2) or with an elbow
bent to a right angle (e.g. B1.17). All these statuettes have a certain degree of
contraposto with the same *Standbein* and *Spielbein* (reversed in Matern's subordinate type), but that is hardly remarkable. In short, I would argue that what
Matern regards as an astonishing lack of variation is nothing more than the
result of artists' adherence to the clear iconographic norms for the depiction of
Sol. The wide variation of depictions of Sol *within* the established iconographic
limits makes it unlikely that the artists producing these images were dependent on an actual statue or image as the dominant prototype.

C1a. Pediment Reliefs

On pediment-reliefs, Sol occurs mainly together with Luna as a subsidiary figure (C1a.2, 3, 5, and 9, probably 6 as well). Usually they are corner figures with
Sol emerging in the left corner and Luna descending on the right. This schema
was already used on the East pediment of the Parthenon. In Rome it was a feature of the pediment of the temple of Jupiter Capitolinus, certainly after AD 82
(restoration of Domitian), and quite possibly earlier. The evidence is provided
by a Trajanic relief, now lost, and a relief from the Arch of Marcus Aurelius
(C1a.3), supplemented by seven sarcophagus reliefs (C3b1.1–7), two terracotta
lamps (G1d.1–2), and certain coins. The reliefs of Trajan and Marcus Aurelius
both depict the Capitoline temple in the background of their main scene. It is
hexastyle on the former and tetrastyle on the latter relief, and in both cases the
minute figures of the pediment sculpture are rather sketchily rendered. While
both depict the three figures of the Capitoline Triad in the centre, they differ
significantly in the positioning of the other figures of the pediment. On the
panel relief of Marcus Aurelius (C1a.3b), Sol is in the right half of the pediment,
moving left towards the centre, and Luna is to the left, also moving left, away
from it. On the drawings of the Trajanic relief, the two are on the opposite sides
(Sol left, Luna right) and both are moving towards the centre. These differences
may be the result of artistic license, may reflect a renewal of the pediment
sculpture at some point between the reigns of Trajan and Marcus Aurelius, or
may indicate that the respectively tetrastyle and hexastyle temples on these
reliefs are not actually both the same temple. Whatever the case, these reliefs
document Sol and Luna as flanking figures of the Capitoline Triad on one or
more temple pediments in Rome in the second century AD.

   This combination is also found on the seven Antonine sarcophagi. Here we
find the Capitoline triad flanked by Sol on the left in his *quadriga* and Luna

on the right in her *biga* with both Sol and Luna moving to the right. On the two lamps we also find Sol on the left, Luna right, both moving to the right on their respective chariots. These images are not uniform, as various other figures may be depicted alongside the Triad as well.[61] Thus they do not offer direct evidence for the composition of the pediment reliefs of the temple, but do confirm that the image of the Capitoline triad flanked by Sol and Luna had wide currency in Rome by the 2nd c. AD.[62]

Beyond the pediment, the Trajanic relief also depicted the planetary deities standing along the raking sima atop the roof, apparently as full length statues, with Sol on the left end, Luna on the right and Jupiter on the highest point in the centre. When the drawing of this part of the relief (since lost) was made in the sixteenth century, Luna, heading left up the roof in her *biga* and Mars, nude, helmeted, holding an upright spear were still well-preserved, Mercurius and Jupiter were already too much damaged to be easily recognizable, and Venus, Saturn and Sol had disappeared completely.

Sol was also a prominent figure atop the temple of Apollo on the Palatine (A2a.1), and two small pediments (C1a.2, C1a.6), both thought to be of shrines, and both probably from Rome, also depict Sol emerging in the left corner. In both cases the right corner, presumably with Luna, has been lost.

In other parts of the empire, notably in the East, Sol alone (C1a.1, 7, 8) or Sol and Luna (C1a.5, 9) could be depicted as the main decoration of temple pediments. In one case Sol is depicted on one pediment and Luna on the other (C1a.5), in the other both are on the same pediment.

C1b–C1f. Other Architectural Reliefs

Sol is not a common figure in other architectural contexts, and in most cases very little is known about the original context of the architectural fragment on which Sol occurs.

On the Arch of Constantine (C1e.3), Sol is depicted five times, and in all cases on reliefs of Constantinian date rather than reused older ones. Three times Sol is depicted as one of the two *dei militares* of Constantine's army, the other being Victoria. A large relief on the west wall in the eastern arch depicts Sol opposite a closely similar relief of Constantine on the east wall. A tondo on the eastern, short side of the Arch depicts Sol in his *quadriga*, with a similar

---

61   On the lamps, two Tritons; on the sarcophagi, the two Dioscuri with or without Fortuna (C3b1.1, 2, 4, 5, 6) or the three Parcae (C3b1.3).

62   The provenance of most sarcophagi and one of the two lamps is unknown, but when the provenance is known it is the city of Rome and its immediate environs and a similar provenance is likely in most other cases.

tondo depicting Luna on the west side. This prominence of Sol on the Arch connecting him with the army, with Constantine, and with the Arch itself, is clear evidence that he remained important to the official imperial message after the battle at the Milvian bridge.[63]

No clear patterns emerge from the other reliefs in these sections. They range from mythical depictions of Phaethon or the gigantomachy to generic depictions of Sol alone or Sol and Luna, come from all parts of the Empire, and vary in date between the late second century BC to the fourth century AD. In short, as part of architectural decoration, reliefs depicting Sol were rare, but could occur throughout the empire and throughout the imperial period. They obviously do not form a homogeneous group either in nature or function.

C2a and C2b.Sol (Alone or with Luna)

A relatively small number of votive altars and reliefs are dedicated to Sol himself, and a fair number of these associate him directly with Luna in some manner. A good example is the votive altar of Eumolpus and his daughter Claudia Pallas depicting a bust of Sol, but with an inscription dedicating it to Sol and Luna (C2b.1). Another example are the twin altars from the Aventine Dolichenum dedicated to Sol and Luna respectively (C2b.2).[64] In the case of the latter we would not have known that Sol and Luna were invoked jointly if only one altar had survived. Similar connections with Luna, now lost, cannot be excluded for some of the other reliefs listed in C2a (Sol alone).

C2c. Mithras.

The rich and complex imagery of Sol in Mithraic contexts is discussed in chapter 4, pp. 153–175.

C2d

In the context of Jupiter Dolichenus, Sol and Luna are most prominent on the distinctive bronze votive triangles of that cult. Relatively few such triangles have survived, but no doubt a great number were melted down to reuse the bronze. The surviving triangles come from the Rhine provinces and the Balkans as well as from Dülük itself, the original home of the cult. It is reasonable to assume that such triangles were a standard element of Dolichenic shrines, and it is clear from the surviving evidence that Sol and Luna were fairly standard figures on such triangles, although there is notable variation both in the figures depicted and in their position. There is no narrative inscribed on the image,

---

63   The Arch was dedicated in AD 315.
64   Cf. CIL III, 14386d; CIL VIII, 1458–9; CIL XIII, 4472 & 4477.

but this does not diminish its rich visual symbolism.[65] Sol and Luna normally appear as busts,[66] that is as less elaborate figures than Jupiter, Juno and Victory, but the depiction of Sol and Luna could take on different forms. The two altars from the Aventine Dolichenum in Rome (C2b.2), dedicated to Sol and Luna respectively, are a good example of their potential prominence.[67]

C2e. Jupiter Columns

Jupiter- and Jupiter-giant columns or pillars, known in German as *Iuppitersäulen* and *Iuppitergigantensäulen* are a strictly regional phenomenon, characteristic of the Rhine border and its hinterland.[68] They were votive monuments to Jupiter Optimus Maximus, in the form of elaborately decorated, freestanding columns supporting a statue of Jupiter, seated, standing, or on horseback. The latter is usually depicted trampling a giant underfoot. A typical monument could consist of a high, rectangular base with a relief carving of a standing deity on each side (often referred to as a *Viergötterstein*), surmounted by a cylindrical, hexagonal, or octagonal socle decorated with the planetary deities or other gods, on which rested the actual column which could be undecorated, patterned (e.g. with a motif of scales or even oak leaves), or decorated with reliefs of deities. The Tuscan, Corinthian or composite capital of the column supported the statue group of Jupiter.

Sol appears on a significant number of Jupiter columns either as bust, standing figure, or charioteer. He can be depicted on the base, the socle, the column drum, or even as part of the capital. Most common is sol as planetary god alongside the other planets.[69] Usually the planets are depicted on the intermediate socle, occasionally on three sides of the rectangular base (two pairs and a trio) with the dedicatory inscription on the fourth side. Alternatively Sol is paired with Luna and they are depicted with other deities on the capital,

---

65   The following figures are depicted on one or more of the surviving votive triangles on which Sol occurs: Jupiter Dolichenus, depicted in various ways, including – in (neo)-Hittite tradition – standing on the back of a bull and brandishing an axe (C2d.1–4, 9, 11–13); Sol, as radiate bust (C2d.1–5, 9–13); Luna, as bust (C2d.1–5, 9–13); Victory, often crowning Jupiter (C2d.3–4, 9, 11–12); Juno Dolichena, depicted in the Hittite tradition on the back of a cow or hind. (C2d.3–4, 9, 11–13); Sarapis (C2d.5); the Diosuri (C2d.4, 11); bearded men emerging from rocks and holding leaves (C2d.3, 13); Hercules (C2d.11, 13); Minerva (C2d.11, 13); Dionysus (C2d.13); eagle (C2d.4, 9–11, 13); peacock (C2d.4).

66   On C2d.9 the two figures on the frontal split *quadriga* may be Sol and Luna.

67   Cf., e.g., K9.18.

68   On Jupiter columns, cf. Bauchhenß & Noelke 1981: Woolf 2001; Noelke 2006, 2010; Blanchard 2015. For distribution maps, Noelke 2010: 367–373.

69   C2e.4–5, 7–8, 9?, 12–14, 16–20, 22–28.

the shaft of the column, the socle, or on two sides of the rectangular base.[70] In three cases not all the figures have been sufficiently preserved and Luna cannot be explicitly identified, so that we cannot exclude that there were a few Jupiter columns on which Sol, but not Luna, was depicted.[71]

A wide range of deities could be depicted on Jupiter columns and none had a fixed place except Jupiter. This makes it difficult to estimate how common Sol was on these monuments. In many cases only one or two sections survive and it is then impossible to establish which deities (if any) adorned the lost parts of the monument. However, Sol and Luna were potential elements of these columns from the outset. They flank Juno at the top of the oldest surviving column (C2e.1) which dates to the reign of Nero. Sol, Luna and the planetary deities would appear to be characteristic of the more elaborate columns, but are usually omitted on less lavishly decorated ones. Thus we may conclude that Sol, with Luna or in the company of all the planetary deities, formed a characteristic, but not essential element of the Jupiter columns.

A full evaluation of Jupiter columns is difficult, given their fragmentary survival and the lack of information on the potentially significant context of these monuments.[72] A further problem is the fact that no trace has survived of wooden columns which may or may not have existed. Some columns make clear reference to oak trees,[73] and although the earliest columns are mid first century there are remarkably few surviving stone columns prior to the second half of the second century. It is worth noting that we do have evidence from some sanctuaries in the region for isolated posts erected without an architectural function. It is not known whether these posts were decorated and we cannot be certain that they had a ritual function, far less that they were related to the stone Jupiter columns.[74] Nonetheless they represent a potential forerunner or parallel.

C2f. The "Danube Riders"

A large number of fairly small lead and marble plaques from the Danube provinces constitute virtually our only evidence for a cult of some regional significance which flourished from the latter part of the second century to the fourth

---

70   C2e.1–2, 3?, 6?, 10–11, 15, 21?

71   The three possible columns are C2e.3, 6, 21. On all three there are the traces of unidentifiable figures who may have been Luna.

72   A good example of the importance of context is the column from Bad Cannstatt (C2e.16). It depicts only six of the seven planetary deities. Saturn is omitted, but was apparently supplied by the context given that an altar to Saturn was found nearby.

73   Green 1992: 152; Espérandieu, *Germanie* 2269.

74   Derks 1998: 132–4, 154–6.

century AD.[75] Almost all aspects of this cult are enigmatic. We do not even know the names of the main protagonists of these reliefs, a woman-priestess or goddess-behind a three-legged table and two riders riding towards her.[76] Virtually no inscriptions are associated with these plaques and they are mostly stray finds so that we also lack potentially informative contextual evidence.[77]

The most comprehensive discussion of these plaques is still that of Tudor (1969). The lead plaques were produced in large numbers from moulds, and the distribution of identical plaques suggests that there were various production centres in the region. Sirmium, for example, was apparently the production centre for most plaques found in Pannonia Inferior.[78] The small marble plaques are less common, but also appear mass-produced, insofar as they can typically be populated by figures that are so summarily carved that they are virtually unrecognizable. Because so few plaques have been found *in situ*, dating them has depended on style and iconography, problematic under the best of circumstances and especially hazardous in the case of such mass-produced, provincial objects.[79] It is generally thought that the aedicula-shaped plaques are the oldest and began to be produced under the Severi, while the round plaques are thought to belong to the second half of the third century and the earlier part of the fourth. The plaques appear to have been bound to person as well as to place. A few were found in military camps, others in small shrines in civilian settlements, and yet others in tombs.[80] In at least one case, discussed by Popovic (1991), a plaque was discovered in the tomb of a woman, indicating that this cult was not limited to men, as Mithraism was. There is also no evidence that it was a predominantly military cult. Suggestions for the origin of the cult range from Dacia to the East.[81]

---

75 A very small number of plaques has shown up outside the Danube region, for instance in Gaul (Popovic 1991, 237) and Britain (Mackintosh 1997, 363). On the provenance of Danubian rider plaques cf. Mackintosh 1995, 58.

76 Ertl (2014, 100–102) gives a good enumeration of all the various figures whom we may, perhaps, be able to recognize on these plaques. For the various proposals concerning the identity of the woman at the centre, cf. Plemić 2013, 60. Almost all suggestions remain tentative, however. This is even true of the horsemen approaching the central woman. They are often identified as the Dioscuri, but on about 15% of the plaques, only one horseman is depicted.

77 Popovic 1991, 235–6. Only eight inscriptions are associated with the cult, of which only three can be satisfactorily deciphered, and none mention the name of a deity. Cf. Mackintosh 1997, 363.

78 Popovic 1991, 241.

79 Tudor 1969: II, 78–84; Oppermann 1981.

80 Popovic 1991: 243–4; Tudor 1969: II, 55; cf. C2f.125.

81 Dacia: Tudor 1969: II, 81; Orient: Popovic 1991: 245.

C2g. Hosios kai Dikaios

In Asia minor we find a substantial number of votive altars and stelai dedicated to Hosios and Dikaios on which Sol is depicted in his canonical Graeco-Roman guise.[82] Only a selection of those is presented here. In eight cases the bust of Sol is depicted,[83] once above four protomes of horses, and in three cases Sol is depicted driving a *quadriga*. Sol is always radiate, sometimes with the addition of a nimbus. In two cases Sol alone is depicted (C2g.2 and C2g.4), and in one case we have a canonical Sol-Luna image (C2g.11). The other eight cases include Sol as one of a number of gods. The range of deities is broad, and there is no apparent pattern. Diana/Artemis occurs once (C2g.3), but not explicitly paired with Sol, and in general Sol is depicted apparently on par with other deities. Hosios (with rod or measuring stick) and/or Dikaios (with scales) are depicted on only three of the ten reliefs, but are mentioned in the inscriptions of all ten.

C2h. Saturnus

Saturnus was an important regional god in the part of North Africa that coincides roughly with Africa Proconsularis and Numidia. He represents a continuation of the Punic cult of Ba'al in this region.[84] From the first century AD (a few perhaps a bit earlier) to the fourth century AD, dedicants erected stelai in honour of Saturnus in a large number of places and in a wide range of styles. Iconographically, the stelai show a significant amount of regional variation as well as some change over time. All have in common, however, that the dedicant is depicted more prominently than the deity. The simplest stelai depict very summarily sketched frontal figures of the dedicant in low relief with round head, rectangular body, and raised arms holding offerings. Above the dedicant we usually find a crescent, sometimes with the addition of a rosette. Such stelai often have no inscription at all, or else have an inscription in either neo-Punic or Latin. On the more elaborate ones, the relief is deeper, with greater volume and far more detail. The iconography is more complex with a greater number of figures, notably deities. We find gabled or round-topped stelai with the dedicant or dedicants in a deep niche framed by columns and deities above the gable and/or in the tympanum, and sacrificial scenes below.

---

82   On Hosios and Dikaios cf. Ricl 1991: 1992; Parker 2017, 91. The radiate horseback rider
       (C2g.11) is not discussed here as he falls outside the canonical image types for Sol.

83   In the case of C2g.2, the bust may not be Sol.

84   On the Saturnus of Africa cf. Leglay 1960, 1966, 1971, 1988; Eingartner 2003; Benseddik &
       Lochin 2005; Wilson 2005; Schörner 2007; McCarty 2013; 2016. Specifically focusing on
       Sol: Ben Abid 2012. On the solar orientation of temples of Saturnus in N. Africa: Esteban
       2014.

On the simpler stelai, Sol and Luna are not depicted, although there is often a crescent, sometimes with a rosette, above the head of the dedicant. The rosette is usually interpreted as a solar symbol, as are various other symbols such as a rayed disc and a star, with varying degrees of likelihood. Their use is not restricted to the less elaborate stelai, but the interpretation of such symbols requires rigorous analysis and careful, critical *Forschungsgeschichte* well beyond anything we can offer here. So we will limit ourselves to the actual images of Sol and will not concern ourselves further with the wide array of potential symbols of the sun.[85]

On the more elaborate reliefs Sol and Luna become the most common added figures, although by no means essential. Sol is almost invariably depicted as a bust (97%), sometimes with whip,[86] and on three stelai from Tébessa above four horses. On over 80% of the stelai on which sol occurs he is depicted together with Luna, usually to either side of Saturnus who himself is depicted either as bust, as seated on a throne or as reclining figure. Sol can be depicted to either side of Saturnus, with a slight preference for the left side (about 60%). On stelai from the sanctuary of Saturnus on the slopes of El Kheneg (castellum Tidditanorum) the bust of Luna is sometimes replaced by a crescent.[87] Sometimes Sol is replaced by a whip, and Saturnus may be represented by his *harpe*.[88] In other cases, the bust of Sol may be depicted alone, for instance in a tympanum.[89] In one case the bust of Sol is in the middle and flanked by Luna and Saturnus.[90] On two occasions, Sol is depicted with the other six planetary deities.[91]

Rare, but quite interesting are the depictions of Sol as standing figure. On a stele from Timgad the depiction is fairly straightforward: Sol (left) and Luna (right) stand to either side of the reclining Saturnus.[92] On a stele in Ksar-Toual-Zammel an enthroned Saturnus is similarly flanked by the standing figures of Sol and Luna, this time with the addition of the two Dioscuri.[93] The Dioscuri also occur on two reliefs from the environs of Tébessa, this time on horseback.[94] On two other stelai, both from Timgad, Sol and Luna are also

---

85   For a few examples of such symbols: C2ha.1–3, 5–6, 8; Leglay 1960, 66; Wilson 2005, 404.
86   E.g. C2h.10, 19, 28, 48, 85, 87, 90–92.
87   C2h.4–7, 21–22, 25.
88   C2ha.4, 7.
89   C2h.24, 78, 79, 89.
90   C2h.13. In this arrangement, the three busts are in the order of the days of the week.
91   C2h.9.
92   C2h.66.
93   C2h.96.
94   C2h.82–3.

depicted as standing figures to either side of Saturnus. Sol is radiate, but in a unique variation of his standard image type, he is holding a horse, as is Luna. There can be no doubt that Sol and Luna are meant (the former is radiate, the latter is definitely female), but the addition of the two horses is clearly intended to recall the Dioscuri as well.[95]

The large variety of the stelai itself also reinforces the symbolic nature of the imagery, while the lack of uniformity suggests that these stelai were not intended to communicate complex or detailed messages. But while the reading may have been fairly straightforward to the dedicants, we should take care not to take the meanings for granted.[96] One potential issue, for instance, is the meaning of the crescent which is sometimes thought to symbolize Ba'al Hammon, while on other occasions it clearly represents Luna. The deployment of other non-anthropomorph symbols also requires closer study. The styles of the stelai may be a fruitful object of analysis as well, in particular in terms of regional variation and the coexistence of different styles.

Dating the stelai is difficult. The traditional, more-or-less style-based dates, which I have perforce accepted here, are due for revision.[97] McCarty, for example, makes a cogent argument for a "centre-periphery" model to explain the stylistic variation, with the more elaborate stelai partaking in an iconographic koine that was transmitted along the major Roman roads and centres of habitation, while the simpler ones were more rural.[98] This subverts the basic rationale behind the dates suggested by Leglay (stylistic evolution over time) but does not (yet) offer clear alternative dating criteria. Be that as it may, the dates suggested in this catalogue, based primarily on Leglay, should be handled with skepticism.

In short, there is a great deal that we can still learn about these stelai and that may shed further light on the meanings of the basic image types for Sol.

C2i. The Planetary Deities

The planetary deities are the gods and goddesses linked to the "wandering stars" or planets: the Sun, the Moon, Mercury, Venus, Mars, Jupiter and Saturn. They occur with reasonable frequency in Roman art, and the reliefs collected in this section represent only a small proportion of the total number images when all media and contexts are taken into account.[99] Precisely when and how these

---

95   C2h.65, 71.
96   On the social status of the dedicants, cf. Wilson 2005: 407.
97   Wilson 2005: 403.
98   McCarty 2010.
99   For other depictions of the planetary deities cf. A1a.3, A2d.1, C1a.3a, C2c.29, 54, 67, C2e.4–5, 7–8, 12–14, 16–20, 22–27, C2h.9, D2.1–5, E3.1–4, F1b.7, F3.1–2, 4, F4.4, G1f.1, H1ok, J2b.1, 8–9, J2e.1, J3.3–4, J6.1, K5, K6.1, K9.34.

deities became attached to their specific planet is not certain, but it was probably not long after the wandering stars were recognized as a separate group.[100]
The Greeks acquired this knowledge from the Babylonians quite early, and the
connection between these gods and their planets is certainly pre-Classical. It
was maintained throughout the Hellenistic and Roman period, with some variation of deities. This should not be surprising, for throughout this period the
divinity of the planets was relatively uncontested.[101] Nonetheless the concept
of divine planets has troubled scholars because of its perceived un-Greek irra-
tionality. Some therefore suggest that under the impetus of Hellenistic science
the connection between the planets and their deities was downplayed and a
more "objective" rather than religious nomenclature was sought. Following this
scientific phase there was then a revival of what is termed "planetary religion"
from the end of the first century AD.[102] But as Beck points out, the names of the
associated deities were almost always mentioned with "their" planet throughout the Hellenistic period.[103] Furthermore, the notion that the planets were
divine was not a voluntary article of faith, but a widely accepted philosophical
tenet or, in anachronistic terms, scientific fact. We will return to this divinity
of the planets in chapter 4. It is pure chance that sections C2i and C2ia each
contain seven entries, not by design.

C2j to C2x. Varia

The remainder of section C2 of the catalogue is devoted to isolated cases:
deities with whom sol is normally not associated, groups of deities not commonly depicted together in this manner, or deities who are altogether rare in

---

100   Delattre 2013; Beck 2007, 72–3; Eilers 1976; Cumont 1935.

101   Beck 2007, 72.

102   Wallraff (2001, 92–3), citing Cumont and Gundel, claims that the planets were not directly
named as Saturn, Jupiter, Mars, etc. (rather than "planet of Saturn etc.") until the first
century BC in Latin and the second century AD in Greek ("Im lateinischen Sprachraum
werden die Götternamen ohne weiter Zusätze erst am Ende der römischen Republik zur
Bezeichnung der Planeten verwendet, im griechischen Sprachraum sogar erst ab dem 2.
Jh. n.Chr." – the latter is not actually what Cumont (1935, 37) says, as the Greek papyrus of
the 2nd c. AD that he quotes is, according to Cumont, definitely a copy of a text composed
"à une date plus ancienne"). This argument is not entirely clear but appears to be that
naming the planet directly by its deity's name is the result or an exponent of the renaissance of planetary religion, while speaking of the "planet of [deity]" is less religious. I do
not find this distinction convincing, because I don't understand which problem it is trying
to solve. It is clear that Cumont (1935) feels that divine planets were not consonant with
the "rationalisme scientifique" of Alexandrine scholarship, but as Beck points out, this
idea is anachronistic. There is no reason to assume that the divinity of the planets would
be considered irrational among Alexandrian scholars, as the concept had impeccable
philosophic credentials.

103   Beck 2007, 73 n.3.

art. This section further illustrates how widely the image types for Sol could be deployed, but does not otherwise hold surprises for us.

C3. Funerary Reliefs

Section C3 lists reliefs from funerary contexts on which Sol occurs, i.e. sarcophagi, stelai, and other funerary monuments. Sol does not commonly figure on such reliefs, but is not a negligible figure either.

The majority of the sarcophagi on which Sol appears are decorated with mythological scenes, namely the myths of Phaethon (C3a1.1–13), Endymion (C3a2.1–7), the adultery of Mars and Venus (C3a3.1–3), Prometheus (C3a4.1–3), Ariadne (C3a5.1), Meleager (C3a6.1), Paris (C3a7.1), Protesilaos (C3a8.1), and Rhea Silvia (C3a9.1).[104] Of the other sarcophagi, two groups are noteworthy: a group of Antonine sarcophagi with the Capitoline Triad, Sol, and Luna on the side of the lid (C3b1.1–7) and sarcophagi with masks of Sol and Luna as corner figures of the lid (C3b2.1–5). The remaining sarcophagi vary in type. Five of these depict Sol and Luna (C3b3.1–5) and range from the elaborate Velletri sarcophagus of the mid second century (C3b3.1) to a simple strigillated sarcophagus of the mid third century (C3b3.4). Two others depict only Sol, as (tiny) element of complex scenes (C3b4.1–2). The sarcophagi are predominantly from Rome and Italy; a small number come from France,[105] and one from Turkey.[106]

The funerary stelai gathered under C3c are a mixed batch. On eleven of the stelai Sol but not Luna is depicted, usually as a minor figure, but once as the main figure. On the other three, Sol and Luna are depicted together. Most of the stelai are from Asia Minor, a few are from France.[107] The remaining monuments in section C3 include the tomb of the Haterii in Rome (relief of the Rape of Persephone), the large funerary monument of Igel near Trier, and a relief in a cliff face near Cadenet in France. Of the final two monuments, the funerary altar of Julia Victorina, does not belong in the catalogue, but sheds such interesting light on the Sol-Luna symbolism that I have incorporated it anyway.

In many cases we are dealing here with typical depictions of the image type Sol, often together with Luna, and often as minor figure (alone as well as with Luna). Sol is not a common figure on sarcophagi and funerary stelai, and therefore the same issues arise as discussed above with regards to the reliefs C2j to C2x: Sol does not contribute to the construction of a pattern, but (usually)

---

104   On Roman sarcophagi and their meanings, cf. Zanker & Ewald 2004.
105   C3a2.7, C3a4.1, C3b2.3, C3b4.
106   C3b3.5.
107   C3c.4, 8, 13.

represents a variation or anomaly of the normal pattern in these cases. We would need to study those patterns or groups in which Sol is normally not represented to see how the insertion of Sol affects the iconographic schema. That is beyond the scope of this study.

C4. Other Reliefs and Reliefs of Unknown Function

Only a few of the objects listed here require further discussion. The *iovila* from Capua (C4.1) is a small votive plaque of the third century BC dedicated by the family of the Kluvatii on the occasion of a festival known as the *pumperiae*. The facing head of Sol with a full circle of rays is a good example of a Sol image type current in Italy until the late Republic, when it was gradually displaced by the radiate bust. The head of Sol on Roman unciae of the late third century BC is closely related to this type.[108]

The terracotta disc in the archaeological museum of Brindisi (C4.2) is almost certainly late Hellenistic, and not third century AD as Yalouris proposes in the LIMC.[109] It is thus an early non-numismatic example of the Sol-Luna imagery. The astrological context is noteworthy.

On the well-known Decennalia base (C4.21) we again find Sol and, possibly, Luna. The base supported one of the columns erected in 303 to commemorate the twentieth year of Diocletian's rule and the tenth year of the tetrarchy. Four columns bore statues of the tetrarchs while a fifth, larger column was surmounted by a statue of Jupiter. On one side of the surviving base a sacrifice is depicted attended by, among others, Roma seated at the far right. Her head is lost, but still partially preserved next to it is a bust of Sol in the fold of her billowing cloak; his face has been damaged, but the rays are still clearly visible. In the 16th century, when the base was discovered, Sol's head was less damaged and there were reportedly still traces of a female bust next to it, suggesting Sol and Luna may have been depicted together.[110] I see no trace of Luna on the sixteenth-century drawing in the Codex Coburgensis, however, and no real space for her either, so that on balance I think it more likely that Sol alone was depicted here.[111]

In section C4 we also find a number of images from the Near East of which the identity is problematic (C4.25–7). Local solar or sun-related deities in the Roman Empire generally had their own distinct iconographies, and this was certainly true in Asia Minor and Syria. Nonetheless, confusion is possible,

---

108   L1.1; Cf. Schauenburg 1955.
109   Cf. LIMC Semele 23.
110   Wrede 1981: 122 n. 78.
111   For the Codex Coburgensis drawing see arachne.dainst.org/entity/1223840.

particularly in Syria, where the use of the most distinct iconographic attribute of Sol, rays, extended well beyond local solar deities. Various non-solar deities are also depicted radiate, gods as well as goddesses. This increases the possibility of confusion, in particular when only a radiate bust is depicted without any further defining attributes, and the context is unknown. In their present state these busts fall within the definition of the basic image type Sol. But in Syria, perhaps more than in other parts of the empire, context may have provided visual evidence that a different deity was meant, and that the adherence to the norms of the image type Sol is a result of a lack of detail, not artistic choice. The issue is an iconographic one. I am not arguing that all cases of the image type Sol automatically depict the same god. The *interpretatio romana* of local deities often resulted in a Roman form for a local god. But in the Near Eastern context of a range of potential radiate deities, the lack of additional defining attributes leaves these busts underdefined to a greater degree than they would have been in other parts of the Empire.[112]

C5. Not or Probably Not Sol

The images collected here give an impression of Hellenistic and Roman image types that were akin to Sol, but with essential differences.

In the Hellenistic period in particular, Apollo may be depicted radiate as the sun god, but with attributes of Apollo as well, such as a quiver and bow or a cithara (C5.1–3). In the late Republic and the Augustan era, this solar Apollo was common in Roman art as well, but after that he recedes from art. Throughout most of the imperial period, the basic image types sol are used to depict the sun god. Apollo is still considered to be the sun, but no longer depicted in a manner that competed with Sol. Consequently the solar Apollo of Augustus came to be associated with the image types Sol and with their preference for Sol, both Aurelian and Constantine can represent themselves as heirs of Augustus and his Actian Apollo.

Most of the other examples in C5 are of regional solar deities with particular attributes or other iconographic characteristics that differentiate them from the basic image types Sol. The list is by no means exhaustive. In the Near East, the most obvious iconographic difference between local solar deities and Sol is the practice to depict the former in battle dress rather than nude or with a

---

112   Canonical images of Sol certainly existed in this region, at times prominently. On coins of Tripoli in Phoenicia, for example, a tetrastyle temple is depicted with in the central intercolumnal space the burning altar of Zeus Hagios; in the space to the left a statue of Sol, radiate, nude, right hand raised is depicted on a pedestal. In the corresponding space on the right, Luna. Cf. Matern 2002: 299 M185a–d (Julia Domna, Caracalla, Heliogabalus, Julia Soaemias); *CIL* 03, 14386d.

chiton (C5.4–9, 12, 14, 16). Such solar deities as Shamash, Iarhibol, or Malachbel are warrior gods and are hence depicted fully armed throughout the period of Roman rule.[113] These depictions betray a significant degree of Roman influence. The armour that these gods wear, for instance, is of the standard Roman type and in the later Empire the gods may also echo Sol's typical gesture of the raised right hand.[114] This means that the differences in iconography of these gods, notably their armour, was purposeful and served to differentiate them from the standard image types Sol of the Graeco-Roman art of imperial Rome. These images make quite clear that they do not depict Sol or Helios, but a different god. And yet these local deities were so closely related to Sol that they sometimes echo the Graeco-Roman type to a striking degree. These are not different sun gods in the (obviously impossible) sense of different suns. There is only one sun and these gods represent different manifestations or traditions of sun worship.

But that alone may be too simple an explanation for the differences (and similarities) in iconography between these deities and the image types Sol. In the mingling of local and Roman elements we see a reflection of the process of positioning these local deities and the religious traditions they represent within the broader context of the Roman Empire. That process was neither straightforward nor easy, and the outcome was by no means always the same. In dealing with local religions, Roman practice ranged from the outright banning of cults, rites, or priesthoods to the introduction of previously local cults into other parts of the Empire, not to mention the imposition, locally, of imperial cults. Local approaches to coping with the new, imperial situation ranged from the continuation of traditional cult practices unchanged, to the promotion of redefined local cults and the adoption of imperial ones. The politics of religion were complex and formed a major part of the process of empire-building, for religions and religious traditions loomed large in the socio-political discourse of imperial identities and power-relations.[115] Viewed from this perspective such local images as the Near Eastern sun gods in their Roman armour form

---

113 Cf. Matern 2002: 120–122.

114 Cf. Matern 2002: 241, I58 and I59, bronze statuettes in the Louvre (BR 344) and a private collection.

115 For a good, recent case study of "the dynamic way in which the people of the provinces negotiated their way through the new imperial context" in religious terms, cf. Revell 2007. Her focus is on two sites in Britain and the Roman province of Baetica respectively. More work has been done on religion and Empire in the Western provinces than in the East, but cf. Price 1984, Woolf 1994 or Lozano's (2007) interesting study on the differences between the *Divi Augusti* of Rome and the *Theoi Sebastoi* of the Near East. Cf. Also Sweetman's (2007) more general discussion of Roman Knossos. Cf. Webster 2001; Woolf 2001; Price 2012; and various contributions to Kolb & Vitale 2016.

interesting documents of a complex discourse. Studying such images in terms of identity, power, and empire would be worthwhile but again – it is a *Leitmotiv* of this book- that is beyond the scope of this study.

The same is true with most of the other images in this section: the Egyptian Souchos can be almost indistinguishable from the standard image type Sol, but for his crocodile (C5.10). In other cases a sun god is depicted on horseback (C5.20) or on a chariot drawn by eagles (C5.19). There are other examples as well of such iconographic variations which clearly differentiate the depicted figure from the standard image types Sol, but also quote or recall aspects of the Graeco-Roman Sol. But this was not invariably the case with local solar deities. Elagabal, for instance, was normally "depicted" aniconically, as a conical rock.

D. Mosaics and Opus Sectile

The number of mosaics on which Sol is depicted is not large. The themes are primarily cosmological: Sol-alone or with Luna-and the zodiac (D1a.1–7, D1b.1–2), Sol and the planetary deities (D2.1–5), Sol and the seasons (D3.1–2), and other cosmological scenes such as the famous mosaic in Mérida (D5.1). A small number of mosaics depict myths (D4.12. D5.8–9), and the others simply the bust of Sol (D5.2, 4–7). On the so-called Christ-Helios mosaic of mausoleum M in the Vatican necropolis (D5.3), see chapter 9. For synagogue floor-mosaics depicting Sol, see chapter 4, pp. 142–9.

E. Wall-Paintings and Stucco Decorations

The images gathered in this section offer few surprises. One group of images is new, namely the Fall of Icarus (E4a.1–5), while the rest all follow patterns we have already encountered and discussed. The fresco of Sol (?) and Luna from the Farnesina deserves mention because of its date (28 BC) and iconography. Tunica, lance, boots and nimbus are all elements that are not in line with the iconography of the standard image types for Sol, but the whip is closely associated with Sol and there can be no doubt that his counterpart is Luna. Bearing in mind that if this is Sol it is the oldest surviving example of Sol as standing figure without his chariot, this may be an image that antedates the coalescing of clear iconographic norms for the depiction of the image type sol as standing figure.[116]

---

116   The Colossus of Rhodes was presumably a standing figure, but we know nothing of its iconography. On certain Bactrian coins of the 2nd century BC the sun god is depicted as a standing figure, cf. Matern 2002: 86–7. On the Farnesina paintings in general, see Moormann 2008.

The fresco in the *ala* of Pompeii IX 7,19 (E2.3) is a good example of how closely Sol and Apollo were identified in the first century AD. The radiate nimbus, whip, and *chlamys* clearly identify the male bust as Sol, but his counterpart is described as Diana the huntress with two javelins. Thus this image conflates the Apollo-Diana and Sol-Luna imagery visually, much as Horace does in his *Carmen Saeculare* (cf. chapter eight). Nearby in Pompeii we find the canonical Sol-Luna imagery (E2.2). In general, the iconography of Sol in Pompeii adheres to the iconographic norms set out in chapter two.[117]

The groups of planetary deities are somewhat surprising. The tondi from the Insula Occidentalis follow the normal pattern for the planets as markers of the days of the week (E3.1). In the house of the *Caccia Antica*, however, only six planets are depicted (E3.2), of which four as busts in tondi, while Venus and Jupiter are represented by more elaborate panels. Mars appears to be absent. Venus and Jupiter are the two most beneficial planets, which may explain why they receive more elaborate treatment, and Mars is the most malefic, which may explain why he is omitted, but the order of the images is also not "planetary" and a convincing interpretation of this cycle is difficult to give. Whether the four busts at the *Officina Quactiliaria* represent Sol, Luna, Jupiter and Mercury as planets is not certain (E3.3).

The depiction of Sol and Luna in the Via Latina catacombs (E6.1) in the scene of Joseph's dream (*Gen.* 37, 9) is appropriate,[118] and that the sun and the moon are depicted in their anthropomorphic form along the established lines of Graeco-Roman iconography is not surprising. As in the case of the synagogue floors discussed in chapter 4, this image is evidence that the image types for Sol were signs in the semiotic sense, not icons of the Graeco-Roman sun god. The other images in this section do not need further discussion here.

F. Plates and Vessels

Iconographically, this section of the catalogue offers little that is new. What makes it noteworthy is the early date of many of the objects listed here.

The black gloss relief wares from Cales (F1a) represent the oldest objects in this section, and among the oldest in the catalogue as a whole. Cales was a Campanian town on the site of Calvi Risorta, just to the North of Capua, on the Via Latina. After conquering it in 335 BC, the Romans made it an important centre for the Roman administration of Campania. It was settled almost

---

117 See in particular E1a.1–2.

118 "Then he dreamed another dream, and told it to his brothers, and said, 'Behold, I have dreamed another dream; and behold, the sun, the moon, and eleven stars were bowing down to me.'"

immediately by Roman and Latin colonists, was the seat of the quaestor for Southern Italy, and rapidly developed into a major Roman city.[119] It also became an important centre for the production of relief-decorated black-gloss ware imitating silver vessels. Calenian relief ware was produced and exported on a significant scale by the first half of the third century BC and continued to be produced until about 180 BC.[120]

On Calenian vessels, in particular omphalos bowls, busts of Sol were depicted regularly, though not with particular frequency. The frontal bust of Sol is normally accompanied by two horses or two pairs of horses jumping up to either side.[121] This image conflates two of the standard image types sol (radiate bust and charioteer respectively), and remained a common way to support the identity of the radiate bust until Late Antiquity.[122] Normally four horses are depicted, but sometimes the image is so sketchy that only two horses are shown, without meaning that in these cases Sol was driving a *biga*. On occasion Sol is depicted without horses.[123] The bust of Sol above a crescent with stars within a zodiac circle is noteworthy as a particularly early example of this type of astrological imagery in the Roman world.[124] The presence of the Dioscuri as an integral part of a number of designs is also noteworthy, as the Dioscuri are often found in the company of Sol.[125] We should note, lastly, that Apollo with the rays of the sun, but identified as Apollo by his lyre, also occurs.[126]

Of the images of Sol on Calenian ware, most fit what was to become standard in the Roman world. Only the radiate Apollo with a lyre would disappear in the course of the first century AD. Calenian pottery thus gives us quite early examples of Roman images of Sol. These are by no means Roman inventions, of course. The Greek centres to the South as well as the Etruscans to the North had longstanding traditions of depicting their sun god, Helios and Usil respectively.[127] Roman art inherited sol from both traditions, but tracing that process is as difficult and, frankly, as meaningless as tracing the beginnings of

119 Cornell 1995: 352.
120 Pagenstecher (1909) still provides the most comprehensive study of Calenian ware but his dates are a bit too late (cf. Jentel 1976: 31–3; Pedroni 2001). Of course, in view of the Latin potters' inscriptions production cannot have begun before the late 4th c. BC. The most richly decorated ware is the oldest.
121 F1a.2(?)11.
122 Cf. e.g. C2c.13, 68 (2 horses), C2g.4, C2n.1, C3d.2, C4.16, J1.2, 4, L1.5.
123 F1a.1, 13.
124 F1a.13.
125 F1a.6–7, 9, 11. Cf. C2d.4,6–7,11, C2e.1, C2h.65, 71, 82–4, 96, C2n.1, C2w.4, 11, C3a1.3, C3b1.1, 4–6, C3b3.2, C3c.6, F1b.1(?), F4.2, H4f.1, H10g.1, J1.6, J3.3.
126 F1a.1417.
127 Cf. LIMC Helios and LIMC Helios/Usil.

"Roman" art in general. In the case of Calenian ware, I have taken the nature of the town, which was a Roman administrative centre where Latin was spoken by a population descended in significant numbers from Roman and Latin colonists, to be "Roman" enough to designate its products as "Roman". What that tells us is that by the third century BC, stock image types of Sol were incorporated in Roman art as a matter of course. This is in line with the numismatic evidence of Roman Republican coinage and as such need not surprise us. It is also in line with the Romans' own assessment of Sol as one of the traditional deities of the Roman pantheon.[128] For the purpose of this study of the Roman image types for Sol that is all we need to establish.

Of the other pottery vessels, a substantial number is Mithraic in origin, but generally speaking Sol was not a frequent figure on these vessels, or indeed on vessels of any kind. On three of the five bronze vessels he is one of the planetary gods.[129] On the other two, both sixth century censers, we have another example of the continuity of the Sol-Luna imagery into Christian contexts. In this case they are depicted to either side of the crucifixion of Christ, not uncommon in (early) medieval art.[130]

The silver cup from Kertsch (F4.1) does not really belong in this catalogue, but is a beautiful example of the fully established image type of Sol as charioteer in Hellenistic art, and as such can serve to support our contention, outlined above, that "Roman" art such as that in Cales produced images of Sol along typological lines that by this time were already well-established. The undocumented silver bowl auctioned by Christie's in 2010 (F4.5) is without iconographic parallel. If authentic, it serves as a reminder how rich and varied the range of scenes was in which Sol occurred.

We close our discussion of this section with a brief glance at a silver plate from Boscoreale now in the Louvre (F4.2). It is decorated with the high relief bust of a woman wearing an elephant headdress. To the right is a cornucopia topped by a lunula, and decorated with a radiate bust of Sol, an eagle, and two star-topped caps of the Dioscuri. Numerous other symbolic images and animals are crowded around the bust as well. The presence of the lunula, the bust of Sol and the caps of the Dioscuri as decorative elements on the cornucopia by the main figure – probably the personification of Africa – is clearly symbolic in nature and reinforces the evidence for a highly symbolic use of the image type Sol already at this early date. For the plate must date to before AD 79, when the villa in which it was found was buried by the eruption of the

---

128 See chapter 2.
129 F3.1,2,4, cf F4.4.
130 Déonna 1948.

Vesuvius, and may well be considerably older. Roller suggests the personifica-
tion of Africa may actually be Cleopatra Selene (40 BC–5 BC?), daughter of
Marc Antony and wife of Juba II (48 BC–AD 22), client king of Mauretania.[131]
An even earlier date is not impossible either.

G. Lamps

With this section on Roman lamps with depictions of Sol we turn our attention to a group of simple, mass-produced objects that reached broad layers of
society in all corners of the Empire. Most lamps were undecorated, utilitar-
ian and made of terracotta, but significant numbers of terracotta lamps were
decorated to varying degrees, primarily on the disc or the handle, with a wide
range of images. The invention of a double matrix system of mass production
(one matrix or mould for the bowl of the lamp, a second for the covering) in
the Hellenistic era made it easy to produce closed lamps on a large scale. This
type of lamp generally had only two small openings, one in the spout and
one in the disc covering the bowl, which had the advantage of keeping the oil
cleaner. The disc, of course, provided an excellent space for decoration and the
matrix process enabled factories to produce lamps with relatively high quality
relief decorations at relatively little additional cost. It is hence reasonable to
assume that such decorated lamps entered the dwellings of a broad segment of
Roman society. In addition to these common, industrially produced lamps the
Romans also could have luxury lamps of bronze, often decorated, to enhance
more prestigious spaces. We find images of Sol on terracotta as well as bronze
lamps which is as one would expect, given the range of images with which
lamps were adorned. Indeed, as source of light sol is perhaps a "logical" decorative element for lamps, but he is not an especially common one, although he is
not particularly rare either.[132]

Lamps provide useful information about the chronology of depictions of
sol. A glance at the catalogue reveals that a relatively large number of lamps
date to the first or early second century AD, and that likewise a surprisingly

---

131   Roller 2003: 141–2. Della Corte (1951: 35–7) interprets it as a portrait of Cleopatra VII, her
      mother.
132   On the social role of figurative imagery on lamps, see Bielfeldt 2014 (with thanks to
      M.J. Versluys for alerting me to this article). She presents a fascinating picture, based pri-
      marily on literary sources, of lamps as objects entangled in webs of active and reflective
      seeing of self and others, webs of light and darkness in which lamps are at once silent wit-
      nesses and active enablers, etc. She cites passage after passage in which lamps are imbued
      with a notable amount of agency in a surprising range of situations, making it clear that
      even such mundane objects as lamps could and did have very different "social lives" in
      antiquity from today. On the most common deities on lamps, Bielfeldt 2014: 202 n. 21. On
      Luna, Bielfeldt 2014: 227–230.

large number of lamps, all from Greece, are from the fifth and sixth century AD. In this sense lamps as a category differ markedly from most other groups in this catalogue, in which most images are dated to the second and third century AD, and only a smaller minority date to the first century AD or earlier. One reason for this difference could be that in the case of lamps, dates are not based on the image but on the lamp-type. That would imply that in at least some of the other cases (reliefs, statuettes, and the like) the accepted dating – more likely to be based on the image, i.e. Sol – is too late, and that a larger percentage belongs to the early Imperial period. But other factors can play a role as well. Changes in tastes and practices in lamp-designs may have had an effect, for instance, so that industry-related factors are reflected in the chronological distribution of lamps on which Sol is depicted, rather than the popularity of the image itself and the concepts it represented. We see something like this in Roman imperial coinage, in which the chronological distribution of images of sol is wholly atypical when compared to other groups in the catalogue. Clearly one cannot postulate a direct correlation between the occurrence of image types within a specific category of material (lamps, coins) and the general popularity of that image type in society at large.

While lamps alone, then, cannot offer a picture of the relative popularity of the image types sol from century to century, the fact remains that they can often be dated typologically with considerable accuracy. The relatively large number of lamps from the first century AD is thus further confirmation of the fact that the image types Sol were well-enough established to be deployed routinely by the beginning of the imperial period. The lamps likewise confirm the uninterrupted use of these image types until well into the Byzantine era in at least certain parts of the ancient world.

Particularly noteworthy, in this regard, are the late lamps from Athens, Corinth, Delphi and Phthiotic Thebes.[133] It is tempting to link these late lamps to lingering pagan sentiments, well-documented in particular in Greek philosophical circles, but we must be careful not to do so based simply on the image on these lamps. We have already come across various post-pagan depictions of the image types Sol in contexts which cannot possibly be defined as pagan, such as the Visigoth church in Spain (C4.28), the crucifixion scene on a bronze censer (F3.3), and a number of synagogue mosaics (D1a2, 4–7), and more examples could be given.[134] Thus we have already established that the image types Sol were not intrinsically religious or exclusively pagan. They

---

133   G1a.71–109. These lamps were produced in Corinth and a were of a specific type that was otherwise used only for Luna.

134   Cf. K6.9.

simply depict the sun, or some directly or indirectly associated concept. As already stated the sun is a fairly logical motif for the decoration of a lamp, and quite possibly that is all there was behind this choice of motif by the early Byzantine lamp makers in Greece.

That is not to say that the lamps could not attain considerable added significance in specific contexts, but such added significance was then provided by the context, not inherent in the lamp itself. The cave of Pan at Phyle on the Parnitha above Athens is a good example of such a potentially significant context, for the practice of leaving votive lamps in such caves was certainly not, in origin at least, a Christian one. But even here we should take care not to read too much into the evidence. Many lamps with Christian symbols also ended up in the cave. This does not mean that it had become a Christian place of worship, but rather suggests that the correlation between the cult in the cave and the imagery on the lamps could be quite tenuous.[135] It is therefore best not to view the early Byzantine Greek lamps decorated with a bust of sol as signs of lingering pagan sentiment *per se*, but to see them instead as lamps with the generic depiction of the sun.[136]

Iconographically the images on the lamps listed here adhere to the standard image types for Sol. Most common are busts of Sol, but a few lamps depict him on his *quadriga* or as full-length figure. Generally he is without an attribute except rays and sometimes nimbus, but on occasion he is depicted with a globe, a whip or both, and sometimes with a raised right hand.[137] Only a relatively small number of lamps depicts Sol and Luna together (G1c.1–20; G1d.1–2; G4.1), but on a fair number of other lamps the bust of Sol is depicted above an upturned crescent with two stars,[138] maintaining the close link between Sol and Luna. Other, more complex images incorporating sol are rare on lamps. Of these the lamps depicting Sol, Luna and the Capitoline Triad have already been mentioned. A few individual lamps have interesting designs, such as the lamp in the British Museum on which the profile bust of Sol is being crowned by a

---

135   G1a.108–109. On the cave of Pan at Phyle and similar caves in Attica see Fowden 1988b, 55–7; cf. Larson 2001, 231.

136   The significance of lamp decorations has not received much consideration, and Stewart (2003, 195) notes that images on lamps are often dismissed as essentially meaningless decoration. He offers a number of cogent arguments against this straightforward dismissal (Stewart 2003, 195–207). Particularly relevant to the analysis of the image types Sol on lamps are his remarks on the problems of establishing and defining the context of lamps and the importance of admitting inconsistency of use (Stewart 2003, 196–7).

137   *Quadriga*: G1b.1–3; G1d.1–2; full-length standing figure: G1c.5; G4.1; whip: G1a.7–10, 55, 64, 69, 70, G1c.5; G3.4; globe: G1a.28, 58, 62, 64; G1c.2, 5, 6, 10, 17, 19; G3.2, 3, 5; G4.1; raised right hand: G1d.1, 2; G3.2, 3,5; G4.1.

138   G1a.6, 30, 33, 40, 42, 47, 51, 67, 120, 127, 130, 139–142; G1g.2; G2a.1–3, 6, 8, 10–14, 16–17

small winged Victory (G1g.2). Finally, the use of multiple lamps in a single context also offered the opportunity for more complex iconographies to enhance the associated meanings. The ephemeral nature of such groups makes it hard to document this, but we have at least one clear example of lamps actually being produced to be used together. The fact that lamps of the type listed under G1a.71–109 could only depict either Sol or Luna, and no other images, surely must mean that they were meant to be used jointly as the Sol-and-Luna image type rather than in isolation, as Sol or Luna only.

H. Intaglios

Depictions of Sol are not rare on intaglios, but not frequent enough to be considered common either. The images adhere well to the established image types and illustrate the wide range of depictions possible. As engraved ringstones were quite widely distributed in society, this fairly rich array of gems with images of Sol gives a good idea of how widely the iconography of the sun was known and understood. For an extensive discussion of the intaglios see chapter three, pp. 115–134.

J. Jewellery, Costume, and Other Adornments

This is a rather heterogeneous group of objects, ranging from adorned statues to gold earrings, and there is certainly a degree of arbitrariness in its composition. This is particularly the case with the decision, for instance, to include decorative elements of *ependytes* in this section but decorative elements of armor in the next. That arbitrariness need not concern us. Our aim was to produce a catalogue that organized the material with a degree of logic but without concern for the manner in which the image types Sol were deployed. It is important, therefore, that all *ependytes* end up in the same section, but does not matter if all armour is catalogued under a different heading.

The variety of images again illustrates how widely the image types Sol were deployed, and reminds us not to discount rare contexts as anomalies or chance occurrences. For example the votive reliefs to Sabazius from the Balkans (C2t) depicting Sol and Luna do not stand alone, but find *comparanda* in bronze foil plaques of diadems found in Rome (J1.6, cf. K9.45). Other contexts are more familiar. We find the planetary deities, in the order of the week starting with Saturn, as well as the Sol-and-Luna pair, of course, sometimes with the Dioscuri, and the like.[139] The objects come from most parts of the Empire and span its full history. Dates and provenances contain few surprises although the earrings from Bolsena, dated to the first century BC or earlier may be

---

139   Planetary deities: J2b.1,.8–9, J2e.1, J3.3–4, J6.1; Dioscuri: J1.6, J3.3.

noteworthy if Sol is indeed depicted with a raised right hand on one of them
(J5.1).

K. Minor Objects

This section of the catalogue presents a wide array of objects and concludes
our survey, leaving only coins and medallions to be discussed in section L. It
contains few surprises, but gives a further impression of the wide reach of the
image types Sol and the long period of time during which they were current.

The appliqués gathered under K1 are depictions of Sol of various types and
materials gathered here because they were originally attached to, or part of
some other object, the nature of which can no longer be established. Some
of the bronze appliqués may be the heads of bronze statuettes, others may be
parts of vessels (terracotta, bronze, or silver), decorative elements of furniture,
and the like. All objects gathered in this section are typical of an image type
Sol, but it cannot be excluded that lost elements or context originally modi-
fied this. A beardless, radiate bronze head may originally have been part of a
cuirassed statuette for instance, or one with some other attribute or attributes
incompatible with the image types Sol.

In section K2a we find a number of statues of Roman generals with images
of Sol on their breastplates. The majority of these are Julio-Claudian, including the most famous one, the statue of Augustus from Primaporta. The *loricati*
come from as far afield as Cartagena, but are mostly from Italy itself. A breastplate from Ritopek (Castra Tricomia) in Moesia Superior, dated to the third
century on the grounds that Sol is depicted on it, but quite probably earlier
in date, should also be mentioned here. It depicts Mars between two sets of
three planetary deities (K2.14). Sol also occurs as decorative element on other
parts of Roman military attire, such as helmets and a *cingulum*, as well as the
parade harness of a horse. The decorative elements of chariots listed under
K3 may also be from a military context, although this is by no means certain.
The image types Sol are not a common element but clearly not an anomaly
either in this context. The early dates of these depictions – over half date to the
first century AD – is worth noting. In view of these dates, it seems likely that
the pole of the *signum* carried by Flavinus, the *signifer* of the *ala Petriana* in
Britain, on his funerary stele was surmounted by the radiate head of Sol, rather
than the radiate head of the emperor as is sometimes suggested (K2b.1).

Sol would seem a logical decorative element for sundials (K4.1), but this was
apparently not the case. On *parapegmata*, peg-calendars with holes for pegs
to mark the correct day, depictions of Sol and the other planetary gods could
be included whenever the calendar incorporated the seven-day week (K5a
and b). This was not necessary of course, and section K5c lists parapegmata

incorporating the seven-day week, but without images. The early date of the parapegma from Posilippo (first century BC) shows that the concept of a seven-day week was part of public life in the Roman world by the reign of Augustus, if not earlier.

It is difficult to evaluate the data in the next section, K6. The metal fittings of boxes and chests gathered here come predominantly from Hungary, four sets from Intercisa along the Eastern Danube frontier South of Aquincum, and two sets from Császár, West of Aquincum and also close to the Danube. Whether this means very much is hard to say, for to what extent it is simply chance that such fittings were preserved at Császár and Intercisa (at least partially in tombs) and found their way into museum collections is not clear.[140] There is nothing to indicate that the imagery is specifically local. The other figures depicted are either Graeco-Roman or, interestingly, Christian (K6.1–2), and aside from generic compositions such as Sol and Luna or the planetary deities there are no indications that the figures were combined with special care or had a significance much beyond the decorative. This is particularly clear in the case of the fittings from Intercisa listed under K6.2, with its corner strips decorated with repeated, identical figures of Mars, Jupiter and Sol. This repetitive depiction of these pagan deities is meaningless, but striking nonetheless in view of the main scenes, which are, in part at least, Christian.[141] The central band on the front of the box depicts Lazarus, Moses striking the rock, the Good Shepherd, the sacrifice of Isaac, Jonah, and the healing of the blind. The corresponding section of the lid, on the other hand, is decorated with a roundel depicting Orpheus, and with four smaller roundels at the four corners of the scene in which Sol (upper left), Luna (upper right), the chi-rho (lower left) and an eagle (lower right) are depicted. Without attempting an exegesis of the iconography of this chest as a whole, it seems to me that we need not ascribe any particularly profound meaning to the haphazardly placed, repeated figures of Sol, Mars, and Jupiter along the corner strips.

This apparently random use of these figures suggests that they were generic to the point of being meaningless in this decorative context. That in turn suggests that they were common enough not to attract notice as decorative components of chests or boxes. One would then assume that chests decorated in this fashion were common, but that they have a very low survival rate in

---

140 Metal fittings of this type have not received much attention and do not loom large in the visible sections of museum collections. It is worth noting that both Letta (in the LIMC) and Matern (2002) have overlooked the fittings published by Buschhausen (1971).

141 Mars, Jupiter and Sol have in common that they are planetary gods, but with the other four planets missing completely, any connection with days of the week or planets strikes me as tenuous.

the archaeological record. Wood decays and the fittings, of course, are easily melted down and reused. It is well possible, therefore, that the fittings listed in K6 are only the tip of an iceberg with two factors contributing to their low number and misleadingly regional character in this catalogue: a poor rate of preservation in the archaeological record and a low profile in museum collections. The final entry in this section, a tenth century copper box with ivory panels in Braunschweig (K6.9), is listed to illustrate the continuing popularity of the image type Sol & Luna long after the end of antiquity.

Little need be said about the weights in section K7. The late Etruscan mirror reputedly discovered in or near Cosenza and now in the Museum of Fine Arts in Boston (K8.1) is listed here only *exempli gratia*. Similar Etruscan mirrors can be found in Rome and I have included this one as illustration of the iconographical context within which Rome's own imagery of Sol evolved. The final section (K9) illustrates again how far flung the standard images in Graeco-Roman style of Helios and Sol were. There are no specific groups in this section and I will not comment on the objects individually.

L. Coins, Medallions, Contorniates and Tesserae

The catalogue lists the main coins depicting Sol issued by the official Roman mints in the Republic and Empire. The list is presented here only for indicative purposes. It is not exhaustive and issues by provincial and autonomous mints have not been included at all,[142] for it is not my aim to discuss these coins in any detail. Most of the work on this part of the catalogue was carried out by Dr. Tracene Harvey, and I owe her great thanks for this. She has attempted to identify all major variations of images of Sol on the coins of each minting authority (Republican magistrate or imperial ruler), with under each variant a list all the coins of that ruler on which that variant occurs. The information has been drawn almost exclusively from the RRC and RIC respectively. It was exceedingly rare for a non-Roman deity to appear on Roman Republican or Imperial coins (see p. 7, n. 6), so that we can state with certainty that all these coins were understood to depict Sol of Roman tradition. One can turn to Berrens (2004) for an extensive exploration of imperial Roman coins depicting Sol that is far more detailed than what I could offer here,[143] although his interpretations and conclusions should be treated with care.

There can be no question that coin-imagery was meaningful to Romans. The sheer variety of images as well as the large numbers of different coins issued

---

142   Matern (2001: 285–301) provides an extensive, but by no means exhaustive list of local issues, as does Yalouris in the LIMC s.v. Helios.

143   On Republican coins depicting Sol, cf. Ryan 2005.

make this abundantly clear. It is no chance, for instance, that Sol dominated the coinage of Aurelian in the last year of his reign. His government intended to convey certain meanings with those repeated depictions of Sol and the intended audiences could no doubt readily read those messages. But we lack much of the information and knowledge on which they could draw to do so. Hence while there can be no doubt that studies of the deployment of the image types Sol on Roman coins have great potential, we need to know much more about the coins than we do at present for that potential to be fully tapped.

Often the knowledge we lack is not for want of data but simply for lack of analysis. Coins were usually not minted in isolation, for example, but as as a group with an aggregated message to which each coin of the emission contributed its part. The early emissions of Alexandria under Nero, discussed in chapter six (pp. 913–918) are an excellent example of this. Here we see not only how the coins contribute jointly to a detailed dynastic definition of Nero's position, we also see how studying the imagery of the individual coins within the context of the emission as a whole, significantly facilitates their interpretation. Without the context of the emission, at least one of the coins is somewhat ambiguous in its meaning, but within the group its place is clear and the ambiguity disappears.[144] In other ways as well, knowing the place of an individual coin within the overall production can be quite telling.

Much has been made in the past of the Aurelian bronzes proclaiming *Sol dominus imperii Romani*.[145] These coins have been taken to be conclusive evidence that Aurelian elevated the sun to supreme deity of Rome. Thanks to the MER-RIC project, we can now can state definitively that these coins were minted only once, at one mint (Serdica) and in such low numbers that they constitute less than 0.02% of the total number of coins issued under Aurelian (which in turn was only a fraction of the total number of coins in circulation during his reign). We can state with confidence, then, that a Roman had far less than a one in ten-thousand[146] chance of seeing one of these bronzes. We cannot postulate a religious revolution on the basis of such exceedingly rare coins, not even an unsuccessful one, but that is not my point here. We always knew that the Sol Dominus coins of Aurelian were rare, but it is only thanks to the MER-RIC project that we can confidently state just how rare. The MER-RIC project bases its data on a thorough analysis of 104,000 individual coins

---

144   This does not mean that the ambiguity of the coin, when seen alone, was unintentional, but merely adds to the its polyvalence.

145   L2.87–89.

146   One in five-thousand coins of Aurelian, doubled to account for the total number of coins in circulation. That number is still too low, but how much too low is hard to say.

currently in public or private collections, all dating to the nine years between
AD 268 and 276 and all minted at Roman imperial mints. Of every Roman coin
issue during this brief period we now know when (often to the month), where,
and in what numbers it was minted. To the best of my knowledge we do not
have information this detailed for any other period of Roman coinage – yet.
But at some point we will, and once we do, we will be in a far better position
to analyze coin-images within the context of any issue they may have been
part of, and with a strong sense of the overall number of coins involved. That
in turn should allow us to have at least some idea of the intended audiences
and perhaps related events. In short, we will be in a much better position to
understand the non-monetary roles and impact of coins.

The local coinage minted by numerous cities in, especially, the Eastern half
of the Empire adds a few extra layers of complexity to this already complex
field. What was the purpose of these locally minted coins? Cities regularly
allowed years, even decades to pass without exercising their right to mint, and
recent research into the volume of output of local mints draws into question
their economic role. Hale Güney (2015), for example, calculates the coin output of Nicomedia in 59/8 BC at about 33.000 drachmai worth of tetrachalkons.
That is the equivalent of the annual wage of 165 soldiers, hardly an impressive
amount of money, especially if we take the longer view and factor in years
that cities like Nicomedia did not mint coins at all.[147] Güney cites research
showing that over the course of 200 years of imperial rule, Amasea on average
minted about the number of coins it would take to pay the basic wages of five
soldiers per year.[148] This was no mean city. Heavily fortified with impressive
walls and a strong fortress, this home town of Strabo had been the residence of
the Mithridatids before it was conquered by the Romans in 70 BC. It was still
Metropolis of the region well into the Byzantine era. A major coast-to-inland
trade route passed right through the city, crossing the river Iris over an arched
stone bridge within the town walls. It is hard to see what economic impact
such a paltry sum of money could have had on such a city.

Of course we may be assuming too much when we take the role of these coins
to have been monetary. The inclusion of a separate category "medallions" (L3)
raises similar questions. We may agree that Roman medallions were coin-like
objects with primarily non-monetary functions, but the problem we then face
is that there are no hard-and-fast criteria by which we can distinguish Roman

---

147   The city did not mint any coins during the first decade of Nero's rule, for example, accord-
      ing to the RPC, which dates all Neronian coins of the city to "after 63".
148   Güney 2015: 44. She gives various other, comparable examples as well.

medallions from Roman coins.[149] Both medallions and coins served to disseminate messages, the basic difference being that coins were primarily intended to function as currency, while medallions were primarily intended to function as gifts. Hence an important criterion for the identification of medallions is their size and weight. Any coin of a standard size and weight is a coin, but multiples or (more rarely) fractional coins are deemed to be medallions. But as Toynbee's discussion of the rare Aurelian Sol Dominus coinage illustrates, there are (or appear to be) too many coin-sized medallions and medallion-sized coins for even this distinction to work well.[150] In a recent thorough review of the issue Mittag (2012) stresses again that the difference lay in the primary or intended function of the object (monetary or not), but establishing that was far easier for the Romans than for us. Following Toynbee, I have tended to list coin-like medallions as coins, leaving section L3 to those medallions that were clearly not intended to have a monetary function, for instance because their weight was at variance with the closest standard. But that still leaves us with a number of medallions that could equally well have been listed as coins, and vice versa.

Tesserae, finally, have been included mainly as a reminder that they exist, and that Sol could be depicted on them. I have limited myself to lead tesserae, but the array of objects to which the term can apply is quite large, as is the range of materials from which they could be made. The number of potential functions of these tesserae was equally diverse.[151] I am not aware of any evidence suggesting that depicting Sol on a tessera in any way restricted or defined the tessera's use or purpose.

In conclusion, then, the state of our numismatic knowledge is nowhere near where it could be, and where it should be to answer the types of questions we would ask of coins, medals, and tesserae. It does not mean that we should just ignore them in this type of research, but it does mean that we should recognize that any coin catalogue we make now has a far greater likelihood of being outdated within the decade than the general catalogue of this study does. This is particularly the case with Roman provincial coins. As long as the RPC is still incomplete, any catalogue we produce will be so uneven that it will be useless as soon as the RPC is finished.

---

149   Toynbee 1944: 1. Krmnicek (2016, 5–9) discusses the identification and study of medallions and contorniates in a useful introduction to the topic.

150   Toynbee devotes all of her chapter 3 to this problem, using the Sol Dominus coins (L2.87–89) as an example of coins/medallions that do not fit well in either category.

151   NP s.v. "Tessera."

Printed in the United States
by Baker & Taylor Publisher Services